W9-CDL-848

Legendary Checklist

Equipment Screen Items

Name	Location	Got It?
Wallet	N/A	❑
Fish Journal (chart)	Ordona Province; Ordon Village	❑
Wooden Sword	Ordona Province; Ordon Village (Link's House)	❑
Ordon Shield	Ordona Province; Ordon Village (Jaggle's House)	❑
Ordon Sword	Ordona Province; Ordon Village (Rusl's House)	❑
Vessel of Light	Faron Province; Faron Woods (Faron Spring)	❑
Hero's Clothes	Faron Province; Faron Woods (Faron Spring)	❑
Hidden Skills (chart)	Faron Province; Faron Woods	❑
Fused Shadow #1	Dungeon 1: Forest Temple	❑
Heart Container	Dungeon 1: Forest Temple	❑
Letters (chart)	Faron Province; Hyrule Field (South)	❑
Golden Bugs (chart)	Faron Province; Hyrule Field (South)	❑
Youth's Scent	Eldin Province; Hyrule Field (Kakariko Gorge)	❑
Hylian Shield	Eldin Province; Kakariko Village (Malo Mart)	❑
Wooden Shield	Eldin Province; Kakariko Village (Malo Mart)	❑
Quiver	Dungeon 2: Goron Mines	❑
Fused Shadow #2	Dungeon 2: Goron Mines	❑
Scent of Ilia	Lanayru Province; Hyrule Field (North)	❑
Big Wallet	Lanayru Province; Castle Town (Agitha's Castle)	❑
Zora Armor	Eldin Province; Kakariko Village (Graveyard)	❑
Fused Shadow #3	Dungeon 3: Lakebed Temple	❑
Poe Souls (chart)	Lanayru Province; Castle Town (Jovani's House)	❑
Master Sword	Faron Province; Sacred Grove	❑
Big Quiver	Lanayru Province; Castle Town (STAR Tent)	❑
Magic Armor	Lanayru Province; Castle Town (Malo Mart Castle Branch)	❑
Poe Scent	Dungeon 4: Arbiter's Grounds	❑
Reekfish Scent	Lanayru Province; Zora's Domain	❑
Mirror Shard #2	Dungeon 5: Snowpeak Ruins	❑
Giant Wallet	Lanayru Province; Castle Town (Agitha's Castle)	❑
Mirror Shard #3	Dungeon 6: Temple of Time	❑
Medicine Scent	Lanayru Province; Castle Town (Borville's Office)	❑
Mirror Shard #4	Dungeon 7: City in the Sky	❑
Giant Quiver	Lanayru Province; Castle Town (STAR Tent)	❑

Ⓑ Button Items

Name	Location	Got It?
Fishing Rod	Ordona Province; Ordon Village	❑
Bottle #1	Ordona Province; Ordon Village (Sera's Sundries)	❑
Bee Larva	Ordona Province; Ordon Village (Sera's Sundries)	❑
Milk	Ordona Province; Ordon Village (Sera's Sundries)	❑
Slingshot	Ordona Province; Ordon Village (Sera's Sundries)	❑
Lantern	Faron Province; Faron Woods	❑
Lantern Oil	Faron Province; Faron Woods	❑
Red Potion	Faron Province; Faron Woods	❑
Bottle #2	Faron Province; Faron Woods	❑
Gale Boomerang	Dungeon 1: Forest Temple	❑
Fairy	Dungeon 1: Forest Temple	❑
Ooccoo	Dungeon 1: Forest Temple	❑
Ooccoo Jr.	Dungeon 1: Forest Temple	❑
Iron Boots	Ordona Province; Ordon Village (Bo's House)	❑
Red Chu Jelly	Lanayru Province; Hyrule Field (Great Hylian Bridge)	❑
Purple Chu Jelly	Lanayru Province; Hyrule Field (Great Hylian Bridge)	❑
Hot Springwater	Eldin Province; Kakariko Village	❑
Hero's Bow	Dungeon 2: Goron Mines	❑
Bombs	Eldin Province; Kakariko Village (Barnes' Bombs)	❑
Hawkeye	Eldin Province; Kakariko Village (Malo Mart)	❑
Blue Potion	Eldin Province; Kakariko Village (Goron Vendor)	❑
Yellow Chu Jelly	Eldin Province; Hyrule Field (Kakariko Gorge; Lantern Cavern I)	❑
Bomb Bag #2	Lanayru Province; Upper Zora's River (Iza's Boat Ride)	❑
Giant Bomb Bag	Lanayru Province; Upper Zora's River (Iza's Boat Ride)	❑
Bottle #3	Lanayru Province; Fishing Hole	❑
Bomb Bag #3	Lanayru Province; Zora's Domain (Throne Room)	❑
Clawshot	Dungeon 3: Lakebed Temple	❑
Rare Chu Jelly	Ordona Province; Ordon Village (Ranch)	❑
Bomblings	Eldin Province; Kakariko Village (Barnes' Bombs)	❑
Bottle #4	Lanayru Province; Castle Town (Jovani's House)	❑

Name	Location	Got It?
Great Fairy's Tears	Lanayru Province; Castle Town (Jovani's House)	❑
Auru's Memo	Lanayru Province; Lake Hylia	❑
Spinner	Dungeon 4: Arbiter's Grounds	❑
Ashei's Sketch	Peak Province; Snowpeak (Entry Area)	❑
Coral Earrings	Eldin Province; Kakariko Village (Graveyard)	❑
Simple Soup	Dungeon 5: Snowpeak Ruins	❑
Good Soup	Dungeon 5: Snowpeak Ruins	❑
Superb Soup	Dungeon 5: Snowpeak Ruins	❑
Ball and Chain	Dungeon 5: Snowpeak Ruins	❑
Dominion Rod	Dungeon 6: Temple of Time	❑
Renado's Letter	Eldin Province; Kakariko Village (Shaman's House)	❑
Doctor's Invoice	Lanayru Province; Castle Town (Telma's Bar)	❑
Wooden Statue	Lanayru Province; Hyrule Field (South Gate)	❑
Ilia's Charm	Eldin Province; Hidden Village	❑
Ancient Sky Book	Eldin Province; Hidden Village (Impaz's House)	❑
Double Clawshot	Dungeon 7: City in the Sky	❑

Pieces of Heart

Name	Location	Got It?
Piece of Heart #1	Faron Province; Faron Woods	❑
Piece of Heart #2	Dungeon 1: Forest Temple	❑
Piece of Heart #3	Dungeon 1: Forest Temple	❑
Piece of Heart #4	Faron Province; Hyrule Field (South)	❑
Piece of Heart #5	Eldin Province; Hyrule Field (Kakariko Gorge)	❑
Piece of Heart #6	Ordona Province; Ordon Village (Ranch)	❑
Piece of Heart #7	Dungeon 2: Goron Mines	❑
Piece of Heart #8	Dungeon 2: Goron Mines	❑
Piece of Heart #9	Eldin Province; Kakariko Village	❑
Piece of Heart #10	Eldin Province; Kakariko Village	❑
Piece of Heart #11	Eldin Province; Kakariko Village	❑
Piece of Heart #12	Eldin Province; Death Mountain (Trail)	❑
Piece of Heart #13	Eldin Province; Hyrule Field (Bridge of Eldin)	❑
Piece of Heart #14	Eldin Province; Hyrule Field (Kakariko Gorge; Lantern Cavern #1)	❑
Piece of Heart #15	Lanayru Province; Lake Hylia	❑
Piece of Heart #16	Lanayru Province; Lake Hylia (Lantern Cavern #2)	❑
Piece of Heart #17	Lanayru Province; Fishing Hole	❑
Piece of Heart #18	Lanayru Province; Castle Town	❑
Piece of Heart #19	Dungeon 3: Lakebed Temple	❑
Piece of Heart #20	Dungeon 3: Lakebed Temple	❑
Piece of Heart #21	Faron Province; Sacred Grove	❑
Piece of Heart #22	Eldin Province; Hyrule Field (Bridge of Eldin)	❑
Piece of Heart #23	Lanayru Province; Lake Hylia (Lanayru Spring)	❑
Piece of Heart #24	Lanayru Province; Lake Hylia	❑
Piece of Heart #25	Eldin Province; Hyrule Field (Bridge of Eldin; Lava Cavern)	❑
Piece of Heart #26	Desert Province; Arbiter's Grounds (Exterior)	❑
Piece of Heart #27	Dungeon 4: Arbiter's Grounds	❑
Piece of Heart #28	Dungeon 4: Arbiter's Grounds	❑
Piece of Heart #29	Eldin Province; Hyrule Field (Bridge of Eldin)	❑
Piece of Heart #30	Lanayru Province; Hyrule Field (East Gate)/ Hyrule Field (North) Path	❑
Piece of Heart #31	Dungeon 5: Snowpeak Ruins	❑
Piece of Heart #32	Dungeon 5: Snowpeak Ruins	❑
Piece of Heart #33	Peak Province; Snowpeak (Snowboard Area)	❑
Piece of Heart #34	Lanayru Province; Hyrule Field (North)	❑
Piece of Heart #35	Dungeon 6: Temple of Time	❑
Piece of Heart #36	Dungeon 6: Temple of Time	❑
Piece of Heart #37	Faron Province; Sacred Grove	❑
Piece of Heart #38	Eldin Province; Hidden Village	❑
Piece of Heart #39	Faron Province; Faron Woods	❑
Piece of Heart #40	Eldin Province; Hyrule Field (Bridge of Eldin)	❑
Piece of Heart #41	Dungeon 7: City in the Sky	❑
Piece of Heart #42	Dungeon 7: City in the Sky	❑
Piece of Heart #43	Eldin Province; Hyrule Field (Kakariko Gorge)	❑
Piece of Heart #44	Dungeon 8: Palace of Twilight	❑
Piece of Heart #45	Dungeon 8: Palace of Twilight	❑

Contents

Acknowledgements

This guide would not have been possible without the tireless help and support of everyone at Nintendo of America. In particular, we would like to thank the following people:

Gail Tilden, Damon Baker, Seth McMahill, Kyoko Grant, Thomas Hertzog, Brian Carlson, Jeffrey Storbo, Scott Olson, Danny Yi

David Bueno created the map images for this guide

PRIMA Official Game Guide

Written by

David S. J. Hodgson

Stephen Stratton

Product Manager: Mario De Govia
Senior Project Editor: Brooke N. Hall
Editor: Amanda Peckham
Manufacturing: Stephanie Sanchez
Design & Layout: Bryan Neff, Paul Smith, Scott Watanabe, Jody Seltzer

ISBN: 978-0-7615-5571-1
Library of Congress Catalog Card Number: 2006937819
Printed in the United States of America

06 07 08 09 LL 10 9 8 7 6 5 4 3 2 1

Prima Games
A Division of Random House, Inc.
3000 Lava Ridge Court, Suite 100
Roseville, CA 95661
1-800-733-3000
www.primagames.com

Author Bios

David Hodgson - Originally hailing from the United Kingdom, David left his role as a writer of numerous British video game magazines (including *Mean Machines*, *Computer & Video Games*, and the *Official Nintendo* and *Sega Saturn* magazines) and a bohemian lifestyle on a dry-docked German fishing trawler to work on the infamous *GameFan* magazine in 1996. David helped to launch the fledgling GameFan Books and helped form Gamers' Republic in 1998, authoring many strategy guides for Millennium Publications, including *The Official Metal Gear Solid Mission Handbook*. After launching the wildly unsuccessful incite Video Gaming and Gamers.com, David found his calling, and began authoring guides for Prima Games. He has written over 50 Prima strategy guides, including *The Godfather: The Game*, *Knights of the Old Republic*, *Perfect Dark Zero*, *Half-Life 2*, and *Burnout Revenge*. He lives in the Pacific Northwest with his wife, Melanie, and an eight-foot statue of Great Cthulhu.

We want to hear from you! E-mail comments and feedback to dhodgson@primagames.com.

Stephen Stratton has worked on more than 30 projects in his five years of writing strategy guides for Prima. His repertoire of mastered games includes *Counter-Strike: Condition Zero*, *Rome: Total War*, *Mercenaries: Playground of Destruction*, *The Legend of Zelda: The Wind Waker*, *Super Mario Sunshine*, *Hitman: Contracts*, and *Splinter Cell: Chaos Theory*.

Steve is a lifelong video gamer who attended the Rochester Institute of Technology in Rochester, NY. In addition to his Prima Games guides, he also held a staff position with Computec Media and managed the strategy section of their incite.com video game website.

We want to hear from you! E-mail comments and feedback to sstratton@primagames.com.

Training

Link's Moves and Abilities

When exploring the shadowy caverns and uncharted corners of Hyrule, survival is never guaranteed. Link's world is full of all sorts of dangers, and the first step to ensuring a long life in the adventuring business is to master all of the moves and abilities your survival may hinge upon.

Human Form

▲ Link's most versatile form is his normal, everyday self. In human form, Link can wield a sword and defend himself with a shield. He also has access to all of the different items and tools he has acquired during his travels, which are often used to overcome a variety of obstacles. Most importantly, Link can talk to people he meets while in human form.

Walking and Running

▲ Push ◎ in any direction to make Link run in that direction. Gently push ◎ to make Link walk, which is handy when navigating narrow ledges and the like.

Jumping

➤ No specific button is required to make Link jump; simply run off the edge of any ledge or precipice and Link automatically leaps into the air. Practice jumping about with Link early in the adventure to get a feel for how far he can travel through the air.

Tip: Before making a tricky jump, always press Ⓩ to center the camera behind Link. This allows you to line up the jump properly and run straight ahead.

Rolling

➤ While running, press Ⓐ to make Link tuck and roll. This simple move causes Link to move a bit faster, so it's common to roll over and over when traveling long distances on foot. Link is also a much smaller and more agile target when rolling, so abuse this handy maneuver when you need to quickly move out of harm's way.

Tip: Rolling into objects can have surprising results. Try rolling into the tall trees in the Ordon Woods!

Human Form Combat

◄ Now we're getting to the good stuff! Link lives in troubled times, where knowing how to defend oneself is one of the most vital skill sets to master. Let's take a look at the many offensive and defensive moves that are available to Link in his human form.

Ⓩ Targeting

➤ This is where it all begins! Targeting hostile creatures is *absolutely vital* to succeeding in combat. Whenever you encounter a creepy creature, press and hold Ⓩ to target it. Link's attention then becomes focused on the enemy, keeping it in his view at all times.

▲ Understand that Link's movements revolve around his current target. When you push ◎ to move about, Link now sidesteps around his targeted foe.

▲ The function of Ⓐ also changes when you're targeting an enemy. While moving to one side or the other, pressing Ⓐ causes Link to perform a quick lateral hop. This is an effective way to avoid linear attacks, and can even help you flank your foe!

➤ Holding Ⓩ to target is also how you raise Link's shield to defend against incoming attacks. Blocking with a shield can be extremely useful, especially when you're faced with a new enemy whose attacks are unfamiliar, or when up against overwhelming odds. Link can defend just about any attack by blocking; don't overlook this handy ability!

➤ Press Ⓐ while moving backward to execute a hasty retreat in the form of a backflip. This is a fast way to put some distance between you and your target.

Tip: Backflip multiple times to retreat as far as you like without losing track of your target.

◄ Link's accuracy is second to none while Ⓩ targeting! Lock-on to an enemy and then use any long-range item, such as the Slingshot, Gale Boomerang, or Hero's Bow. The attack flies straight at the enemy, almost always finding its mark! This is much easier than manual aiming, which there often isn't time for during the thick of battle.

Jump Attack

➤ Once you've targeted an enemy, remain stationary and press Ⓐ to make Link leap forward and execute his powerful jump attack! This move works great against flying enemies, but it leaves Link open to counterattack for a few seconds. Use the jump attack only when you see an opening, and avoid using it when enemies swarm in.

Sword Combos

◄ Swing the Wii Remote back and forth to make Link draw his sword and begin hacking and slicing! This is the most common way to tear through your foes. Remember to Ⓩ target your enemies to take the guesswork out of aiming!

➤ Link can also execute a running barrage of sword strikes. Start running, then begin swinging the Wii Remote to make Link slash from side to side. This is a fast way to clear out fields full of tall grass, or to soften up groups of enemies before making a more calculated assault.

Spin Attack

➤ This ferocious 360-degree sword strike is Link's bread and butter when enemies swarm in. Shake the Nunchuk to make Link spin around with his sword arm extended, slashing through everything nearby. The range on this attack is surprisingly long, allowing you to eliminate whole groups of enemies with a single attack.

Note: After performing the spin attack, you must wait a few seconds until it recharges. Link's sword flashes and the distinctive sound of steel being drawn emanates from the Wii Remote's speaker when the move is once again available.

Ending Blow

➤ Link encounters a fearsome-looking Spirit Wolf on his way to the Forest Temple, but the wolf isn't a threat. Instead, it transports Link to an ethereal realm, where the skeletal form of the Hero's Shade materializes and teaches Link his first Hidden Skill, the ending blow.

▲ The ending blow allows you to quickly defeat a tough enemy that you've knocked to the ground. When this move becomes available, the "Finish Ⓐ" icon appears at the bottom of the screen. Quickly press Ⓐ to execute the ending blow; Link leaps through the air and comes crashing down on his target, sword-point first! No matter how much fight a monster may have left, the ending blow ensures that its lights go out!

Note: The ending blow is just one of seven incredibly useful Hidden Skills that Link can learn over the course of the adventure. Refer to the Walkthrough section to learn when and how to acquire each one, including detailed tips on how they're best used.

Wolf Form

➤ As a wolf, Link has access to a whole new range of talents and abilities, but he loses many of the skills he possesses in human form. While he can still walk and run about as normal, Link cannot wield a sword or shield or use any items; wolf paws weren't designed for such work! It's also impossible for wolf Link to speak with humans he meets; they usually just cower in fear, not understanding that he's really a heroic, good-natured kind of wolf. But these are small prices to pay for the sheer thrill of letting one's inner animal run free!

Dashing

➤ Walking, running, and jumping remain exactly the same between Link's wolf and human forms, but his bipedal roll ability becomes replaced by a short dash that works in much the same way. Press Ⓐ while running to dash forward a few paces, getting an extra boost of speed to help speed up travel and avoid hostile attacks.

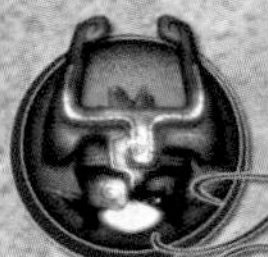

Tip: Dash just before running off a ledge to jump a bit farther than normal.

Sensing

➤ Being a wolf has its advantages. In wolf form, Link has access to heightened senses, which he can turn on and off at will. Press ✚ or ✚ to activate and deactivate Link's lupine sense view and see the world in an entirely new way.

➤ As you might expect, Link's wolf sense has a variety of different uses. With sense view engaged, he can follow scent trails, become aware of invisible characters and enemies, and even detect soft spots in the ground where items lie buried!

Digging

➤ All kinds of neat things end up in the soil: Hearts, Rupees, you name it. Whenever Link's wolf sense detects a soft patch of earth, he sees the area as a dark, shimmering circle, which is known as a **dig spot**. Approach a dig spot and the "Dig ✚" icon appears at the bottom of the screen. Press ✚ to dig into the soil and excavate whatever goodies were buried there.

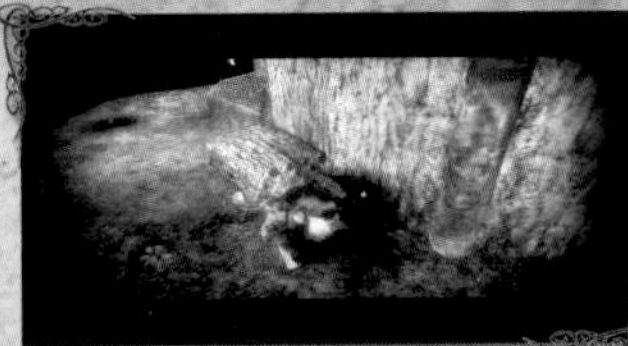

➤ Some dig spots appear larger than others. These large dig spots indicate an underground route that can be used to reach a new area. Tunnel into large dig spots and see where you end up!

Midna-Jump

➤ Midna finds it easier to control Link when he travels in wolf form. At certain areas in Hyrule, she can help him leap great distances to reach new areas and progress through the environment. Whenever this is an option, an icon of Midna's head appears at the bottom of the screen, and a giggling sound emanates from the Wii Remote's speaker. Press ✚ to summon Midna and initiate a Midna-jump.

➤ Midna zips over to the ledge you can leap to. Hold Ⓩ to target her, then press Ⓐ to have her pull you across the wide gap. Sometimes you can make multiple jumps in quick succession; just keep holding Ⓩ and pressing Ⓐ until you reach the end of the line.

Howling

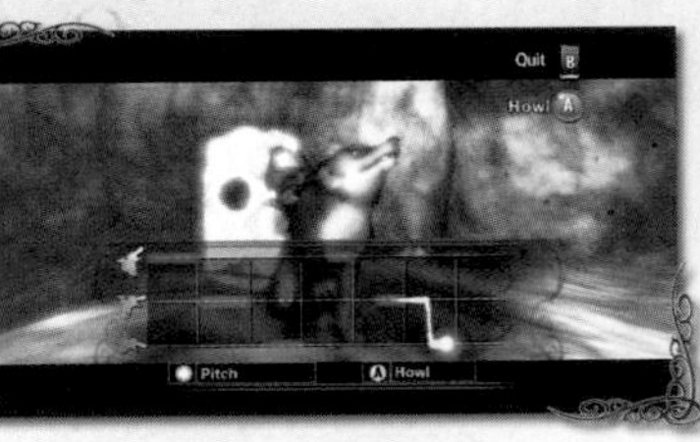

➤ When Link assumes his lupine form, the spirit of the wolf runs deep within him. While standing near certain objects, such as Hawk Grass or a Windstone, the "Howl Ⓐ" icon appears at the bottom of the screen. Press Ⓐ to begin listening to the object's tune, then use ◎ to howl along, imitating the pitch of the notes that form the song. Do so correctly and something special will happen!

Note: Howling the tune of Hawk Grass summons a Hawk, which Link may speak with in his wolf form. Hawks usually have helpful advice, so call on them whenever you need a tip!

Note: Howling the tune of a Windstone summons a Spirit Wolf at a certain place in Hyrule. Each Windstone summons a certain Spirit Wolf, who you may then visit to learn a new Hidden Skill! Refer to the Walkthrough section for the locations of each Windstone and Spirit Wolf in the game.

Speaking with Animals

➤ Link's wolfish appearance frightens most humans, but animals are a bit more intuitive and don't scare so easily. As a wolf, Link can speak to all manner of woodland creatures, including Cuccos, squirrels, frogs, ducks, and more! When traveling in Link's wolf guise, speak with every animal you see for unique advice and offbeat conversations.

Wolf Form Combat

Wolf-based combat is surprisingly similar to that of Link's human form. Though you have no sword or shield, Link is far more agile as a wolf, and his razor-sharp claws and fangs cut as swift and sharp as nearly any sword. Targeting also works just the same as it does when Link moves about on two legs; hold Ⓩ to keep a lock on your foe, and your movements become relative to the current target.

Jump Attack

➤ Link's patented jump attack gets a nasty new twist when he employs it as a wolf. Instead of the single (and somewhat slow) leaping strike that human Link performs, wolf Link springs through the air with great speed, snapping his fangs around his adversary! If the initial bite doesn't defeat the enemy, you can usually rapidly press Ⓐ and make Link chomp away four or five more times!

Bite Combos

➤ Link's standard sword barrage is replaced by a series of vicious bites when you wiggle the Wii Remote in wolf form. These quick nips have a shorter range than the human form sword strikes, but they're a bit faster to execute.

Spin Attack

➤ Even without the cutting edge of Link's sword, this wolfish spin attack is an extremely powerful and versatile combat maneuver. Employ it when faced with multiple enemies, or as an addition to other wolf-based attacks.

Note: As with Link's human form spin attack, you must wait a few seconds between each use to let the attack recharge.

Energy Field

➤ When you're feeling the urge for widespread destruction—and in Link's wolf form, you should always be feeling this urge—press and hold Ⓑ to charge up a crackling energy field. A circle of pure energy encompasses Link, automatically targeting each nearby enemy. Release Ⓑ to make Link fly about, ripping through each targeted enemy in turn. Few monsters can withstand the might of this brutal assault!

Tip: In wolf form, the area-effect attack is the best way to deal with those pesky Twilit Messengers. Defeat all but two of them, then target both inside an area-effect attack to drop them fast!

Riding Epona

➤ Hyrule is a vast land filled with dangerous creatures—not exactly the kind of place you want to be exploring on foot! Fortunately, you usually have the option of riding Link's faithful steed, Epona. Venturing through fields of Hyrule on horseback is the only way to go; it's faster, safer, and way more fun!

Note: Needless to say, you can't ride Epona in wolf form!

➤ Approach Epona and press Ⓐ to climb onto her back. Press Ⓐ again while stationary to slide back down to the ground. And if you're in a hurry, approach Epona from the rear and press Ⓐ; Link leaps into the saddle and dashes off at great speed!

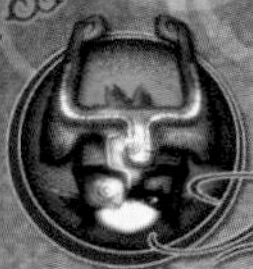

IF YOU NEED A RIDE BUT EPONA'S NOWHERE TO BE FOUND, PLUCK UP SOME HORSE GRASS AND GIVE A WHISTLE. SHE COMES RUNNING!

➤ While riding Epona, notice the six spur icons at the bottom of the screen. These let you know how many times you can press Ⓐ to make Epona dash forward at high speed. Each time you press Ⓐ, one of the spur icons disappears. The icons regenerate over time, but try not to waste them; you never know when you might need that extra boost of speed!

➤ Epona won't run off cliffs or sudden drops, but she'll happily bound over short obstacles. When approaching a low wall, fence, or gate, press Ⓐ to spur Epona and make her gallop at high speed. Run straight at the obstacle you wish her to leap, and Epona gracefully jumps over it in stunning fashion!

◄ Controlling Epona is a bit tricky at first. This lady likes moving forward, and fast; turning and backing up aren't exactly her favorite maneuvers! Gently press ◎ backward to make Epona back up slowly. Press ◎ backward with more force to make her neigh and spin around 180-degrees.

Horseback Combat

◄ Fighting your foes on horseback while galloping along at high speed across a vast, rolling plain; what more could you ask for? Link's sword works wonders from horseback. Make him slash to either side by swinging the Wii Remote, or execute a powerful horseback spin attack by shaking the Nunchuk!

➤ While Ⓩ targeting can be a help during horseback combat, it's not quite as useful as it is on foot. That's because Epona is oblivious to your target and won't chase after it; only Link's attention becomes focused on his prey. Still, if you want to launch a long-ranged assault, there's no better way to ensure hits than to target your enemies with Ⓩ!

➤ Epona isn't without offensive capabilities, either. Steer her into an enemy and she'll bump it, doing a bit of damage. Hit Ⓐ to spur her along and she smashes through foes, knocking them clear out of the way!

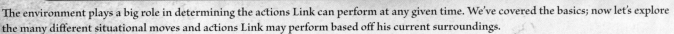

Environmental Effects

The environment plays a big role in determining the actions Link can perform at any given time. We've covered the basics; now let's explore the many different situational moves and actions Link may perform based off his current surroundings.

Common Interactions

Link can interact with a variety of different environmental objects. All of these actions are initiated in the same way: by moving close to the object and then pressing Ⓐ to interact with it. Here are some of the many actions Link can perform in this manner:

Speaking with characters

Talking to animals

Throwing pots, rocks, and other objects

Pushing movable blocks

Reading signage

Lifting pots, rocks, and other objects

Opening doors

LADDERS, LEDGES, AND VINES

◄ Link's world is vast in all directions, including up and down. Very few areas in Hyrule are completely flat; just about every Overworld region and dungeon chamber features something that can Link can climb onto. No special button presses are required to make Link grab hold of a ledge, ladder, or collection of vines. Simply move Link toward any of these objects and he'll perform the appropriate action automatically.

➤ Move Link toward a low block or ledge and he'll automatically vault up onto it. If the ledge is a bit too high, Link may jump up and grab onto its edge. Then press the appropriate direction to make him climb up the rest of the way.

➤ While hanging from the edge of a ledge, you can make Link shimmy sideways in a hand-over-hand fashion. This can be useful when you need to cross a ledge that's too narrow to stand atop.

◄ If you want Link to drop off a ledge instead of leap, push ◎ gently so that he walks over the edge. Link automatically spins as he falls and grabs hold of the ledge on his way down. Then press Ⓐ to drop to the ground, or move ◎ in the appropriate direction to shimmy sideways, or climb back up.

➤ When climbing ladders and vines, simply use ◎ to move about. Link's not the fastest climber, but he gets to where he's going eventually! If you decide not to make the trip, press Ⓐ to let go and drop to the ground below.

Note: YOU CANNOT ATTACK OR USE ANY ITEMS WHILE CLIMBING OR HANGING FROM A LEDGE.

➤ Once you acquire the Clawshot, you can scale vines much faster than normal. Target a patch of vines with the Clawshot and then fire to zip up as far as you can.

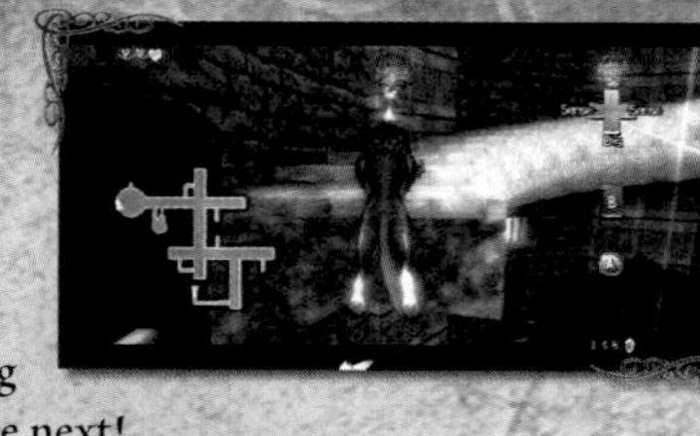

➤ Link can't climb ladders and vines in wolf form, but he can grab hold of ledges if need be. This is especially useful when jumping from one ledge to the next!

◄ In wolf form, Link has the advantage of being able to traverse wire-thin tightropes with exceptional balance—an ability he's never mastered as a human. Use this trait to your advantage to help reach otherwise inaccessible areas.

WATER AND SWIMMING

➤ Link is an accomplished swimmer. When he enters a deep body of water, he naturally begins swimming about its surface. Press Ⓐ to make him swim a bit faster.

◄ Link can't hold his breath for long and won't dive underwater on his own at first. Once you find the Iron Boots, you can put them on to make Link sink to the bottom of the ocean floor. Keep a close eye on Link's oxygen meter when you do this, however. The gauge rapidly depletes until you return to the surface, and it's lights out for Link if you don't get there in time!

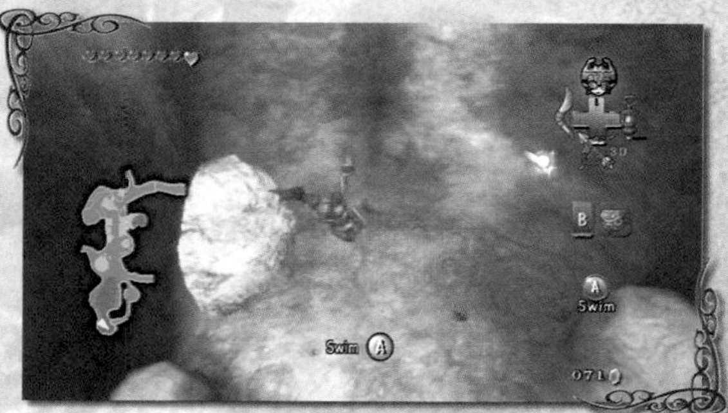

▲ Once you acquire the Zora Armor, Link can swim about underwater like a fish. He no longer runs out of oxygen and can dive down as deep as he pleases.

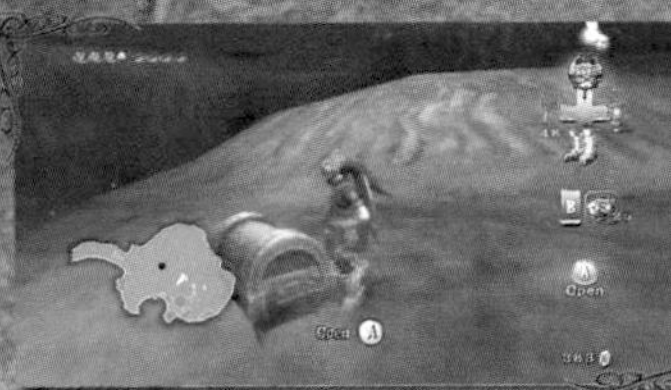

➤ Still, to perform any underwater actions, Link must don his Iron Boots so he can stand up straight on the ocean floor. With the Iron Boots equipped, Link can open submerged treasure chests, use Water Bombs to clear away underwater Bomb Rocks, lift sunken rocks and pots, and so on.

Long Drops and Short Stops

➤ It doesn't take long for Link to encounter areas of the Overworld that are so high up that a fall would be fatal. In most cases, when Link plummets into a bottomless chasm, he's returned to the point from which he fell, with one less Heart in his Heart meter.

FALLING INTO A DUNGEON'S PIT USUALLY RESULTS IN BEING RETURNED TO THE POINT FROM WHICH YOU ENTERED THE CHAMBER.

➤ Not every fall is a fatal one, of course. A long drop onto solid ground may sting a bit, but it usually isn't fatal. In fact, Link can plummet quite a surprisingly long distance before the impact starts to inflict damage.

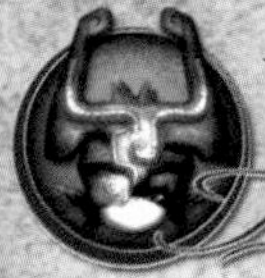

WHEN FALLING FROM A GREAT HEIGHT, PUSH AND HOLD ◎ FORWARD TO MAKE LINK ROLL WHEN HE LANDS. THIS OFTEN SOFTENS THE IMPACT, RESULTING IN NO LOSS OF HEALTH!

Fire and Lava

➤ Link starts feeling the heat when he nears the top of Death Mountain. Fire becomes an enemy all itself, with giant flaming boulders cascading down all around him. But things really get toasty once Link enters the Goron Mines, where lakes of lava and columns of searing flame are all too common.

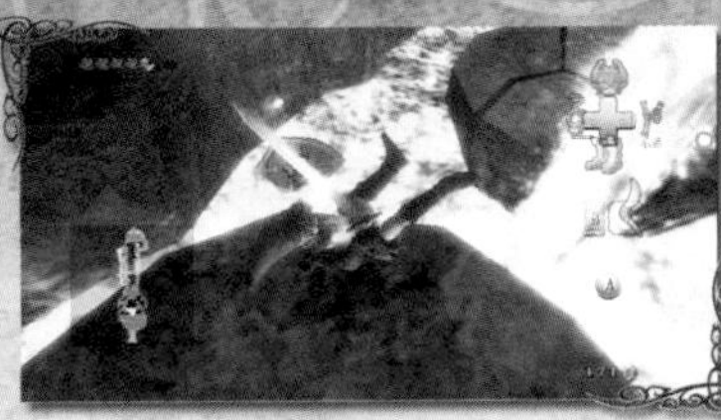

➤ Running into a fiery spire is never a good idea, but taking the plunge into a molten inferno is about the worst thing that can happen! The effect is very similar to slipping into a bottomless pit; Link restarts at the point from which he entered the chamber, sans two Hearts.

➤ It may seem obvious that items made of wood are flammable, but the reality can be shocking when your Wooden Shield unexpectedly burns up due to a nasty dose of a Dodongo's flame breath! Make sure to bring a metal shield when exploring areas in which fire is part of the natural feng shui.

Waking the Wind

➤ It's everywhere, and although you can't see it, you'll eventually learn to respect the raw power displayed by a forceful gale of wind! Depending on the current situation, powerful drafts can be obstacles to overcome, or methods of reaching otherwise inaccessible areas. When faced with an overwhelming gust of wind that's blowing you away, slap on those Iron Boots and do your best to hang in there!

➤ Looking to rise to new heights? With a Cucco or an Oocca at hand, updrafts become virtual elevators, allowing you to reach tall platforms and progress to unexplored areas. Handy!

Snow and Cold

➤ Some areas of the Overworld are hostile by themselves, with or without the monsters that lurk there! Peak Province is one such place. The icy waters you must traverse in the entry area aren't meant for swimming. Don't even try it!

TRAVERSING DEEP SNOW IS SLOW GOING IN HUMAN FORM. CHANGE INTO A WOLF TO DASH ALONG MUCH FASTER!

➤ Naturally, monsters who give off a freezing aura are similarly chilling encounters. Being touched means getting frozen for a few moments, during which your health slowly melts away. Keep your distance from such cold-hearted foes and do your best to avoid this frosty fate!

Weapons & Equipment

Common Items

Common items are everywhere. Find them by smashing open pots and crates, cutting down tall grass, lifting rocks, and so on. You can also purchase some common items from various shops.

Arrows

Arrows provide ammunition for the Hero's Bow. You can't fire the Hero's Bow without them!

Fairies

Fairies are tiny, helpful creatures that replenish up to eight Hearts when you touch one. Capture a Fairy in a Bottle to save it for future use!

Hearts

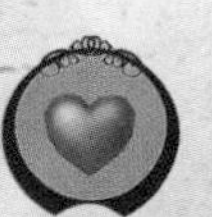

Collect Hearts to replenish Link's Heart meter. Each one you grab restores one full Heart.

Rupees

Rupees are the currency of Hyrule. Collect them to store them inside your wallet, then use them to purchase items from shops. There are seven different types of Rupees:

Green (1) Blue (5) Yellow (10) Red (20)

Purple (50) Orange (100) Silver (200)

Seeds

Seeds are used as ammunition for the Slingshot. You can collect them by smashing the pumpkins at Ordon Village or by defeating Deku Baba enemies and then breaking apart the large Deku nuts they leave behind.

Collectible Items

There are many different types of collectible items throughout your adventure. You don't have to hunt these items, but it's often worthwhile to seek them out!

Fish

Cast your Fishing Rod's line into deep bodies of water to catch some fish! The largest fish you catch while bobber-fishing are recorded in your Fish Journal. There are six types of fish to land; some appear only in certain areas:

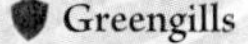

- Greengills
- Hylian Loach
- Hylian Pike
- Hyrule Bass
- Ordon Catfish
- Reekfish

Golden Bugs

Twelve species of Golden Bugs exist throughout Hyrule, and each species features male and female varieties. That makes 24 Golden Bugs for you to catch! Each Golden Bug you collect is recorded in your Golden Bugs chart; give them to Agitha at Castle Town for huge rewards!

Pieces of Heart

Forty-five Pieces of Heart are scattered across the land. Seek them out while exploring the Overworld and delving into dungeons. Some people will give you Pieces of Heart as rewards for good deeds. Collect five Pieces of Heart to form a new Heart Container and extend Link's Heart meter by one full Heart!

Heart Container

Where to Get: Varies

How to Get: Defeat the bosses of each dungeon up through Dungeon 8: Palace of Twilight

Uses: Collect to add another full Heart to Link's Heart meter

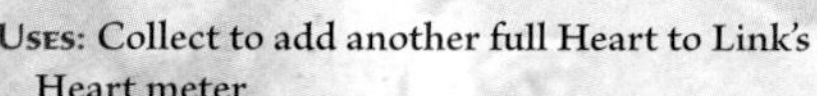

Poe Souls

A man named Jovani lives in Castle Town and sold his soul for a vast amount of wealth, becoming cursed. When you finally meet Jovani, he asks that you find and bring him 20 portions of his soul, which are guarded by Poes and Imp Poes—evil ghosts that can't be seen by human eyes! Defeat each Poe and Imp Poe you encounter to claim the Poe Souls they guard. Though Jovani asks you to find only 20 Poe Souls, there are 60 to collect in all!

Dungeon Items

The following items are commonly found within dungeons. Some of these items are optional and simply make exploring dungeons a bit easier. Others are required to progress through dungeons and reach their bosses.

Big Key

The Big Key exists in most dungeons. Its purpose is to open the Big Key locked door, behind which lies the dungeon's boss. Find the Big Key and use it to gain access to the boss chamber.

Compass

The Compass shows the locations of all treasure chests within the current dungeon, along with any objects of interest. After you acquire the Compass, check your Dungeon Map to find the locations of these items.

Dungeon Map

The Dungeon Map reveals the entire floor plan of the current dungeon. This includes the rooms you've visited and all the rooms featured in the dungeon. Combined with the Compass, the Dungeon Map can be a great help in determining where you need to go next.

Ooccoo and Ooccoo Jr.

Ooccoo is found within many dungeons. Use this odd, chickenlike creature to warp out of the current dungeon so you can stock up on items, potions, and the like. When you use Ooccoo to warp outside, Ooccoo Jr. travels along with you. Use Ooccoo Jr. to warp back into Ooccoo so you may continue where you left off.

Small Key

Small Keys are found within most dungeons. Use them to open locked doors within the dungeon. It's often impossible to progress through a dungeon without collecting its Small Keys.

Quest Items

Link finds the following items over the course of his adventure. Some of these are gained through battle or exploration, while others must be purchased from certain shops.

Ancient Sky Book

Where to Get: Eldin Province; Hidden Village

How to Get: Show Impaz the useless Dominion Rod

Uses: Shad uses it to recharge the Dominion Rod; Link uses it to record "sky characters" from owl statues

Ashei's Sketch

Where to Get: Peak Province; Snowpeak (Entry Area)

How to Get: Speak with Ashei

Uses: Convinces Prince Ralis to give you the Coral Earring

Auru's Memo

Where to Get: Lanayru Province; Lake Hylia

How to Get: Speak with Auru

Uses: Convinces Fyer to send you to Desert Province via cannon

Ball and Chain

Where to Get: Dungeon 5: Snowpeak Ruins

How to Get: Defeat the dungeon's midboss

Uses: Smashes away ice blocks; defeats enemies

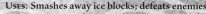

Bedroom Key

Where to Get: Dungeon 5: Snowpeak Ruins

How to Get: Find and open the third treasure chest that Yeta marks on your map

Uses: Opens the door to the Yeti's bedroom, where the second Mirror Shard is kept

Bee Larvae

Where to Get: Varies

How to Get: Purchase from shops; knock down Hylian Hornet nests and scoop remains into a Bottle

Uses: Fishing bait; health restoration

Big Quiver

Where to Get: Lanayru Province; Castle Town

How to Get: Win STAR Tent minigame, level one

Uses: Increases quiver capacity to 60 arrows

Big Wallet

Where to Get: Lanayru Province; Castle Town

How to Get: Give Agitha her first Golden Bug

Uses: Increases wallet capacity to 600 Rupees

Blue Chu Jelly

Where to Get: Varies

How to Get: Defeat a Blue Chu, then scoop its remains into a bottle

Uses: Drink to replenish all Hearts

Blue Potion

Where to Get: Varies

How to Get: Purchase from shops

Uses: Drink to restore all Hearts

Bomb Bag #1

Where to Get: Eldin Province; Kakariko Village

How to Get: Purchase from Barnes' Bomb Shop

Uses: Holds Bombs

Bomb Bag #2

Where to Get: Lanayru Province; Upper Zora's River

How to Get: Help Iza by destroying rockslides along Zora's River.

Uses: Holds Bombs

Bomb Bag #3

Where to Get: Lanayru Province; Zora's Domain

How to Get: Destroy the giant underwater Bomb Rock in the center of the Zoras' throne room pool

Uses: Holds Bombs

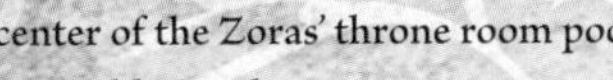

Bomblings

Where to Get: Varies

How to Get: Purchase from shops

Uses: Destroying Bomb Rocks; opening paths; harming enemies

Bombs

Where to Get: Varies

How to Get: Purchase from shops; find within treasure chests

Uses: Destroying Bomb Rocks; opening paths; harming enemies

Bottle #1

Where to Get: Ordona Province; Ordon Village

How to Get: Catch a fish for Sera's cat, then visit Sera's Sundries

Uses: Holds a variety of useful items, including potions, Fairies, and Lantern oil

Bottle #2

Where to Get: Faron Province; Faron Woods

How to Get: Purchase from Coro

Uses: Holds a variety of useful items, including potions, Fairies, and Lantern oil

Bottle #3

Where to Get: Lanayru Province; Fishing Hole

How to Get: Bobber-fish in the small pool off the west wooden bridge's west side

Uses: Holds a variety of useful items, including potions, Fairies, and Lantern oil

Bottle #4

Where to Get: Lanayru Province; Castle Town

How to Get: Visit Jovani after acquiring 20 or more Poe Souls

Uses: Holds a variety of useful items, including potions, Fairies, and Lantern oil

Clawshot

Where to Get: Dungeon 3: Lakebed Temple

How to Get: Defeat the dungeon's midboss

Uses: Latching on to Clawshot medallions and vines; reaching otherwise-inaccessible areas; pulling distant objects toward you; stunning and defeating enemies

Coral Earrings

Where to Get: Eldin Province; Kakariko Village (Graveyard)

How to Get: Show Ashei's Sketch to Prince Ralis

Uses: Allows you to catch Reekfish at Zora's Domain

Doctor's Invoice

Where to Get: Lanayru Province; Castle Town

How to Get: Give Renado's Letter to Telma

Uses: Convinces Doctor Borville to help you track down Ilia's Wooden Statue

Dominion Rod

Where to Get: Dungeon 6: Temple of Time

How to Get: Defeat the dungeon's midboss

Uses: Allows you to control the movements of certain carved statues,

including the overworld Owl statues

Double Clawshot

Where to Get: Dungeon 7: City in the Sky

How to Get: Defeat the dungeon's midboss

Uses: Allows you to travel from one Clawshot medallion to the next without touching the ground

Fairy

Where to Get: Varies

How to Get: Move into contact or scoop into a Bottle

Uses: Restores up to eight Hearts; when carried in a Bottle, automatically revives you if your Heart meter becomes empty

Fish Journal

Where to Get: Ordona Province; Ordon Village

How to Get: Catch your first fish with the Fishing Rod

Uses: Keeps a record of the number, size, and types of fish you've caught while bobber-fishing

Fishing Rod

Where to Get: Ordona Province; Ordon Village

How to Get: Return Uli's lost cradle to her

Uses: Allows for bobber-fishing

Frog Lure

Where to Get: Lanayru Province; Fishing Hole

How to Get: Win Rollgoal minigame board 1–8

Uses: Helps you catch fish, including the legendary Hylian Loach, while lure-fishing

Fused Shadow #1

Where to Get: Dungeon 1: Forest Temple

How to Get: Defeat the dungeon's boss

Uses: Helps Midna combat Zant

Fused Shadow #2

Where to Get: Dungeon 2: Goron Mines

How to Get: Defeat the dungeon's boss

Uses: Helps Midna combat Zant

Fused Shadow #3

Where to Get: Dungeon 3: Lakebed Temple

How to Get: Defeat the dungeon's boss

Uses: Helps Midna combat Zant

Gale Boomerang

Where to Get: Dungeon 1: Forest Temple

How to Get: Defeat the dungeon's midboss

Uses: Retrieves distant items and objects; stuns enemies; activates weathervanes; extinguishes torches

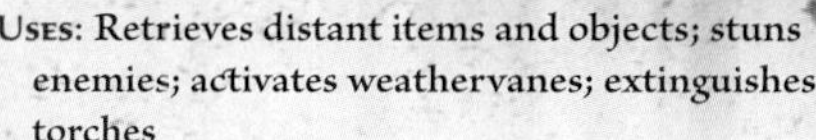

Giant Bomb Bag

Where to Get: Lanayru Province; Upper Zora's River

How to Get: Score 25 points or more at Iza's Rapid Ride minigame

Uses: Doubles the storage capacity of all your Bomb Bags, including any you obtain in the future

Giant Quiver

Where to Get: Lanayru Province; Castle Town

How to Get: Beat STAR Tent minigame, level two

Uses: Increases quiver capacity to 100 arrows

Giant Wallet

Where to Get: Lanayru Province; Castle Town

How to Get: Give Agitha all 24 Golden Bugs

Uses: Increases wallet capacity to 1,000 Rupees

Golden Bugs (Chart)

Where to Get: Varies

How to Get: Catch your first Golden Bug

Uses: Keeps a record of the Golden Bugs you've caught, as well as the ones you've given to Agitha

Good Soup

Where to Get: Dungeon 5: Snowpeak Ruins

How to Get: Give Yeto the Ordon Pumpkin, then scoop some of his soup into a Bottle

Uses: Drink to restore up to four Hearts

Great Fairy's Tears

Where to Get: Varies

How to Get: Visit Jovani after collecting 20 Poe Souls; complete the Cave of Ordeals; speak with the Great Fairy at any province spring after completing the Cave of Ordeals

Uses: Drink to restore all Hearts, and gain a temporary boost to attack speed and power

Hawkeye

Where to Get: Eldin Province; Kakariko Village

How to Get: Purchase from Malo Mart (only available after you complete Malo and Talo's archery challenge)

Uses: Lets you zoom in on distant objects; can be combined with the Hero's Bow for precise long-range shooting

Hero's Bow

Where to Get: Dungeon 2: Goron Mines

How to Get: Defeat the dungeon's midboss

Uses: Fires arrows over great distances to defeat enemies from range or activate out-of-reach switches, etc.

Hero's Clothes

Where to Get: Faron Province; Faron Woods

How to Get: Fill the Vessel of Light for Spirit Faron

Uses: Legendary adventuring attire that's well suited to all combat scenarios

Hidden Skills (Chart)

Where to Get: Faron Province; Faron Woods

How to Get: Learn your first Hidden Skill from the Hero's Shade

Uses: Keeps a record of the Hidden Skills you've learned, detailing how to perform them

Hot Springwater

Where to Get: Varies

How to Get: Stand in a hot spring and scoop its water into a Bottle; purchase from the Goron Vendor in Castle Town

Uses: Drink before it cools to replenish all Hearts; Cooled springwater, and water you scoop from rivers, have no beneficial properties

Hylian Shield

Where to Get: Eldin Province; Kakariko Village

How to Get: Purchase from Malo Mart

Uses: Legendary shield that can deflect most attacks; resistant to fire

Ilia's Charm (AKA Horse Call)

Where to Get: Eldin Province; Hidden Village

How to Get: Show the Wooden Statue to Ilia, talk to Impaz, then show the charm to Ilia

Uses: Restores Ilia's memory; allows Link to call Epona from just about anywhere

Iron Boots

Where to Get: Ordona Province; Ordon Village

How to Get: Defeat Mayor Bo in a sumo-wrestling contest

Uses: Equip to increase Link's weight, letting him activate pressure switches on the floor, sink to the bottom of bodies of water, walk along magnetic tracks, and much more

Key Shards

Where to Get: Dungeon 2: Goron Mines

How to Get: Visit each of the Goron Elders within the Goron Mines

Uses: Collect all three Key Shards to assemble the Big Key and access the dungeon's boss

Lantern

Where to Get: Faron Province; Faron Woods

How to Get: Speak with Coro

Uses: Lights up dark areas; lights torches; burns away thick spiderwebs; keeps some enemies at bay

Lantern Oil

Where to Get: Varies

How to Get: Purchase from shops

Uses: Keeps the Lantern burning brightly

Lent Bomb Bag

Where to Get: Lanayru Province; Upper Zora's River

How to Get: Speak with Iza and agree to help clear the rockslides from Zora's River

Uses: Temporarily gives you another Bomb Bag to hold extra Bombs

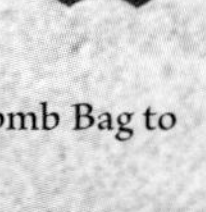

Letters (Chart)

Where to Get: Faron Province; Hyrule Field (South)

How to Get: Encounter the Postman for the first time

Uses: Keeps all the letters Link has received so he can read them again at any time

Magic Armor

Where to Get: Lanayru Province; Castle Town

How to Get: Purchase from Malo Mart Castle Branch

Uses: While equipped, Link loses Rupees instead of Hearts when hit by enemies in combat (also steadily consumes Rupees)

Master Sword

Where to Get: Faron Province; Sacred Grove

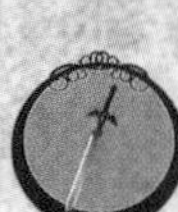
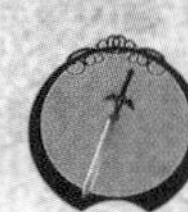
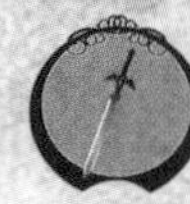

How to Get: Solve the Event of Giants puzzle; pull the Master Sword from the ground

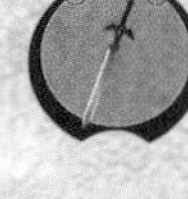

Uses: Legendary sword of unrivaled power; carves through enemies in short order

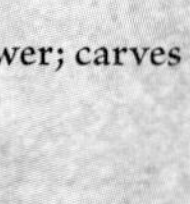

Milk

Where to Get: Varies

How to Get: Purchase from shops

Uses: Drink to replenish up to three Hearts; two servings are stored in one Bottle

Mirror Shard #2

Where to Get: Dungeon 5: Snowpeak Ruins

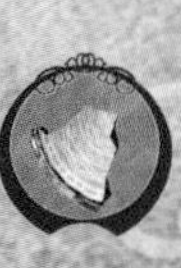

How to Get: Defeat the dungeon's boss

Uses: Helps open the way to the Twilight world

Mirror Shard #3

Where to Get: Dungeon 6: Temple of Time

How to Get: Defeat the dungeon's boss

Uses: Helps open the way to the Twilight world

Mirror Shard #4

Where to Get: Dungeon 7: City in the Sky

How to Get: Defeat the dungeon's boss

Uses: Helps open the way to the Twilight world

Ordon Goat Cheese

Where to Get: Dungeon 5: Snowpeak Ruins

How to Get: Find and open the second treasure chest that Yeta marks on your map

Uses: Can be added to Yeto's Good Soup to create Superb Soup

Ordon Pumpkin

Where to Get: Dungeon 5: Snowpeak Ruins

How to Get: Find and open the first treasure chest that Yeta marks on your map

Uses: Can be added to Yeto's Simple Soup to create Good Soup

Ordon Shield

Where to Get: Ordona Province; Ordon Village

How to Get: Enter Jaggle's house; dash into the wall to knock down the shield

Uses: Allows Link to block most attacks, but it can't withstand fire-based attacks

Ordon Sword

Where to Get: Ordona Province; Ordon Village

How to Get: Enter Rusl's house and retrieve it

Uses: A standard metal sword that lets Link slice through enemies

Purple Chu Jelly

Where to Get: Varies

How to Get: Defeat a Purple Chu, then scoop its remains into a Bottle

Uses: Drink to either gain or lose Hearts (effect is random)

Quiver

Where to Get: Dungeon 2: Goron Mines

How to Get: Defeat the dungeon's midboss. Quiver acquired when you obtain the Hero's Bow

Uses: Stores up to 30 arrows for the Hero's Bow

Rare Chu Jelly

Where to Get: Varies

How to Get: Defeat a Rare Chu, then scoop its remains into a Bottle

Uses: Drink to replenish all Hearts and temporarily increase attack speed and power

Red Chu Jelly

Where to Get: Varies

How to Get: Defeat a Red Chu, then scoop its remains into a Bottle

Uses: Drink to replenish up to eight Hearts

Renado's Letter

Where to Get: Eldin Province; Kakariko Village

How to Get: Speak with Renado after completing Dungeon 6: Temple of Time

Uses: Convinces Telma to give you the Doctor's Invoice

Simple Soup

Where to Get: Dungeon 5: Snowpeak Ruins

How to Get: Scoop some of Yeto's soup into a Bottle

Uses: Drink to restore up to two Hearts

Sinking Lure

Where to Get: Lanayru Province; Fishing Hole

How to Get: Catch all types of fish while lure-fishing; leave the Fishing Hole through the main door; return and bobber-fish off the northwesternmost bank

Uses: Attracts fish like pins to a magnet, making lure-fishing extremely easy; can help you catch the legendary Hylian Loach

Slingshot

Where to Get: Ordona Province; Ordon Village

How to Get: Purchase from Sera's Sundries

Uses: Fires seeds over long distances; stuns most enemies and defeats weak enemies; knocks down Hylian Hornet nests

Spinner

Where to Get: Dungeon 4: Arbiter's Grounds

How to Get: Defeat the dungeon's midboss

Uses: Lets you ride along Spinner tracks to reach otherwise-inaccessible areas; can help you cross quicksand without sinking

Superb Soup

Where to Get: Dungeon 5: Snowpeak Ruins

How to Get: Give Yeto the Ordon Goat Cheese, then scoop some of his soup into a Bottle

Uses: Drink to replenish up to eight hearts

Telma's Invoice

Where to Get: Telma's Bar, Castle Town

How to Get: Talk to Telma after handing her Renado's Letter

Uses: Allows access to Doctor Borville's Clinic

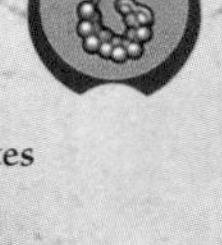

Vessel of Light

Where to Get: Varies

How to Get: Speak with the spirits that reside in each province

Uses: Stores the Tears of Light you acquire after defeating Twilit Parasites

Wallet

Where to Get: Link has this from the get-go

How to Get: N/A

Uses: Holds up to 300 Rupees

Water Bombs

Where to Get: Varies

How to Get: Purchase from shops; find within treasure chests

Uses: Destroy underwater Bomb Rocks to clear passages, etc.

Wooden Shield

Where to Get: Varies

How to Get: Purchase from shops

Uses: Allows Link to block most attacks, but it can't withstand fire-based attacks

Wooden Statue

Where to Get: Lanayru Province; Hyrule Field (South Gate)

How to Get: Defeat a large pack of Stalhounds

Uses: Helps Ilia regain some of her memory

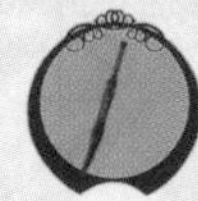

Wooden Sword

Where to Get: Ordona Province; Ordon Village

How to Get: Obtain the Slingshot, then visit Link's house

Uses: A dull wooden sword that can defeat weak enemies

Worm Bait

Where to Get: Varies

How to Get: Defeat a Bomskit, then scoop its remains into a Bottle

Uses: Bait for bobber-fishing

Yellow Chu Jelly

Where to Get: Varies

How to Get: Defeat a Yellow Chu, then scoop its remains into a Bottle; can also be found by the signposts and other features in the Fishing Hole

Uses: Fuels the Lantern, just like Lantern oil

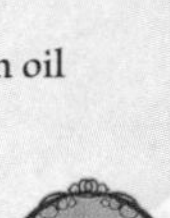

Zora Armor

Where to Get: Eldin Province; Kakariko Village (Graveyard)

How to Get: Speak with Rutela after you escort Prince Ralis to Kakariko Village

Uses: Allows Link to swim and breathe underwater, just like a Zora

Friends & Fiends

Characters

Many unique individuals reside in Hyrule and the lands beyond. Some of these beings are kind and generous; others are cowardly or cruel. Link encounters lots of new faces over the course of his adventure, and a few familiar ones as well. Here we detail each of the characters he meets.

Ashei

She is around 24–25 years old, and one of the members of the resistance. Her father was a soldier for the Hyrule royal family, but he left the kingdom due to trouble with a superior. She has learned combat skills from her father, and hearing the gossip that the Hylian soldiers are weak and powerless, she decides to visit the kingdom. Currently, she's studying about a small tribe of Yeti that inhabit Snowpeak mountain. Stronger than most men, with a slender physique, Ashei is a cavalier, but quiet. She favors strong, muscular men as companions.

Auru:

Between 60 and 70, Auru is a senior member of the resistance, a group of people seeking to restore the kingdom. Auru used to be the royal family's tutor, then he retired and kept his distance. He recognized that something unsettling was occurring, so he came back to offer his aid. He knows about the royal family, and their past history with an ultimately evil entity called Ganondorf. Though aged, Auru remains in good physical condition and is a very skillful fellow.

Barnes:

He's somewhere between 30 and 40 years old. He lives in Kakariko Village and runs a bomb shop. Barnes is quick to panic and has a blabbermouth, speaking first and thinking about it later. This sometimes annoys Renado, but Barnes is a jovial fellow and fine jester.

Beth:

One of the young girls (between 8 and 11 years old) in Link's village, she is the daughter of Hanch and Sera. Too grown-up, she's a sassy madam, and she thinks the other children in the village are babies. She has a crush on you, and she also dreams of a city life, away from all these goats.

Borville:

Borville is the town's medical doctor who has excellent credentials and is a regular at Telma's Bar. Where he falters is his bedside manner. He has stormed out of the bar when he was summoned to diagnose a problem with a Zora prince; these aren't his specialty! Some say his rudeness to all his patients is actually a defense mechanism and that he's really a coward.

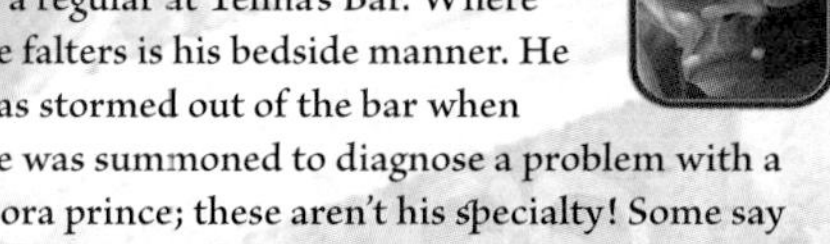

Charlo:

Charlo stands near the goat pens and collects donations and offers devotions for a charge. Some think this is some kind of scam, but to those with deep pockets, he offers a special reward....

Chudley:

About 30 years old, Chudley runs a very swanky store in Castle Town. He looks down on you as if you're simply too common to be coming into an emporium as elegant as his. If you're one of the Hyrule high rollers, though, he's a simpering fool.

Colin:

The son of Rusl and Uli, Colin is between 7 and 10 years old. He is meek, mild, and timid, but good-natured, like his parents. The other village children look down on him. He adores both you and Ilia, and he follows her wherever she goes.

Coro:

A gatekeeper living in a cottage and eking out a subsistence in the woods, Coro is content with his primitive surroundings. He's between 15 and 16, and he loves the animals and birds of the woodland. City dwellers refer to him as a "bumpkin." Coro is the younger brother of Iza and the older brother of Hena. He's a little timid, but jocular.

Darbus:

Leader of the loincloth-wearing rock creatures known as Gorons, Darbus is a towering and muscular figure. Although he has strength unimaginable to most humans, he is on friendly terms with the nearby villages and wishes to create a joint society with them. At least this was his goal until a king named Zant transformed him. Darbus is between 30 and 40 years old.

Eldin:

The embodiment of the land of Eldin, this magical spirit takes the form of a bird and resides in the spring near Kakariko Village. It seeks the light.

Epona:

Link's favorite horse, Epona has been an integral part of your adventures in the past, but she's now the favored steed for rounding up wayward goats at the pasture you tend with Fado. Epona is resilient but sometimes restless, until Ilia soothes her.

Fado:

A friend of yours and around your age (about 17), Fado works with you in the same farmhouse. Fado is an easygoing, down-to-earth type of fellow, but he has a somewhat childish side and sometimes goads you into reckless behavior, before receiving a scolding from Ilia.

Falbi:

Somewhere between 20 and 30 years old, Falbi is a former circus member and is very tall, especially compared to the short Fyer down below. He's begun a small business awarding fabulous prizes for those who can grab a Cucco by the legs and pilot it to a small platform down on Lake Hylia. Overly cheerful, he loves to gesticulate wildly and coax customers in for a ride.

Faron:

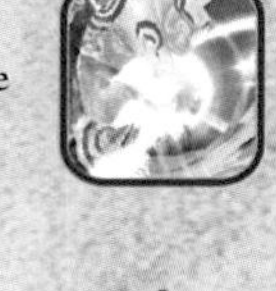

The embodiment of the land of Faron, this magical spirit takes the form of a monkey and resides in the spring near Faron Woods. It seeks the light.

Fyer:

Although he looks much older, Fyer is between 20 and 30 years old and is a former member of the circus. Short, hunched, and lazy-looking, he's recently started his own small business firing folks from a cannon, although there's limited potential on the floor of the lake! He's a great mechanic, however, and specializes in rebuilding old cannons.

Ganondorf:

A leader (and demon thief) of a band of thieves who invaded Hyrule to hold dominion over the Sacred Realm, Ganondorf was a powerful magician who used his abilities to thwart and terrify. But he was blind to danger, and was subdued, and brought to justice. However, by some divine prank, Ganondorf had been blessed with the **chosen power of the gods**, and breaking free of imprisonment, he escaped into the Twilight world. There, his vile influence grew, eventually consuming those without the courage or wisdom to see through his falsehood, just as it had in the world of Light.

Gengle:

Jovani's cat is his best friend, but Jovani's greed has turned the feline into a cat-sized rock of gold, now perched on his head. The other cats in town are worried about where Gengle's got to. Gengle is immobile, but knows he wants to rid himself and his master of all riches as soon as possible!

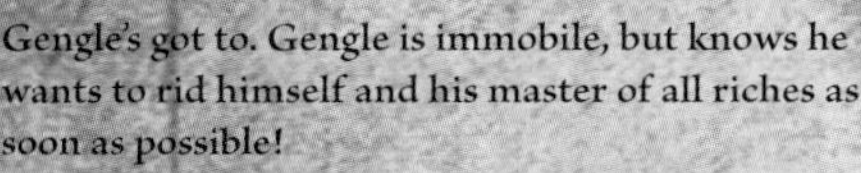

Gor Amoto:

Incredibly ancient, Gor Amoto appears to you only briefly. Shaky, and emitting steam from his head and back, he is the fourth most powerful elder in Goron society. He is easygoing and short, and he carries a device to help you on your way.

Gor Coron:

Gor Coron is an ancient Goron, and the most important elder of the four senior Gorons living within Death Mountain. He is responsible for isolating his tribe from the humans of the village below, as he doesn't wish them to know the fate of their tribal leader, Darbus. Gor Coron partakes in wrestling to judge strength, and he opens his heart to you after your victory. He is easygoing, but he speaks quickly and vigorously, commanding fear and respect from his brethren.

Gor Ebizo:

Countless years have rendered the long-haired Gor Ebizo old and frail. He is the second most powerful elder in Goron society. He is also easygoing and short, and he carries a device you need to assemble. His fondest wish, is to work with some type of young entrepreneur selling wares to adventurers. Perhaps his wish will come true some day.

Gor Liggs:

Another old Goron is the third most important one, Gor Liggs, who spends his time listening to trancelike, melodic beats in his meditation chamber. He doesn't take life too seriously and is a mellow fellow, but his attitude shows he has had fascinating life experiences. He believes in one love and in the potent healing powers of Hot Springs Water.

Gorons:

Living in the Death Mountain area are hard-as-stone creatures with incredibly thick and tough hides adorned with multiple ceremonial tattoos. They usually mine and sell trinkets down in the Kakariko Village. After the twilight descended, the Gorons have refused to deal with humans and have blocked off communication.

Great Fairy:

A magical creature born of purity and light, the Great Fairy exists to support those who cast aside fear and demonstrate their courage through deeds of selfless valor. Residing within the Gerudo Desert, the Great Fairy has fashioned a harrowing Cave of Ordeals, in which the bravery of those who would seek her aid is put to the ultimate test.

Hanch:

Beth's father and Sera's husband, the dejected-looking Hanch is between 30 and 40 years old. He runs the only commodity shop in the village. He has a meek and timid demeanor and cannot oppose his overbearing wife. He seems to be slightly unlucky.

Hena:

Hena is between 10 and 20 years old and is sister to Iza and Coro. She takes an active and healthy enjoyment in fishing, caring for fish in her tank, keeping a photographic record of the largest past catches, and renting out boats (and her advice) to those who wish to fish!

Hero's Shade:

A spirit covered in armor, the Hero's Shade lives in a visionary world and teaches the art of weapon-play to you. He talks politely and classically, like an old-fashioned master of the sword.

Hylian Soldiers:

These soldiers comprise the military force that protects the kingdom of Hyrule. They have fought bravely in the past, but once the kingdom fell to the twilight, the soldiers became fractured. You'll encounter sorrowful mourners, cowardly quitters, and the brave knights who still wait for a hero to rise.

Ilia:

An attractive young woman of about 16 years, Ilia is the charming daughter of Bo, the mayor of Ordon Village. Beloved by all who know her and fast friends with Link, Ilia is always cheerful and active. Even after falling victim to severe memory loss, Ilia's kind and gentle nature never changes.

Impaz:

About 70 years old, Impaz is an aged woman living in fear in the hidden village where Ilia was locked away. It comes to pass that Impaz played a part in freeing Ilia. Impaz is the last of her tribe, which used to live in this village. She is kind and speaks with a thin but firm voice. She thanks you profusely for saving her.

Iza:

In her 30s, Iza is the eldest of three children. Coro and Hena are her siblings. She runs a boat rental shop in the usually wild rapids of the Upper Zora's River. She is frank and open-hearted but is rather gruff.

Jaggle:

The father of Talo and Malo and Pergie's husband, he lives in your village and is in his 30s. He's a farmer, although he frequently works on his hobby: crafting items out of wood. A strong-headed but laid-back fellow, Jaggle doesn't care about the details, and neglects his duties to take a nap.

Jovani:

About 40 years old, Jovani made a deal that was shortsighted and greedy, and sold his soul to an evil spirit, which has rendered him (and his cat) immobile. He asks you to reclaim his soul from the Poes. He hopes his girlfriend will still remember him!

Kili, Hanna, and Misha:

These three 10-year-old girls are always out in a group, and they're all in love with the same boy. Whoever can muster the nerve to complete the challenges inside the tent will win a fabulous prize!

Lanayru:

The embodiment of the land of Lanayru, this magical spirit takes the form of a snake and resides in the spring near Lake Hylia. It seeks the light.

Link:

You're a young man who is around 17 years old. You are a wrangler in a quiet village tucked away in the Ordon Woods, in a far corner of the kingdom of Hyrule. Away from Castle Town, you lead a quiet life and are a constant source of amusement among the village children. You are cheerful and truthful, but with a mischievous side, and you're often admonished by Ilia, your childhood friend and daughter of the village mayor.

Louise:

A Persian cat and resident of Telma's Bar, Louise is spoiled by her owner, Telma. But she's always a pleasant kitty and could be a great ally if you could speak to her in an animal tongue.

Luda:

About 10 or 12 years old, she is the daughter of Renado of Kakariko Village. Luda is compliant, polite, and reliable, and she acts very mature for her age. She is the most grown-up of the children. Like Renado, she enjoys taking care of children such as Colin.

Madame Fanadi:

Somewhere between 40 and 50 years old (even Fanadi herself is unsure, despite her supposed powers), Fanadi sits in her mansion, waiting for patrons to cross her palm with Rupees before she recalls some mostly dubious information for them. However, she can sometimes be accurate, if you can understand the doublespeak she mutters!

Malo:

The youngest boy in your village, Malo is the child of Jaggle and Pergie, and Talo's brother. Oddly mature, especially when compared to his overly excitable brother, Malo is only around 4–6 years old. He seldom speaks, but when he does, he speaks incisively and sternly as if he were an adult. Malo is a true champion of commerce and hopes to run a successful store one day.

Malver:

Things change quite drastically at the Chudley's Emporium after Malo takes ownership and opens his Malo Mart Castle Branch. Prices plummet, folks are more cheery, and the formerly-pretentious shopkeep, Chudley, changes his entire image; he even changes his name! Now going by the handle of Malver, Malo Mart Castle Branch's #1 salesperson just lives to see his customers smile.

Mayor Bo:

A portly but muscular fellow in his mid 40s, Bo is the mayor of this hamlet and the father of Ilia. He has personally chosen you as an envoy to send into the kingdom to befriend the neighboring villages and countries. He cherishes you as if you were his own son. Although appearing organized, he's a little scatterbrained, which can cause arguments with Ilia.

Midna:

A genie-like pixie with a childish proportion, only four feet high. She is arrogant and scornful to you and seems to be seething with anger at an injustice inflicted upon her by evil and unknown forces. She is somehow linked to the strange twilight that has descended upon the land. What are Midna's real secrets? Who is she really?

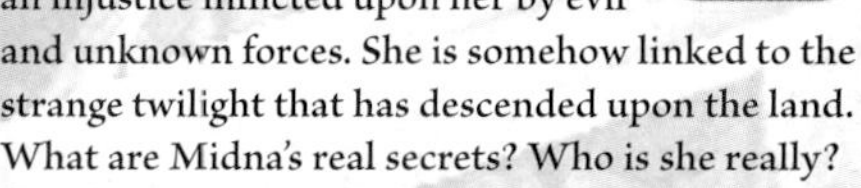

Oocca:

You'd swear Ooccoo must be one-of-a-kind—you may even pray it—but you'd be wrong! Ooccoo is just one of an entire race of beings called Oocca, who live high above the clouds of Hyrule, in the spectacular City in the Sky. The Oocca have fallen under hard times ever since Zant's evil goons took over their city. Work with them and see what you can do to set things right.

Ooccoo:

Although it's difficult to tell, Ooccoo seems around 40 years old. She lived in a great city in the sky, but she fell to Hyrule after strange events befell her home. She is hoping to find something she lost. Although she's short, with baleful eyes, she's friendly and has a great gift for you.

Ooccoo Jr.:

The bodiless offspring of Ooccoo, Ooccoo Jr. is a fledgling Oocca with mysterious magical abilities. When Link needs to quickly exit a dungeon, all he needs to do is speak with Ooccoo; Ooccoo Jr. then appears and whisks Link away so the brave lad can restock his items and equipment.

Ordona:

The embodiment of the land of Ordona, this magical spirit takes the form of a goat and resides in the spring near Ordon Village. It seeks the light.

Pergie:

The mother of Talo and Malo, Pergie is married to Jaggle and is in her 30s. Due to her slothful husband, she's always working and constantly struggling to deal with her mischievous sons. But, although she's tough, she loves and supports her brood.

Plumm:

A female myna bird that works hard at her balloon-popping attraction, which she invites only those in wolf form to see. Plumm appears at two spots in Lake Hylia, ready to take your money in exchange for a shot at this minigame. She's great friends with Trill.

Postman:

Onward to mail! Hyrule's one and only Postman may seem like an odd fellow at first, but no one could be more dedicated to bringing folks their letters in a timely fashion. Lacking any means of transportation, the Postman runs about Hyrule Field on foot, carrying out his solemn duty; come rain, come sleet, or snow. Later in the adventure, Link spots the Postman catching breaks in a variety of unusual places, including Telma's bar and the Elde Inn.

Prince Ralis:

About 10 years old, this boy is part of the Zora tribe and was on a mission to deliver a message from the Zoras' queen (his mother) to Princess Zelda when dark forces waylaid him. Ilia rescued him. He has received a fine upbringing and speaks politely. He is reliable but worries he won't be able to fulfill his eventual destiny as the leader of the Zora tribe.

Princess Agitha:

Around 10 years old, Agitha is a princess and lives alone in a tiny castle in town. She is an avid butterfly collector. She dresses in cutesy gothic fashions and firmly believes she is living in a fantasy world, where she's the queen of the insects. She giggles, is excitable, and loves presents, especially if they're creepy and crawly!

Princess Zelda:

Princess Zelda is about 20 years old, and is the queen-in-waiting of Hyrule. Her kingdom was taken over by a strange man clad in shadow armor, who in exchange for the lives of her people, banished her to this castle. Zelda speaks with an intellectual and serene confidence, even in this darkest hour. She is strong and brave, and she would give up her life to bring peace to her kingdom. Like you, she has a strange power, known as the Triforce, that only a chosen one can achieve.

Purlo:

About 20 years old, Purlo builds temporary, circus-style tents in Castle Town and attracts customers to his games. He speaks in a pretentious and slightly odd tone. Although he's not obvious about it, his game is so difficult that he's sure no one can claim the large money prize he offers.

Renado:

Somewhere between 30 and 40 years old, Renado is the village shaman, or priest. He is Luda's father. He hides the children from the darkness inside his sanctuary. He is always wise, calm, and collected. He possesses experience and grace, treating everyone evenly. He talks politely to everyone, even children and you. He is a kind-hearted soul.

Rusl:

A resident of Ordon Village, where you also reside, Rusl is between 20 and 30 years old. He is pregnant Uli's husband, and Colin's father. Rusl has a frank personality, but he's an honorable soul and many people think of him as the village leader. He is the only swordsman around. He regards you as his younger brother.

Rutela:

When alive, she was between 20 and 30 years old. She and her king were executed by the mad king of shadows, named Zant, and her tribe was frozen in a deep, difficult-to-reach pool in the northern province that shares the tribe's name. She is ethereal and elegant, and seeks help for her son.

Sages:

Approximately 50 years old, but with a strange ethereal power masking their true age, there are seven sages of ancient times who succeeded in capturing the mad warrior magician known as Ganondorf. Executing him with a ceremonial blade, they attempt to keep the world of Hyrule at peace. They don't possess physical bodies, and have graceful, poetic movements.

Sera:

The mother of Beth and wife of Hanch, Sera is a rotund and jolly lady of 30-something years old. However, she can be unpleasant and haughty to her husband, Hanch. She loves her cat very much; in fact, many in the village say she treats her cat better than her husband.

Shad:

Between 18 and 20 years old, Shad is another member of the resistance. He's a handsome city boy, with glasses. When Shad was a child, his father (who was a butler with the royal family) told him a tale about a city floating in the sky. Since this time, Shad has studied about this city, and he realizes that a secret pertaining to its origin is somewhere under the graveyard in Kakariko Village. With the current terrors Hyrule faces, he believes the airborne people (the first Hylians to roam the land) could help the cause.

Soal:

A small boy who makes a little cash by polishing shoes in the Castle Town streets. He's making a good living since the celebrated store owner Chudley came to town with his exclusive wares and ludicrous prices!

Talo:

He is between 8 and 11 years old, and shares similar features with his mother and father, Jaggle and Pergie. He's Malo's elder brother. Talo is a scamp who longs for a chance to receive sword-play instructions from you. Immature, even at this age, Talo also looks down on the shy Colin.

Telma:

Between 30 and 40 years old, Telma runs a bar in Castle Town. She is bossy but obliging. With an unyielding spirit, Telma is actually the leader of a resistance force, a group that wants to restore the kingdom. She is hoping to find a worthy man to recruit to help her forces.

Trill:

This intelligent myna bird, owned by Coro, watches over the unattended shop in the Faron Woods. Trill is friends with Plumm, another myna bird who lives somewhere near the great lake Hylia.

Twilis:

A unique race of beings who reside within the Twilight world, the Twilis have been cursed by the wicked king of shadows, Zant. After succeeding in his treacherous coup on Princess Midna—the rightful ruler of the Twilight domain—Zant subjugated the Twilis, forcing the poor shadowlings to do his bidding. But because the worlds of Twilight and Light are so closely connected, Link may yet find a way to save these unfortunate souls.

Uli:

The wife of Rusl and mother of Colin, Uli is in her 20s and heavily pregnant with the family's second child. She is relaxed, affable, and beautiful, and she has an air of generosity and caring.

Yeta:

Yeta is about 30 years old in Yeti years, and is the wife of Yeto. They both live in an old house, surrounded by snow. She recently received a present from her husband; a piece of an ornate mirror; and ever since she's felt strange. Sometimes angry, sometimes tired, she isn't her old self. She spends her time resting near the fire, and eating comfort food prepared by Yeto.

Yeto:

About 40 years old, Yeto is a male yeti, with a massive frame. He is very cheerful and happy, and husband to Yeta. They both live in and old mansion on a remote and snowy clifftop. Yeto was out hiking one day, and found a shard of mirror. He didn't know it was cursed, and gave it to Yeta, who has been feeling ill ever since. When you meet Yeto, he's carrying a fish home, and hoping his cooking will improve Yeta's health.

Zant:

The false leader of the Twilight world and driving force behind its incursion into the world of Light, Zant is the self-proclaimed king of shadows who cursed Princess Midna and cast her out of her own realm. When Midna's father—the true Twilit king—chose not to name Zant as his successor, the evil shadowling became maddened by an uncontrollable rage. He cried out in anguish to the gods, begging that his vengeance be granted. His plea was heard by a god of unholy power, who offered Zant the chance to fulfill his lust for supremacy.

The Zoras:

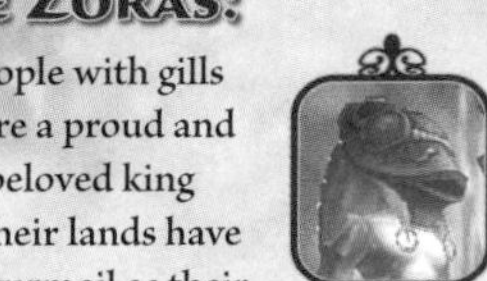

An aquatic tribe of people with gills and lungs, the Zoras are a proud and ancient race, led by a beloved king and queen. Recently their lands have become embroiled in turmoil as their water supply has dwindled. Now full of melancholy, they wish for happier times.

Enemies

Link has plenty of friends in Hyrule, but there are also scores of fiends who wish him harm. Studying the strengths and weaknesses of every villainous creature is vital to survival in Link's world. Here you'll find the quick breakdown of the foes you'll face. The walkthrough will have even more details on how to best these creatures and keep Link intact.

Aeralfos

Threat Meter

- Winged, flying lizard-beast armed with a sword and shield
- Z-target when airborne, wait for it to raise its shield, then fire the Clawshot to latch onto its shield and ground it
- Punish Aeralfos with fast attack combos once it's grounded
- Don't Clawshot its shield while it's grounded or you're pulled toward it and exposed to counterattacks

Encountered In: Dungeon 7: City in the Sky

Armos

Threat Meter

- The Armos is impervious to frontal attacks
- Roll around to its weak spot, then execute an attack
- When the Armos begins to glow, get away quickly because it is about to explode
- Alternately, run behind it without targeting and use Hidden Skill #5 to quickly dispatch the Armos

Encountered In: Dungeon 6: Temple of Time

Baba Serpent

Threat Meter

- The Baba Serpent's head is invincible
- Wait for the creature to rise up and expose its neck, then slice it or fire at it with a ranged weapon
- After you separate the Baba Serpent's head, shoot it again or finish it with sword swipes
- If you're caught in its mouth, you can escape with a spin

Encountered In: Dungeon 1: Forest Temple

Baby Gohma

Threat Meter

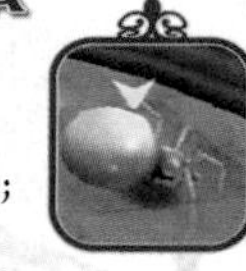

- Baby Gohmas are not aggressive; in fact, they run directly away from you
- Bomb Arrows or the Clawshot will dispatch them
- Slashing with the sword while running forward also proves effective

Encountered In: Dungeon 6: Temple of Time

Bari

Threat Meter

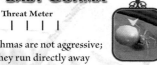

- The Bari is impervious to most attacks
- The Clawshot is the most effective; target the creature and fire for interesting results

Encountered In: Dungeon 3: Lakebed Temple

Beamos

Threat Meter

- The Beamos shoots a jet of fire from its "eye" that will damage and stagger you
- On your first encounter, the Beamos are impervious; use your shield to block their attacks and get by them
- Once you receive the Hero's Bow, you can target the eye and defeat the Beamos with a shot

Encountered In: Dungeon 2: Goron Mines

Beamos (White)

Threat Meter

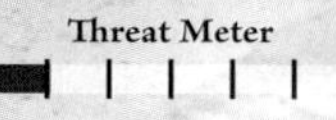

- The pink laser the Beamos fires will drain your energy
- Step back out of the laser's range and fire a regular arrow
- You cannot harm the White Beamos until it activates

Encountered In: Dungeon 6: Temple of Time

Big Baba

Threat Meter

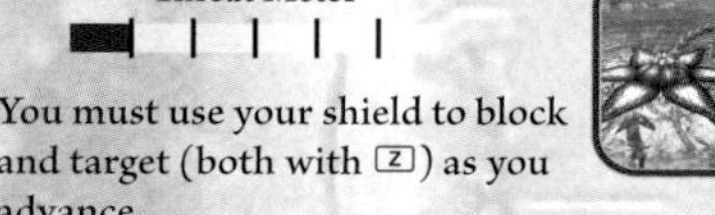

- You must use your shield to block and target (both with Z) as you advance
- Sidestep when the Big Baba's head strikes at you, then spin or slice it
- When the head is destroyed, throw a Bombling (target with Z) to blow up the creature

Encountered In: Dungeon 1: Forest Temple

Bokoblin

Threat Meter

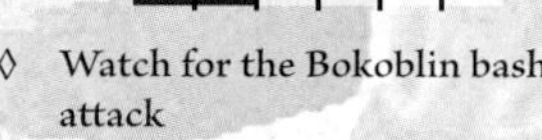

- Watch for the Bokoblin bash attack
- Target a Bokoblin and use a four-hit combo
- If several attack, use your spin move

Encountered In: Ordona and Faron Provinces

Bombfish

Threat Meter

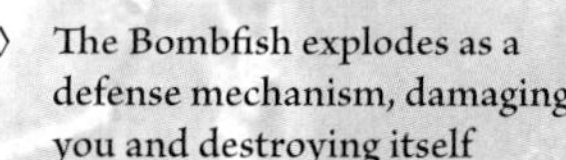

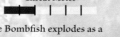

- The Bombfish explodes as a defense mechanism, damaging you and destroying itself
- Attack from dry land, or underwater with your Iron Boots on, and Z-target with your Clawshot
- If you lure the fish to you, it can explode nearby features

Encountered In: Dungeon 3: Lakebed Temple

Bombling

Threat Meter

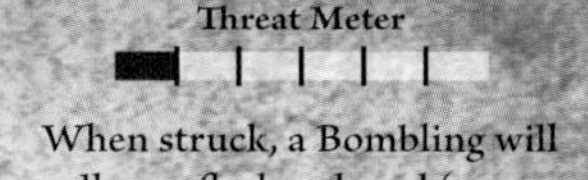

- When struck, a Bombling will collapse, flash red, and (seven seconds later) explode
- Use Bomblings to clear obstacles or defeat tough enemies
- They pose no threat if you stay away from them

Encountered In: Dungeon 1: Forest Temple

Bomskit

Threat Meter

- Bomskits pose no threat if left alone, though they will drop bombs if chased
- Use a projectile weapon to dispatch a Bomskit
- When defeated, the Bomskit's remains can be scooped to get Worm Bait for fishing

Encountered In: Hyrule Field

Bubble, Fire Bubble, Ice Bubble

Threat Meter

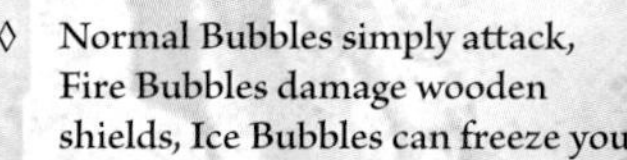

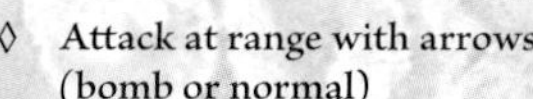

- Normal Bubbles simply attack, Fire Bubbles damage wooden shields, Ice Bubbles can freeze you
- Attack at range with arrows (bomb or normal)
- Avoid finishing moves, as the Bubbles usually dodge, leaving you stuck for a moment and vulnerable

Encountered In: Hyrule

Bulblin Infantry

Threat Meter

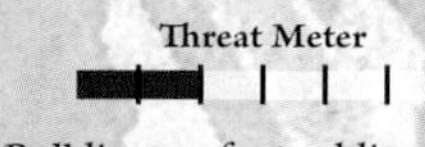

- Bulblins are foot soldiers that carry primitive clubs
- Use your shield and Z-target to push back the initial attack, then counter with three regular slices, comboed into a spin to finish them off
- Multiple Bulblins can be simultaneously defeated with this technique
- You can also knock a Bulblin back with your shield, leaping and slicing, then (with the Bulblin lying on its back) finish it with your first Hidden Skill

Encountered In: Dungeon 2: Goron Mines

Bulblin Riders

Threat Meter

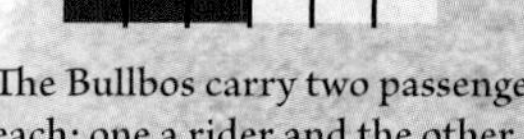

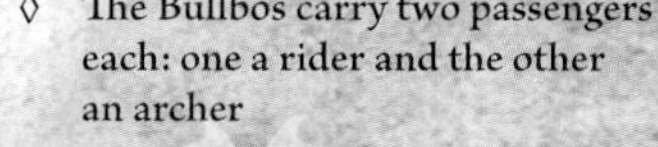

- The Bullbos carry two passengers each: one a rider and the other an archer
- Use your spurs to catch up, draw your sword, then hack away to slice rider and archer in one swipe
- Charging in, using the spin attack, and charging away is the other option

Encountered In: Kakariko Village

Bulblin Warrior

Threat Meter

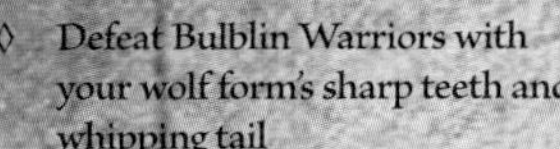

◊ Defeat Bulblin Warriors with your wolf form's sharp teeth and whipping tail
◊ Target one and leap for a bite, follow up with a spin attack to strike more than one
◊ When a Bulblin's knocked down, pounce on it to finish it off

Encountered In: Ordona and Faron Provinces

Chilfos

Threat Meter

◊ A difficult enemy, the Chilfos uses a thrown spear that knocks you down and leaves you vulnerable
◊ From long range, fire two Bomb Arrows in rapid succession
◊ At close range, slice rapidly until the spear breaks, then spin attack, and use more slashes to defeat the creature

Encountered In: Snowpeak Mountain

Chu

Threat Meter

◊ Chus come in various colors, denoting the healing properties their remains have
◊ Sword strikes work well against the creatures
◊ Scoop Chu remains into a bottle for later use

Encountered In: Lanayru Province

Chu Worm

Threat Meter

◊ The worm's Chu Jelly bubble is impervious to your sword strikes, but not Bomb Arrows
◊ Use Z-target and launch a Bomb Arrow, then use sword swipes to finish it
◊ The Clawshot also proves effective against the Chu Worm

Encountered In: Dungeon 3: Lakebed Temple

Darknut

Threat Meter

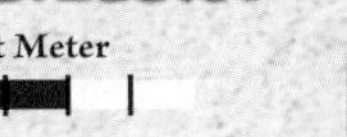

◊ Slow-moving, heavily armored knight with powerful attacks
◊ Z-target and backflip to dodge its attacks, then quickly follow up with a jump attack (3), and repeat
◊ After taking heavy damage, Darknut sheds its armor, becoming more agile and dangerous
◊ Use the back slice maneuver to stagger an unarmored Darknut, then quickly follow up with fast attack combos
◊ In groups, try to defeat each Darknut in turn

Encountered In: Dungeon 6: Temple of Time

Deku Baba

Threat Meter

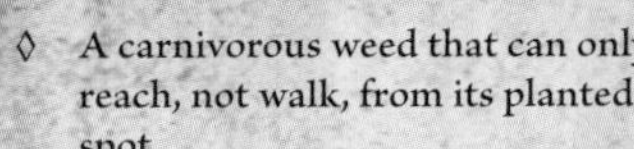

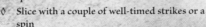

◊ A carnivorous weed that can only reach, not walk, from its planted spot
◊ Slice with a couple of well-timed strikes or a spin
◊ Find Deku nuts, for your Slingshot, in the Deku Baba's head

Encountered In: Ordona and Faron Provinces

Deku Like

Threat Meter

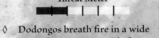

◊ The Deku Like can be harmed only if it swallows something explosive
◊ Find a Bombling to drop into the Deku Like's mouth from above

Encountered In: Dungeon 1: Forest Temple

Dodongo

Threat Meter

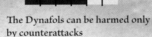

◊ Dodongos breath fire in a wide arc and are impenetrable from the front
◊ To defeat Dodongos with your sword, circle around to target the tail
◊ Three slices at the tail finish off this scaly threat
◊ A spin attack works well at hitting multiple Dodongo tails

Encountered In: Dungeon 2: Goron Mines

Dynafols

Threat Meter

◊ The Dynafols can be harmed only by counterattacks
◊ Wait for the monster to make a swing, block it, and immediately retaliate with a spin attack or helm splitter
◊ Back striking the creature's tail also works
◊ It takes three or four successful attacks to defeat a Dynafols

Encountered In: Dungeon 6: Temple of Time

Fire Keese

Threat Meter

◊ Deal with Fire Keeses the same way as the other Keeses
◊ Use the Z-target and slice, or shoot with a ranged weapon

Encountered In: Dungeon 2: Goron Mines

Fire Toadpoli

Threat Meter

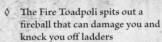

◊ The Fire Toadpoli spits out a fireball that can damage you and knock you off ladders
◊ Raise your shield and Z target the Fire Toadpoli, when it spits the fireball, knock the fireball back with your shield (move your Nunchuk forward)
◊ Time it early for best results; one fireball strike will defeat the beast

Encountered In: Dungeon 2: Goron Mines

Freezard

Threat Meter

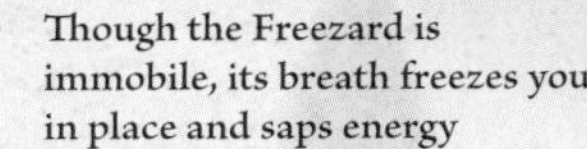

◊ Though the Freezard is immobile, its breath freezes you in place and saps energy

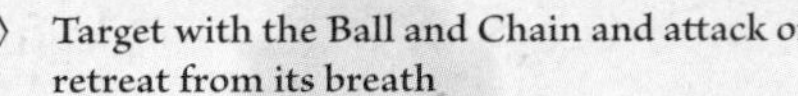

◊ Target with the Ball and Chain and attack or retreat from its breath
◊ Beware other enemies in the same area, because if you are frozen, they'll take advantage of your vulnerability

Encountered In: Snowpeak Mountain

Ghoul Rat

Threat Meter

◊ The Ghoul Rats don't actually do damage
◊ The Ghoul Rats cling and slow you down, making you vulnerable to other monsters
◊ Transform into a wolf, turn your sense view on, and spin attack to shake them off, then bite

Encountered In: Dungeon 4: Arbiter's Ground

Guay

Threat Meter

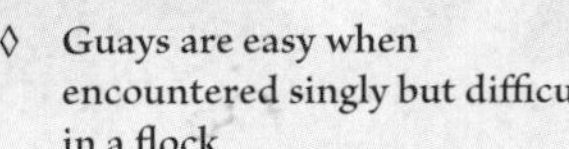

◊ Guays are easy when encountered singly but difficult in a flock

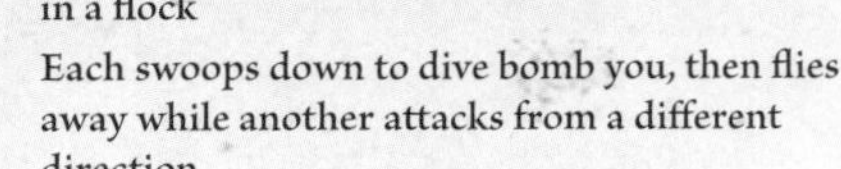

◊ Each swoops down to dive bomb you, then flies away while another attacks from a different direction
◊ Block with your shield, then slay the Guay as it flies away
◊ After you gain the **Hero's Bow** or **Clawshot**, auto-target each bird and fire

Encountered In: Kakariko Village

Helmasaur

Threat Meter

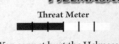

◊ You cannot hurt the Helmasaur by hitting it from the front or sides

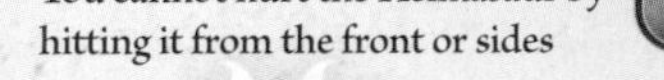

◊ It can push you back even if you're blocking
◊ Target the Helmasaur, maneuver to face its rear, then strike (with spin attack, or Hidden Skill #3)
◊ The **Clawshot** is very effective against the Helmasaur

Encountered In: Dungeon 3: Lakebed Temple

Helmasaurus

Threat Meter

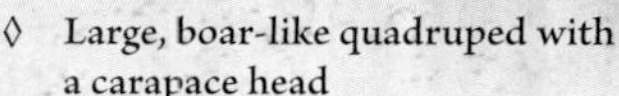

◊ Large, boar-like quadruped with a carapace head

◊ Charges forward and attacks by ramming into you

◊ Ⓩ-target and jump to one side to avoid charge attack, then attack the Helmasaurus's vulnerable backside

Encountered In: Dungeon 7: City in the Sky

Hylian Hornet

Threat Meter

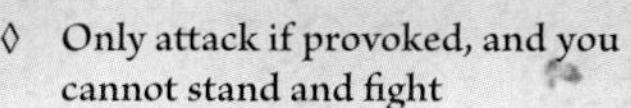

◊ Only attack if provoked, and you cannot stand and fight

◊ Run away from them and they give up after five seconds

◊ Or you can dive into water to avoid them

Encountered In: Ordona and Faron Provinces

Ice Keese

Threat Meter

◊ Small winged enemy

◊ Similar to normal Keese, but this version emanates a frosty aura

◊ Easily defeated with just about any form of attack

Encountered In: Peak Province; Snowpeak

Imp Poe

Threat Meter

◊ The Imp Poe is invisible to your human form; you must use sense view to see them

◊ The Imp Poes attack with a sickle weapon

◊ Pounce on the Imp Poes to defeat them and reveal the Poe Soul

Encountered In: Lanayru Province

Kargarok

Threat Meter

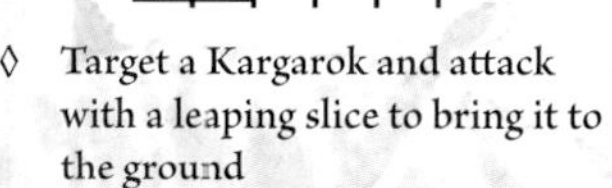

◊ Target a Kargarok and attack with a leaping slice to bring it to the ground

◊ Finish it with a strike

◊ Beware: If you miss the finishing blow, your sword gets stuck, allowing the Kargarok a free attack

Encountered In: Hyrule Field

Keese

Threat Meter

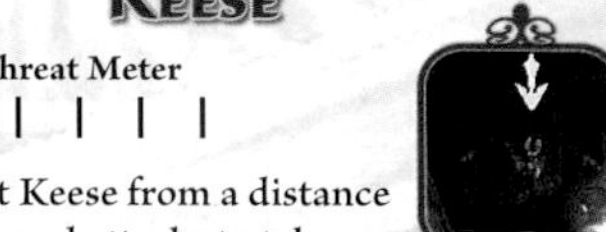

◊ Try to spot Keese from a distance and use ranged attacks to take them down

◊ If a Keese attacks, target with Ⓩ, then swipe or jump and swipe

◊ Auto-target incoming Keese with ranged weapon (can be tricky)

Encountered In: Ordona and Faron Provinces

Leever

Threat Meter

◊ A ring of Leevers rotate and move around you, then converge and strike

◊ Stop, stand still, and as the Leevers surround and come in for the strike, execute a spin attack and defeat them all

◊ Projectiles (or running away) are also effective

Encountered In: Hyrule Field

Lizalfos ("Axe-tail")

Threat Meter

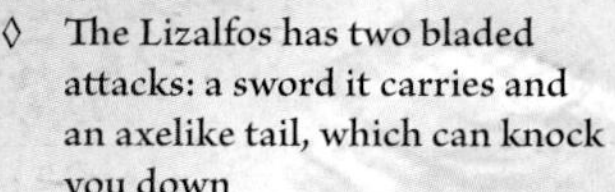

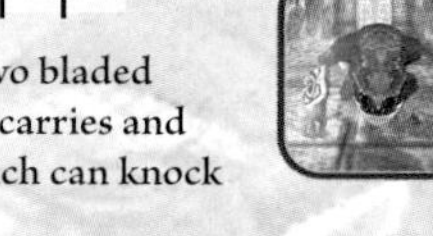

◊ The Lizalfos has two bladed attacks: a sword it carries and an axelike tail, which can knock you down

◊ The Lizalfos is skilled in defense, so multiple simple sword strikes are required to down it

◊ It's more effective to shoot Bomb Arrows or Ⓩ-target the Lizalfos, ram it with your shield, then roll around with Ⓐ and slice its back

Encountered In: Dungeon 3: Lakebed Temple

Lizalfos ("Skull-face")

Threat Meter

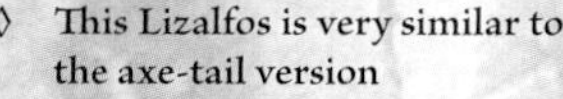

◊ This Lizalfos is very similar to the axe-tail version

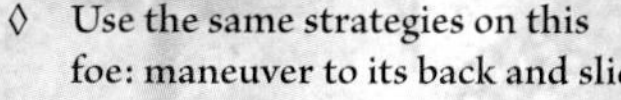

◊ Use the same strategies on this foe: maneuver to its back and slice

Encountered In: Dungeon 3: Lakebed Temple

Mini Freezard

Threat Meter

◊ If they strike you, Mini Freezards encase you in ice, leaving you vulnerable

◊ Strike with you sword, block, and then strike a second time to defeat them

◊ If facing a group of Mini Freezards, concentrate on one at a time

◊ The Ball and Chain weapon is the most effective, though you don't have it during your first Mini Freezard encounter

Encountered In: Snowpeak Mountain

Moldorm

Threat Meter

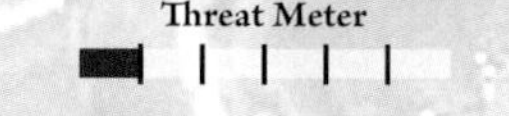

◊ Moldorms burrow and pop out to take quick attacks

◊ Sword attacks alone are usually futile

◊ Use the Clawshot to pull them from the ground and then dispatch them with your sword

Encountered In: Hyrule

Poison Mite

Threat Meter

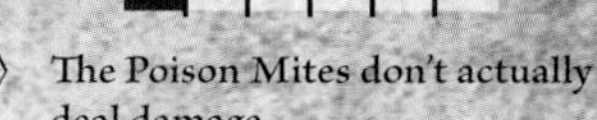

◊ The Poison Mites don't actually deal damage

◊ The mites slow you down in sinking sand, threatening to pull you down

◊ Do not fight until you reach solid ground, or shine your Lantern to scare them off

Encountered In: Dungeon 4: Arbiter's Ground

Puppet

Threat Meter

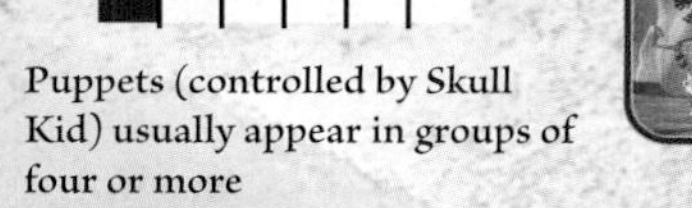

◊ Puppets (controlled by Skull Kid) usually appear in groups of four or more

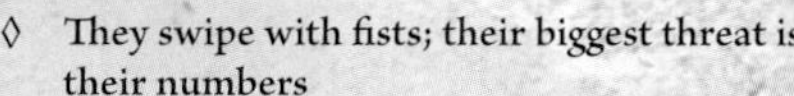

◊ They swipe with fists; their biggest threat is their numbers

◊ A spin attack takes out Puppets with one go

Pygmy Skulltula

Threat Meter

◊ A mid-sized Skulltula that hangs from a thin web

◊ Drops down from above just as you're about to jump across a small gap; harms you if you leap into it

◊ Slowly move forward until it descends, then defeat it with the Slingshot from a safe distance

Encountered In: Dungeon 1: Forest Temple

Encountered In: Faron Woods

Rat

Threat Meter

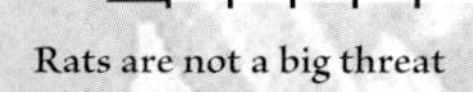

◊ Rats are not a big threat

◊ In the dark, listen for their squeaking, and use Ⓩ to target them

◊ Slice or jump in and slice

Encountered In: Ordona and Faron Provinces

Redead

Threat Meter

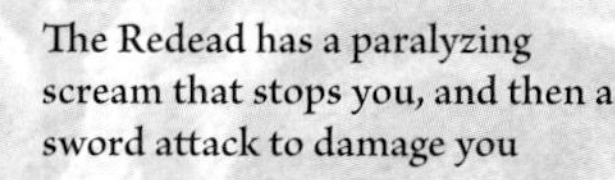

◊ The Redead has a paralyzing scream that stops you, and then a sword attack to damage you

◊ Use Bomb Arrows from range

◊ Alternately use your wolf form and bite the Redead

Encountered In: Dungeon 4: Arbiter's Ground

Shell Blade

Threat Meter

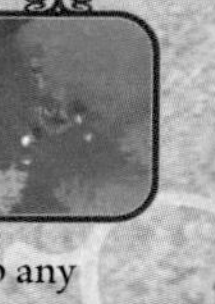

◊ The Shell Blade is impervious to vertical slashing moves

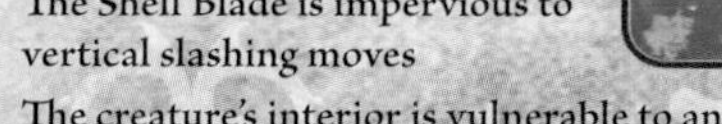

◊ The creature's interior is vulnerable to any horizontal slice

◊ The spin attack is excellent against the Shell Blade

Encountered In: Dungeon 3: Lakebed Temple

Skullfish

Threat Meter

- There are many ways to defeat Skullfish, such as the Gale Boomerang, Clawshot, or dropped bombs when you're on dry land
- If in the water, use the Iron Boots and sword or simply swim away from them
- Catching a Skullfish with the Fishing Rod rewards you with a Heart but you must throw the Skullfish back

Encountered In: Dungeon 3: Lakebed Temple

Skulltula

Threat Meter

- The Skulltula cannot be defeated head on
- Use Ⓩ to block the leg attacks, move to either side, then strike with a combo of slashes
- When the beast collapses, finish it with a **leaping strike** and press Ⓐ when prompted to complete combat

Encountered In: Dungeon 1: Forest Temple

Stalfos

Threat Meter

- The Stalfos is an undead monster invincible to most attacks
- Use Bomb Arrows or other explosive
- Repeat as necessary

Encountered In: Dungeon 4: Arbiter's Ground

Stalhound

Threat Meter

- These undead beasts dig up from the ground below, attack, then burrow down back, only to reappear from the same place again
- Two spin attacks or a couple of leaping strikes will defeat them
- Stalhounds tend to drop Rupees, too

Encountered In: Hyrule Field

Stalkin

Threat Meter

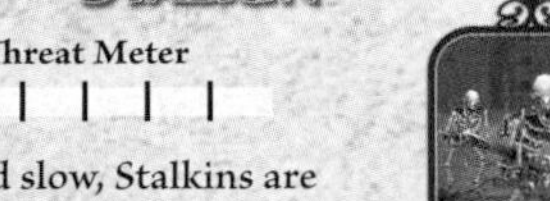

- Brittle and slow, Stalkins are not particularly frightening or dangerous
- They can attack in large numbers
- A single spin attack will defeat all of them in a group

Encountered In: Dungeon 4: Arbiter's Ground

Staltroop

Threat Meter

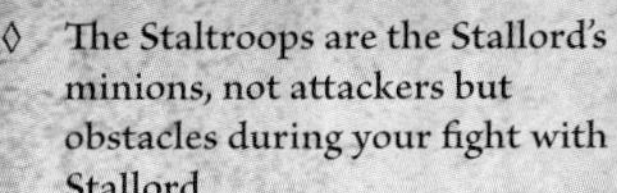

- The Staltroops are the Stallord's minions, not attackers but obstacles during your fight with Stallord
- Avoid the Staltroops and don't stop moving when on the sand

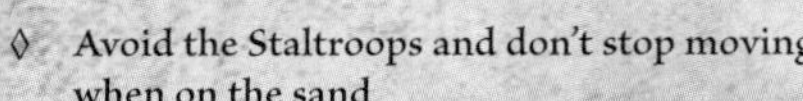

- Spinning into them with the spinner will defeat them

Encountered In: Dungeon 4: Arbiter's Ground

Tektite (Red and Blue)

Threat Meter

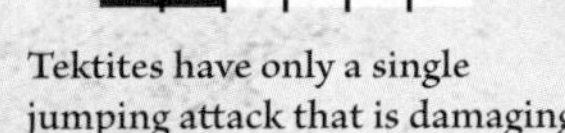

- Tektites have only a single jumping attack that is damaging
- Let the Tektites congregate around you
- When the first one jumps, execute the spin attack as it descends to finish all of them

Encountered In: Dungeon 2: Goron Mines

Tile Worm

Threat Meter

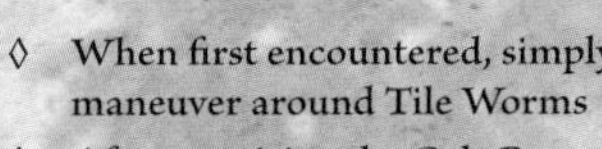

- When first encountered, simply maneuver around Tile Worms
- After acquiring the Gale Boomerang, target the tile the Tile Worm is under, and attack
- Once the Tile Worm is exposed, finish it with regular attacks

Encountered In: Dungeon 1: Forest Temple

Toado

Threat Meter

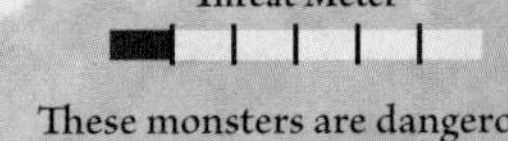

- These monsters are dangerous only in large numbers
- Defeat Toadoes with a single spin attack
- Try to keep your back to a wall to avoid being surrounded, use spin attacks and then slashes to defeat groups

Encountered In: Dungeon 3: Lakebed Temple

Torch Slug

Threat Meter

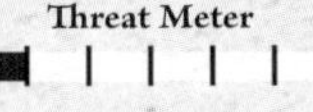

- Torch Slugs are harmless until you near them
- Combat them with a quick sword attack (not a leaping attack, as they can repel you)
- They're also found on cave ceilings, dropping to startle you, so use a ranged weapon from afar

Encountered In: Dungeon 2: Goron Mines

Twilit Baba

Threat Meter

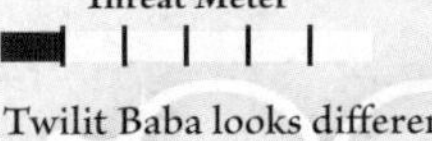

- The Twilit Baba looks different from the Deku Baba but behaves similarly
- It cannot attack beyond the length of its reach
- In wolf form, bite twice or use a spin attack

Encountered In: Ordona and Faron Provinces

Twilit Bulblin

Threat Meter

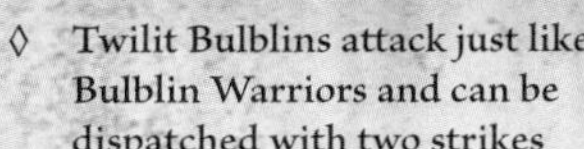

- Twilit Bulblins attack just like Bulblin Warriors and can be dispatched with two strikes
- If you knock them onto their backs you must wait because the wolf doesn't have a finishing move
- Defeat Twilit Bulblins with a couple of bites, spins, or Midna's energy crackle

Encountered In: Faron Woods

Twilit Bulblin Archer

Threat Meter

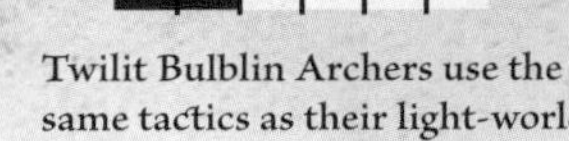

- Twilit Bulblin Archers use the same tactics as their light-world counterparts
- They can make life difficult for a wolf, so make these enemies a priority
- Charge with your speed boost, avoid running directly at them, jump and bite, wait for them to rise, and bite again

Encountered In: Lanayru Province

Twilit Kargarok

Threat Meter

- This creature's attack deals half a Heart's worth of damage
- Wait for it to dive, while keeping a constant lock-on, and then leap and bite the bird
- It takes two strikes to defeat a Twilit Kargarok

Encountered In: Castle Hyrule

Twilit Keese

Threat Meter

- Similar to regular Keeses, but longer
- One strike will slay a Twilit Keese
- Spin attacks also work if the Keeses are flying near you

Encountered In: Castle Hyrule

Twilit Messenger

Threat Meter

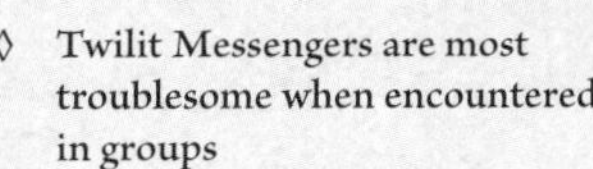

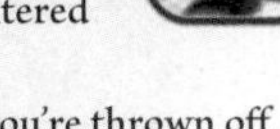

- Twilit Messengers are most troublesome when encountered in groups
- Target one and bite until you're thrown off
- Then finish it off with a spin attack

Encountered In: Ordona and Faron Provinces, Lake Hylia

Twilit Parasite

Threat Meter

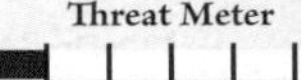

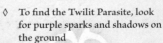

- To find the Twilit Parasite, look for purple sparks and shadows on the ground
- Sixteen of them roam the land; they can hide inside walls, floors, the ground, or out of reach

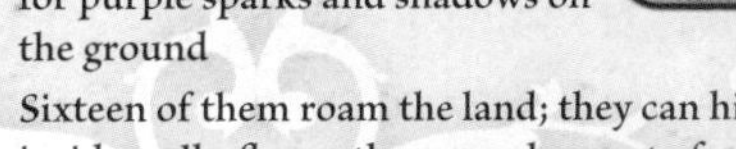

- Use Ⓩ to target these foes then pounce with one attack

Encountered In: Ordona and Faron Provinces

Twilit Vermin

Threat Meter

- The Twilit Vermin attack mercilessly
- It is very weak, so a single strike will defeat a Twilit Vermin
- However, while swimming, you can't attack them, but they can attack you, so seek dry land

Encountered In: Castle Hyrule

Walltula

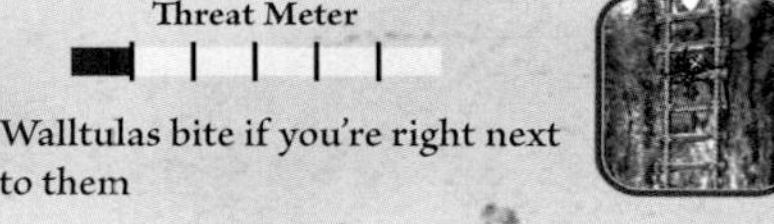

Threat Meter

- Walltulas bite if you're right next to them
- Use your Slingshot from range
- Only one hit defeats them

Encountered In: Ordona and Faron Provinces

Water Toadpoli

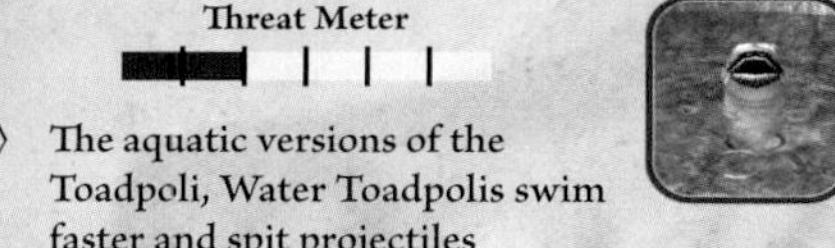

Threat Meter

- The aquatic versions of the Toadpoli, Water Toadpolis swim faster and spit projectiles
- Shield block and wait to bounce back the spitball
- You can also shoot an arrow, which is faster

Encountered In: Dungeon 2: Goron Mines

White Wolfos

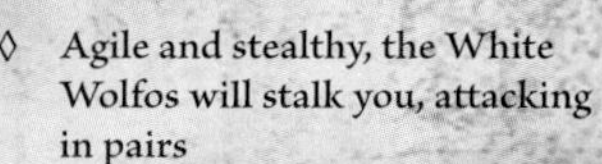

Threat Meter

- Agile and stealthy, the White Wolfos will stalk you, attacking in pairs
- Shield block the first one and strike the second with a well-timed blow
- You can also ignore them, run by them quickly, or go after them in wolf form

Encountered In: Snowpeak Mountain

Young Gohma

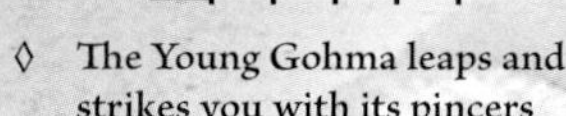

Threat Meter

- The Young Gohma leaps and strikes you with its pincers
- Two sweeping sword strikes will defeat this foe

Encountered In: Dungeon 6: Temple of Time

Zant Mask

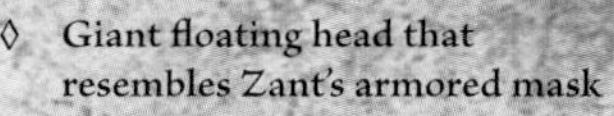

Threat Meter

- Giant floating head that resembles Zant's armored mask
- Immobile but can teleport about
- Attacks after teleporting by firing purple orbs, which can be deflected via the shield attack maneuver
- When they appear, simply attack them with relentless combos

Encountered In: Dungeon 8: Palace of Twilight

Zant's Hand

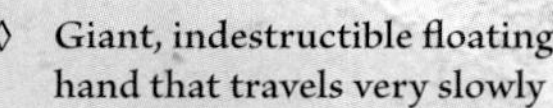

Threat Meter

- Giant, indestructible floating hand that travels very slowly
- Doesn't attack you directly, but chases after the Sol Orbs you take from it
- When positioned directly above the Sol Orb, it slams downward to grab it, harming you if you're caught
- If it grabs the Sol Orb, use the Clawshot to steal it back

Encountered In: Dungeon 8: Palace of Twilight

Bosses

The Big Battles

Here we give you an overview of the meanest and most difficult enemies you'll come across: the bosses. In this section you'll get your first look at them, a quick overview of what they're about, and where you'll encounter them. Find the detailed, nuts-and-bolts strategy for dealing with these bruisers in the walkthrough. There we'll provide you with rock-solid tactics for defeating these aggressive beasts.

Ook

Threat Meter

Ook is a crazy baboon who's mad for dancing and has a weapon you need. There's a trick to defeating him that brings him down from on high and lands you the Gale Boomerang, a very useful tool for your adventures. Knock into Ook's perch and you'll soon get him on your level.

Encountered In: Dungeon 1: The Forest

Twilit Parasite Diababa

Threat Meter

This deadly creature comes in two forms, and neither is happy to see you. It takes some coordination between you and an earlier enemy to take down this out-of-control weed, but when it's down, it divulges a Heart Container and a piece of Fused Shadow for your troubles.

Encountered In: The Forest Temple

King Bulblin

Threat Meter

King Bulblin is a thorn in your side throughout the game. You encounter him time and again in various guises and for each fight he has some new trick. It's fitting for you to keep jousting with this evil beast as he was the one who first broke the calm pattern of your once-peaceful life!

First ***Encountered In:*** Ordona Province

Dangoro

Threat Meter

The way past Dangoro is through his stomach. It'll take a lot of skills when you face off with him. You'll have to use sword, sumo, and shoes to best this hulking brute—and not necessarily in that order. It's a chance to show off what you've learned in the various arts of battle.

Encountered In: Dungeon 2: Goron Mines

Twilit Igniter: Fyrus

Threat Meter

Fyrus is a huge beast whose body is a raging inferno. His blasts of heat and fire can be lethal if you get caught napping. It takes a lot of footwork and some decidedly accurate bow shots to defeat this twilit nightmare. And it takes several tries before he's down for the count.

Encountered In: Dungeon 2: Goron Mines

Twilit Carrier Kargarok

Threat Meter

This enemy is a combo of archer and giant flying beast. You have to dodge and duck missile fire before getting a chance to retaliate. Be patient, wait for your moment, and then pounce!

Encountered In: Lanayru Province

Twilit Bloat

Threat Meter

Disturbing as it may seem, you have to defeat this bloated creature with bite attacks. It will be a true measure of your heroism. And it's the only way to fill the Vessel of Light to restore the spirits!

Encountered In: Lanayru Province

Deku Toad

Threat Meter

The Deku Toad is a vile beast and it has vile little beasts to send after you while it readies its attack. You'll not only have to fend off minions but when the big beast leaps, watch the skies! Luckily the Deku Toad doesn't have much energy and needs to take a breather after each attack. And that is the perfect time to strike!

Encountered In: Dungeon 3: Lakebed Temple

Twilit Aquatic Morpheel

Threat Meter

This sneaky monster has a two-stage attack, and both stages are deadly. Just when you think you've got a handle on things, the Morpheel proves that you should always look below the surface. You'll be tested on your targeting abilities and your swimming control. Stay the course and you'll come out on top.

Encountered In: Dungeon 3: Lakebed Temple

Skull Kid

Threat Meter

The unsettling Skull Kid has creepy Puppets at his command and he seems bent on having them bring you harm. When you finally confront the puppet-master, you have to keep a sharp eye out for him while dodging or destroying his grisly toys. The Skull Kid pops from one location to the next as he torments you, so react quickly when you see him!

Encountered In: Faron Woods

Twilit Fossil Stallord

Threat Meter

No one said that saving the kingdom would be easy. The Stallord tests your mettle as you negotiate the Spinner around the arena, dodge the Staltroops, weave away from the monster's purple toxins, and smash into the creature's back. You'll get the hang of it, or you'll pay the price! And even then, it's not over. The Stallord has an evil surprise for you just when he seems defeated. This battle will challenge your endurance as well as your skill.

Encountered In: Dungeon 4: Arbiter's Grounds

Death Sword

Threat Meter

This undead creature won't fall without the abilities of both your forms. You need the sharp eyes, and teeth, of the wolf as well as the quick sword and bow of the boy who would be a hero. It's about speed and accuracy when facing off against Death Sword. During this battle you'll find out if you're lacking in either.

Encountered In: Dungeon 4: Arbiter's Grounds

Darkhammer

Threat Meter

The wicked Ball and Chain of Darkhammer can quickly be your undoing if you're not careful. Judicious use of the Clawshot or your roll move can keep you out of harm's way, but you have to exploit the monster's weakness (in the form of an exposed tail) to stop his onslaught. It can be a long fight, but wait for the right moment and then strike!

Encountered In: Snowpeak Mountain

Twilit Ice Mass Blizzeta

Threat Meter

Blizzeta has control over ice, and she uses it with deadly purpose. Between her dangerous shards and frozen minions you have to make good use of the Ball and Chain to stay alive. Fight ice with steel and bash away at Blizzeta's weapons before taking the fight directly to her.

Encountered In: Snowpeak Mountain

Darknut

Threat Meter

Simply attacking Darknut will not win this battle. You need quick reflexes and patience to properly disassemble this armored foe. Throwing yourself at him will only get you hurt. It's all in the timing and the rolling. If you do it right, Darknut won't be able to land a single blow on you.

Encountered In: Dungeon 6: Temple of Time

Twilit Arachnid Armagohma

Threat Meter

Armagohma is a fierce arachnid with the power to make your time with her memorable, though not pleasant. With rays of fire and fearsome offspring, this arachnid monster will harry you about her lair. You need a steady bow hand and some fast sword work to make it through. And if you do, you'll be rewarded with a Mirror Shard and a Heart Container.

Encountered In: Dungeon 6: Temple of Time

Aeralfos

Threat Meter

You encounter your first Aeralfos about halfway through the City in the Sky dungeon. This guy's tricky at first, but once you figure out his weakness, he's easy to ground-and-pound! Defeat this mid-boss to claim the awesome Double Clawshot, which allows you to move about the City in the Sky more freely.

Encountered In: Dungeon 7: City in the Sky

Argarok

Threat Meter

This massive black dragon has taken over the City in the Sky and is terrorizing the poor Ooccas who live there. It is well-armored and tough to track, but the Double Clawshot provides a way for you to bring this flying monstrosity to the ground.

Encountered In: Dungeon 7: City in the Sky

Phantom Zant

Threat Meter

You combat Zant's phantasmal form on two separate occasions during your trek through the Palace of Twilight before reaching the final showdown against him. Phantom Zant doesn't combat you directly; instead, he summons hordes of twilit fiends to do his dirty work for him! Track his movements carefully and interrupt his summoning attempts at every chance.

Encountered In: Dungeon 8: Palace of Twilight

Zant

Threat Meter

Though Zant torments you at numerous points throughout the adventure, you don't actually get to fight him until you infiltrate the Palace of Twilight and breach his throne room. A powerful being of shadow and deception, Zant uses a variety of nefarious tactics to assault you over the course of the battle. Keep an eye on your surroundings and remember all that you've suffered through, and you'll find a way to see through his every guise.

Encountered In: Dungeon 8: Palace of Twilight

Possessed Zelda

Threat Meter

Ganondorf's villainy knows no bounds. After you storm Hyrule Castle and threaten him with the might of the Master Sword, Ganondorf possesses Princess Zelda, using her body as a host for his wicked soul. Turn the possessed princess's light-based attacks against her to rid her of Ganondorf's vile influence.

Encountered In: Dungeon 9: Hyrule Castle

Ganon

Threat Meter

A massive, hulking pig-beast, Ganon is the physical embodiment of Ganondorf's unbridled power and rage. In this terrible form, Ganon can teleport about at will and attack without warning. Track his movements carefully and have the courage to stand him down!

Encountered In: Dungeon 9: Hyrule Castle

Ganondorf

Threat Meter

The epic final battle against Ganondorf occurs in two stages. In the first, you face the demon thief on horseback, and must rely on Princess Zelda's help to slow him down. The second stage of the fight is a one-on-one duel to the finish; bring all the techniques you've learned to bear against Ganondorf and defeat him to save Hyrule from the darkness he represents!

Encountered In: Dungeon 9: Hyrule Castle

How to Use This Walkthrough

The walkthrough contained within this book not only provides you with a complete journey across your entire adventure, but also reveals the optimal times to gather all the optional items, chests, hidden prizes, and other goodies! This walkthrough has the advantage of informing you of hundreds of important events. The following list details just some of the major ones:

- When you have the first opportunity to visit each area, dungeon, hidden area, side-dungeon, Lantern Cavern, and other major location.
- When to collect all 45 Pieces of Heart and 8 Heart Containers, so you can enter later dungeons with excellent energy levels!
- When and where to begin (and complete) your collection of all 24 Golden Bugs, which allows you to increase your Rupee count and Wallet size!
- When and where to begin (and complete) your collection of all 60 Poe Souls, which allows even more Rupees.
- Where every single item in the game, from the Small Key to the Double Clawshot, can be located, and how best to access everything.
- How to battle the numerous fiends and beasts that roam and prowl the wild lands, dark dungeons, and misty woodlands of Hyrule!
- You'll also learn when you can purchase, find, fish for, or grab the many super-secret items, including the Magic Armor!

The Pages

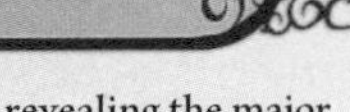

There are two parts to every section in this Walkthrough. The first is the Introduction, which lets you know what to expect in the coming parts of your adventure. Here's how it all breaks down:

1. **Heart Energy Bar:** Throughout the entire walkthrough, the optimal number of Hearts you have is shown here. This means you can quickly check to see if you've grabbed all the Heart Containers and Pieces of Heart at the earliest possible moment. It also tells you how far you are through your adventure.
2. **The Map:** The large poster of the Hyrule Overworld reveals the locations of all the major items in the world, but each section's map delves a little deeper, showing you (in Overworld sections) the major sites of interest and items, and (in dungeons) all the treasure chests, bosses, and other areas of note.
3. **The Overview:** A quick explanatory paragraph revealing the major accomplishments you must attempt in this section.
4. **The Task Bar:** This shows the (usually) eight major tasks you must complete, and the order to complete them, for this particular section. If you're only interested in completing the adventure in the fastest time possible (which is just over eight hours!), you can easily skip a task or two, and focus on the area you may be stuck in.
5. **Denizens:** This shows the land of Hyrule's many friends, fiends, and foes, and specifically shows the new entities you'll encounter in this section.
6. **A Link to the Present:** This reveals what your Collection screen should look like if you obtained all the items, objects, and equipment upgrades at the earliest possible moment. Compare this to your

Collection screen! As important elements appear (such as your first Golden Bug collection), this is referenced at the start of the next section.

7. **Items to Obtain:** Vitally important to many an adventurer are lists of items that must be found during an exploration. Fortunately, we've listed every single non-Rupee item, so you can make sure you've thoroughly explored every area. The items are shown in the order you receive them.
8. **Your Current Location:** This reveals where you are currently, and each dungeon is color-coded so you can flip through the book to easily find a specific section.

The second part is the main walkthrough itself, which gives you a thorough explanation of everything you can do during that specific part of the adventure:

9. **Characters and Enemies:** Over on the extreme left and right edges of the page are the characters and enemies you're currently interacting with on the specific page of the walkthrough. If you want to know (for example) when you fight King Bulblin, look for his picture, and you'll see! This also shows you when a new character or enemy is encountered.
10. **Task Title:** Every time a new task begins, you'll see this title; you can then check it against your progress, and the Task Progress Bar at the bottom of the page (#13).
11. **Information Box:** This walkthrough has many different Information Boxes. There are many other types of Information Boxes, such as:
    - **Author:** How the authors reacted to certain parts of the game.
    - **Hidden Skills:** Instructions on when you receive and how you learn each Hidden Skill.
    - **Weapons:** Revelations on how to use each major item and weapon you receive.
    - **Portals:** References to every new warp portal that opens up.
    - **Mid Boss and Boss Battles:** Tactics on battling the toughest beasts of Hyrule.
    - **Stores:** Showcases the goods and prices of stores throughout the Kingdom.
    - **Golden Bug:** Reveals where all of Agitha's insects are found.
    - **Poe:** Shows where every one of the 60 roaming Poe foes are encountered.
    - **Missing Links:** Reveals the hidden, cool, and otherwise odd stuff you can do.
    - **Postman:** Showcases when the Postman arrives, and where he's found.
12. **Frame-by-frame Action:** Where appropriate, battles or other visual elements are shown in a series of screens, which make for spectacular viewing!
13. **The Task Progress Bar:** Running along the base of each page is this bar, which shows the current task you're on (this is written on the right side of the right page, too). As you complete consecutive tasks, the progress bar fills up until you complete a section.
14. **Notes, Tips, and Cautions:** Throughout the walkthrough, whenever there are additional points to make (Notes), tactics to try or knowledge to impart (Tips), or warnings to deliver (Cautions), these appear.
15. **Item Box:** Whenever you receive an item in the adventure, the walkthrough shows it too; this way you can keep track of exactly what you got, and when!
16. **Item Progress Bar:** Cunningly slotted in on the right side of each page is this bar. When you receive an item, it appears. All the items are shown top to bottom, in the order you receive them, so you know when to expect to find the next big item (such as a new weapon or key).

The time to enter the world of Hyrule is upon you! Good luck, and happy adventures!

Overworld: Ordon Village; Tranquility Before the Twilight

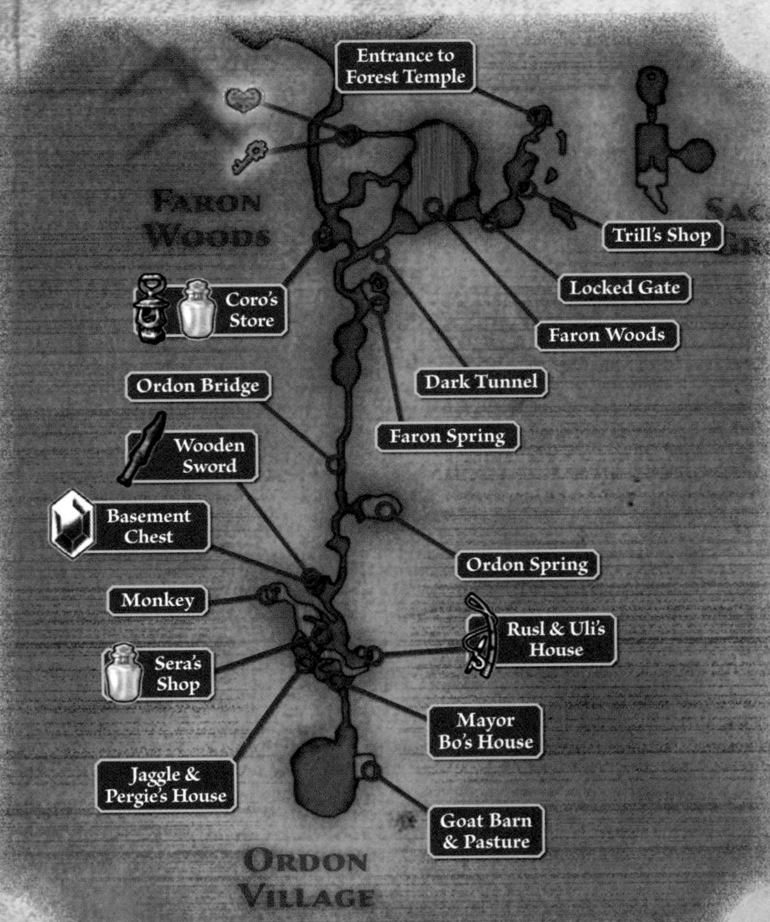

Ordon Village; Tranquility Before the Twilight: Overview

You have a peaceful life as a goat herder, animal wrangler, and keen friend of the forest, and the tiny community you call home is filled with cheer. When you're not riding your faithful steed Epona and rounding up those wayward goats in the pasture, you're using the famed whistling grass to summon a hawk, or wishing you had a Fishing Rod; the Greengills are biting at this time of year! But the mayor of Ordon has something special for you: you are to be an envoy to Castle Town, across the Hyrule Field, and present a specially forged sword at a ceremony. You must leave your tranquil life, after finishing up your chores naturally, and begin to explore the world around. The arrival of a pesky monkey from nearby Faron Woods is but a tiny prelude of the adventure to come!

Enter Ordon Village

Explore Ordon Village

Rescue the Cradle from the Monkey

Remove Buzzing Threat from Tall Tree

Items to Obtain

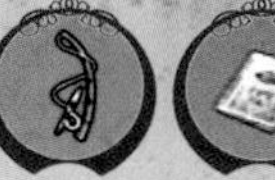

Blue Rupee (5) | Fishing Rod | Fish Journal | Yellow Rupee (10) | Milk in a Bottle | Slingshot

Milk | Bee Larva | Seeds | Wooden Sword | Lantern | Lantern Oil

Purple Rupee (50) | Small Key | Piece of Heart

A Link to the Present

Heart Pieces: 0 (0 Total)

Wallet

Overworld Denizens

Characters

Link

Rusl

Epona

Uli

Colin

Fado

Hanch

Sera

Beth

Mayor Bo

Ilia

Talo

Malo

Jaggle

Pergie

Coro

Trill

Enemies

Hylian Hornets

Walltula

Deku Baba

Keese

Rat

Bokoblin

5 Leave Your Home, Explore Faron Woods pg 42

6 Investigate the Dark Tunnel pg 44

7 Unlock Gate to Forest Temple Woods pg 48

8 Return to Ordon Village, Prepare for Big Day pg 49

Characters Encountered

Rusl

Epona

Uli

Colin

Fado

Ilia

Task 1: Enter Ordon Village

Sunset at the Spring

Near the settlement of Ordon Village, you sit and admire the serene view. "Tell me..." Rusl asks you, "Do you ever feel a strange sadness as dusk falls?" But enough of this melancholy! Rusl is delivering something to the royal family of Hyrule in two days' time.

Rusl encourages you to explore the kingdom and the world around it. You lead your horse, Epona, who is carrying some bundles of kindling you both gathered, over the Ordon Gorge Bridge. Rusl locks the bridge gate.

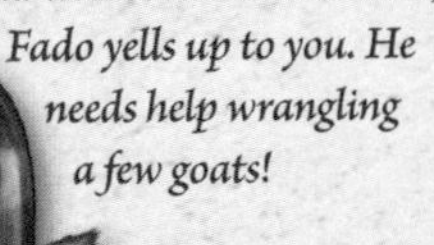

Rusl rejoins his family, Uli and Colin. He leaves you and Epona at your woodland home, and heads to the village entrance. Colin takes Epona's reins and leads her off to rest. You climb up into your home. A moment later, Fado yells up to you. He needs help wrangling a few goats!

Link:

You're a young man who is around 17 years old. You are a wrangler in a quiet village tucked away in the Ordon Woods, in a far corner of the kingdom of Hyrule. Away from Castle Town, you lead a quiet life and are a constant source of amusement among the village children. You are cheerful and truthful, but with a mischievous side, and you're often admonished by Ilia, your childhood friend and daughter of the village mayor.

Rusl:

A resident of Ordon Village, where you also reside, Rusl is between 20 and 30 years old. He is pregnant Uli's husband, and Colin's father. Rusl has a frank personality, but he's an honorable soul and many people think of him as the village leader. He is the only swordsman around. He regards you as his younger brother.

Epona:

Link's favorite horse, Epona has been an integral part of your adventures in the past, but she's now the favored steed for rounding up wayward goats at the pasture you tend with Fado. Epona is resilient but sometimes restless, until Ilia soothes her.

Uli:

The wife of Rusl and mother of Colin, Uli is in her 20s and heavily pregnant with the family's second child. She is relaxed, affable, and beautiful, and she has an air of generosity and caring.

Colin:

The son of Rusl and Uli, Colin is between 7 and 10 years old. He is meek, mild, and timid, but good-natured, like his parents. The other village children look down on him. He adores both you and Ilia, and he follows her wherever she goes.

1

2

3

4

5

6

Fado:

A friend of yours and around your age (about 17), Fado works with you in the same farmhouse. Fado is an easygoing, down-to-earth type of fellow, but he has a somewhat childish side and sometimes goads you into reckless behavior, before receiving a scolding from Ilia.

➤ Head on over to Fado when the opportunity presents itself, and speak to him (Ⓐ). He tells you to hurry up and bring Epona with you. You saw Colin leading Epona down the forest path to the right of your house, so go this route.

Note: When you are near a person, and a yellow arrow is pointing down on their head, the option to "Speak" appears. Chat with anyone and everyone you can. Important information is in colored text. You can talk to everyone a second time for further (or repeated) information!

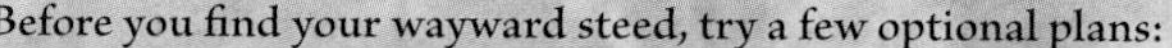

Missing Links

Before you find your wayward steed, try a few optional plans:

1. Treetrunk Call

Turn around and inspect the sign by the ladder. It reads "Link's House." Inspect your abode by climbing the ladder and entering the door under the fluttering banner.

Inside the front door is your home's main level. Check out the fireplace and two ladders: one near the entrance heading up, and another at room's far end, heading down.

Caution: Going down into the basement at the moment isn't wise because the room is pitch-black! Return with a Lantern to see what this chamber contains.

Note: We'll return to this place soon. Don't peek until you want to know what's down there!

Missing Links (cont'd)

Climb the ladder up from the main floor to reach a balcony, with a bookcase and various objects. Did you spot a picture of Epona? Climb the next ladder up.

This leads to the observation deck, where you can check the hole with Ⓐ. Press ◁ and ▷ on your Nunchuk to look out over Ordona Province. Watch the soaring hawk!

Note: There's a picture of Fado and a picture of a goat on the ground floor cabinet. Check it before you leave. Interesting....

2–5. Grounds for Exploration

2. While Fado stands around, check the forest glade in which you're standing. A cute squirrel skips around. You can't catch him, though. If only you could talk to animals....

3. A target dummy—part scarecrow, part stress-reliever—stands near your home. You can lock-on to him, but you don't have a weapon yet.

4. Search the glade to find boulders that are small enough to lift. Grab each one. You may find Rupees, Hearts, or nothing! Place a rock down with Ⓐ. Throw a rock so it smashes by running, then pressing Ⓐ.

Note: Rocks shatter only when they hit a tree or wall. Otherwise, they remain intact. Shatter some rocks for items.

5. Clumps of reeds and grass sway in the breeze. They also contain Rupees and Hearts if you run through the center of each clump.

Characters Encountered

Colin

Epona

Rusl

Ilia

Fado

Uli

Hanch

Sera

Beth

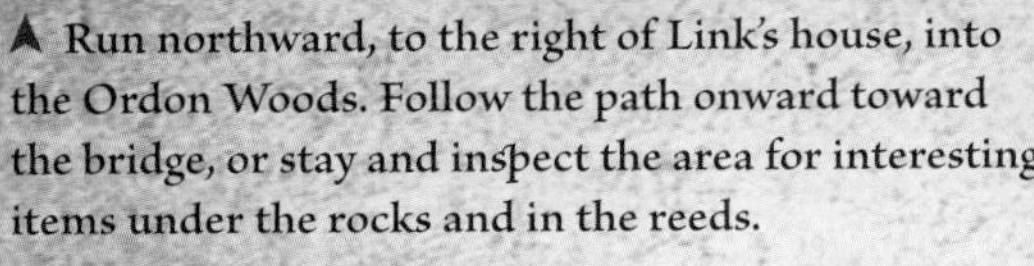

➤ Run northward, to the right of Link's house, into the Ordon Woods. Follow the path onward toward the bridge, or stay and inspect the area for interesting items under the rocks and in the reeds.

Tip: While you're roaming without a steed, roll everywhere, using Ⓐ.

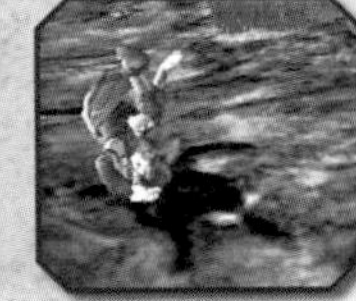

➤ You're looking for a way to the Ordon Spring, where Colin has taken Epona. As you reach the bridge, you'll see Rusl has locked it, and you cannot move farther northward. Instead, choose one of two paths to the spring: one is hidden, the other not.

➤ **Follow the Path:** Follow the main path northward, then turn right at the sealed bridge entrance. The radiant spring is inside this entrance.

➤ **Warren Peace:** A sneaky way of entering the spring is to backtrack to the grassy wood area and check the eastern bank. Among the gnarled tree roots and grass is a small warren! Press Ⓐ to enter when you're near.

Note: If you want to interact with an area, such as this warren hole, press Ⓐ when you're given a prompt. If the prompt doesn't appear, you cannot access this area, although an item in your inventory could do the trick!

➤ Crawl along this tunnel until you reach the corner, then make the turn when you're prompted. You shuffle 90 degrees and continue your progress. Keep on crawling until you reach the light at the end. Step out into the spring, and head for your horse.

Missing Links

1-2. Woodland Wandering

1. Inspect every clump of grass, and turn over every rock before you meet Epona. You can find Rupees if you look hard enough!

2. Rupees aren't only on the ground. Roll and knock yourself into the tree. Sometimes a Rupee is dislodged, and falls to the ground. Try this on every tree you see!

Author Note

We're not ashamed to say we completed the entire adventure a couple of times before we found this method of Rupee-collecting. Naturally, we did this by accident, too!

You step into the pool, and watch as a girl steps forward toward Epona. It is Ilia. She looks radiant in this dappled light. She's washed your horse for you. You smile at her. When you catch your breath, head on over and talk to her.

➤ Epona is ready for you to ride. Ilia reminds you that you have work to do at the ranch; Fado will be getting antsy. You should also pick up a piece of grass shaped like a horseshoe, also known as Horse Grass. There are two clumps on either side of the spring entrance. You play a sweet melody, and Epona canters to you.

➤ Get onto Epona by moving to her side and pressing Ⓐ. Dismount by pressing the same button, but only when Epona isn't moving! Trot back the way you came. Head out of the spring.

➤ Turn left, heading south toward your home. Pass the woods and your house, and head straight for the entrance to Ordon Village to the south. Spur Epona with Ⓐ if you require extra speed.

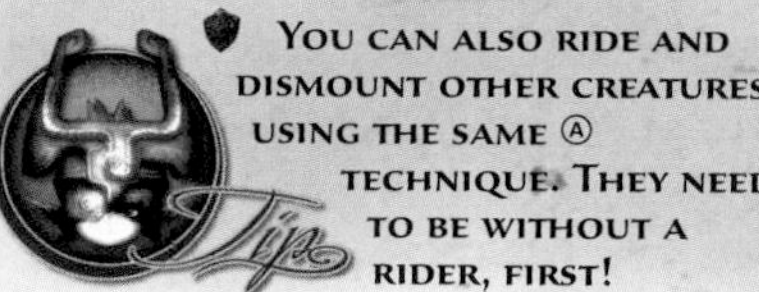

This Horse Grass is scattered in clumps throughout Hyrule. When you need Epona, pick some and play the melody.

Tip: You can also ride and dismount other creatures using the same Ⓐ technique. They need to be without a rider, first!

Horseplay

- Spur Epona onward by pressing Ⓐ. You dig your heels into her hide, and she speeds up. This is useful for traversing long distances, or areas with long, straight paths. You travel faster but can't corner as easily.
- Don't overdo the spurring! If you use up all six instances (shown at your screen's bottom), you must wait a few seconds for Epona to recover. Spur her every few seconds, with a second or two of normal speed in between, for best results.
- Stop Epona, then pull ♀ softly to pull her backward or pull hard to turn her around. This is useful if you ride into a wall or dead end, and during combat.

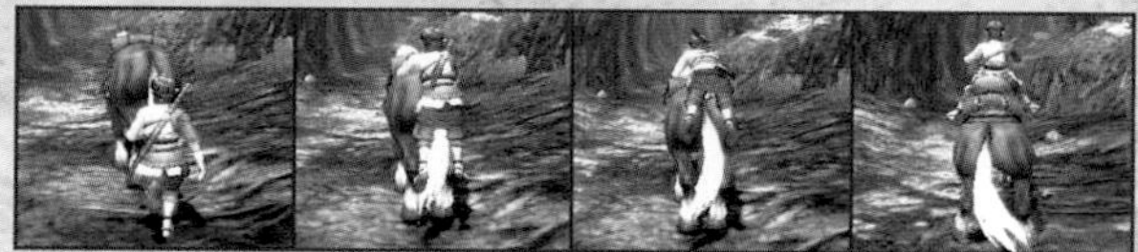

Tip: To quickly mount Epona, approach her from behind, then dash toward her and press Ⓐ. You leap over her tail and land in the saddle. This gives you momentum and is great for speeding away from areas.

Task 2: Explore Ordon Village

Ordon Village at Sunset

Welcome to Ordon Village! The people are friendly, unless you're out to destroy their pumpkins.

As twilight leads to night, you enter Ordon Village and watch the villagers as they stand around, talking. By a shallow stream, Rusl practices his sword-swinging while Uli and Colin watch. In the distance, a large man is waiting at the goat enclosure entrance. Dismount from Epona if you wish.

Note: You can try a host of activities at the village, but it's quicker to head to the goat pasture. However, if you're taking your time, talk to everyone you can and explore the area. The optional activities are shown in this guide after you meet Fado and help him with the goats.

◄ Get off your horse, and speak to the trio of villagers standing near the first house on the right. The man, Hanch, and his jolly wife Sera, tell you of the mischievous monkeys pilfering from the village.

➤ Everyone's locked their homes and businesses because of this simian stealing. Sera and her daughter Beth admonish Hanch for his inability to catch the monkeys.

Hanch:

Beth's father Sera's husband, the dejected-looking Hanch is between 30 and 40 years old. He runs the only commodity shop in the village. He has a meek and timid demeanor and cannot oppose his overbearing wife. He seems to be slightly unlucky.

Characters Encountered

Sera

Beth

Hanch

Colin

Uli

Rusl

Mayor Bo

Ilia

Fado

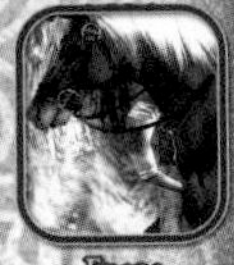
Epona

Sera:

The mother of Beth and wife of Hanch, Sera is a rotund and jolly lady of 30-something years old. However, she can be unpleasant and haughty to her husband, Hanch. She loves her cat very much; in fact, many in the village say she treats her cat better than her husband.

Beth:

One of the young girls (between 8 and 11 years old) in Link's village, she is the daughter of Hanch and Sera. Too grown-up, she's a sassy madam, and she thinks the other children in the village are babies. She has a crush on you, and she also dreams of a city life, away from all these goats.

Tip: All of the village dwellings are locked, to keep out those pesky monkeys. When Ordon is a monkey-free zone, try entering each of them. Continue with your meeting and greeting. You can climb and explore the village too; all of the items and out-of-the-way areas are revealed in this guide after you finish your goat wrangling.

➤ Move down the main village path and stop when you see Colin, Uli, and Rusl at the shallow stream jetty. Speak to Colin and he tells you he's making you a **Fishing Rod.**

➤ Rusl, who's nearby, testing the metal of a sword, also lets you know about Colin's **Fishing Rod.** It should be ready for you tomorrow. When you're done talking, optionally explore the area more before heading south toward the exit.

➤ Crossing the stream leads you to an imposing fellow with a frankly incredible moustache. This is Mayor Bo, who's standing outside his impressive hut. His dwelling is sealed.

Mayor Bo:

A portly but muscular fellow in his mid 40s, Bo is the mayor of this hamlet and the father of Ilia. He has personally chosen you as an envoy to send into the kingdom to befriend the neighboring villages and countries. He cherishes you as if you were his own son. Although appearing organized, he's a little scatterbrained, which can cause arguments with Ilia.

➤ There's much you can do in the village, but it's easier to perform these feats in daylight. Refer to the next Missing Link section for details.

Instead, return to your steed, and ride her south, past the mayor's house, and up the narrow banked path to the goat pasture at Ordon Ranch.

A Goat of a Chance: Herding Time

➤ When you arrive at the goat pasture, Fado greets you. He needs you to herd 10 of the goats into the barn. Agree to this task, or you can't progress.

➤ After you begin the task, a running total of how many goats you have successfully herded into the barn appears at your screen's bottom. You also have a new tactic: the "whoop." Press Ⓐ to let out a sharp yell. This gets the goats moving quickly!

Goat herding goes fast if you follow these techniques:

1. Start your herding away from the barn, and concentrate on the goats farthest away.

2. Ride Epona so you're on the far side of the goat and the barn. Don't ride in-between the barn and the goat! Follow a general looping pattern.

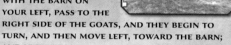

3. As you near a goat, or group of goats, they move away from you. If you're riding with the barn on your left, pass to the right side of the goats, and they begin to turn, and then move left, toward the barn; and vice versa.

4. As the goats begin to turn in the general direction of the barn, let out a whoop. This startles the goats, and they speed up. They move toward the barn but may not enter yet. Don't worry; concentrate on getting goats near the barn first, *then* into it.

5. Herd groups of goats. Wrangle single goats based on where they are; clear the upper area first, then move down to the pasture's middle and lower parts.

6. After the remaining goats are in the lower part of the pasture, finish the job.

Tip

- Watch out! Herding takes much longer if you pick a group of goats and herd them all the way to the barn. The goats you haven't herded yet tend to bolt, so concentrate on the entire herd, moving them nearer the barn door, instead of groups within the herd.
- Follow any wayward goats bolting away from the barn immediately; maneuver around and behind in a semicircle, rather than heading straight into them.
- Keep your herd near the barn. Epona always should be the farthest animal from the barn during this wrangling. If she isn't, you'll spook goats and they'll flee to all sides!

Caution

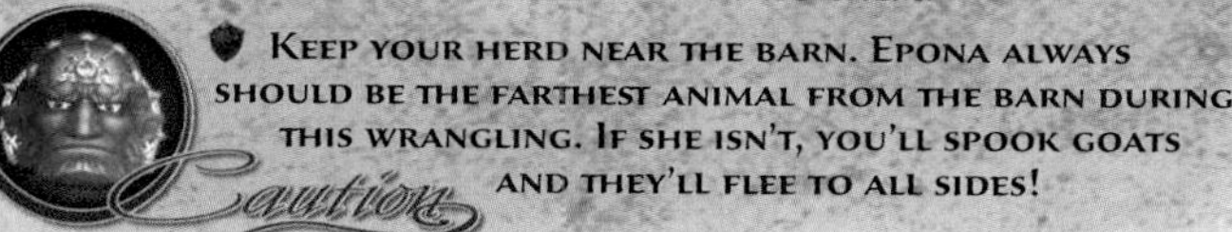

Author Note

Those goats definitely got the better of us the first time we tried wrangling, but this was due to overuse of the whoop button. Goats scattered to the rocky sides of the pasture, and it took a few attempts to finally get this wrangling sorted. We got most excited when multiple goats headed into the barn: we had a five-hit "Goat In!" combo at one point! This was also the place where we practiced controlling Epona before taking her out into the wilds of Faron Woods.

◄ Take as long as you like with the herding. After you're successful, Fado comes in and thanks you for your help. He says he can handle wrangling duties tomorrow while you head toward the main city with that gift Rusl is making.

► Fado sets up some fences for you to leap over. Make sure Epona is facing the fences directly, and not approaching from the sides or an angle, or she refuses to jump. Use the spurs (Ⓐ) to gain enough speed to leap each fence. There are two in the pasture. When you're finished, bound over the fence leading back to the village, and to your home.

Missing Links

1. Barn Storming

Before you leap, you can optionally explore the ranch barn, where you herded all the goats. Fado secured them in stalls where they remain, happily bleating. Interestingly, that ground looks soft enough to dig...if you had the right implement for the job.

You are prompted to save. It is always wise to do this. Make sure to save before and after exploring a difficult area also.

Tip

Characters Encountered

Beth

Talo

Malo

Colin

Epona

Rusl

Jaggle

Pergie

Hanch

Fado

Sera

Task 3: Rescue the Cradle from the Monkey

Monkey Business: Ordon Village Objectives

You awaken the next morning. Three children shout to you from in front of your house. Optionally, you can peer through your upper window at the view.

Head down two ladders to the main floor, and exit your home. Beth is here along with two young tykes, Talo and Malo. Talo explains with glee that there's a **Slingshot** for sale at the store!

Leave those three to argue, and talk to Colin, who's tending to Epona near your house. He's finished the **Fishing Rod**, but you'll need to find Rusl to get it.

Talo:

He is between 8 and 11 years old, and shares similar features with his mother and father, Jaggle and Pergie. He's Malo's elder brother. Talo is a scamp who longs for a chance to receive sword-play instructions from you. Immature, even at this age, Talo also looks down on the shy Colin.

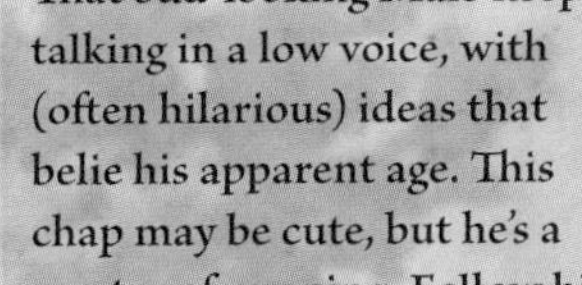

Malo:

The youngest boy in your village, Malo is the child of Jaggle and Pergie, and Talo's brother. Oddly mature, especially when compared to his overly excitable brother, Malo is only around 4–6 years old. He seldom speaks, but when he does, he speaks incisively and sternly as if he were an adult. Malo is a true champion of commerce and hopes to run a successful store one day.

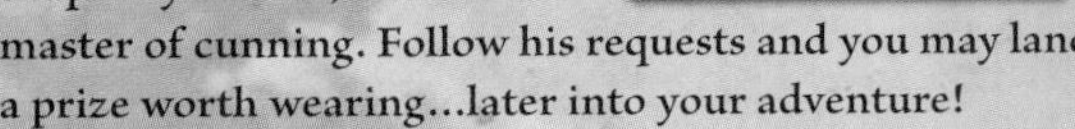

Missing Links

Along with the squirrel-watching, horse-inspecting, scarecrow-targeting, and grass-running, there are a few other matters to optionally watch for while you're here:

1. The Machinations of Malo

That odd-looking Malo keeps talking in a low voice, with (often hilarious) ideas that belie his apparent age. This chap may be cute, but he's a master of cunning. Follow his requests and you may land a prize worth wearing...later into your adventure!

2. The Five Rupee Rock

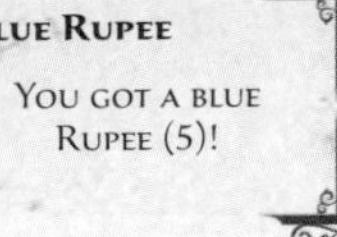

One of the rocks, hidden in the middle of the patch of long grass behind where Epona stands, awards you with a blue Rupee (5), multiple times!

Blue Rupee

You got a blue Rupee (5)!

Note: This is the first time you secure a blue Rupee (worth five green Rupees). Unlike the green Rupee, this denomination is large enough to show up as an in-game cutscene. Blue Rupees become more plentiful later on.

Hive Inspection, and Hawk Summoning

➤ Run down the path to the village, and spot Hanch looking up at the tree above Fado's house. Head on over and speak with him. He has to restock the store and he has spotted some Hylian Hornets nestled in the branches.

➤ The moaning and groaning doesn't end there, either! The family cat hasn't come home since yesterday, and Sera's in a bad mood. Hanch is thinking the Hylian Hornets might help his situation, as he can at least return to Sera with **Bee Larva**. Use your free-look and check out the **hive**.

Free-Looking

When you want a full view of the area around you (including areas above and below you), enter this viewing mode. Use ⓒ, then ○ or the Wii Remote to look around with the cursor. If you're stuck, check your surroundings with free-look to help your predicament.

Note

◀ Keep the hive on your mind, then ignore Fado's house (it's locked) and run across to **Sera's Sundries: One-Stop Shopping**. There's a sign to one side and a cat-flap next to the door; you can't miss it. Open the door, and head inside to meet Sera.

Sera is draped over the table, looking at a **Bottle** of Milk. She scolded the family cat, and he hasn't returned. She's so fraught, she has exhausted herself. Leave the shop; she isn't in the mood to sell the **Slingshot**, pot of **Bee Larvae**, and **Bottle of Milk**.

➤ Exit Sera's house and inspect the main sign in town, then inspect every part of the village you can. There's a wide variety of extra fun to be had (see the Missing Links list nearby). On your way to checking the area out, move to the pumpkin patch. You'll hear a hollering!

◀ It's Jaggle! He's standing on a nearby rock between the waterwheel and Sera's Sundries. Follow his instructions, and talk to him by Z targeting, then pressing Ⓐ. He asks you to do the same with Talo and Malo.

Jaggle asks you to climb the vine up to the top of the rock he's standing on. Once you're up there, he points down to the creek near his house (the one with the waterwheel) at the cat. He wonders if the cat can catch a fish....

Tip

Talking to folks from a distance saves you time, but Z targeting is also important for targeting enemies. You automatically face them as well, making combat easier. Learn this technique now!

Jaggle:

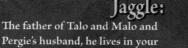

The father of Talo and Malo and Pergie's husband, he lives in your village and is in his 30s. He's a farmer, although he frequently works on his hobby: crafting items out of wood. A strong-headed but laid-back fellow, Jaggle doesn't care about the details, and neglects his duties to take a nap.

◀ The cat isn't Jaggle's reason for getting you here, however. He points to some **Hawk Grass** growing out of a nearby rock. He tells you to hop across the rocks to check it out. Use Ⓐ to jump the gap.

Tip

When you're jumping across gaps, you automatically make the leap. There is no "jump" button to press. However, it is wise to re-orientate the camera directly behind you with Z so you move in a straight line!

➤ Head to the rock with the **Hawk Grass**, then pick it and blow it. A hawk (the one you saw from your window earlier) swoops down and lands on your arm. You can now rotate your view, and use the **red target** to line up a location for the hawk to fly to when you set him free (with Ⓐ).

Characters Encountered

Fado

Sera

Beth

Jaggle

Pergie

Rusl

Uli

Colin

Ilia

Mayor Bo

Talo

Malo

Face the tree above Fado's house. You can see the Hylian Hornets' hive from here. Line up the hive and set the bird free. It flies at the hive, knocking it to the ground and smashing it. This is the first method of dealing with the Hylian Hornets.

Tip: To summon the hawk, locate a patch of Hawk Grass, pick it, and blow on the grass to summon the bird for another target. If the hawk can't interact with the target, it flaps its wings and leaves. The friendly hawk is useful for striking down troublesome insects and cradle-snatching monkeys.

Missing Links

The hamlet of Ordon Village is brimming with entertainment to keep you occupied for hours! Try some or all of the following:

1. Sera's Sundries: What a Cat-astrophe!

Free-look survey the inside of Sera's store, and you'll spot not only the three items behind Sera, but her cat in pictorial form. There are three pictures of her feline friend here; two more than of her own daughter, Beth!

2. Cucco Catching

There's a strutting, squawking Cucco in the area between Sera's Sundries and the pumpkin patch. You can pick the bird up and run around carrying it above your head! When you're done, throw (while moving) or place (while halted) it on the ground.

3. Cucco Flying

Another amusing diversion is taking to the skies as the Cucco flaps manically to stay in the air. Leap off a low rock and you'll glide to the ground in a second. Jump from the roof of Fado's house, under the Hylian Hornet tree, and you'll glide for more seconds! This trick comes in handy later, so practice it.

Tip: You can let go of the Cucco at any time and drop to the ground. If you're dropping from a great height, press to roll and keep running. If you don't do this, you'll land heavily and slow down.

4. Hawk vs. Cat

When you've talked to Jaggle and summoned the hawk for the first time, you may be tempted to launch it down at Sera's cat. Alas, a battle between bird and feline doesn't break out.

5. Pulverizing Pumpkins

The village has four pumpkin patches: one by Jaggle's rock, one near Jaggle and Pergie's house, one in a fenced area near the mayor's home, and one next to Rusl and Uli's house. They each release a different item in each specific location (a Heart, a Rupee, or nothing).

Missing Links (cont'd)

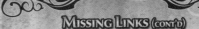

6. Jaggle's Pumpkin Surprise

Jaggle doesn't take kindly to complete pumpkin patch devastation; if you destroy all four pumpkins in the patch near the rock he's standing on, he shouts at you for your lack of vegetable respect.

5. Pumpkin Slingshot Seeds

When you obtain the Slingshot, you can gather 50 seeds from any nearby pumpkin patch. Some pumpkins release seeds, but only after you obtain the Slingshot.

The Monkey and the Cradle

➤ When you learn to summon the hawk, head to the stream in the village center and speak with Uli. Rusl has already left the village with the sword. But Uli seems worried; she's lost a **cradle** made from finely woven tree bark. She made it when Colin was born, and she cherishes it.

➤ It's time to look for the cradle! First though, as you're near the mayor, head over and talk to him. He's fearful of Fado handling the goat ranch today. He's right to be nervous!

◄ A goat bounds down the path toward you both. It's up to you to stop it! Move left and right so you're blocking the goat's path, then grab it using Ⓐ. You automatically swing it around, throwing the goat to the ground.

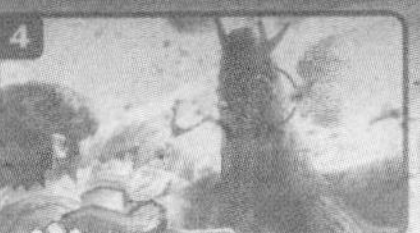

The mayor thanks you for stopping the goat. If you try to enter the mayor's house, he tells you Ilia is inside, working like crazy on something. You can't disturb her, so head toward the house with the waterwheel on the side of it.

➤ Enter the home of Jaggle, Pergie, Talo, and Malo and after optionally inspecting the residence, walk over to Pergie and talk to her. She says Jaggle's probably asleep somewhere (he's actually on that rock), and he's making a shield for Rusl.

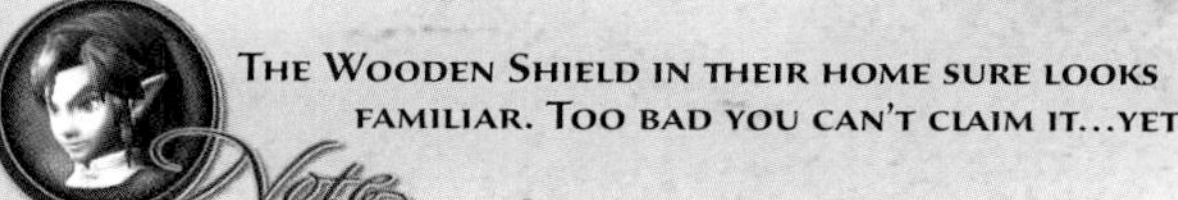

The Wooden Shield in their home sure looks familiar. Too bad you can't claim it...yet!

Note

Pergie:

The mother of Talo and Malo, Pergie is married to Jaggle and is in her 30s. Due to her slothful husband, she's always working and constantly struggling to deal with her mischievous sons. But, although she's tough, she loves and supports her brood.

➤ Head out of Pergie's home, and climb up on the rock where Jaggle is standing. Hop across the flat rocks, onto the roof of Sera's Sundries, then to the rock in the middle of the pond, heading northwest. Check the narrow stream ahead.

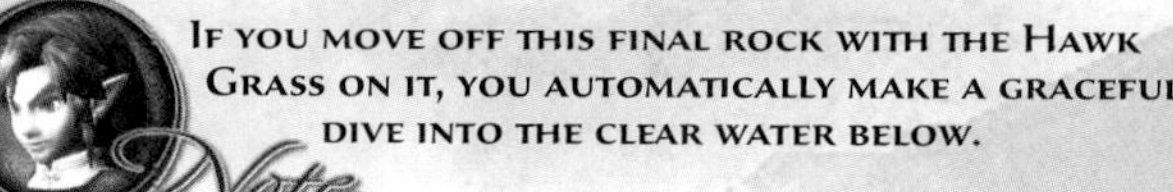

If you move off this final rock with the Hawk Grass on it, you automatically make a graceful dive into the clear water below.

Note

➤ Optionally, you can investigate the leaping figure atop a rock ahead of you. Dive into the water, and swim up the narrow gap between the hillsides. As you close in on the figure, you can hear eeping and monkey calls. It's the cheeky monkey!

➤ Swim left and clamber onto the pond-side bank. That monkey is leaping up and down, carrying Uli's cradle. This will not do! Optionally inspect the rocks for Rupees (one has a blue Rupee), then swim to the jetty where the cat waits. She runs when you approach her.

➤ Run to the rock on which Jaggle is standing. Return to the end rock, and use the clump of Hawk Grass to summon the hawk. During the cutscene, carefully look for the 10-Rupee piece. It's on a tree somewhere. You'll get that in a moment.

You can get the cradle thanks to the hawk! All you need now is a lady who's a fan of intricate woven furniture.

▲ Although you can't hit the Hylian Hornets from here, you can strike something equally important: that pesky monkey! You can't attack or approach him from the ground or water, so aim and send in the hawk. The bird steals the cradle back from the monkey, and drops it at you. You catch it. Now return (carefully) to Sera's roof, and drop down to the grass below. You can fall into the pond, but you need to push the cradle to shallow water.

Characters Encountered

Uli

Colin

Rusl

Jaggle

Pergie

Talo

Malo

Mayor Bo

▲ Head toward Uli's location and give her the cradle. She's thankful and realizes she needs to give you something. She wants you to accompany her to her home. Follow slowly behind, or run up and around to the front door.

▲ Uli presents you with the rod Colin made. It is simple (it lacks a reel), but finely crafted. Set it to Ⓑ on your Main Items screen. When it's equipped, press Ⓑ to hold it. Lower the Wii Remote to cast your line into the water. Raise the Wii Remote to pull the line in, like a real rod!

Fishing Rod

You got a **Fishing Rod**! It's simple and has a bobber.

Note: This is your first "real" item! Many items stay with you throughout your adventure. Some are upgraded. Others are stolen, or downgraded! Your items are accessed on the Main Items screen by pressing ⊖ on your Wii Remote.

Missing Links

There are still more interesting asides to find around in this village. Why not try the following, while you look for the cradle?

1. Rusl and Uli's House: One-Eyed Rocking Horse

After speaking with Uli, run up to her house (behind her and up the path to the left, and open the door. Inside, amid the finely woven cushions and well-made sofas is a scary-looking rocking horse with one eye! This must be Colin's.

2. Rusl and Uli's House: Wall Art and Equipment

Survey the room (with ◎) to notice a piece of wall art drawn by Colin showing the family (is the second child you?), a Fishing Rod, and a helmet and bladed implement. Unfortunately, none of it can be taken.

3. Rusl and Uli's House: The Pumpkin Patch and Dirt Patch

Head outside, and optionally devastate the two pumpkins growing at the dwelling's side. A patch of earth near the stacked logs looks like it could lead somewhere, if you could dig it up. Hmmm....

4. Frogs, Fish, and Rupees in the Stream

Head down to the stream below Rusl and Uli's house, and wade in. Turn left and at the end of the stream are a couple of Rupees that are easily missed. There are also tiny frogs leaping near the stream, and fish in this area.

5. Goat Petting

After you stop the goat from charging, pet it when you're close, and it calms down, bleating with delight!

6. Jaggle and Pergie's House: Rupee Collecting

Don't forget the pumpkin patch, tree to roll into, grass to inspect, and rocks to throw near the picnic table and waterwheel home of Jaggle and Pergie. You can watch tiny birds, too!

7. Jaggle and Pergie's House: Puppy Love!

An adorable puppy wags his tail and follows you around the house when you enter it. You can pick him up, but unfortunately, you're cannot leave the building with this playful pooch.

8. Jaggle and Pergie's House: Straw Dolls

The evidence of the unruly Talo and strange Malo are scattered around the house; a straw doll lies on the floor, and three more are propped on the upper bunk bed if you climb the ladder to check.

Missing Links (cont'd)

9. Jaggle and Pergie's House: Pumpkin and Pottery

The biggest surprise comes from the pumpkins. There are Rupees in some of the four near the fireplace (the ones on the table don't break), and there are two pots to smash, too. The one near the chest and shelves gives you five Rupees.

10. Mayor's House Roof: Up on Top

Get a great view of the village by climbing the ladder near the pumpkin patch leading to Jaggle and Pergie's house. At the top, head left to claim Rupees from two pumpkins, roll into the tree, then climb the crates and hop onto the roof.

11. One Giant Leap

A long ladder leads up onto the dwelling's top, and this leads to a narrow roof area with a great prize: a yellow Rupee (10)! Claim it, look around (you can spot the hive), then peer over the edge. You can make the drop to the ground without getting hurt. Don't forget to roll!

Yellow Rupee

You got a yellow Rupee (10)!

Note: This is the first time you secure a yellow Rupee (worth 10 green Rupees). Unlike the green Rupee (1), this denomination is large enough to show up as an in-game cutscene. Yellow Rupees become more plentiful later.

12. Ten Rupee Wrangling

While on the upper roof, look to your right, and take the Hawk Grass from the clump at the edge of the roof. Summon a hawk. The hive is too far away to hit, but the hawk is the key to obtaining the 10 Rupee piece you can see on the hillside.

Normally you can't reach this hillside, but if you locate the Cucco below you on the right side, and aim the hawk at it, the bird of prey grabs it and brings it back to you! Take the Cucco, fly over to the hillside, and claim your Rupee prize! Check the rocks for a five Rupee piece, too!

Author Note

That yellow Rupee (10) had us stumped for some time. We tried launching the hawk at the Rupee. Nope! We leapt up at the hillside, jumped from the roof. We even shouted at the screen. It didn't help. In the end, we spotted the Cucco, and all was well. But how would we fare when the puzzles were actually difficult, later in the adventure? It didn't bode well....

Task 4: Remove the Buzzing Threat from the Tall Tree

Slingshot Shenanigans

◄ Optionally try out your Fishing Rod at the shallow hillock's bottom. Stop at the stream edge and test the rod. If you're patient, you can catch a **Greengill** here. This is one of three good fishing spots in the village.

► Now to befriend the cat! Move to the fishing spot behind Jaggle and Pergie's wheelhouse, and stand at this jetty's edge. Cast your line, and wait for a moment or two. The bobber slowly sinks until it's vertical. Wait for it....

Fish on! Pull the rod up (using the Wii Remote; move it so it's vertical) and gently pull back when the floater bobs down slightly in the water. If you miss, re-cast your line. Keep this up until you land a fish! This is likely to be a moderately sized Greengill.

◄ When you reel in your first fish (from any location), Sera's cat can smell it! The cat now becomes much more friendly. Now reel in a second fish from where the cat is by the wheelhouse jetty. The cat plays with your prize, then scampers away with it, all the way to the cat-flap at Sera's house!

Sera

Hanch

Fun with Fishing

Remember these tips for hours of fishing frivolity:

- You receive a Heart for each fish you catch.
- Later in your adventure you can obtain different lures.
- When you're near a body of water, check it for fish, then cast your line.
- Fish aren't in all areas; don't bother fishing at a spring for example.
- There are monstrous specimens to land later on!
- All the different types of fish you catch, and their size, are recorded.

Note: Your Fish Journal keeps track of only the fish you catch using a bobber.

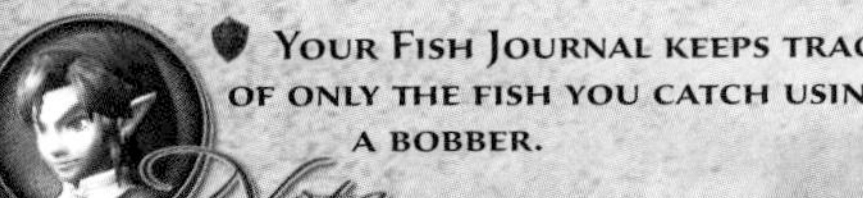

Author Note

Did you hear that chime when Sera's cat entered the cat-flap? It's the classic sound you've heard every time Link has unlocked secrets in games past. This time though, we were excited to hear it on the Wii Remote thanks to the tiny built-in speaker when we played the Wii version. The Wii Remote also has sword-slashing, rod-reeling, bowstring tightening, and loads of other sounds to hear! You might want to stock up on AA batteries though; we went through three sets during one playthrough. Better yet, use rechargable batteries.

▲ Head to Sera's Sundries! Sera is inside, both surprised and delighted. That cat "brought a fish back with him. He was worried about me being angry!" She's feeding the cat some Milk, but she kindly gives you the dregs in a Bottle for free. How kind!

Milk Bottle
You got Milk in a Bottle! But this Bottle's half-empty!

Tip: The Milk isn't important; the Bottle is the most important item. Finish the Milk. There are four Bottles to find during your adventure, and the healing liquids you can carry in them are critical to your survival. It may not seem like it at first, but the Bottle is an amazing gift!

Note: Swap Set Items by positioning each one from the ⊖ menu screen, then setting them by pressing ✜, ✜, or ✜ on your Wii Remote. Just press the direction your item is positioned on to access it, and Ⓑ to use it. Some items are used automatically when you press the ✜; don't worry, we'll tell you when!

◄ Set your Bottle to ✜, swig the Milk (even if you have full health), and then inspect Sera's Sundries, as she's happy to sell you some items. The three in question are all behind her. Use ◎ to access them.

Store

Sera's Sundries

Item	Name	Price	Effect
	Milk	10 Rupees	Two helpings; each replenishes 3 Hearts
	Bee Larva (10)	10 Rupees	Fishing bait, minimum life energy gain
	Slingshot and 50 Pellets	30 Rupees	Projectile weapon

Don't buy the jug of Milk. It fills up the Bottle, and you need it empty later. You also must keep the Bee Larvae in a Bottle, so they aren't ideal, either (and you can claim free Larvae in a moment). However, purchase the **Slingshot.** Hand over the 30 Rupees; it's worth it!

Tip: You don't have enough money? What have you been doing? We've just shown you loads of places to find Rupees. Check back and read up on all the hidden places. We managed to arrive at Sera's with 83 Rupees! Can you do better?

Slingshot
You got the **Slingshot**! Children LOVE this item. You can hold up to **50** pellets.

Milk Bottle
You got **Milk**! One Bottle holds **two** helpings!

Bee Larva
You got the **Bee Larva**! Fish love these, but you can eat them too.

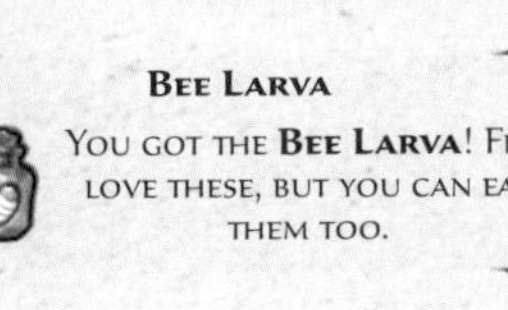

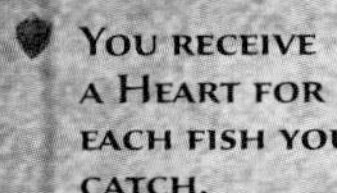

Bee Larva

- If you purchase or locate Bee Larva, you must use the Bottle to capture 10 Larvae.
- Each is either used to bait your Fishing Rod hook (the fish are more attracted to this new lure, but they eat one larva each time they bite).
- Or, you can eat larva to recover one-quarter Heart per larva. That means that chomping down all 10 gives you only two and a half Hearts!

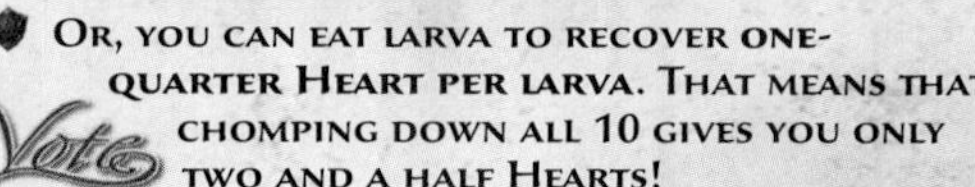

Note

The best way to use Bee Larva is to scoop some up from the broken hive shortly, instead of paying for it. Don't use them to increase your health. Bait your hook with one, test it out, then ignore this item after you finish fishing here. There are better ways to increase your health, and better things to use as bait!

Tip

Slingshot: Your First Weapon

Set the Slingshot to Ⓑ on the ⊖ menu screen. Use the Wii Remote to move the red target until you're over your target. Press Ⓑ to fire. Lock on to your target with the Ⓩ button on your Nunchuk.

When you're aiming, remember that your pellets travel in an arc, and they will fall to the ground, rather than travel in a straight line like an arrow. This means you should aim at distant targets (like the hive, in a moment) higher than dead-center, to adjust for the trajectory.

You can refill your Slingshot with pumpkin seeds!

Hornet Keeping

Head out of Sera's shop, and walk to where Hanch is standing. It's time to bring an end to these pesky Hylian Hornets. Achieve this in one of three ways:

Plan 1: Hawk Strike

➤ You may have launched your bird of prey at the hive from the flat rock near Sera's store roof, aiming at the hive. The bird knocks the hive down, and the Hylian Hornets are far enough away to dissipate.

Plan 2: Slingshot Strike

◄ The second plan is to stand by Hanch and aim up at the hive with your Slingshot, whacking it with a pellet until the hive falls and smashes. The Hylian Hornets don't take too kindly to this and swarm you. Run!

Plan 3: Headbutt Strike

➤ A final plan, which is only slightly less insane than it sounds, is to head around and up to the vines on the tree, climb them, and head up, dislodging the Hylian Hornets with your head! You'll lose about one Heart dropping and fleeing the swarm.

Hylian Hornets

Threat Meter

Hylian Hornets are angry only if provoked. If you find yourself surrounded by them, you cannot stand and fight. One option is to run away from them. Five seconds into your flight, the Hylian Hornets give up the chase. The second option is to dive into water, to where the Hylian Hornets cannot fly. You can be stung and defeated by Hylian Hornets, but only if you wait around while they attack!

▲ After the hive explodes, talk to Hanch, who was throwing stones at the nest ineffectually. Head up to the hive's remains. Empty your **Bottle** and stand near the nest. Use Ⓐ to **scoop Bee Larvae** into your Bottle. That way, you get these for free! Don't pay Sera's outrageous prices!

Enemies Encountered

Hylian Hornets

Characters Encountered

Rusl

Uli

Jaggle

Pergie

Talo

Malo

Beth

Return to Ordon Village and the hive reappears. Knock it down just like you did, and capture 10 Bee Larvae, and you'll have more than you need. Inspect the tree from top to bottom for Rupees (see Missing Links), then optionally destroy pumpkins and take your first pumpkin seeds (these are available from some pumpkins now that you have the Slingshot).

Tip

Pumpkin Seeds

You got **pumpkin seeds (50)**! Use them with your Slingshot.

This is the first time you secure pumpkin seeds. Explode more pumpkins to gather additional seeds, up to the maximum of 50.

Note

Missing Links

Once again, there's much to do in the village, especially now that you're able to fish.

1. Fishing Hole #1

Start at the shallow stream below Rusl and Uli's house. You catch **Greengills** here.

2. Fishing Hole #2

Another fishing hole is where the cat was prowling, behind Jaggle and Pergie's waterwheel home. You catch **Greengills** here, too.

3. Fishing Hole #3

Another good spot to fish is the narrow bank protrusion at the pond's far end, near where the monkey was standing. You can catch **Ordon Catfish** here!

4. The Hornet Tree: Two Green Rupees and a View

Head right up the narrow bank to a small promontory and great view of the village. Find two Rupees here, and this is a great spot for Cucco flying!

5. The Hornet Tree: 15 Rupees and a Great View

After the hive is downed, climb the tree vine all the way to the top, then edge along the main branch to claim two precariously positioned Rupees, a 5 and 10 on each smaller branch. Enjoy the highest view of the village from here!

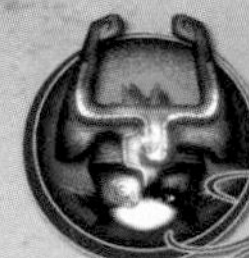

Leap from these branches, and you can land without hurting yourself. Remember to roll (press ⓐ).

Tip

6. Pumpkin Pulverizing: From Range

Remember you can strike items that explode, like pumpkins, from a distance now that you have the Slingshot. Practice on those pumpkins, and don't forget the seeds!

Task 5: Leave Your Home, and Explore Faron Woods

Slicing Mr. Scarecrow

◀ Leave the village by the only exit, and meet Rusl at the woodland glade where your home is. He tells you he's delivered something to your room. Before you find out what it is, head to Talo, Malo, and Beth, who are waiting near that scarecrow. They've spotted your **Slingshot** and want a demonstration of its power!

◀ Use Ⓩ to target the scarecrow, then fire at him. Blam! That pumpkin head is split wide open. Beth and Talo are wowed. Use ◁ and ▷ to look around.

◄ Now spend some time shattering a second scarecrow that's appeared, and then use your ◎ to manually aim at the collection of five targets on the trees. Pan left to spot them all, with your Slingshot out. Then fire! Speak to the children, and they pester you about that present Rusl left for you. Check your home, but remove the arachnid pests, first.

Tip: THE TARGETS HAVE REAPPEARED: SHOOT THEM AGAIN TO ENSURE THAT YOU'RE FAMILIAR WITH MANUALLY AIMING!

Walltula

Threat Meter

Two Walltulas are scuttling on your treehouse's side. These nasty little critters cling to vertical surfaces and bite if you're right next to them. Aim your Slingshot from ground level, using Ⓩ trigger to auto-aim, and take down the one on the ladder. Look up onto your roof, and manually tackle the one up there. Both require only one hit, and each gives up a Rupee when it explodes.

With the Walltulas defeated, climb the ladder, and enter your home. Inside the main level, a chest has appeared! Open the chest, and you'll discover your second weapon: it's the **Wooden Sword** that Rusl made for you!

OVERWORLD CHEST #1: WOODEN SWORD

WOODEN SWORD
YOU GOT THE **WOODEN SWORD**! IT WAS RETURNED TO YOU FULLY REPAIRED. IT'S EASY TO USE: SWING THE WII REMOTE!

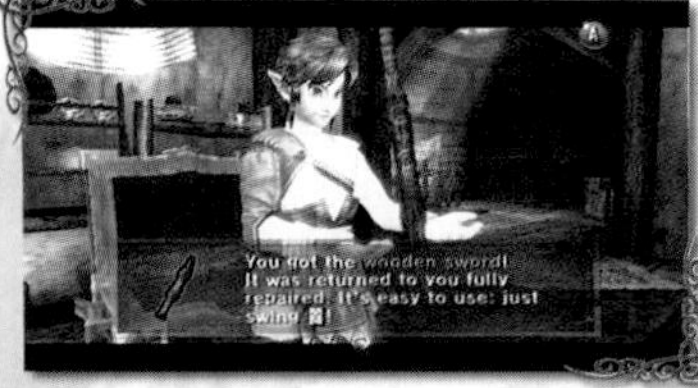

◄ Exit your house, and spend more time with the trio of tykes. Talo is excited about your sword; he wants to use it on some troublesome monkeys who've been seen in the woods. Agree to teach them how to use your sword, and in turn, learn yourself.

The Wooden Sword

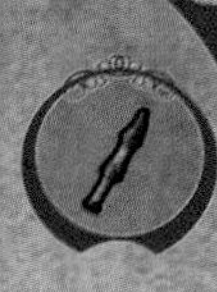

Talo asks you to show off a slice move on the scarecrow. Waggle the Wii Remote to unsheathe your sword. Swing the Wii Remote from left to right (or right to left) to execute a **horizontal slice**.

Use Ⓩ to target the scarecrow, then swing like you did before. Although Beth wants to see a stab, try the vertical slice first.

Tip: USE THE SWING AGAINST SINGLE FOES IN QUICK SUCCESSION WITH MANY OTHER SWINGS.

Attempt a stronger attack, the **stab**. Start by targeting a foe with Ⓩ, press ✥, then swing your Wii Remote.

Tip: USE THE STAB ON SINGLE FOES YOU WANT TO DEFEAT QUICKLY.

Beth asks you to show off your spin attack. Malo murmurs that it's easy to pull off. Lightly shake the Nunchuk from side to side to launch it. A couple of seconds later, your sword recharges, and you can try again.

Tip: USE THE SPIN ON MULTIPLE ENEMIES, OR FOR QUICK TAKEDOWNS. WATCH THE RECHARGE TIME! THIS IS AN EXCEPTIONAL MOVE SO USE IT OFTEN.

Talo isn't ready to let you leave before you show him the **jump attack**. Malo mutters that it's achieved with Ⓐ while you target with Ⓩ.

Tip: USE THE JUMP ATTACK ON ENEMIES AS YOU CLOSE IN FOR A QUICK INITIAL STRIKE.

Enemies Encountered

Walltula

Characters Encountered

Colin

Epona

Beth

Talo

Malo

Coro

➤ The children are impressed, you just learned all the main sword strikes. They spot a monkey nearby and run after it, leaving you alone.

Spend some time practicing the four techniques shown on the scarecrow. Be sure you can remember how to damage foes in those four different ways. When you're done, speak to Colin, who's standing at the village entrance. He tells you the children have run into the forest.

◄ Chase after them. Mount Epona, and head northward, down the woodland path. You can't take Epona into the village, as Colin stops you. Remember to sparingly use the spurs to increase Epona's speed. In the next glade, Beth is waiting to the side. Talo and Malo have both gone on ahead, and she can't catch up to them. Chase down those troublesome tykes after optionally checking the glade for items. In the next glade, the weird Malo tells you Talo went across the bridge. Follow him!

◄ Gallop over the now-unlocked Ordon Bridge after passing the spring, and don't stop. Epona isn't going to leap off the bridge's sides, so don't worry about falling. Continue to the other side, into the more dangerous hillocks and glades of Faron Woods....

Caution

Epona won't leap off the bridge, but you can! Don't get too close to the sides or jump off the bridge if you're on foot, or you'll plummet to a nasty end. You'll lose a Heart of life and appear at the glade where you met Beth.

Missing Links

1. Horsing About in the Grass

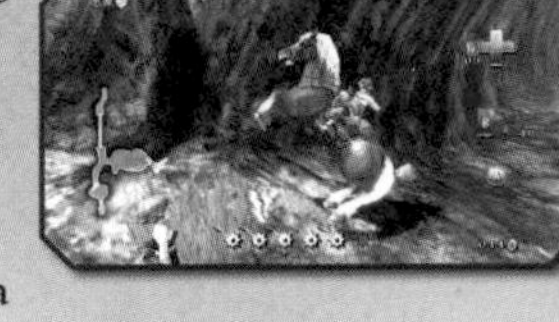

You don't need to dismount when investigating grassy areas; running through them with Epona usually results in hidden items appearing.

2. Sword Swiping in the Grass

As soon as you're granted the **Wooden Sword**, you can swipe at long grass instead of running about in it. Run, and swing the Wii Remote from side to side. For some real grass clearing, try a cool **spin attack** (rock the Nunchuk side to side).

Task 6: Investigate the Dark Tunnel

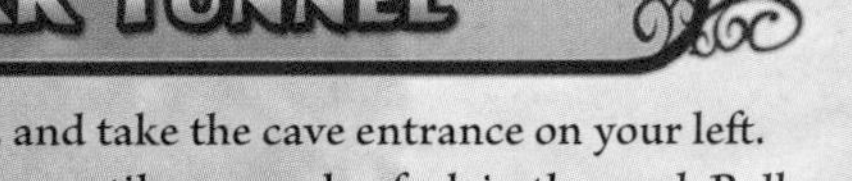

Wander into Faron Woods

▲ Speed up from a canter to a charge and steer Epona through the glade, and into a smaller glade with a low fence ahead of you. Spur Epona on, and leap the fence. Make sure you're dead-on, or Epona refuses to jump. After the jump, you land near Faron Woods Spring.

Ignore the spring for the moment, and take the cave entrance on your left. Gallop through the tunnel-like cavern until you reach a fork in the road. Pull up beside the sign and read it. You need light before you venture farther!

➤ Turn left, and head down the sunlit trail to a clearing. A chap with excellent hair is sitting near his campfire. Dismount and head over to talk to him. This guy's name is Coro, and he wrote the sign at the junction. He warns you not to venture around these parts without illumination, even in the daylight. After this warning, he gives you a special gift.

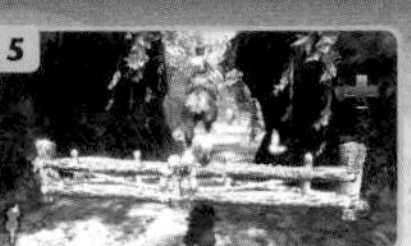

Coro:

A gatekeeper living in a cottage and eking out a subsistence in the woods, Coro is content with his primitive surroundings. He's between 15 and 16, and he loves the animals and birds of the woodland. City dwellers refer to him as a "bumpkin." Coro is the younger brother of Iza and the older brother of Hena. He's a little timid, but jocular.

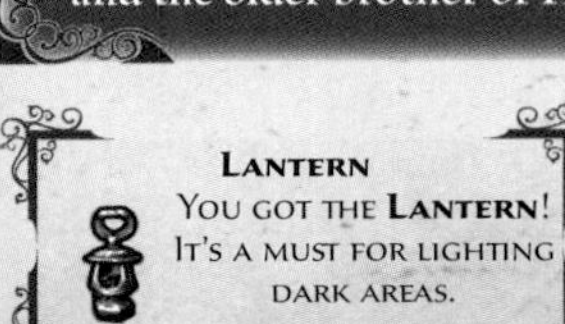

Lantern
You got the **Lantern**! It's a must for lighting dark areas.

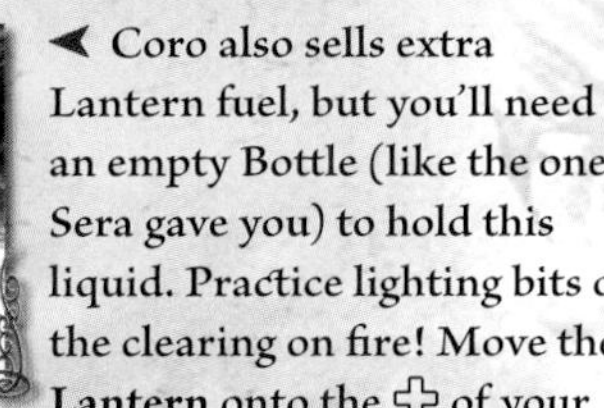

Tip: Set the Lantern to Ⓑ on the ⊖ menu screen and press Ⓑ to use it. It uses up fuel, so make sure you stand still, and *then* press Ⓐ to snuff the light out!

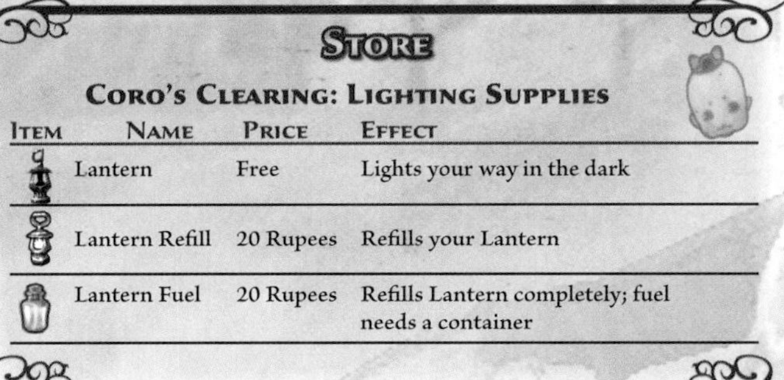

◄ Coro also sells extra Lantern fuel, but you'll need an empty Bottle (like the one Sera gave you) to hold this liquid. Practice lighting bits of the clearing on fire! Move the **Lantern** onto the ✣ of your Wii Remote. Access it using one of the ✣ directions. Press Ⓑ and light the stove. Now make sure you keep a lookout for the Lantern fuel meter under your Hearts. It is slowly depleting, so don't hold your Lantern for long.

Store

Coro's Clearing: Lighting Supplies

Item	Name	Price	Effect
	Lantern	Free	Lights your way in the dark
	Lantern Refill	20 Rupees	Refills your Lantern
	Lantern Fuel	20 Rupees	Refills Lantern completely; fuel needs a container

Lantern Fuel
You got Lantern fuel! It refills your Lantern if you select it, then press Ⓑ.

Tip: Use your Lantern sparingly. Refill the Lantern only when it's really low on fuel because any excess liquid is wasted. It is more cost-effective to fill the Bottle and refuel during an exploration, so empty it of Milk or Bee Larva, and fill it with Lantern fuel.

➤ After you light the stove, and Coro congratulates you, move to one of the two unlit torches on the clearing's opposite side. Practice your lighting skills by waving the Lantern at both of them. When you're done, put the Lantern away (stand, then Ⓐ).

Optionally explore the clearing. Currently, the place is a dead end. At the clearing's northern end is a vine-filled gate preventing your progress. On the east side, a **boulder** stops your path. Head back to Coro.

▲ If your Lantern is near full, and you've bought more fuel and filled your Bottle, it's time to investigate that dark, dank tunnel! Head to the long grass and sign, and bring out your sword. A **Deku Baba** plant rears up and tries to strike you! Fight back, then enter the cave, or head back to your house.

Deku Baba

Threat Meter

The Deku Baba is a weed that's grown out of control, and it hungers for anything nearby, including you! Fortunately, it isn't hardy when struck by a sword, and your makeshift weapon is adequate for the job. Ⓩ target the Deku Baba, and slice it with a couple of well-timed strikes or a spin. It collapses, and you can open the head for Deku nuts, which you can use with your Slingshot.

This large man-eating plant with a vicious mouth needs battering with something sharp. Pulverize it with your sword.

Enemies Encountered

Deku Baba

Characters Encountered

Coro

Missing Links

1. Grass, Trees, and Rock Inspection

Inspect the first and second glades in Faron Woods, plus the spring and Coro's clearing. You'll get Rupees, Hearts, and other items from horseback or by rolling into trees, picking up rocks, and sword slicing through the grass.

2. Coro's Clearing: Scarecrow Tactics, and Low Ramp

Investigate the area southwest of where Coro sits to get more practice time with a scarecrow. A ramp leads up to a corner and an upper window into Coro's house, but you can't reach there for the moment.

3. Coro's Clearing: Deadheading Flowers

You've tried slicing through the long grass with your Wooden Sword, but those small patches of white flowers are impervious to your swings. However, if you use the spin attack, you'll deadhead the flowers. This is the only way to cut into them!

4. Inside the Hut

Coro is a messy little pup, as a quick peek inside his home will tell you. Garbage, old lanterns, drapes, and other debris is scattered about here. Unfortunately, none of it is useful.

5. Dark Tunnel Entrance: Spinning in the Grass

The Dark Tunnel entrance is the best spot to execute a few good 360-degree spins, as the amount of grass you cut is more than with slashing. Grab those Rupees!

Note: You now have illumination! Remember the pitch-black cellar of your treehouse? This is the earliest opportunity to see what's down there. There's a better time to investigate your home in a few minutes, but if you must know what's down there, read on!

Returning to Link's House: Basement Investigation

◄ Head to Ordona Province and your treehouse, enter it, and run to the ladder leading to the dark basement. Remember to equip your **Lantern**! Step forward and turn your Lantern on. The room illuminates, revealing a chest ahead. Open it! The prize is well worth it. Now head back to the Dark Tunnel.

Overworld Chest #2: Purple Rupee (50)

Purple Rupee

It held a **purple Rupee (50)**!

Note: This is the first time you receive a purple Rupee, worth 50 green Rupees!

Missing Links

1. Link's Looking Lovely

Before you leave, check out the basement more thoroughly. Amid the supplies and debris is an old mirror. Step up to it to inspect yourself. (Use Ⓒ for a close up!)

The Dark Tunnel

▲ After you defeat the Deku Baba, you can enter the Dark Tunnel. Note the suspicious patch of earth to the gate's side. Don't worry about it now. There's also a play Wooden Sword. It's Talo's and you can't pick it up, so enter the cave tunnel.

▲ Inside, the cave is gloomy, so edge forward and press Ⓑ to swing your Lantern near a torch, lighting it. Put your Lantern away to conserve fuel. Optionally slash the nearby grass for Hearts and Rupees before you continue. Up ahead, you can hear a squeak and flapping!

Keese

Threat Meter

The Keese is a vicious little airborne rodent who loves to swoop and nip at you. Retaliate in one of two ways. If you spot a Keese (or a group) sleeping upside down on a cave ceiling, use your **Slingshot** and target each one. Close in to auto-target for easier takedowns. If one is attacking, target with Ⓩ, then swipe or jump and swipe. You can easily slay them. You can also auto-target incoming Keeses with your Slingshot, but you may miss.

The Keese is a brown bat with piercing yellow eyes. It's more of a nuisance than a threat. Swipe once to keep it at bay.

◄ Engage the Keese, then run to the next torch and light it with your **Lantern**. You have plenty of fuel left, so keep the Lantern out, produce your sword, and head up the tunnel. As it bends to the right, a Deku Baba rises to scare you. Battle back with sword swipes!

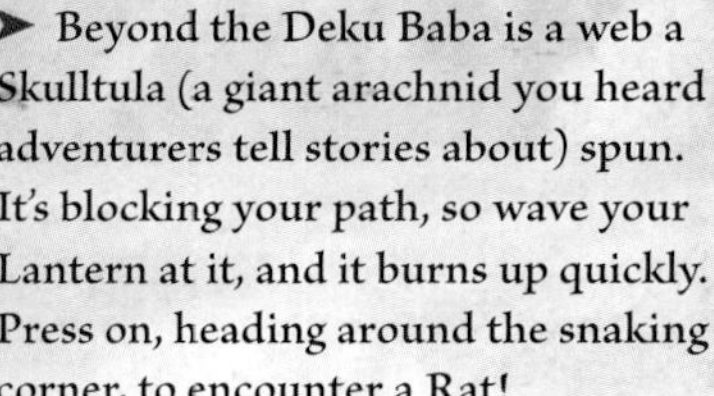

➤ Beyond the Deku Baba is a web a Skulltula (a giant arachnid you heard adventurers tell stories about) spun. It's blocking your path, so wave your Lantern at it, and it burns up quickly. Press on, heading around the snaking corner, to encounter a Rat!

Rat

Threat Meter

Rats are the least of your worries on this adventure. Listen for them squeaking, produce your sword, and press Ⓩ to target. This works well because you'll face your target even in the darkness! Slice or jump in and slice.

Rats are scuttling creatures who live in shadows and emerge to give you a nasty nip. Return the favor with one sword slice!

▲ The Rat was guarding a junction in this Dark Tunnel. Swipe the torch and put your Lantern away for a moment. Interestingly, there are two suspended pots and the entrance to a side tunnel and two more behind you. Shoot them with your Slingshot to retrieve a total of 12 Rupees.

▲ Investigate the side tunnel on the right wall, and bring out your Lantern and sword as you enter this dark place. A Deku Baba halfway up here needs trimming! Then immediately slice into a Keese. Remember that you can also mow the grass with your blade, too!

➤ The side tunnel ends abruptly, but don't head back until you light the torch and check out the object next to it. This is a small chest, but it contains a few Rupees. Kick it open, then head to the junction and make a right. Slicing grass on the way yields a Heart.

Overworld Chest #3: Yellow Rupee (10)

▲ Bring the Lantern out and burn through a large web. This is the final part of the Dark Tunnel, and you can see the forest ahead of you. Dash out, and remember to put away your Lantern (stand still and press Ⓐ).

Enemies Encountered

Deku Baba

Keese

Skulltula

Rat

Task 7: Unlock the Gate to the Forest Temple Woods

Fighting Fiends in Faron Woods

After you emerge from the Dark Tunnel, you can explore the first large environment away from your village. The Faron Woods area is large, but safe if you keep your sword ready and your Slingshot as backup. Head northeast to encounter a Deku Baba.

◄ In the middle of this woodland is a giant tree, with two large stump platforms on which you can climb. Although there's nothing interesting here at the moment, make a mental note of where these stumps are because you'll be returning here later!

➤ Move to the eastern part of the woods to encounter your first two Bokoblins guarding a gate that's firmly locked. The sign points to the Forest Temple ahead. The gate seems to require a key, so now you know what to do next. Well, apart from battling these two fiendish foes!

Bokoblin

Threat Meter

Bokoblins are sly and stupid, and they love to bash you. Bring out your sword, and strike them four times in a combo after targeting them. If several attack, use your spin move.

➤ Head to the western part of the woods, and you'll encounter another Bokoblin! These purple fiends are nasty, and they love to club innocent villagers who've strayed too far from home. In your case, they've made a terrible mistake!

If you head along the western edge of the woods, there's a small hillock and an overhang you can leap off. Look back with Ⓒ to spot a chest sitting high out of reach; you won't claim this until later. Drop and fight a Keese!

➤ Fight around the large central tree; there are openings to scoot through, and a couple of Keese and a Bokoblin to target. Try using your Slingshot on a Keese; it's a quick hit that works well if you auto-target. When a second Bokoblin comes at you, don't use the Slingshot because it takes eight or nine shots to bring him down!

Explore the northeast corner of the woods. Find three Deku Babas and some nesting Keeses to slice and dice. Fire a Slingshot into a Deku Baba. It stuns the plant, after which you can follow up with a sword to finish!

▲ It's time to enter the tunnel at the north end of the woods to search for a key. Expect a Deku Baba and one or two Bokoblins to greet you. After you dispatch them, bring out your Slingshot, and tag the three nesting Keeses at the tunnel entrance.

◄ As you emerge in the tunnel's far end, you'll spot a dead end, and an incoming Bokoblin. He's not tough if you slash and bash him with your sword. Then tackle a Keese who's flapping in your face. The Bokoblin seemed to be guarding that small chest. Open it!

Overworld Chest #4: Small Key

Small Key

You got the **Small Key**! This key opens the gate to Faron Woods.

Enemies Encountered

Deku Baba

Bokoblin

Keese

◄ Although there doesn't seem to be anything else to do here, wait a moment. Try bringing out your **Lantern** and lighting those two torches! Once both are lit, a previously invisible chest in the alcove above and behind the first appears! Open it immediately!

Overworld Chest #5: Piece of Heart

Piece of Heart

You got a **Piece of Heart**! Collect **five pieces** to form a new Heart Container and increase your life energy! Piece of Heart #1 of 45.

▲ With the Small Key (which appears on your screen above the Rupees you've collected) stored, and your first Piece of Heart found, run to the eastern part of the Faron Woods. Slay or avoid the woodland foes on the way. Move up to the gate and unlock it. Defeat the Bokoblin inside.

Missing Links

1. Larking in the Long Grass

There's grass to cut, and Rupees plus Hearts to harvest. Watch you don't stand on a Deku Baba, as they lurk near patches of grass, too! You can turn Deku Babas' heads into Slingshot ammunition, so pick them up and break them after combat.

Check your Collection menu, where your Piece of Heart is now visible. You need four more for an additional life energy Heart! You can have a theoretical maximum of 20 Hearts of life energy. Here's how this breaks down:

Location	Pieces?	Total
Starting Life Energy	—	3 Heart Containers
In Dungeons (Pieces)	2 x 8 Pieces	3 1/5 Heart Containers
In Dungeons (Containers)	—	8 Heart Containers
In the Overworld	29 Pieces	5 4/5 Heart Containers
Grand Total	45 Pieces + 8 Heart Containers	20 Life Energy

Note

Task 8: Return to Ordon Village, and Prepare for the Big Day

Deeper into the Faron Woods

◄ You emerge from a short tunnel into a large curved clearing where two Bokoblins are talking. Ready your sword's spin attack, and engage them in combat. If you need healing, seek out a Heart in the grass clump at the foot of the large tree to your left. Continue northward.

▲ Attack another Bokoblin, before a bird with the biggest head you've ever seen beckons you over! This is Trill, and his forest store is a perfect place to spend those Rupees you've been unearthing.

Characters Encountered

Beth

Trill

Coro

Plumm

Talo

Rusl

Epona

Fado

Ilia

Mayor Bo

Uli

Pergie

Malo

Jaggle

Hanch

Colin

Store

Item	Cost (Rupees)	Notes
Red Potion Refill	30	A blend of mushroom and herbs replenishes 8 Hearts. Bottle needed.
Lantern Oil Refill	20	The woods are dangerous at night! This fills your Lantern or Bottle. Bottle or Lantern needed.

Trill:

This intelligent myna bird, owned by Coro, watches over the unattended shop in the Faron Woods. Trill is friends with Plumm, another myna bird who lives somewhere near the great lake Hylia.

➤ Check your Lantern oil levels. You should be close to empty with your Lantern, but still have a full Bottle of fuel. Either pour the fuel into the Lantern and use the Bottle to store the Red Potion, or dip the Lantern in and refill it yourself, and ignore the Red Potion.

Before you leave the store, pay up! There's an honor system in play, so cycle through how much you want to pay, and Trill tells you if you've paid too much or too little. Pay the rest if you shortchanged the bird, or he'll peck you the next time you use the shop!

Tip: If you follow the advice in this walkthrough, you'll fill your wallet to 300 Rupees easily. This is fine, until you head into a dungeon, where chests remain unopened if you can't fit Rupees inside your wallet. One way of solving this problem is to overpay Trill. You don't get the money back, but you can check off the chests in a dungeon without going back there again! Neither affects your ultimate goals, however.

➤ After you finish shopping, slash by heading north and west toward a patch of long grass. A Deku Baba is hiding inside. Not for long! Find Rupees and Hearts in the grass around here, as usual.

➤ Now head northeast to spot a winding road leading northward. However, to your right is a patch of grass with a Deku Baba to slice up and a small chest to open! Remember this area for later; this is the entrance to the Sacred Grove, but you can't enter it yet.

Overworld Chest #6: Yellow Rupee (10)

➤ Move to the entrance of the winding path northward. At the foot of a giant tree, you spot Talo and that cheeky monkey placed in a cage! Perhaps the monkey isn't to blame after all! Draw your sword, race up the winding path, and sure enough, strike down the two Bokoblins guarding the pair. Use a spin attack to smash the wooden cage!

Author Note

With the boulders in the background and those two short, stone columns on either side of the cage we spent several minutes attempting to find a tricky lever to free our friends. After jumping on the columns in different orders and hacking at the boulders to no avail it was frustration that led us to slash at the cage...and find the solution.

Missing Links

1. Thieving from Trill Part 1

This doesn't affect anything during your adventure, but you can steal from Trill by walking away from the store after filling a Bottle! Trill calls you a thief, but nothing happens. You can escape!

2. Thieving from Trill Part 2

That is, until you enter the fence. Trill launches an attack, and he's deadlier than any foe you've faced thus far! He can take a quarter of a Heart life energy every couple of seconds. Pay what you owe, and he halts his pecking!

3. Thieving from Trill Part 3

Or, ignore Trill's pecking, run in, scoop up the Red Potion, restore eight Hearts, and leave with minimal damage! This isn't heroic, but it's possible!

Ordona Province: A Big Day of Transformations

Walk Talo out of the Dark Tunnel, and he begs you not to mention this to his dad. He runs off, and Rusl strolls in and greets you. He mentions how strange the woods feel. He wishes you luck tomorrow; you might even meet Princess Zelda!

◄ The next day, Fado asks you to finish the chores at the ranch. Use the **Horse Grass** to call Epona and wrangle those goats using the techniques taught earlier. A time of 26–30 seconds is excellent. The best time on record? **23 seconds!** Try it when you wrangle goats here a second time. When you're done, leap over the northeast corner's fence.

Author Note

A peaceful starting village, complete with a working ranch, brought us back to the days of *The Ocarina of Time*, although Fado's idiosyncrasies and his goats aren't quite as strange as that sleepy-head Talon and the Lon Lon Ranch. Remember how you had to wake him up with an egg that hatches into a Cucco?

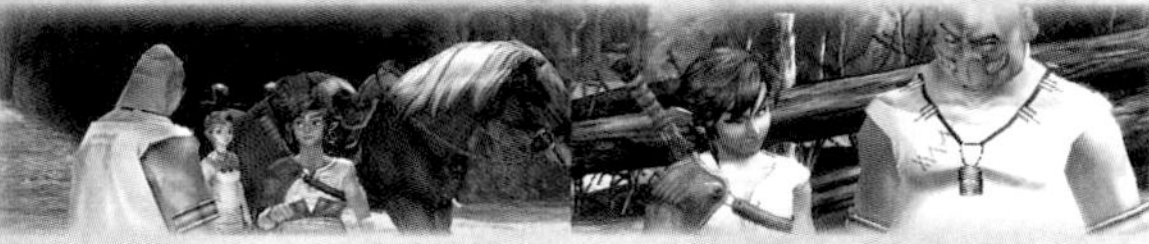

You ride down to meet Ilia and Mayor Bo. Everything is ready and the royal gift is here. Ilia isn't happy, and she scolds you for pushing Epona too hard! Then she scolds her father for sticking up for you. She takes Epona to the spring; that's where you'll find her!

◄ When you finish talking with the mayor, Fado yells. Another goat is loose! Stand and move left or right to catch it, then press Ⓐ to toss it. Optionally pat it afterward so it bleats happily. Say good-bye to the mayor (his house is locked).

◄ Run to Rusl and Uli's house, where Uli asks you to take care of yourself. Rusl is practicing sword moves; he's impressive! He offers to teach you when you return.

You can also visit Pergie in her house, and she thanks you for rescuing Talo and Malo. Up on the flat rock with the vines stands Jaggle, who tells you to have a safe trip! You can even speak to miserable Hanch. He is spending his day stocking shelves! Hanch's wife hears the city stores are really ritzy! Buy her wares if you need them.

Missing Links

1. Cucco or Cuckoo?

This is the first time you've encountered a Cucco while carrying a sword. If you're feeling malicious, you can run after a Cucco, slicing it with your blade! Feathers fly off everywhere, and it squawks like mad. Spend too long striking a Cucco, and something strange happens: you become the Cucco! You have 10 seconds' worth of flying, dashing, and flapping until you return to your human body.

◄ Head out of the village, and speak to Colin, who isn't being let into the woods by Talo and Malo. Optionally speak to Beth, then entertain Talo and Malo by giving them the Wooden Sword when Talo asks for it. You can't enter the woods otherwise!

Talo screams with joy, and the brothers head off to the scarecrow. Colin asks if you could teach him to ride a horse sometime, then he disappears into the woods. Follow him to the spring. This time, don't miss a couple of squirrels scampering about. Head to the gate.

➤ The gate to the spring is locked, and so is the one to the bridge! Ilia isn't letting you in, and Colin says he'll talk to her about you rescuing Talo. Colin tells you to try the tunnel entrance (which you found earlier). Head to the woodland glade and enter the narrow tunnel on your knees. Collect a couple of Rupees on the way. Exit and meet up with Ilia.

Ilia realizes that you helped Talo, and she tells you Epona is feeling better. But she wants you to promise her not to try anything out of your league! Suddenly, Epona lets out a startled whinny!

A massive Bullbo crashes through the gate with two Bulblin Riders. One strikes Ilia with an arrow. You fall, clubbed in the head! The riders gather up the bodies of Ilia and Colin. The raiding party is joined by a massive Bulblin on Bullbo-back!

This is King Bulblin riding Lord Bullbo! He blows a huge horn, and something strange appears out of the sky. You waken, run to the bridge, and an inky black arm pulls you into another world!

A strange and alien being holds you by the neck. This is a Twilit Messenger. Your Triforce glows. The Messenger flees. Your body twitches. You scream, and transform into a black-and-white wolf! You collapse and the Messenger slowly drags you away. Silently, a strange figure watches....

Enemies Encountered

Deku Baba

Bokoblin

Bulblin Rider

Bulblin

King Bulblin

Lord Bullbo

Twilit Messenger

Task #8
Return to Ordon Village, and Prepare for the Big Day

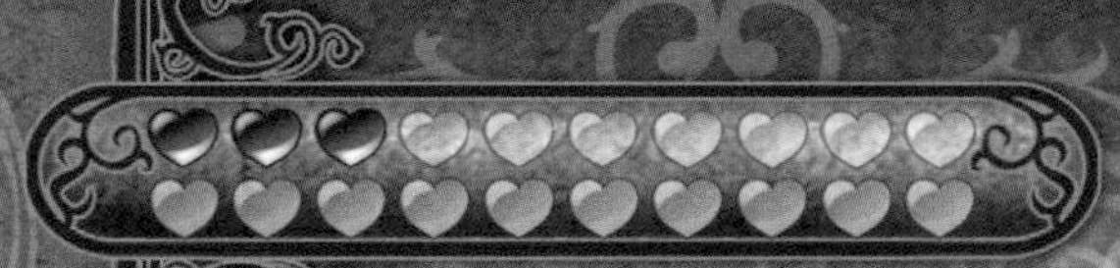

Overworld: A Wolf Howls in the Twilight

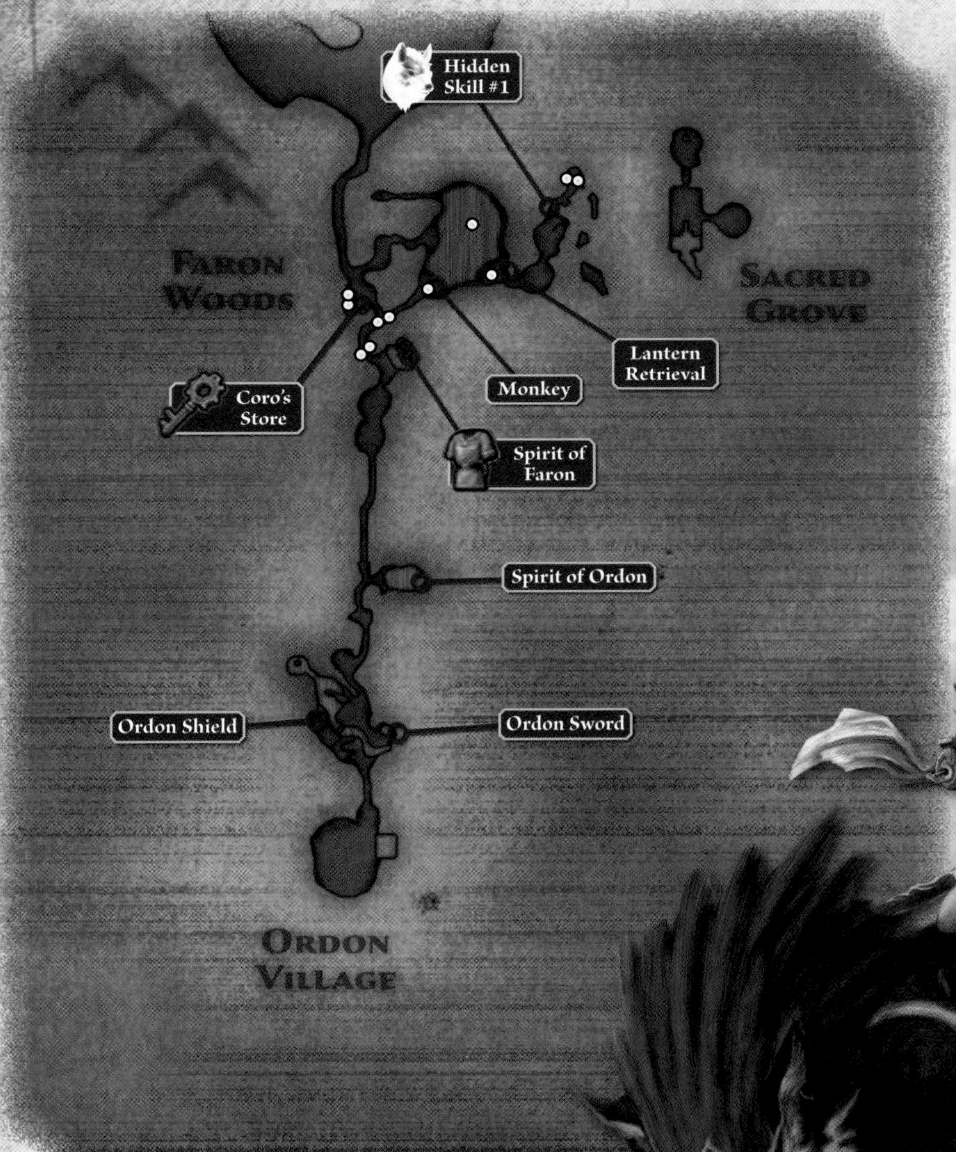

Hidden Skill #1

Faron Woods

Sacred Grove

Lantern Retrieval

Monkey

Coro's Store

Spirit of Faron

Spirit of Ordon

Ordon Shield

Ordon Sword

Ordon Village

Legend

Twilit Parasite

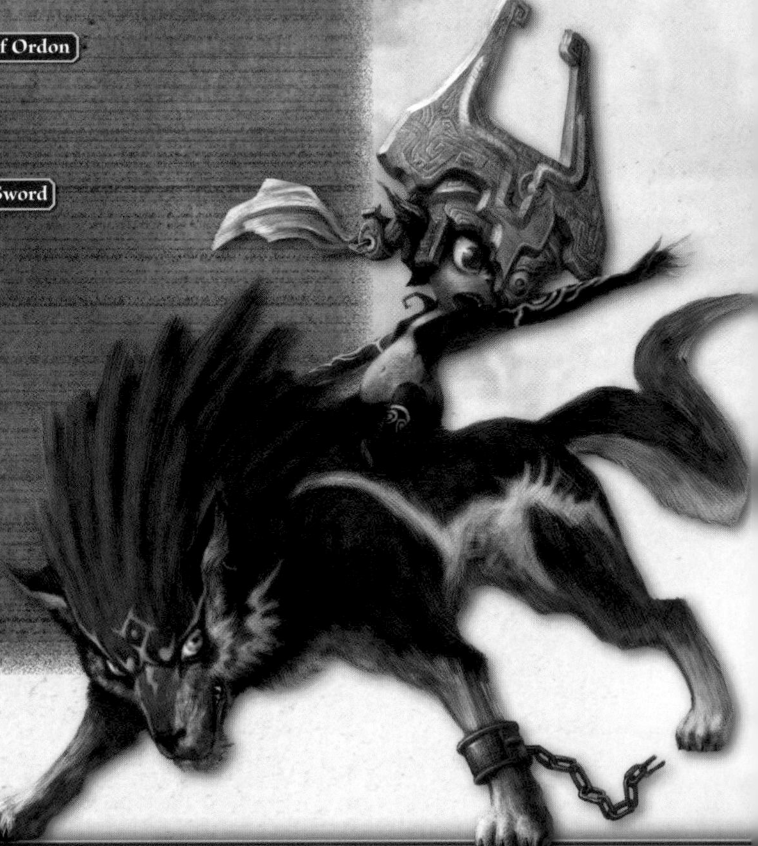

1

pg 54
Escape to the Castle Tower

2

pg 56
Gain an Audience with Twilight Princess

3
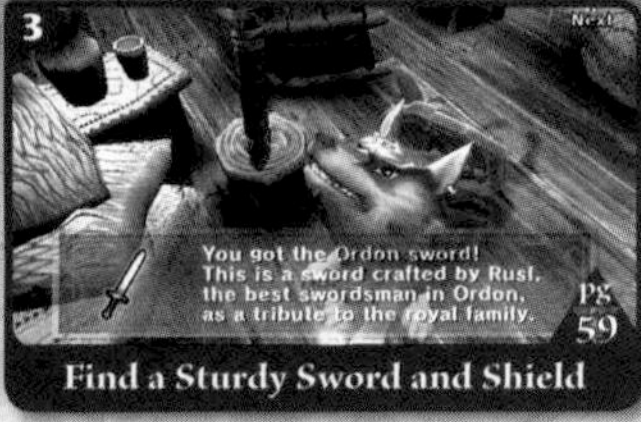
You got the Ordon sword!
This is a sword crafted by Rusl,
the best swordsman in Ordon,
as a tribute to the royal family.
pg 59
Find a Sturdy Sword and Shield

4

pg 61
Speak with the Spirit of Faron Spring

A Wolf Howls in the Twilight: Overview

After a startling transformation into a wolf, and an even stranger meeting with an impish creature of the twilight, you begin an uneasy alliance with your new rider: a shadow creature named Midna. She rides you through a series of sewers, a tower, and up through the battlements of what appears to be Castle Hyrule, to gain an audience with the Twilight Princess. It seems the King of Shadows has spread twilight across the realm, turning people into spirits and casting the world into permanent gloom. But a hero shall rise, learning the old ways to triumph over this menace, once the light has been restored to three provinces: Faron, Eldin, and Kakariko. Your epic quest has only just begun, but the heroic outfit you're about to be given has been passed down through generations....

A Link to the Present

Overworld Denizens

Items to Obtain

Ordon Shield, Ordon Sword, Vessel of Light, Hero's Clothes, Small Key, Lantern, Hidden Skill #1

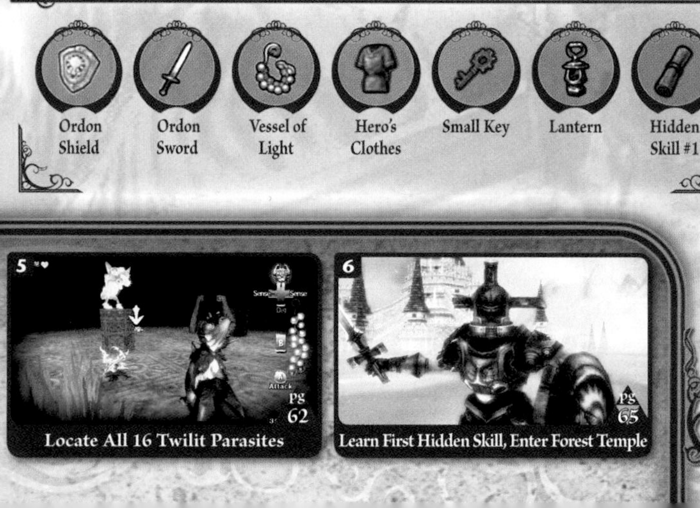

Characters Encountered

Midna

Task 1: Escape to the Castle Tower

Imprisoned in the Sewers

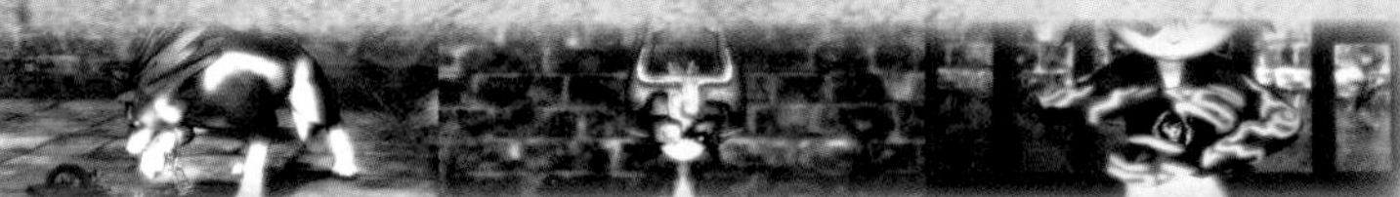

You awaken in wolf form, chained to the ground. You're in a cell, deep inside a dungeon catacomb. You look up to see a strange, cherubic figure floating near you.

You must be obedient! After some teasing, she severs the chain link and makes you a deal. If you can reach her, she'll tell you what the deal is!

◄ The weird little imp has a giant pink arm flailing out of her helm, and if you talk to her, she hints there's a **hole** you can squeeze through. It's in the front-right area of the cell, blocked by a crumbling crate. Move to this area, and execute a spin attack. This occurs with your tail now, instead of a sword! Then press ✚ to dig under the bent bars, and scramble out of your prison.

Author Note

In what turned out to be an incredible brain-teaser, we spent literally half an hour rampaging through this cell, trying everything to escape, **except** (of course) the spin or normal attack to shatter the crates. We suggest you learn from our mistake!

You reach the jail corridor, and Midna disappears, then sits on your back. You're captured and must obey her! Should you need her advice, press ✚ for information. "Are we clear?" she asks. "Good! Now get moving!"

Midna:

Midna is a genie-like pixie with a childish proportion, only four feet high. She is arrogant and scornful to you and seems to be seething with anger at an injustice inflicted upon her by evil and unknown forces. She is somehow linked to the strange twilight that has descended upon the land. What are Midna's real secrets? Who is she really?

◄ Midna has ordered you to escape, but the door at the south end of the corridor is firmly sealed. Instead, open the door to the adjacent cell, and enter. Inside is a long chain with a pull-handle at the end. Midna requests to speak with you, telling you to press Z. This locks onto the chain, and you can walk around it, while Midna's strange ethereal arm grabs and grasps. When you "bite" with Ⓐ, you grab the chain and pull it down. This releases the small barred gate leading to a sewer channel. Run south, down there.

Missing Links

1. Hay, Will You Look at This?

Even the jail cells in this place hold a little cash. Dig into the piles of hay and straw scattered about; almost all of them contain a green Rupee (1).

Castle Sewers

◄ Scamper down the narrow outlet, into the main catacombs area, and stop to check the strange light in the corner of the first passage. Use either ✚ or ✚ to view your world through an ethereal sense. You'll see the spirit of a castle guard! He talks about something chasing him! This is a **spirit** and others are around....

Tip — Sense View: Your sense view allows you to see spirits and scents that appear throughout the land. However, your view is limited so it's often better to switch back and forth to see where you're going. The sense also allows you to find "dig spots," or sparkling patches of earth you can dig in to find Hearts, Rupees, and even hidden rooms in the ground!

◄ For now, turn and face north. You're in a castle of some kind, and a sewer channel stretches off to a T-junction at the far end. Drop into the shallow water (you can run through it), and investigate the black blob moving around ahead. What is this creature?

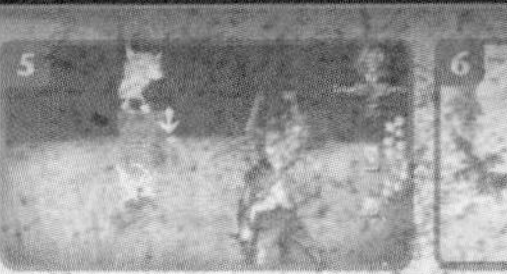

Twilit Vermin

Threat Meter

The Twilit Vermin is a vicious little mite that seeks a victim and attacks mercilessly. However, it is very weak. Target it with Z immediately, then bite or spin attack it. A single strike defeats it. The only time to worry about Twilit Vermin is if you're swimming—while swimming, you can't attack them, but they can attack you! Seek dry land, and then retaliate.

The Twilit Vermin is a shadow creature that doggedly attacks, but it can be dispatched easily with a single bite. Watch out for ambushes, though!

➤ At the T-junction, make a right turn, and trot to the end of the sewer passage. Midna's giant arm appears, indicating that there's a chain to pull nearby. It is on the southern side of the sewer channel. Pull it, then leap into the conduit nearest the end of this passage. The chain has opened it up, and at the far end is a small crate to destroy. Inside the crate is a blue Rupee (5)!

➤ The other three arched conduit channels are sealed, so dash westward to the T-junction, and head through the open barred door. Midna speaks to you, telling you to use your attacks. Stop at the next conduit on the north wall. Pull the chain, leap into the now-open channel, and bite the Twilit Vermin inside! Smash the skull for a Heart, then head back to the main sewer.

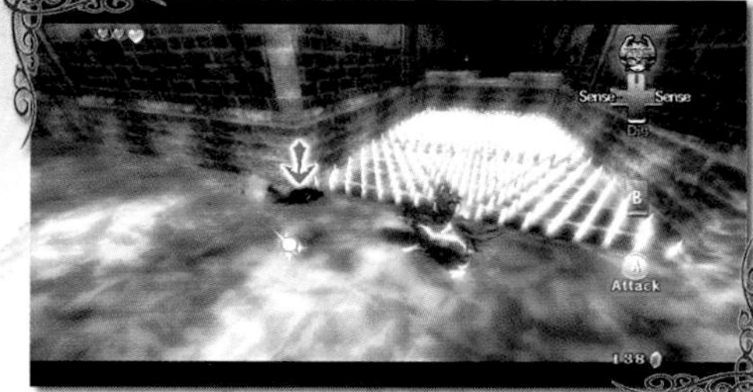

➤ You reach a crossroads, with a nasty set of spikes on the floor to your right. Don't stand on them! Instead, try your spin attack on a roaming Twilit Vermin in the shallow water. Then dash to the western end of the sewer area and smash a couple of skulls.

➤ In the southwestern corner of this area is another chain to pull. It releases a Twilit Vermin, so dodge its leap, then devour it! The channel is now open, and it bends around to the east. Jump inside, then flick your sense view on and you'll see a patch of sparkling black earth. This is a **dig spot!** There's another around the corner. Dig up both spots for a green Rupee (1) and Heart.

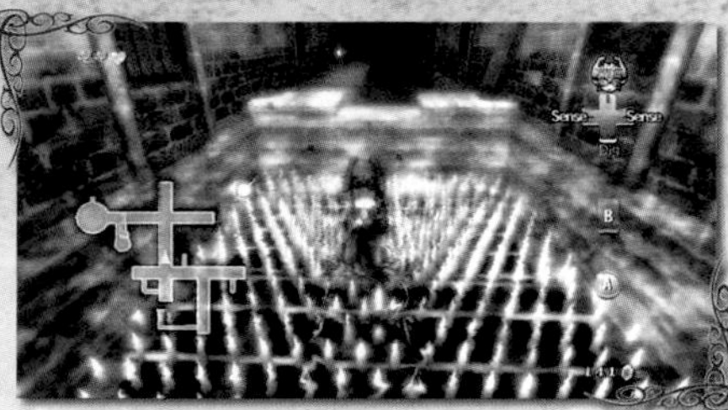

➤ Flick your sense view back to normal and investigate the southern end of the crossroads, opposite the spiked floor. Near a skull on the right walkway is a chain. Pull it and a metal dam wall rises up, filling the sewer with water! You can now dog-paddle northward, over the spikes, to the northern part of the sewer system. Stand on the ground and wait for a swimming Twilit Vermin to meet you, then defeat it. Remember that when you swim near a Twilit Vermin, you are defenseless.

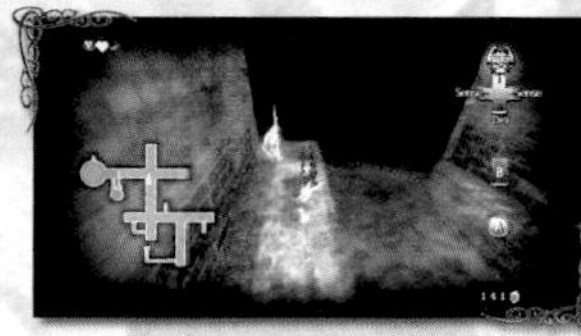

➤ With your sense view engaged, run to the northern crossroads along the walkway to the side of the sewer, and look for the floating light. It is another guard. Now turn right at the crossroads, and pull the chain on the southern side.

➤ This opens a small conduit next to the chain, and two Twilit Vermin spring out! Don't follow them into the water; either attack them from land or ignore them until later. Check the conduit for items and dig spots.

Enemies Encountered

Twilit Vermin

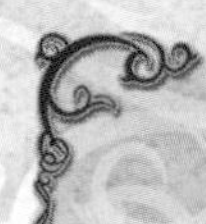

Midna

➤ Move to the northwestern end of this sewer area and Midna departs from your back and goes through a barred fence. She wants you to follow her. There's a small passage under the water, just below and left of the fence. You need to drain the water.

◄ Do this by trotting all the way back to the opposite end of this east-west passage, then grabbing the chain near a second metal dam wall. It empties the water from this area. A second yank on the chain refills the area. A cowering spirit of a soldier in one corner warns you about monsters!

If you're having problems battling the Twilit Vermin, yank this chain as soon as you can, dropping the water as soon as you cross the spiked floor. This way, you can attack these foes in shallow water where your attacks are effective, instead of in deeper water where you're vulnerable.

Tip

➤ With the water level dropped, move westward, optionally pausing in the northernmost point to grab a final chain, releasing two Vermin and allowing access to a final conduit containing a crate with a Rupee inside.

➤ Head back to Midna and peer down to locate a narrow tunnel. Midna leaves you for a moment, so enter it and you emerge in a small earthen area leading around to Midna herself. Use your sense view to crack more than Hearts from skulls. There are two dig spots near another cowering soldier—expect a Heart and a blue Rupee (5) for your troubles. Now bound out of the earthen ground to meet Midna, and move west.

Missing Links

1. Skull Smashing

Scattered about the sewers are the skulls of an unknown, but not quite human, creature. You can pick up the skull with your teeth, then throw and smash it, or destroy the skulls where they sit. They give you Rupees, Hearts, or nothing at all!

Task 2: Gain an Audience with the Twilight Princess

Climbing the Castle Tower

◄ You arrive at the base of a tall tower with a winding staircase around the perimeter. First, optionally attack two Twilit Vermin splashing in the water at the tower's base. Stay on the steps, wait until they leap on dry land, then snag them!

Follow the staircase upward, around the tower perimeter, and leap to a piece of loose masonry that collapses. Retrace your steps and stop at the edge. Midna decides to guide you. **Target** her with Ⓩ, then press Ⓐ to follow her. You leap across easily. Do this twice.

Using Midna to leap gaps is an incredibly important technique. Listen for her laugh at an area you can't normally maneuver across. Then leap across as quickly as possible. Hold down Ⓩ and you auto-target the next leaping spot. Press Ⓐ quickly to complete the leaps fast; this prevents you from falling during a complex jump or climb.

Tip

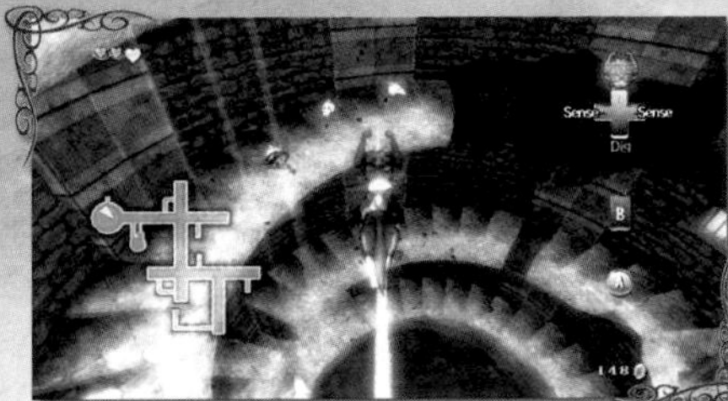

◄ Continue to bound up the tower, leaping a couple of small gaps on your own, then using Midna again on a piece of fallen stairs to reach an upper area. Stop when you see a rope stretching out to the side.

This rope leads to the section of staircase you just avoided. Position yourself facing the rope directly, then walk onto it. Continue to the lower end of the staircase, then break the skulls and slay the Twilit Vermin. You can target it and leap from the rope if you're daring! Find the Rupee prize in one of the skulls, then head back up the rope, and continue to ascend to a skull with a Heart in it, and a second rope.

1 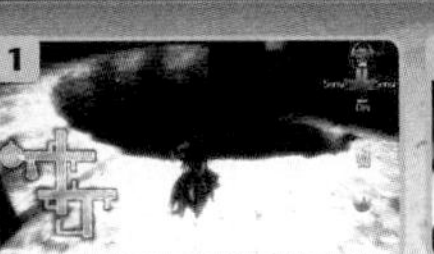
2 
3 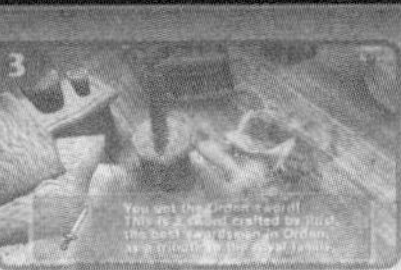
4 
5 
6 

➤ Cross the second rope, bound up and around the top of the staircase again, and use Midna to jump three long gaps until you reach the tower's exit. Climb around the fenced stairs to the base of the tower parapet. A couple of dark, bat-like things appear!

Twilit Keese

Threat Meter

These are Twilit Keeses. Target them at once, then leap back and forward to grab each of them. It only takes one bite to slay them. Spin attacks also work, providing the Keeses are flying near you.

The Twilit Keese is longer and more fear-inducing than the regular Keese, but just as easily defeated!

➤ Spend some time smashing crates for Rupees and a Heart, and then inspect the door. It is firmly shut. Climb onto the rubble to the right of the door, hold Ⓩ, and make a five-stage series of jumps up to an open door high above you.

Castle Hyrule Battlements

◄ You're traveling to another tower, where Midna wants to introduce you to someone. Bound out and down, onto the parapet. You can optionally turn south and head down the stairs to smash a skull or two for a Heart.

Head north. You can spend some time peering across to the castle's main central keep. When you're done, head to the corner of the dilapidated parapet section, where a soldier spirit waits to wail about monstrous birds. He confirms where you are: Castle Hyrule!

➤ Midna urges you to the tower. Push the crate forward so it reaches a wooden blockade, then climb up and onto it, and drop onto a second stone parapet. Drop into the hexagonal stone area, and press Ⓩ to target a massive, flapping monstrosity!

Twilit Kargarok

Threat Meter

This wretched creature swoops in to attack, delivering a nasty swipe or nip that deals half a Heart's worth of energy loss. Wait for this dive, while keeping a constant lock-on, and then leap and bite the bird. It lets out a yelp that sounds like a horn! It comes back for seconds, so strike it again, either with a leaping bite, or a spin attack (which is less effective). The horn noise is higher-pitched this time, so you know you've defeated it. Keep away from the sides when you're attacking. Wait and let the Twilit Kargarok come to you, or you may leap to a bottomless plummet!

An otherworldly version of a hated Hyrulian carrion, the Twilit Kargarok should be struck twice. Listen for the horn!

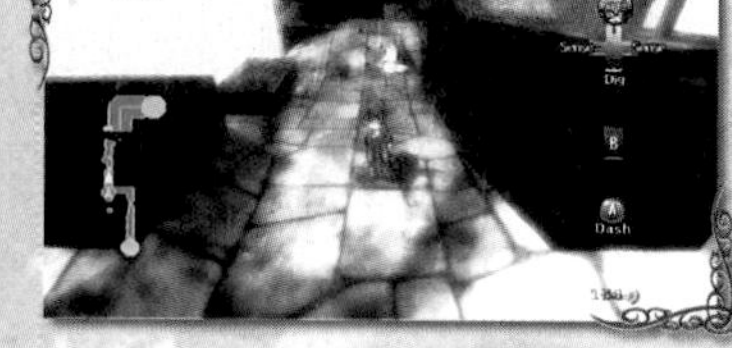

➤ With the beast defeated, smash a skull, then ignore the small square tower with crates on it because it's too far away to reach. Face north and walk along another crumbling parapet until the strange music sounds the arrival of another Twilit Kargarok. Stay away from the edge of the parapet as you defeat it!

◄ Continue to the far northern end of the parapet, where you can see another small square tower that cannot be reached because the bridge is out. Look right and smash the skull for a Heart. Midna offers to help you leap across to the rooftop nearby. Execute a quick three-jump maneuver.

Enemies Encountered

Twilit Vermin

Twilit Keese

Twilit Kargarok

Characters Encountered

Midna

Princess Zelda

Cucco

Jaggle

Mayor Bo

Hanch

Now on a roof, canter forward, following the gable and making a turn before you're assaulted by two Twilit Kargaroks. Stay in the upper middle part of the roof, and leap to grab both of them. Once they're defeated, head directly to the ledge. Climb up and into an open doorway.

Missing Links

1. Up on the Roof

Clusters of crates dot this roof. Check for two sets to the left of where you landed, skulls on the small roof windows, and crates along the wooden fence perimeter. All carry Rupees, Hearts, or nothing!

Princess Zelda's Private Quarters

You appear in a small window halfway up a spiral staircase. Drop down and optionally head downward; there's little here except a sealed door. Move to the top of the staircase, break open two small crates for Hearts, and nuzzle open the large arched door.

A hooded figure is watching the enveloping twilight. The figure turns. "Midna?!" she says. The figure kneels down next to you. Midna tells her she should explain what she managed to do.... "Twilight Princess!" she finishes.

The figure explains that the kingdom of Hyrule has been transformed by the king that rules the twilight. She recalls how Princess Zelda and her troops valiantly defended the throne from the creatures of shadow.

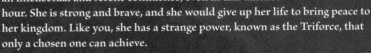

A figure strides to the throne, dressed in shadow armor and flanked by two Twilit Messengers. Princess Zelda drops her sword. The Triforce is cast in shadow. Castle Hyrule burns as the townsfolk turn to spirits.

The figure removes her hood, declaring "I am Zelda." The princess explains that shadow beasts are looking for her. You must find a way to remove this permanent twilight!

Princess Zelda:

Princess Zelda is about 20 years old, and is the queen-in-waiting of Hyrule. Her kingdom was taken over by a strange man clad in shadow armor, who in exchange for the lives of her people, banished her to this castle. Zelda speaks with an intellectual and serene confidence, even in this darkest hour. She is strong and brave, and she would give up her life to bring peace to her kingdom. Like you, she has a strange power, known as the Triforce, that only a chosen one can achieve.

Although you can speak to Princess Zelda, she tells you to leave quickly before the guards arrive. She doesn't mind you climbing on her bed, checking the book on the table, or even dousing the fire with a spin attack to claim a yellow Rupee (10)! Now leave, heading down the spiral steps.

A guard is coming! Midna transports you across the castle roof, where she asks you what you want to do next. Quickly transforming into the terrified forms of Colin and Ilia, Midna supposes you'll want to help them. She'll help, as long as you do exactly what she says! You land back at the Ordon Spring, still in the shape of a wolf!

1 
2 
3 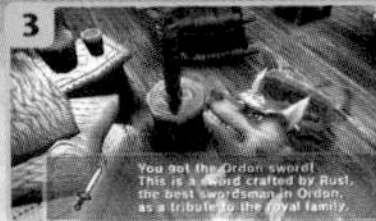
4 
5 
6 

Task 3: Find a Sturdy Sword and Shield

Ordon Province: Roaming in Wolf Form

➤ You cannot count on the help of your village friends, as you're a fearsome furry beast, but you do have an extra sense to help you! Use it to find multiple dig spots at the springs, each containing a Heart! Then exit via the gate. Midna appears. She wants a **sword** and **shield** that suit her. She's very demanding! Check the dig spot near the bridge, then head south. There's another dig spot in the clearing. A Bulblin warrior wanders around—target and bite or spin attack it. Move to your home, and more appear!

Bulblin Warrior

Threat Meter

Bulblin warriors are roaming your woods, but defeating them is straightforward with your sharp teeth and whipping tail. Target the nearest one as soon as you can, then leap in and gnaw on him. Follow this up with a spin attack to strike more than one foe. Pounce on the foe as he lies on the ground to finish him off.

The Bulblin warrior isn't something to fear when encountered on its own. Your wolf form can attack and defeat it in seconds!

➤ When you're done, head toward the village. A voice thanks you for dealing with those Bulblins. It's the squirrel! It seems you can talk to animals in wolf form; try this out on every animal you spot! Now head into the village itself.

Missing Links

1. Going Underground

The area outside your house, near the scarecrow, around the trees, near the Ordon Village entrance, and various other areas have dig spots; unearth Hearts and Rupees from them.

➤ Enter Ordon Village. All the homes are locked up. The pasture is closed. But there's a Cucco to speak to, clucking near the mayor's house. It tells you of a **ruckus** in the village: monsters stole the children!

You can talk to the frogs at the stream or more Cuccos, but the most interesting area is the ground near the waterwheel, where Jaggle and the mayor are asking about the **shield** and **sword**. Listen to them explaining where these items are. They spot you and flee inside the house.

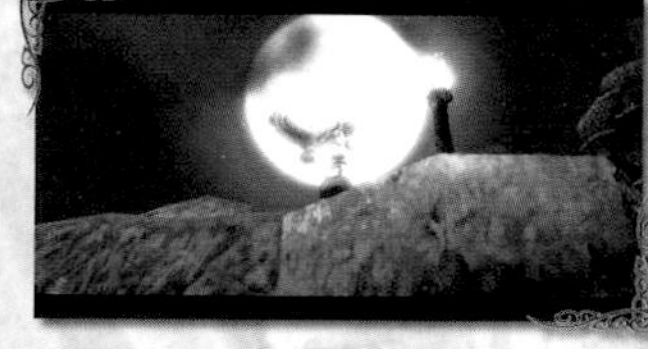

➤ Midna tells you that the village is full of idiots. There's an entrance left open on the roof of the waterwheel house. Run back over the bridge, and move toward the pumpkin patch. Hanch now notices you and summons the hawk! It swoops down and knocks you about!

➤ The hawk can seriously devour your energy, so move back to the village entrance, out of range of its talons, and stand on the small rock jutting out of the grass. Midna appears, and so does Sera's cat! She tells you to sneak up and scare Hanch!

Use Midna to double-jump onto the roof of the store, then leap across two flat stone pillars and land on the one Hanch is standing on. He jumps into the pond while the hawk flies off. You can optionally stop here and summon the hawk with your howl. Or, you can use Midna to jump onto the waterwheel, then the roof beyond.

➤ Enter Jaggle and Pergie's house and drop down to the ground. Optionally smash the pumpkins and pots as before, then stand on the main table. Midna wants you to find the shield. It's up on the eastern ledge. Use Midna to bound up there, then dash into the wall to dislodge the shield, and again to drop it. Pick it up.

Enemies Encountered

Twilit Kargarok

Bulblin Warrior

King of Shadows

Characters Encountered

Midna

Rusl

Uli

Ordona

Ordon Shield

You got the **Ordon Shield**! Press Z to defend yourself, but beware: If it is touched by fire, it will burn.

➤ Midna thinks the shield looks cheap, but it'll do for the moment! Exit the house via the open window on the right wall, just along from the shield on the upper area. You land in the pond. The sound startles Rusl, who is arriving at his house with Uli. He tells her to go inside while he checks the area for beasts! Swim to the bank, then run south and east toward the house. Rusl stops you!

➤ He waves his torch and sword at you, which is a good deterrent; you can't harm him, and he can strike you back! Run around Rusl, and optionally approach Uli. She screams, and Rusl leaps in front of her and viciously swipes at you! Back up, away from both of them!

➤ You need some way to enter Rusl's house, so head around the right side of it, near the small pumpkin patch, and switch your sense view on. There are a couple of dig spots, and a larger dig area near the stack of logs. Dig down under the house, and you appear inside! Quickly search around and you discover the **Ordon Sword** on the sofa! Midna appears and tells you to head back into the woods.

Ordon Sword

You got the **Ordon Sword**! This is a sword crafted by Rusl, the best swordsman in Ordon, as a tribute to the royal family.

➤ Carrying both shield and sword on your back, emerge from Rusl's house. "Foul beast!" he shouts, and swings his weapon at you. Avoid him, and dig around for Hearts if your energy is low. Then flee back to the area near your house (there's grass to slice for Hearts and Rupees), and dash into the woods.

Missing Links

1. Frog Fanfare

Move to the stream near Rusl and Uli's home and locate a tiny frog hopping around. He tells you he's living in paradise and that there are some sparkling patches of ground to locate. A second frog also tells you to dig around for some buried items or clues. The third frog? He just ribbits.

2. Puppy Love

The cute puppy dog you hugged earlier is roaming around outside near the waterwheel house. He is happy to tell you he loves digging. Definitely use your sense view here; the village is full of places to dig!

Note: Also remember that many of the locations where you found Rupees the first time, such as the rocks near the round rock the monkey was standing on, can be accessed for more Rupees and Hearts!

3. Digging for Victory Part 1

Turn your sense view on and you'll discover multiple dig spots where the frogs are, at the bank of the stream. Some are near the path to Rusl's house, too. Don't forget the big dig spot below the tree the hive was stuck to! As with all dig spots, Hearts or Rupees of various denominations are your reward.

4. Digging for Victory Part 2

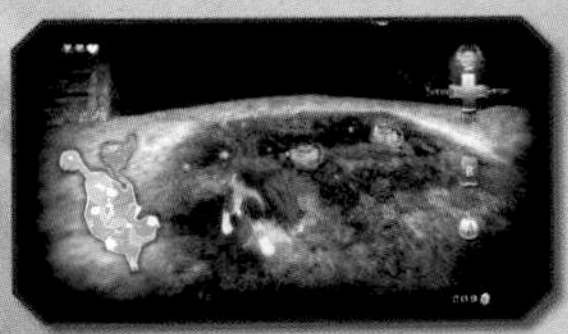

There are two dig spots near the village entrance and Fado's house. Four spots are by the water to the right of Sera's store. Find some in the pumpkin patch on the other side of Sera's store, near the waterwheel. The pumpkin patch here has multiple spots to dig, too. Finally, the ground near the western jetty where you caught fish for the cat has dig spots.

5. Howling for the Hawk

You can summon the hawk in wolf form, as well as Epona (once you find the Horse Grass). This isn't much use, as there's little for the hawk to do, except chat with you. But he does tell you he might be able to help you in the future!

Task 4: Speak with the Spirit of Faron Spring

Enemies Encountered

Twilit Messenger

The Spirit of Ordon Spring

Run as far north as you can go, to the bridge. Then a strange voice calls you into the springs. It is the spirit of Ordon Spring. Too late, it realizes a shadow being approaches! Black, glowing monoliths fall to earth. A portal above you appears! A Twilit Messenger falls out of the sky!

Twilit Messenger

Threat Meter

Sinewy and alien, with pulsating veins of pink in an otherwise inky black hide, the Twilit Messenger is most troublesome when encountered in groups. But for now, target this foe and when prompted, tap Ⓐ multiple times to latch on, and bite the Twilit Messenger until you're thrown off. Then finish with a spin attack.

This frightening ghoul from the netherworld is thankfully easy to slay if you bite down hard!

Warp Portal

Twilit Messengers always announce the arrival of an area of ethereal instability in the area. Usually, after they are defeated, Midna can create a warp portal at this point. Whenever you see Twilit Messengers, fight them as soon as possible to open up more warp portals!

The beast dematerializes and is sucked back into a differently colored glowing portal vortex. Out of the pool comes a ball of light energy that takes the form of a goat. It is **Ordona***, one of four* **light spirits***.*

Ordona's brethren have started to lose their power thanks to attacks from these shadowy Messengers. The kingdom is now a netherworld of darkness!

And yet, a hero has risen who can revive the light from the three remaining spirits. Your true power has not been revealed yet, but a journey to **Faron Woods***, and the revival of the light spirit there, should lead you on your path.*

Ordona:

The embodiment of the land of Ordona, this magical spirit takes the form of a goat and resides in the spring near Ordon Village. It seeks the light.

➤ Optionally dig for Hearts in the spring, heal, then leave and journey north, across the bridge (watch you don't fall off the side!), and dash into Faron Woods. The realm has been transformed with twilight hues and echoing sounds of darkness!

Tip: Remember that you can still check for dig spots, Rupees in the grass, and additional items during your run through here!

➤ When you've finished foraging, move into the next glade and watch as three Twilit Messengers fall from the sky! Midna flees your back, leaving you to fend for yourself!

▲ Fighting three Messengers at once isn't as difficult as you'd expect. However, there's a special stipulation for dispatching all of them: you must defeat the last two Messengers at exactly the same time! Otherwise the last Messenger left alive shrieks to bring the others back, and combat begins anew! Start with a spin to stop all three, then gnaw on one with multiple bites. Keep fighting until Midna appears. She helps you by giving you a new attack. Hold down Ⓑ for an energy field. Enclose all the enemies in it (so they sparkle with pink charges), then release the button!

Midna

Coro

Vessel of Light
You got the **Vessel of Light**! Use this to collect the tears that cut through the darkness.

When the Messengers are defeated, continue your journey northward to Faron Spring. There are numerous dig spots to find here. When you've had your fill, move to the ball of spirit energy in the middle of the pool near the waterfall. The spirit gives you a **Vessel of Light**. Set off, following the path to the northwest.

Note: The Vessel of Light now appears on your in-game screen, and you must locate the evils that consume the tears. Find them by using your sense view. The evils take the form of small winged insects. Check your map, or the one in this guide, to locate all 16 of the Twilit Parasites.

Task #5: Locate All 16 Twilit Parasites

Locating Twilit Parasites #1 and #2

Note: The 16 Twilit Parasites can be gathered in any order. The following route provides the quickest method.

Twilit Baba

Threat Meter

Taking the place of the Deku Baba in the ground where you previously encountered this plant is the Twilit Baba, with a dark serpentine stalk and strange pink and black head. Fortunately, it attacks and is snipped in the same manner as the Deku Baba. As a wolf, simply leap and bite the plant twice, or spin attack.

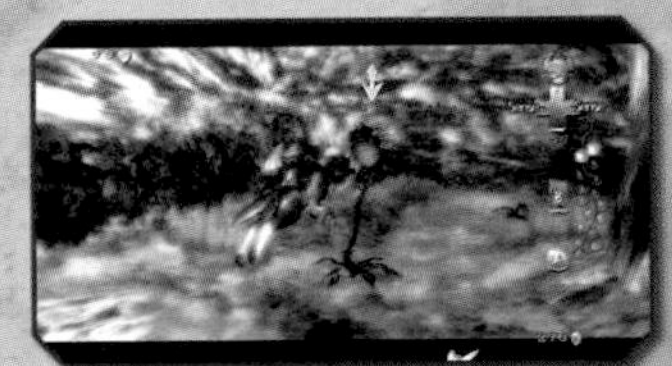

The shadow version of the Deku Baba is monstrous, but ineffectual at harming you as long as you bite and spin!

Twilit Parasite

Threat Meter

The Twilit Parasites hold the tears needed to rejuvenate the spirit of the spring, so look for purple sparks and shadows on the ground in the area where the white dots are marked on your map. Sixteen of these insects roam the land, and they can hide inside walls, floors, the ground, or out of reach. Target these foes with Z and then pounce with one attack. The insect explodes, and an orb of tears appears. Wait for it to float down, then run into it.

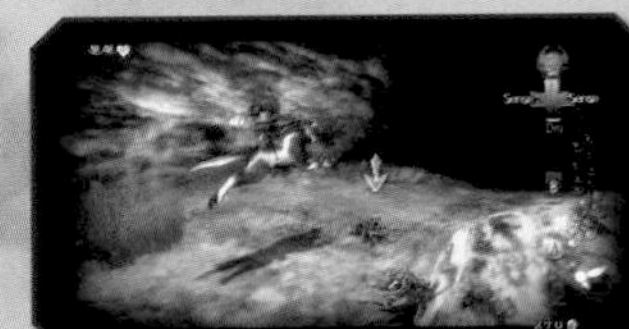

Only small purple sparks of electricity can be seen, until you use your sense view. Then pounce and bite!

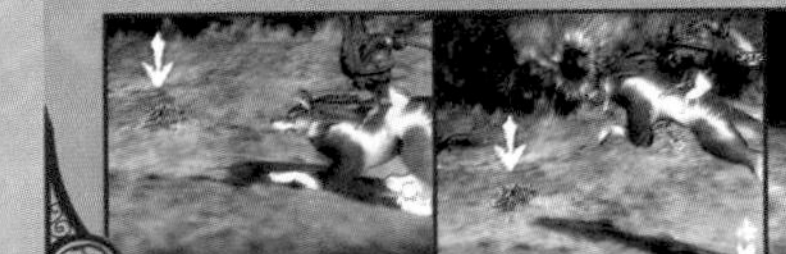

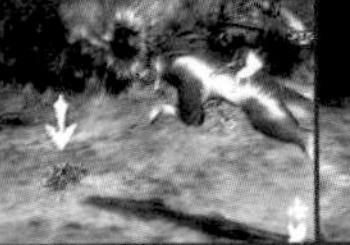

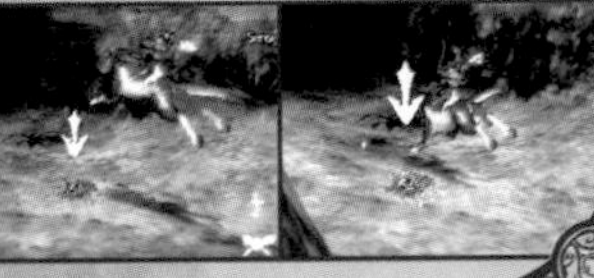

The first two Twilit Parasites are scuttling about the path next to the Twilit Baba. Just target and pounce on each of them and secure your first tears. Once they appear on your Vessel of Light, continue along the path. Dispatch two more Twilit Babas.

Twilit Parasites #3 and #4

◄ Move to the Dark Tunnel entrance. The gate is locked again, so return here in a moment. For now, turn and visit the area where Coro resides. Head around and up the ramp, passing the scarecrow. At the end of the ramp, Midna appears to allow you to leap into Coro's hut!

► Leap down into the interior of the hut and use your sense view to make out the ghostly form of Coro. He's freaking out about the bugs! Two of them appear, buzzing with electricity and scuttling about the floor. With your sense view on, leap at them; you can defeat both with one jump! After they explode, Coro is even more puzzled! Take the orbs of tears, then exit the way you came in, climbing up the furniture and out the window.

Twilit Parasite #5

▲ Journey around to the north (far) side of Coro's house, past the campfire, and check the wall. A Twilit Parasite is crawling around here. Target it with your sense view, and grab it!

Twilit Parasites #6 and #7

► Journey back to the entrance to the Dark Tunnel. If you inspect the gate, you'll see it is firmly closed. However, there's a dig spot just to the right of the gate, allowing you to tunnel under the gate. Crawl out, into the tunnel entrance, and target the two Twilit Parasites maneuvering about in this area. Bite them, and collect those orbs of tears!

Twilit Parasites #8 and #9

◄ You can use the tunnel shortcut (see Missing Links), or run through the twilight version of the Dark Tunnel. The creatures (Deku Babas and Keeses) have been replaced with twilit versions that are just as easy to defeat. Collect the Rupees from the usual places.

Emerge into Faron Woods, and you'll see the lower area has been completely submerged in thick, evil, purple mist. Move to the northwestern side of the higher ground you're standing on, and locate the two Twilit Parasites on the rock wall. Now defeat them without accidentally leaping into the mist! Wait for each Twilit Parasite to descend if they start to fly.

Twilit Parasites #10, #11, and #12

◄ There must be some way to cross the mist-filled woods, and there is. Move to the flat stump at the northern part of the wood entrance, and Midna appears. She can transport you across to higher ground after a three-leap maneuver. Don't forget to hold Ⓩ to target her!

► Run to the top of the overhang in this western part of the woods. Summon Midna, then leap three times to the inside of a giant tree in the middle of the woods. Three Twilit Parasites are in here. Don't leave until you collect all three orbs!

Twilit Parasites #13 and #14

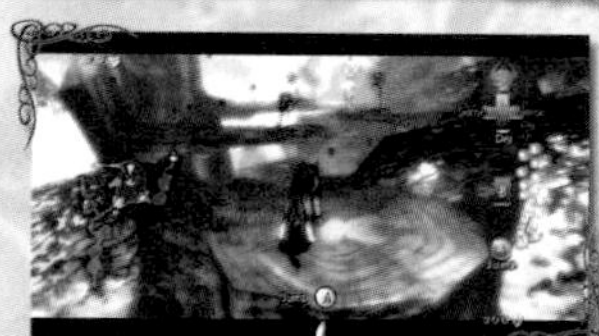

◄ Now for a giant series of leaps! Use Midna and hold down Ⓩ to jump eight times across the tree branches to the top of the Faron Wood trees. Jump another four times, avoiding three Twilit Babas (if you're too slow, you'll be knocked off the branch and into the mist).

Enemies Encountered

Twilit Baba

Twilit Parasite

Twilit Keese

Characters Encountered

Midna

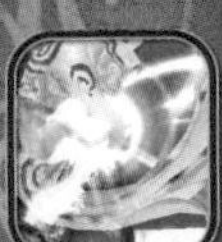

Faron

Fado

Sera

Hanch

Jaggle

Pergie

Rusl

Uli

Coro

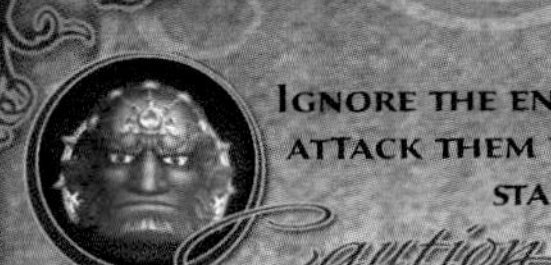

Caution

Ignore the enemies here. It is impossible to attack them without landing on the mist and starting this area over again!

➤ Move to the other end of the massive tree stump and use Midna again to leap across a large gap, after the swinging log has passed to one side. Make seven more leaps down some trunks and platforms to reach the southeast exit.

➤ Here, you can spot two more Twilit Parasites, but they are traveling through the earth. You must target them, then run to where they are buried, and dig them up! Once they surface, attack them. When you collect both orbs, you can search for the final two Twilit Parasites!

Author Note

It was at this point that we looked at our Twilit Parasite tears collection, and found we'd missed the one outside of Coro's hut! Curses! How do we get back? Fortunately, we stood at the end of the wooden pier, leapt easily back to the Dark Tunnel, and backtracked.

Twilit Parasites #15 and #16

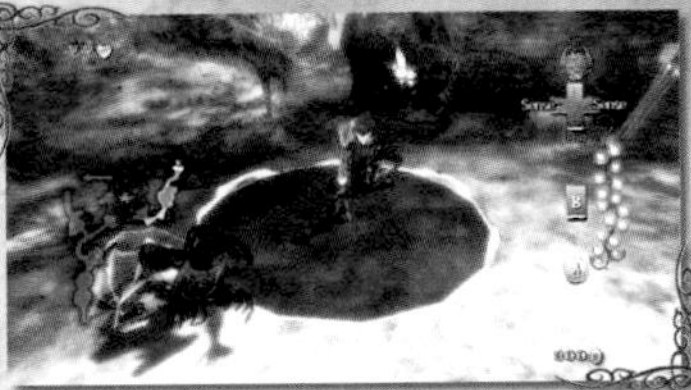

➤ Step out of the tunnel and you'll notice that the energy walls of the Twilit Messengers have appeared, and three of them are advancing on you! Target, leap, and grab the nearest one, and pummel him with teeth and tail until he falls. Then press and hold Ⓑ for Midna's energy attack, targeting the final two. Catch them both, and all three disappear.

Tip

After the fight, make a mental note that a portion of a bridge has appeared here, propped up against the far rock wall. This comes in handy later!

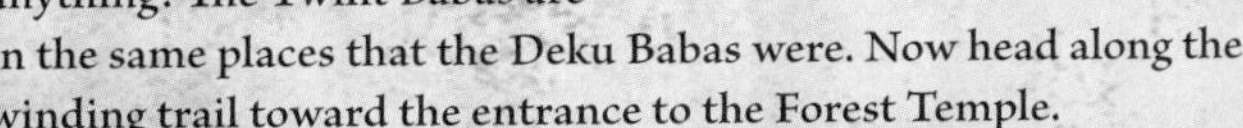

➤ The three Twilit Messengers form a portal in the sky, and you're free to continue. Trill's Shop is completely empty, but you're a wolf and can't steal anything! The Twilit Babas are in the same places that the Deku Babas were. Now head along the winding trail toward the entrance to the Forest Temple.

➤ As you reach the entrance to the Forest Temple, you see a monkey spirit standing in fear on one of the short columns. Target the final two Twilit Parasites and bite them to complete your **Vessel of Light** collection. The monkey is astonished, and as a wolf, you can understand her! She is relieved, although "ever since the **boss** went funny in the head, there's been scary monsters everywhere," she says.

Missing Links

1. Going Underground

You can optionally find dig spots that house either a Rupee or a Heart in the following places:

- The winding path and long grass near the Dark Tunnel
- The sign to the Dark Tunnel
- Near the campfire around Coro's house
- The north side of Coro's house
- The tree opposite Coro's house
- The south entrance to Faron Woods
- The western wall, near the overhang
- Behind the sign at the southeast exit to Faron Woods—a yellow Rupee (10)
- Next to the propped-up bridge near Twilit Parasites #15 and #16
- At the foot of the large tree opposite the propped-up bridge
- At the foot of the large tree opposite Trill's Shop
- At the start of the winding trail to the Forest Temple (near the opened chest)
- On either side of the opened chest

2. Dark Tunnel Shortcut

There's actually a shortcut that (in wolf form) allows you to ignore the entire Dark Tunnel area! Dig in the left wall behind the first unlit torch as you arrive in the tunnel.

You appear out of a dig hole in the right side of the wall by the north exit, or entrance if you're traveling south. This is quicker than traipsing through the tunnel.

1 

2 

3 

4

5 

6 

Task 6: Learn Your First Hidden Skill and Enter the Forest Temple

The Light Returns to Faron Province

As soon as the last Twilit Parasite is captured, no matter where you are, you're whisked back to the Faron Spring. The spirit thanks you and Midna leaves you. Then the spirit returns in the form of a giant monkey. Your own form has changed, too!

The green tunic that is your garb once belonged to the ancient hero chosen by the gods. Now that hero is you! You must now attempt to seek a forbidden power deep inside the Forest Temple. Midna returns to push you toward that Forest Temple.

Faron:

The embodiment of the land of Faron, this magical spirit takes the form of a monkey and resides in the spring near Faron Woods. It seeks the light.

Hero's Clothes

You got the **Hero's Clothes**! It is said that these clothes were worn by the hero who long ago saved Hyrule from danger.

◄ Head to the Forest Temple entrance at your earliest convenience. If you decide to return to Ordon Village, you can visit Fado in the pasture, but Epona cannot be summoned. Fado remarks on your outfit and tells you to find the children. The rest of the villagers have the same request.

► Sera, in the shop, is worried about Beth. Hanch is on the rock, fearful of the fate of the tots.

Jaggle is standing by his bench, and Pergie is sitting dejected in her house. Even the puppy is yelping!

Rusl and Uli are inside their house. They remark on your clothing, as Rusl is nursed back to health. They're happy you managed to get the sword back from that evil wolf who stole it!

Into the Murky Mists, and an Audience with an Old One

▲ The mayor is away, so head north, over the bridge and into Faron Province. When you're battling the Deku Baba in the winding path to the Dark Tunnel entrance, Midna tells you how to block with your shield: hold Z. Try it! It makes combat much easier, as the Deku Baba usually hits your shield and is stunned. Finish it easily, and the two others!

▲ The gate to the Dark Tunnel is locked, and you can't use the dig hole as Link, so head toward Coro and speak with him. He looks you up and down. You seem to be ready for the challenge, so he hands you a Small Key that opens the gate to the Dark Tunnel leading to Faron Woods. If you need Lantern oil, now's not the time to buy it.

Tip: Your Lantern is about to be stolen by a monkey! As long as there's some fuel left in, don't put any more in, as the monkey uses the entire Lantern's fuel supply during the next woodland romp.

Small Key

You got a **Small Key**! This opens a locked door, but only in this area.

Enemies Encountered

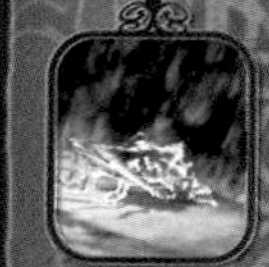
Twilit Parasite

Twilit Messenger

Twilit Baba

Deku Baba

Characters Encountered

Midna

Hero's Shade

▲ You can't head north (Midna doesn't let you), so unlock the Dark Tunnel entrance and head inside. The same enemies and tactics apply during this run-through of the area. Keep moving and take the left fork to appear at Faron Woods.

▲ The lower ground is still filled with mist! Bring out your Lantern. As soon as you do, that cheeky monkey grabs it and waves it about. She hasn't stolen it; she's beckoning you to follow her! Drop off the wooden pier and draw your sword. Carefully follow the monkey northward, into the woods.

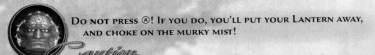

▲ The monkey takes you on a long route, around the left side of the giant tree. On the other side, tackle a Keese, then keep up with the monkey. She runs through the arch in the tree and is scared by a Keese. Keep going, and defeat a Deku Baba. Do not try leap attacks that take you into the mist, or you'll have to retrace your steps!

➤ The monkey throws the Lantern down and escapes toward the Forest Temple. Pick up your Lantern again. It is empty, so head directly toward Trill's Shop. Slay two Bokoblins along the way, then dip your Lantern into the oil, and optionally fill your bottle. Don't forget to pay the bird!

Lantern

You got the **Lantern** back! It ran out of oil while you were following the monkey around.

◄ Did you notice a chest that appeared in Faron Woods? It was on the upper of the two stump platforms on the giant tree in the middle. It wasn't there before! If you're after every chest, head back to the mist-filled woods, bring out your Lantern, and wave it using Ⓑ. Step into the mist!

Caution

Do not press Ⓐ! If you do, you'll put your Lantern away, and choke on the murky mist!

➤ Follow the path the monkey made in reverse. Move left around the base of the giant tree, then to the edge of the mist that has receded, and wave your Lantern again. Keep this up until you reach the two stump ledges. Climb to the upper one, and open the chest.

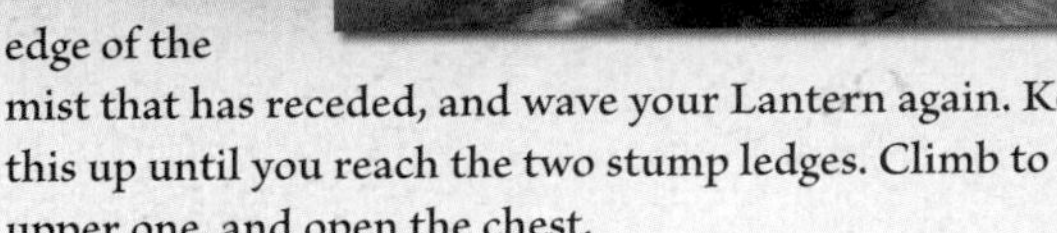

Overworld Chest #7: Red Rupee (20)

➤ You can actually leap off and succumb to the mist now! You'll teleport to the entrance to the Forest Temple and Trill's Shop, and lose only a quarter Heart energy! Or, drop slowly down, wave the Lantern, and carefully head southeast out of here! Head back toward the Forest Temple immediately!

Hidden Skill: Ending Blow

As you reach the entrance trail to the Forest Temple, you spot a ghostly White Wolf with red eyes. It looks fearsome, but strangely, you feel you know this creature! It pounces on you, and you both disappear into the ether! You are transported into a strange, cloud-like area with Castle Hyrule partially submerged in the distance. The White Wolf has turned into a heroic, armored skeleton of old. Could this be a past adventurer, appearing from beyond the grave to teach you new combat techniques?

Target the undead hero, and attempt to strike him. You are knocked back. "A sword wields no strength unless the hand that holds it has courage." But you are still ready to learn the ending blow.

"Enemies that are filled with energy will quickly recover and attack again even when stunned by a powerful strike. The ending blow is a secret technique you can use on stunned enemies to end their breath before they spring back into action." Knock the undead hero on his back or front, then complete this technique.

Ending blow: press Z to target and then press A when an enemy is stunned on the ground.

Ending Blow

You learned the first Hidden Skill, the **ending blow**! Hidden Skill 1 of 7.

Hero's Shade:

A spirit covered in armor, the Hero's Shade lives in a visionary world and teaches the art of weapon-play to you. He talks politely and classically, like an old-fashioned master of the sword.

▲ Run up the trail to the Forest Temple entrance, and attack two Bokoblins. Try knocking them off their feet with an **ending blow**. Then burn the Skulltula web with your Lantern, and enter your first dungeon, the dank and murky **Forest Temple!**

Enemies Encountered

Keese

Deku Baba

Bokoblin

Dungeon 1: The Forest Temple

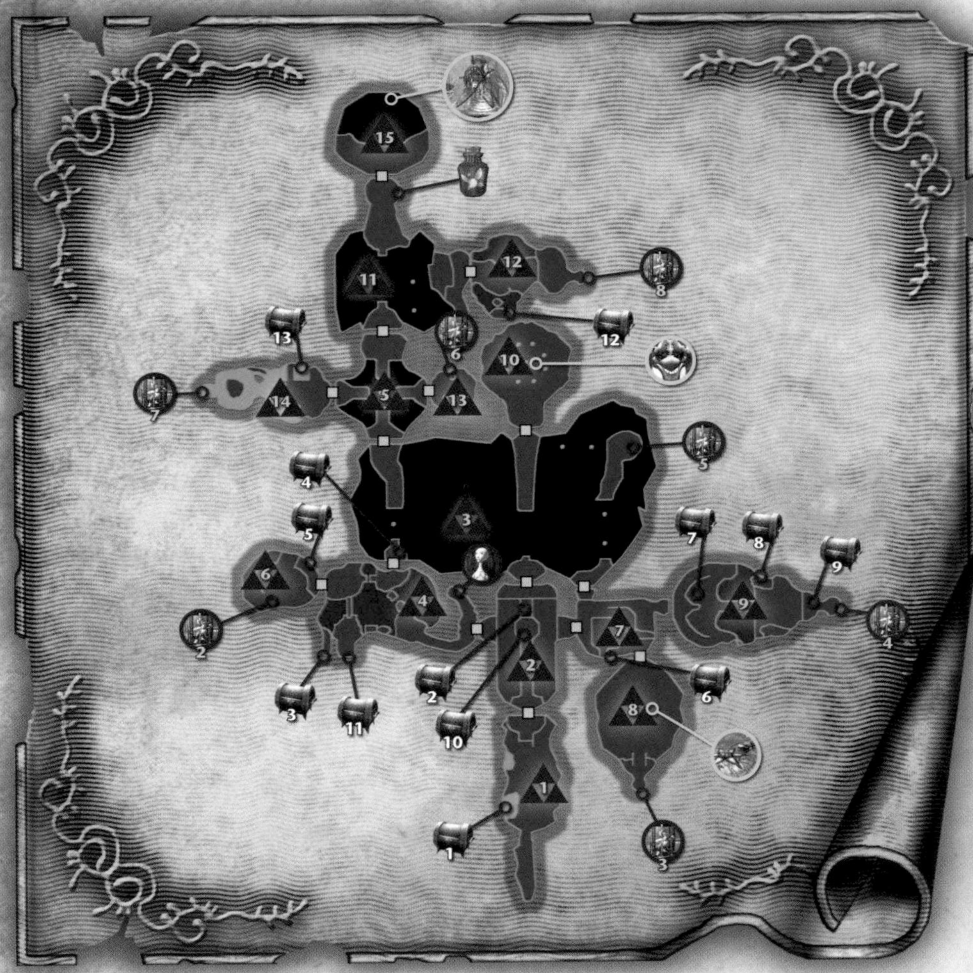

Legend

Room Legend

1. Entrance
2. Crossroads Hub
3. Wind Gorge
4. Step-stones Cavern
5. Wind Bridge Crossroads
6. Totem Pole Cage Room
7. Staircase Cavern
8. Lair of Big Baba
9. Room of the Tile Worms
10. Cavern of Ook
11. The Giant Forest Tree Chasm
12. Waterlogged Cavern
13. Nest of the Skulltulas
14. Small Cave Maze
15. Boss Battle! Twilit Parasite Diababa

Number of Treasure Chests: 13

1. Yellow Rupee (10)
2. Red Rupee (20)
3. Yellow Rupee (10)
4. Small Key
5. Yellow Rupee (10)
6. Piece of Heart
7. Small Key
8. Red Rupee (20)
9. Piece of Heart
10. Compass
11. Big Key
12. Small Key
13. Red Rupee (20)

Items

- Fairy in a Bottle

Characters

- Monkey
- Big Baba
- Ook
- Twilit Parasite Diababa

The Forest Temple: Overview

Your first dungeon is only a single level deep, but it has many confusing, interconnecting chambers filled with fearsome-looking foes that require cunning as well as brute strength to defeat. The monkey that led you here expects you to rescue her seven brethren, each either locked inside a wooden cage or behind a barred or sealed doorway. You must backtrack through previously explored rooms several times before you can obtain the more useful items—the Dungeon Map and Compass—after which you can easily locate all 13 of this dungeon's chests. This dungeon also holds your first, and extremely useful, new weapon: the **Gale Boomerang** (pried from the hands of a bad baboon named Ook). Finally, after all monkeys are freed, they allow you access to the boss room, where you face your first creature of the twilight! Good hunting!

1 Secure the Second Monkey Pg 70

2 Free the Third and Fourth Monkeys Pg 78

3 Battle the Bad Baboon named Ook Pg 83

4 Find the Fifth Monkey Pg 85

Dungeon Denizens

Characters

Ooccoo

Midna

Monkey

Enemies

Walltula

Deku Baba

Skulltula

Bombling

Keese

Bokoblin

Baba Serpent

Deku Like

Big Baba

Tile Worm

Bosses

Mid Boss: Ook the Baboon

Big Boss: Twilit Parasite Diababa

A Link to the Present

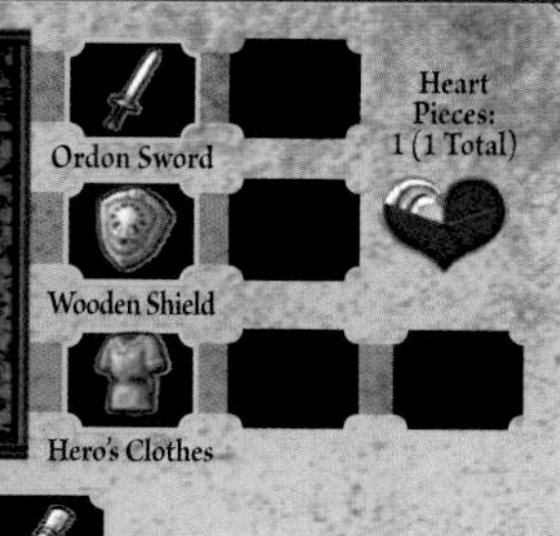
Ordon Sword

Wooden Shield

Hero's Clothes

Heart Pieces: 1 (1 Total)

Wallet

Hidden Skills: 1 (of 7)

Fish Journal

Items to Obtain

Dungeon Map

Ooccoo

Small Key (1st)

Piece of Heart #2

Small Key (2nd)

Small Key (3rd)

Gale Boomerang

Piece of Heart #3

Compass

Big Key

Small Key (4th)

Fairy in a Bottle

Heart Container #1

5 Obtain the Big Key pg 86

6 Save the Sixth Monkey pg 88

7 Escape with Monkeys Seven and Eight pg 90

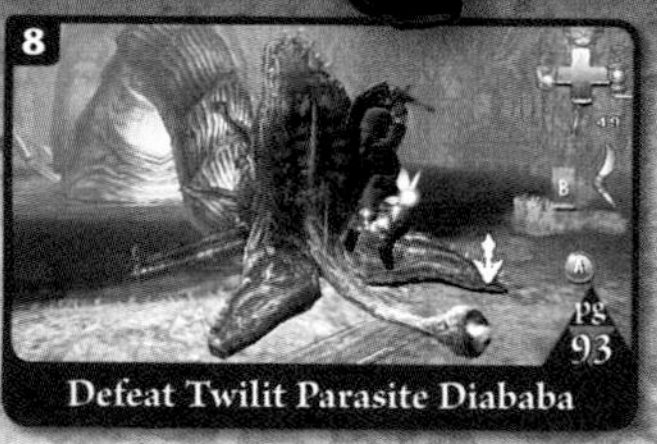
8 Defeat Twilit Parasite Diababa pg 93

Characters Encountered

Midna

1st Monkey

Task 1: Secure the Second Monkey

Chamber 1: Entrance

➤ Once through the large cobweb, step into the dark, rocky corridor, and bring out your sword. A roving Keese flutters into your face; Z target, then slash it out of the air. Move past a couple of small boulders on your right, and into the first large chamber.

➤ You hear scratching and movement around you, coming from a Walltula on the left wall, scuttling around some vines. Ignore it for now, and pass between the two large totem poles. A Deku Baba springs from the ground. Slay it by cutting the stalk from the head, then check the area of vines to the side; there's some climbing to do.

➤ **Treasure Chest:** Before you continue, aim your **Slingshot** up the vine-covered wall, and shoot down two Walltulas crawling on it. After both explode, head into the vines and climb up them, then shift along the rock wall before dropping onto a small rock ledge. There's a chest here. Open it and claim the yellow Rupee (10) inside.

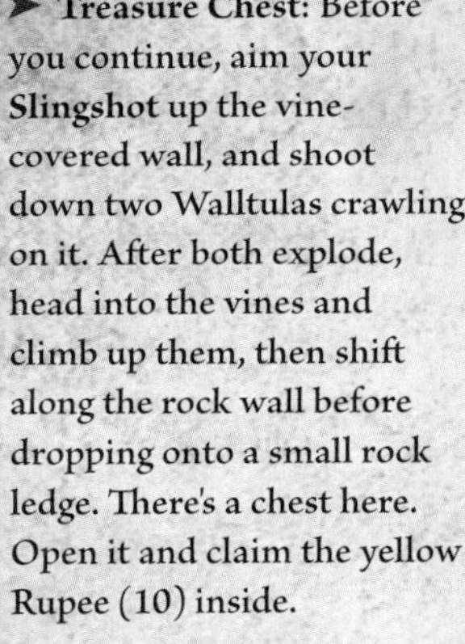

Treasure Chest #1
Yellow Rupee (10)

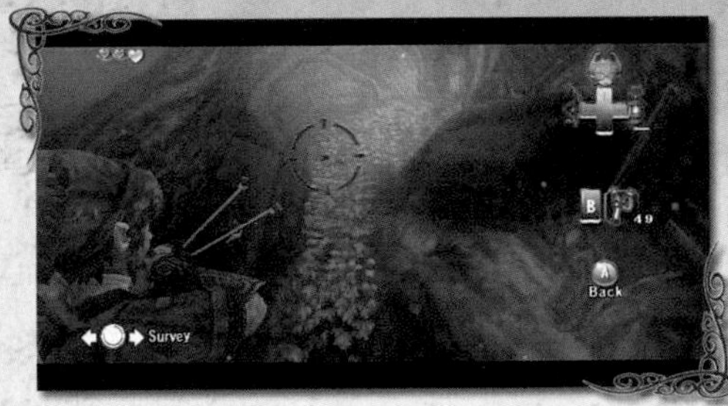

▲ Drop off the platform and head north, until you spot a monkey in a cage below a vine wall. As you pass by the second set of totem poles, watch for the Bokoblin and a Deku Baba; slay both with a spin or your preferred slashing.

A spin attack makes short work of a wooden cage. Multiple sword swipes take longer.

▲ Head to the monkey cage, and help the hairy simian out by demolishing her cage. Execute a quick spin attack to destroy the bars. The monkey scrambles up the vines, and beckons you onward. Midna tells you this is the monkey who stole your Lantern!

▲ Step back from the vines, and (if you haven't already), aim your Slingshot at the two Walltulas, dropping both before you climb. If you don't, you'll be bitten and fall. Once at the top, the monkey urges you to open the round dungeon door. Oblige her.

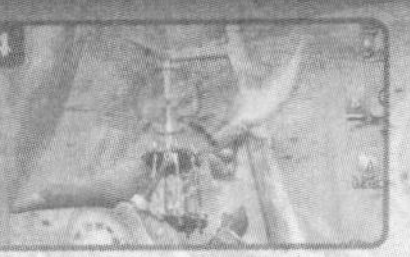

Missing Links

1. Totem Pole Roll

Roll into each of the four totem poles in chamber 1A, and they will shake. This dislodges pots on top of two of them. Each pot contains a blue Rupee (5).

Tips: Position your roll properly: if you roll toward the chamber wall, the pot falls and smashes on the wall, and the Rupee may be inaccessible. The pot should topple into the flat floor, away from the sides.

2. Dungeon Grass Slashing

As usual, there are goodies in the grass: the right-side clump holds a Rupee, and the grass in the upper floor near the dungeon door yields a Heart and two Rupees.

3. Out-of-Reach Pottery

If you're checking this chamber carefully, you'll see a group of pots up on a high ledge. They all hold blue and yellow Rupees, but you can't get them yet! Return here later.

4. Within-Reach Pottery

Clay pots are atop the vine wall near the dungeon door; head left before you exit, and smash a couple for a Heart and a Rupee.

Chamber 2: Crossroads Hub

➤ Head down the rickety steps and reconnoiter this room. It has three exits (north, east, and west) not including the one you came in from. Amid the grass on the lower ground area is a Deku Baba waiting to be ripped apart; he's on the right in the grass.

Skulltula

Threat Meter

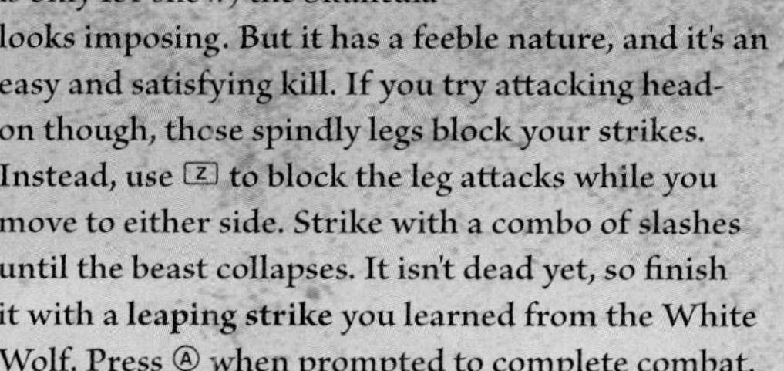

With a fearsome countenance and skull-shaped thorax (which is only for show) the Skulltula looks imposing. But it has a feeble nature, and it's an easy and satisfying kill. If you try attacking head-on though, those spindly legs block your strikes. Instead, use Ⓩ to block the leg attacks while you move to either side. Strike with a combo of slashes until the beast collapses. It isn't dead yet, so finish it with a **leaping strike** you learned from the White Wolf. Press Ⓐ when prompted to complete combat.

The fearsome Skulltula is a scuttling fiend with angry mandibles, but it has a softer side too (and that's where you should stick your sword).

▲ Move up to the steps where you fought the Skulltula, and survey the scenery. The two doors on each side of you require a jump that's too far to currently attempt. The way lies forward, but there's a sizable gap to overcome. First, check down below; there's an odd creature in the left corner.

Enemies Encountered

Keese

Walltula

Deku Baba

Bokoblin

Skulltula

Characters Encountered

Midna

1st Monkey

Bombling

Threat Meter

This odd creature is a Bombling, a stationary spider standing straight up on its legs, over a hole. Move forward and slash it once or twice. It collapses and flashes red. Seven seconds later, it explodes with a force that can damage you. After that, another Bombling appears from the hole on which the first was standing. Replacement Bomblings continue to appear.

If you're slaying Bomblings, strike them, and move on. You can also near them, and back away slowly, and they scuttle toward you a few feet before returning to their hole. Bomblings are more useful than a menace, as they appear near an impassible rock or foe that requires an explosive solution. In this instance, pick up the flashing Bombling and place it in front of a large boulder. Move back!

Creepy, crawly, and explosive: the worst kind of spider is the most helpful, as long as you're quick when you're carrying it!

Treasure Chest: The explosion you caused by placing the Bombling in front of the boulder reveals a small alcove under the upper north exit area. Drop and open the chest; there is a red Rupee (20) inside. Return to the central platform.

Treasure Chest #2
Red Rupee (20)

Red Rupee
You got a red Rupee (20)!

Optionally look up at the suspended chest (you need other means to retrieve the item inside), then figure out how to advance into the next dungeon chamber. Achieve this by retrieving your **Lantern**, and moving to each of the four torch stands. Light two stands and you can summon Midna. She convinces you to light the place up. After the fourth torch stand is burning, a set of **heavy wooden steps** appears!

Note

These heavy wooden steps prevent you from opening the alcove blocked by the boulder below. Use the Gale Boomerang (which you'll find later) to snuff out the torches. The steps recede, allowing you access to the boulder, if you didn't explode it already.

Run up the steps toward the northern dungeon door. Before you exit however, inspect the large chest to your left: it holds an incredibly useful piece of parchment; the Dungeon Map. Now you know how many floors the Forest Temple is, and which rooms you've explored. Head through the door the monkey is near.

Dungeon Map
You got the Dungeon Map!

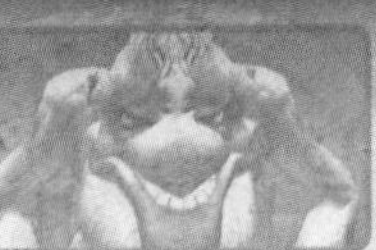

Using the Dungeon Map

Press ① to view the map and ② to toggle the minimap on and off. You've visited green rooms. The **yellow arrow** shows your current location. Tilt the analog stick and x to change floors. The **blue arrow** shows where you entered the current room. Combine this with the **Compass** to reveal the location of all the chests and the dungeon boss (shown by a skull icon).

Note

Missing Links

1. Dungeon Grass Slashing

This chamber is also filled with grass, which yields a Rupee piece or Heart refill for each large clump. Locate them before you face the Skulltula. There are more near the Bombling, and on one side of the northern exit.

2. Hanging Around: Cobweb Pottery

Hanging above the central platform are three pots and a treasure chest—and all are out of reach. Bring out the Slingshot though, and you can smash the pots, retrieving a blue Rupee (5) from two of them. You cannot drop the chest yet.

Chamber 3: Wind Gorge

The next chamber is a large gorge complete with wooden platforms that turn when the wind blows through fans connected at each platform's top. Your new monkey friend races to a rope bridge and begins to cross, but stops short.

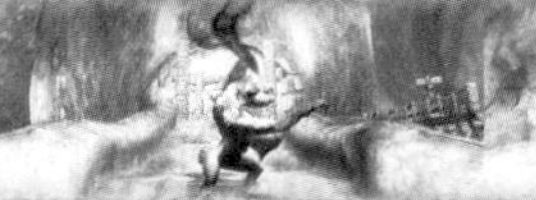

A huge white baboon, known as Ook, raises from the opposite ledge, and launches a large Gale Boomerang! This severs the bridge supports, and the structure comes crashing down. The monkey scampers back, while the bad baboon pats his buttocks with joy!

The monkey grabs onto the falling bridge's boards and returns to you. That baboon leaves the scene, and Midna appears. She advises you follow the monkey, who's telling you to head into the Crossroads Hub. Follow that advice and retrace your steps.

Chamber 2: First Return to Crossroads Hub

▲ Follow that crazy monkey to the rope span on the chamber's west side, and watch as she leaps and hangs from the middle of it. Line yourself up behind her, then run off the wooden platform. You'll automatically jump, and she catches you.

▲ Then it's a simple matter of letting go using Ⓐ as you're swinging forward. Time this correctly, or you'll land short or end up back on the platform. Press Ⓐ after Link swings upward.

Enemies Encountered

Deku Baba

Skulltula

Bombling

Ook

Characters Encountered

Midna

1st Monkey

Ooccoo

➤ You'll land on a small ledge. On the nearby wall is an area of vines you can climb; however they don't lead anywhere. Ignore the torches on either side of the door. Open the door, enter the Step-stones Cavern, and make a right.

Note: Use the Clawshot on this vine wall to hook and propel yourself if you return to this dungeon later (once the dungeon is completed, the monkeys are gone) to collect any chests you missed the first time around.

Chamber 4: Step-Stones Cavern

➤ Draw your sword and head over to a Bombling. Slice it once, pick it up, then move and place it next to the rock wall behind it, to the north. Back away, and the boulders explode when the Bombling detonates, revealing a secret alcove!

◄ A couple of the pots contain Rupees, but one is of particular interest. It is moving, and there's a head popping out! Smash it, and this weird Cucco-like creature appears, but with a human head! This is Ooccoo, who's lost in the dungeon, too!

Ooccoo

Although it's difficult to tell, Ooccoo seems around 40 years old. She lived in a great city in the sky, but she fell to Hyrule after strange events befell her home. She is hoping to find something she lost. Although she's short, with baleful eyes, she's friendly and has a great gift for you.

Ooccoo

You met Ooccoo! If you call her in a dungeon, she will let you out and allow you to return when you want.

Note: Ooccoo is an item whom you carry throughout each dungeon, after you find her. She leaves you when you finish a dungeon. However, she's helpful in that she can teleport you out of a dungeon, then back in at the same place you left. Do this to visit a shop and purchase an item to complete part of a dungeon, or to halt your game. If you save without using Ooccoo, you begin your dungeon trek at the entrance after you reload (although all the dungeon's doors and chests you unlocked are still open).

▲ Place Ooccoo in your inventory (✚) for easy access, then turn and follow the cavern tunnel around to a large Skulltula web blocking your path. Access your **Lantern** and wave it at the web to burn it, then continue into the cavern.

Caution: Although you should be stocked with Lantern fuel, each time you wave the Lantern, it uses up more energy that letting it burn. Wave your Lantern only to light webs or torches, or to clear the murky air!

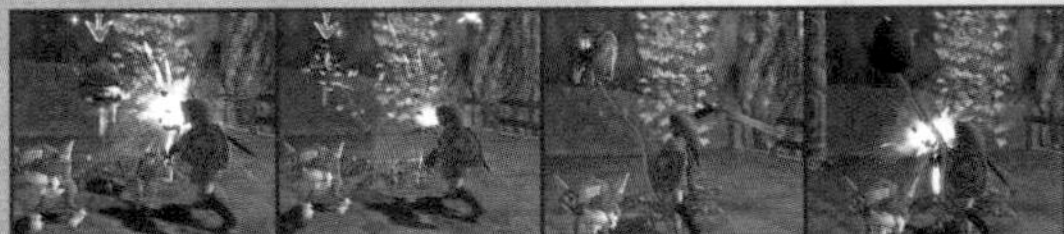

Slice and dice that Deku Baba, but don't use a jumping attack. Then collect those Slingshot nuts!

▲ While the monkey cowers, inspect that patch of weeds, and slay the Deku Baba that appears from it. There's a dormant Deku Baba against the wall; burst open the head for a Rupee! After you're done, survey the room; there's a vine wall, and a bridge with gaps in it.

◄ Take the bridge ahead and slightly to the right of you. Follow that monkey across (you don't need to press a button to jump; Link automatically leaps). Stop at the doorway. It is unlocked, and you can continue, but it's better to inspect this chamber first.

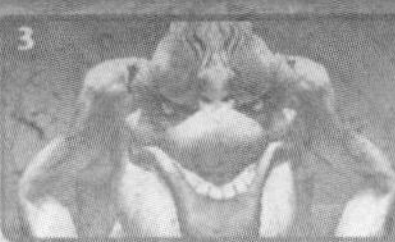

The monkey cowers in fright at the pygmy Skulltula hanging from the ceiling on a string of web. She's blocking your path to a locked door. You can draw your sword and attempt to attack, but you can't reach, and you're likely to end up in the water after a nasty nip! Instead, bring out your **Slingshot** and tag that pygmy Skulltula. She falls, then scuttles toward you...and off the ledge into the water! An excellent dispatch!

The monkey bounds across to the locked door on the chamber's western side. Alas, you don't have a key yet, so ignore her. Instead, cross the rope bridge to the left. This allows you to inspect the room's southwest part.

Look closely, as you'll see you can reach this area via the vines (but the bridge is quicker). This area contains a locked gate with a massive chest behind it. There are four fan contraptions but none of it can move. You won't be raiding this yet!

Tip: Did you notice the "Z" on the floor, running between the fans? That's a clue you need when you come back here....

Treasure Chest: Before you leave via the north wall's unlocked door, dive into the water and swim around, under the rope bridge, and toward the southwest area's watery part, right of the locked gate. Swim through a gap below a tree trunk, and go up a small dirt ramp. A hidden chest in here contains 10 Rupees to pilfer!

Treasure Chest #3
Yellow Rupee (10)

You can use the **vines** to the small rope bridge's left to climb up, or the steps up from the shallow water near your Deku Baba fight. Exit this place via the door in the north wall. You'll appear in the Wind Gorge, but on the western side.

Missing Links

1. Lily Pad Larks

Swimming in this chamber nets you Rupees when you move through the middle of the lily pads dotted around, so check all of them! Climb out in the southeast corner after your swim.

2. Deflowered Deku Babas

The Deku Babas aren't hardy enough for this dungeon, and some have withered away. Pick up their heads to find nuts (for your Slingshot), Hearts, or Rupees.

3. A Vine Time

Use your Slingshot on the Walltula, then climb up on the vine wall, slowly moving to the small wooden ledge, then leaping to the locked gate. Why is this necessary?

4. Bridge Demolition

Because if you slash the rope supports on the bridge, it collapses, and the only way to the locked gate is via the vines! It isn't wise to demolish the bridge if you want a quick exit.

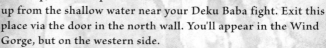

Enemies Encountered

Ook

Bombling

Deku Baba

Walltula

Pygmy Skulltula

Characters Encountered

Midna

1st Monkey

2nd Monkey

Chamber 3: First Return To Wind Gorge

➤ Away from the massive middle gap, the gorge's western portion is safe. Wait for the wind to spin the rickety platform bridge to link both sides, then roll across. Stop at the other side, produce your Slingshot, and Ⓩ target those pesky Keeses as you did in the misty woods of Faron Province. Run to the door in the north wall, and open it.

Tip: Any Keeses who are too far to auto-target with Ⓩ can be aimed at manually. This is important because you must master this technique! You can move if you hold down Ⓩ and use Ⓑ!

Chamber 5: Wind Bridge Crossroads

➤ **Treasure Chest:** The door leads to a large airy chamber with a chest to your right. Open it; it contains a **Small Key!** You can use this to open the locked door in the Step-stones Cavern. You can't progress farther, so head back the way you came, through the Wind Gorge.

Treasure Chest #4
Small Key

Small Key
You got a Small Key! This opens a locked door, but only in this area.

Tip:

- Small Keys open doors only in the dungeon in which you currently are.
- You can't transfer Small Keys between dungeons.
- The locks they open are all the same, like the one in the Step-stones Cavern.
- Look above your Rupee count to see a Small Key icon. This is handy because it tells you how many keys you possess.
- Each Small Key is discarded after it opens one door.

Missing Links

1. Pot Smashing

Shatter the trio of pots opposite the chest as you enter this room! There's a tiny amount of money to be found.

2. Bokoblin Bashing!

You can't turn the bridge platform yet, but you can attack the two Bokoblins guarding it! Pull out your trusty **Slingshot** and hit one, then watch as it trots toward you and falls into the bottomless pit.

Chamber 3: Second Return To Wind Gorge

➤ Head south, back to the western side of the Wind Gorge, and bring down the couple of Keeses who have returned to bug you. Wait for the bridge platform to connect with the ground you're on, then run and open the south door.

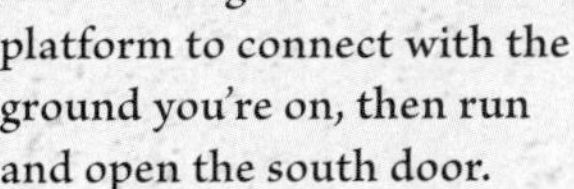

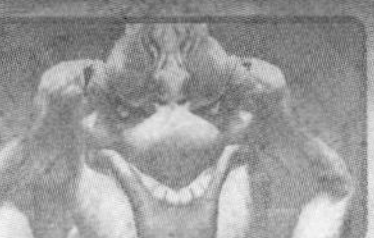

Enemies Encountered

Keese

Bokoblin

Skulltula

Chamber 4: First Return To Step-stones Cavern

▲ Enter the Step-stones Cavern, and make an immediate right. If the Skulltula hasn't been defeated, it needs a Slingshot and a dip in the water. Jump the gap automatically, then run up and unlock the door with Ⓐ. Push the door open.

Chamber 6: Totem Pole Cage Room

▲ Step into a large oval chamber where an imprisoned monkey sits in a cage atop a totem pole. Your first monkey friend leaps over and rocks the cage, but it won't open. It's time to help! Head around to the shaky bridge, ignoring the vines. When you cross the bridge, it collapses!

▲ You can't go back, so either drop, or follow the wooden path down past the tree roots, to the main grassy area. That eeping is getting louder, so head over to the totem pole and check it out. It's too high to reach with your sword. You need a better plan.

➤ **Treasure Chest:** First, however, inspect your surroundings. Check the area under the bridge, directly under the vine wall, right next to a post, for a chest that's easy to miss. Open it and grab your cash prize!

Treasure Chest #5
Yellow Rupee (10)

▼ It's time to free the second monkey! After watching the first monkey roll into the totem pole, try this yourself. Attempt another afterward (do this quickly or the cage rocks, but doesn't fall), and the cage comes crashing down! Your monkey collection is increasing.

Follow the clue the first monkey gave you and roll into that totem pole twice; it's the only way to get out of here!

◀ This monkey-freeing attracts the attention of two Bokoblins, who jump down. Assault them with a sword spin and hacking; wait for them to arrive and dispatch both with one spin. Follow the monkeys around and up the path.

➤ Back at the small collapsed bridge, the monkeys swing from the rope above, creating a precarious path for you to swing across! Press Ⓐ quickly when Link is swinging upward. Do this twice, then exit the chamber.

Missing Links

1. Mowing the Lawn

Cut the grass for Hearts and Rupees, and return here with the Gale Boomerang to rake up those patches of leaves.

Characters Encountered

Midna

1st Monkey

2nd Monkey

Task 2: Free the Third and Fourth Monkeys

Chamber 4: Second Return To Step-stones Cavern

▲ With two monkeys in tow, leap across the gap where you fought the Skulltula, and ignore the door leading to the Wind Gorge. Instead, move southward, slaying the reappearing Deku Baba and heading out of the Step-stones Cavern the way you first came in.

Chamber 2: Second Return to Crossroads Hub

▲ Your monkey chums arrive at the hub with you, and one makes a swing so you can get back onto the middle platform (or drop and run around, and up the steps). The second monkey attaches to the rope leading across a gap to the east. Swing across, and bring out your Lantern. Burn the web, then open the door.

Chamber 7: Staircase Cavern

Baba Serpent

Threat Meter

Head down into this large open chamber with a giant staircase in front of you. Move along the path, then be ready to attack a larger, more ferocious Baba plant; the Baba Serpent! This fearsome foe's head is invincible—no amount of hacking stops it. Instead, wait for the creature to rise up and expose its neck, then either slice it with your sword, or fire at it with a ranged weapon.

Meet the Baba Serpent! Separate the stalk from the head, or your combat never ends.

After you separate the Baba Serpent's head, shoot it again, or finish it with a flurry of stabbing sword swipes. If you're caught in its mouth, as shown above, the damage is light, and you can escape with a spin. There are two Baba Serpents in this chamber; watch for the one in the long grass to your right!

➤ Complete a check of the ground level, and you'll notice a second strange creature: the Deku Like. It's in front of a chest in this room's southern part, and it's impervious to your sword and Slingshot. You must defend it in another manner.

➤ Climb the stairs to discover a second of these stationary creatures. Ignore it for the moment, turn left and run up these stairs, taking care to dodge around the Bombling. The Bombling is your clue to finishing these Deku Likes.

Deku Like

Threat Meter

The Deku Like can't move and you can harm it only if it swallows something explosive. Use the nearby Bombling. Slice it until it forms into a bomb, pick it up, and carry it to the wooden structure's edge, above the second Deku Like you saw.

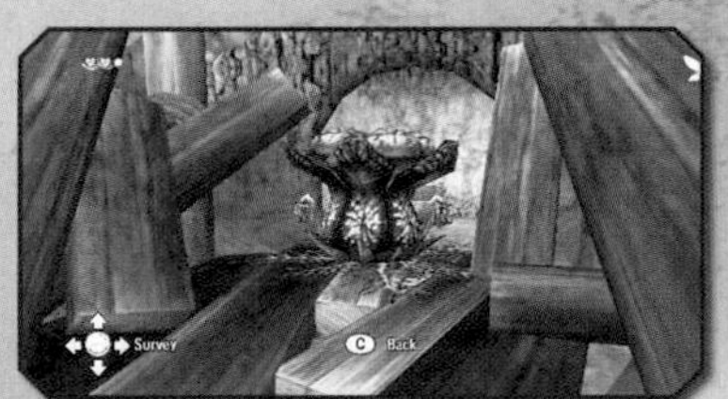

The Deku Like ("Like" is Hyrulian for "eat") is a plant impervious to slicing. It loves to feast on adventurers!

Drop the Bombling into the Deku Like's gaping maw. It chews on it, then succumbs to indigestion! Any other plan—like using your sword, flinging projectiles, or jumping the gap—results in a quick meal at your expense. Collect the three Hearts the Deku Like emits after it explodes.

▲ **Treasure Chest:** Drop from this ledge (press on the analog stick to roll), and enter the small alcove you couldn't reach earlier. Ignore the Bombling here and open that chest! Inside is a **Piece of Heart**. The Deku Like slaying was well worth it!

Treasure Chest #6
Piece of Heart

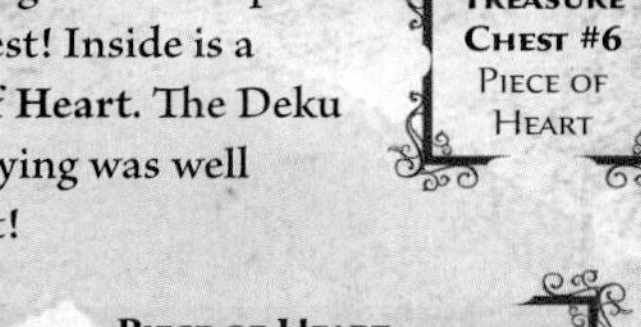

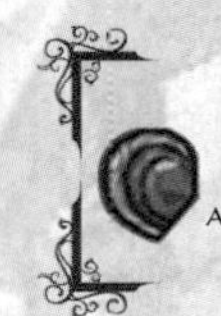

Piece of Heart
You got a Piece of Heart! Collect three more for another full Heart Container. Piece of Heart #2 of 45.

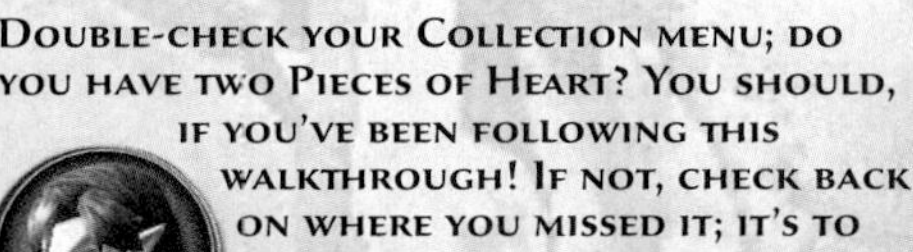

◄ After you take out the Deku Like on the upper area, jump over the gap to the rocky ledge in the chamber's northeast corner. A boulder blocks a cave entrance. Return here in a moment; there's a second Deku Like to tackle! Turn and face south, and check out the vine wall. Produce your Slingshot and drop the two Walltulas, then jump and climb up.

Note: Double-check your Collection menu; do you have two Pieces of Heart? You should, if you've been following this walkthrough! If not, check back on where you missed it; it's to your advantage to collect Pieces of Heart as early as possible.

Tip: Drop and collect the items the Walltulas drop if you wish.

► Don't exit via the southern upper door yet! Instead, face west and chop down a nearby Bombling. Pick it up as it's flashing, and walk forward to the gap at the ledge's edge. Drop the Bombling onto the first Deku Like you saw. That's both of them defeated!

▲ Now comes the tricky part: which exit to choose! To complete this dungeon in the fastest time, either destroy the boulder blocking the northeast corner's door, or head through the upper door in the southeast corner, at the top of the long vine climb. Do one, then the other.

Enemies Encountered: Deku Baba, Baba Serpent, Deku Like, Bombling, Walltula

Characters Encountered

Midna

1st Monkey

3rd Monkey

Missing Links

1. Grass, Pots, and Deku Nuts

As usual, the grass can be cut down for some Rupees (and to help spot that Baba Serpent). Also smash the pots (for Rupees) and slice grass on the western wooden platform. On the eastern side, there are Deku nuts to smash, too.

Chamber 8: Lair of Big Baba

As you enter this large, arena-like chamber, you spot a monkey imprisoned behind a locked door. The key is on the ground in front of you, but the biggest Deku plant you've ever seen swallows it; the beast drops the key into its massive sack. Welcome to the home of the fearsome Big Baba!

Big Baba

Threat Meter

Step 1: Fighting Big Baba means using your shield to block and target (both with Z). With your shield out, advance on this frightening foe, and sidestep when it slams its head at you. Block, and as the head reaches the ground, spin or slice it!

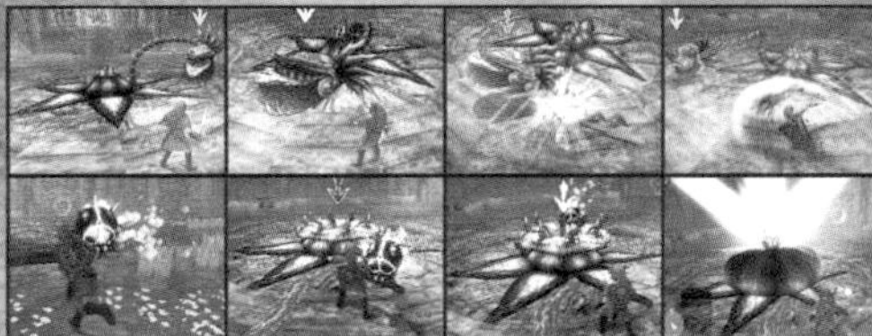

With the head destroyed, the sack shuts and refuses to cough up that key. However, two Bomblings stand at the room's southern end. Slice one, pick it up, and carry it toward the sack. Then Z target, and throw the bomb into the maw. The beast gets blown up, and the key is yours!

A giant among Baba plants, this big boy is slain in the usual way: slice the stalk and head, then bomb the base!

Author Note

Throughout the adventure, we were constantly attempting to make our explorations even tougher, so we instigated a "manual targeting" policy, where anything that required throwing couldn't be Z targeted. Of course, we missed the open maw numerous times, leading us to question our gaming prowess!

Small Key
You got a Small Key! This opens a locked door, but only in this area.

➤ Pick up the Small Key from Big Baba's remains. Run south and use it to unlock the door to the captured monkey. After it's freed, you can both leave via the north door. It's time to locate your next trapped simian.

Missing Links

1. Grass and Pottery Slicing

Before you leave the room, or during the fight with Big Baba, scour the perimeter. There are pots with Hearts in them, and grass to mow down. The cave the monkey was held in has pots containing Rupees.

Chamber 7: First Return to Staircase Cavern

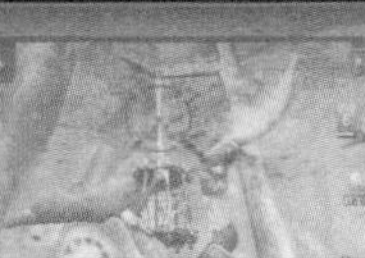

➤ Your next task is to secure another monkey. This one is trapped in the room east of you. Return to the Bombling on the wooden plank platform and slice it. Pick it up and run along the wooden platform. Leap the gap while carrying the Bombling, then lob it so it lands on the upper ledge, right next to the boulder. This might take a few tries! As long as the Bombling lands next to the boulder, both explode, allowing you access to a previously hidden door.

Author Note

We spent an inordinate amount of time stuck on this puzzle, until we realized we could leap that gap with Bombling in hand! We blew ourselves up countless times, but our favorite demise came when we were caught in a Bombling explosion, flew off the side of the ledge, and got eaten by a Baba Serpent.

Small Key
You got a Small Key! This opens a locked door, but only in this area.

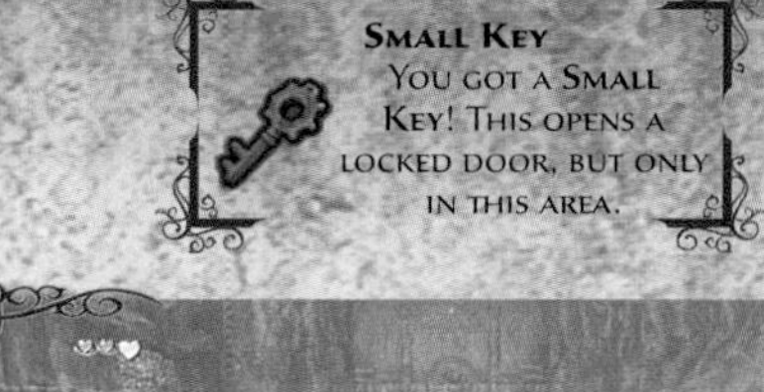

▲ Your eyes didn't deceive you; some of those tiles up ahead seem to be moving! Three of them on the passage between the pools of water have a nasty new critter—the Tile Worm—lurking beneath them. You can easily ignore them by running along the right side of the three-tile wide passage!

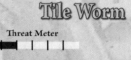

Caution
The tiled passage between the water hides three Tile Worms. There are two on the left line of tiles (one under tile #1, and one under tile #10) and one under tile #5 in the middle line of tiles.

Enemies Encountered: Baba Serpent, Big Baba, Bombling, Tile Worm

Chamber 10: Room of the Tile Worms

➤ You enter a green and dank chamber, with two bodies of water on each side of a tiled path. Take a moment to oversee the entire area. The steps across the way lead to a locked door with a monkey behind it. Most interesting though, is that chest!

➤ **Treasure Chest:** Did you see it? The chest is on top of that totem pole! Drop down and then roll into the pole to dislodge the chest. It comes crashing to the ground. Open it up to discover a **Small Key**. Grab this before proceeding.

Treasure Chest #7
Small Key

Tile Worm

Threat Meter

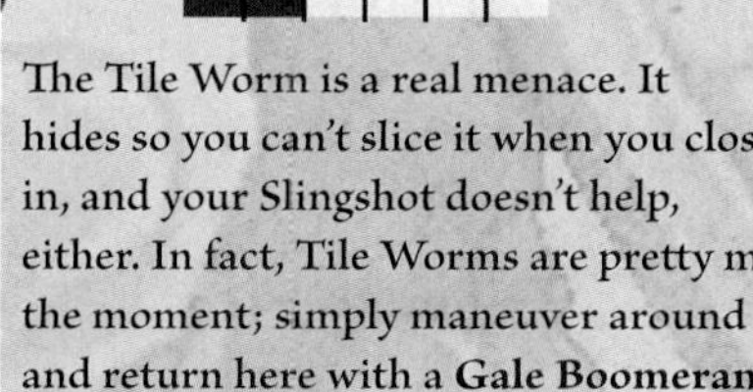

The Tile Worm is a real menace. It hides so you can't slice it when you close in, and your Slingshot doesn't help, either. In fact, Tile Worms are pretty much invincible at the moment; simply maneuver around the moving tiles, and return here with a **Gale Boomerang** for a spot of revenge!

Don't stand near this sneaky snake; he knocks you high into the air and disorients you!

Characters Encountered

Midna

1st Monkey

2nd Monkey

3rd Monkey

4th Monkey

Once on the other side of the tile passage, don't stand on the ground tiles with the four torches at each corner. This avoids the waiting Tile Worms entirely. Instead, bring out your Lantern, and light the two unlit torches. This raises the large set of steps at the far end of the room. Leave the remaining two lit torches untouched.

Run around the tiled floor avoiding the lurking Tile Worms, or pass through the middle of the floor (there are none there), and clamber up onto the giant steps you just raised. On the way, notice a chest behind these steps, and a Skulltula hanging from the ceiling above the locked door.

You can't access the chest yet, so return here later. However you can shoot the Skulltula from the steps with your Slingshot, or attack it when it drops to the ground. Be sure to finish with a leaping stab!

Use the **Small Key** you grabbed from the chest you knocked off the totem pole to free the fourth monkey, and retrace your steps out of the room. Make a mental note to return here later to collect the items you left.

Treasure Chest: Before you leave this chamber, get the one chest you can reach. Near the torches and tiles on the left side of the room is a vine wall. Climb it and edge along, then go down onto a curved platform. After smashing some pots for Rupees and a Heart, open the chest for a cash infusion.

Treasure Chest #8
Red Rupee (20)

Tip

You may be experiencing "full wallet syndrome," as you fill up your wallet and can't carry any more Rupees. This means leaving dungeons with chests still unclaimed! This isn't a problem, but if you really need to complete each dungeon and ransack every single chest, try the following:

- Donate more than you should to Trill the bird in Faron Woods before entering this dungeon.
- Don't pick up any stray Rupees that fall from pots, grass, or monsters.
- Locate a larger wallet as soon as possible; visit Princess Agitha with an insect in the city.

Missing Links

1. Ground Floor Grass

As usual, there's grass everywhere to slice and dice, including near the tile floor.

2. Totem Pole Pottery

One of the totem poles has a chest, and the other holds a pot with a blue Rupee (5) inside. Simply roll into the totem pole and grab the Rupee after the pot falls and smashes.

3. Pulverizing Pottery

Numerous pots are scattered about here, including some near chest #8, some on the opposite earthen ledge, also accessed via a vine, and some in the alcove you freed the monkey from.

Task 3: Battle the Bad Baboon named Ook

Chamber 7: Second Return to Staircase Cavern

◄ With your monkeys in tow, having rescued both of them, head back to the Crossroads Hub. You can optionally take the only exit you haven't investigated yet; it leads back to the Wind Gorge (1C), but you can't proceed. You head through this door in the opposite direction later in this expedition.

Chamber 2: Third Return to Crossroads Hub

► Back in the Crossroads Hub, your quartet of cackling chimps beckons you to swing across to the middle platform and then up the shallow steps to the northern door. Oblige them, as this leads to the Wind Gorge. Make sure you have all four monkeys before continuing!

Chamber 3: Third Return to Wind Gorge

▲ You're now in the middle section of the Wind Gorge, with a massive gap, thanks to the baboon's bridge-cutting skills. Watch as each monkey creates a swinging handle for you, then take a deep breath; you need to swing four times across the gorge, and land on the other side! As always, time this carefully, pressing Ⓐ about once a second to ensure a safe trip.

◄ Once on the other side, climb up the steps leading to the unlocked door. Although you can turn east and try leaping across the bridges to rescue a monkey, it's better to wait for a moment. Slice the Deku nuts by the door, and then enter.

Chamber 10: Cavern of Ook

You enter Ook's cavern, and the door seals shut behind you! Ook is crazy, and he's wielding a deadly Gale Boomerang! He throws the weapon and it slices off two Baba Serpent heads from the ceiling. Patting his bare bottom in satisfaction, Ook prepares a second Boomerang swing for you!

Ook

Threat Meter

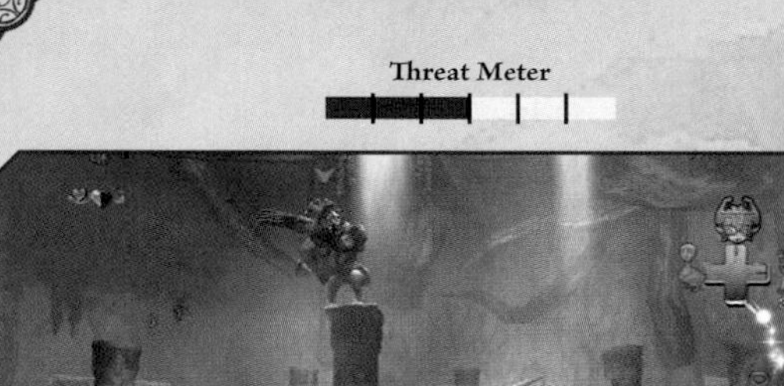

Ook likes to dance. Fortunately, he's at the top of a highly unstable totem pole. Bring that buttock-patting ape down for a spanking!

Begin by executing a perfect spin attack on the two advancing Baba Serpent heads; this stops Ook's first attack. Now run forward, and watch as the manic simian leaps from totem pole to totem pole. He then stops and launches the Boomerang.

Enemies Encountered

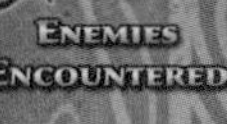

Tile Worm

Skulltula

Deku Baba

Ook

Baba Serpent

Characters Encountered

Midna

5th Monkey

Ook (cont'd)

Keep your eye on Ook, and run around to avoid the Boomerang, and any more Baba Serpent heads he cuts from the ceiling. He launches the Boomerang and is dancing on the totem pole, waiting for it to return, then the returning Gale Boomerang hits the totem pole and knocks him down!

Then execute a flurry of sword slashes, Ⓩ targeting Ook's posterior! Slash that backside until Ook stands up, clutches his buttocks, and leaps back up on the totem pole! That'll teach this unruly ape! Now continue this tactic two more times. After you knock him off the totem pole (remember: roll twice into it quickly!), and slash his bottom two times, he cuts down two more Baba Serpents. Deal with them immediately, so they don't clamp their jaws around you.

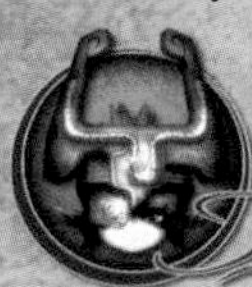

Tip: If you need to refill your health during the fight, smash pots around the room's perimeter for Hearts.

After a final ignominious buttock bashing, Ook gives up his Boomerang, knocks himself out on his own totem pole, and squirts out the parasite beetle responsible for his manic antics!

After Ook realizes his antics, his bottom is flush with embarrassment, and he hops out of a hole in the cavern. You can't follow him, so instead, you step over to the **Gale Boomerang**. *A voice whispers "I am the Fairy of Winds who resides in this boomerang." She instructs you to use the weapon she's bound to, and focus her power!*

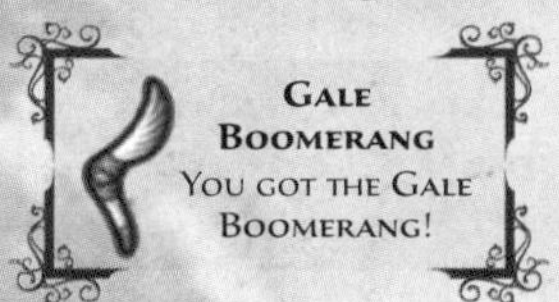

Gale Boomerang
You got the Gale Boomerang!

Gale Boomerang

The Gale Boomerang houses the Fairy of Winds. On the minus screen, set it to Ⓑ. Use the Wii Remote to find targets and press Ⓑ to throw it and suck things up with gale force. Lock on to objects with a yellow target by pressing Ⓩ while holding Ⓑ. You can lock on to and strike as many as five things at once!

Set the item to your Ⓑ, and test it out. Don't forget you can keep Ⓩ targeting up to five times before you release! Remember to press Ⓑ first. Here are some tips for using the Gale Boomerang:

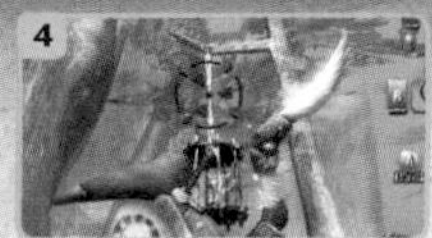

Gale Boomerang (cont'd)

Gale Boomerang tips:

- Sweep up leaves with this weapon to unearth items such as Rupees.
- Fire this manually, or target it. You can auto-target at close range, too.
- It dazes foes caught in the wind. Follow this up with sword strikes.
- Target a distant item, such as a pot or Heart Piece, then launch the Gale Boomerang. It picks up the item and brings it back to you!
- Breakable objects are smashed if they hit scenery on the way back. Otherwise, you can lift and use the item as if you just walked up to it.
- Double-target a pot near a wall. Use the Boomerang to pick it up and smash it and the second target to bring the contents back!
- The Gale Boomerang also snuffs out torches and turns wind fans.

Tip

➤ Test out your new weapon on the bars that are preventing you from exiting. Z lock on to the fan above the door, and target five times. Launch the Boomerang, and the fan spins long enough to raise the bars. If you target the fan only once, the bars don't lift high enough. Exit via this south door.

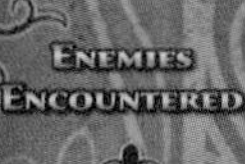

Ook

Baba Serpent

Bokoblin

Keese

Task 4: Find the Fifth Monkey

Chamber 3: Fourth Return to Wind Gorge

▲ Back in the Wind Gorge, you can finally head east, brandishing your Gale Boomerang. Target the fan atop the rotating bridge platform, and use the wind of the Boomerang to activate it. The platform turns. Run onto it. Then run onto the second platform (assuming it is lined up east to west), and continue to the exposed rock platform ahead.

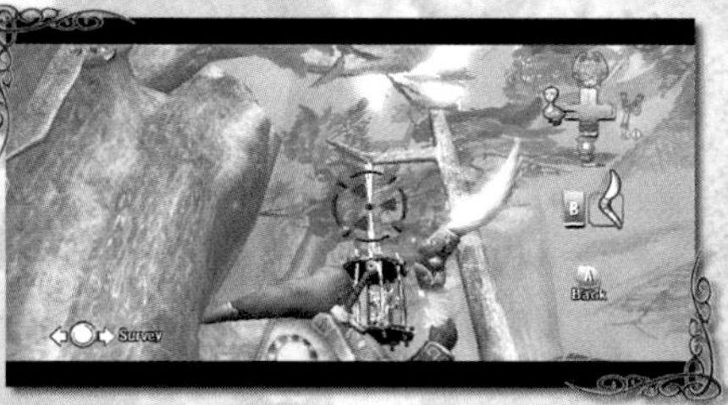

➤ Bring out your sword, and defeat the Bokoblin guarding another cage, with your fifth monkey friend inside. Once you've defeated the enemy, step back and use the Gale Boomerang to target the Skulltula web holding the cage. Slice the web and the cage falls, shattering and freeing the fifth monkey. This one leaps west, across the rotating bridge platforms. He's waiting for you at the northwestern rocky ledge you haven't explored yet. Head there shortly.

Be careful traversing the bridge platforms! The wind still rotates the fans and you can run off into the bottomless chasm if you're not careful!

Caution

◄ For the moment though, head south, back to the room with the Tile Worms in it (11). Head south, traversing two bridge platforms, and optionally slicing or targeting the Keese with your Boomerang. Open the door in the southeast corner.

Midna

5th Monkey

Task 5: Obtain the Big Key

Chamber 7: Third Return to Staircase Cavern

◀ This door leads you into the Staircase Cavern. From here, drop down onto the wooden platform, make a left. Pass the Bombling, leap the gap, climb onto the higher ledge, and exit via the door in the northeastern corner.

▶ Before you leave this cavern, try using your Gale Boomerang. You can target a Bombling at range, but the one near the wooden railing always explodes. Or, try targeting both Walltulas and the Deku nuts. The Gale Boomerang strikes them all with a single whirl!

Chamber 9: First Return to Room of the Tile Worms

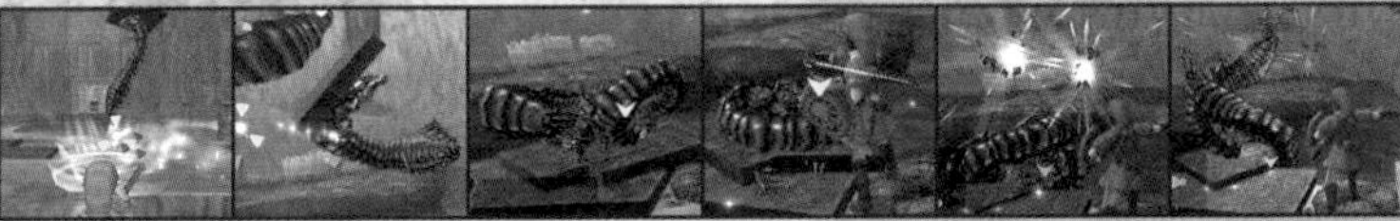

▲ Head back to the room where the Tile Worms were mocking you earlier. It's time for some payback! Bring out the Gale Boomerang, and target the tile the Tile Worm is under. Launch the Boomerang, and watch as the Tile Worm is ripped out and spun onto the ground. Now attack with your sword, finishing the otherwise annoyingly defensive foe. Repeat this tactic until all Tile Worms are defeated, if you wish.

◀ **Treasure Chest:** Now for the real prize this room holds! Step over to the tiled ground (ideally with no remaining Tile Worms), and target the two lit torches with your Gale Boomerang. Blow both of them out, and the entire large staircase recedes. You can now reach the previously hidden alcove and open the chest. The prize is well worth your backtracking trouble!

Treasure Chest #9
Piece of Heart

Piece of Heart
You got a Piece of Heart! Collect two more for another full Heart Container. Piece of Heart #3 of 45.

Chamber 7: Fourth Return to Staircase Cavern

▲ Head out of the Tile Worm chamber, and back into the Staircase Cavern. You should have cleared all chests in this area, so drop down (watch those respawning Baba Serpents!), and head through the door in the west wall.

Chamber 2: Fourth Return to the Crossroads Hub

▲ **Treasure Chest:** Now swing back into the Crossroads Hub, and tackle the 10th chest in this dungeon: the one hanging above the middle wooden platform. A simple targeting of the web string with your Gale Boomerang drops the chest. Inside is a Compass!

Treasure Chest #10
Compass

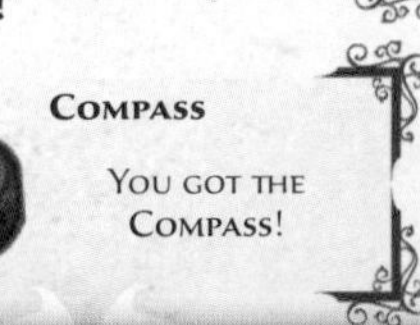

Compass
You got the Compass!

The Compass is a handy tool that shows you where to find objects hidden in this dungeon. Check the map screen and you'll see the following additional information: The floor and location of each remaining chest (including ones you opened but couldn't take the Rupees if your wallet was full), and the location of the dungeon boss (represented by the skull icon).

Chamber 1: Return to the Entrance

◄ Optionally, from the Crossroads Hub, you can travel southward, back to the entrance, now that you're armed with the Boomerang. You can knock Walltulas off the vines easily and grab the pots on the tiny platforms you can't reach by jumping.

Chamber 4: Third Return to Step-Stone Caverns

► Head north, then west, back to the Step-stone Caverns via the monkey swing, and past the area where you found Ooccoo. Watch the returning Deku Baba! When you're done with combat, head to the barred gate via the vines or the rope bridge. Your key awaits!

◄ With the Gale Boomerang, you can now open the barred gate! Naturally, the process is tricky, but the backward "Z" in the floor provides the clue. Target each of the four fan pillars, starting with the far right. Then the far left. Then the near right. Then the near left. When you're done, launch the Boomerang! The Boomerang must connect with all four fans in this order for the gate to open.

▲ With the gate open, roll forward and move directly to the ornate chest, and open it up. You've discovered the **Big Key**; this leads to the most important room in the dungeon! Take it, then exit via the door in the northern wall.

Treasure Chest #11
Big Key

Big Key

You got the Big Key! Use it to gain access to the lair of this dungeon's boss!

The Big Key is big news to a dungeon explorer. Always lying inside the largest and most ornate chest type, the Big Key allows access to the lair of the dungeon boss. There's only one Big Key per dungeon, and the key unlocks only the boss's room of the dungeon you're currently in.

Enemies Encountered

Bombling

Walltula

Tile Worm

Baba Serpent

Deku Baba

Task 6: Save the Sixth Monkey

Characters Encountered

Midna

1st Monkey

2nd Monkey

3rd Monkey

4th Monkey

5th Monkey

Chamber 3: Fifth Return to the Wind Gorge

➤ There's no need to produce your Boomerang here; the wind moves the platform to allow north-south access, so run northward, and meet up with the fifth monkey you saved over on the east side of this gorge. Follow him to the door and enter.

Chamber 5: First Return to the Wind Bridge Crossroads

➤ Pass the open chest, and optionally smash the pots, then stand at the edge of the wooden platform, with the gap in front of you. Don't fall off! Bring out the **Gale Boomerang**, target the fan atop the bridge platform, and spin it 90 degrees to connect the north-south route.

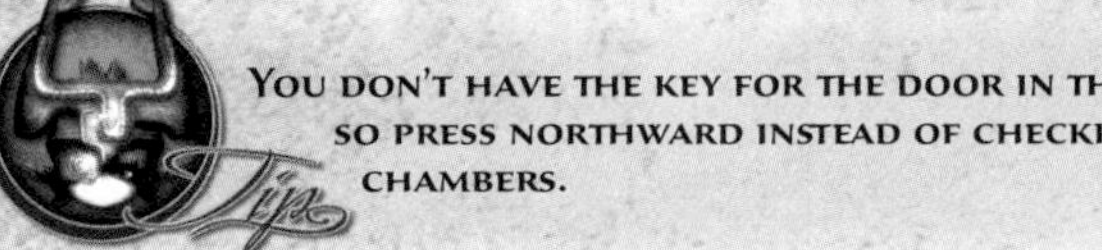

◄ Ignore the two Bokoblins on either side of you (or shoot them with your Slingshot), and race northward so you have an open view of the platforms and doors to the east and west. Now take out the Gale Boomerang and mess with those Bokoblins. Target one to draw their attention, and watch as it runs at you and falls off into the inky darkness! Now exit via the north door.

Tip: You don't have the key for the door in this chamber yet, so press northward instead of checking out the side chambers.

Chamber 11: The Giant Forest Tree Chasm

◄ Enter a huge and cavernous chasm, where the monkeys you've assembled have leapt to a gigantic tree, and are sitting on the large fungal growths waiting for a complete collection! The way north is completely blocked, so turn right.

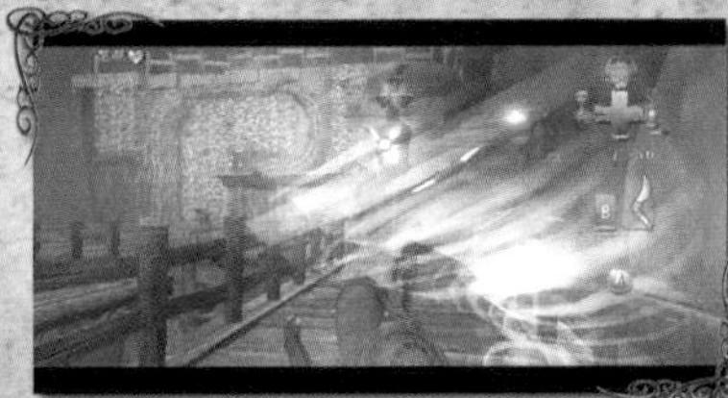

◄ Head onto the bridge platform, and spin the fan once with your Gale Boomerang. Next, run onto the second bridge platform, then use the Boomerang to spin this second structure so it faces east to west, allowing you access to a cliffside and large vine wall.

➤ Hop off the bridge and assault the Bokoblin at the base of a large vine wall, then bring out the Gale Boomerang once again, and target up to three Walltulas on the vine wall. Scrape them off with a thrown Boomerang, then begin to climb the wall.

Tip: If you want to grab the items each Walltula drops, target the last one twice, or wait until you're near the wooden ledge before you dispatch it.

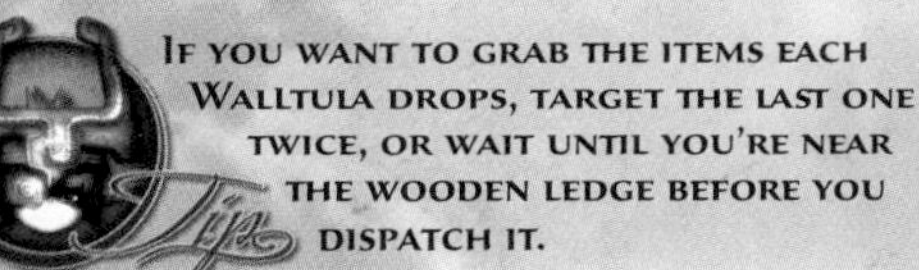

Caution: A vine wall leads down off the edge of the lower deck you're standing on—beware! This leads to a long drop into the bottomless pit! There's no way to reach the northern area currently.

➤ Climb up the vine wall, sidestepping, then dropping down to the ledge. Take care of the third Walltula if you didn't already, then climb up the smaller strip of vines. Struggle to the grassy rock ledge at the top, and optionally survey the chamber from here. Then engage a lone Bokoblin in a bout of swordplay before finally exiting via the eastern door.

1

2

3

4

5

6

Missing Links

1. Grass and Pottery Slicing

As with many of the other dungeon rooms, this one has grass and pots, both on the rock ledge before you exit. Rupees and Hearts are available here.

Chamber 12: Waterlogged Cavern

▲ Enter this oddly quiet, waterlogged chamber, and bring out your sword; two Baba Serpents must be defeated! Once you've slashed them into the ground, stop and check out the area to your right. A Deku Like sits on a small stepping stone.

◄ The stepping stone leads to a ledge that's too high to reach from the water if you swim there, so removing the Deku Like is your priority. Fortunately, there's a Bombling peering out of a tiny island on the other side of the chamber! You can't stand on the island, but you don't need to. Simply target the Bombling with your Gale Boomerang, bring the bomb back to your hands, turn, and throw it quickly into the Deku Like (don't forget to Z target)!

◄ Treasure Chest: Whooph! The Deku Like explodes, allowing you to cross onto its stepping stone, and onto the ledge with a treasure chest on it. The prize is well worth your effort: a Small Key that can open the door back in Wind Bridge Crossroads (1E).

Treasure Chest #12
Small Key

Small Key
You got the Small Key! This opens a locked door, but only in this area.

▲ You can now visit the rest of this chamber, heading over the wooden bridge, and bringing out your sword to administer a beatdown on a nasty Baba Serpent.

► Next comes another puzzle; a small vine wall leading to a boulder blocking your path. With your knowledge of Bomblings, solving this is easy; target the same Bombling hole you did earlier, but manually target the boulder with a second lock-on. Launch the Gale Boomerang and watch the bomb head from the island and explode into the boulder!

Enemies Encountered

Bokoblin

Walltula

Baba Serpent

Deku Like

Bombling

Characters Encountered

Midna

Monkeys 1-6

7th Monkey

➤ With the boulder shattered, climb the vine wall, and enter a wooden grotto area. Head straight for the Bokoblin and slice it down, then watch out for your first fight with a Baba Serpent peering down from the ceiling! Execute a couple of jumping attacks to separate the stalk from the head, or back up and target the stalk (not the head) with your Gale Boomerang. There's a second Baba Serpent on the opposite side of the grotto.

➤ A monkey is behind that rock doorway, and the only way to free him is to bomb it open. However, if you target the Bombling, then the doorway, the bomb explodes en route.

▲ Instead, stand at the edge of the grotto, and just target the Bombling, catch the bomb, then run and lob it at the door. This does the trick, and the grateful monkey scampers out to greet you!

Missing Links

1. Pottery and Deku Nut Pulverizing

This chamber has Deku nuts on the far side of the bridge near the last Baba Serpent, plus many pots in the grotto. Don't forget the yellow Rupee (10) inside the monkey alcove! Unfortunately, the lily pads don't usually give up any cash if you swim through them.

Task 7: Escape with Monkeys Seven and Eight

Chamber 11: First Return to the Giant Forest Tree Chasm

➤ Backtrack to this tree and chasm, and run left along the rock ledge to the vines, grab hold, then drop down to the wooden deck below. Step down to face the nearest platform bridge.

➤ Use the Gale Boomerang to activate the bridge, step onto it, then target both bridge fans with a single Boomerang spin, and activate the second bridge. They both turn simultaneously, allowing you to run across. Then turn the second bridge again, and leave.

Chamber 5: Second Return to the Wind Bridge Crossroads

▲ Head south, entering the Wind Bridge Crossroads, and spin the bridge platform so you can enter it, and again so it faces east to west. Now investigate both of the side rooms, in either order. Don't forget to tackle the Bokoblins if you didn't knock them off the wooden platforms earlier! In this case, we headed east.

Chamber 13: Nest of the Skulltulas

➤ The webs on the floor should be a clue. Arm yourself with the Boomerang, and target the bodies of two Skulltulas before they descend to ambush you. Fight them one at a time, or both at once, using swordplay.

Spin to catch both Skulltulas off guard, then execute a leaping stab to pierce arachnid flesh!

➤ Now inspect this chamber, and you'll notice three holes in the ground. Two have webs covering them, so move to the hole in the north of the room, bring out your **Lantern** and swing it, burning the web and dropping you down. You'll land (if you chose the correct hole) on a giant tree stump. Smash that cage with a spin, and set the monkey free!

➤ If you used another method (dropping down the hole, or burning the south web hole), prepare for battle with a Skulltula! Finish it off, then use the Bombling to blow up the Deku Like if you wish; it holds a red Rupee (20). When you're finished, climb the vine and exit the chamber.

Missing Links

1. The Seven Hanging Pots

Be sure you cut down more than just the Skulltulas; seven pots are suspended by webs, and many contain Hearts and Rupees. Target the web string, not the pot.

2. Scattered Skulls

The lower portion of this lair has ape-like skulls scattered about the floor. These are like rocks; pick them up and toss them at walls and they explode. Or simply slice them; they sometimes contain goods.

Chamber 5: Third Return to the Wind Bridge Crossroads

▲ Now investigate the locked chamber on the opposite side of the crossroads. Dash across the bridge platform, and use the **Small Key** you found in the Waterlogged Cavern (1L) to open the door. This leads to a long, irregular chamber.

Chamber 14: Small Cave Maze

➤ Enter the chamber, and concentrate on targeting the Tile Worms hiding on the floor in front of you. Unearth three using the Gale Boomerang. Finish the first two off with swords, then move forward and right for the third.

Enemies Encountered

Bokoblin

Baba Serpent

Skulltula

Deku Like

Tile Worm

Characters Encountered

▲ You can't climb the giant wooden supports, so head west, and find the tunnel entrance in the northwest corner. Head on through to a small sunken chamber with a nasty Skulltula to fight! Bring out your Gale Boomerang, stun the spider with a single hit, then leap in and finish the beast with your sword!

◄ Knock the Walltulas off the vine wall with your Boomerang's ranged attack, then climb the vine wall to the upper cavern area. Face east (back toward the Wind Bridge Crossroads chamber), and chop the stem off a Baba Serpent using the Boomerang. Finish it with your sword.

▲ Now turn and face the opposite direction. With all beasts defeated, aim at the two fan columns on either side of the locked gate where you can see a shrieking monkey. The Boomerang spins the fans and opens the gate, freeing your final monkey!

► Before you leave, head to the upper part of the tiled room. Now on the wooden platforms, you should see a treasure chest on a platform along the north wall. Head around and leap across, grabbing the platform and pulling yourself up. Then open your 13th chest before leaving.

Treasure Chest #13
Red Rupee (20)

Missing Links

1. Retiling the Floor

As well as defeating the tiresome Tile Worms, you can lift all the brown tiles off the floor, leaving the green tiles where they are. That way, you know no Tile Worms remain.

2. Grass and Pottery Pulverizing

Slice the grass near the monkey doors and the pottery behind the monkey and under the wooden platform supports for various small Rupees and Hearts.

Chamber 5: Fourth Return to the Wind Bridge Crossroads

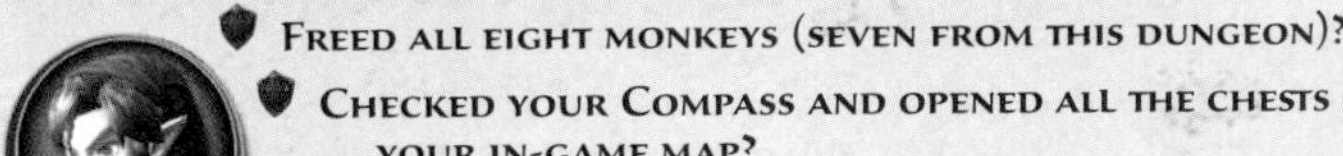

Check your status! Have you:

- Acquired the Big Key from the Step-stones Cavern (1D)?
- Freed all eight monkeys (seven from this dungeon)?
- Checked your Compass and opened all the chests on your in-game map?

Note: If so, head northward!

► After checking that you've accomplished all your previous tasks, enter the Wind Bridge Crossroads. Step onto the bridge platform, spin it to face north-south, move onto it, then go through the door into the Giant Forest Tree Chasm.

Chamber 11: Second Return to the Giant Forest Tree Chasm

➤ Enter the chasm with all monkeys freed, and they excitedly leap along the huge branch of the giant forest tree to make an eight-strong single monkey rope!

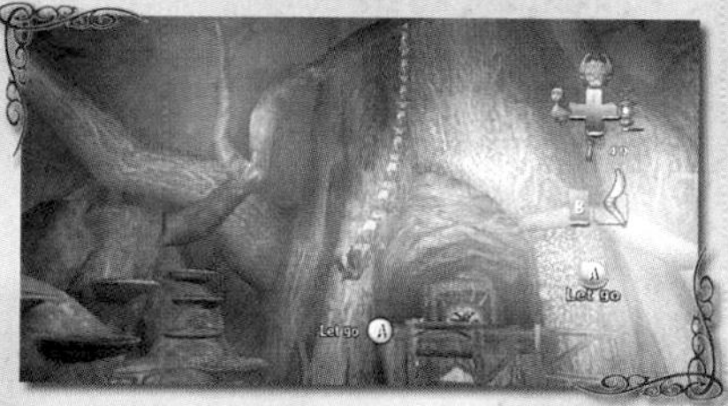

◄ Move off the north-facing platform in front of you (you'll automatically jump and grab) when the monkey chain is swinging toward you. Let go when the chain swings near the north wooden platform. This is easier than it sounds!

➤ Then run toward the locked door ahead of you. Produce the **Big Key**, optionally smashing pots on the left side, but don't open the door yet!

➤ Empty the Bottle if it contains potions or Lantern fuel. The reason is simple: there's a Fairy in the pot to your far right. Make sure you have the empty Bottle selected (with Ⓑ), smash the pot, and swipe the Fairy with your Bottle!

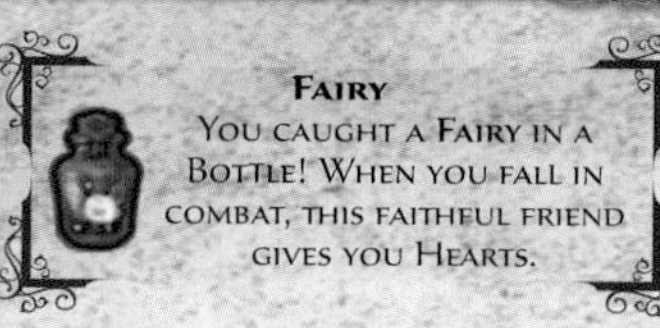

Fairy
You caught a Fairy in a Bottle! When you fall in combat, this faithful friend gives you Hearts.

The Fairy is an excellent healing device. Heed these instructions!

1. Press ✚ to place the Fairy Bottle back into your item inventory.
2. Immediately swap the Fairy Bottle with the Gale Boomerang so you don't accidentally use it!
3. The Fairy gives you eight Hearts worth of healing and does this automatically when you reach zero Hearts during a battle. Effectively, it resurrects you.
4. Because you have only three Hearts in your health bar so far, you'll receive only your maximum health.

Note

➤ With Boomerang at the ready, move to the huge door and unlock it. Don't attempt this until you've secured the Fairy and cleared this room, or you'll face a fearsome foe without additional Fairy help!

Enemies Encountered

Skulltula

Walltula

Baba Serpent

Tile Worm

Twilit Parasite Diababa

Task 8: Defeat Twilit Parasite Diababa

Chamber 10: Boss Battle! Twilit Parasite Diababa

Threat Meter

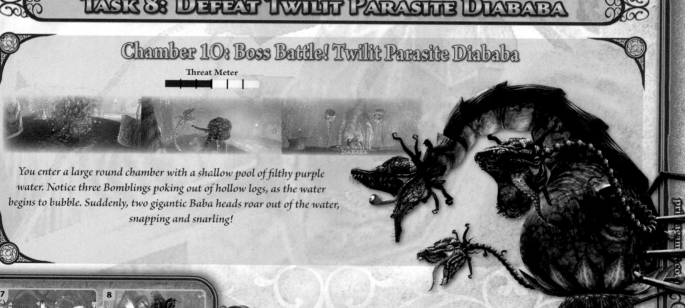

You enter a large round chamber with a shallow pool of filthy purple water. Notice three Bomblings poking out of hollow logs, as the water begins to bubble. Suddenly, two gigantic Baba heads roar out of the water, snapping and snarling!

Ook

Midna

Boss Battle! Twilit Parasite Diababa (cont'd)

Form 1: Twin Diababa Serpents

The biggest mouths are also the hungriest. Make sure their meal consists of Bombling, not heroic adventurer!

The twin Diababa Serpents are surprisingly easy to slay; bring out your **Gale Boomerang** and target any of the three Bomblings resting on the logs. Bring the Bombling back, target either Diababa head, and send the bomb spinning into that maw for a spot of deadly indigestion! The head sinks back into the mire. Repeat this plan for the second head. You can target the Bombling and head in a single throw if you wish.

Form 2: Twilit Parasite Diababa

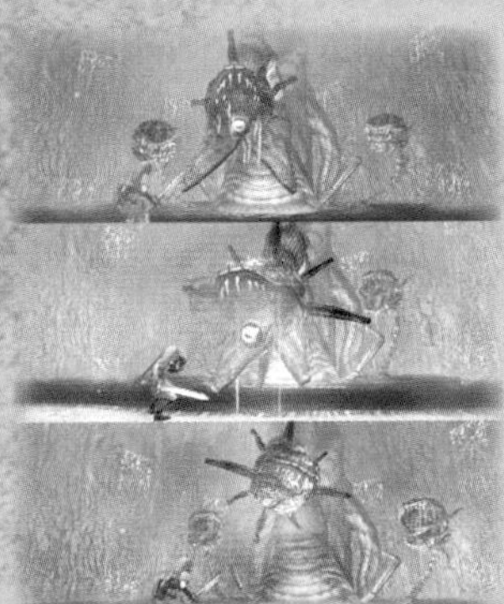
Both heads sink back into the water. Wait, what's that rumbling sound? The entire chamber shakes and the water boils before a massive snaking head, flanked by the Diababa Serpents you just defeated, emerges from the murk and roars in your face!

The Twilit Parasite Diababa is a fearsome and nearly invincible foe, but it still can't digest bombs!

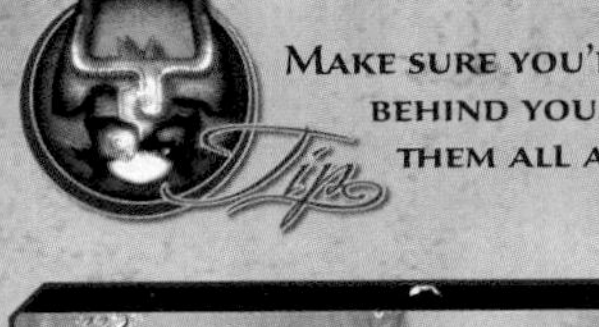
Tip: MAKE SURE YOU'RE SMASHING THE POTTERY TO THE SIDES AND BEHIND YOU. THEY CONTAIN HEARTS, BUT DON'T GRAB THEM ALL AT ONCE!

Step 1: First, a Baba Serpent head snaps its mouth then lunges at you. Look for the mouth movement, then roll out of the way, or block with your shield (Z). Next, the other Serpent does the same. Roll away from this attack, too.

Step 2: You won't have harmed this deadly monstrosity yet but don't worry; help is on the way! Ook swings in from an upper (and unreachable) entrance, and produces a Bombling!

Step 3: Now concentrate on slaying either Baba Serpent (which is optional, but helps you concentrate on the main threat) or the Parasite itself. Defeat the Baba heads in the same way as before, except you're targeting Ook's Bombling as he swings back and forth on a rope.

Step 4: The Parasite is your real concern. Target Ook with your **Gale Boomerang.** Then select the maw of the Parasite with the second target, before you launch the attack. Your timing has to be just right!

Step 5: Make sure you launch the Boomerang when Ook is just about to leave his perch on either side of the chamber and swing into the middle. This catches the Parasite in the side of its head. If you launch the attack at any other time, the Parasite shrugs off the attack! When you're successful, the Parasite's snaking head lolls about, then collapses onto the ground near you.

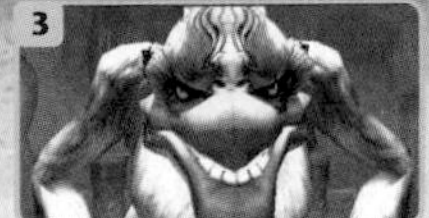
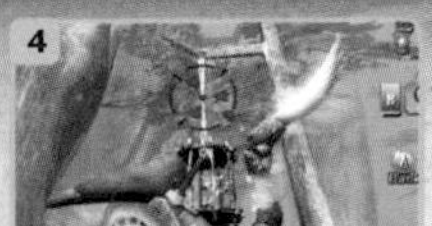

Boss Battle! Twilit Parasite Diababa (cont'd)

Step 6: Make short work of this fiend by targeting the odd eyeball-like appendage that's now exposed, and spin attack, stab, or better yet, launch a leaping finishing move. The beast is badly wounded the first time you try this, then it rises up for a new attack!

Step 7: The Parasite now sprays your grassy outcrop with purple ooze that's damaging. Simply roll out of the way, or throw the Boomerang at the beast's mouth to halt it.

Step 8: Victory! Repeat steps five and six once again, and the second series of stabs should finish this fearsome foe off for good!

Enemies Encountered

Bombling

Twilit Parasite Diababa

*The monster shrivels up into an emaciated tube before dropping its "eye"-like appendage. Inside is a prize worthy of this dungeon trek; a Heart Container! The creature then explodes into shards of twilight. These coalesce into a piece of strange-looking armor. Midna appears and explains this is a piece of **Fused Shadow**.*

*"Do you remember what the spirit said?" Midna asks you. "About how you had to match the **power of the King of Shadows**?" This is your key to victory, and there are three Fused Shadows to find. Midna tells you more only if you help her find the two other Fused Shadows.*

◄ Midna creates a **warp portal** and is waiting for you to join her. Before you do, be sure you pick up the **Heart Container**; this increases your life energy by an entire full Heart, permanently!

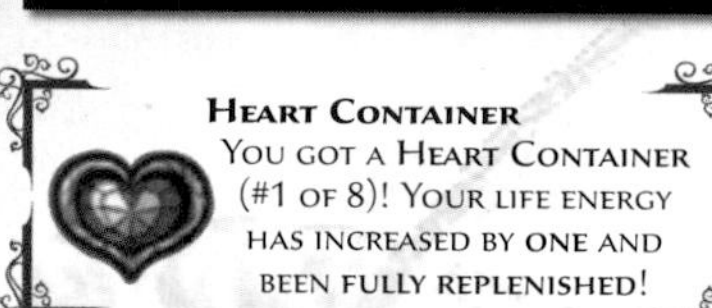

Heart Container
You got a Heart Container (#1 of 8)! Your life energy has increased by one and been fully replenished!

Heart Containers are the grand prize. There are eight: you get one for each main dungeon boss slain in the first eight dungeons. The other method to increase your energy is by locating the 45 Heart Pieces. Collect five pieces to increase your energy by one. Therefore, you can acquire a maximum of 20 energy (45 divided by 5 = 9 Heart Containers from collecting pieces; plus 8 for the dungeon boss fights, equals 17, and you started with three Hearts' worth of energy).

Note

◄ Midna offers you a warp portal to exit the dungeon. If you're ready, take it. If chests still remain unopened, backtrack for them or re-enter the dungeon at a later time using Midna's portal. Save your game!

► You appear at the Faron Woods Spring. A voice of the spirit Faron calls you: "Do not think that Hyrule is now saved from the spread of twilight!" it says. You are to travel to the land protected by **the Eldin spirit**. Midna also informs you that you're looking for portions of Hyrule covered in twilight.

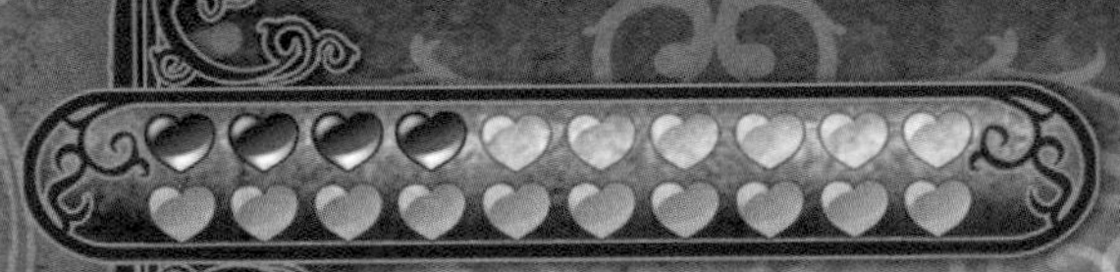

Overworld: From Faron Province to the Goron Mines

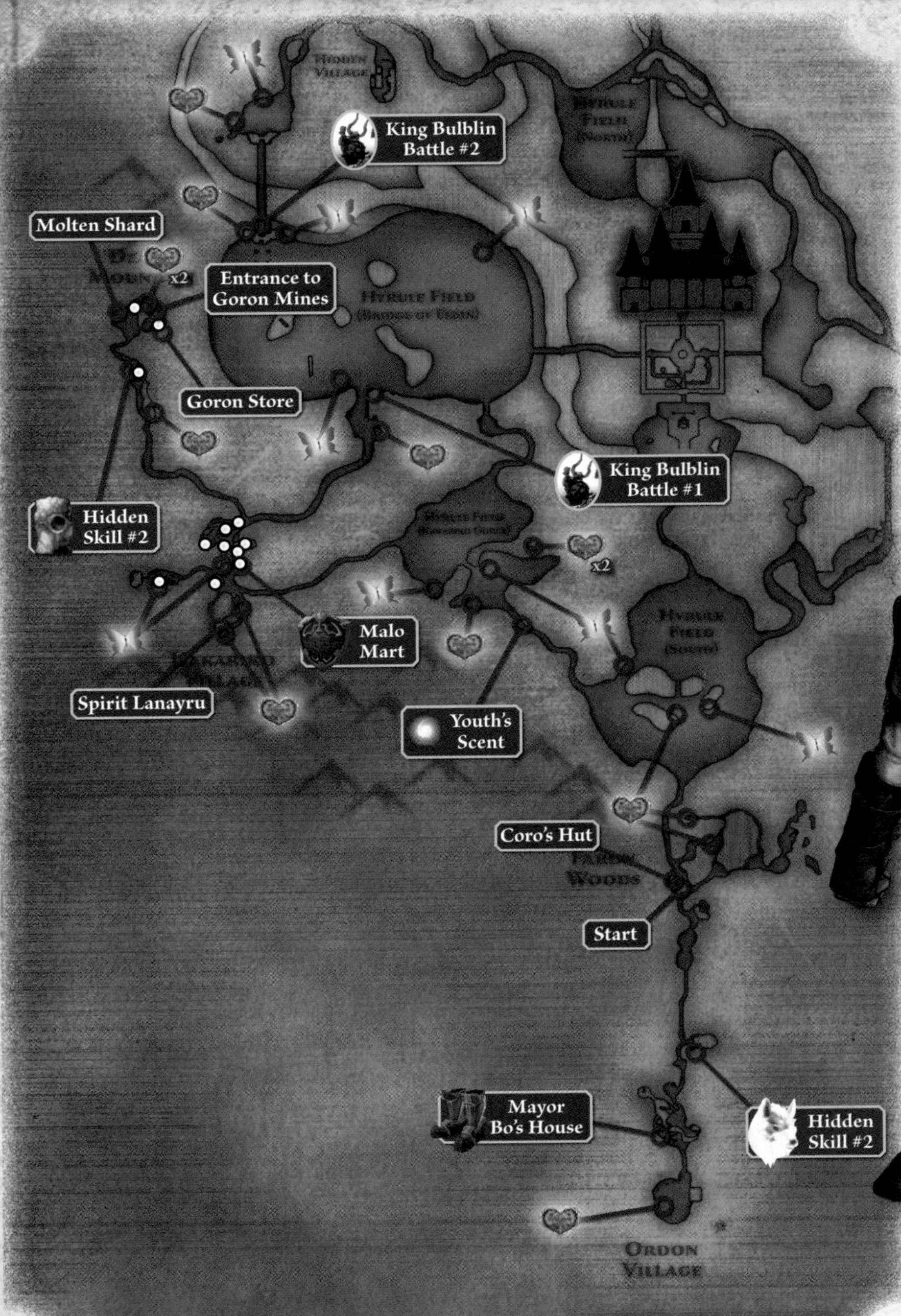

Legend

- Piece of Heart
- Golden Bug
- Twilit Parasite

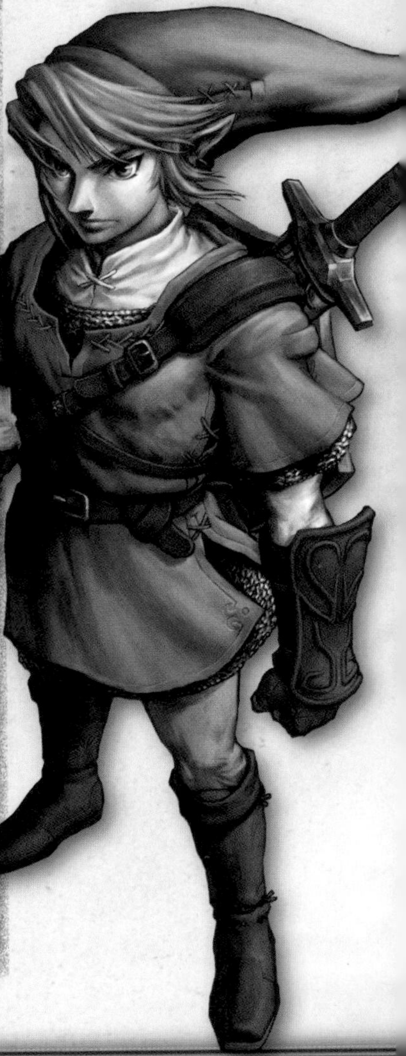

King Bulblin Battle #2

Molten Shard

Entrance to Goron Mines

Goron Store

King Bulblin Battle #1

Hidden Skill #2

Malo Mart

Spirit Lanayru

Youth's Scent

Coro's Hut

Start

Mayor Bo's House

Hidden Skill #2

Ordon Village

pg 98
Smell the Scent, Learn of Danger

pg 102
Explore the Twilight Village of Kakariko

pg 104
Fill Vessel of Light with Tears from Parasites

pg 113
Find the Location of the White Wolf

The Epic Journey Begins—From Faron Province to the Goron Mines: Overview

Your real adventuring starts now! You successfully completed the Forest Temple, and your tasks now become incredibly wide-ranging as you begin to explore the lands of Hyrule. Start by wandering through the south Hyrule Field, until you reach (and learn) the scent of the children missing from your village. After you explore the field, a large gorge, and the twilight village called Kakariko, the Eldin spirit summons you to fill the Vessel of Light. Once Kakariko Village is back to normal, you must learn how to fight with a tribe of mountain-dwellers known as the Gorons; surprisingly, your friend Mayor Bo shows you how! After learning a second Hidden Skill, return to find the village in turmoil; the hideous Bulblin king has kidnapped Colin! Fight for his return, obtain a shield worthy of a hero, and learn the secrets of the Gorons by climbing their fearsome mountain!

A Link to the Present

Overworld Denizens

Characters

Renado, Luda, Barnes, Gorons, Eldin Spirit, Gor Coron

Enemies

Kargarok, Stalhound, Bomskit, Twilit Bulblin, Crow, Bulblin Rider, King Bulblin, Lord Bullbo, Leever

Items to Obtain

Letter #1

Female Beetle

Male Beetle

Worm Bait

Piece of Heart #4

Youth's Scent

Vessel of Light

Male Ant

Female Ant

Letter #2

Female Pill Bug

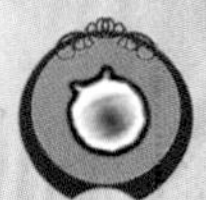
Male Pill Bug

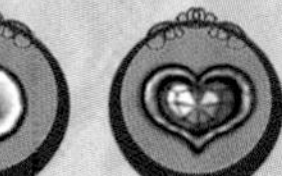

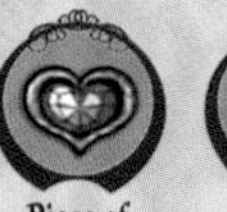
Piece of Heart #5

Hidden Skill #2

Iron Boots

Piece of Heart #6

Hylian Shield

Letter #3

Male Grasshopper

Female Grasshopper

Male Phasmid

Female Phasmid

5 — Find Mayor Bo, and Learn Secrets of Sumo — Pg 117

6 — Defeat King Bulblin and His Hordes — Pg 118

7 — Obtain the Hylian Shield — Pg 120

8 — Meet Gor Coron, Gain Access to Goron Mines — Pg 123

Task 1: Smell the Scent, Learn of Danger

Entering Hyrule Field (Faron Province)

➤ You're at the Faron Woods Spring and can optionally bathe here to restore your energy to full (four Hearts, as you've just slain the dungeon boss!). Epona is still nowhere to be found (the Horse Grass has no effect), so set off toward the only unexplored area: the open gate north of where Coro is selling his oil. Optionally buy some if you wish.

Missing Links

1. Cutting Coro's Grass

As with all areas you've previously visited, you can run around, slashing grass, hitting scenery, and generally disturbing the area where Coro resides to obtain the odd additional Hearts and Rupees.

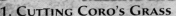

➤ Leave Coro's hut behind and venture onward, into a long narrow grass-filled path toward the huge, open Hyrule Field. This is the northern part of Faron Province, and the path is guarded by a couple Bokoblins. Bring them down with some sweeping swordplay.

Then you enter Hyrule Field (Faron Province) itself! In the distance, the evil glow of twilight pervades the lands. Slice at a roaming Bokoblin!

Begin to wander through this open expanse of area. The Missing Links section shows exactly what you'll find during this investigation of the large new area. As you reach the middle of the field, however, your progress is halted by a thin man in very tight attire. He's yelling at you! This must be the Hylian Postman!

He tells you to go no farther, as a black wall blocks the path ahead! He then introduces himself and hands you your **first letter**. Press ⊕ to open your **Collection** screen and select the letter. The letter is from the Postman himself, telling you not to flee when you see him approach at high speed!

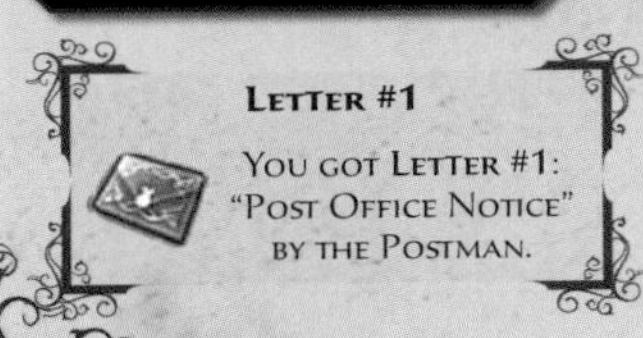

Letter #1

You got Letter #1: "Post Office Notice" by the Postman.

Kargarok

Threat Meter

If you're traveling along the main path, you're usually set upon by a couple of Kargaroks: giant, bony birds with a nasty bite that can be troublesome if you're not defensive with your posture. Target each bird one at a time, somersault back, then attack with a leaping slice. This sends the flapping foe down to the ground. Finish him here with an ending blow, or wait for multiple Kargaroks to flap about and then use your always-dependable spin attack. Watch the ending blow though; if you miss, your sword gets stuck in the ground, and the Kargarok gets a free attack!

Auto-target each monstrous bird, leap back, and attempt a jumping strike. Then locate the fallen flying fiend and finish him!

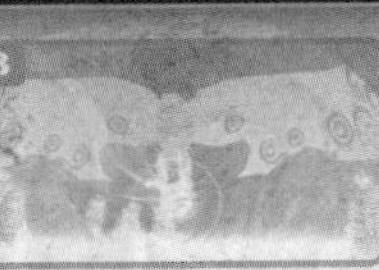

Stalhound

Threat Meter

As night is falling, you'll also encounter a couple of skeletal dogs known as Stalhounds. These undead beasts dig up from the ground below, follow you and attack if you engage them or slow down, then burrow down back, only to reappear from the same place again. Two spin attacks are all that's needed, but a couple of leaping strikes also provide an entertaining way to rid yourself of these bony brutes. They tend to drop Rupees, too.

The Stalhound is an undead dog with a bark far worse than its bite. Slash it twice, and it crumples into dust!

➤ Move to the middle of this area and look west, to a group of trees on a bank you can't climb. Do you notice something twinkling or glowing on one of the trees?

Golden Bug: Female Beetle

Collection: 1 (of 24)

Yes, there's definitely something sitting on the side of that tree! Bring out your **Gale Boomerang** and aim it at the insect. The wind brings the bug back. Put the Gale Boomerang away and look for the bug flitting about nearby. Walk slowly toward it, waiting for it to descend, and when the "Pick up" message appears, grab it!

Female Beetle

You caught a **Female Beetle**! Bug fans love that golden color!

Golden Bug: Female Beetle (cont'd)

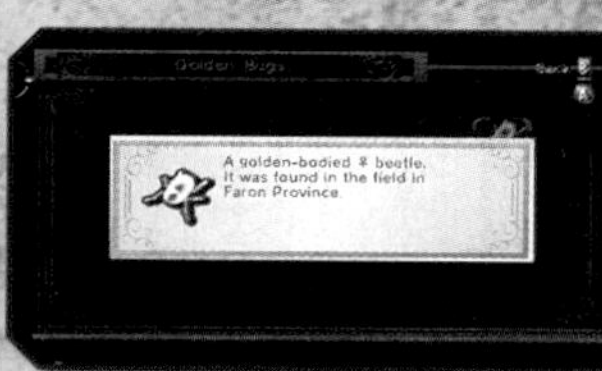

Your Collection Inventory has another space filled in. The Golden Bugs icon is now active! Press Ⓐ to see spaces for 24 different bugs. Inspect the one you've caught by highlighting it; information tells you where it was found.

Golden Bugs are scattered throughout Hyrule, and it's your (optional) job to find them all! Here are some bug-hunting tips:

- Male and female bugs are always in the same general area. Find one, and you should find the other!
- Bring out-of-reach bugs to your feet using the Gale Boomerang.
- Each bug type always appears in exactly the same place. There are 12 male and 12 female bugs to find.
- The same bugs reappear in the same area even after you've caught them; there's no need to capture any a second time (although you can!).
- It is easier to go bug-hunting at dusk, night, or at dawn. The bugs glow so they're more visible during these times.

Tip

A strange little princess who lives in Castle Town is looking for bugs to add to her creepy-crawly collection! There are some great prizes if you can help!

➤ Continue maneuvering around the Hyrule Field and you encounter a few more flapping Kargaroks, plus a rise of trees, a shallow lake, and a bridge you can cross over and run under. Move into the southeastern area of the field. A stone ground slopes gradually into the shallow lake, and there are a couple of Bokoblins to take down.

Enemies Encountered

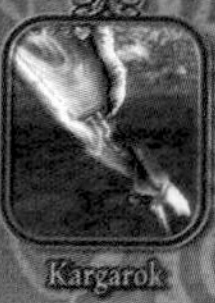

Kargarok

Stalhound

Golden Bug: Male Beetle

Collection: 2 (of 24)

Sitting on a tree within reach, near where the two Bokoblins roam, is a Male Beetle! It buzzes and flits away as you near, so follow it slowly, watching it as it lands in the grass a little ways away.

Male Beetle
You caught a **Male Beetle**! Bug fans love that golden color!

You've found a pair! This gives you an additional reward if you can find someone interested in insects!

Tip

Bomskit

Threat Meter

Now move into the south and eastern part of Hyrule Field, and you spot another strange critter. This one is really odd—a two-legged, scaly, bug-eyed foe that scuttles away from you as soon as it sees you! It drops a series of exploding organic bombs that cause minimal damage. Mainly defensive in nature, the Bomskit flees when you near; you can't catch it unless you auto-target and run it into a wall so it turns and tries to escape near you. Simply hit it with any projectile weapon if you want to dispatch it, but there's no need because these aren't that aggressive.

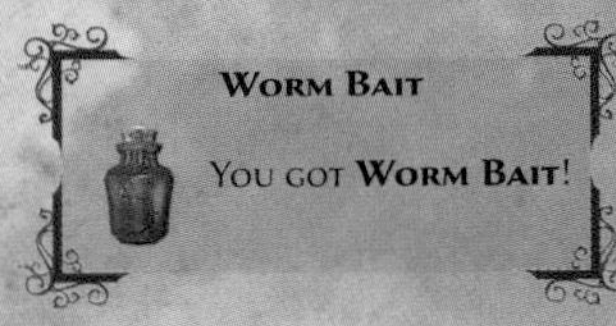

Worm Bait
You got **Worm Bait**!

However, something the Bomskit carries is of particular use to you. If you're carrying an empty **Bottle**, when you finish off a Bomskit, quickly scoop up (using Ⓑ) the remains of the Bomskit. These turn into Worms you can use to bait your Fishing Rod! Wait too long, and the Worm burrows into the earth; use your wolf form to dig it up again!

▲ Continue your exploration of Hyrule Field (south) by walking back to the main path and locating the southern end of the bridge, near the paths. Look for a tree to the left of the entrance. Did you spot something rotating on one of the branches? It looks like a **Piece of Heart**! Bring out your Gale Boomerang and target this object. The wind whipped up by the Gale Boomerang brings this item back to you. Excellent!

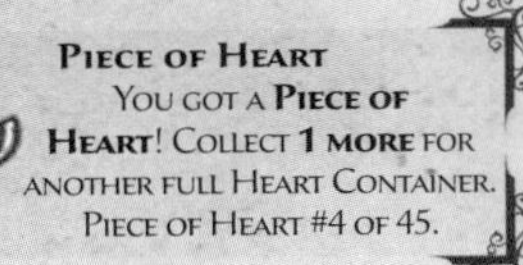

Piece of Heart
You got a **Piece of Heart**! Collect **1 more** for another full Heart Container.
Piece of Heart #4 of 45.

▲ With this valuable item stored in your Collection menu, move around the eastern side of the field, keeping a close watch on the fearsome foes that reappear after a while. Dish out sword damage to two more Stalhounds and Kargaroks.

➤ Head northward, optionally following the path, and you discover that the path heading to the northeast is sealed by a Bulblin gate. Two warriors guard this area with their lives, which you should cut short. Afterward, journey west, across the grass. Your trek continues as you cover the remaining area after a thorough search of this field. Defeat a Bokoblin near the path that winds north. Move across to this path. The northern path is blocked by a rock fall.

Journey northward to see a firmly sealed gate guarded by a couple of none-too-bright Bulblins. Ending blows seal the victory!

➤ The far western part of Hyrule Field is the only available exit, so move to the path and run (and roll) out of here. The path closes in on both sides, before you reach an imposing black barrier. Walk forward, and Midna appears. She tells you it's a good idea to head this way, but you'll transform into a wolf. Head toward the wall.

Missing Links

1. Hyrule Field: Southwest Area

This part of the field is a gently rolling hill with a copse of trees to your right, and a small clump of grass or two on the edge to slice. This is a shortcut to the western path.

2. Western Path

As the sun sets, check out the western path. Some clumps of grass near the trees reveal multiple Rupees with a single slash. Rolling into trees doesn't seem to offer any more money, though.

3. The Middle of the Field

Aside from a roving Bokoblin, there's little to trouble you here. Some grass gives multiple Hearts near the shallow lake and large tree. Check the shallow lake for Bomskits to scoop.

4. Under the Bridge

Closely inspect the bridge and you'll see a large chest underneath the southern end! Alas, you can't reach it yet, and there's some strange gold medallion on the underside of the bridge, too. Perhaps you need the fabled **Clawshot** for this?

5. The Northeast Area

Exploring the northeastern part of Hyrule Field nets you little except sore feet after a lengthy walk, but there are some small patches of grass near the Bulblins' gate.

Missing Links (cont'd)

6. The Ring of Grass

As you cross from east to west, over the large mound of grass, notice a ring of grass in the middle of this section. Be on the lookout for these; although they don't offer anything at the moment, a wolf could have fun digging here!

7. By the Black Barrier

The patch of grass near the black barrier, on the western exit path, is filled with a Rupee and three Hearts; this is a great place to re-energize!

A Wolf in Eldin Province: The Scent of Danger

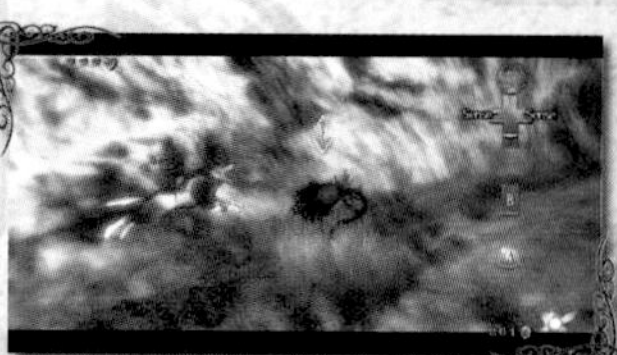

➤ Midna asks if you wish to enter the twilight. Agree, and you're grabbed by her giant orange hand and pushed through the wall of twilight. You're transformed into a wolf and cannot return, so proceed up the winding path. Attack the Twilit Baba on the way.

Youth's Scent

Continue to the top of the pathway, and sniff the Wooden Sword that's stuck in the ground. Use your **sense view** to discover a yellow mist emanating from it! This is a scent; the smells of Talo, Malo, Beth, and Colin! That Wooden Sword is the one you gave to Talo.

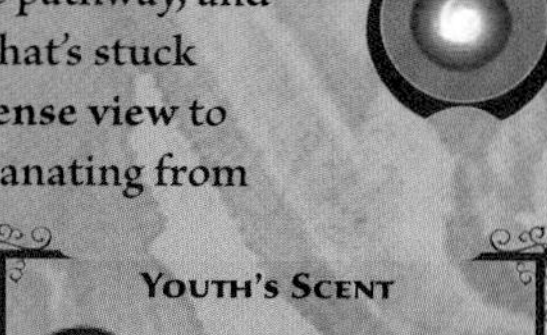

Youth's Scent

You learned the **Youth's Scent**!

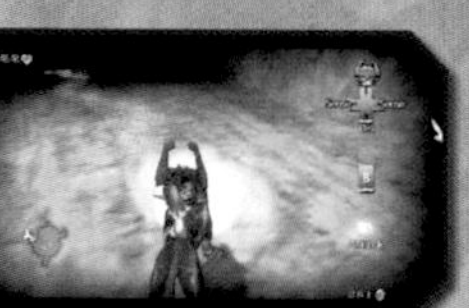

Sense view: the scent is a misty line for you to follow.

Throughout your adventure, and only in wolf form, you can learn a number of different scents, one at a time. Wherever the scent is in the land, it appears as a colored mist. Following it to the source usually helps you progress. Press ✚ or ✚ to activate your sense view.

Enemies Encountered

Bomskit

Stalhound

Kargarok

Bokoblin

Twilit Baba

Midna

Task 2: Explore the Twilight Village of Kakariko

Onward to Kakariko Village

Journey into the Eldin Province to a place called Kakariko Gorge, which is almost as large as the previous section. The scent trail leads down the path, but you don't have to follow it. Stop and defeat the Twilit Baba to the side of the path, then survey this large open expanse.

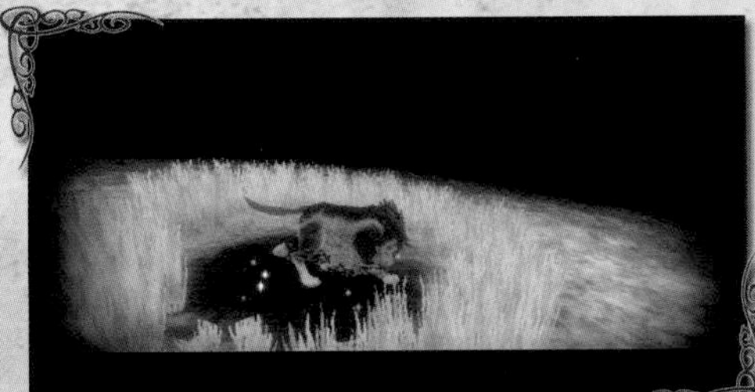

Warp Portal

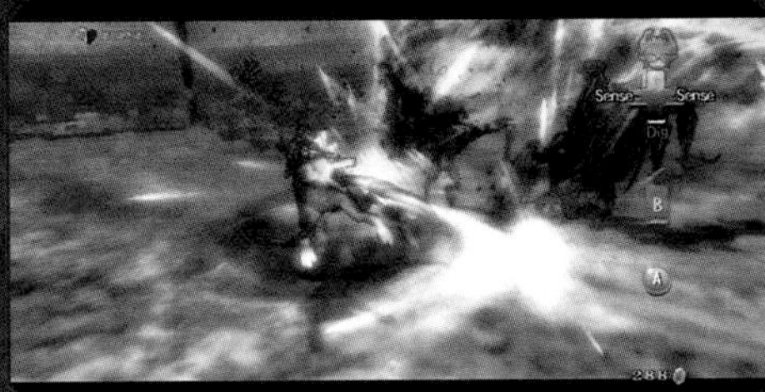

The forces of darkness are intent on stopping you. Let the light shine, especially from your brutal tail attack!

When you've finished patrolling the left and right areas on this side of the bridge, head down the main path, where the scent trail is leading you, and stop as three Twilit Messengers bind you into combat with them. Pick one and attack it until it falls. Use the clamping jaw technique (leap onto its hide and tap Ⓐ). When only two are standing, use Midna's area-of-effect attack to drop them, and free yourself from the force field.

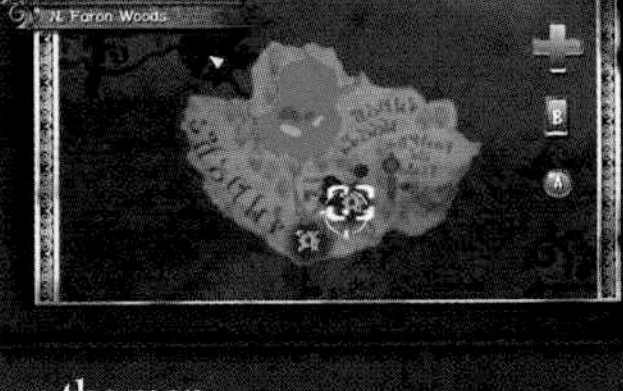

Another strange warp portal appears above you. Midna appears and notes that the bridge ahead has completely disappeared! She beckons you to check your map for clues. Whenever you destroy those creatures from the darkness, a warp portal opens that looks like this on the map.

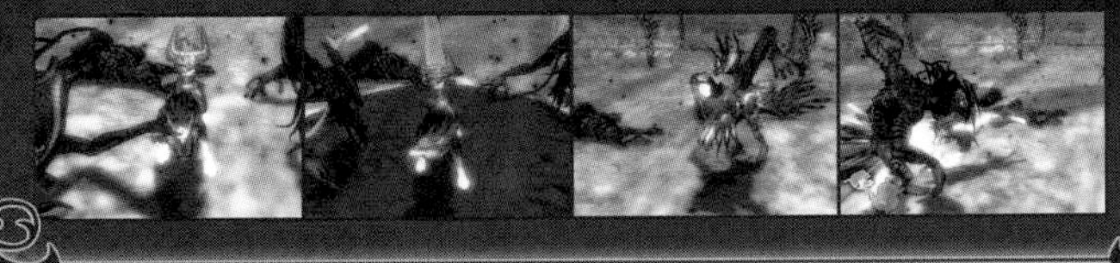

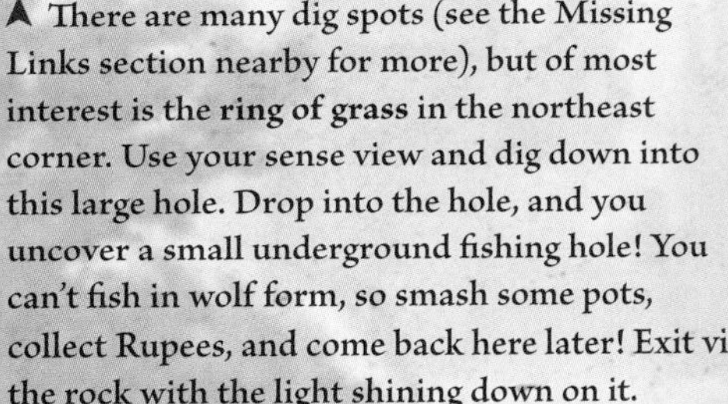

▲ There are many dig spots (see the Missing Links section nearby for more), but of most interest is the ring of grass in the northeast corner. Use your sense view and dig down into this large hole. Drop into the hole, and you uncover a small underground fishing hole! You can't fish in wolf form, so smash some pots, collect Rupees, and come back here later! Exit via the rock with the light shining down on it.

Warp to North Faron Woods. The bridge propped against the rock wall is perfect! Speak to Midna, and select Kakariko Gorge. This is the correct place, as Midna summons her powers and teleports you and the bridge, and lays it across the gorge!

◄ Choose to teleport to the North Faron Woods warp portal. If you choose another area, you can optionally look about as the wolf. As you've already been throughout Ordona and Faron Provinces, try entering South Faron Woods and bounding into Hyrule Field.

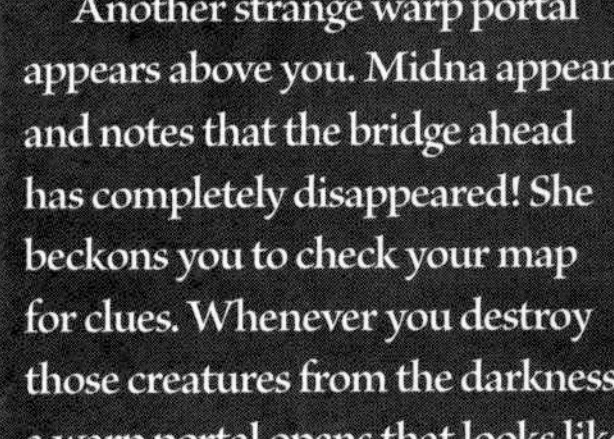

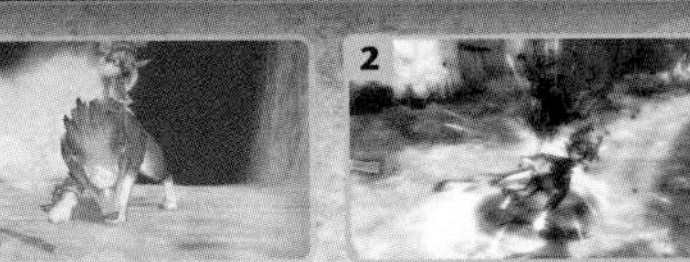

Twilit Bulblin

Threat Meter

Head over the bridge. At the junction where the path splits, you face down two new foes: the Twilit Bulblins. These attack just like Bulblin Warriors and are dispatched with two strikes. You have to wait if you knock them onto their backs, as the wolf doesn't have a finishing move. Quickly defeat them with a couple of bites, spins, or the over-the-top Midna energy crackle!

Twilit Bulblins may wear fearsome masks, but they're still easily dispatched, thanks to your wolf's nasty bite!

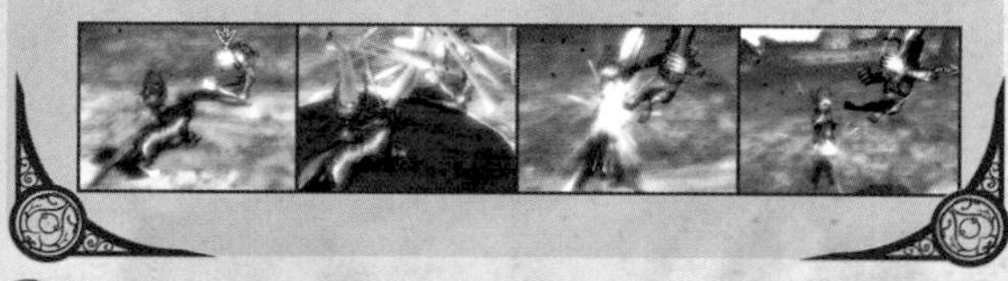

➤ There are two exits in the northern part of this gorge. If you ignore the scent and head east, you can locate the path and bound up and around to the northern passage. The way is completely blocked by rocks. Head back the way you came.

➤ Take the path after the bridge, optionally pausing to dig at the dig spots near the path junction. The road heads west. Follow the scent all the way to a large gate. The Youth's Scent continues through the gate. This looks sturdy, so locate the dip in the earth on the left and burrow under.

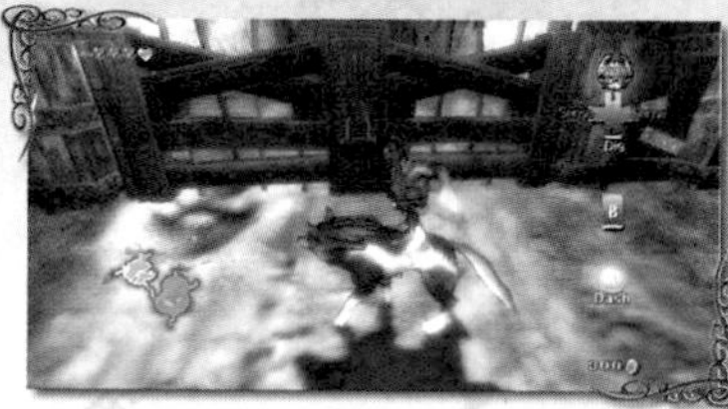

➤ Once on the other side, prepare to tackle two Twilit Bulblins with your favorite offensive move. Then journey along the path with the high rock walls on either side, into Kakariko Village.

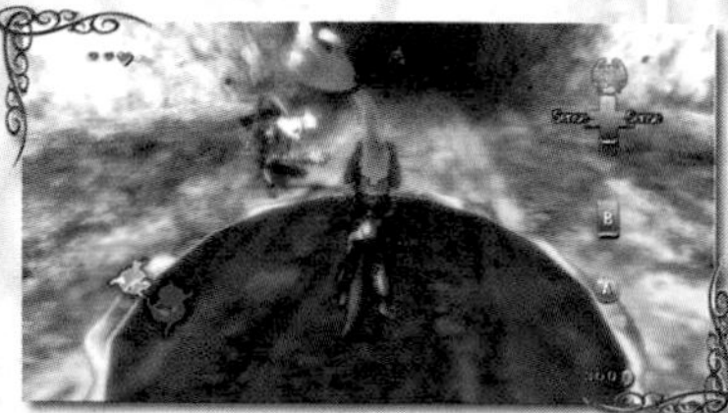

Missing Links

1. Kakariko Gorge: Lashing Out in the Long Grass

Your wolf form can methodically cut the grass in this pathway. Find some Hearts in the grass opposite where the Twilit Baba appeared. Check all clumps!

2. Kakariko Gorge: The Southeastern Rise

Head right, off the path as you enter the Eldin part of Hyrule Field, and check the raised area. There's a tree with a number of dig spots. Also check the far eastern edge for a lone Bomb Rock.

3. Kakariko Gorge: The Southwestern Field

An interesting Bomb Rock embedded in the left wall glows a faint blue. Perhaps something is behind there? Come back with explosives to find out! Don't forget the dig spot in the far left corner near the fence!

4. Other Warp Portal Locations

If you choose to visit Ordona or the South Faron Woods when looking for the bridge, you can romp around each area, digging up holes and (for example) sniffing around Coro, who doesn't mind a new, more-ferocious friend. When you're done looking, talk to Midna and warp to the other Faron Woods area.

5. Hyrule Field (South): Dig Spots

There are dig spots all over Hyrule Field (South). You can check them out now, but it's preferable to do so when you can change to and from a wolf at will.

6. Kakariko Gorge: Northwest Section

Check the northwest section of the gorge for a couple of dig spots along the north wall, near a clump of standing rocks. In the corner there's a clump of trees with a Twilit Baba to snap at.

7. Kakariko Gorge: Northeast Section

The opposite northern side of this gorge is a large sloping field, with a strange little raised section at the very north end. An odd owl statue stands here, but you can't use it yet. There's a Bomb Rock in the northeast corner.

8. Kakariko Gorge: Western Gorge Edge

You can also follow the edge of the gorge all the way to the bridge. There's a rock in the middle of the gorge. Look closely to see a Piece of Heart and a chest on it! Return here later.

Enemies Encountered

Twilit Baba

Twilit Messenger

Twilit Bulblin

Kakariko Village in Twilight

Characters Encountered

Midna

Eldin Spirit

Beth, Talo, Colin, Malo

Luda

Renado

Barnes

Warp Portal

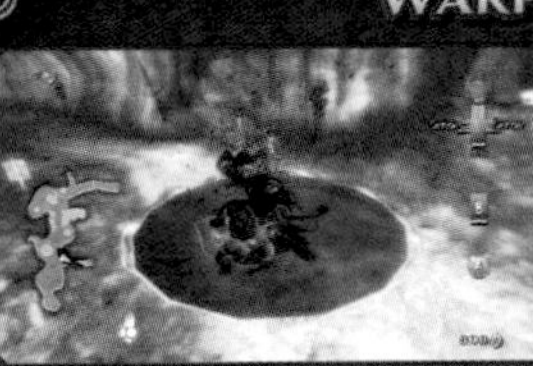

As soon as you enter Kakariko Village, three Twilit Messengers turn and attack you. Combat begins as normal, but you need two Messengers to fall at exactly the same time. This fight is a little trickier, because it's difficult to round up two foes to stand near each other for Midna's area-of-effect attack (B). A better plan is to run to the Messenger prowling the far part of the energy field, drop him, and then slam into both remaining Messengers. A new warp portal forms over Kakariko Village!

Note: On most occasions, you can now speak to Midna and ask her to warp you to or from here.

When the energy field dissipates, the **Eldin spirit** has enough light force to speak to you from the Springs, on the village's western side. Trot over to the faint mass of glowing matter, and it gives you a **Vessel of Light** with which to collect tears. Just as before, 16 Twilit Parasites have appeared, and you must search for each of them!

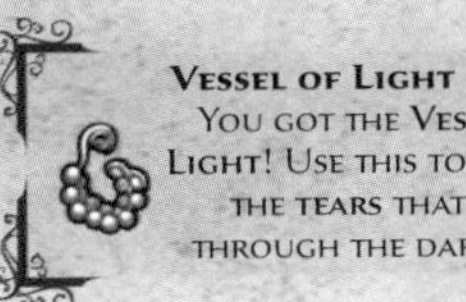

Vessel of Light
You got the Vessel of Light! Use this to collect the tears that cut through the darkness.

Task 3: Fill the Vessel of Light with Tears from Parasites

The Sanctuary: Twilit Parasites #1, #2, and #3

Follow the **Youth's Scent** in a winding path, and it ends at the front doors of what looks to be the home of the village shaman. Use your sense view and you can see an odd-looking man staring nervously out of the window. Make a quick sweep of the village, learning what the nearby signs say.

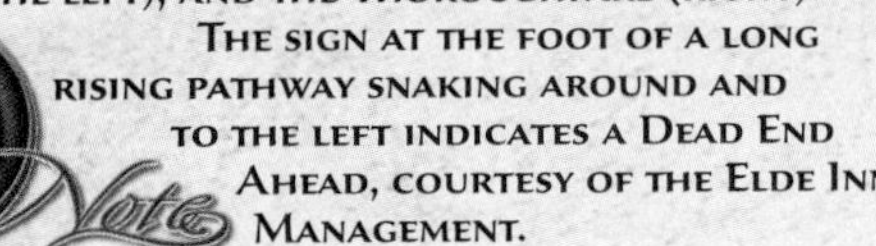

Note: The sign by the entrance to the village shows directions to the Sanctuary (ahead), the Springs (to the left), and the Thoroughfare (right). The sign at the foot of a long rising pathway snaking around and to the left indicates a Dead End Ahead, courtesy of the Elde Inn Management.

The time has come to find another way into this sanctuary. (Notice the bell on top of the structure? You might want to ring that later!) Move around from the front door to a dead tree. Midna can transport you to the roof of the structure with a triple lock-on leap. Once you're up here, find the loose boards and fall through a hole in the ceiling.

Turn your sense view on, and the many spirit flames turn into recognizable people inside the sanctuary. Beth, Talo, and Colin are sitting next to another girl and a tall man with long braided hair; he must be the shaman. An agitated fellow at the window says he doesn't see any shadow monsters nearby.

The shaman gently reminds Talo that he is safe inside this structure. The mechanic isn't sold on this idea. The beasts weren't affected by his bombs! The lady at the general store has disappeared (Malo looks interested at this point). The mechanic thinks the sanctuary is next!

1

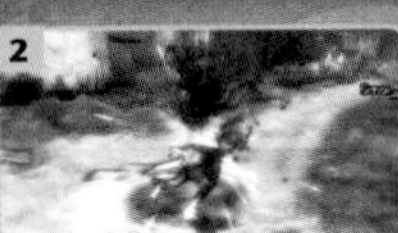
2

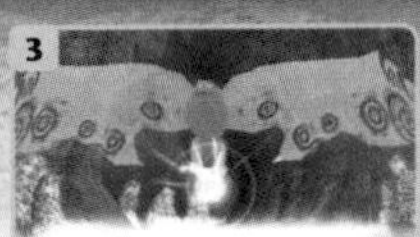
3

4

5

6

"Barnes!" the shaman roars, as Beth begins to sob. Barnes gets down on all fours: "Renado..." he says, "it's risky here!" Renado, the shaman, mentions that a cellar exists under the building, for additional protection. The entrance opens only after all the candles are lit.

Barnes grabs a torch and is about to start lighting the candles when Renado's daughter speaks up. She warns Barnes that there were Twilit Parasites appearing down there too. Colin comforts Beth. He's sure Link is coming to save them all. Well you are, aren't you?

Renado:

Somewhere between 30 and 40 years old, Renado is the village shaman, or priest. He is Luda's father. He hides the children from the darkness inside his sanctuary. He is always wise, calm, and collected. He possesses experience and grace, treating everyone evenly. He talks politely to everyone, even children and you. He is a kind-hearted soul.

Luda:

About 10 or 12 years old, she is the daughter of Renado of Kakariko Village. Luda is compliant, polite, and reliable, and she acts very mature for her age. She is the most grown-up of the children. Like Renado, she enjoys taking care of children such as Colin.

Barnes:

He's somewhere between 30 and 40 years old. He lives in Kakariko Village and runs a bomb shop. Barnes is quick to panic and has a blabbermouth, speaking first and thinking about it later. This sometimes annoys Renado, but Barnes is a jovial fellow and fine jester.

◀ Your map indicates that a Twilit Parasite is around here. The best way to locate it would be to try to reach the cellar. Beforehand, you can activate your sense view and bound across the room to listen to Renado again, as well as Barnes, who isn't overly confident in your skills!

➤ As an invisible wolf, you have a distinct advantage! Start by grabbing the piece of wood lying next to the flaming torch. Light both ends on the torch, then climb up the steps to the ledge surrounding the room. Leap around this ledge, remaining as close to the wall as possible, and you'll light all four candles. Do this in any direction. If the wood burns out, light it again.

▲ After the fourth candle is lit, the massive owl carving in the middle of the sanctuary slides across the room, revealing a hole in the floor. Bound down, and drop into the hole.

➤ You appear in a long and very thin passage, ending in a small antechamber with another of those odd owl statues in it. Note the flashes in the air; turn on your sense view and you'll discover three Twilit Parasites scuttling about here! Jump and chew on each of them, and fill the first three container sections of your Vessel of Light.

➤ Optionally take some time digging up sparkling earthen areas, then head north to the opposite end of the cellar corridor. Midna can help you climb up the scaffolding. Auto-target her and make the jumps, up and out of the sanctuary. You appear out of a well-lit tube in the village graveyard. Continue your Twilit Parasite search!

Enemies Encountered

Twilit Messenger

Twilit Parasite

Task #3

Fill the Vessel of Light with Tears from Parasites

CHARACTERS ENCOUNTERED

Midna

Barnes

THE GRAVEYARD: TWILIT PARASITE #4

➤ Prowl the graveyard, because your map indicates there's a Twilit Parasite somewhere around here. To begin with, target and chew up the Twilit Keeses fluttering about here so they don't bother your investigation. Then move to the gravestones. Some of them can be pushed (they have a stone base)!

➤ The Twilit Parasite isn't under a gravestone though; it's buried in the mound of graves in the middle of the yard. Switch on your sense view and locate its shadow, then unearth it and target the scuttling scarab! Bite down and then collect your fourth set of tears.

◄ There's little else to do in the graveyard, besides inspect the area. There are two unlit torches in the southwest corner, and an odd rock in the west wall. Are those Zora carvings on it? Then leave via the path to the east.

LOOSE ROOF BUILDING: TWILIT PARASITE #5

➤ Scamper back into the village and head to the north-south thoroughfare. There's little point in investigating the town until all the Twilit Parasites are captured, so find them in this order: stay on the left side and leap onto this Cucco coop. Then scramble onto a series of low rooftops, heading north. Jump the gaps!

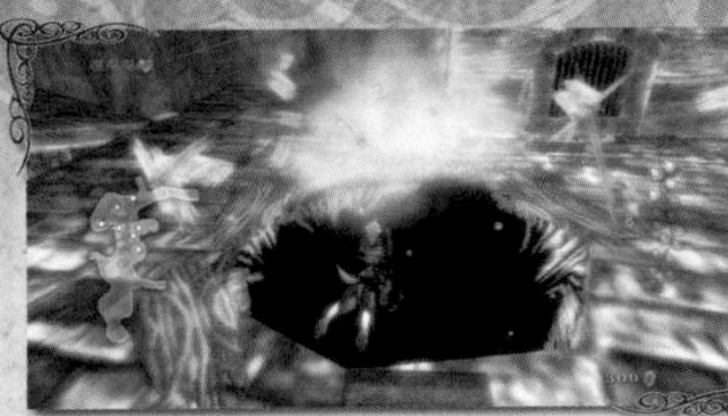

◄ Continue heading north to the rooftop where two Twilit Keeses threaten you. Keep the jumping to a minimum so you don't fall off and have to retrace your steps! Then stand on the middle of the roof. The debris gives way and you drop into the building.

➤ This single-room dwelling is unused and musty, but your map indicates there's a bug loose somewhere around here! Switch on your sense view, and you realize the bug is trapped under the crate. Push the crate toward the wall and the Twilit Parasite scuttles out. Jump on him and secure another orb of tears for your Vessel. Summon Midna to escape this building by jumping on the wardrobe.

BARNES' BOMB SHOP: TWILIT PARASITE #6

➤ Although you can locate the Twilit Parasites in any order, it's easy to find them by completing a clockwise tour of Kakariko Village. The next stop is Barnes' Bomb Shop. The front door is locked, so climb the small outbuilding to the right and leap through the window. Line your jump straight on or you won't make the jump!

▲ Barnes isn't kidding about the explosives in his shop. Read any of the notices to learn that Lanterns are strictly prohibited. What happens when you light one? Find out later! Climb the stairs to the left of the main store, which is currently empty (Barnes is hiding in the sanctuary).

◄ When you reach the top of the steps, run around to a ladder and a wardrobe. With your sense view, you can see that the Twilit Parasite is inside the wardrobe, so run into it. It topples over, freeing the bug. Target and leap at it, then collect the orb of tears it leaves behind. Continue upward by jumping on the fallen wardrobe, then onto the table with the rug on it, onto the platform with the ladder, and finally out of the door.

Above Barnes' Bomb Shop: Twilit Parasites #7, #8, and #9

◄ Run out onto the roof of Barnes' Bomb Shop and turn around. Follow the shallow steps up and onto a number of high ledges overlooking the village. A screeching announces the arrival of a Twilit Kargarok. Attack it away from the edge, so you don't fall back down to the ground below.

Caution

There's good news and bad news regarding falling from heights in Kakariko Village. The good news: you almost never lose any energy, and all drops are fine to try. The bad news: you have to retrace your steps to get back up here, at least until you're in Link form and can find a Cucco to help you get about!

▲ Head to the south and west along the path to an upper corner of the large promontory, where Barnes has built a bomb storage shack! He's written a sign telling you of the danger. He's also secured the area completely—well, except for the hole in the side of the building! Position yourself in front of it and enter the hole. Once inside, you can optionally smash a pot opposite you for Rupees and a Heart.

► The Twilit Parasite isn't budging from the stove, and you can't strike it, so pick up a piece of wood near the stove (in the southwest corner) and bring it across to the small fire that's burning. This smokes the Parasite out, but the sparks it generates set the entire building on fire. Midna leaves you, and you have moments before the building explodes! Quickly run to the hole in the north wall.

◄ Bang goes the bomb storage! Barnes may be furious, but you should be happy; there were actually three Twilit Parasites hiding in the building! Collect the three orbs of tears from the rubble. Dig in the middle of the rubble if you wish to find Hearts and a Yellow Rupee (10). You're halfway through your hunt!

Lookout Shack: Twilit Parasite #10

▲ While you're on this upper area, head north and look for a ramped pathway winding higher. Follow it past a dead tree overlooking the destroyed shack, and up to a quick combat with a couple of Twilit Keeses. Cross a wooden ledge heading up to a lookout shack. Ignore the dig spots and stand on the wooden platform. There's a great view of the village. Now move back to the corner and look for the hole. Dig in!

Enemies Encountered

Twilit Keese

Twilit Kargarok

Twilit Parasite

➤ Once inside the lookout shack, check the map to see the Twilit Parasite hiding in a group of pots in the room's northeast corner. Use your spin attack to smash them all, then chase down and grab the Twilit Parasite. Ram the wall to knock any remaining pots, then leave via the same hole you came through.

Elde Inn: Twilit Parasites #11 and #12

◄ Exit the lookout shack and check your map. You have only three white dots left to find! Descending via the promontory and rooftops takes too long, so simply leap off the wooden platform. Don't worry; you don't take any damage. Run southward to the shaman's sanctuary, but stop short of that place, and instead make a left turn up the supposedly dead-end path. A Twilit Kargarok flaps into view; make short work of it before you continue.

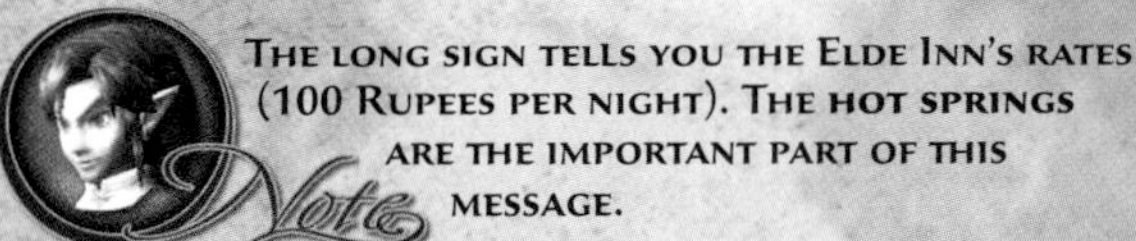

Note: The long sign tells you the Elde Inn's rates (100 Rupees per night). The **hot springs** are the important part of this message.

➤ Run up and along the curved path above the closed store until it ends abruptly, with a sign telling you the management accepts no responsibility for jumping accidents. Jump across to the wooden platform and enter the arched doorway.

➤ Enter the ledge above the storage room inside the Elde Inn and drop down, optionally shattering the two pots for a couple of Hearts. Pick up the piece of wood from near the stove, then jump on the table and light the wood with the candle near the door. Run to the fireplace in the southeast part of the storeroom and light the fire. The Twilit Parasite sparks, and you can defeat it in this room.

◄ Now investigate the rest of the Elde Inn. Step through the doorway into the saloon, bound over or around the bar, and attack two Twilit Bulblin Warriors milling about. Use bites and the spin attack for an easy takedown. Then search the room. Amid the breakable scenery, there's a chest under the stairs. Don't forget it!

Overworld Chest #8: Red Rupee (20)

➤ Gallop up the steps to the second floor of the inn and engage a vicious Twilit Bulblin on the balcony above the bar. There's little else here to interest you, except a gap in the balcony fence allowing you to quickly leap downstairs.

➤ Move to the wardrobes propped up against the balcony's northeast corner and ram into both of them. This dislodges another Twilit Parasite, but it moves into an adjacent room. Claim the blue Rupee (5), then dart into the north doorway to the bedrooms. The Twilit Parasite is flying about near the beds to your right. Target and grab it! Then head back to the storeroom and climb up the shelves, leaving the same way you came in.

General Store: Twilit Parasite #13

Note: The next sign in the village showcases the amazing items inside the general store. Unfortunately it has closed, and the proprietor has vanished!

➤ Check the map; the only available white dot in the village is somewhere inside the general store. The door is locked, so head around the side, below the curved dead-end road. Struggle into a small hole in the base of the wall, near an empty crate you can smash.

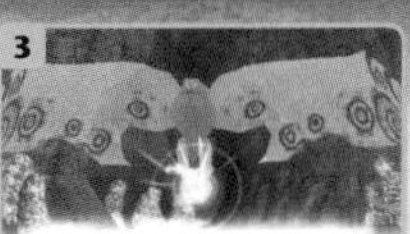

➤ Climb up behind the store counter and begin to ascend to the top of the room, heading to the southwest corner where the Twilit Parasite seems to be lying low. You can smash pots and crates on the way. The bug is on the wall and remains still. Use your sense view, target, and dispatch! Then exit via the same hole you crawled in from.

Author Note

This Twilit Parasite took more than a few minutes of puzzle solving. We thought the metal pipes, lighting, crates, and exterior walls were part of the problem. Of course, we were being zapped by the bug throughout this time. It was only after three good punishing hits from the bug that we realized we just had to look for him! Over-thinking puzzles is a common mistake....

Kakariko Village: Final Exploration

◄ All of the Twilit Parasites seem to have been nullified in Kakariko Village, so take a little extra time to run up the dead-end curved road, leap onto the Elde Inn roof, then use the exterior staircase and ramps to scramble all the way to the top of the village on the east side. The final ramp leads to the hot springs, which is currently empty. Now that you've seen most of the village, check your map. The final Twilit Parasites are north of the village. Drop down and scamper north until you see a rocky cave mouth. Read the sign: straight ahead is Death Mountain, and Hyrule Field is to your right. Death Mountain? That doesn't sound too encouraging!

◄ Before you attempt the treacherous route up toward Death Mountain, check the main road to your right toward Hyrule Field. Unfortunately, this route is also blocked by two Twilit Bulblins. These are easily crushed, but that gate is much more solid—impenetrable, in fact.

Missing Links

1. Bomb Rock Wall

Check out the rock wall near the southern exit and the Eldin Springs as soon as the Twilit Messengers are defeated. A Bomb Rock here definitely needs exploding.

2. Kakariko Village Dig Spots

Kakariko Village has a number of dig spots. Here are some general places to look:

- The western bank of the springs, up on dry land (Hearts)
- In the owl room of the cellar, under the sanctuary (Rupees and many Hearts)
- By the northwest tree in the graveyard (Hearts)
- In the northwest corner of the village, ground level
- At both sides of Barnes' Bomb Shop (multiple green Rupees and one blue Rupee)
- In the rubble after you destroy Barnes' bomb storage shack (multiple Hearts, yellow Rupee)
- By the dead tree on the winding ramped path overlooking the bomb shack (Heart)
- By the dead tree on the "dead-end" path above the store (Rupees)
- Just to the right of the Elde Inn, below the curved dead-end road (Hearts and Rupees)
- By the dead tree and fence, next to the hot springs above Elde Inn (Rupees)
- By the sign for Death Mountain (Rupees)

3. Kakariko Graveyard: Gravestone Pushing

During your Twilit Parasite search, and any time afterward, you can push some of the gravestones and discover Rupees inside. There may even be a nasty spirit known as an Imp Poe in one of them, but he isn't here yet.

4. Kakariko Promontory: Bomb Storage Crates

Just before you accidentally demolish Barnes' bomb storage shack, try breaking open the crates along the western wall area. There are Rupees and Hearts to gather.

Enemies Encountered

Twilit Kargarok

Twilit Bulblin

Twilit Parasite

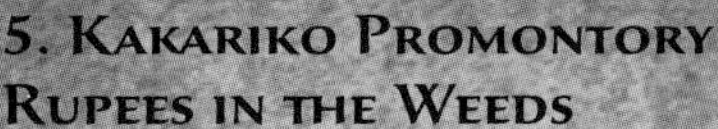

Goron

White Wolf

Missing Links (cont'd)

5. Kakariko Promontory: Rupees in the Weeds

Usually, the weeds don't produce that many rewards, but a clump on the winding path to the lookout shack offers four green Rupees (1).

6. Kakariko Lookout Shack: Pot Luck

Apply this excellent technique whenever you see pots out of reach on a shelf above you. Simply ram into the wall, shaking the pots loose. There are 11 Rupees here!

7. Kakariko Elde Inn: Cracking Crates and More

During your stay at the Elde Inn, stop hunting for Parasites for a moment and smash the crates near the central wooden support beam for Rupees. Find more in the northwest and southeast corners. There are even more in the upstairs bedroom, and wardrobes to ram and topple for Rupees, too.

Death Mountain Trail: Twilit Parasite #14

◀ Enter the trail, and Midna spots a spirit atop a large chain mesh wall. She reckons the way forward is impassable, but step onto the shallow rock ramp on the left side of the area, then leap up twice to the trail itself.

➤ Jump up, switch your sense view on, and listen to the large, orange Goron speak about the troubles between the villagers and his tribe. It looks like they need to co-exist peacefully. Run past the three rocks (you can nudge them if you wish), heading north. You encounter three Twilit Vermin. Defeat them before continuing; spin attacks work well.

Gorons:

Living in the Death Mountain area are hard-as-stone creatures with incredibly thick and tough hides adorned with multiple ceremonial tattoos. They usually mine and sell trinkets down in the Kakariko Village. After the twilight descended, the Gorons have refused to deal with humans and have blocked off communication.

◀ Follow the trail as it winds northward, until you reach a long left-turning bend, where you must engage a couple of Twilit Keeses in combat. Then use the scenery and climb up and over the second mesh wall. Continue north until you reach a series of steam vents and a wider clearing. Climb up the long step to the upper area and dodge between the vents, or you'll take slight damage and get knocked back.

▲ Now search for the next Twilit Parasite. He's under the ground in this plateau area. Dig to free him, using your sense view constantly, and then grab him and collect those tears, all the while avoiding the scalding vents.

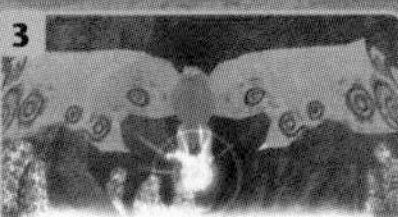

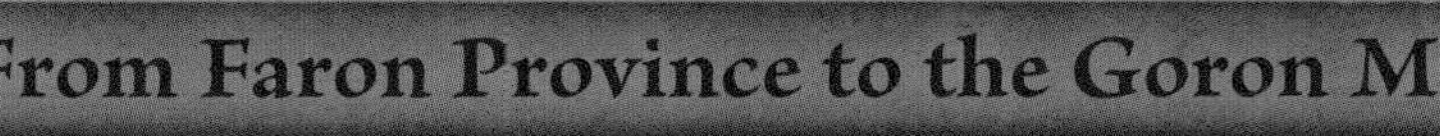

Howling for the White Wolf

Hidden Skill

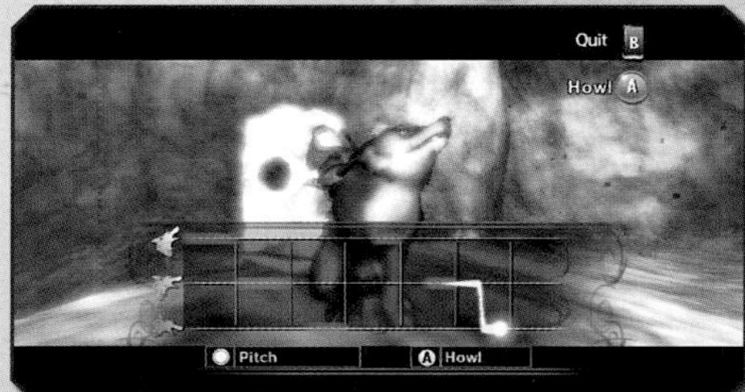

Note: You have summoned the White Wolf! He is currently waiting for you at the Ordon Springs. You must head here as Link and learn your next Hidden Skill! The walkthrough tells you the earliest point that this is possible.

Before you continue, it is vitally important that you investigate that strange ceremonial stone on the rocky clearing you're standing on. Listen and the wind whistles a tune through the hole in the rock. You must now recite the tune. Watch the tune, then replicate it. The pitch is as follows: High, Middle, Low (hold), High, Middle, Low. Use ⊙ to howl high and ⊙ to howl low. For mid-range howling, don't move the stick.

You appear as a wolf, high in the heavens near Death Mountain. The White Wolf appears at the end of a leafy edge, on the opposite side of the world. You howl the tune again and both of you continue to yelp. When you finish, the White Wolf tells you "Let teachings of old pass to you...." The wolf leaps down into the land.

Enemies Encountered

Twilit Vermin

Twilit Keese

Twilit Messenger

Twilit Parasite

Death Mountain: Twilit Parasite #15

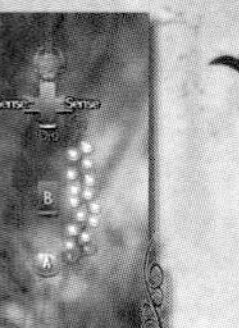

▲ You're very far from the White Wolf, so finish up the hunt for Twilit Parasites first. Continue up the winding path, avoiding the steam vents, and after the sharp corner, bound down the rocky steps, all the way to two crates containing Hearts.

Warp Portal

You've reached the base of Death Mountain itself! Bound down to the base of the mountain and begin combat with four Twilit Messengers. Be cunning, however. Ignore the three Twilit Messengers in the main area, move around the small opening, and attack the lone Twilit Messenger in this alcove first.

Then gather the remaining three Twilit Messengers into a huddle, and defeat them with a devastating area-of-effect salvo! The Twilit Messengers depart and form another warp portal. You can now teleport to the base of Death Mountain.

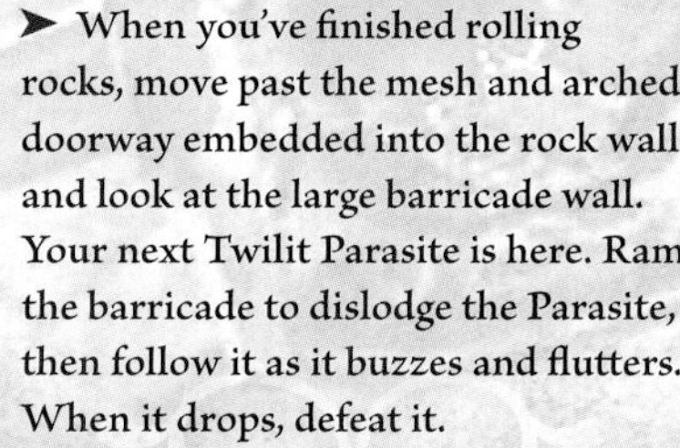

➤ When you've finished rolling rocks, move past the mesh and arched doorway embedded into the rock wall and look at the large barricade wall. Your next Twilit Parasite is here. Ram the barricade to dislodge the Parasite, then follow it as it buzzes and flutters. When it drops, defeat it.

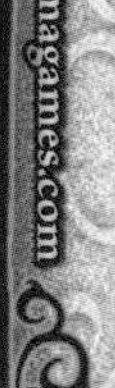

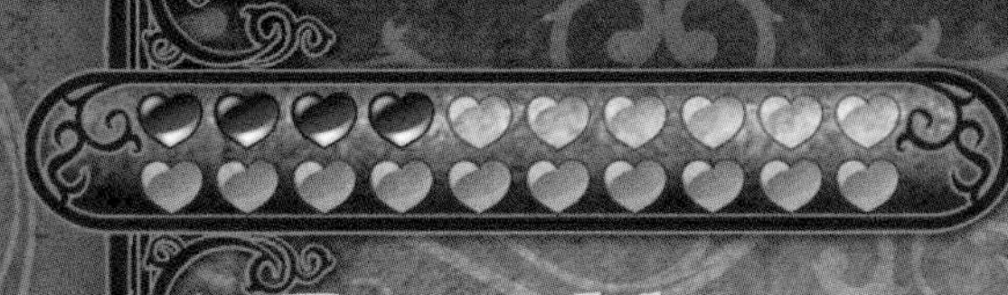

Characters Encountered

Midna

Goron

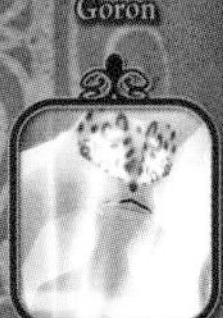
Eldin Spirit

Renado

Luda

Colin

Death Mountain: Twilit Parasite #16

Use Midna to jump up onto the barricade, and listen to the Goron moaning about being left out of the way, and at the bottom of the hill. Then run along the rock ledge, listening for falling lava rocks as the volcano rumbles in the distance. Steer clear of the steam vents, too.

Run along the first rock ledge, then onto the crumbling wall near a large, wooden support piece. Use Midna and leap directly up onto the support platform.

◄ Flick on your sense view and run to the next Goron, who's standing by some steaming vents (watch out for them). He's stuck where he is, but the Twilit Kargarok isn't. It attacks! Counter it in the open area behind where the Goron is standing.

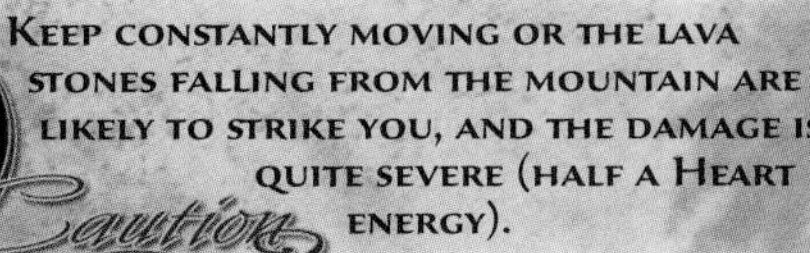

Keep constantly moving or the lava stones falling from the mountain are likely to strike you, and the damage is quite severe (half a Heart energy).

Caution

► Leap off the rise and into the hot springs to the north. This is the location of the final Parasite! It's near a group of five Vermin; tackle the Vermin first, then shake the Parasite down, but only after you investigate the hot springs area itself.

The hot springs are dry and there are two suspicious-looking Bomb Rocks in the northern area; you'll have to see what's behind there later. Quickly enter the tunnel to see a dig spot and a ceremonial stone you can't move at the far end. Perhaps it needs approaching later, from the opposite direction?

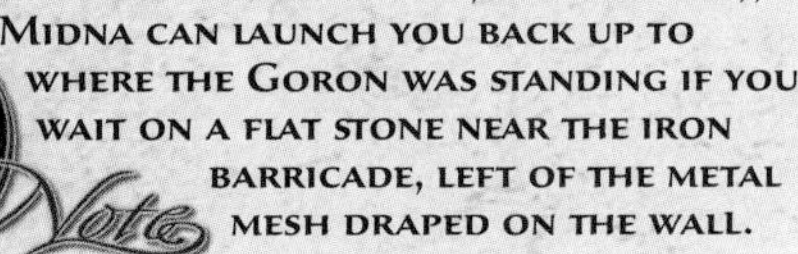

If you wish to leave the hot springs (if you missed a previous Twilit Parasite, for example), Midna can launch you back up to where the Goron was standing if you wait on a flat stone near the iron barricade, left of the metal mesh draped on the wall.

Note

Missing Links

1. Death Mountain Trail: Dig Spots

The following places along Death Mountain are good for locating dig spots:

- The dead tree below the mesh wall at the base of the trail
- Right below the second mesh wall (Rupees)
- The path just after the whistling rock, between Parasites #14 and #15 (Hearts)
- The eastern base wall of Death Mountain (Rupees)
- At the foot of the large wooden support and crumbling wall, first rock ledge (Rupees)
- Behind the Goron overlooking the hot springs
- Inside the small tunnel to the ceremonial rock (hot springs; Rupee)

2. Death Mountain Trail: Rock Nudging

The following places along Death Mountain allow you to push rocks and look for items underneath:

- The start of the trail, just beyond the first Goron guard (Heart)
- Below the second mesh wall, where the Twilit Keeses are (Rupee)
- Right above the mesh wall (Heart)
- Just south of the first steam vent (Rupee)
- On the right side of the steam vent clearing
- The eastern base wall of Death Mountain (Heart)
- The northern base wall of Death Mountain (Heart)
- The first rock ledge near the barricade and Goron (Rupee)

3. Death Mountain Trail: Weed Ripping

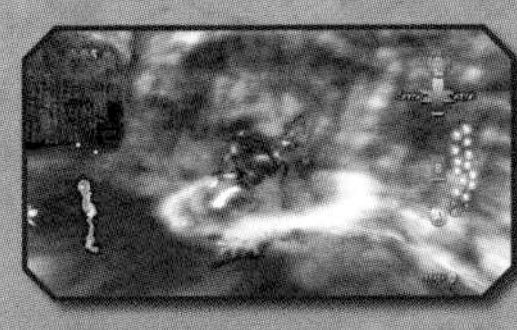

Along Death Mountain trail, search the clump of grassy weeds along the right bank, where Twilit Keeses were fought (Heart).

4. Death Mountain: Roll out the Barrel

At the far end of the first rock ledge, inside the crumbling wall area, are two barrels to shatter with a spin attack. Both contain Rupees. Crates on top of the rock ledge hold a Heart and Rupee. Two crates to the left of the Bomb Rocks in the hot springs hold a Heart.

The Eldin Spirit Awakens

As soon as the 16th Twilit Parasite has shed its tears into your Vessel, you're transported back to the springs inside Kakariko Village. You are transformed into human form, and the spirit takes the form of a giant bird. Eldin tells you a great power awaits in the sacred grounds of the Gorons. Eldin disappears into a shower of light.

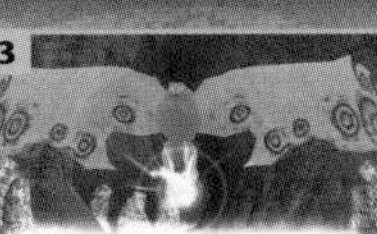

You stride out of the Kakariko Village springs and the sanctuary door opens. Renado introduces his daughter and Colin explains that the shaman saved them. The experience has been a nightmare; a regular occurrence these days.

Even stranger is the turn of events with the Gorons; they treat the villagers as foes. Perhaps it is their mines that are cursed?. Renado wants you to take the children back to Ordon Village, while he hopes there might be something he can do to help the Gorons.

Eldin Spirit:

The embodiment of the land of Eldin, this magical spirit takes the form of a bird and resides in the spring near Kakariko Village. It seeks the light.

▲ The children have other ideas; they want you to help Renado! Speak to everyone, then optionally dip your toes into the village spring to rejuvenate your health. Now that you're human, you can do some additional searching in Kakariko Village.

Enemies Encountered

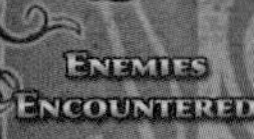

Twilit Kargarok

Twilit Vermin

Guay

Twilit Parasite

Task 4: Find the Location of the White Wolf

Hunting Through Kakariko Village

By now, you know the village's layout, so return to the various areas, starting with the graveyard. Push gravestones back and forth, run around the yard, and when you're done, investigate the far end and steps.

▲ Bring out your **Lantern** and move to the unlit torch to the left of the set of steps. Light both the torches, and a previously invisible chest appears from the ether! Open it to claim your cash prize. Climb the steps.

Overworld Chest #9: Purple Rupee (50)

Guay

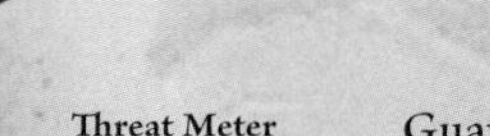

Threat Meter

Guays are easy to defeat when one or two are encountered, but these usually fly in a flock. Each swoops down to dive-bomb you, then flies away while another attacks from a different direction. This keeps you constantly looking around, and the ambushes can take their toll. React by blocking with your shield, then slay the Guay as it flies away. Easier still, after you gain the **Hero's Bow** or **Clawshot**, auto-target each bird and fire!

The Guay is a slow-moving dive bomber who is difficult to slay when out of sword range, unless you use a projectile!

Note: Flocks of Guays leave a scattering of Rupees, usually valued at around 30–40, after you defeat every bird in the flock. If the Rupees haven't appeared, auto-target and search for the stragglers!

Characters Encountered

Barnes

Goron

Renado

Midna

Golden Bug: Male Ant

Collection: 3 (of 24)

While you're on the graveyard's raised western part, check the tree on which some of the Guays were sitting. There's a Male Ant sitting on the base of the trunk. Pocket it, and continue to build your Golden Bug collection!

Male Ant

You caught a Male Ant. Bug fans love that golden color!

Head into the village, and go north along the thoroughfare. Visit the general store and the Elde Inn. Both are empty, but you can manhandle any items you missed or want to rummage in (such as crates or wardrobes). You can't jump over the counter in the general store, though.

Golden Bug: Female Ant

Collection: 4 (of 24)

Run across to the thoroughfare's other side, and enter the small building with the hole in the roof that you made earlier when searching for Twilit Parasites. On the floor in the middle of the room is the female partner to the Male Ant you found in the graveyard. Smash some crates in this room for Rupees afterward.

Female Ant

You caught a Female Ant! Bug fans love that golden color.

Head into the village and continue northward, and visit Barnes' Bomb Shop. Barnes is there, but he's complaining that his storage shack was recently destroyed. It's going to be a little while before he can sell you his wares. Fortunately, he's blaming the explosion on the twilight beasts, which is true, technically!

Test of Strength at the Trail

◄ There's little else to do in the village until you return here later in your adventure, so head toward Death Mountain at the trail's foot. Run until you reach the giant barricade with the mesh on it. Climb to the top, and walk up the trail. A **Goron** at the top blocks your path. "The elder said no humans may pass!" he shouts, then he rolls into a ball and tumbles into you. The force knocks you off the trail, down to the barricade's base! Your way is blocked. Retreat!

Author Note

We didn't take "no" for an answer. Through judicious skipping of cutscene information, we ignored the hints and continued to scale the mesh barricade (an agonizingly slow ascension), and tried to dive, catch, whack, and shout at the rolling Goron. We're embarrassed to say that we did this 15 times until we decided that yes, perhaps it was better to leave....

◄ Head toward the village. You meet Renado at the junction, who explains humans can never beat a Goron in a rolling battle! In fact, only one person has been able to earn their trust: **Mayor Bo** from your village! He asks you to return to your village, talk to Bo, and tell the villagers their children are safe and will be returned after a horse and cart are found. Move into the village.

Horseplay

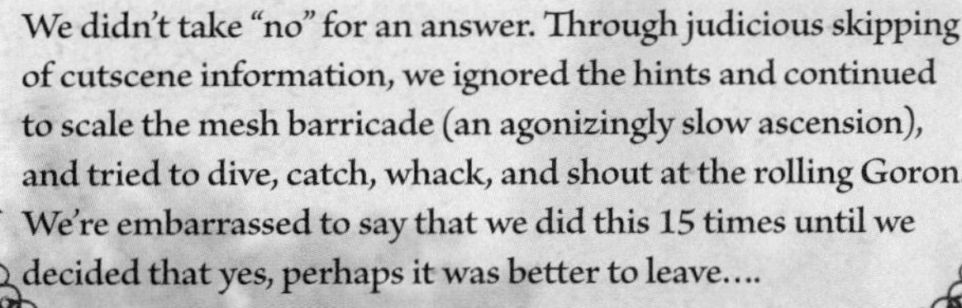

You hear a faint whinnying. Epona gallops down the rocky path to the village, with two Bulblins hanging on for dear life! The Bulblins go flying as Epona shoots toward you at a strong gallop. You have no choice but to dive to the side, then grab Epona's saddle and ride this bucking bronco!

◄ You must calm Epona down by remaining on her back while she bucks and gallops uncontrollably. Leap on and ride and immediately press ◄...

...then press ◎ when you reach here and ◎ again when you reach the short waterfall...

...and ◎ after you emerge from the spring...

...and finally ◎ again after you head north into town. Epona calms down and stops outside the sanctuary. Well done—you're quite the wrangler!

Midna thinks so too, and Epona will make returning to Ordon Village quicker. You can't warp there, and there are a few special items to pick up on the way back, so race out of the village, and vault over the spiked gate, into Kakariko Gorge (face straight ahead and travel as quickly as possible; use the spurs).

A Thorough Search of Kakariko Gorge

"WAAAIIIT!" shouts the Postman, jogging toward you when you land in Kakariko Gorge. The Postman has a letter for you. Open it up and read it. It's from Ooccoo, that strange bird you found in the Forest Temple. She's off on a journey, and she also has a son!

Letter #2

You got Letter #2: "Dear Adventurer" by Ooccoo.

Dash around the rest of Kakariko Gorge. There are Kargaroks to fight from horseback (draw your sword, and use the spin attack, then slow down, auto-target, and finish them). Ride about the gorge, then head to this area's western part.

Golden Bug: Female Pill Bug

Collection: 5 (of 24)

Ride to the small copse of trees, and halt your horse. Dismount and rummage around in the grass near the rock side. Something shiny is near the grass clump. Grab it, or cut the grass and stoop to take it. You've snagged your first Female Pill Bug! Ride to the bridge.

Female Pill Bug

You caught a Female Pill Bug! Bug fans love that golden color.

Golden Bug: Male Pill Bug

Collection: 6 (of 24)

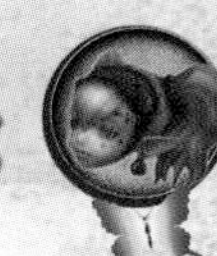

When you ride over the bridge to this area's southern part, halt your gallop and dismount. There's a Golden Bug in the grass. Face north, and it's just right of the path, near the bridge.

Male Pill bug

You caught a Male Pill Bug! Bug fans love that golden color.

Before you leave for Faron Province, ride to Kakariko Gorge's southeastern part, and look out over the large rock formation rising from the bottomless chasm. Defeat any Bokoblins or other foes in the area, bring out your **Gale Boomerang**, and target the **Piece of Heart** stuck atop the grassy rock. Throw the Gale Boomerang, and it brings this right back to you!

Piece of Heart

You got a Piece of Heart. You collected five pieces and formed a new Heart Container. It also filled your life energy! Piece of Heart #5 of 45.

Enemies Encountered

Kargarok

Bokoblin

Characters Encountered

Coro

Sera

Hanch

Jaggle

Pergie

Mayor Bo

White Wolf

Hero's Shade

◄ Optionally, you can recheck this section of Hyrule; Kakariko Gorge looks the same as when you entered it in wolf form (except the twilight has receded). The only difference is the arrival of a few Bokoblins scattered about the path. Optionally tackle them, either on or off your horse. Some Bomskits are also scuttling about here. If you need Worms for your hook, attack from range, or corner them with your sword.

Southward, Back to Your Home

► Locate your horse (use the clumps of Horse Grass if you lose her), and ride southeast, into Hyrule Field (south), aiming for the southern exit that takes you into Faron Woods.

Tip: When you're spurring your horse onward, and know you're about to enter a "loading" area (when the game loads between zones), spur Epona as fast as possible. Even if you empty your spurs meter, it is full when you enter the next area!

▲ Head into Faron Woods, and pass Coro (you can refill your Lantern fuel if you wish). Follow the woodland path southward, snaking past the Dark Tunnel and Faron Woods Springs, and crossing the long bridge into Ordona Province.

Once over the bridge, check your map. You should see that the White Wolf, whom you summoned on the Death Mountain trail when collecting tears from Twilit Parasites, is waiting for you. If he isn't, go howl at the Death Mountain trail whistling rock the next time you're in wolf form; you're at a disadvantage if you don't learn this second Hidden Skill right now!

Hidden Skill #2: Shield Attack

Head into the Ordon Spring, and look to your right, in a small alcove near the tiny tunnel entrance. The White Wolf waits for you to come, sword in hand! He growls at you, and you draw your sword. He pounces! You awaken in the ghostly ether. The undead hero forms and asks you if you wish to learn your next skill. The answer is yes!

First, your teacher wants to verify that you learned the previous Hidden Skill correctly, and he tells you to come at him with the ending blow. Slash or spin attack until he falls, then target with Ⓩ and press Ⓐ.

"Excellent!" remarks the warrior. "Let the **shield attack** be hewn into your mind!" This technique is useful if your foe is clad in armor and bears a shield. When facing such a foe, lock on with Ⓩ and thrust the **Nunchuk** forward to push your **shield** against your enemy's defenses. Attack with any sword technique you wish. Try it!

Shield Attack: Press Ⓩ to target, then thrust the Nunchuk forward to shield bash your enemy. Follow up with sword play.

Shield Attack: Execute the same move when being struck by magical projectiles. Bounce them, and other ranged attacks, at the enemy. Thrust the Nunchuk early for best results!

Hidden Skill
You learned the second hidden skill, the Shield Attack.
Hidden Skill 2 of 7.

Task 5: Find Mayor Bo, and Learn the Secrets of Sumo

Enemies Encountered

Bokoblin

Bomskit

Wrestling with Mayor Bo

▲ Follow the advice of Renado the shaman, and inform each of your village's inhabitants that their children are safe. Start with Sera in her sundries store. Don't forget the miserable Hanch on the flat rock outcrop above the pumpkin patch!

◄ Head over to Jaggle and inform him next; he says he'll talk to the mayor about getting the kids back where they belong.

◄ Pergie is sitting in her waterwheel house, worried sick. Her demeanor changes when you tell her those tykes are OK!

As you move across to Rusl's house, Mayor Bo calls you over and beckons you inside. He's thankful the children are safe, but he's worried that Ilia isn't among them! He hears that you need his secrets to defeat Gorons in ceremonial combat. He agrees, as long as you promise to tell no one! You're led into the back room, where Bo teaches you of the basics of sumo wrestling.

Sumo wrestling techniques:

1. The first fella to push his foe outside the arena wins.
2. Step forward and grab your foe with Ⓐ.
3. Strike a fleein' foe with your Wii Remote.
4. Sidestep an attackin' foe with ◁ or ▷.

Note: Master all three techniques and you'll be shovin' folks out of the arena in no time, lad!

Ready? Fight! Use all three of the techniques on Mayor Bo, then grab and wrench him out of the ring to complete your training. He sets up a second match and is more difficult to defeat. You must learn which techniques to try.

1. Use the strike on a foe trying to sidestep.
2. Use the grab on a foe trying to strike.
3. Use the sidestep on a foe trying to grab.
4. Always use a grab and push to secure victory.

* Vary your tactics when encountering Goron challengers.

Execute these moves as you see an enemy's action, and you'll win every time!

Tip: If you need further guidance, run into the sumo room, and look for the three notes (called "The Way of Sumo") pinned to signs; they reinforce these techniques.

➤ After the second bout, you can practice again, before the mayor leads you into the main room and tells you another secret: you need additional weight to beat the heavy Gorons in sumo wrestling! Your prize is in the chest.

Overworld Chest #10: Iron Boots

Characters Encountered

Uli

Beth

Talo

Colin

Barnes

Renado

Iron Boots

You got the Iron Boots! Wear these and you'll become so heavy that not even a Goron can move you.

THE IRON BOOTS ARE USEFUL, SO KEEP THEM READILY AVAILABLE. PLACE THEM IN YOUR INVENTORY SO WHEN YOU PRESS ✚, THEY SLOT ON AND OFF YOUR FEET. YOU DON'T USE Ⓑ TO ACTIVATE THEM, AND YOU CAN USE OTHER ITEMS IN CONJUNCTION WITH THE IRON BOOTS. HOWEVER, THEY SLOW YOUR MOVEMENT, SO WEAR THEM ONLY WHERE NECESSARY. THEY ARE ALSO MAGNETIC.

Note

➤ Head out of the mayor's house, and across to Rusl and Uli's place. Uli is inside, and she thanks you for letting her know Colin is safe and sound!

◄ Your next port of call is important; you must ride Epona up into the pasture area and speak with Fado. He needs his goats herded. Agree, and follow the previous strategies for maneuvering these stubborn creatures into the barn.

Providing you complete this task, Fado offers you an excellent reward for your wrangling! Pick up this Piece of Heart from him before you leave Ordon Village.

Piece of Heart

You got a **Piece of Heart**! Collect **five pieces** to form a new Heart Container. Piece of Heart #6 of 45.

Missing Links

1. Mayor Bo's Body of Work

When you're seeking sumo guidance from the mayor, check out his place, including Ilia's bedroom upstairs, and the sumo dojo. Notice the fancy wrestling sketches on the wall, too!

Task 6: Defeat King Bulblin and his Hordes

Kidnapped by King Bulblin!

◄ It's time to leave Ordon Village again. Return the way you came, northward toward Faron Woods, then across Hyrule Field and into Kakariko Gorge, before leaping the spiked gate and arriving in Kakariko Village.

Before you arrive, Beth and Talo are playing in the thoroughfare when they hear hoofbeats. The massive Lord Bullbo roars into town, carrying the mighty King Bulblin! Talo turns in terror, but Beth is transfixed as the massive creature bears down upon her.

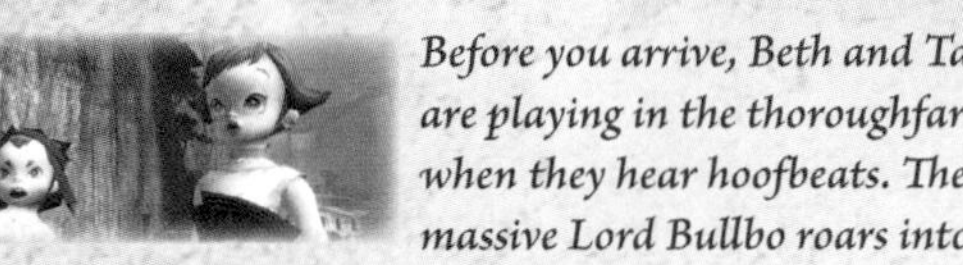

Colin leaves Malo at the sanctuary door, and runs out to save Beth, pushing her out of harm's way. But he's directly in line of the stampede! Barnes appears, and King Bulblin stares him down, carrying Colin's limp body in his giant fist.

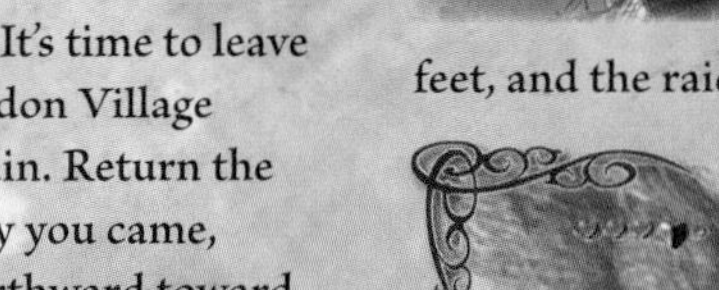

◄ You arrive in time to see the end of this terrible raid by King Bulblin and his cohorts; the king lifts Colin above his head and roars, then stomps Lord Bullbo's feet, and the raiding party gallops northward away from the village.

▲ The raiders are getting away! You can catch them, even after stopping Epona, turning around and talking with Beth, who's lying on the ground (but OK), Malo, who's standing in the thoroughfare (and as OK as he normally gets), and Talo (who's dumbstruck, hiding behind the Cucco shack).

Charge! You must follow the evil raiding party and rescue Colin before darkness devours him. Gallop northward, and make the long turn, heading past Renado at the Death Mountain trail entrance, then increase your speed and leap over the spiked gate.

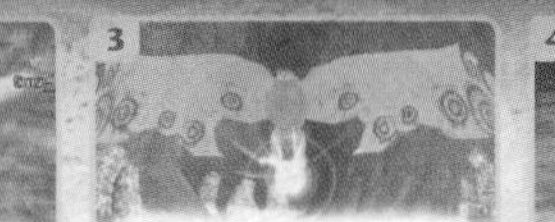

Battle in the Flat Field

Once in a giant flat field, west of Castle Hyrule, King Bulblin awaits. Colin is tethered to the king's banner, and the king beckons you to fight him! You unsheathe your sword, and the king blows a mighty horn. Five Bulblin riders and their archers gallop to his side!

Bulblin Riders

Threat Meter

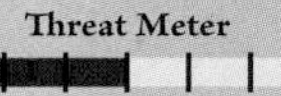

A massive melee begins with you and Epona pitted against five Bulblin Riders and their archers and King Bulblin. Your tactics should begin with the Bulblin Riders; they are fast, and the Bullbos they ride carry two passengers: one a rider and the other an archer. To deal with them, use your spurs to catch up to enemies ahead, or speed away from foes behind you.

You're jostled and struck multiple times. Bring out the blade, and lay waste to these Bulblins with quick slashes and the spin attack!

Draw your sword early, and as you reach your target, optionally Z target (although this isn't useful as there are too many foes), then hack away. Slice off both rider and archer with one swing! Charging in, using the spin attack, and leaving is the other option. Don't concern yourself with the Bulblin Riders exclusively; more appear when you defeat the ones currently surrounding you.

King Bulblin Riding Lord Bullbo

Threat Meter

Fracas in the Field

Step 1: This battle rages for minutes. You must deal with the regular Bulblin Riders, then gallop to catch up with King Bulblin. He's dashing around the expansive field and you must keep up with him, even over low fences and walls!

Step 2: Replenish your health during the battle by riding through the small unlit campfires for Hearts.

Step 3: When you're out of spurs and waiting for Epona, slow down and defeat Bulblin Riders, but keep a lookout for King Bulblin. When you have enough speed, dash for the king and match his speed. Spur Epona two or three times to reach the same velocity.

Step 4: As you arrive, be sure your sword is drawn, execute a couple of slices, then a spin attack on King Bulblin. This shatters some of his armor before he gallops away. Slow down, deal with the Bulblin Riders, and repeat steps 3 and 4.

Keep up the attacks on King Bulblin five or six additional times, until daylight comes and you knock King Bulblin's horn from his hand!

Caution: Do not ram the low walls at an angle, or you may fall off your horse. Always get back up on Epona; fighting on foot is impossible!

Battle on the Bridge

King Bulblin has no horn to call his shock troops; instead he gallops to the Bridge of Eldin. As you enter, a Bulblin Archer sets fire to a barricade at each end. King Bulblin and Lord Bullbo rear up, then charge for you, on the bridge!

Step 1: Unsheathe your sword, and trot (but don't charge) toward King Bulblin. Strike him before he hits you and you plummet off the bridge!

Move Epona to one side, running at King Bulblin.

Enemies Encountered

Lord Bullbo

King Bulblin

Bulblin Rider

Bulblin Archer

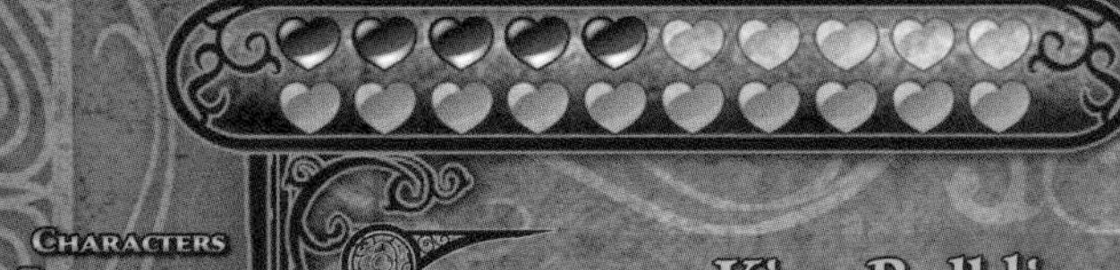

Characters Encountered

Colin

Renado

Talo

Beth

Luda

Barnes

King Bulblin Riding Lord Bullbo (cont'd)

Step 2: As you both near each other, move to one side, dodging him (always toward the middle of the bridge). At the same time, slice with your sword. Time this correctly, and you knock another piece of armor from the king.

Step 3: Gallop to the bridge's end, then rein in Epona and turn her around. You're about to go for a second strike! Follow the same plan: keep your speed low (if you charge, there's less time to strike). Keep to the side.

Cut in at the last moment, and slice with your weapon! After a second successful strike, King Bulblin falls off his mount.

A hit knocks the mighty Bulblin off his steed, and into the gloom of a plummet to a doom. Your mount rears up and you raise your sword in triumph! King Bulblin could never have survived that fall....

You pick up Colin, and bring him to Kakariko Village. Colin is wounded, but he knows what his father meant when he told him to be strong. Beth has been saved, and while Colin recuperates, you turn your attention to that rumbling volcano. It's time to pay the Gorons a visit!

Task 7: Obtain the Hylian Shield

Village Exploration, and Making a Deal with Malo

After Renado takes care of Colin, and brings him into the Elde Inn for recuperation (the hot springs will help), move into the southern springs, and regain your energy. Epona has done her job, but you'll need her in a moment, so bring her along.

▲ You can move into the thoroughfare and speak to Talo, who's surprised at Colin's bravery and even more shocked that his brother hasn't come out of that closed-up general store.

Store

Check the old store to see that it's under new management! Malo's face is plastered all over the old signage, and after you enter the place, you can see Malo's been hard at work, importing items from around the realm. He's behind a Wooden Shield. Check out his wares.

Malo Mart

Item Name	Price	Effect
Red Potion	30 Rupees	This replenishes eight life energy: keep it in an **empty Bottle**.
Wooden Shield	50 Rupees	A simple shield. Made of wood, it will burn if touched by fire.
Hylian Shield	200 Rupees	Limited supply! Don't let them sell out before you buy one.

Ignore the Red Potion (you don't need it unless you've finished the bottle you purchased at Trill's Shop) and the Wooden Shield (you already have one). Instead purchase the **Hylian Shield**! This is the only place to buy it, and it's expensive.

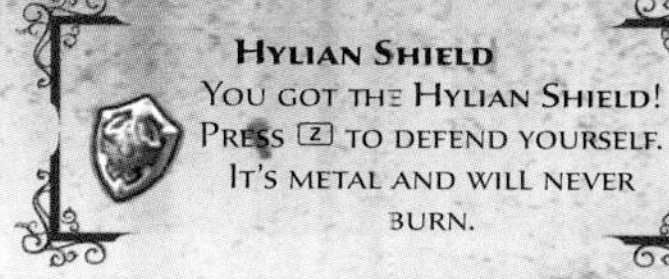
Hylian Shield
You got the Hylian Shield! Press Z to defend yourself. It's metal and will never burn.

> **Note:** You're about to enter a fire-filled mountain mine, so pony up the Rupees for that Hylian Shield! The only reason to buy the Wooden Shield is that there's a different design on it, and you must burn your original Wooden Shield first.

◄ Leave the Malo Mart. If Malo can't be a hero, he can help equip one! Move along the thoroughfare, and enter the Elde Inn to check up on a couple of folks inside.

The first is rather surprising! Enter the main bar area, then head right, into the storage room. Sitting on his haunches, complaining that he got a letter wet in the hot springs and is drying it out, is the Postman. After you find him, head into the bar, and go upstairs.

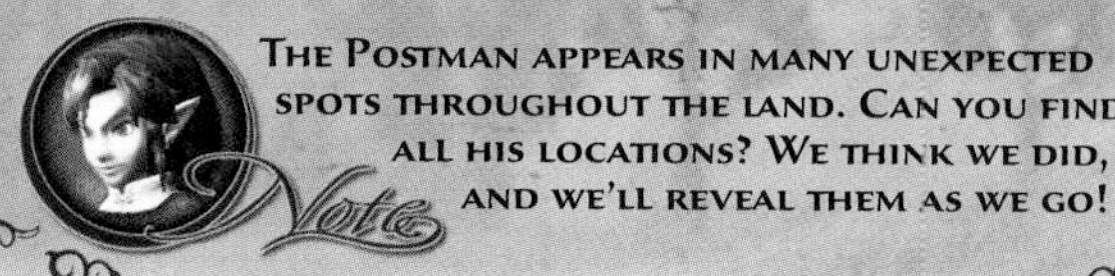
> **Note:** The Postman appears in many unexpected spots throughout the land. Can you find all his locations? We think we did, and we'll reveal them as we go!

➤ Move past the balcony, and into the bedroom, where Beth and Luda are wrestling Colin for his attention, while Renado looks on. He tells you that Colin will awaken after rest. Head onto the thoroughfare, and go northward to Barnes' Bomb Shop.

➤ Barnes still hasn't opened the store, unfortunately, but if you climb up the interior stairs, he's shoveling volatile gunpowder into a bucket! He relies on the Gorons for the raw materials.

There's nothing you can do to help Barnes. Investigate the rest of the village if you wish, then take Epona and gallop north, past the Death Mountain trail entrance, and leap the spiked gate. Head into the flat field, known as Hyrule Field (west).

Missing Links

1. Lantern's Out!

When you're inside Barnes' Bomb Shop, ignore his warnings and take your Lantern out. When you do, Barnes lets out a yelp and douses you with water from a secret ceiling sprinkler system!

Bug-Hunting in the Flat Hyrule Field

When you enter the field's rocky outcrop (where there is a chest on a ledge), that crazy Postman appears once again! He gets around, and he's ready to deliver your third letter. It's a letter from Malo, who's letting you know about the new goods in the village shop. As you've been there, pocket the letter.

Letter #3
You got **Letter #3**: "URGENT NOTICE!" by Kakariko Goods.

Golden Bug: Male Grasshopper

Collection: 7 (of 24)

Enter Hyrule Field and slow your horse to a canter. You can pick up another couple of Golden Bugs from this area! Deal with the Kargaroks flying about, then look for the shiny bug west of the southern entrance. It's a Male Grasshopper!

Male Grasshopper
You caught a **Male Grasshopper**. Bug fans love that golden color!

Enemies Encountered

King Bulblin

Kargarok

Gorons

Leever

Threat Meter

While you're searching for the Grasshopper, you may stumble upon a ring of green, spinning, plant-like beasts known as Leevers. They rotate and move around you, then converge and strike you. The clue to dispatching them is in their name: leave them alone and don't chase them. Stop, stand still, and as the Leevers surround and come in for the strike, execute a spin attack and defeat them all. You can also run away, or attack with projectiles!

The Leever won't leave you alone! Let the strange spinning plant come to you; then spin yourself.

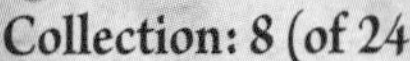

Golden Bug: Female Grasshopper

Collection: 8 (of 24)

With the Leevers a constant source of annoyance, journey to Hyrule Field's northeastern part, and search for a second Grasshopper in the ground here. Pick it up, and add it to your collection.

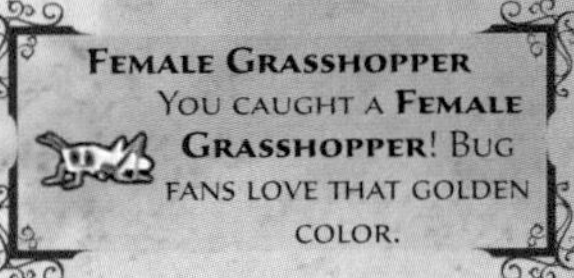

Female Grasshopper
You caught a **Female Grasshopper**! Bug fans love that golden color.

Golden Bug: Male Phasmid

Collection: 9 (of 24)

Keep that collection going by heading to the northwestern bridge area, and riding to the Bridge of Eldin's south entrance. There's a sparkling little bug on the wall! Bring out your Gale Boomerang and target this one, scraping him off the wall and onto your feet. Pick him up.

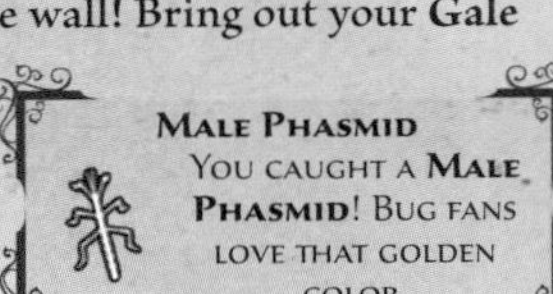

Male Phasmid
You caught a **Male Phasmid**! Bug fans love that golden color.

➤ The bug collecting doesn't have to end there, either! You can cross the bridge now that the fiery barricades have gone. It's eerily quiet here, but don't be scared. Gallop across the bridge, and make an immediate left turn.

Golden Bug: Female Phasmid

Collection: 10 (of 24)

Stop by what looks like a Bomb Rock, dismount, and bring out the Gale Boomerang. Look for the bug on a ledge up from you. You can't reach this ledge by foot, but you can target the bug (get the yellow target marker). Bring the Phasmid back and add her to your collection.

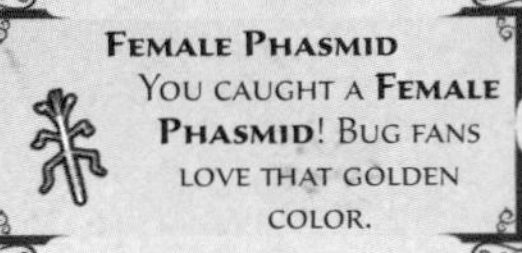

Female Phasmid
You caught a **Female Phasmid**! Bug fans love that golden color.

With a strong collection of bugs, back up across the bridge. You can look around this area, but the road to the north is blocked. The bridge has interesting vines and an owl statue, and the north end has that ledge and Clawshot points. Return to Kakariko Village.

1

2

3

4

5

6

Task 8: Meet Gor Coron, and Gain Access to the Goron Mines

Enemies Encountered

Leever

Bulblin Archer

Up the Death Mountain Trail (Again)

◀ The time has come to test your strength against the Gorons! Leave Kakariko Village and head up the Death Mountain Trail's start, to the large barricade with the mesh wall. Climb to the top, and ready yourself for Goron combat!

The Goron is surprised to see you again, but he begins his roll just as before. Put your **Iron Boots** on (set them so you press ✚ to access them on and off), then press Ⓐ to catch the Goron, and throw him off the barricade!

◀ Take your boots off and continue up the path. When you see a second Goron rumbling your way, put the boots back on, catch him, and throw him as you would an Ordon goat! Catch a third Goron, then a fourth as you reach the second barricade. Flick those Iron Boots on and off, or you'll be knocked flying.

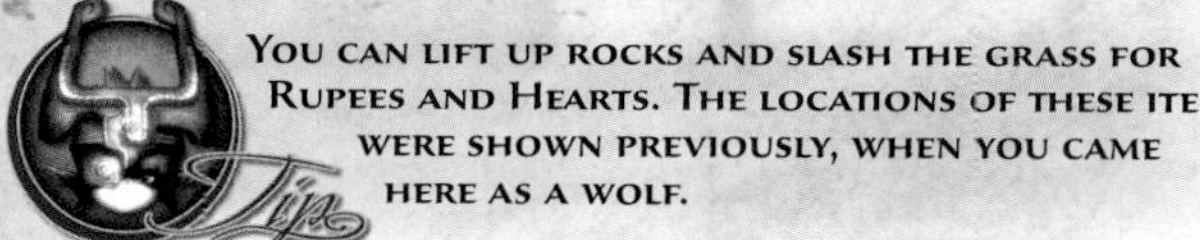

Tip: You can lift up rocks and slash the grass for Rupees and Hearts. The locations of these items were shown previously, when you came here as a wolf.

➤ Reach the second barricade, and use the large steps on the right side to clamber on. Once at the top, run away from the barricade's edge, put those boots on, then catch and lob another Goron. If you're too close to the barricade edge, you get knocked back and off, boots or no boots! Run into the rocky clearing.

➤ Nasty Bulblin Archers are up ahead, and you don't have the necessary ranged weapon to deal with them… or do you? Move to this patch of Hawk Grass, and blow on it. Your hawk friend soars down and lands on your arm. Target the five Bulblin Archers with the bird, and knock them off their perches!

➤ Or, you could bring out your Slingshot. It may not work as well as a bow (which you'll find soon) would, but you can strike the nearer Bulblins with this weapon. If you're out of ammunition, or want to use the hawk, there's a second grass patch near the whistling rock. Target the last Bulblin in the alcove entrance with the hawk.

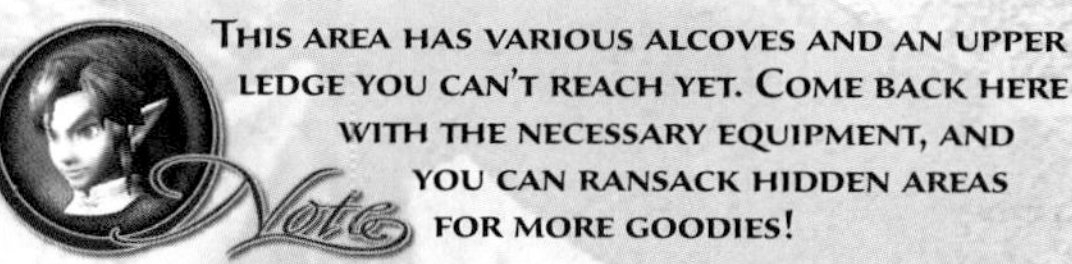

Note: This area has various alcoves and an upper ledge you can't reach yet. Come back here with the necessary equipment, and you can ransack hidden areas for more goodies!

◀ Leave the rocky clearing, avoiding those steam vents, and follow the rubble-strewn trail as it winds northward. Follow the erratic steps to the base of Death Mountain. Now you must negotiate the Gorons and find an entrance!

Entering Death Mountain

Jump down to the lower flat area, as Gorons propel themselves up and into an arched iron entrance at the top of the section you're viewing. A Goron advances on you. Use your shield attack (Hidden Skill #2) to buffet him back. Watch out for the falling magma rocks, though! Raise the Hylian Shield, and even this strike won't harm you.

A giant shadow appears above you, and you leap away as a huge shard of molten rock falls from the skies and imbeds itself in the flat area where you once stood! Remember the location of this molten shard for later!

7

8

Characters Encountered

Gorons

Gor Coron

➤ You need a way to ascend the exterior of the mountain; either move to one of the less-aggressive Gorons, or use your shield attack to strike one so he curls up into a ball. Move and leap on his back, and when he unravels, you're propelled high into the sky. Make sure the camera shows the upper ledge, and land on it!

◄ Route #1: Either turn left, or in this case, right, and run along the ledge to the crumbling wall and wooden support. Use a shield bash and a sword bonk to persuade the waiting Goron to curl up and propel you onto the next upper level. From here, you can investigate the Goron hot springs.

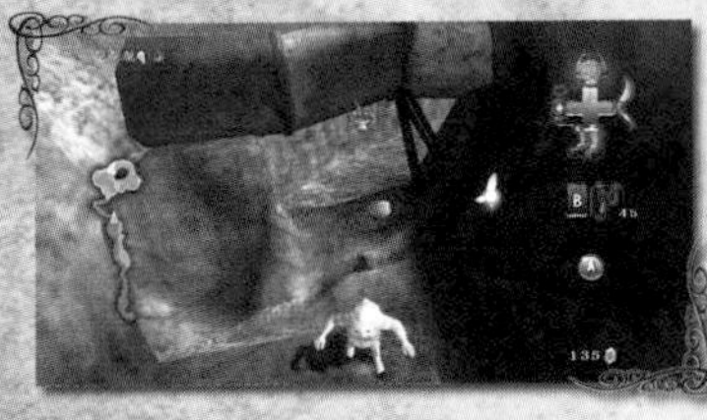

◄ Route #2: Or, you can turn left, and persuade this Goron, standing near a barricade, to propel you up and onto a large iron pipe conduit. From here, you can drop to a path you haven't explored before. Behind you are two barrels; smash them both for a Heart and Rupees. Run around the steaming vents, heading along the path.

➤ This brings you in above the Goron hot springs. The Gorons can't get enough of the warm water and volcanic bubbles! You have to drop down to visit them, as a steaming vent blocks your path.

You can negotiate the steaming vent if you face it, raise your shield, and sidestep into the vent's steam. The steam knocks you backward, but you can drop and hold onto the ledge, then hand-over-hand past the steam itself! You can also navigate the steam vents by wearing the Iron Boots.

Tip

A Dip in the Hot Springs, then Skyward

▲ Speak to the Gorons in the water and they're more amiable. There's no need for combat. The Gorons tell you the water can imbue you with **energy** although there's not enough to bottle currently! Visit the northern shop.

Store

Item	Name	Price	Effect
	Arrows (10)	10 Rupees	There are few ships in the area. If you use a bow, carry lots of arrows.
	Lantern Oil	20 Rupees	The mountains are dark at night!
	Wooden Shield	50 Rupees	It is wood, so if it catches fire, it may burn.
	Milk (2 servings)	20 Rupees	Chugging a glass of Milk after soaking is popular!

There's no need to purchase any of these items: If you're low on Lantern fuel, purchase some, but don't buy Milk. Your Hylian Shield is better than the Wooden one. And arrows are plentiful inside the Goron Mines, after you find the **Hero's Bow**!

However, you're about to enter another dungeon, and there are many treasure chests to kick open. If you're full of Rupees, you won't be able to loot everything inside the dungeon, so buy everything you can if you want to ransack every dungeon chest!

Tip

◄ When you finish in the hot springs, move to the sitting Goron near the mesh draped over the wall, and climb up and out. Avoid or use the shield block and hand-over-hand technique at any steaming vents shooting out to the sides. At the next rocky outcrop, fight another Goron so he knocks you skyward even farther, as shown.

1 
2 
3 
4 
5 
6 

◄ Run around the corner to another steaming vent. Block with your shield, then walk forward so the steam pushes you over the ledge; grab onto it. Then hand-over-hand to the left, past the steam. Climb onto the iron fencing, and drop on the ledge.

You can avoid the remaining steam vents easily, so continue around the fenced ledge to a cave in the mountain. When you see three barrels ahead of you, don your **Iron Boots**, catch another rolling Goron, and throw him to the side.

▲ There are two more Gorons to battle into balls before you can enter Death Mountain. Strike the first one, then head onto his hide, but turn to face the mountain before he shoots you upward. This way, you'll reach a hidden ledge with three yellow Rupees (10) on it!

► You can stand on the narrow ledge, take the Rupees, then edge left, to the iron archway and dungeon entrance. Or, you can drop, fight the final Goron, and propel yourself up and onto the entrance platform. Either way works, but don't forget to break out that barrel near the doorway for a Heart.

Missing Links

1. Rock and Roll

You should have learned which rocks hide Rupees and Hearts when you climbed around here as the wolf. However, after you negotiate the hot springs and reach the dungeon entrance, check this rock for Rupees. Don't forget the ledge of yellow Rupees (10), too!

Gor Coron's Wrestling Ring

You step into the iron archway entrance, and six Gorons roll up and propel toward you! "ENOUGH!" a smaller, more wizened Goron calls out. The Goron elder, known as Gor Coron beckons you over. The Gorons part to let you through.

He is impressed that you made it this far. However, the mines are sacred to his tribe. "Outsiders are not allowed, unless..." Gor Coron smiles.

Gor Coron waddles onto the wrestling stage, and prepares for the bout. Ready? Fight!

◄ If you begin the match without donning the **Iron Boots** you acquired from Mayor Bo, Gor Coron slaps you out of the ring! There's no time to grab or return any techniques, so stand up, **put your boots on**, move back to Gor Coron, and request a rematch.

► The match is a more frantic version of the training you received under Mayor Bo. You must choose a technique out of three possible moves, and hope Gor Coron doesn't offer up a defense. You or your opponent may elect not to make a move, in which case any of the three attacks will work.

7

8

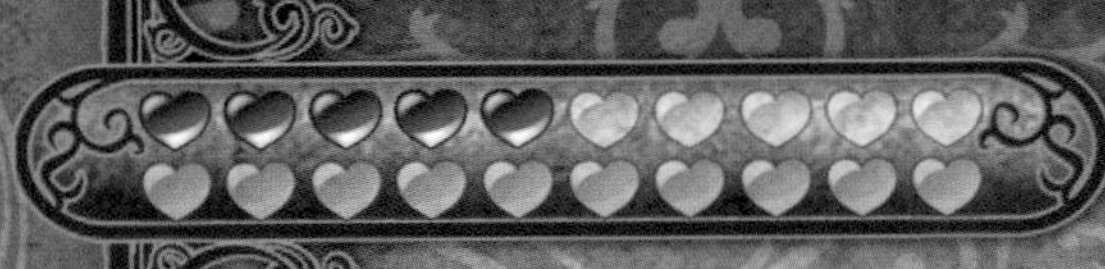

Gorons

Gor Coron

If you both attack with the same technique (in this case, the grab), you'll both knock each other back.

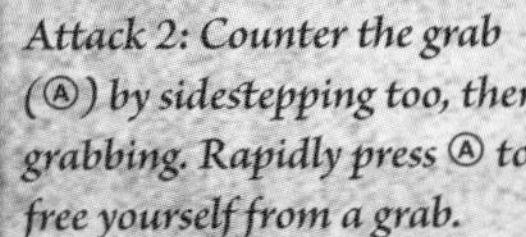

Attack 1: Counter the strike (Wii Remote forward) by sidestepping, then grabbing Ⓐ.

Attack 2: Counter the grab (Ⓐ) by sidestepping too, then grabbing. Rapidly press Ⓐ to free yourself from a grab.

Attack 3: Counter either a grab or a strike with the sidestep (◄ or ►).

◄ Combat may take a while, so sidestep, then either strike or grab. Keep this up while evading Gor Coron's attacks, and wear those Iron Boots, and you'll eventually (using the grab) push him off the ring, winning the bout, and his respect.

Gor Coron:

Gor Coron is an ancient Goron, and the most important elder of the four senior Gorons living within Death Mountain. He is responsible for isolating his tribe from the humans of the village below, as he doesn't wish them to know the fate of their tribal leader, Darbus. Gor Coron partakes in this wrestling to judge strength, and he opens his heart to you after your victory. He is easygoing, but he speaks quickly and vigorously, commanding fear and respect from his brethren.

Gor Coron speaks about a **treasure** that must be protected, and that Darbus reached for it and was transformed into "an unspeakable monster"! Gor Coron begs you to aid Darbus and find some way to transform him back. The two Gorons guarding the inner entrance step aside.

Note: You can speak to every Goron in this chamber (all 10), including Gor Coron again and the two Gorons who blocked the entrance, for additional information.

▲ Before you journey into the mountain's belly, run to the Goron on the chamber's east side, who steps aside to let you use an elevator. Wear the **Iron Boots** and stand on the middle of the elevator floor switch.

▲ You appear outside the dungeon, on the Death Mountain trail, near the hot springs. But you can't reach there yet. Step right, remove your boots, and push the ceremonial rock along the floor indent. This opens the small tunnel.

Tip: Do you remember the rock with the carvings on it from your exploration of the Death Mountain trail hot springs area? This is the only way to remove it, allowing access in and out of the dungeon easily!

1

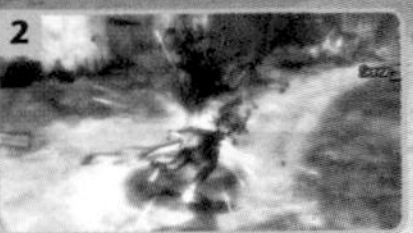

2

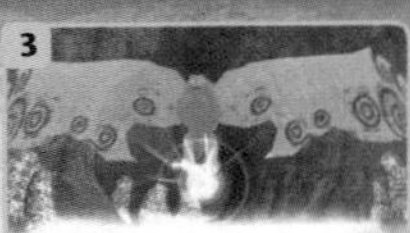

3

4

5

6

◄ Run through the tunnel and outside into the hot springs. Now that Gor Coron has welcomed you, the Gorons are relaxing, and their shop has reopened. Check out the wares (they are listed after this dungeon), head into the elevator shaft area, and move to the opposite side.

▲ A narrow ramp zigzags down to a partially crushed mine cart. Jump or run down the ramp, and inspect a second ceremonial rock blocking another entrance. Push this rock out of the way, as before. When you're done, head through the entrance to another narrow tunnel. This one leads almost to the mountain's base, to the molten shard impact area!

Tip: Now, if you wish to return here (and you will, as there's a chest in this dungeon you cannot reach yet), reach the meteor impact area, climb the net, enter this tunnel, and run up to the elevator. This shaves minutes off your usual ascension!

Tip: Although you can't currently tell, there are small dig spots in the elevator area. Return here in wolf form to unearth additional treasure!

▲ Step through the entrance to the Goron Mines and begin an epic dungeon quest to save the Goron tribe from its possessed and frightening leader, Darbus.

Missing Links

1. Hands Up

During your look around the wrestling room, you can speak to the Gorons for additional information, check the viewing seats, and spot Goron hand prints in the victory plaques around the arena.

Dungeon 2: Goron Mines

1F

2F

Legend

Rooms

1. The Lava Pit
2. Volcano Forge (1F and 2F)
3. Domain of the Dodongos
4. Magnetic Pool
5. Gor Amoto's Shrine Room
6. Diamond Switch Chambers
7. Mine Loading Docks
8. Mine Reservoir
9. Gor Ebizo's Shrine Room
10. Dangoro's Stomping Grounds
11. Dangoro's Treasure Hole
12. Beamos Star Chamber
13. Gor Liggs's Shrine Room
14. Stalactite Cavern
15. Grand Volcanic Passage
16. Boss Battle! Twilit Igniter: Fyrus

Number of Treasure Chests: 17

1. Red Rupee (20)
2. Small Key
3. Dungeon Map
4. Red Rupee (20)
5. Piece of Heart
6. Small Key
7. Red Rupee (20)
8. Piece of Heart
9. Purple Rupee (50)
10. Small Key
11. Yellow Rupee (10)
12. Yellow Rupee (10)
13. Hero's Bow
14. Compass
15. Purple Rupee (50)
16. Purple Rupee (50)
17. Purple Rupee (50)

Characters

- Gor Amato
- Gor Ebizo
- Gor Liggs
- Dangoro
- Twilit Igniter Fyrus

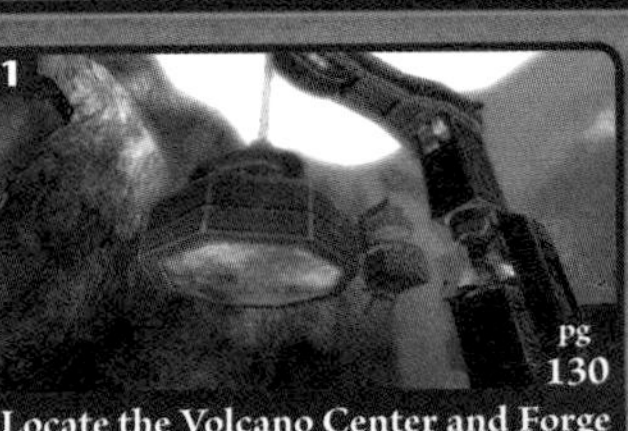
1 Locate the Volcano Center and Forge
Pg 130

2 Find the 1st Key Shard from Gor Amoto
Pg 133

3 Journey to the Mine Loading Docks
Pg 137

4 Obtain the 2nd Key Shard from Gor Ebizo
Pg 141

Dungeon Denizens

Characters

Midna

Gor Amoto

Ooceoo

Gor Ebizo

Gor Liggs

Darbus

Enemies

Fire Toadpoli

Torch Slug

Bulblin

Dodongo

Fire Keese

Tektite

Beamos

Water Toadpoli

Bosses

Mid Boss: Dangoro

Big Boss: Twilit Igniter: Fyrus

A Link to the Present

Ordon Sword

Heart Pieces: 1 (6 Total)

Wooden Shield

Hylian Shield

Hero's Clothes

Wallet

Quiver

Golden Bugs: 10 (of 24)

Hidden Skills: 2 (of 7)

Youth's Scent

Fish Journal

Letters 3 (of 16)

Fused Shadow Pieces 1 (of 3)

Items Already Acquired

Iron Boots

Gale Boomerang

Lantern

Slingshot

Fishing Rod

Bottle #1

Bottle #2

Items to Obtain

Small Key (1st)

Key Shard (1st)

Dungeon Map

Ooccoo

Piece of Heart #7

Small Key (2nd)

Piece of Heart #8

Purple Rupee

Small Key (3rd)

Key Shard (2nd)

Hero's Bow

Compass

Big Key (3 Key Shards)

Fairy in Bottle

Heart Container #2

The Goron Mines: Overview

The interior of Death Mountain, used as mines by the Gorons until their leader Darbus fell under a mysterious spell, is a series of large chambers, many filled with molten lava that saps your energy and forces you to begin again. Take your time as you journey into Death Mountain's center, locating three Goron elders hidden from their patriarch, who each carry a portion of the only key that allows access to Darbus's chamber. The Goron leader was chained and sealed after the twilight possessed him. Defeat a similarly confused Goron hulk named Dangoro to obtain an excellent new ranged weapon—the **Hero's Bow**—and learn to use it quickly, as you must employ it when you face your fiercest boss enemy yet!

5 Battle Feared Goron Dangoro for Hero's Bow PG 144

6 Complete the Key Shard from Gor Liggs PG 146

7 Search for the Great Volcanic Passage PG 148

8 Change Fate of Gorons: Fight Fyrus! PG 151

Goron

Task 1: Locate the Volcano Center and Forge

Chamber 1: The Lava Pit

Tip

Before you enter these mines, bring along the following:

- A Bottle filled with a Red Potion.
- Your Iron Boots positioned on ✚ so you can slip them on and off quickly.
- A Lantern and Slingshot within easy access.
- Carry the Gale Boomerang as your main Ⓑ item.
- The Hylian Shield; purchase it from Kakariko Village.

➤ Ahead of you, lava jets rise and fall, and molten ooze burns in a large pool beneath you; you'll succumb to the flames if you fall in, and restart this chamber with less health, so stay away from the hot stuff! You can, if you wish, follow the Goron rolling track in the earth down to this pit's edge, and position yourself near the rock platform.

◄ Or, you can leap from the top of the initial ground, straight over the winding path, and land near the edge. Place yourself on one of the metal beams sunk into the ground.

◄ Make a quick leap onto the first platform. You don't need to press a button—you'll leap automatically. Once on the first platform, you can turn either left or right.

➤ The route is similar; jump past a lava plume, onto the next stone platform. If you judge the distance well, you can leap to the side of the plume while it's still jetting upward! However, it is better to wait until the jet subsides.

Caution

Being caught in a lava jet knocks you back to the platform you were on, and you lose a quarter of a Heart. If you're jumping at an angle, you're sometimes knocked straight into the lava instead. Not good! If you land in the lava, you restart this room, with two Hearts of energy lost.

➤ Move to the next platform edge, then line up your jump so you're leaping straight over the gap. If you approach at an angle, you may miss the area of flat rock ahead and hit the lava. Either side leads you to the same spot, although the right route is easier. Wait for the lava jet to stop, and make the jump.

➤ Run along the flat stone ground, and into a cagelike corridor on your left. This is an old mine structure, and a feeble attempt was made to block your path. A quick spin or some sword hacking breaks the wooden beams stopping you from continuing.

Author Note

This chamber was a brutal challenge to begin with, so don't feel bad about falling in the lava more than a few times; we fell many times. The trick here is to keep steady and not rush any of the sections; dashing to the middle of the room usually results in a misstep and fiery plunge!

◄ After a small left turn, you come to a second set of wooden beams blocking your way, and a massive fire jet belching from a furnace along the left wall. Draw your sword and smash this set of beams, but don't continue yet!

➤ After you smash the doorway blockage, move to the floor switch, and stand on it using your **Iron Boots.** This switches off the fire jet for five seconds. Take off your boots (you don't want to clump slowly along this gantry), and run past the furnace wall.

1

2

3

4

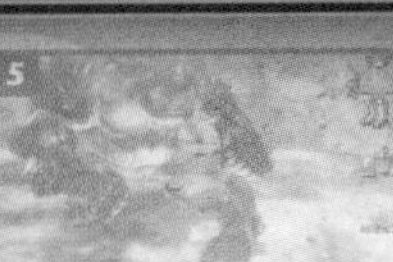
5

6

▲ Stop at a second floor switch, near a small rock (you can pick up and smash the rock, but no items fall out). You must tame another belching fire jet, so put on your **Iron Boots**, switch off the jet, take the boots off, then run along this next gantry area. Jump across onto a lower, open gantry as you pass the furnace wall. Stop for a moment.

Caution: What happens if you're caught by the fire jet? You're launched into the lava pit and must begin this chamber again, with two fewer Hearts in your energy bar!

▲ Survey the scenery. A door is to the north. Your map indicates that this is the only exit, so you must reach there, but the lava pit is blocking your path! Optionally climb the ladder to your left. If you do, you must backtrack and shut down the second fire jet again.

▲ The best plan is to activate the second floor switch. Roll and leap past the deactivated jet, then turn right and run over the small exposed gantry heading south. Stop before you reach the gap. You're now south of the jet, but on the gantry's middle edge. Turn to face a new foe in the pit.

Fire Toadpoli

Threat Meter

There's a lurking beastie in the lava! Your Slingshot and Boomerang don't affect him, and he spits out a fireball that can damage and knock you off the ladder you'll climb in a minute. It's better to face this foe down, as long as you've negotiated the fire jet first! Raise your shield and Z target the Fire Toadpoli in the lava. When he spits the fireball, knock it back with your shield (move your Nunchuk forward). Time it early for best results. Stay at the edge, near the Toadpoli, because if you just block the fireball, you're knocked back. One rebounded fireball is all it takes to defeat this fiendish foe!

The Toadpoli spits and belches out fireballs. Return the favor for a permanent case of indigestion!

◄ Jump the gap, move to the ladder, and climb to the top of the caged gantry area. From here, optionally turn and walk north, and drop to the left to investigate the pots above the second fire jet. This isn't necessary, so head south instead.

◄ Position yourself south, and run forward atop the cage. You leap the gap over the first jet and come eye-to-eyestalk with a new lava lurker: the Torch Slug!

Torch Slug

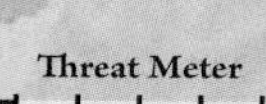

Threat Meter

Torch Slugs are slow-moving, docile creatures until you near them. Then they emit a small puff of fire that can damage you. Combat them by executing a quick sword attack (but not a leaping attack, as they can repel you). The only problem you may have is that they also like to sit on cave ceilings, dropping to startle you. If this occurs, bring out a ranged weapon and deal with them before you near.

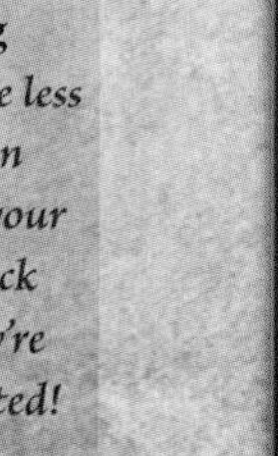

These slugs are less menacing than Hanch from your village! A quick slice, and they're done and dusted!

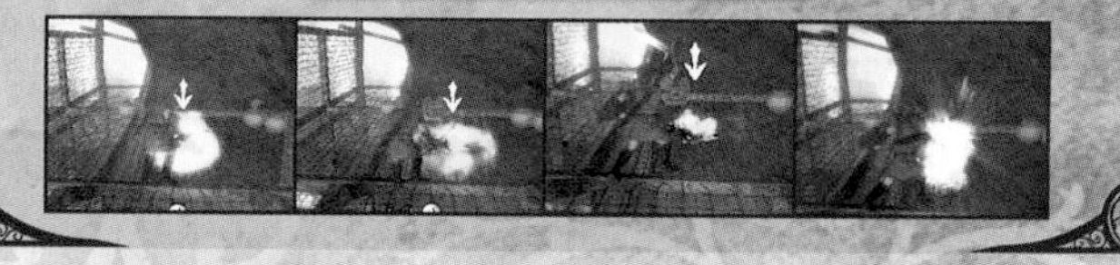

Enemies Encountered

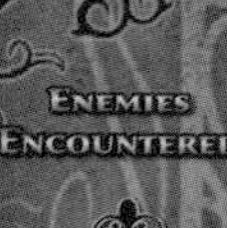

Fire Toadpoli

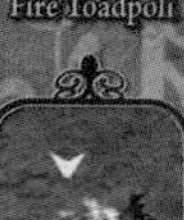

Torch Slug

➤ Treasure Chest: With the Torch Slug slugged, break the pots (for Rupees and a Heart), then claim the real prize—the first treasure chest in this dungeon. There's a red Rupee (20) inside. Turn and face north, and leap the gap between cages.

Treasure Chest #1: Red Rupee (20)

◄ When you make the jump, turn to face east and you'll notice a stone platform allowing you access to a high northern ledge. Point yourself at the platform, then leap to it, and again to the long ledge.

◄ Turn south, as a third fire jet prevents you from continuing farther north. Leap across the ledge's gap, and look for the floor switch. However, also watch out for the Torch Slug dropping from the ceiling. Hit it with a Slingshot or Boomerang, or edge forward until it drops, then slay it with your sword.

➤ With the Torch Slug out of the way, face north, stand on the floor switch, then put your **Iron Boots** on. The third jet of fire stops belching from the ledge's north end, and you can escape this infernal chamber! Take off your boots, hug the right wall, and run along the ledge. Watch out!

➤ As you reach the final jump to the fire grating, a Torch Slug drops from the ceiling. Stay to the right and avoid the beast, keeping your speed up! Or, look up and left before you activate the switch, and tackle this foe from a distance. When you've dodged the Torch Slug, leap the gap, and round the right corner before the fire reactivates.

Caution

Do not stop to slash at the Torch Slug; if you do, the counter finishes ticking down, and the jet of fire blasts you! Even if the Torch Slug hits you when it falls, there's still time to escape. Ignore this creature.

➤ Once away from the fire jets (the reactivated third one blocks your way back), head around and onto a small metal gantry. Ahead is a steel door. First, however, drop and defeat the Torch Slug and his two friends who fall from above.

◄ You can't open this door by hand, so climb up to the small metal gantry, turn and face the platform to one side of the door, and leap across to it. Your weight doesn't shift this platform until you wear your Iron Boots. Don these, the platform descends, and the door opens. Inside is a dungeon door; open it.

Missing Links

1. A Heart in the Right Place

You can smash the three boxes on the entrance's left side as you enter this chamber. The far one contains a Heart!

2. Ladder to Pulverizing Pottery

Climb the ladder past the second furnace fire vent to a small alcove containing two pots; one carries a Rupee and Heart. Drop by the ladder, or fall into or behind the vent you leapt past!

3. Rock Bashing

There's a plentiful supply of small rocks in this chamber, but none of them reveal an item when you lift or smash them against a wall. You can use them to smash other scenery, such as barrels.

4. Roll out the Barrel

At this pit's north end, near the exit door, are three wooden barrels, one containing a Heart; rip through them with your sword if you need the additional energy.

1

2

3

4

5

6

Task 2: Find the First Key Shard from Gor Amoto

Enemies Encountered
Torch Slug 
Bulblin Infantry 

Chamber 2: Volcano Forge

▲ You emerge inside the active volcano, with the Hylian sky visible above you! A giant forge the Gorons constructed, now populated by the hated Bulblins, is ready for you to traverse it. After you take in how huge this volcano is, head up the metal ramp.

▲ Make a left turn at the octagonal platform at the ramp's end. There are Bulblins here—green-skinned fellows with an evil temperament. You can target them with the Boomerang, but it's best to leave them alone for the moment. Your stay in this active volcano is brief, for now.

▲ Turn left and head onto the gantry that slopes down, near the initial ramp. Follow it as the gantry turns right, then descends to the lava surface! Draw your weapon as you head onto this platform; Bulblins are here.

Bulblin Infantry

Threat Meter

Bulblins are devious, stupid humanoids who love to inflict pain. They took Ilia from the Ordon Spring earlier and haven't learned any manners since then. These foot-soldiers carry primitive clubs. Attack them with a flurry of regular sword slices.

As the heat intensifies, bring out your sword and begin to slice some Bulblin hide!

Use your shield and Z target, and push back the initial attack. Counter with three regular slices, comboed into a spin to finish them off. You can take down two or more Bulblins at once with this technique.

Or, you can knock the Bulblin back with your shield, leaping and striking with a sword slice, then (with the Bulblin lying on his back) finish him with your first Hidden Skill; a nasty skewer! Combat with Bulblins is entertaining and easy.

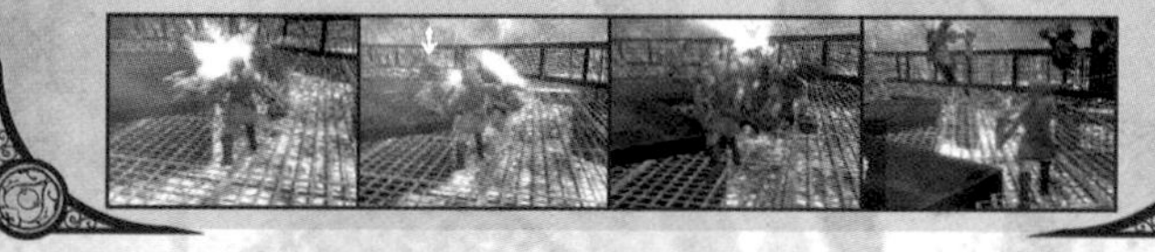

◄ **Treasure Chest**: See what those Bulblins were guarding. After barrel bashing and pot smashing (for Rupees and Hearts), inspect the chest between the two torches. Inside is a handy key.

Treasure Chest #2: Small Key

Small Key
You got a **Small Key**! This opens a locked door, but only in this area.

◄ Run up the gantry to the octagonal platform, and straight across, with the entrance ramp on your right. Head up a second, ascending gantry that turns right almost immediately. After an incline, it turns left.

➤ You're now in the southeast part of the volcano forge, and you must traverse two rotating platforms. Stand on the gantry platform's left side, and move forward after the platform completes a rotation. Hop on, then off. Stop at the small gantry platform, wait for the second platform to finish a 180-degree turn, then hop on and off it.

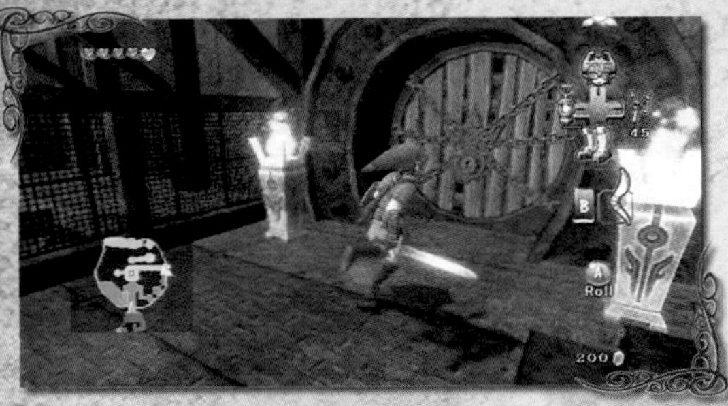

▲ Once past both the rotating platforms, you reach a locked door with a torch near it. Fortunately, you took the **Small Key** from the chest the Bulblins were guarding, so use it to exit.

Chamber 3: Domain of the Dodongos

▲ You appear in a smaller chamber. There is a fearsome lizard-like creature scuttling about below. This is the deadly, fire-breathing Dodongo! Turn right, and run down the ramp to the earthen floor to engage this menace.

Note

Look closely at this chamber's ceiling to see that sections of it are turquoise colored. You'll find out why in the next room.

Dodongo

Threat Meter

The Dodongos are a real problem when you don't have room to maneuver, as they breath fire in a wide arc toward you. They are impenetrable from the front, too; many an unwary adventurer has paid the price for doggedly attacking the head, when the tail is this beast's weak spot!

Until you receive a powerful ranged weapon, you must finish Dodongos with your sword: use the Z to target; you can target either the head or the tail. Choose either, then circle around the Dodongo. Retarget the tail.

The Dodongos have an Achilles heel, although it's actually their tail. Hack there for best results!

Three slices at the tail finish off this scaly threat, and you can round behind, then target, or jump or walk around while targeting. A spin attack works well at hitting multiple Dodongo tails. Keep targeting the back ends of the beasts!

Caution

The reason to enter the Goron Mines with the Hylian Shield becomes obvious if you try to attack a Dodongo using the Wooden Shield. After a couple of fiery attacks, the shield burns to a crisp, leaving you defenseless!

◄ With your first Dodongo finished, move to the metal plate embedded in the rock, and leap across the gap to the first of three round islands in the middle of this lava. Wait for the lava fountain to subside, and leap to the second island. Turn right, locate the metal plate, and leap from there to island platform three. Hop to an upper metal platform, where you fight a Dodongo; defeat him before you continue.

Tip

The difference between a Wooden Shield and the Hylian Shield are obvious. The Hylian Shield remains intact under even full heat and halitosis of the Dodongos' most vicious attacks. Shield block with impunity!

Note: Look toward the room's eastern part from here to see a large stone wall blocking your path. Head around this for the moment.

➤ Face east from the Dodongo platform and jump to a new island, wait for a final magma plume to fall, then land on solid ground in this chamber's northeast corner. There's a Heart in one of the crates on either side of this area.

◄ Spend a few moments introducing a Dodongo to the sharp end of your sword, and after the coast is clear, check the chain handle sealed into a large wall chunk. Grab it, and pull it backward. The wall moves along the groove in the ground! Let go, and the wall moves back to where it was originally. Pull the wall back as far as it can go.

▲ When the wall is back in the groove, let go, turn right and run to the metal plate, leaping to the island, and onto the platform where you fought the second Dodongo. Jump off this platform's southeastern corner, onto the third island, then turn left 90 degrees, and leap across to the central corridor, looking for metal strips in the earth to guide you.

➤ Roll down this corridor, keeping to the right so you squeeze past the spike-tipped wall before it closes. If you aren't fast enough, retrace your steps and try again. Once past the moving wall, open the door and exit.

Traversing the islands while the lava fountains spit is treacherous. Here are some plans to help you:

1. The lava fountains erupt at the same time, for five seconds. They are dormant for three.
2. Look through the grated window when you've pulled the wall all the way back.
3. Three seconds into the eruption, let go. Run and you'll leap across the islands as the eruption finishes.
4. Waste no time in getting to the door. The wall takes 12 seconds to close. Keep rolling; you can make this with at least two seconds to spare!

Tip

Missing Links

1. Barrel and Crate Bashing

There are rocks, crates, and barrels on the way to the first Dodongo, and on the flat area nearby, as well as by the moving wall. Expect small cash prizes and Hearts as your reward for hitting the barrels and crates.

Chamber 4: Magnetic Pool

➤ Step through into a small connecting chamber containing water in front of you. A sturdy metal fence prevents you from swimming to the other side. Step off the metal platform's end, and into the water, and swim to the fence.

➤ Your way forward is blocked, so you must locate a different path by heading downward. Without a suit of Zora armor, you cannot swim underwater, so put on your **Iron Boots** and sink to the pool's bottom! Slowly clump through the gap in the fence.

◄ An oxygen meter appears below your energy bar, but don't worry about that yet; you have plenty of time. You can't access the door on this room's opposite side if you swim to the surface, so clump forward, toward a ground switch. Take off your boots if you're moving too slowly, then put them on when you're over the switch.

Enemies Encountered

Dodongo

Characters Encountered

Gor Amato

Ooccoo

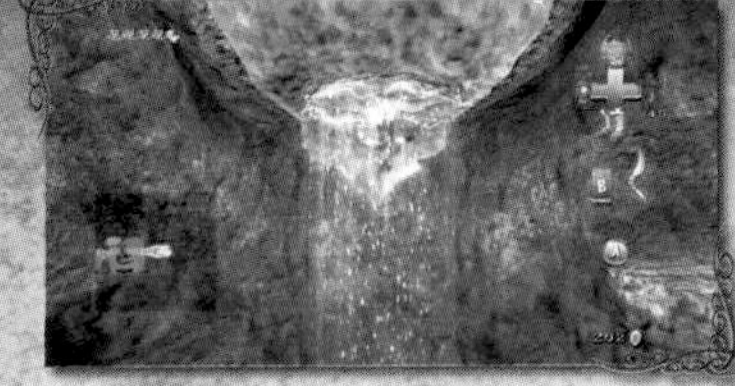

➤ The switch activates a magnetic beam that sucks you up and onto the turquoise channel on this room's ceiling. This is also magnetic, and you can walk here, upside down, as long as you're wearing the boots. Don't take them off! Walk up and around to the exit door so you're standing right side up, and head into the elder's chamber.

Chamber 5: Gor Amoto's Shrine Room

◄ Step forward into the chamber, which has the familiar look of Gor Coron's wrestling ring. An exceptionally old Goron is standing with the help of a cane. His head has taken the shape of a tiny, steaming volcano! This is the room of Gor Amoto, Goron elder.

Gor Amoto:

Incredibly ancient, Gor Amoto appears to you only briefly. Shaky, and emitting steam from his head and back, he is the fourth most powerful elder in Goron society. He is easygoing and short, and he carries a device to help you on your way.

◄ Speak with this steaming Goron and the fine old fellow wishes you well on your quest. In fact, he's extra helpful, as he provides you with a **Key Shard** after you talk to him! The others are entrusted to the two other elders you've yet to meet.

Key Shard
You got a **Key Shard**! You need all three Key Shards to return the Big Key to its original shape.

◄ After you take the Key Shard from Gor Amoto, he says you must merge it with two others to form a key that opens the room where **Darbus** is being held. You can find the Key Shard, and how many of the three pieces you've collected, on your **Dungeon Map** menu.

Treasure Chest: When you finish with Gor Amoto, step off his ring and open that chest behind him. You now can pore over both floors of this dungeon using the map.

Treasure Chest #3: Dungeon Map

Dungeon Map
You got the **Dungeon Map**!

◄ **Treasure Chest:** Hold on! Gor Amoto has a second chest in this room, too. Behind the first chest, head up the three steps onto the wooden shrine platform, and check out the chest in front of the hieroglyphic wall. Open it for a Rupee reward!

Treasure Chest #4: Red Rupee (20)

➤ The shrine holds a brightly colored gem, but you can't grab it, no matter how hard you try! It's time to leave this place, but you must climb up to the second floor. Use the ladder to the shrine's right.

➤ Climb to the top, and turn right. Run along the upper ledge, overlooking the wrestling ring, and inspect the pots by the upper exit. One of them is shaking suspiciously. Pick it up to discover that strange old bird, Ooccoo, again! When you're done, exit via the doorway to the right of her pot.

Ooccoo
You reunited with **Ooccoo**! This kind character can let you out of dungeons and return you to where you were.

Missing Links

1. Pottery Pulverizing
Although Gor Amoto doesn't allow weapons in this room, you can still smash his collection of pots to the right of the shrine. There's a Heart in one of them. Up by Ooccoo, one of the pots holds a green Rupee, too!

2. Rock and Roll!

Finally! After receiving nothing from most of your previous rock lifting, if you pry up the rock near the upper exit, you discover three Hearts inside! What a bonus!

1 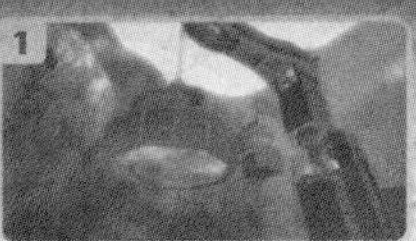
2 
3 
4 
5 
6

Task 3: Journey to the Mine Loading Docks

Enemies Encountered

Torch Slug

Chamber 4: First Return to Magnetic Pool

➤ You're above the lower entrance to Gor Amoto's shrine room, and that rumble you hear is the magnet working. This allows you to scale the magnetic walls on either side of the chamber. Don your **Iron Boots**, and walk on either side of the wall!

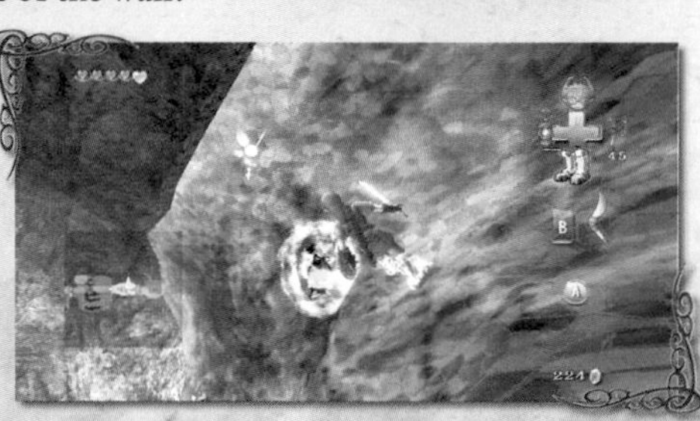

➤ During your stride along the wall, keep the boots on, or you'll fall into the pool and have to retrace your steps. One wall has two Torch Slugs, while the other has one; choose either. Target the first of these creatures, and hack it with your sword. Firing at it from range is ineffective; you'll put the Torch Slug out for a few seconds with the Boomerang, and there's no effect from the Slingshot.

Tip: To walk faster along the magnetic strips lining much of this dungeon, Z target an enemy, and sword-swing. Unlike your walking, this doesn't slow down, and you can move slightly faster. But only slightly!

➤ When you finish traversing the magnetic wall, put away your boots (make sure you're on firm ground, or can slide there), and open the upper door.

Chamber 3: First Return to Domain of the Dodongos

➤ You're on the roof of the corridor where you pulled the moving wall. Optionally break open a barrel for an additional Heart, then run forward to the roof's end, where there's a floor switch. Do **not** drop down, or you'll have to journey back here! When you're at the roof's end, step onto the floor switch, use your boots, and you're flipped upside down, onto the magnetic ceiling.

Tip: Keep those boots on! Don't take them off until you reach the upper exit of this chamber, or you'll fall.

➤ As you're upside down, you may be disorientated, but don't worry; target the Torch Slug and head for it with your sword waving! Head north, past the magnetic beam toward two more Torch Slugs, and give them a taste of cold steel.

➤ **Treasure Chest**: This trail of Torch Slugs is the clue to locating a chest, in the northwest alcove, accessible only via the magnetic ceiling. When you can drop onto the metal floor, do so. Then open that chest: the result is well worth it!

Treasure Chest #5: Piece of Heart

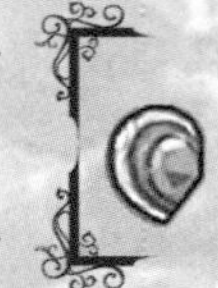

Piece of Heart
You got a **Piece of Heart**! Collect **three more** for another full Heart Container.
Piece of Heart #7 of 45.

➤ With the Piece of Heart stored, don't make the mistake of dropping off this ledge! You must exit via the ceiling, so put your **Iron Boots** back on and walk up the wall next to the chest, around and onto the ceiling. Then swing the camera behind you.

➤ Slowly stomp to the magnetic beam in the middle of the ceiling, then past it, heading in a southeasterly direction. Any other route stops at a dead end. You'll spot a Torch Slug in the corner; target and slice it!

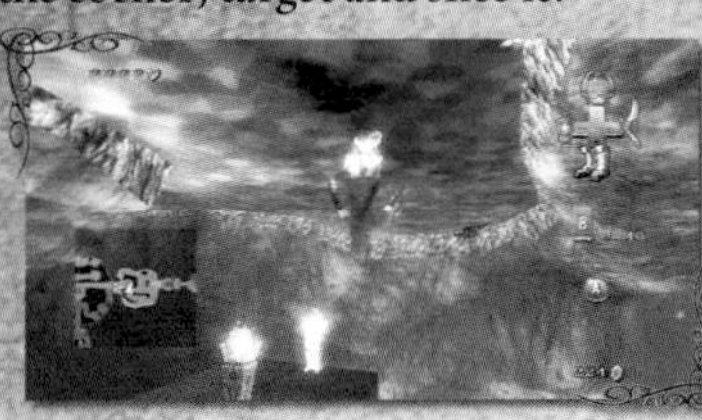

◄ Continue around the corner until the path splits. Take the right heading in a curve toward the western middle exit; target a Torch Slug to slice, then keep your boots moving as you slowly curve to the right. You're heading for a small platform with two bright torches burning. Slay the nearby Torch Slug first, if you wish. Steer yourself above and between the torches, and drop. Don't do this too early and fall to the first floor! Now you can exit via the second floor door.

Chamber 2: First Return to Volcano Forge

◄ Although still counted on your map as being on the first floor, this is the upper section of the Volcano Forge you couldn't reach earlier. Make short work of the barrels next to the entrance door (they are empty), then run forward, toward the gantry ramp and central magnet.

A massive spin slices into four Bulblin warriors at once! This is the only way to teach these fiends a lesson.

Head down the ramp and around to the floor switch guarded by four Bulblins. Bring out your sword and begin a frantic battle, remembering to block, and using that spin attack! Finish your foes with a leaping strike, then move over to the floor switch.

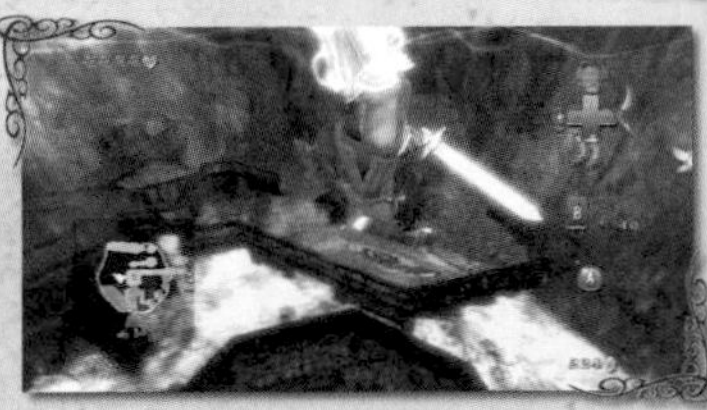

➤ Don those Iron Boots and activate the floor switch. A massive **magnet crane** grinds into action above you, moving around the volcano interior in a half-circle. Take your boots off, and run west to the octagonal platform, then put your boots on again. The magnet swings around and picks you up. Don't fall!

◄ Face east and when the magnet swings to the north, lose your boots and drop onto the octagonal platform in the volcano's north part. Draw your sword, and stride up the ramp.

◄ Two Bulblin warriors guard a large octagonal platform linked to the one you landed on; storm this area with your sword drawn, and make short work of them. A shield bash followed by a leaping skewering is another great way to finish these foes.

Fire Keese

Threat Meter

It's easy for you to ignore or deal with the Fire Keeses who are flapping about this chamber; the tactics are identical to defeating them as they were when you faced the non-fiery cousins in Faron Province; Ⓩ target and slice, or shoot with a ranged weapon.

Attack the Keeses along with the Bulblins; ranged combat or jumping slices are effective.

◄ Stand on the floor switch the two Bulblins were guarding, and activate it with your **Iron Boots**. Another giant magnet crane rumbles into life. Stay where you are, and the crane lifts you upside down and swings around to this zone's second floor part.

Chamber 2: Volcano Forge (Second Floor)

Note: This is the same chamber as you were previously in. The difference is that you're higher up, on the second floor.

➤ Drop on the north metal ledge, and face off with two more Bulblin warriors. Slash them to dispatch them, then optionally tackle the breakable scenery. Exit via the door in the north wall. There are still unexplored areas above you to access later.

Missing Links

1. Pots, Barrels, and Crate Smashing

The various scenery hides useful items; mainly on the north gantry ledge near the exit. The barrel and pots to the right yield a Heart, while the cluster of objects on the other side give you a Heart and a blue Rupee (5).

Chamber 6: Diamond Switch Chambers

▲ You enter one chamber split into two segments with a sealed door between them. Investigate the southern chamber first, which is waterlogged and features a series of stepping stone islands leading to a sealed door of metal and blue-gray stonework. First though, fend off a Tektite attack!

Tektite (Red and Blue)

Threat Meter

Tektites can skate across bodies of water despite their size, but they aren't intelligent. They have only a single jumping attack that is damaging. Wait for the Tektites to congregate around you, and when the first jumps, execute the spin attack as it descends to knock it back and strike the nearby Tektites. One spin is all it takes to finish these foes! Expect blue Rupees (5) or Hearts from them.

Avoid the Tektite's dangerous leap that's tricky to dodge, or counter it with your finest swordplay—the spin attack!

Tip: Tektites in Hyrule Field are a good source of Heart-shaped energy if you run low.

◄ **Treasure Chest:** After you defeat the Tektite menace, check the room. The door ahead is closed, but there's something interesting in the pond's northwestern corner. Swim and drop using your **Iron Boots** to uncover a chest!

Treasure Chest #6: Small Key

Small Key

You got a **Small Key**! This opens a locked door, but only in this area.

➤ You can't strike the diamond-shaped switch above and left of the door by your Slingshot or Boomerang, so stay in the water, and swim to the southeastern area, where a large mesh fence stops you. Drop using your boots, and swim through the hole. There's no need to push the submerged metal crate; swim around the left side for a gap big enough to squeeze through. Then surface.

Enemies Encountered

Torch Slug

Bulblin Infantry

Fire Keese

Tektite

➤ Try some barrel and crate smashing, then climb up onto the higher rock floor and stomp on the floor switch with your boots. A magnetic beam activates near where you surfaced. Stride back there, and head up onto the ceiling.

➤ Stride northward while upside down and stuck to the ceiling, until you're above the metal floor, then drop to land on it. Run to this floor's edge, to the middle of the chamber, and activate a second floor switch near a small gantry plank.

Author Note

We attempted to hone our depth perception by dropping Link onto the upper metal floor as close to the edge as possible, and failed three times in succession. It's always better to estimate where the floor is, then take three more steps forward, as we found at great cost.

➤ The second floor switch creates another magnetic beam, but this is different from the ones you previously encountered. It shoots horizontally from the west wall. The trick here is to move to the gantry plank's edge, put your boots on, then fall off. The boots cause the beam to suck you into the wall, instead of falling into the water.

➤ **Treasure Chest:** Walk right along the crescent-shaped magnetic wall area, and remove your boots to land atop the blue-gray stone wall, on a metal roof. Next to a torch is a small chest; open it to claim the red Rupee inside.

Treasure Chest #7: Red Rupee (20)

➤ You can smash the adjacent pot, but the real point of taking this laborious path is to stand near the diamond switch, currently colored blue. Slash the switch with your sword, and it turns yellow, indicating the door in the north wall is opening. You have five seconds, so run!

Jump off the metal roof onto the rocky ground where the door has opened, and dash through. If you fall into the water, or stand around, the door closes after five seconds, and you must slash the diamond switch again, which could result in retracing your steps!

➤ The door closes behind you, and you're in this chamber's northern part. There's another diamond switch in the southeast corner if you wish to head back south, but that isn't necessary. Instead, concentrate on slicing and dicing the two incoming Bulblin warriors.

Beamos

Threat Meter

The two Bulblin warriors aren't the real threat in this chamber. More worrisome are the rotating stone monoliths at the top of the ramp. These are guardian creatures called Beamoses. When the "eye" spots you, it launches a fire jet that can hurt and knock you off balance! Swords, Slingshots, and Boomerangs are all ineffective. Beamoses are currently indestructible. Don't head up the ramp yet, and if you do, use your shield to block their attacks. Use this time to figure out how far the fire beams come out at you; around 10 feet. You're safe if you stand beyond this range, or if the Beamos is looking away from you.

Currently, Beamoses are indestructible and fire a concentrated beam of fire at you. Block with your shield, and find some way to shut down those eyes!

▲ **Treasure Chest**: Ignore the Beamos duo and head east instead to the magnetic wall area. Don those Iron Boots, and trek up the wall, before making a right turn and striding south. You're looking for a chest in the chamber's corner, on a small metal ledge. The result is worth your slow stomping!

Treasure Chest #8: Piece of Heart

Piece of Heart
You got a **Piece of Heart**! Collect **two more** for another full Heart Container. Piece of Heart #8 of 45.

➤ The time has come to escape! Drop to the ground, climb back up the magnetic wall, but turn left this time, and drop onto the metal ledge running along and above this chamber's northern part. Jump the gap to smash the pots, then draw your sword and slice the ropes holding the drawbridge up. Drop, head over the drawbridge, and use the Small Key you found back in the water to open the door.

Missing Links

1. Bashing Barrels and Floating Crates

South room: the barrels under the magnetic beam are mostly empty, save one with a Heart. Two of the floating crates though, which you can shatter only with the Boomerang, hold blue and yellow Rupees!

2. North Chamber Pottery

North room: the second of the two chambers where the menacing Beamoses reside has a cluster of pottery in the northwest area; this contains some Rupees and a Heart. Above this, on the upper ledge, is a second cluster of Rupee-holding pots.

Enemies Encountered

Bulblin Infantry

Beamos

Bulblin Archer

Task 4: Obtain the Second Key Shard from Gor Ebizo

Chamber 7: Mine Loading Docks

▲ You step into an extremely large, open area. So large in fact, that Bulblin archers, armed with flaming arrows, have taken up defensive positions on upper ledges. Optionally slice up a barrel to your left for a Heart, then head toward the gantry. Use the spin move to smash the rickety wooden planks preventing your progress.

◄ Ascend to the middle of the dock, walking along the wooden gantry. In the distance, Bulblins attempt to strike you with arrows. Their range is limited, so don't worry about them yet. Optionally head left to smash some pots.

◄ Now sidestep east to the ladder's top, and leap off into the water. You must thoroughly search this area, so run around the gantry's support struts, so you're facing west at water level, then jump into the water just right of a second ladder.

Gor Ebizo

➤ **Treasure Chest:** Ignore the arrows (unless you're remaining still, then shield block), and dive into the water. Use your Iron Boots to sink to the bottom, and investigate the underwater area's northwestern corner. Smash the wooden beams to gain access to a chest hidden under the supports of a small gantry island, and claim your prize!

Treasure Chest #9: Purple Rupee (50)

Purple Rupee

You got a **purple Rupee (50)**!

Note: You may not have the room to carry this purple Rupee in your wallet. Collect those bugs and visit Agitha in Castle Town to increase the girth of your wallet!

➤ Leave the chest, rise to the surface without your boots, and clamber back on the water-level platform, then climb up the nearby ladder facing south, or the other ladder toward the east. If you took the longer ladder, you're on the east-west wooden gantry within Bulblin archer range, so bring out your shield!

➤ Run up the wooden gantry ramp to a small rocky alcove where a Beamos is guarding a door. You can't reach the door or push the Beamos along the groove on which it sits. Instead, you must shield yourself or roll away from the beams it fires.

➤ **Treasure Chest:** Ignore the Beamos because you cannot defeat it. Instead, move right while facing it, to the alcove's corner, where you can kick open a chest to reveal a Small Key.

Treasure Chest #10: Small Key

Small Key

You got a **Small Key**! This opens a locked door, but only in this area.

▲ This key opens the door in the west wall, on the main gantry platform's far end. Head across there from this alcove, traversing the three narrow planks. Before you exit, turn north and check out the three Bulblins. If you haven't already, draw your Slingshot near the metal crate in the middle of the gantry platform, and arc in shots to hit each Bulblin, defeating them. You need to aim above their heads for the arcing shots to strike.

Caution: If you're standing behind a wooden object, such as the small crates on the platform near the exit, these catch fire and burn if a Bulblin arrow strikes them, as does your Wooden Shield. Tackle these archers from far range, where they can't reach you!

Caution: Before you leave, stand on the platform to this exit door's right, and look up at a high wooden structure above the heads of the Bulblins. There's mesh netting draped over the side. This is the location of a treasure chest that cannot be accessed at any time during this dungeon exploration. You must return to this dungeon with the Clawshot (which you receive in Dungeon 3) to access this area.

Missing Links

1. Barrels, Boxes, and Pottery Breaking

The scenery here is an excellent source of small Rupees and Hearts (and arrows after you pick up the Hero's Bow). Check them near the southern entrance, the gantry's western part. There are pots on either side of the Beamos, and two small crates on a small platform near the exit door (one holds a Heart).

1 2 3 4 5 6

Chamber 8: Mine Reservoir

➤ Unlock the door, and enter a large, rectangular chamber containing a couple of massive rotating platforms slowly turning. Don't investigate them yet. Turn right and jump off into the water; there are lower level items to locate! Swim around and climb on the reservoir's north bank, and defeat two Tektites.

Fishing

This is optional, but you can take a break from exploring and cast a fishing line into the reservoir from the eastern bank facing west. There are only Greengills to catch, but you can grab a Heart for each one you reel in!

➤ When you finish fishing, run up the metal ramp, optionally smashing the barrels and crates for a Rupee and Heart, and head to the entrance area. Stand between the two torches, wait for the rotating platform to stop, then hop on, and head across to the other side.

➤ The exits to this chamber are on the west and south wall, but you can't reach them yet. Instead, turn right and head up the metal ramp, then turn and stand on the small rusting platform overlooking a giant rotating platform filled with Goron symbols. Stop right there!

➤ You need to cross this platform heading west, but you cannot run to the other side without the platform rotating. Fortunately, there are magnetic squares embedded into the platform for you to stick to. The optimal method to cross is:

➤ Step 1: Run on the platform as it finishes rotating; dash early, and make sure the platform side shows the single magnetic square in the middle. The other side shows two magnetic squares, but this takes longer to traverse.

➤ Step 2: Run to the metallic square's edge, then put on your boots as the platform rotates. Stop where you are. When the platform rotates right side up, take off your boots early so you can run before the platform finishes rotating.

➤ Step 3: Run ahead, but aim for the platform's left corner, as this rotates up rather than down, giving you a spare second to reach the door at the opposite end. Run onto the solid metal floor, and enter this door.

Chamber 9: Gor Ebizo's Shrine Room

➤ Roll down the passage into the chamber, which has the familiar look of Gor Coron's wrestling ring. A hunched elderly Goron is standing with a weary expression on his face, and his back is slowly turning to stone! This is the room of Gor Ebizo, Goron elder.

Gor Ebizo:

Countless years have rendered the long-haired Gor Ebizo old and frail. He is the second most powerful elder in Goron society. He is also easygoing and short, and he carries a device you need to assemble. His fondest wish, is to work with some type of young entrepreneur selling wares to adventurers. Perhaps his wish will come true some day.

Enemies Encountered

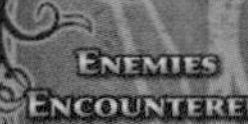

Beamos

Bulblin Archer

Tektite

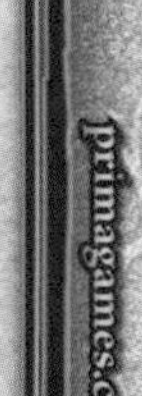

Task #4

Obtain the Second Key Shard from Gor Ebizo

Gor Ebizo

➤ Speak with this stone-cold Goron and you'll find he's still sprightly. He offers you good luck on your quest. In fact, he's extra helpful, as he provides you with the second Key Shard after you talk to him! You only need one more.

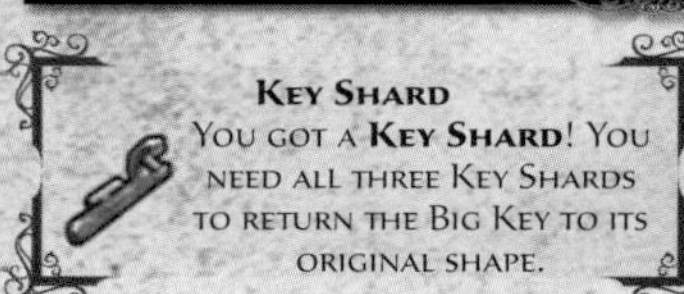

Key Shard
You got a **Key Shard**! You need all three Key Shards to return the Big Key to its original shape.

◄ **Treasure Chest**: When the conversation with Gor Ebizo ends, step off his ring and run around his chamber's left edge, onto the shrine platform's far side, and open a chest!

Treasure Chest #11: Yellow Rupee (10)

➤ Depart this shrine room by climbing up the ladder to the right of the shrine. At the top, turn right. Run along the upper ledge, overlooking the wrestling ring, and exit via the upper door.

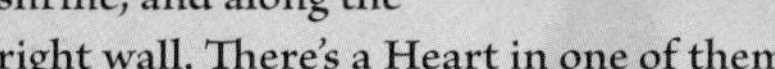

Missing Links

1. Pottery Pulverizing

Although Gor Ebizo doesn't allow weapons in this room, you can still smash his collection of pots to the right of the shrine, and along the right wall. There's a Heart in one of them.

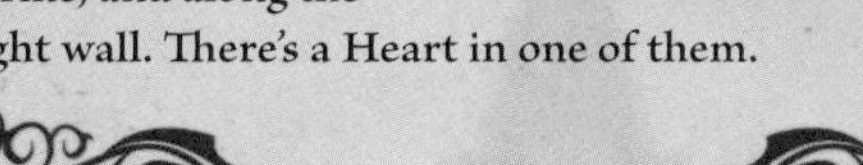

Task 5: Battle the Feared Goron Dangoro for the Hero's Bow

Chamber 8: First Return to Mine Reservoir

➤ You're back inside the large Mine Reservoir, but on an upper doorway ledge. The only place to explore is the door on the southern wall, so don your Iron Boots and stride along the magnetic wall to the corner. Drop down; don't waste time trudging to the magnetic strip's end.

Author Note

Once again, removing our Iron Boots too soon resulted in Link landing not on the southern ledge, but in the water. We then had to repeat the maneuvering across the rotating platforms to Gor Ebizo's shrine and back again. Don't repeat our mistake!

◄ **Treasure Chest**: Land on a wooden ledge right next to a chest and kick it open; the prize isn't going to set your heart a-flutter, but you're still making money in this expedition. Head along the ledge toward the south wall's exit, and open the door.

Treasure Chest #12: Yellow Rupee (10)

Missing Links

1. Barrels and Crate Smashing

If you're looking for a couple of extra energy Hearts, spin into the scenery on this exit ledge before you leave.

Chamber 10: Dangoro's Stomping Grounds

◄ Enter this circular lava pit, but beware of the great Goron awaiting on the opposite side! Optionally bust the pots and wooden containers, and do it now, as you won't be able to return here in a moment. Stride toward the circular arena, and watch as the massive Goron, who obviously didn't get the Gor Coron memo, rises up to challenge you, then butt-stomps the arena into the lava pit below!

1

2

3

4

5
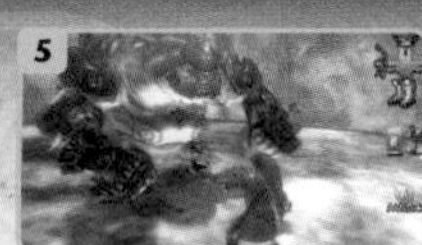
6

Dangoro

Threat Meter

He's powerful and coated in armor, but he feasted too heavily on Bullbo. Dangoro's weak spot is his stomach!

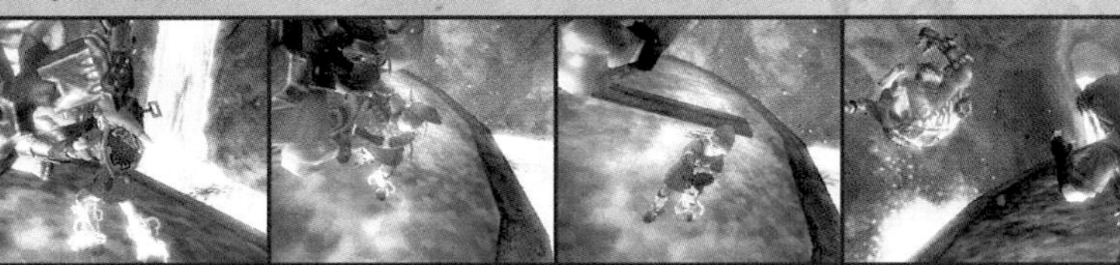

Step 1: Fighting Dangoro is all about timing. Run within sword-swiping range, and block his attacks. When he raises both arms, target and slash that stomach with three strikes, and finish with a spin attack. If you hit with all attacks, Dangoro spins into a ball.

Step 2: Don your **Iron Boots** or you won't have a hope of defeating this hulking brute! When Dangoro rolls into a ball, he attempts to rumble straight over you. When you're prompted, grab Dangoro with your boots on, swing him around, and throw him across the arena! He flies off to the arena's edge. Combat begins again.

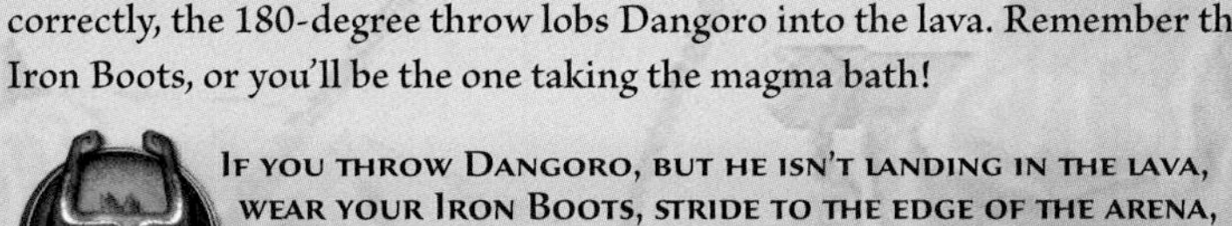

Step 3: Run to the arena's edge, and turn so your back is to the edge of it and you're near the lava pit below. Dangoro raises one arm for a massive punch attack; this is your cue to attempt a second four-hit combo with the spin finish! After Dangoro rolls into a ball, grab and throw him; if you positioned yourself correctly, the 180-degree throw lobs Dangoro into the lava. Remember those Iron Boots, or you'll be the one taking the magma bath!

Tip: If you throw Dangoro, but he isn't landing in the lava, wear your Iron Boots, stride to the edge of the arena, turn and face Dangoro, then attempt the takedown steps shown.

It takes three dips in the lava pool for Dangoro to realize who he's dealing with! Dangoro's helmet flies off, and he understands why you're here: to reach and help the Goron patriarch. He offers you a weapon in exchange for your help, then raises the arena to connect with the path.

▲ You may be disorientated after this battle, so check your map to ensure you're heading south, and stride off the arena, through the door that's now unlocked. Or, head north to claim the three Hearts from the scenery, if you need them.

Chamber 11: Dangoro's Treasure Hole

▲ **Treasure Chest**: Step into a small, circular lava pool with a narrow stone pathway. There is a treasure chest in its center. Dangoro wasn't kidding; pry open the chest for a piece of useful equipment!

Treasure Chest #13: Hero's Bow

Hero's Bow
You got the **Hero's Bow**! This Goron treasure once belonged to a hero of legend.

Enemies Encountered

Dangoro

Characters Encountered

Gor Liggs

The Hero's Bow

The Hero's Bow is one of the most useful and important pieces of equipment you'll ever receive! Set it to Ⓑ on the ⊖ screen. When you wish to use the Hero's Bow, press Ⓑ. Aim at targets by moving the Wii Remote, then press Ⓑ to shoot. You can hold up to 30 arrows.

With the new Hero's Bow in your inventory, you may be tempted to use it on the Torch Slug that dropped from the ceiling, but sword slashes are easier. Destroy the crates for a Rupee and Heart too. The Torch Slug gives you more arrows. When you're done, exit via the south door. Aim your target at either piece of rope, and fire an arrow to cut the drawbridge down.

Here are some useful tips for using the Hero's Bow:

- Practice using the Hero's Bow immediately. You have an exceptional range, but using this is like using the Slingshot.
- Your range is longer than enemies with bows, such as the Bulblins. This means you can stay at range and fire without being struck.
- You can fire at nearby foes by Ⓩ button targeting them with your Hero's Bow equipped. This is an excellent way to shoot foes who are near, but you can't reach (such as those above you).
- Learn how to move in first-person aiming view! Enter this viewpoint, then hold down Ⓩ. Keep it held to move left and right. You automatically stop at the edges of platforms, too!
- First-person aiming and moving is the key to using this item. It means you can dodge a foe firing at you, while keeping it targeted and at range!
- Later into your adventure, you can combine arrows with bombs for an explosive projectile.

Tips

- You can also find "big" and "giant" quivers that hold 60 and 100 arrows respectively. This won't happen for a while though!

Task 6: Complete the Key Shard from Gor Liggs

Chamber 12: Beamos Star Chamber

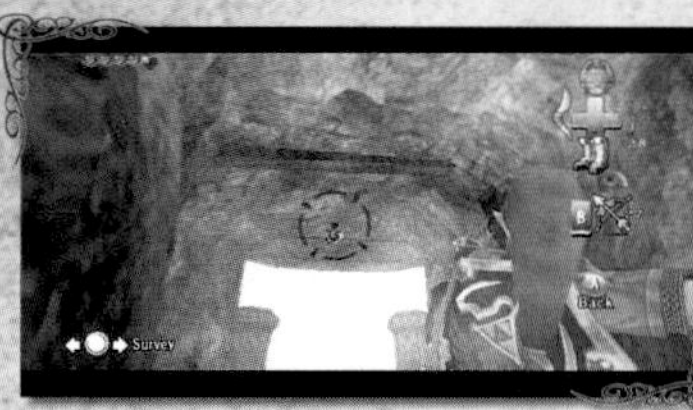

➤ Step over the drawbridge, and check the ceiling of the room ahead. A Torch Slug offers archery practice. Drop it, then run into the star-shaped chamber. Beamos monoliths block each "point" of the star, so head north.

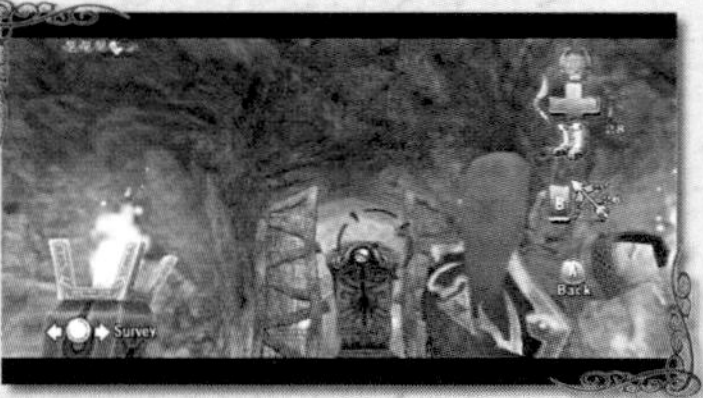

➤ The Beamoses are dormant. That is, until you reach the one inside the small northern tunnel. Head toward him until he wakes up, then step back a few feet, and raise your Hero's Bow. Make sure you're out of his beam range, then fire an arrow into that eye! This is the preferred method of dispatching Beamoses!

Tip

Whenever you encounter these foes from this point forward, bring out your Hero's Bow.

➤ Turn south, and stop at this chamber's entrance. The beams of the two nearest Beamoses can't reach you if you're standing in the middle (as shown). Take aim and shoot each of the seven Beamoses from this position until all are smoldering! Enter the chamber and ransack the goods the Beamoses were guarding; push or pull the Beamoses in front of the points, and run around them.

1

2

3

4

5

6

➤ **Treasure Chest:** The items in the northeast, northwest, southeast, and southwest corners are all optional, but you should definitely move the Beamos out of the way in the chamber's eastern point. A chest holding the **Compass** is here.

Treasure Chest #14: Compass

Compass
You got the **Compass**! This handy tool shows you where to find objects hidden in this dungeon.

➤ Move to the opposite side and maneuver the western Beamos out of the way. He was blocking a doorway, which is your next chamber to visit.

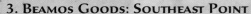

Missing Links

1. Beamos Goods: Northwest Point

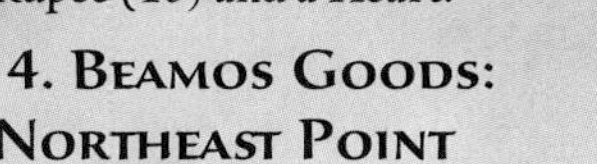

There are four barrels to smash. One holds a yellow Rupee (10).

2. Beamos Goods: Southwest Point

Push the Beamos out of the way. Barrels and pots hold a single green Rupee (1).

3. Beamos Goods: Southeast Point

Push the Beamos out of the way. Barrels and a pot hold a yellow Rupee (10) and a Heart.

4. Beamos Goods: Northeast Point

Two barrels and a Torch Slug are here. A Heart is in one of the barrels.

Chamber 13: Gor Liggs's Shrine Room

➤ Roll down the passage into the chamber, which has the familiar look of Gor Coron's wrestling ring. A thin and elderly but sprightly looking Goron with tribal paint and tattoos is meditating. This is the room of Gor Liggs, Goron elder!

Gor Liggs:

Another old Goron is the third most important one, Gor Liggs, who spends his time listening to trancelike, melodic beats in his meditation chamber. He doesn't take life too seriously and is a mellow fellow, but his attitude shows he has had fascinating life experiences. He believes in one love and in the potent healing powers of Hot Springs Water.

➤ Speak with this meditative elder, and he provides a Key Shard and assembles the **Big Key** for you!

Big Key
You collected all three Key Shards and completed the **Big Key**! Hurry to the boss.

➤ **Treasure Chest:** When the conversation with Gor Liggs finishes, he returns to his meditation, and you can step off his ring and run forward up the ramp, then to the middle of the shrine platform to open another chest! Leave this chamber the way you came.

Treasure Chest #15: Purple Rupee (50)

Missing Links

1. Pottery Pulverizing

Although Gor Ebizo doesn't allow weapons in this room, you can still smash his collection of pots left and right of the shrine. There's a Heart in one of them. You can also smash the rocks near the seating, but they don't hold anything.

2. Dodongo Wall Skins

During your pottery-smashing, did you notice that Gor Liggs has covered parts of his wall in Dodongo skins? They make the perfect addition to a Goron shrine! He also has additional hand print plaques.

Enemies Encountered

Torch Slug

Beamos

Task #6
Complete the Key Shard from Gor Liggs

Task 7: Search for the Great Volcanic Passage

Chamber 12: First Return to Beamos Star Chamber

➤ Exit into the Beamos Star Chamber, and head south, toward the last Beamos you haven't moved yet. Grab and shift it so you can squeeze in the doorway behind the monolith, and open the unlocked door beyond.

Chamber 14: Stalactite Cavern

➤ Upon entering this irregularly shaped cavern, you spot groups of Torch Slugs stuck to the ceiling, and a diamond switch inside a small grotto on a far-off wall. Step forward, walking along toward a square-shaped piece of mesh wall. Spin attack three Fire Keeses.

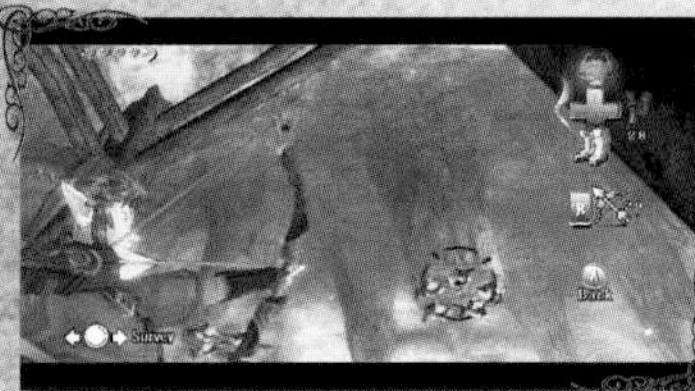

➤ When you defeat the Keeses, bring out your **Hero's Bow** and aim it up at the flat stalactite in the middle of the chamber. There are five Torch Slugs here; hit each one with an arrow. Move left and drop five more Torch Slugs on another stalactite. Aim at the curved rock wall beyond that and dispatch two final Torch Slugs.

➤ Roll or spin into the square piece of fence, and it falls forward, allowing you to reach the initial passage's far end. Turn left, then look up, and fire at three Torch Slugs. Or, leap across to the rock ledge, bring out your shield, and spin attack when they drop.

Watch out! These Dodongos are difficult to dispatch on the tiny rock island. You may be knocked about if you don't dispatch one from range!

➤ Take out your Hero's Bow and target the tail of one of two Dodongos prowling the stone island in the middle of the cavern. Dispatch one with arrows, then jump and defeat the second with your usual tail-end tactics. Providing you shot all the Torch Slugs on the ceiling, continue across.

➤ Leap and cling to the edge of the next, smaller island, then climb onto it and jump to the northern part of the cavern's ledge. The exit is sealed using the same mechanism you saw earlier; you need to activate a diamond switch to leave.

➤ Run past the sealed exit to the southeastern corner. Stand on the floor switch, bring out those trusty Iron Boots, and activate the magnetic beam. After you're on the ceiling, spin the camera around to see where you're going.

➤ Those Dodongos have learned new tricks! One is advancing toward you on the ceiling, so draw your **Hero's Bow** and fire it three times at the tail. The Dodongo is struck, loses grip, and drops (upward) to the ground below! Of course, you could aim at the Dodongo from the ground, but that isn't quite as satisfying.

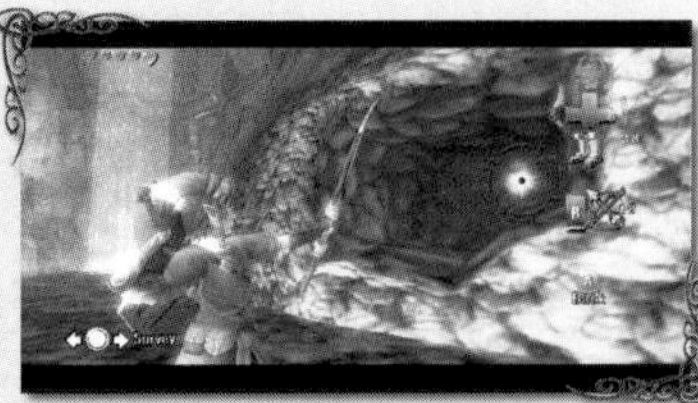

➤ Clump along in your Iron Boots until the grotto opening appears on your right. Spin the camera around and locate the diamond switch. Draw your **Hero's Bow** and fire at the switch. It turns yellow. You have only five seconds to exit before it turns back again! When you fire, lose the boots, drop, and move to open the door.

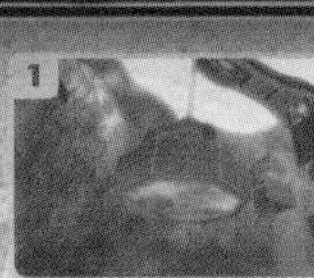

Missing Links

1. Barrels of Fun

The barrels near the entrance hold a Heart and arrows. Fire at the Torch Slugs before you break these open, and you'll obtain more arrows. The Barrels after the mesh fence also hold a single Heart. The barrel in the north wall's alcove holds a blue Rupee (5). The barrel and pots near the exit have two Hearts to claim.

Chamber 2: First Return to Volcano Forge (Second Floor)

➤ **Treasure Chest**: Although this is the fourth time you've been in the volcano's crater, it's only the second time at this height. You arrive at the topmost part of the chamber, along the west wall. Turn right and leap the gap. Optionally smash pots for a Heart and arrows, then pry open your next treasure chest.

Treasure Chest #16: Purple Rupee (50)

➤ Leap back and run past the entrance door, to a jutting ledge, and look across at a drawbridge. Bring out that **Hero's Bow** and aim it at the rope, dropping the drawbridge. Head across, and once again, use the Iron Boots to summon a magnet.

➤ Ride this magnet crane (the third in this chamber) 90 degrees to the north ledge where you were dropped off earlier. Check your map to spot a couple of chambers in the northeast part of this dungeon you couldn't reach. No so with the Hero's Bow! Optionally smash the pots and barrels for Rupees and Hearts, and attack the two reappearing Fire Keeses. Leave via the north door.

Chamber 6: First Return to Diamond Switch Chambers

➤ Enter the chamber with the diamond switch, and prepare for combat! Not with the Tektites, who have disappeared, but with two large Water Toadpolis.

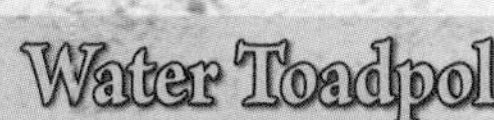

Water Toadpoli

Threat Meter

The aquatic versions of the Toadpoli, Water Toadpolis swim faster but can be dispatched in the same way. Shield block and wait until the Water Toadpoli spits out its projectile, then bounce it back. Or, use an arrow, which is faster, but less satisfying!

Yes, you can maneuver about for minutes, attempting to bounce spitballs back at a Water Toadpoli, or you can pierce his belly with an arrow!

➤ Hop over the stepping stones after you defeat the Water Toadpoli. Stop at the sealed door entrance. Use your **Hero's Bow** to activate the diamond switch for a quick exit!

Author Note

Naturally, we forgot about the ranged power of the Hero's Bow and trekked across the entire room using the Iron Boots and the magnetic ceiling.

Enemies Encountered

Beamos

Torch Slug

Fire Keese

Dodongo

Water Toadpoli

➤ Head into this linked chamber's northern part, and bring the full weight of your sword into the hides of the two Bulblins who challenge you. Stop at the foot of the ramp.

➤ The Beamoses, who troubled you earlier, are no match for your **Hero's Bow**, so fire a shot into each eye, and stroll between their steaming hulks, up to the drawbridge, and exit.

Author Note

Quick challenge: Fire at and strike one in the eye, then the other, before they both rotate their eyes out of your range. You need quick reflexes!

Chamber 7: First Return to Mine Loading Dock

➤ Smash the barrels for Hearts and arrows, then head up the wooden gantry ramp with your sword drawn. A Bulblin prowls this area, and he may surprise you. Continue up the gantry, and stop at the first left turn.

➤ It's time for precision shooting! There are more Bulblin archers here this time, so aim and dispatch them before they even know you're here. From the gantry's lower part, turn and aim up and right at the Bulblin archer on the metal structure. Turn and aim at the second archer on the metal structure of the west rock wall.

You can stay in this position, without any of the archers seeing you, and aim from right to left at the Bulblin to the right of the magnet arm, the group of three on the upper wooden platform, and the Bulblin left of the trio.

➤ The scenery has reappeared since your last visit, and the pots on the western end of the docks now break open to reveal arrows. Grab these, then stop at the dock junction area where the two small crates are. Two explosive crates have appeared. Detonate them from range with one arrow; don't strike them with your sword.

One in the eye for the denizens of the dark! You can finally shift that Beamos.

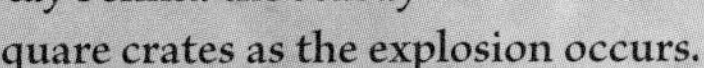

➤ Move up to the dock's upper part, at the same level as the western exit. Turn right and stop at the alcove containing the rotating Beamos. Strike it down with one arrow, then move in and grab the defunct monolith, pulling it out of the way. A rock wall behind it rumbles open to reveal a new path!

➤ Run to the ramp's top, appearing on the loading area's eastern part, and watch out for two Bulblin archers. Their first shots strike an explosive crate. Stay behind the sturdy square crates as the explosion occurs.

➤ Aim at the explosive crate that's behind the two Bulblins, and shoot one arrow straight and true. It lodges in the crate and explodes, dispatching both Bulblins, who fall off the rise on which they were standing. Head northward, toward the giant magnet crane. There's a Heart in a pot at the foot of where the Bulblins fell.

➤ You've found the floor switch for the magnet crane in this area! Use your Iron Boots to stomp on it. The crane arm rumbles into life. It spins back and forth, so head west, and jump off the gap in the metal fence, landing on the square platform. Put your boots on, and you're sucked up onto the magnet.

1  2  3  4  5  6 

➤ Turn and look at the giant drawbridge in this area's northeast corner, and aim an arrow at it as you travel upside down to this new area. Rip the rope with an arrow, and the bridge falls, allowing you access out of here! If you drop down without activating the drawbridge, you land in the water and have to retrace your steps.

➤ Move to the northwestern dirt area, opposite the drawbridge, and rummage around smashing pots and obtaining Hearts and arrows. One of the pots in the far-right corner contains a Fairy! Capture it with an empty Bottle; you should have two Bottles handy. Exit via the door behind the fallen drawbridge.

Fairy

You caught a **Fairy** in a Bottle! When you fall in combat, this faithful friend gives you Hearts.

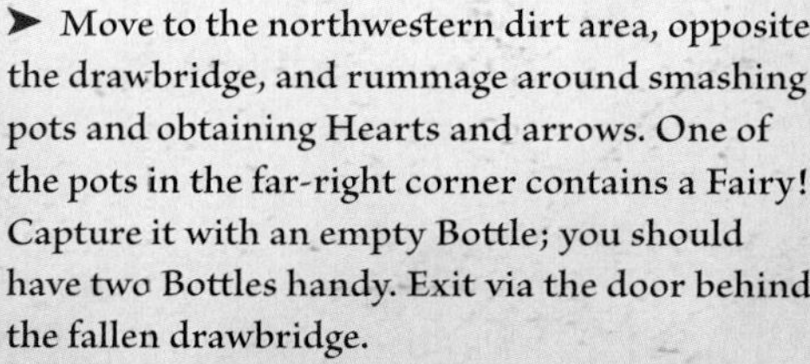

Note: Your Compass may be telling you there's still a chest you haven't opened in this area, and this is true. However, you cannot currently access it. It is high above you, and you must return here after Dungeon 3 with the Clawshot to obtain the item inside!

Enemies Encountered

Bulblin Archer

Beamos

Task 8: Change the Fate of the Gorons: Fight Fyrus!

Chamber 15: Grand Volcanic Passage

◄ Stride into a lava pool with a metal ledge wrapping around it, and smash the pots as you enter. A Heart and arrows fall out, allowing you to use the **Hero's Bow**. Aim, then **hold** Z so you can move and aim.

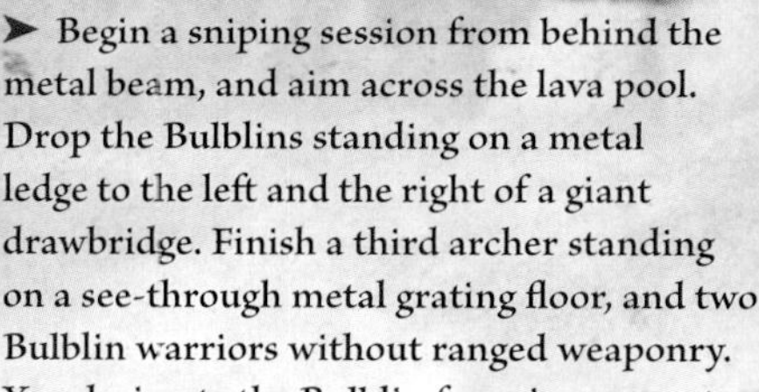

➤ Begin a sniping session from behind the metal beam, and aim across the lava pool. Drop the Bulblins standing on a metal ledge to the left and the right of a giant drawbridge. Finish a third archer standing on a see-through metal grating floor, and two Bulblin warriors without ranged weaponry. You decimate the Bulblin force in moments using this plan!

➤ Run down the ramp, smashing pots on the way for more arrows and a Heart. Find more arrows in one of two pots just right of the drawbridge entrance. When you're standing on the see-through metal grate floor, look south, and look up!

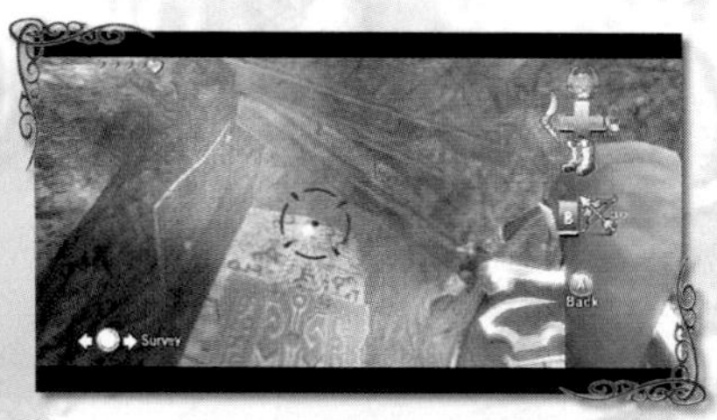

◄ Pierce the rope with an arrow to drop the drawbridge, then adjust your aim as seven Bulblin solders trot toward you. It's a trap! If you're fast, you can rattle off arrows and catch them before they reach you. You can Z target and run about them, plugging them with arrows! Or, switch to your trusty sword and slice your way out of this fix.

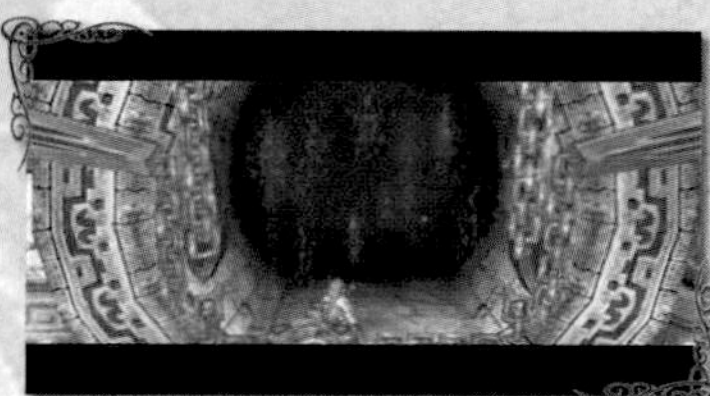

▲ After you defeat the Bulblin welcoming committee, head up the passage to the giant door and produce the **Big Key** you assembled earlier. The lock spins apart and drops, and the door is shoved open. It's time to face the possessed patriarch!

Missing Links

1. Pulverizing Pottery

There are four groups of pottery in this last grand entranceway, behind the columns. They yield a couple of Hearts and some arrows, so grab them before you engage the boss.

Characters Encountered

Midna

Darbus

Chamber 16: Boss Battle!

Twilit Igniter: Fyrus

You enter a serene and green circular chamber, where you can hear some monstrously heavy breathing. Restrained by two huge chains is a black form. Only a tusk-shaped carapace head can be seen. A gem in the carapace glow. The beast awakens!

Roaring and growling, the monster struggles at the huge chains before bursting out of them and bellowing in rage at you. The previously dark form bursts into fire, with flames coursing up and down the massive figure. Fyrus, the twilit alter ego of Darbus, is here!

Step 1: Approach combat with Fyrus methodically, and use the **Hero's Bow** almost exclusively. First, flee the beast as he strides forward toward you. When he stops, he lets out a fire wave that burns you and can destroy the pots surrounding the combat arena.

Step 2: Get far enough away, but face Fyrus, then aim one arrow into that brightly lit gem between his eyes. You can tell when you hit, as he reels back and the gem sparkles.

Step 3: While he's stunned and stumbling about, run to Fyrus's feet, and pick up one of the trailing chains with your hands. When you grab it, don your **Iron Boots** or he'll toss you around. Pull back in the opposite direction.

Step 4: Fyrus takes a tumble and falls onto the floor for a moment or two. Seize this chance!

Step 5: Remove your boots, run around to the fallen Fyrus, and begin a sword combo targeted at the gem on his carapace head. Continue this until the beast rises to his feet.

Threat Meter

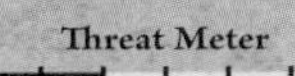

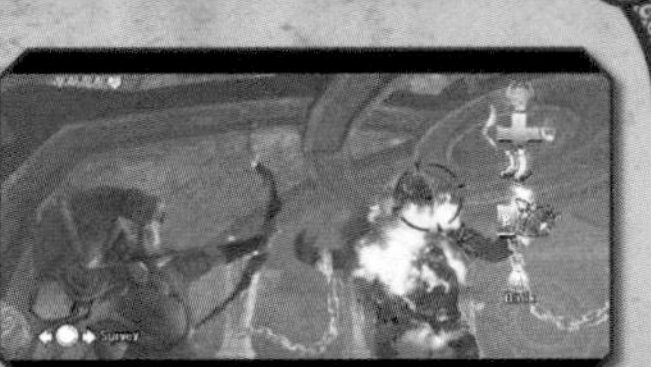

Rage and heat may be consuming this bellowing fellow, but he's confused by ranged attacks on his twinkling weak spot.

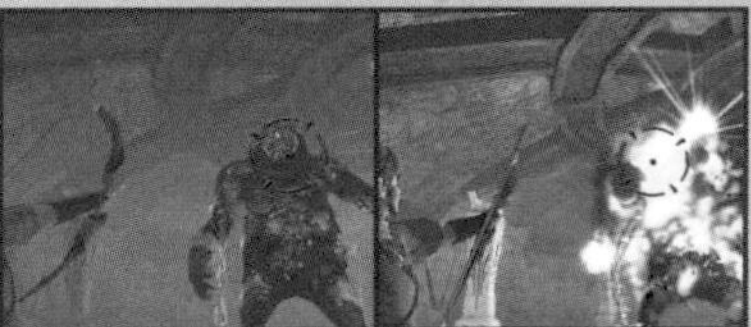

Step 6: To defeat Fyrus with extreme skill, watch him as he sets himself aflame, but have your **Hero's Bow** already targeted at the gem weak spot. When Fyrus regains strength, the gem glows orange. This is the first opportunity to stick an arrow in there!

Repeat steps 3, 4, 5, and 6. If you're quick with your arrow shooting, Fyrus can't attack you! As long as you combo the gem with your sword as Fyrus lies on the ground, it takes three rounds to defeat him.

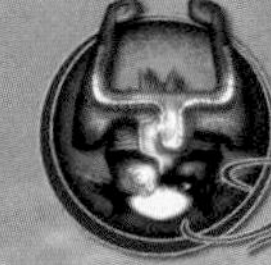

Tip

You should have a **Fairy** to help you if you lose all your energy. Or find and smash pots around the arena's perimeter for Hearts and arrows.

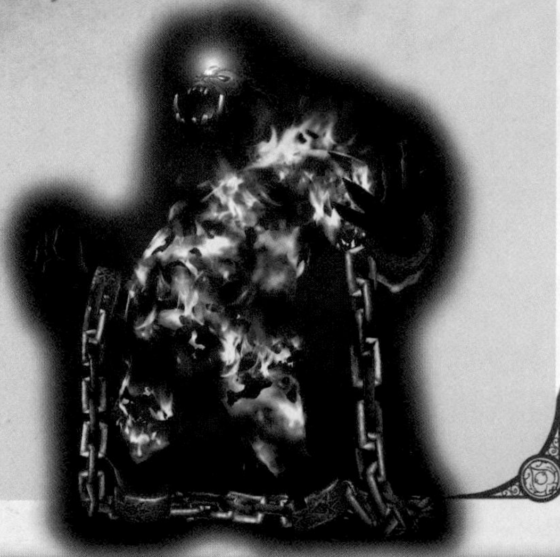

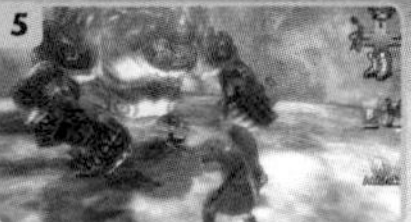

Enemies Encountered

Twilit Igniter: Fyrus

Bulblin Infantry

Fyrus staggers back after your third barrage of sword strikes. The gem on the carapace helmet glows before Fyrus explodes into shards of twilight, and a Heart Container falls at your feet!

The Fused Shadow's second part coalesces in front of you. On cue, Midna appears, and tells you a story. A **King of Shadows** *named* **Zant** *has cast this pall of shadows over your world. Midna has nothing but scorn for him, much as she has for Princess Zelda.*

Two **Fused Shadows** *have been collected. Midna forms a portal, as the last of the twilight drains from the defeated Fyrus, now changed to* **Darbus**.

▲ With combat over, inspect the arena chamber as there are pots full of Hearts and arrows to collect. Ignore them unless you need more arrows, and instead pick up the **Heart Container**! You're now at six Hearts' worth of energy.

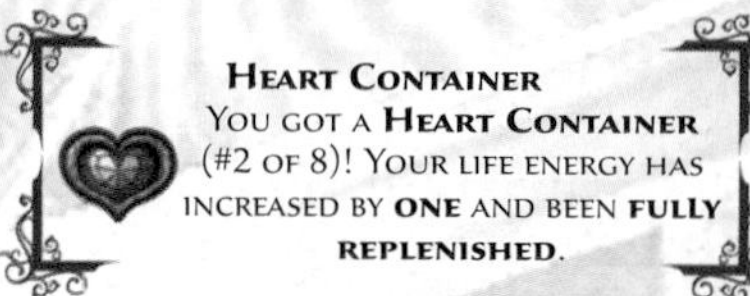

Heart Container
You got a **Heart Container** (#2 of 8)! Your life energy has increased by **one** and been **fully replenished**.

➤ Before you warp out of here, move to the groggy Darbus, and speak to him. The Goron can't remember anything, except that he's been in constant pain and his head hurts. However, the patriarch has been saved, and you'll gain your thanks if you revisit the top of Death Mountain.

Darbus:

Leader of the loincloth-wearing rock creatures known as Gorons, Darbus is a towering and muscular figure. Although he has strength unimaginable to most humans, he is on friendly terms with the nearby villages and wishes to create a joint society with them. At least this was his goal until a king named Zant transformed him. Darbus is between 30 and 40 years old.

◄ After speaking with Darbus, use Midna to warp out of here and save your progress. You return to the Kakariko Springs. The spirit calls to you, telling you that **north** of here, past a great stone bridge, lies the lands guarded by the **spirit Lanayru**. You shall find the one you seek there.

The Final Dungeon Chest Chamber 7: Second Return to Mine Loading Dock

Note: You cannot retrieve this chest until you obtain the Clawshot! Also note that this is the only chest you cannot reach on the first playthrough of a dungeon; you can open all other chests in every other dungeon the first time you play.

➤ After you receive the Master Sword, return to Death Mountain (the exact time is shown later in this walkthrough). Locate the mesh draped over the upper platform in the Mine Loading Dock near the western exit, and defeat all Bulblins.

➤ Clawshot your way up to the platform, scramble onto it, and run to the chest. It opens easily, and the prize inside may not be worth the effort it took to get here!

Treasure Chest #17:
Purple Rupee (50)

Overworld: Journey Through Lanayru Province

Legend

- Piece of Heart
- Golden Bug
- Twilit Parasite
- Bomb Rock

Journey through Lanayru Province—Pushing Back the Twilight: Overview

With a brand-new **Hero's Bow** that is possibly the most useful ranged weapon in Hyrule, you can spend some time investigating the nooks, crannies, and secret Cucco locations in Kakariko Village. After you've bought your first bombs and used them wisely, you must enter a new area of the land: the Lanayru Province, where you find the Scent of Ilia. Follow the scent to Castle Town; there, Ilia tends to a sick Zora prince named Ralis. His tribe needs your help. You must journey to their domain and find a way to return water to the once-expansive Lake Hylia. When the spirit cave at the lake is accessible, the final twilight blighting the land can be forced back and some truly shocking secrets are revealed!

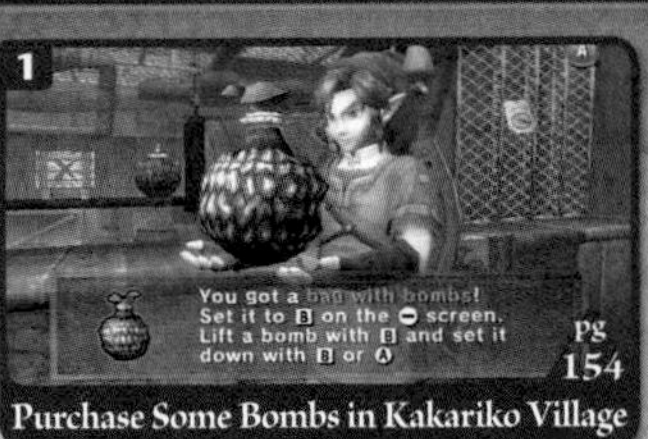

Purchase Some Bombs in Kakariko Village

Retrieve All Newly Available Items & Treasure

Find the Scent of Ilia

Locate Telma's Bar in Castle Town

Overworld Denizens

Characters

Purlo

Telma

Prince Ralis

Hylian Soldiers

The Zoras

Fyer

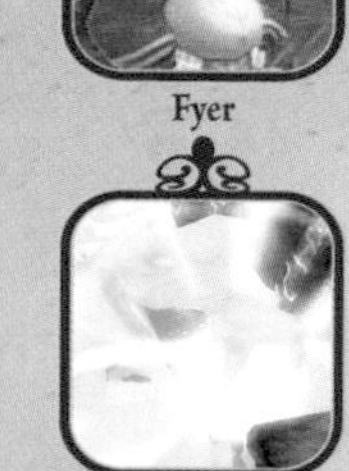

Iza

Rutela

Spirit Lanayru

Enemies

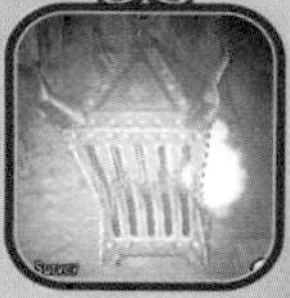

Imp Poe

Yellow Chu

Twilit Bulblin Archer

Twilit Carrier Kargarok

Twilit Bloat

A Link to the Present

Ordon Sword

Heart Pieces: 3 (16 Total)

Wooden Shield

Hylian Shield

Hero's Clothes

Wallet

Quiver

Golden Bugs: 10 (of 24)

Hidden Skills: 2 (of 7)

Scent (Youth's)

Fish Journal

Letters 3 (of 16)

Fused Shadow Pieces 2 (of 3)

Items to Obtain

Hot Springwater

Piece of Heart #9

Hawkeye

Bag with Bombs

Bombs (30)

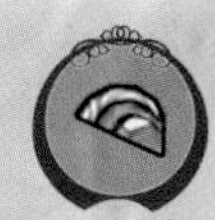

Piece of Heart #10

Piece of Heart #11

Orange Rupee (100)

Blue Potion

Silver Rupee (200)

Piece of Heart #12

Letter #4

Piece of Heart #13

Piece of Heart #14

Scent of Ilia

Vessel of Light

5 Journey to the Domain of the Zoras — Pg 168

6 Restore Warmth to Zora's Domain — Pg 171

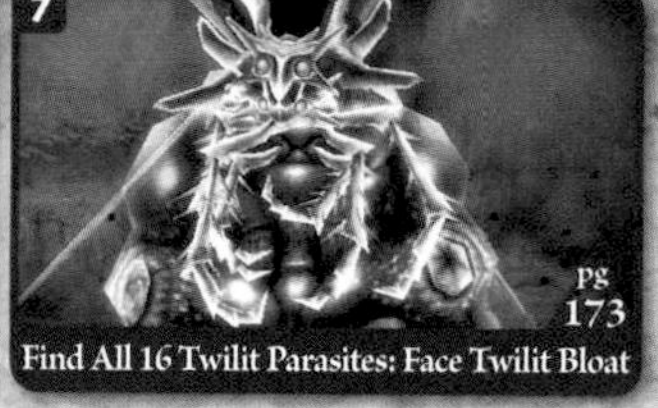

7 Find All 16 Twilit Parasites: Face Twilit Bloat — Pg 173

8 Learn the Secrets of the Goddesses from Lanayru — Pg 179

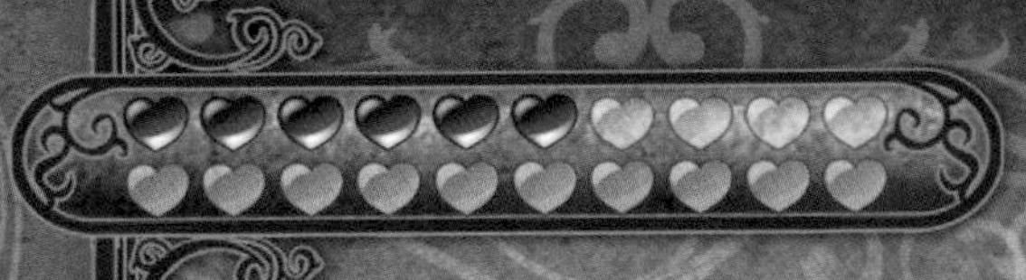

Characters Encountered

Goron

Barnes

Renado

Malo

Talo

Colin

Beth

Luda

Task 1: Purchase Some Bombs in Kakariko Village

Down from Death Mountain

◄ Back at the village, you can now visit the hot springs above the Elde Inn, where two Gorons are bathing and relaxing. They have brought down some supplies for Barnes, and the smaller Goron is setting up shop on the thoroughfare opposite the bomb maker's place. Additionally, if you have an empty Bottle, you can dip it into the hot springs.

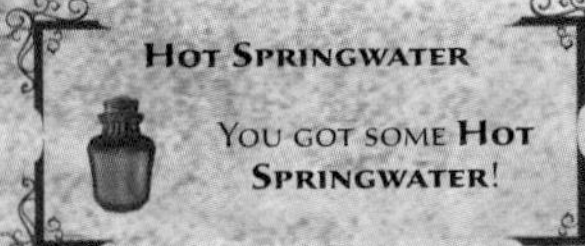

Hot Springwater
You got some Hot Springwater!

Hot Springwater has some incredible rejuvenating powers, which refill all Hearts and have a slight power boost. However, after about a day of travel, the water cools, so consider using other methods to heal yourself.

Note

◄ You can attempt a little item-grabbing with your Gale Boomerang. Stand on the roof of the Elde Inn and double-target the small crate on the tiny ledge to your right. Release the boomerang. The first hit bursts the crate, and the second hit brings back a yellow Rupee (10). However, there's a better way to attempt this later on. When you're done here, drop to the thoroughfare.

➤ Run to the thoroughfare's southern area, where you catch Renado near Malo Mart. He tells you that life is returning to normal and that Talo has become the village lookout, spending his time standing atop the lookout shack.

➤ Renado reckons you should speak with Talo, so head up the thoroughfare, pausing to talk to another Goron who is returning from the mines. He offers to propel you up to the hot springs. This is the short way to reach the hot springs, so accept his offer if you want.

◄ Continue up the thoroughfare if you didn't accept the Goron's offer, and you encounter another Goron who's ecstatic to be back and on speaking terms with the humans of Kakariko Village. He can propel you to the roof of Barnes' Bomb Shop. This way, you don't need to climb the store's interior!

The Goron you spoke to in the hot springs has a store opposite this Goron, but the store is only open between dusk and dawn. Conversely, Malo Mart is open from dawn until dusk, so know what you're shopping for before coming here during the night or day!

Note

➤ You should accept this Goron's offer and land on Barnes' store roof. Climb the promontory to the lookout shack where another Goron is checking out the view. Propel yourself up to the shack's roof by climbing on the Goron's back, landing on the ledge with the door, then ascending the ladder to the roof.

➤ When you reach the roof, don't talk to Talo immediately; instead, peer over the edge, to the right of the rickety fence. Below is a chest on a precarious ledge, but it's almost impossible to reach from here. Note this chest and come back to the town when Cuccos are clucking around. Now speak with Talo, and he begs you to show off your bow-and-arrow skills.

◄ You instantly arrive back at the thoroughfare, where Malo has some training requests for you to show off those skills. The first is an easy target he's erected on the thoroughfare's left side. Aim and fire!

The second target requires more dexterity. It's above Malo Mart. Ready? Aim and fire!

➤ From the top of the lookout shack, Talo asks you to strike the pole on the right corner of the shack. Take a steady aim, then fire.

Continue targeting the pole until you hit it; you can fire as many times as necessary (it usually takes only one or two tries). Malo is almost impressed. He's happy to help bring your energy levels up with a **Piece of Heart.**

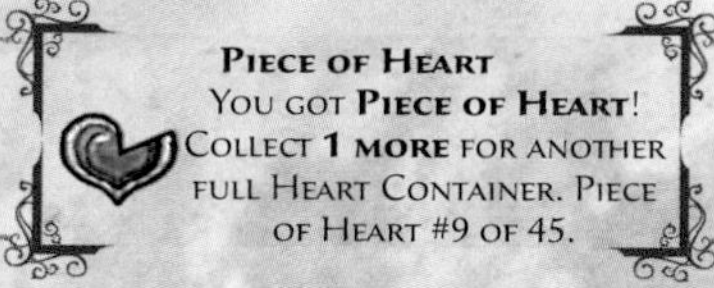

Piece of Heart
You got **Piece of Heart**!
Collect **1 more** for another full Heart Container. Piece of Heart #9 of 45.

➤ Now head into Malo Mart and check out the wares. There's a new item you should have: the Hawkeye. It is purely optional, but it will help you spot those hard-to-see treasure chests!

Store

Malo Mart (Second Visit)

Item	Name	Price	Effect
	Hawkeye	100 Rupees	This eyewear allows you to see distant objects as if with the eyes of a hawk.
	Wooden Shield	50 Rupees	A simple shield made of wood; it will burn if touched by fire.
	Red Potion	30 Rupees	This replenishes eight life energy: keep it in an **empty Bottle.**

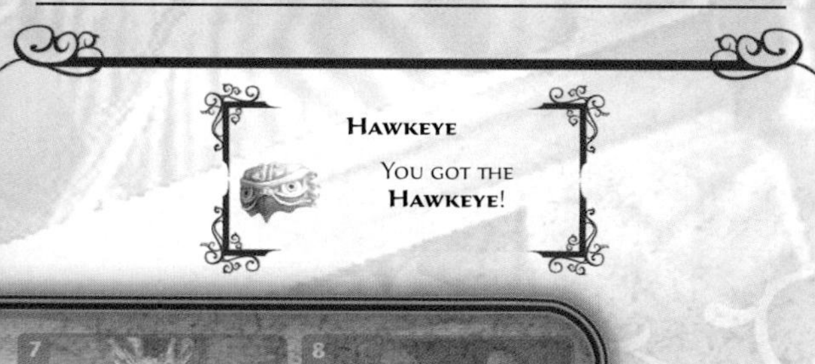

Hawkeye
You got the **Hawkeye**!

Tip: The Hawkeye is available as soon as you complete Dungeon #2: The Goron Mines. You can buy it only at Malo Mart. In addition to helping you spot treasure chests, it can help your aim during Talo and Malo's bow practicing.

This is your viewing scope from a regular viewpoint, looking at the lookout shack.

This is your viewing scope with the Hawkeye zoomed in all the way. The red cross shows it is combined with the Hero's Bow.

The Hawkeye acts like a telescope. When set to Ⓑ on the ⊖ screen, it can zoom in and out at up to five times normal magnification. Combine it with Ⓩ on the Ⓑ screen and you can fire arrows when using the **Hero's Bow** too!

You can use the blue cursor and place it over the Zoom buttons onscreen, or you can use the ⊖ and ⊕ buttons; these are faster.

Note: Maneuvering with the bow is not easy due to its cumbersome nature, and it is better to only use this telescopic function occasionally in offensive combat.

Note: A frivolous way to spend money is to purchase another Wooden Shield, if the first burned up during your dungeon exploration. Do this to look at the different design on the shield's front.

Note: You can optionally visit Colin in the Elde Inn (and stock up on Rupees and Hearts by smashing stuff). Colin is awake and dealing with two maids, Beth and Luda, fussing over him. Leave them and head for Barnes' Bomb Shop!

▲ Barnes has managed to create some actual bombs after all this time! Bring a full wallet and speak to Barnes. He has only one type of bomb currently available, but he may be able to build two more later.

Task #1
Purchase Some Bombs in Kakariko Village

Characters Encountered

Talo

Barnes

Midna

Store

Barnes' Bomb Shop

Item	Name	Price	Effect
	Bombs (10)	30 Rupees	Sold in packs of 10. You get a slight discount that way.
	Premium Kit	120 Rupees	A Bag with Bombs—a great deal.

Despite the large Rupee expenditure, buy the Premium Kit containing the Bag with Bombs; you now have 30 bombs to place all around the countryside.

Bomb Bag

You got a **Bag with Bombs**!

Bombs

You got **30 Bombs**!

Bombs

Bombs are an integral part of your offensive repertoire. Some creatures are affected only by bombs, and you must blow up many pieces of scenery to advance. For now, set your bombs to Ⓑ on the ⊖ screen. Lift a bomb with Ⓑ, and set it down with Ⓑ or Ⓐ (if you're walking or running, you'll throw it instead of placing it). **Combine** bombs with arrows to make a useful ranged weapon. Combine it with Ⓩ on the ⊖ screen.

Task 2: Locate and Retrieve All Newly Available Items and Treasure

Controlled Explosions in Kakariko Village

➤ Now that you have bombs at your disposal, you can work your way through previously explored areas and destroy any Bomb Rocks you saw. Begin at the village's southern end, adjacent to the spring. Set your bomb down by this rock.

Step back at least 10 feet and watch as the rock disintegrates. You can now investigate the area behind this Bomb Rock.

Inside the Bomb Rock entrance is a small, dark cave where two Cuccos are clucking about. You've freed them from these confines. Smash the group of crates in there to find a blue (5) and a yellow (10) Rupee inside.

➤ The cave continues with a small tunnel that leads to a sparkling pool filled with sacred water! Take a dive or fly off using a Cucco and land in the water. Swim around for a while.

➤ **Overworld Chest:** While swimming, keep your eyes peeled for objects. Look into the water to see something at the pool's bottom. Face south and put your **Iron Boots** on, then aim for the treasure chest down here. Quickly open it. What a prize!

Overworld Chest #11: Piece of Heart #10.

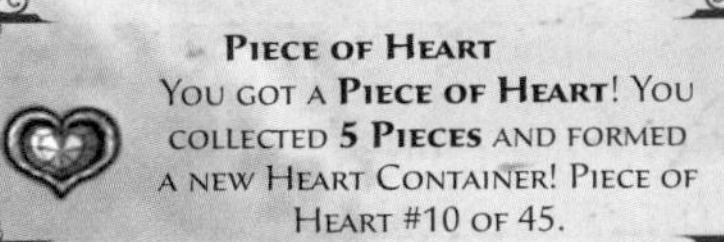

Piece of Heart
You got a **Piece of Heart**! You collected **5 Pieces** and formed a new Heart Container! Piece of Heart #10 of 45.

▲ You've blown up a Bomb Rock using regular bombs. Now you must **combine** a bomb with your arrows. Stand near the Sanctuary and face south. With **Bomb Arrows** selected, aim and fire at the clump of rocks below a dead tree (above the Bomb Rock you just blew up). This destroys the rocks and reveals a **Piece of Heart!** Run forward and use your **Gale Boomerang** to whisk the **Piece of Heart** back to you!

Piece of Heart
You got a **Piece of Heart**! Collect **5 Pieces** to form a new Heart Container. Piece of Heart #11 of 45.

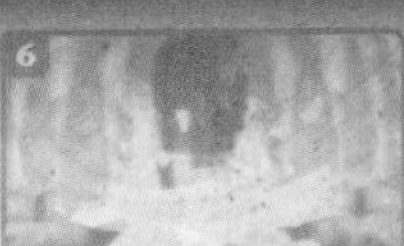

Controlled Cuccos in Kakariko Village

◄ Use the Cuccos in the village to maneuver to difficult-to-reach places. Bring your bird up the dead-end path and fly to the top of the Elde Inn.

When you reach the Inn's top, near the hot springs, fly to the small wooden ledge with the yellow Rupee (10) on your right—if you haven't shattered the crate already. From here, there are two paths to take.

◄ The first is to fly across the thoroughfare and land on top of Barnes' Bomb Shop. Remember to keep hold of your bird! Climb the promontory path to the lookout shack. When you reach the platform outside the shack, run to the far left corner.

➤ **Overworld Chest:** Look around the shack's corner. That chest you may have noticed earlier (when you talked to Talo) is on a ledge you can now reach. Jump off the platform and steer yourself onto the sharp bank near the rock wall. Land right next to the chest and open it up. Your Cucco-flying skills are justly rewarded!

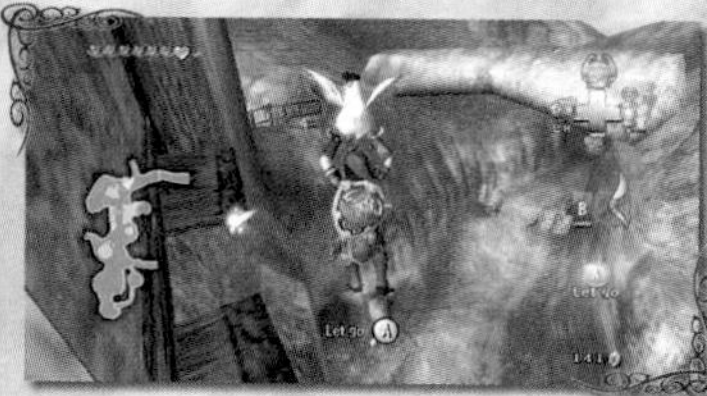

Overworld Chest #12: Orange Rupee (100)

Orange Rupee

You got an **Orange Rupee (100)**!

◄ The second route to take from the hot springs rooftop area is to fly to the small crate on the wooden platforms above the abandoned buildings on the thoroughfare's far side. Land and secure a red Rupee (20) from the crate!

Author Note

Link is wearing a rather fetching waterproof outfit, known as Zora armor. This is because we forgot to fly the Cuccos until after we retrieved the armor. The best time to fly a Cucco is after you free them from behind that Bomb Rock, but prior to entering Dungeon #3.

◄ Return to Kakariko Village at dusk or nighttime and visit the small Goron who's set up his store opposite Barnes' Bomb Shop. He has some interesting elixirs, including the **Blue Potion!** It costs 100 Rupees, so purchase the Red Potion, as you don't have more than eight Heart Containers in your life energy.

Store

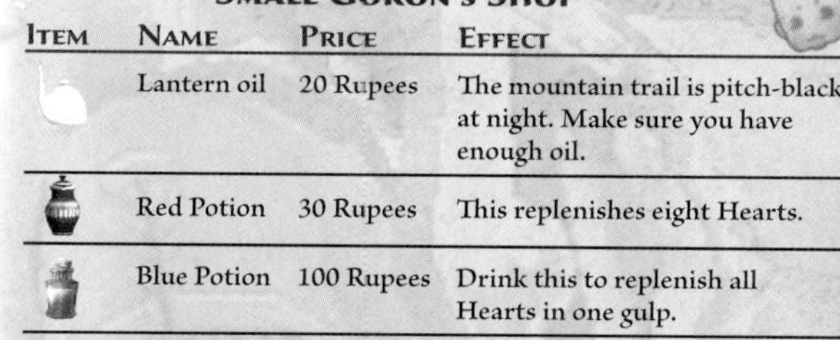

Small Goron's Shop

Item	Name	Price	Effect
	Lantern oil	20 Rupees	The mountain trail is pitch-black at night. Make sure you have enough oil.
	Red Potion	30 Rupees	This replenishes eight Hearts.
	Blue Potion	100 Rupees	Drink this to replenish all Hearts in one gulp.

Blue Potion

You got some **Blue Potion**! Use it to completely replenish **life energy**.

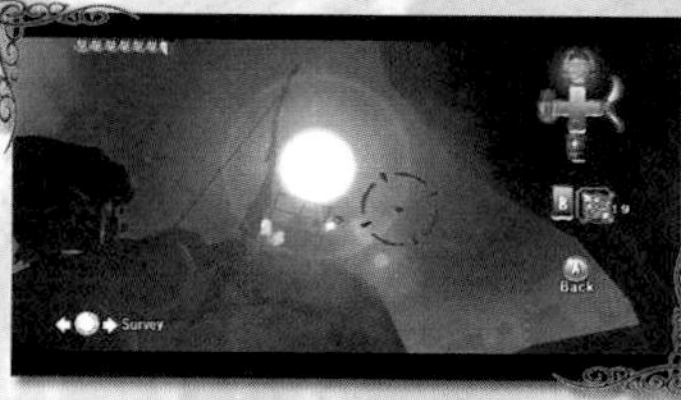

◄ Finally, there's a tricky maneuver to try. Aim a Bomb Arrow at the bell atop the Sanctuary. Something falls out when you strike it. Switch to your Gale Boomerang and target the object before it disappears. If you're lucky, you can grab it and bring it back to you. It is a silver Rupee, worth 200!

Tip: Consider leaving this Rupee until you can transform between Link and wolf form at will, then use Midna to bound to the Sanctuary's roof, which is where the silver Rupee (200) falls. Attempt this every time you appear in Kakariko Village for a constant supply of cash!

Silver Rupee

You got a **silver Rupee (200)**!

Characters Encountered

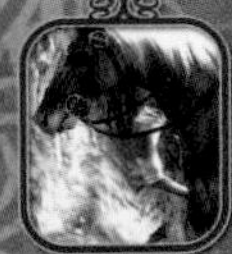
Epona

Goron

Postman

Barnes

Tumbling up Death Mountain Trail

◄ You've exhausted the available options in Kakariko Village, so head north to the Death Mountain trailhead. Leave Epona here and speak to the Goron, who's happy to propel you onto the path.

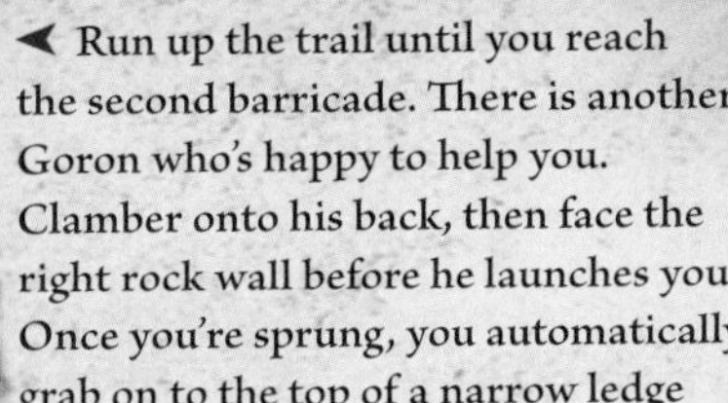

◄ Run up the trail until you reach the second barricade. There is another Goron who's happy to help you. Clamber onto his back, then face the right rock wall before he launches you. Once you're sprung, you automatically grab on to the top of a narrow ledge above. Climb onto here and check out an all-new area of the trail.

► Lift up all four scattered rocks and find a red Rupee (20) under each one! Now turn north, clamber up the large steplike ledges, and run toward a small Goron who's overlooking the clearing below. If you move up to him, he chats to you; he's surprised you saw him all the way up here!

◄ **Overworld Chest:** Talking to the Goron isn't the reason you're here—there's an opening in the rock wall that you just passed. Return here and step inside. There's a drop almost immediately—fall down it, turn around, and locate this chest. The prize inside is just what you've been searching for.

Overworld Chest #13: Piece of Heart #12.

Piece of Heart
You got a **Piece of Heart**! Collect **3 more** for another full Heart Container. Piece of Heart #12 of 45.

► Drop into the clearing. Look west and spot another cave alcove. You can reach this after you gain the **Clawshot**. There is something glistening here; this is a Rare Chu that you can defeat and scoop with Ⓐ, and use to gain energy, but not at the moment.

Galloping around the Great Hyrule Field

◄ If you've followed the walkthrough up until this point, you know there are multiple areas to explore and a correct time to do so. We recommend purchasing more bombs (so you have the maximum of 30); summoning Epona and riding her north and east, out of Kakariko Village; and bombing areas of the Hyrule Field.

As you enter the field (or any other location after you leave the village), the Postman gives you another missive. This one is a letter from Barnes explaining how to combine bombs and arrows. Do this immediately, as you need them shortly.

Letter #4
You got Letter #4: "URGENT! Bomb arrows!" by Barnes' Bomb Shop.

► Trot along the large field's southern entrance and locate the Bomb Rock that's blocking a series of rocky ledges. Choose a bomb or a Bomb Arrow (on horseback, if you really want to show off) and fire, exploding the rock. Dismount from Epona.

◄ Jump and grasp the ledge behind the exploded rock and climb onto an undulating ledge. Follow it to a vine wall, scale the wall, turn left, and look for a gap and another set of vines with a Bomb Rock above them. You *must* use a Bomb Arrow to strike and explode this rock.

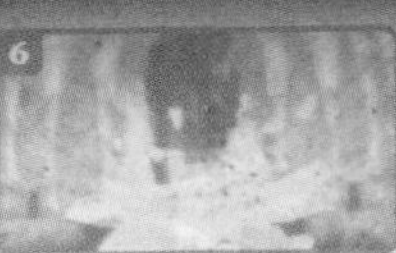

▲ Make a running leap at the vines, grab them, and pull yourself onto the eastern side of the gorge path. Turn left and leap (don't fall onto the road) toward the ledge overlooking an infinite drop. There's a chest to open on this overhang. You can even see Epona from this position.

Overworld Chest #14: Piece of Heart #13.

Piece of Heart

You got a **Piece of Heart**! Collect **2 more** for another full Heart Container. Piece of Heart #13 of 45.

▲ Gallop across the open Hyrule Field to the northwest Bridge of Eldin. Cross the bridge and stop on the north side. Look left, at the area you recently visited to grab that Golden Bug. There's a Bomb Rock here. Destroy it for two yellow (10) and one red (20) Rupees.

Caution

Don't destroy the rock wall that's blocking your route to the north! If you do, you'll begin the next part of the critical path in your adventure and will be unable to return to Hyrule Field or Kakariko Village for a while; it's better to head back there now and grab everything you can.

Explosions Rock the Kakariko Gorge

▲ Before you return to the Bridge of Eldin, head south to destroy all the Bomb Rocks. This is purely optional, but it is your first opportunity to attempt this and to explore new areas away from the critical path. Start in the northern part. There are four blue Rupees (5) and one yellow Rupee (10).

▲ Journey to the edge where you found the Piece of Heart earlier in the eastern part of the Kakariko Gorge. Destroy the Bomb Rock here for two blue (5), one green (1), and one yellow (10) Rupee.

Now move to the western area and locate the Bomb Rock stuck in the rock wall. Destroying this reveals a black cave entrance, which leads to **Lantern Cavern #1**.. You'll find two new enemies in here: the Imp Poe (which you cannot defeat) and a Yellow Chu (whose remains give you Lantern oil). Check your fuel supply, then enter the Lantern Cavern.

Enemies Encountered

Chu (Yellow, Rare)

Imp Poe

Lantern Cavern I

This place isn't called a Lantern Cavern for nothing; you can't get more than a few steps inside before running into a thick spider web. Only the Lantern can remove this obstacle; swing it to burn the web away.

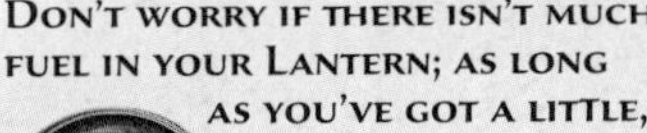

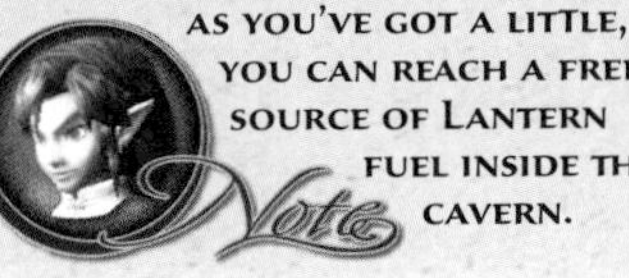

DON'T WORRY IF THERE ISN'T MUCH FUEL IN YOUR LANTERN; AS LONG AS YOU'VE GOT A LITTLE, YOU CAN REACH A FREE SOURCE OF LANTERN FUEL INSIDE THE CAVERN.

Bear right at the fork you come to beyond the web. Head north; a Deku Baba pops up from the ground. Sever its head from its stalk with a few swipes of your sword, then continue onward.

Bear right at the second fork you encounter and continue along until you reach a dead end. Smash the two skulls on the ground for two hearts, but watch out: a Yellow Chu drops from the ceiling above and attacks!

If you're low on Lantern fuel, you've just encountered a free source of it: once defeated, the remains of a Yellow Chu can be scooped into a Bottle, and the Yellow Chu Jelly you get acts like Lantern fuel! Chus are tough to keep track of, so ready an empty Bottle, then use a Spin Attack to splatter this one in short order.

Scoop the remains of the Yellow Chu into your Bottle before they seep into the ground; you've only got four seconds to do so, so act fast!

You've collected Yellow Chu Jelly. Now that you have plenty of fuel for your Lantern, let's explore the rest of the cavern.

Turn around and head back the way you came. Make a sharp right at the fork, then swing your Lantern to burn away the spider web that blocks the north passage.

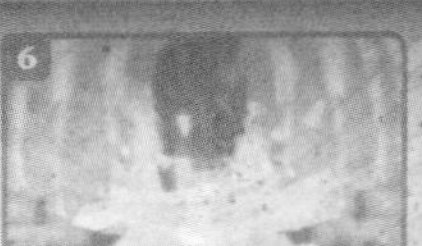

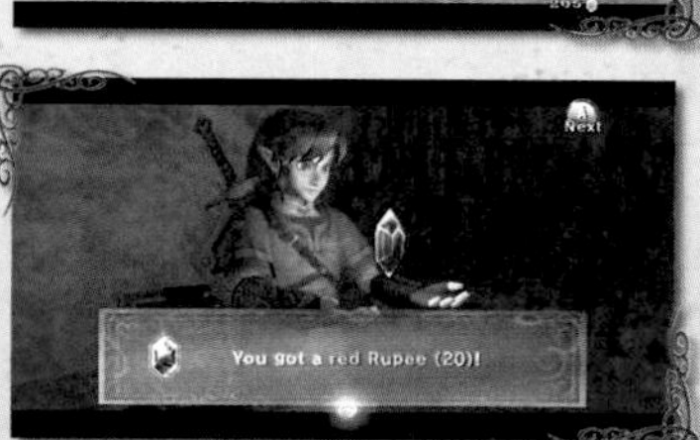

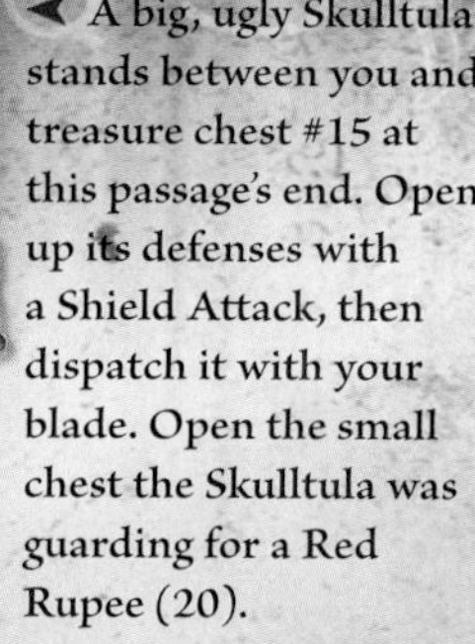

◀ A big, ugly Skulltula stands between you and treasure chest #15 at this passage's end. Open up its defenses with a Shield Attack, then dispatch it with your blade. Open the small chest the Skulltula was guarding for a Red Rupee (20).

Overworld Chest #15: Red Rupee (20)

◀ Backtrack to the first fork you encountered, near the entrance to the cavern. Again, use the Lantern to remove the spider web from your path, then have at the Keese that engages you a short distance ahead.

➤ Continue through the winding passage, ridding the tunnel of Keeses and spider webs as you go. You come to a small chamber, in which you find an unlit torch and two Tektites. Light the torch first so you can put away your Lantern and still see well enough to combat the Tektites; the Spin Attack is your best move in this tight space.

◀ The path forks again west of the torch chamber. Run up the short north trail to find a few goodies inside two skulls, a crate, and a small pot that hangs from a spider web. Use a Spin Attack to get rid of the few rats who attack you here, then collect a heart, arrows, and a Blue Rupee (5) by smashing the aforementioned objects.

◀ Return to the torch chamber and head into the unexplored southwest passage. When the trail splits apart for a second time, use your Lantern to burn away the spider webs so you may continue along the southmost path.

➤ Another Skulltula guards a treasure chest at the southmost passage's end. There's an unlit torch nearby; light it so you may stash your Lantern and conserve its fuel, then punish the Skulltula for standing in your way.

◀ After dealing with the Skulltula, open treasure chest #16 for a Purple Rupee (50). You can also collect a Blue Rupee (5) by smashing the small pot that's suspended by thin webs above the chest, and a Heart by breaking the skull on the ground nearby.

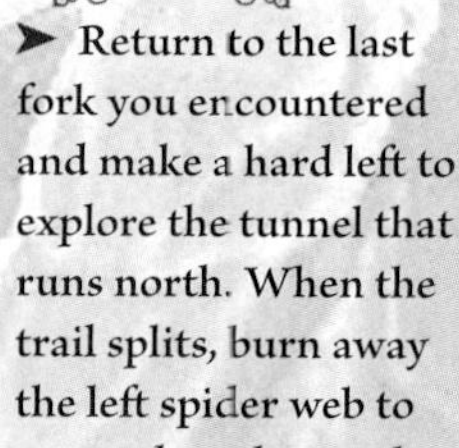

Overworld Chest #16: Purple Rupee (50)

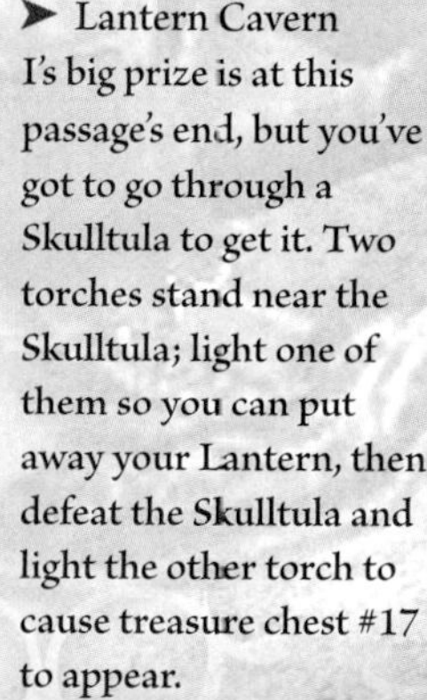

➤ Return to the last fork you encountered and make a hard left to explore the tunnel that runs north. When the trail splits, burn away the left spider web to proceed up the northwest passage.

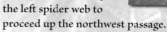

➤ Lantern Cavern I's big prize is at this passage's end, but you've got to go through a Skulltula to get it. Two torches stand near the Skulltula; light one of them so you can put away your Lantern, then defeat the Skulltula and light the other torch to cause treasure chest #17 to appear.

Enemies Encountered

Deku Baba

Yellow Chu

Skulltula

Keese

Tektite

Characters Encountered

Coro

Epona

Midna

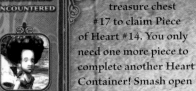

➤ Open treasure chest #17 to claim Piece of Heart #14. You only need one more piece to complete another Heart Container! Smash open the two pots in the webs above the chest for a Blue (5) and Yellow (10) Rupee.

Overworld Chest #17: Piece of Heart #14

Piece of Heart
You got a **Piece of Heart**! Collect **one more** for another full Heart Container. Piece of Heart #14 of 45.

➤ There's only one thing left to do in Lantern Cavern I, and that's explore the tunnel that runs parallel to the east. There isn't much point in doing so unless you're able to transform into wolf form at will, however; all you'll find is an Imp Poe, whom you can't harm in human form.

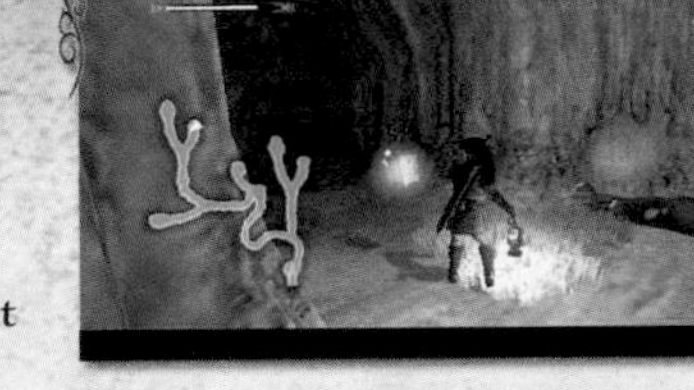

Chu

Threat Meter

That gloopy jellylike entity is a Chu. It bounds along the ground, without aggression. Chus are useful because, like the Bomskit, you can harvest their dispatched forms: scoop an empty bottle when you defeat the Chu to receive a special jelly.

Chu Jelly has a variety of properties:

Chu Type	Properties
Yellow	Lantern Fuel Refill
Red	8 Energy Refill
Blue	All Energy Refill
Purple	Random*
Gold	All Energy Refill, Attack Power Boost

*(*Purple Chu Jelly is potluck; you might gain one, eight, or all your energy. Or you might lose one, eight, or all but one of your energy!)*

Chus Wisely!

- Chus also merge with each other if many are congregating in a chamber; you must strike them multiple times to separate, and finally dispatch them.
- Merged Chus are Purple, and their liquid isn't as valuable. So attack Chus separately, and do not engage differently colored Chus at the same time if you're trying for a specific jelly.
- Chus are on the ground, but also drop from the ceiling. Look up and down!

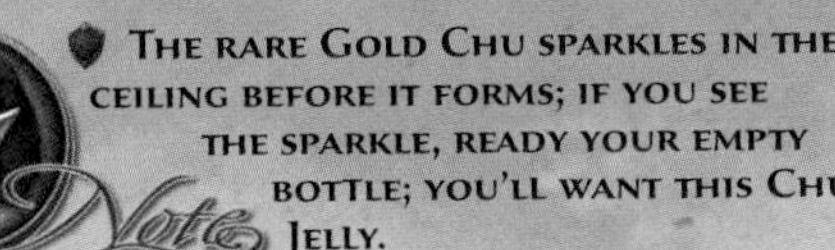

Note

- The rare Gold Chu sparkles in the ceiling before it forms; if you see the sparkle, ready your empty bottle; you'll want this Chu Jelly.

Chus come in Yellow, Blue, Red, Purple, and (in rare cases) Gold colors. If they merge, they become Purple.

Imp Poe

The Poe is a vicious, invisible Imp with a nasty disposition! Back away from this fiend until you figure out a way to take him down.

This is what the Imp Poe looks like! Now you can tell what's striking you; it's an ethereal scythe wielded by a mischevious ghoul.

The floating lantern you encounter in this cavern is the indication of a spirit presence: the Imp Poe. You cannot see the Imp Poe in regular vision; you must see with your sense view on, in Wolf form. The creature appears to you. For the moment, back away, and come back to fight another day!

Threat Meter

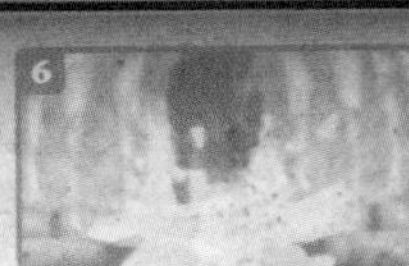

After you emerge from the Lantern Cavern, head back to Faron Province and blow that rock up near Coro's house. Inside is a small woodland dell, with a gnarled tree, a strange owl statue, and some grass you can swipe for various green Rupees (1), and a blue one (5). This area becomes relevant later.

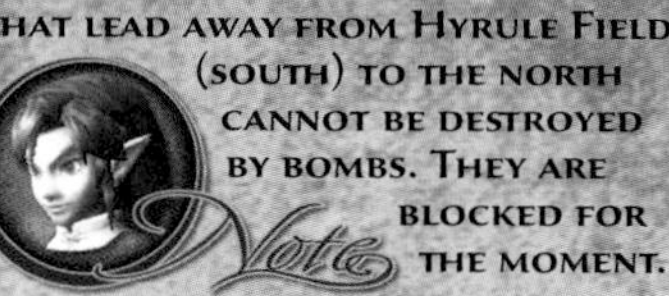

Note: The large, rubble-filled passages that lead away from Hyrule Field (south) to the north cannot be destroyed by bombs. They are blocked for the moment.

Enemies Encountered

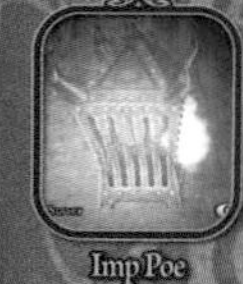

Imp Poe

Bomskit

Chu (Yellow, Red, Blue, Purple, Gold)

Twilit Messenger

Twilit Keese

Task 3: Find the Scent of Ilia

Battle at the Bridge of Eldin

Warp Portal

The entire area you've explored so far has been ransacked of treasure. Head back to the Bridge of Eldin, and gallop across to the north side. Shoot the wall of rocks that blocks the road north. A warp portal appears, and three Twilit Messengers drop onto the bridge. A portion of the bridge also disappears, effectively marooning you on the north side!

Defeating the three Twilit Messengers while on horseback is easier than it sounds. Ride past them to the section of bridge that's disappeared, and turn to the side. Wait for all three to congregate, then strike them all with a spin attack. After a couple of spins, all three should fall. If you're having trouble, dismount and attack them as normal.

Author Note

Be sure you attack these three Twilit Messengers, as this causes a warp portal to open. We didn't do this and consequently spent the rest of the game trying to figure out where to place the missing piece of bridge and taking the long route back to Kakariko Village!

Ride Epona north, along the rocky path that takes you north and east, where the path splits around a hill. You can access the left path only if you're traveling south. The path bends to the east, and you reach a bridge, where two Bulblins and an archer are waiting. Either ride through or stop and hack. The path eventually ends at a thick black wall. This is the last area of twilight!

Pouring Light into Lanayru Province

Midna pulls you into the twilight and you leave Epona behind, transforming into the wolf and running down a rocky path. Along the way, Twilit Keeses swoop down to harass you. Autotarget them and bite down hard.

Continue down the path until you reach an object lying in the road. Turn your sense view on to see a pink scent emanating from it. Sniff it, and you realize this is Ilia's purse! Forget the Youth's Scent, and instead learn **Scent of Ilia**.

Scent of Ilia

You learned the **Scent of Ilia**!

With your sense view on, follow the trail of scent down the hill. On the way, there are four different dig spots and a few Twilit Keeses to gnaw. As the path opens up to Hyrule Field (north), Midna recognizes that castle from your earlier exploits.

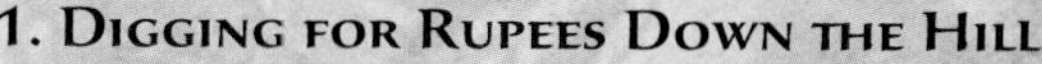

Missing Links

1. Digging for Rupees Down the Hill

The path has three patches of dig holes (Rupees and one eart near the scent) and some weeds on the left side hide two blue Rupees (5). After you pick up the scent, check for dig spot 1 (Rupees), dig spot 2 (Rupees and a Heart), and dig spot 3 (Rupee) before you enter the Hyrule Field (north).

Characters Encountered

Telma

Prince Ralis

Ilia

Goron

Purlo

Task 4: Locate Telma's Bar in Castle Town

Twilight in North Hyrule Field

➤ The path opens up, as you have a gigantic area to cover. Investigate every nook and cranny a little later; instead, head down the stone path, following the scent and periodically pausing to tear a bite out of an incoming Twilit Kargarok and Bulblin. As you near the bridge, two Twilit Bulblin Archers appear.

Twilit Bulblin Archer

Threat Meter

These dark Bulblins exhibit the same tactics as their light-world counterparts, and you must defeat them in the same way: dodge their attacks and strike. It is more difficult as a wolf (you have no shield), so make these enemies a priority. Charge them with your speed boost, and avoid running directly at them or they hit you with a flaming arrow. Then jump and bite, wait for them to rise, and bite again to finish.

➤ Dash across the stone bridge, following the scent as it continues up the main path. This leads you eastward, toward another adjoining area.

Missing Links

1. Digging in the Field

There are Rupees and Hearts to be found if you look hard enough. Find dig spots in the eastern area just after the bridge, near a few clumps of grass (Rupees and a Heart) and in the same area, farther southeast, in the middle of the sloping ground (Rupees and Hearts).

2. Water, Water, Nowhere

This is the only opportunity you have to travel along the riverbed on foot; you can roam around, head under the bridge, and even check out a treasure chest that's currently impossible to reach. It's behind bars at the southern end.

Twilight in the Eastern Field

➤ The scent continues down the path as you emerge into another field, this one with a crumbling wall on your right. Ignore the Bomb Rocks here for the moment. Follow the scent, dealing with any Twilit Babas and Archers as you reach the middle of this open area. The path then bends to the city gates; defeat the Twilit Bulblins coming to welcome you. Cross the wooden bridge and push open the city door that's ajar. Welcome to Hyrule Castle Town!

Missing Links

1. Extra Rupee and Hearts

This zone has a lot of grass to cut and several dig spots. Here are a few of the best ones to find:

Grass: As you arrive, just on the right, near the Bomb Rock (Rupee)

Grass: On the path's left side, halfway up the hill (Rupees and Heart)

Dig spots: Near the second large tree on the path's left side (Rupee)

Grass: With the Twilit Baba to the right of the pathway, just before Twilit Bulblin Archers spot you (Rupees)

Dig spot: Near the same Twilit Baba (Rupee)

Grass: On the right between the path and the castle wall (Heart)

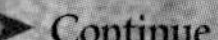

A Ghostly Town—Spirits Are Down

➤ Once in town, you can no longer control the camera, so switch to your sense view and follow the trail to the west. The first spirits you reach speak about a **Zora child**; apparently he has collapsed and has been taken to **Telma's Bar**.

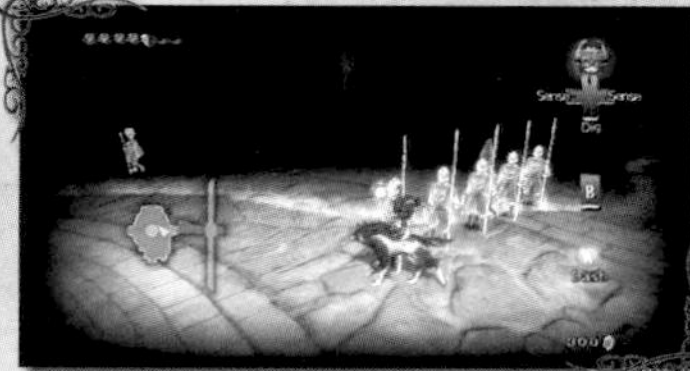

➤ Follow the trail into the central square, where the spirits of patrolling guards roam. You can check out both the guards to the north (one mentions Telma's Bar, the other the fountain to your south). You can optionally run to Hyrule Castle's entrance, but the doors are sealed.

➤ Journey back to the central square, follow the scent to the western side, and walk to the fountain's edge. Listen as townsfolk complain about the **town's water source, Lake Hylia**. You can stop following the scent as it drifts west and investigate the central square. You pass a **store** in the southwest corner. Listen to more complaints about not being able to bathe.

➤ Run to the tea shop in the city's southeast corner, where patrons bemoan their lack of drink. To the side of this place is a large, arched door; go there later for some supplies you can afford.

➤ Head west down the marked road where the scent is still thick. Move down the stairs, around the market stalls, and look at the building the scent moves in and out of. Ilia must have visited here; the sign reads "Medical Clinic." You can also talk to a very bored guard near the gate. When you're done, head south.

You appear on the south road. Run along until you spot an opening in the north wall, then head to a small patch of grass, where you can listen to a group of cats plotting a reconnaissance mission! One is suspicious of a person near a tent on the southeast street. They are waiting outside a locked house belonging to Jovani.

➤ Continue heading in east down this cobbled street, listening to a group of townsfolk telling one another that the Zora boy collapsed. At the junction, the scent runs south; follow it unless you wish to return to the central square.

➤ Continue south, and optionally ignore the scent for a moment as it turns west. There's a path to the east, which passes the mansion of a fortune-teller named Fanadi, a princess named Agitha, and (as you reach the junction where you came in), a tent with a man named Purlo outside. Is this who the cat was talking about? He's a sneaky sort but you can't investigate now, so stand just south in the main market thoroughfare and listen to the Gorons; they're overwhelmed with demand for their Hot Springwater!

Purlo:

About 20 years old, Purlo builds temporary, circus-style tents in Castle Town and attracts customers to his games. He speaks in a pretentious and slightly odd tone. Although he's not obvious about it, his game is so difficult that he's sure no one can claim the large money prize he offers.

➤ When you're done exploring Castle Town, head west down the alley near the Gorons to Telma's Bar. Go down the steps on your right to enter the bar. Before you enter this place, investigate the crates in the top left corner; smash them, and something sparkles! Turn your sense view on to see a Twilit Parasite. This must mean you're close to another Vessel of Light! Dispatch the creature, but ignore the orb—you can't claim it yet.

Missing Links

1. Throw Me a Bone, Here!

Pick up a dog's bone when you're prowling the area near the medical clinic (and the street south of the initial entrance). It doesn't do anything, but it certainly is tasty!

Twilit Kargarok

Bulblin

Twilit Bulblin Archer

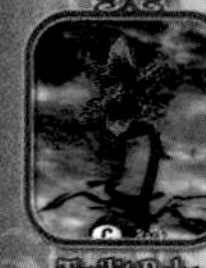

Twilit Baba

Twilit Bulblin

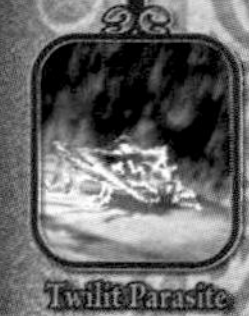

Twilit Parasite

Task 5: Journey to the Domain of the Zoras

Characters Encountered

Telma

Ilia

Prince Ralis

Hylian Soldiers

Goron

Fyer

Falbi

Zora

Lanayru Spirit

The Path to Lake Hylia

Enter Telma's Bar and switch your sense view on. Approach the group of spirits ahead and to the right. It is Ilia! She is watching over the Zora prince, along with Telma, the owner of this establishment. Even though you've found Ilia, she's in spirit form, so you can't speak to her.

Telma:

Between 30 and 40 years old, Telma runs a bar in Castle Town. She is bossy but obliging. With an unyielding spirit, Telma is actually the leader of a resistance force, a group that wants to restore the kingdom. She is hoping to find a worthy man to recruit to help her forces.

Prince Ralis:

About 10 years old, this boy is part of the Zora tribe and was on a mission to deliver a message from the Zoras' queen (his mother) to Princess Zelda when dark forces waylaid him. Ilia rescued him. He has received a fine upbringing and speaks politely. He is reliable but worries he won't be able to fulfill his eventual destiny as the leader of the Zora tribe.

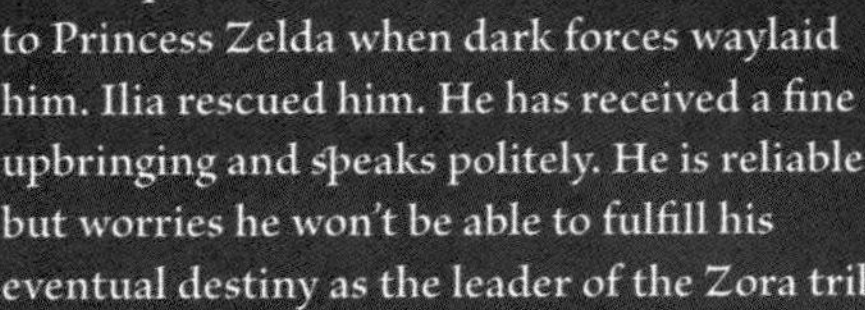

Move to the bar's back room to hear a group of soldiers speaking about their orders. The people can't send prayers to the spring spirit of Lake Hylia, so the sergeant has marked on the table map the area to investigate. Look at the map on the table; a red circle marks the spot.

Hylian Soldiers:

These soldiers comprise the military force that protects the kingdom of Hyrule. They have fought bravely in the past, but once the kingdom fell to the twilight, the soldiers became fractured. You'll encounter sorrowful mourners, cowardly quitters, and the brave knights who still wait for a hero to rise.

Tip: The fabled map of Hyrule is spread over this table in Telma's Bar. Whenever you're stuck, return here and check the map to see where you should head next. After you view the map, the clue also appears on your in-game map. The spring in Lake Hylia shows up as a red circle now. Onward!

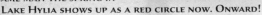

Leave the comfort of Telma's Bar, ignoring that orb for the moment, and leave Castle Town to search for a route to Lake Hylia. The south exit is blocked by people milling about at the Goron's store. The west exit is closed. The only way out is via the door you came from. Back on the bridge, bite and claw at a couple of Twilit Bulblins.

Leave Castle Town and head south and east. Head over the rise to an old stone amphitheater, where you find a chest and two Twilit Bulblins. Defeat the foes but ignore the chest; you can't reach it until much later. You need a rod of some kind here.

Leave the amphitheater and journey northeast, along the side of the zone to the opening in the eastern rock wall; enter the path leading to the bridge overlooking Lake Hylia. This is your first time in this region, so watch for a trio of Twilit Bulblin en route.

Trot forward to the fork in the path. The bridge is to your right. Be aware that **Fyer and Falbi's Watertop Land of Fantastication** is nearby. That sounds wild, as does the main attraction: **Flight-by-Fowl**.

Inspect the area to find a Bomb Rock and an odd alcove to your right and behind you. Ignore this for the moment and run toward the bridge entrance. As you move onto the bridge, notice that the ground is glistening. Continue south.

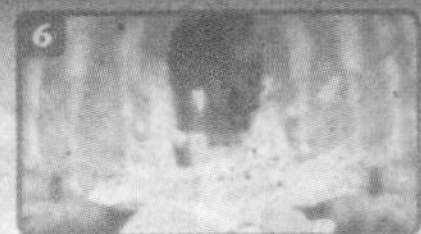

◄ You stop as a Twilit Bulblin Archer fires off a flaming arrow, setting fire to the bridge. You're standing on oil, and there's a fire coming from both ends of the bridge! Sprint past the first two crates and stop at the second set. Move to the crate's base and get on top, then leap to the crenellation on the bridge's side. From there, leap off the bridge to a huge drop below!

Caution

You must find this second crenellation near the box; it is shorter than the rest, which block your path. If the fire catches you, you have to restart your game at the bridge, with three Hearts filled with energy.

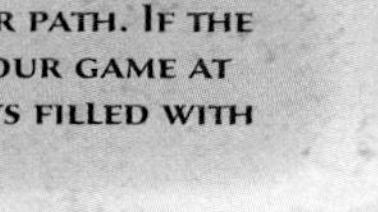

Missing Links

1. Dig Spots and Grass Cutting

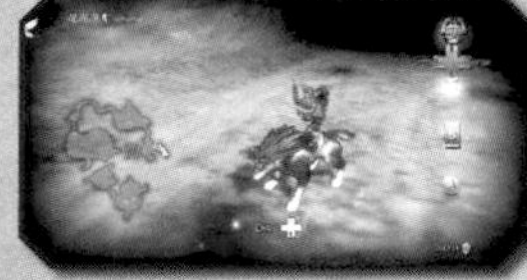

On the earthen road leading to the bridge entrance are three or four dig spots, each containing a Heart. When you reach the fork in the road, cut the grass on the left to find a Heart. For another Heart, cut the grass behind the sign, in the middle of the small boulders. Slice the grass just right of the bridge entrance for loads of green Rupees (1)!

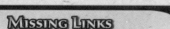

The Dry Lakebed of Hylia

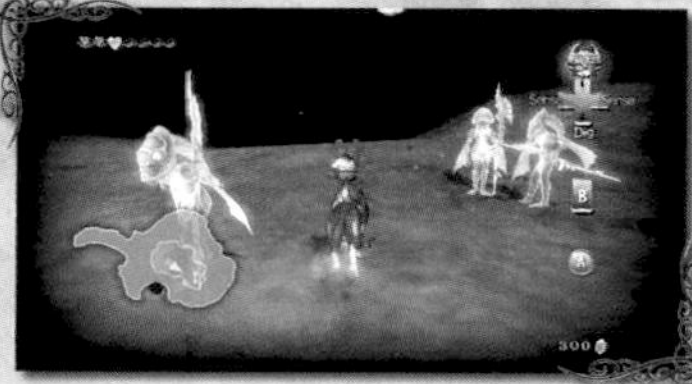

◄ Dog-paddle toward the odd building in the distance and switch on your sense view to check the ghostly floating fires ahead. These change to Zoras, a friendly people now downtrodden by the water shortage. According to the warriors, the problem seems to be coming from the water's source, Zora's Domain.

The Zoras:

An aquatic tribe of people with gills and lungs, the Zoras are a proud and ancient race, led by a beloved king and queen. Recently their lands have become embroiled in turmoil as their water supply has dwindled. Now full of melancholy, they wish for happier times.

Tip

This lakebed is a hot spot for digging. There are at least 40 holes to burrow into for Hearts and Rupees.

▲ After you finish with your big dig, head toward the odd and colorful shack and listen as the depressed owner, Fyer, mumbles about the ruined grand reopening of his fantastication ride. He isn't sure if the Zoras in their domain are to blame or if it has something to do with the Lanayru spirit. He's then spooked by a Twilit Bulblin Archer roaming the lakebed.

Fyer:

Although he looks much older, Fyer is between 20 and 30 years old and is a former member of the circus. Short, hunched, and lazy-looking, he's recently started his own small business firing folks from a cannon, although there's limited potential on the floor of the lake! He's a great mechanic, however, and specializes in rebuilding old cannons.

Enemies Encountered

Twilit Bulblin

Twilit Bulblin Archer

Characters Encountered

Midna

Zora

Fyer

Iza

Coro

Hena

Twilit Carrier Kargarok

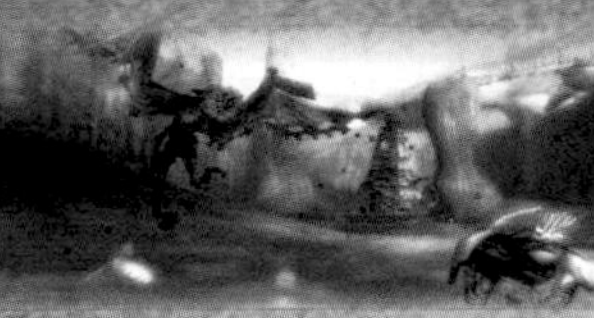

Run across the lakebed to the Twilit Bulblin Archer who's roaming this area. He stops when he spots you, then moves quickly to a patch of grass. After playing an unspeakable tune, a giant Twilit Carrier Kargarok swoops down from the heavens and the archer mounts it!

The Twilit Carrier Kargarok is a strange, giant, mutant version of the Kargaroks you've encountered before, but is covered in Twilit skin. The beast and rider begin with some annoying arrow-firing; you can't reach them, so run away from the arrows. When the rider draws the Twilit Carrier Kargarok down and swoops in on you, be sure you use Ⓩ to target early, then make a leaping jump onto the beast. Tap Ⓐ furiously to bite the Twilit Carrier Kargarok multiple times, until he throws you off. Do this a second time and the Twilit Bulblin Archer falls.

The Twilit Bulblin Archer loves to fire from outside your range, so make the best use of close-combat situations and leap, cling, and bite!

▲ The Twilit Carrier Kargarok is still flapping about as the Twilit Bulblin Archer falls to the lakebed. Target him immediately and finish him off. Then watch as Midna teleports across the skies and lands on the beast's back! She asks if you want to fly to the Zora's Domain. Agree.

Missing Links

1. The Great Lakebed Dig

This is the only time you'll be able to dig (as the lake should be full the next time you visit), so switch on your sense view and prowl the perimeter; there are at least 12 areas around the sides of this bed and Fyer's cannon house. All give you Rupees (mainly green [1] and blue [5]) and Hearts. You'll find them all in about 10 to 15 minutes.

2. Finding Fyer's Funds

After you speak to Fyer, take the Heart and a few Rupees from his collection of pots; there are a few more pots containing a Rupee or two on the other side of his shack.

Flying Up the Riverbed

You're soaring through the great gorge with the riverbed below you, your physical body clamped in the Twilit Carrier Kargarok's claws. You control the winged beast with the Wii Remote—fly in the direction of the light blue target. Dash by pressing Ⓐ.

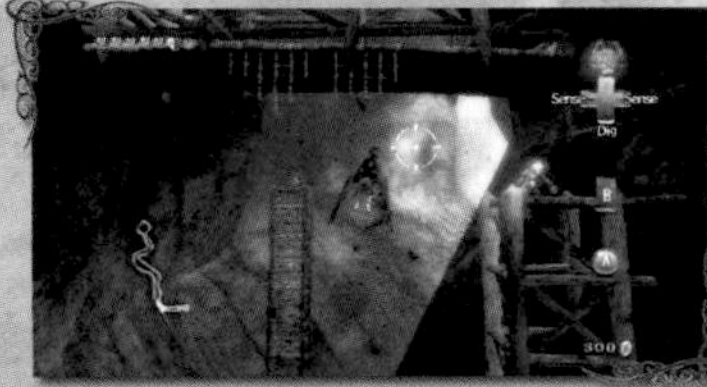

◀ Steer by pointing your target toward the lit areas, and dash between the two long towers that contain archers.

▶ You're traveling directly north; point your carrier up toward the bridge light and dash. Be sure you clear this bridge with archers on it; fly up and dash over.

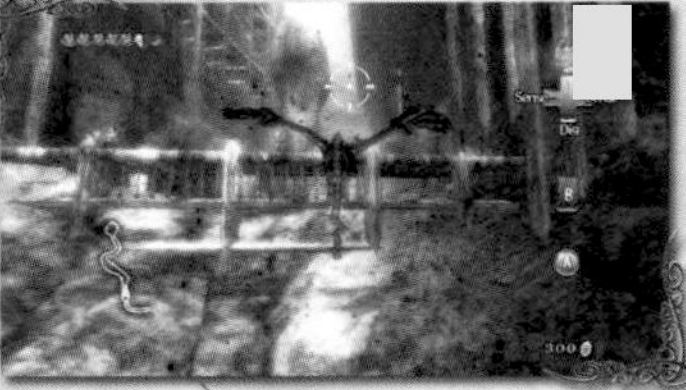

Swoop under each of the detonating rocks that fall to the side and move right when the central rock falls forward.

▶ In the final section of river, fly with periodic dashing, staying in the open and always aiming for the light. Stay to the side of the falling boulders, then aim for the brightly lit exit.

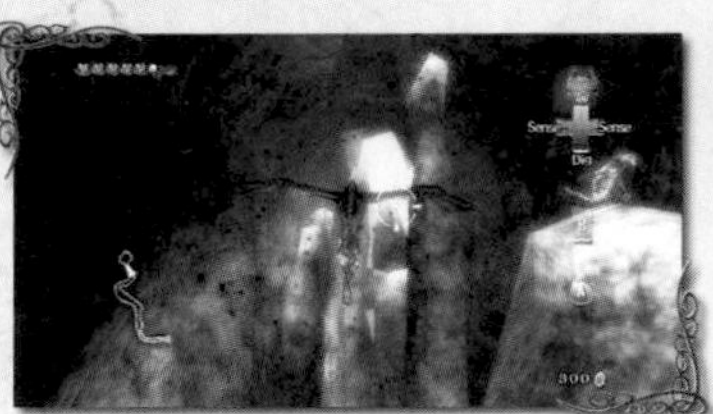

Tip: You can also dash and strike any of the archers that are on exposed rock areas, although this is difficult. It is less dangerous to avoid them by racing by.

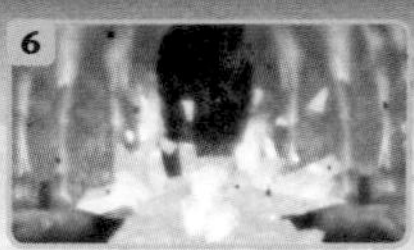

Task 6: Restore Warmth to Zora's Domain

The Cold Shoulder in Zora's Domain

▲ After some scrabbling in the dirt for hidden items, you can investigate the spirit of a woman near the sign for her business, which advertises boat rentals to get from here to Lake Hylia. No wonder she seems so upset—there's no water in the river. Her name is Iza, and she's cold, fed up with the Zoras and their water siphoning, and wants to know what's going on.

Iza:

In her 30s, Iza is the eldest of three children. Coro and Hena are her siblings. She runs a boat rental shop in the usually wild rapids of the Upper Zora's River. She is frank and open-hearted but is rather gruff.

◄ There's little you can do except leap into the dry riverbed from your current location. There's some evidence of ice in the riverbed and two Bomb Rocks (one in the southern area, and the other in the middle part) in the area. The bed seems to get more icy as you head east.

► Head past three thin rocks protruding from the icy riverbed, and continue to run toward the giant ice structure in the middle of this huge cavern. At the base of the ice structure, shatter a little ice for Hearts and gnaw on a few Twilit Keeses.

When you're done exploring the structure's base, find the snowy ramp. Midna says she can help you leap up to the next series of ledges. Jump six times, constantly holding down Ⓩ for best results. Turn right as you reach the ledge.

◄ Walk along the ledge heading east until a shard of ice smashes in front of you. Run and spin attack it, clearing it from your path. Then move around to this point, where Midna recommends you scale the rest of the structure.

Hold Ⓩ, then leap and ascend the structure, which wobbles under your weight. Leap quickly the first three times, and you'll narrowly miss a falling shard. Clamber back on, and stop as you reach the fifth total jump. Let the next shard drop, then make your sixth leap. Grab and hold that next ledge!

Caution: If you're struck by either of the two falling shards on this giant ice platform, you survive the fall but must jump all the way to the top again.

After another four leaps, you make it to the top of the icy tower. Dispatch a couple of Twilit Keeses and maneuver around the icy tundra. There's a rock blocking a path sloping down in the northeastern part of this area.

Warp Portal

Three Twilit Messengers from the world of shadows await your tooth and claw. Head for the Twilit Messenger and bite him or use Midna's area attack. Then trot around the energy fence to where the other two Twilit Messengers are. Position yourself so you can strike them in one energy circle, and let rip.

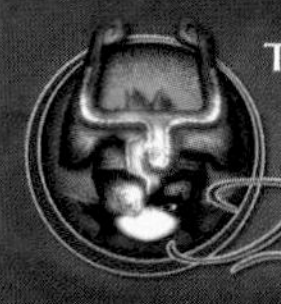

Tip: This battle may take multiple attempts to perfect, as your area attack is stopped if you hit any wall during the takedown. Make sure you're away from walls when you launch this technique.

► A warp portal opens above you. At the same time, you peer down into the ice; dozens of Zoras lie encased in this frozen pool. If only there was some way of melting it...perhaps with a giant molten shard. Hold on....

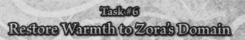

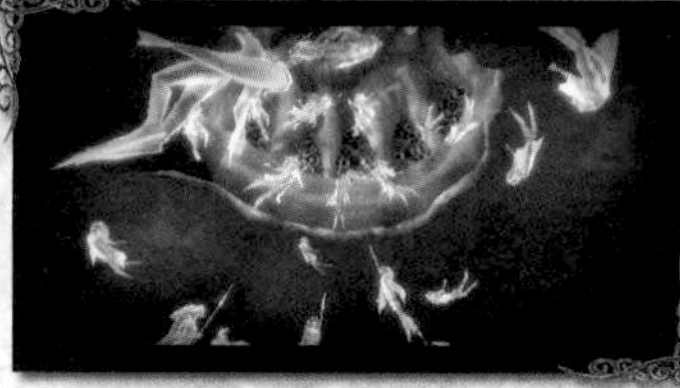

Enemies Encountered

Twilit Carrier Kargarok

Twilit Bulblin Archer

Twilit Keese

Twilit Messenger

Characters Encountered

Iza

Zora

Midna

Rutela

Prince Ralis

Spirit Lanayru

Fyer

Missing Links

1. Grass Slicing and Dirt Digging

You can find many areas where grass and dirt can be disturbed:

Grass: Just north of the landing spot (Rupees)

Grass: Southwest area, just off the promontory (Rupees)

Crates: Just left of where Iza is sitting, by the side of the boathouse (Rupees and Heart)

Dig spots: In the same area as the crates, near the side of the building (Hearts)

Dig spot: Behind the sign, next to Iza

2. Smashing the Ice Stalagmites

There's a couple of large, white ice stalagmites to the east on the riverbed; execute a spin attack when you're near them and they shatter, sometimes giving you a Heart or a Rupee.

A Much Warmer Reception in Zora's Domain

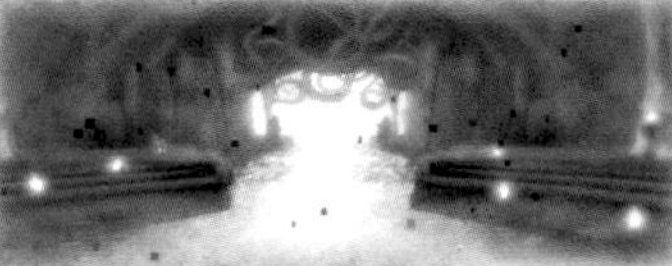

Bring up your map and warp to Death Mountain. Run to the molten shard stuck in the ground and contact Midna. She summons great strength and rips the shard from the ground. Warp back to Zora's Domain. Midna drops the shard into the pool and water begins to flow down the river.

◄ You can now reach the spirit cave and meet the spirit of the lake! Spend a few moments listening to the Zoras as they recover from their forced slumber. They're coughing, murmuring, and wanting to know if their friends in the waterfall pool are okay. Head south.

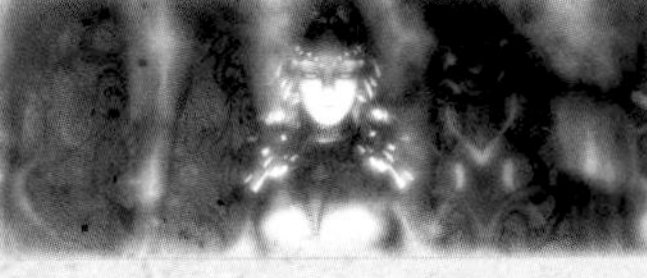

*As you prepare to leave, a voice tells you to stop. Someone can see you. A slender and tall Zora appears in a ghostly pallor. She is Rutela, leader of the tribe. The dark ones executed her, and she sent her son Ralis to warn Princess Zelda. He grows weak. She urges you to help him. If you do, Rutela will bestow **the protection of water** on you.*

Rutela:

When alive, she was between 20 and 30 years old. She and her king were executed by the mad King of Shadows, named Zant, and her tribe was frozen in a deep, difficult-to-reach pool in the northern province that shares the tribe's name. She is ethereal and elegant, and seeks help for her son.

◄ Follow Midna's advice and try to head back to Lake Hylia from this point. Swim along the gushing channel and then leap from a promontory, or over the waterfall; you land in the waterfall pool below and are swept downstream. You awaken at the foot of the cave to the spring of the Spirit Lanayru. Enter.

Missing Links

1. Grassy Ledge, High above the Pool

After you speak with Rutela, but before you leap off the waterfall, check out the area to the east, where you spotted the rock blocking the path before. Crates (Rupees) and grass (Heart) are available now.

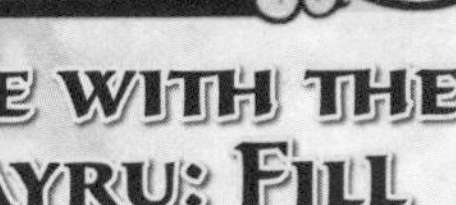

An Audience with the Spirit Lanayru: Fill the Vessel of Light

◄ Once inside the spirit cave, advance forward and speak to Lanayru, the final Spirit of Light. "Collect my light and lift the final cloud of twilight that threatens to cover all of Hyrule!" the entity gasps. You're given a familiar item with which to complete this task. There's little else to do except leave (but first gather a few Rupees from the grass around this pool's edge).

Vessel of Light
You got the **Vessel of Light**! Use this to collect the **tears** that cut through the darkness.

1 

2 

3 

4 

5 

6 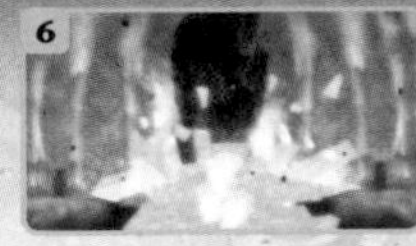

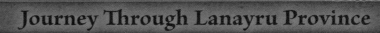

Task 7: Locate All 16 Twilit Parasites: Face Twilit Bloat

Enemies Encountered

Twilit Parasite

Twilit Carrier Kargarok

Twilit Messenger

Lake Hylia: Twilit Parasite #1

◀ Your map now has several white dots indicating the locations of the 16 Twilit Parasites. You begin in Lake Hylia and can attack the Parasites in any order. We chose to head north and west, toward a Zora worried about a strange fluttering foe.

Note: When you reach the small jetty, Midna says you can blow on the Bird Grass over on the small promontory and ride the Twilit Carrier Kargarok up to Zora's Domain. There's no real need to do this, however, as you can warp there.

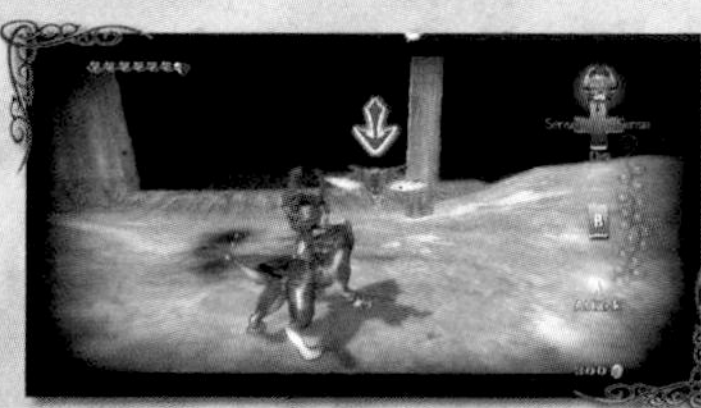

▶ Walk along the series of half-submerged tiny islands that stretch from the spirit cave to this small jetty. Collect items from the grass slicing if you wish, then prepare to fight a nasty Twilit Parasite when you reach this place. Grab the orb it explodes into.

Lake Hylia: Twilit Parasites #2, #3, and #4

▲ Retreat back to the spirit cave entrance, then journey along the wooden bridge to a series of small grassy islands in the lake's southern part. As soon as you leave the wooden bridge sections, you see a Parasite scuttling about. Switch to your sense view, then target and leap on it. Collect your second orb.

Warp Portal

Continue heading toward Fyer's odd-looking hut, and you enter a circular plateau of grass where you hear the familiar sounds of three incoming Twilit Messengers. Run to the fence's opposite side, dispatch the one standing away from the other two, then coax the remaining Messengers closer to each other. Defeat them as normal, using your area attack. You can now warp to and from Lake Hylia.

Tip: The warp portal point at Lake Hylia is one of the most important. You'll use this a lot during your collecting.

◀ Now that the Twilit Messengers have gone, you can concentrate on locating the next Parasite. Wander down the planks linking the islands to Fyer's hut. Ignore Fyer and head around the back of the hut; the Parasite is floating in this area. Wait for it to descend before grabbing it.

▶ Return to the plateau where you fought the Twilit Messengers and take the sloping grass path that's next to the entrance to the wooden bridge area. Follow this around and to the right, then turn south, looking out over a small gap to a protruding island that looks a bit like a mushroom. Line up your position and make the leap, or you land in the water and must swim back to the island near Fyer's hut and try again.

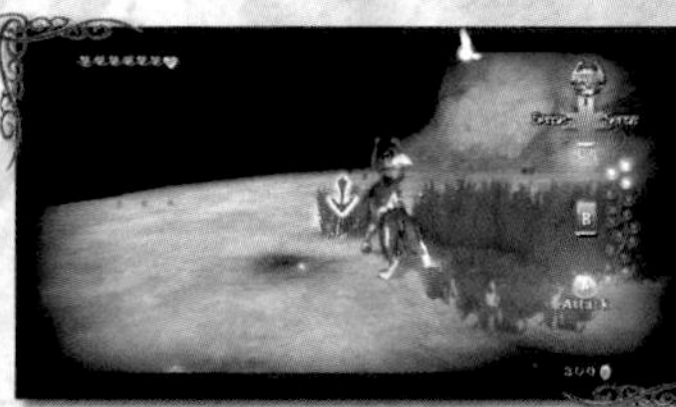

▶ Turn and make another well-positioned jump to a ledge along the southern wall, then work your way around to this set of grass and dig spots. The Parasite is hiding in the grass.

7

8

Characters Encountered

Zora

Fyer

Iza

White Wolf

Prince Ralis

➤ You've removed the Twilit Parasite problem from Lake Hylia, but these vermin appear in other places. The next place to look is up the Zora's River. You must call the Twilit Carrier Kargarok to fly you there. Perform a howling at the tiny island adjacent to Fyer's hut or at the promontory jetty where you found Parasite #1. The pitch is as follows: High, Low, High, Low (hold).

Missing Links

1. Lake Hylia (during the Hunt for Parasites #1–4)

Now you can investigate the upper ground of Lake Hylia. Locate these areas for Rupees and Hearts:

Grass: The mound the Zora is standing on (Rupee) during Parasite #1 hunt

Grass: Half-submerged just west of the Zora during Parasite #1 hunt (Rupee)

Grass: The tiny island west of the Zora, on the way to Parasite #1 (Rupees and Hearts)

Grass: The half-submerged grass at the end of the tiny island's path (Rupee), near Parasite #1

Dig spot: Under the location of Parasite #1 (Rupees and Hearts)

Grass (around four areas): On the grassy ledge, in the western area of Lake Hylia (Rupees and Hearts)

Dig spots: Three or four areas on the western grassy ledge, Lake Hylia (green [1], blue [5], and yellow [10] Rupees)

Dig spots: On the flat plateau the Twilit Messengers appeared on (Rupees and Hearts)

Dig spots: On the smaller connecting island near the wooden walkway to Fyer's hut (Rupees)

Grass and dig spots: There's plenty on the small grassy rock where you dug for Parasite #3 (Rupees and Hearts)

Zora's River: Parasites #5, #6, #7, and #8

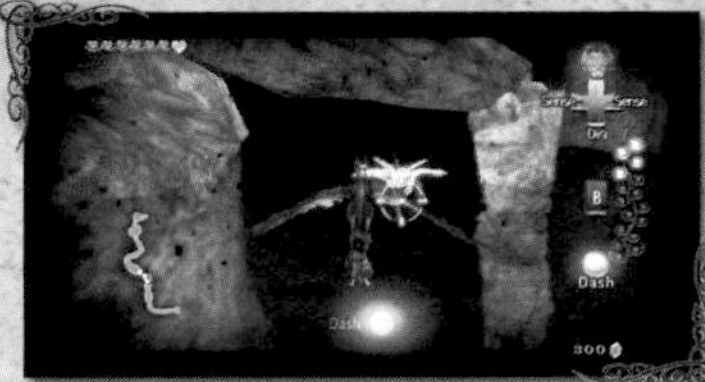

◄ Once on the Twilit Carrier Kargarok, slow down and switch on your sense view right away. The map tells you the four locations you can find each Parasite. To defeat each one, you must dash (Ⓐ) into it. Don't worry if you miss; the Parasites usually fly after you. Simply slow down, wait for the Parasite to pass, then ram it. Continue with this plan until you defeat all four Parasites; the orbs automatically coalesce into you.

Upper Zora's River: Parasite #9

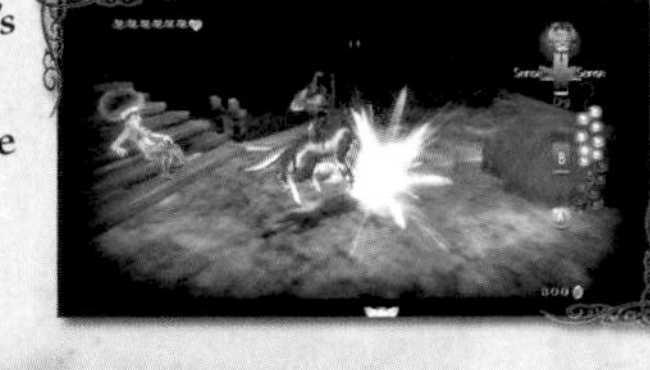

➤ You're back at Iza's dwelling, and she's relaxing on the steps. Speak to her, and the electrical discharge from the Parasite freaks her out. Locate the Parasite, which is behind you, and pounce on it. Iza doesn't know what to make of this sparkling (as you're invisible to her)!

➤ With the water now running through the river, you can access the platform linking the north and south banks of this area. Run across here, and read a sign about the boat trips. Then head down to the north bank and explore; there are the usual spots to locate.

There's an interesting locked door in the north wall. The sign next to it lets you know there's a Fishing Hole beyond. Remember to come back here. A Bomb Rock is on the upper area here as well.

Missing Links

1. Upper Zora's River (after the Hunt for Parasite #9)

The north bank of Upper Zora's River near Iza's hut is packed with goodies:

Grass: Against the rock wall, just to the side of the dwelling (Rupees)

Crates and dig spots: To the side of Iza's dwelling (Rupee and Hearts)

Grass: In the middle of the bank, leading to the Wind Stone (three Hearts)

Dig spot: Behind the sign for the fishing hole (yellow Rupee [10])

Grass: Just right of the path to the fishing hole (Rupees)

Grass: Darker grass on the Wind Stone promontory (Heart)

Dig spots: Under the Wind Stone promontory (Hearts and Rupees)

Dig spots: On the lower bank, near the water's edge, east of the Wind Stone (Rupees)

Grass: Two places before and after the Bomb Rock on the upper ground (Rupees)

1 2 3 4 5 6

Hidden Skill

Howling for the White Wolf

Before you continue, it is vitally important that you investigate that strange ceremonial stone on the nearby rocky promontory. Listen to the tune the wind whistles through the hole in the rock. You must now recite the tune. Watch the tune, or follow the instructions here, then replicate it. The pitch is as follows: Low (hold), Middle, Low, High (hold), Middle, Low. Use ⚪ to howl high and ⚪ to howl low on your ◎. For midrange howling, don't move the stick.

You appear as a wolf near some snowy peaks. The White Wolf appears at the end of a leafy edge, on the world's opposite side. You howl the tune again. When you finish, the White Wolf tells you, "Let teachings of old pass to you...."

Note: You have summoned the White Wolf! He is currently waiting for you on a small stone platform near the east entrance to Castle Town. You must head here as Link and learn your next Hidden Skill. The walkthrough tells you the earliest point that this is possible.

Zora's Domain: Parasites #10 and #11

▲ When you're done howling, move to the far end of the upper bank to the natural bridge, upon which two Zoras stand. They are searching for **Prince Ralis** and dive into the water, where they swim down the stone tunnel with the torches on each side. Don't swim just yet.

◄ Instead head north into Zora's Domain, as there are a few more Twilit Parasites to locate. Move along the eastern bank and listen to the Zoras talk about falling molten shards. Continue farther along to a Zora looking at an icy blockade; the route to **Snowpeak** is impassable!

➤ Drop to the water now and swim into the middle of this area. Use your sense view to locate two Twilit Parasites buzzing about the series of tiny islands here. Climb on an island and be patient.

To target a Parasite, press Ⓩ and flick between the two Parasites until one flies close to you, then leap and strike. If you miss, climb on another tiny island before you're zapped. Keep this up until you defeat both Parasites and you have their orbs.

Zora's Domain: Parasite #12

▲ When you're done with the two Parasites in the middle of the waterfall pool, swim west toward a small and large rock. Climb onto an area of stone. Head up the grassy ramp and locate the shadow in the earth, near a crate. Dig up the bug in the shadow, then pounce on it quickly, or it will fly above you and torment you for several minutes before dropping low enough for you to jump and grab it.

➤ Continue along this sloped ledge, heading north and picking up spare Rupees and Hearts from the Missing Link locations. At the ledge's end, almost hidden behind grass, is a small chest. Open it up for a small reward.

Overworld Chest #18: Yellow Rupee (10)

Enemies Encountered

Twilit Parasite

Twilit Carrier Kargarok

Twilit Messenger

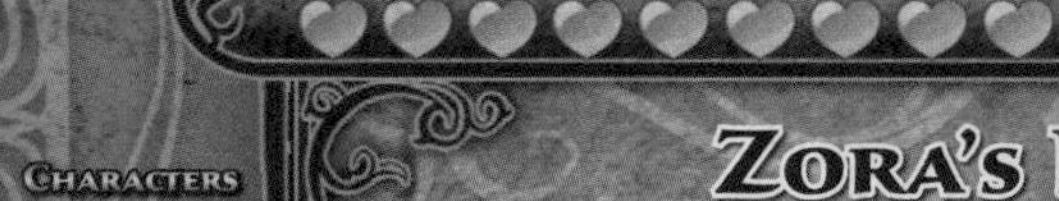

Characters Encountered

Zora

Midna

Telma

Iza

White Wolf

Zora's Domain: Climbing behind the Waterfall for Parasite #13

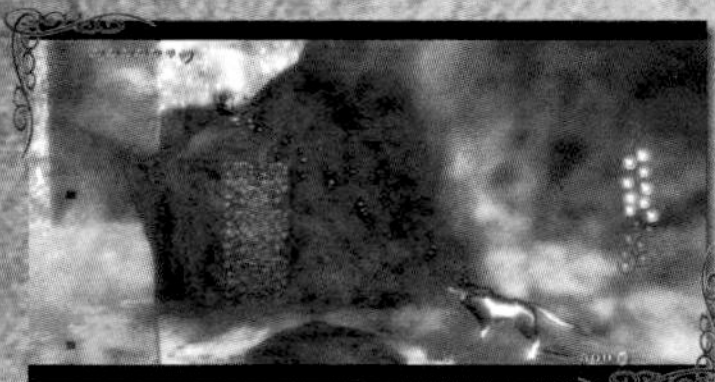

◄ Locate the small grassy ramp to the left of the ice blockade, and utilize Midna to leap onto a ledge. Use her again to leap another gap, then run along the narrow ledge until you're near the waterfall and some aquatic carving on the outside wall.

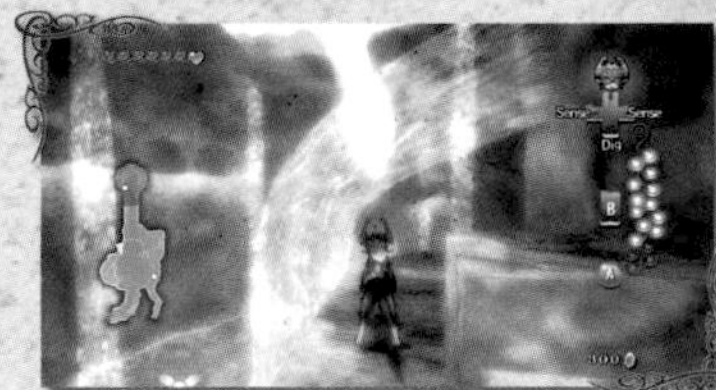

➤ Continue along this ledge's edge to another shallow ramp where you can summon Midna. Leap across to the vine-covered ledge above. Keep going, leaping another couple of very narrow and small rocks protruding from the wall, and you'll be able to head behind the waterfall, along a very narrow stone ledge.

➤ After you pass behind the waterfall, the ledge leads to a sloping grassy ledge that contains a chest at the far end. Break open the chest for a reward.

Overworld Chest #19: Red Rupee (20)

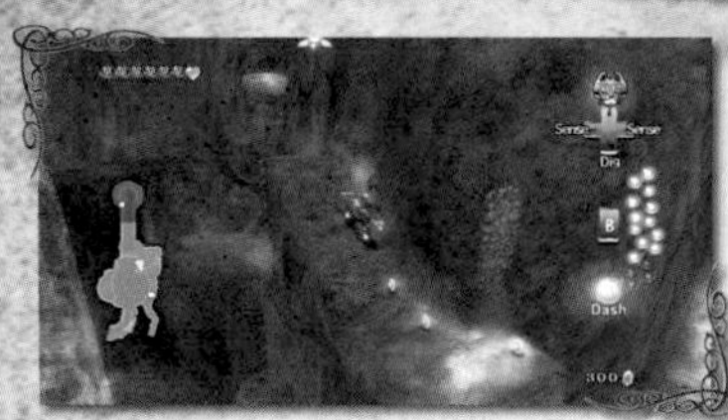

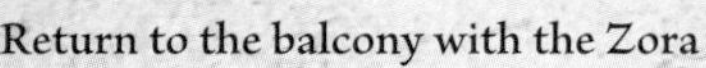

◄ Double back, heading to the narrow stone path with the waterfall. Locate a shallow stone ramp on the inside of the rock wall, and use Midna to leap up to a series of tiny square rock ledges. Leap across them all, and wind your way up along another narrow ledge. Use Midna to leap again, and then run down a grassy ledge, collecting green Rupees (1).

➤ Turn the corner, following the trail of Rupees, and leap onto a rocky balcony area. If you dash north up the stone steps, a rock blocks your way; you saw the other side of this rock earlier at the top of Zora's Domain.

Return to the balcony with the Zora ceremonial columns overlooking the waterfall, and dash along this area heading south. Watch for the Twilit Parasite that's buzzing about here. Dispatch him!

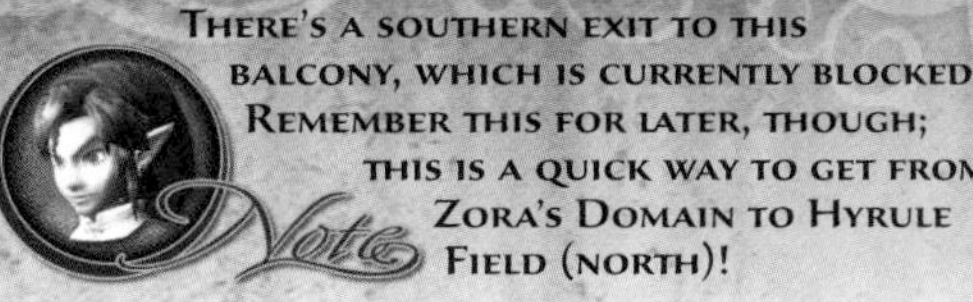

Note: There's a southern exit to this balcony, which is currently blocked. Remember this for later, though; this is a quick way to get from Zora's Domain to Hyrule Field (north)!

Up to the Top of Zora's Domain: Parasite #14

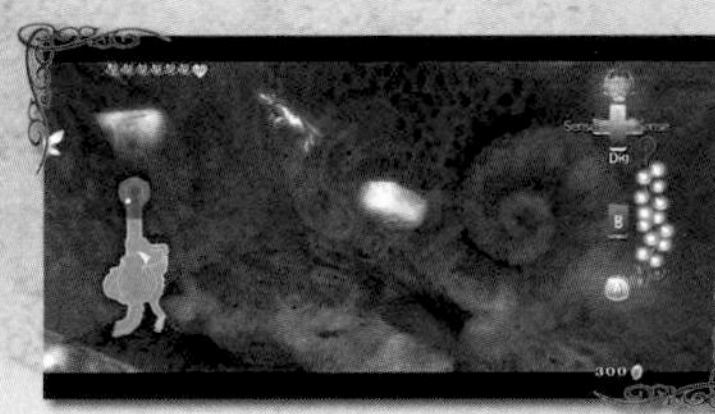

◄ Run north along the balcony, and use Midna to jump back on the narrow grass platform where you collected the green Rupees (1). Run to the top of it, near the giant mollusk fossil on the wall, and use Midna to leap across some tiny protruding rocks.

➤ You finally reach the top of Zora's Domain and can maneuver past the grass and crates you checked earlier. Instead, head to the chamber where the Zoras are recovering. Locate this wall, near an unlit torch and a stretched-out Zora. Charge and ram it! This dislodges the Twilit Parasite that's resting on the surface. Wait for it to descend, then chow down.

Missing Links

1. Zora's Domain (during the Hunt for Parasites #9–12)

As with your previous searches in these areas, check crates, the ground, and grass for the following items:

Crate: Southeast water level ledge (Heart)

Crate: Eastern rock wall, next to ice blockade (Rupee)

Grass and crate: On the far side, near the base ledges where Midna is summoned (Rupees and Heart)

Grass: First ledge, on the way to behind waterfall (Heart)

Grass: Near empty crate where Parasite #12 is dug up (Rupees)

Grass and crate: Western edge, ramped area after Parasite #12 (Rupees)

Grass: On the water's edge side of the ledge right next to chest #18 (Rupees)

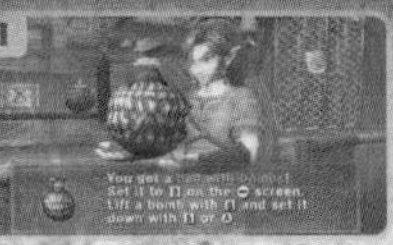
1

2

3

4

5

6

Castle Town: Parasite Found

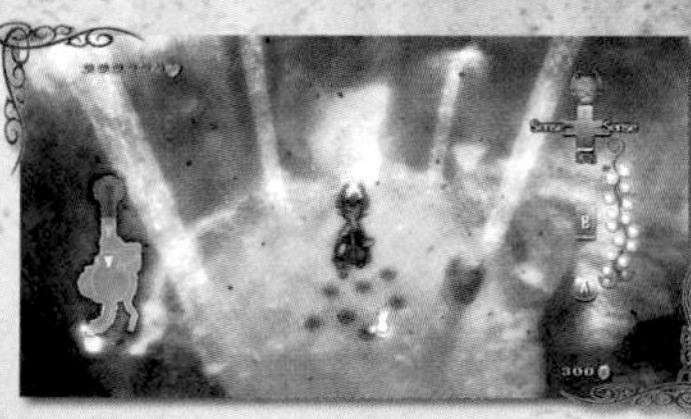

◄ Your last Twilit Parasite is waiting for you in orb form outside Telma's Bar in Castle Town (or behind a crate if you didn't find it when you entered the bar for the first time). Get there as quickly as possible, but definitely try a spectacular leap from the main waterfall.

Swim or run along the ledge and head south, out of the waterfall pool. Follow the advice of the Zora you met near Iza's dwelling and locate the stone tunnel with the torches. Swim into it, going with the current.

► You appear in the water channel on the north part of Hyrule Field with Castle Town in the distance. Swim to a set of steps and climb out. Take the southeast path out of here. Remember there are roaming Twilit Bulblins to slay.

Tip: If you're lost, locate Ilia's Scent and follow it; you're using the same route as before.

◄ Travel into the eastern part of the Hyrule Field next to Castle Town, and enter via the same place as before. On your way, you pass the White Wolf (if you howled at the Wind Stone in Upper Zora's River; if you didn't, do this now!), who is sitting on the vine-covered plinth. Come back here when you're human.

Warp Portal

As you reach the Castle Town entrance bridge, just past the White Wolf, three more Twilit Messengers fall from the sky. Run past the two closest to you, and savage the third near the entrance.

With the first Twilit Messenger down, run around in front of the energy wall and coax the two others together, launching Midna's area attack as soon as you've targeted the remaining two Twilit Messengers. They crumple as you skewer yourself through them. The warp portal to Castle Town is formed.

▲ Travel into Castle Town. Nothing has changed. The area is still bathed in twilight, so head directly south, then around to Telma's Bar via the alley that leads past the tent, Agitha's Castle, and the fortune teller. The orb you formed earlier is still here; grab it.

Note: If there's no orb here, it means you didn't shatter the crates in the far upper corner of the courtyard, releasing the Twilit Parasite. This is where he's hidden.

▲ Gather all the Parasites on the map. There's one that's just appeared in Lake Hylia. Warp there at once, paddle out to its location, and you see something a lot bigger, and a lot more frightening, charging through the waters.

Enemies Encountered
Twilit Parasite
Twilit Bulblin
Twilit Messenger

Characters Encountered

Midna

Spirit Lanayru

The Feeder of Darkness: Twilit Bloat

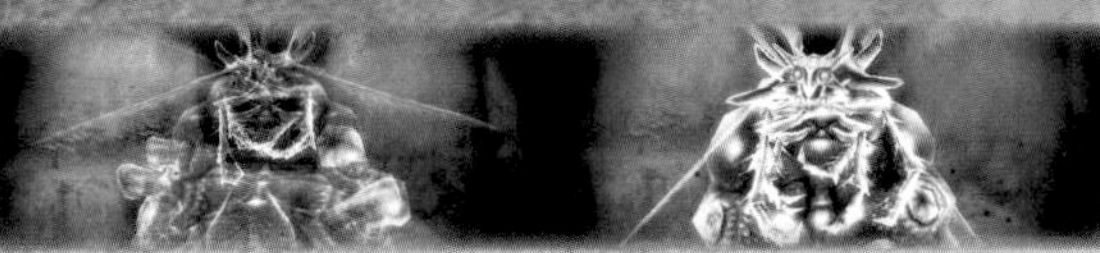

You reach a series of rickety boards bobbing in the lake. Crates begin to shudder as the water bubbles and boils. Suddenly, a massive electrical discharge bursts from the water and takes the form of a gigantic, pustule-ridden parasite!

Threat Meter

Dodge a charge, leap on, and gnaw a pustule-filled tendril. Let the light shine in!

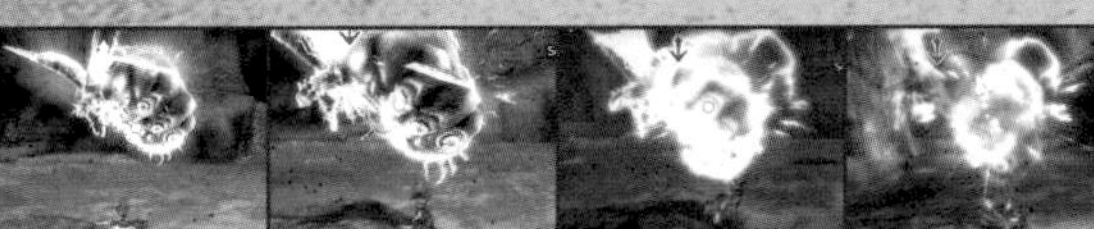

Step 1: This massive pustule with wings immediately begins to aggressively attack, wobbling down through the air and attempting to zap you with an electrical attack (as shown). Simply run around and jump to a different floating platform, away from the attack. As it descends, double back straight at it!

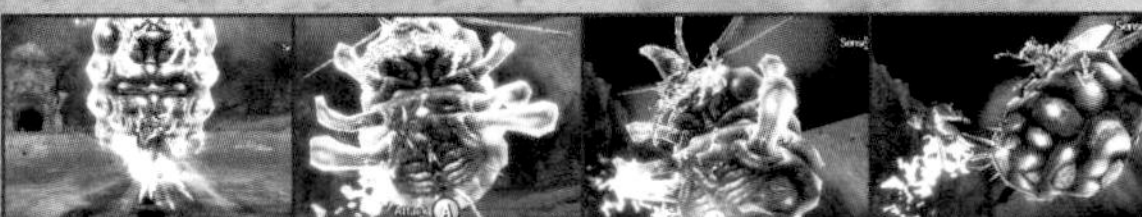

Step 2: The beast takes a short breather. With your sense view on (necessary to target this foe), leap and target Z the beast. Latch on to its disgusting belly. Gnaw on the stumpy tendrils until one bursts and the beast is propelled away from you. Land and secure a Heart from any crate if necessary. The beast is ready to attack again.

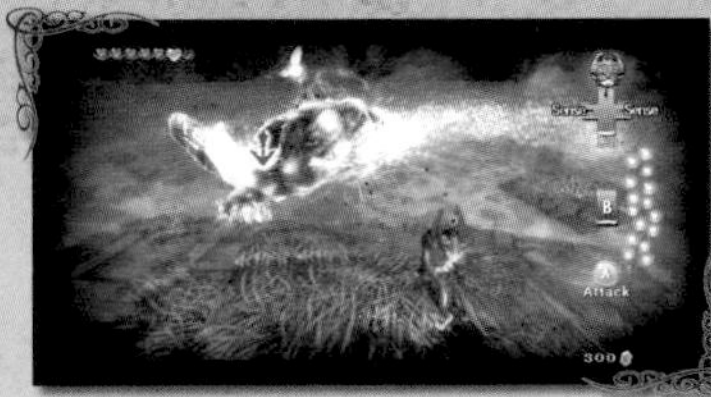

Step 3: The beast now speeds around underwater, circling you. Stay away from the water or you can get zapped by this maneuver. Then the beast rises and attempts to slam into you again. Repeat Steps 1 and 2.

Step 4: After three successful gnawings, the beast gives up and plays dead in the water. Immediately take this opportunity to climb on the thing's belly. Use Midna's area-of-effect attack to cover the entire beast and let go. Each tendril is severed!

The bloated parasite lolls from side to side, hanging upside down, and then deflates slightly, landing on the lake with a dull splash. It then explodes in a shower of shadow. Bound over and collect the final tear. Your Vessel of Light has been filled!

1

2

3

4

5

6

Task 8: Learn the Secrets of the Goddesses from Lanayru

High Spirits and Shocking Secrets

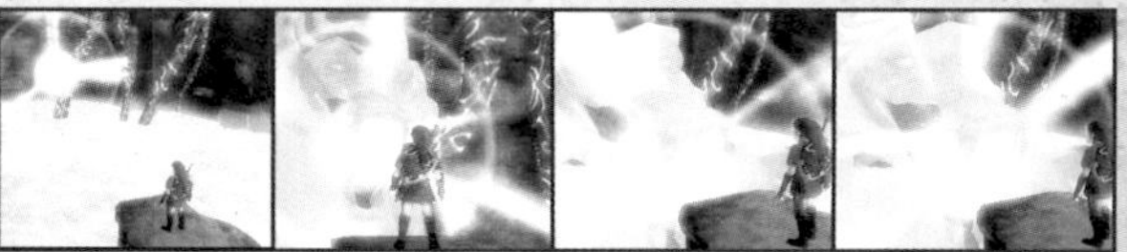

The Spirit Lanayru awakens from a slumber, after Midna leaves to find her Fused Shadow piece. It tells you the dark power you seek awaits in the bed of Lake Hylia. But you must see something first....

When all was chaos, the goddesses descended and gave order and life to the world. They granted power equally to all who dwelt in the light, and then returned to the heavens. These lands became known as the Sacred Realm.

Soon news of the Sacred Realm spread, and a great battle ensued. Among those living in the light, **interlopers** *who excelled at magic appeared and tried to control the Sacred Realm.*

It was then that the goddesses ordered us three light spirits to intervene. We sealed away the great magic those individuals had mastered.

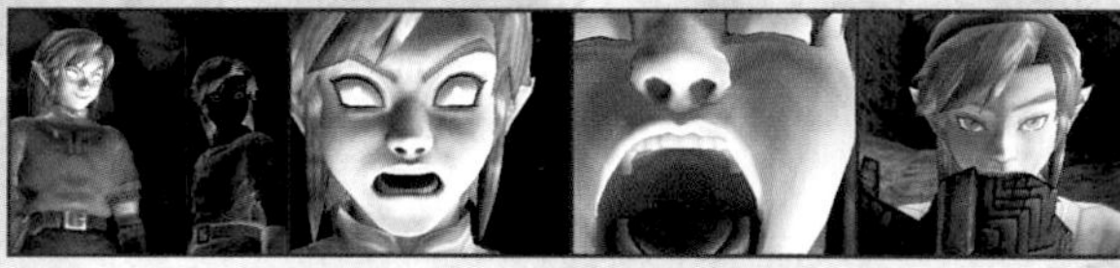

You know this **magic**. *It is the dark power you seek, the Fused Shadow. O hero chosen by the goddesses, beware. Those who do not know the danger of wielding power will, before long, be ruled by it.*

You collapse at the edge of the Lanayru Springs....

Lanayru:

The embodiment of the land of Lanayru, this magical spirit takes the form of a snake and resides in the spring near Lake Hylia. It seeks the light.

Enemies Encountered

Twilit Bloat

Overworld: Thorough Explorations and Saving the Zora Prince

Legend

- Piece of Heart
- Bottle
- Bag of Bombs
- Big Bomb Bag
- Golden Bug
- Bomb Rock
- Underwater Bomb Rock

Zora's Domain
Snowpeak (Entry Area)
Fishing Hole
Molten Shard
Twilit Messenger Fight
Hena's Hut
Iza's Dwelling (Mini-game)
Purlo's Tent
White Wolf
Agitha's Castle
Chudley's Emporium
King Bulblin Battle
Barnes' Bomb Shop
Telma's Bar (Prince Ralis)
Goron's Shop
Fanadi's Flight by Fowl
Plumm
Tired Goron
Telma's Wagon Trail (End)
Fyer's Hut
Zora Armor
Plumm
Lantern Cavern 2
Dungeon 3 Entrance: Lakebed Temple

Thorough Explorations and Saving the Zora Prince: Overview

With a large amount of Hyrule shining brightly in the light, you can now begin a thorough exploration of your surroundings, gathering more Rupees than you ever thought possible, almost completing a collection of Golden Bugs, and finding dozens of chests scattered throughout the land. You can halt your expedition for as long as you like to claim the third Fused Shadow, and attempt to complete minigames, find secret ledges, and bomb multiple Bomb Rocks to uncover the Rupees hidden inside. When destiny finally calls, and you've acquired a bigger wallet, more Bomb Bags, and spoken to a strange little Princess about a Bug Ball, your task is to escort the sickened Prince Ralis to Shaman Renado's healing hands. Only then will a gift from the Zora ghosts be forthcoming and the third dungeon become accessible.

1 — Thoroughly Explore Lake Hylia Pg 182

2 — Learn to Fly by Fowl Pg 183

3 — Complete Lantern Cavern II Pg 185

4 — Thoroughly Explore the Fields and River Pg 191

Items to Obtain

- Piece of Heart #15
- Fairy in a Bottle
- Water in a Bottle
- Piece of Heart #16

- Male Mantis
- Letter #5
- Letter #6
- Red Chu Jelly

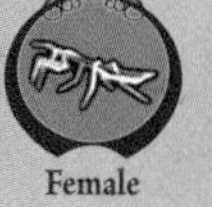

- Blue Chu Jelly
- Purple Chu Jelly
- Female Mantis
- Female Butterfly

- Male Butterfly
- Hidden Skill #3
- Female Stag Beetle
- Male Stag Beetle

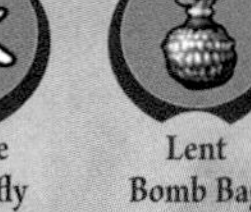

- Male Dragonfly
- Female Dragonfly
- Lent Bomb Bag
- Bomb Bag

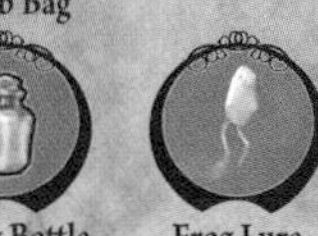

- Giant Bomb Bag
- Piece of Heart #17
- Empty Bottle
- Frog Lure

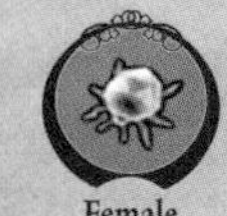

- Sinking Lure
- Big Wallet
- Piece of Heart #18
- Female Ladybug

- Male Ladybug
- Zora Armor
- Water Bombs
- Bomb Bag

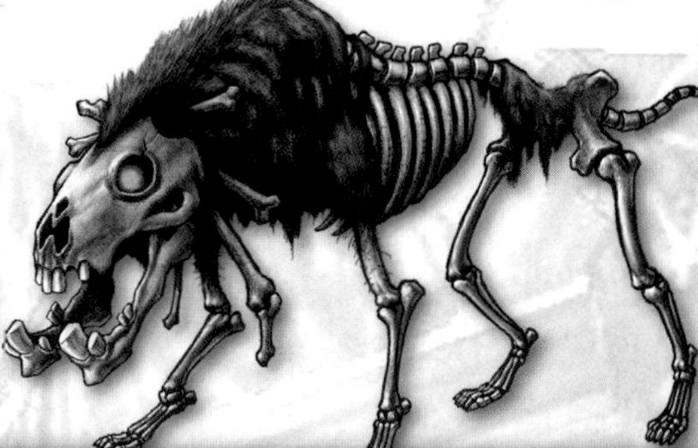

A Link to the Present

Ordon Sword

Heart Pieces: 4 (14 Total)

Wooden Shield

Hylian Shield

Hero's Clothes

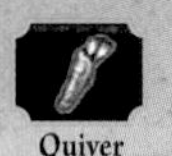

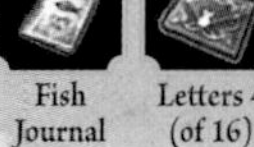

Wallet

Quiver

Golden Bugs: 10 (of 24)

Hidden Skills: 2 (of 7)

Ilia's Scent

Fish Journal

Letters 4 (of 16)

Fused Shadow Pieces 2 (of 3)

Overworld Denizens

Characters

Plumm

Falbi

Hena

Charlo

Soal

Chudley

Kili, Hanna, and Misha

Princess Agitha

Madame Fanadi

Borville

Louise

Enemy

White Wolfos

5 Explore Castle Town and Southern Field — Pg 200

6 Escort the Wagon Safely — Pg 206

7 Obtain the Zora Armor — Pg 209

8 Locate Bomb Rocks, Enter Water Temple — Pg 210

Characters Encountered

Plumm

Zora

Falbi

Task 1: Thoroughly Explore Lake Hylia

A Dive into Lanayru Spirit Cave

Tip: In order to maximize your energy, we're showing you all the incidental items as early as possible. However, Midna may appear from time to time, wanting to press on with the mission to find Rutela's son, the prince. You can start this part of the mission (Task #6) at any time.

◄ Now that the final spirit has spoken to you, you're free to hunt the land for chests, items, and other interesting trinkets before attempting to find the final **Fused Shadow** piece. Begin by diving into the pond inside the spirit cave. Put on your **Iron Boots** so you can sink to a small platform containing a chest, then swim and sink in the pond's eastern part to find a second chest.

Overworld Chest #20: Blue Rupee (5)

Overworld Chest #21: Yellow Rupee (10)

After raiding these two chests, check the pool for some underwater Bomb Rocks, and check the side ledges for grass containing multiple green Rupees (1). Look carefully before you leave to find vine walls, Clawshot medallions, and an upper exit in the south wall you can't reach yet. Return here later.

Exploring Lake Hylia

▲ Without the twilight enveloping the area, you can now investigate every part of the lake. Start with the set of tiny islands and platforms in the southeast. Move to the island near Fyer's house, and chat to a strange bird named Plumm (he doesn't speak to humans, so return as a wolf) and a Zora guard. The other Zoras are on patrol at the lake's bottom.

Plumm:

A female myna bird that works hard at her balloon-popping attraction, which she invites only those in wolf form to see. Plumm appears at two spots in Lake Hylia, ready to take your money in exchange for a shot at this minigame. She's great friends with Trill.

Note: There's a large floating platform (called "The Isle of Riches" by some) tethered to Fyer's hut. It has a pole and a rotating platform at the top; there are a few chests on here. This is a great place to land on, but you can do this only from above.

◄ If you wish to move quickly to the bridge area above Lake Hylia, run toward the hut that Fyer has now opened for business. There's a cannon hut jutting from the rocks next to the bridge, high above the lake's northern wall. The price is only 10 Rupees. Give it a shot and step into the cannon. After the coordinates are measured, and the strange organ with the chirping Ooccoos is wound up, you're fired! You land on a platform that has a giant target painted on it.

Note: This cannon is a great way to reach the Hylian Bridge if Midna isn't able to warp you, or you wish to try an exciting new minigame involving Cucco flying!

1

2

3

4

5

6

Task 2: Learn to Fly by Fowl

Having Some Fun with Flight-by-Fowl

▲ When you reach the perched building high atop the lake, don't enter the door just yet. Instead, take out your **Gale Boomerang** and look around. There's a spinning **weathervane** fan on the building's gable. Aim at it; it spins and halts a **rotating platform** down on the **Isle of Riches**.

Why do this? Because the rotating platform holds a chest with a great prize, and it's easier to land on it if the chest isn't rotating.

Tip

Before you begin your flying, consider spending some Rupees at Trill's, buying bombs from Barnes or items from Malo or the small Goron, or visiting Castle Town to gain a bigger wallet from Agitha. If you don't offload some Rupees or get a bigger wallet, you won't be able to fit all the treasure in your wallet.

Tip

▲ With the rotating platform stopped, enter through the door that leads inside the house. Drop down the ladder to a sloping wooden floor. The exit is up the ramp, to your right and leads to the "fantastication" sign and Hylian Bridge.

◄ Or you can head left, which leads to **Falbi**. He whoops and whistles, beckoning you to pay him 20 Rupees for the chance to fly onto the Isle of Riches to become a wealthy man. Pay up—this will be fun.

Falbi:

Somewhere between 20 and 30 years old, Falbi is a former circus member and is very tall, especially compared to the short Fyer down below. He's begun a small business awarding fabulous prizes for those who can grab a Cucco by the legs and pilot it to a small platform down on Lake Hylia. Overly cheerful, he loves to gesticulate wildly and coax customers in for a ride.

◄ Step #1: Before you grab a Cucco, have your **Iron Boots** close at hand; make sure you can access them by pressing ✚. Then choose a Cucco; they all fly the same, regardless of color. Step off the tiny platform and fly!

Step #2: For your first run, fly through the giant floating Rupee. You receive the amount indicated (the color indicates the amount of Rupees you receive), and the giant floating Rupees show the best landing trajectory to the Isle of Riches. Then swing right and head for the blue Rupee (5). As you arrive, make a strong banking left turn.

► Step #3: Aim for the next giant green Rupee (1). By the time you reach the last giant Rupee, you're too high and will overshoot the tiny rotating platform. You can still land on the lower part of the "Isle of Riches," but where's the fun in that?

Step #4: As soon as you pass through the last giant Rupee, put on your **Iron Boots** and take them off about half a second later. If you wear them too long, you drop too far and miss the top platform. Wear them too briefly, and you will overshoot it. This takes skill and practice, but you can definitely land on the tiny top platform!

If you miss, ride the cannon at Fyer's hut up to the Flight-by-Fowl building and try again. This time, put the boots on during the flight or as you leap, but only very briefly. Then follow the Rupee path. Rotating the fan atop the building to stop the upper platform also makes this much easier.

Tip

Author Note

We managed to land on the uppermost platform using the Iron Boots on our very first attempt! Even more amazing was that we'd forgotten to stop the platform rotating; it is definitely possible, so keep on practicing.

➤ Landing on the platform allows you to ransack all the chests on the Isle of Riches. Begin with the top rotating platform. Kick open this chest for a huge increase in your Rupee collection!

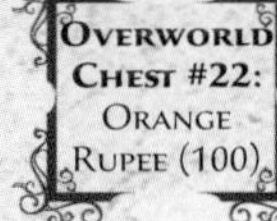

Overworld Chest #22: Orange Rupee (100)

➤ You must now be incredibly careful not to jump off the upper platform and miss the next ledge, or you'll have to complete this flying game again. You must drop off the upper platform's southeast side, hang from it, then land on the next platform below. You must crack open this chest, which is directly under the first.

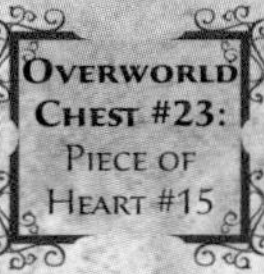

Overworld Chest #23: Piece of Heart #15

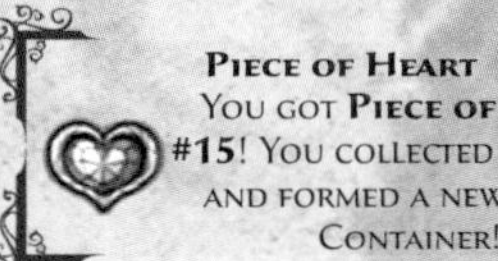

Piece of Heart
You got **Piece of Heart #15**! You collected **5 Pieces** and formed a new Heart Container!

➤ You've increased your energy level by another full Heart Container, but there are more prizes. Drop down from the same corner as you did before, to a larger platform that contains a treasure chest. Pry this open for another Rupee prize.

Drop to the increasingly larger platforms on this isle, and run over to another, smaller chest. The Rupee reward is smaller but still worth your effort. Now jump down to the next platform and avoid the floating lantern—that's an **Imp Poe**. You must return for him when you can transform into a wolf at will. Instead, crack open the next chest.

Overworld Chest #24: Purple Rupee (50)

Overworld Chest #25: Red Rupee (20)

Overworld Chest #26: Yellow Rupee (10)

➤ Despite your ransacking of all the major chests on the isle, there are still more places you can fly to from Falbi's Cucco flying building. Head back here via Fyer's cannon, and start another run.

This time, aim directly at the Lanayru spirit cave entrance. As you near, you'll see two protruding entry pillars, both with chests on them. You can fly and land on one of the protrusions, or fly and land on the middle ledge, grab another Cucco, and land on one. To grab the other chest's contents, repeat the flying. Or wait until you have the Clawshot, which makes reaching the chests a little easier. The western chest has the higher prize.

Overworld Chest #27: Purple Rupee (50)

Overworld Chest #28: Orange Rupee (100)

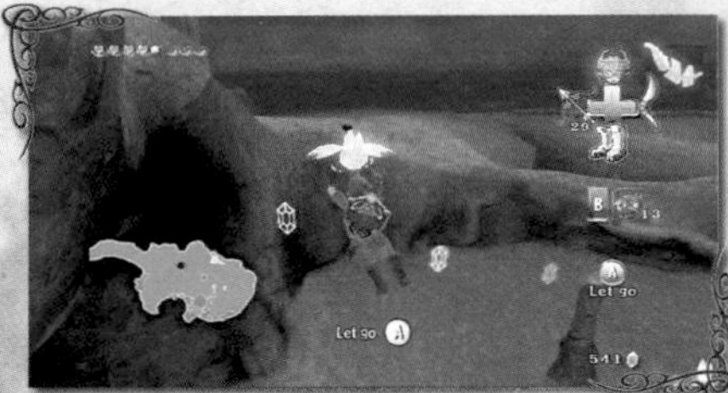

➤ The Rupees don't end there either. Head back up to Falbi again and take to the skies hanging from the Cucco of your choice. This time swing left, and follow the series of giant Rupees down to a long thin rock in the lake's middle. Either drop from the Cucco, or use the Iron Boots to land on the small platform atop a rock pillar.

Note: There's a small ledge directly underneath Falbi's dwelling that you can fly to, but you can't grab the items there yet. Return here with the ability to transform into a wolf—we'll tell you when!

▲ The main reason for landing on this rock is the view, but there's a secondary reason (and a secondary Cucco) too. You can now fly via Cucco to the top of Fyer's cannon hut and inspect the top of the cannon hut from this angle. Land on the cannon roof, then drop to the north side for a red Rupee (20), and then into a boat. Walk along a small crane attached to the hut to obtain two yellow Rupees (10). Then drop to the ground.

Falbi

Task 3: Complete an Exploration of Lantern Cavern II

Exploring the Second Lantern Cavern

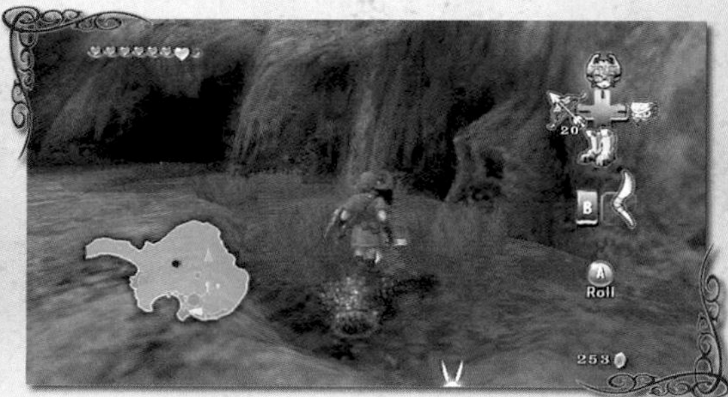

▲ Now explore the area to the south of Fyer's cannon hut. Move to the series of islands and plateaus, and locate the ladder leading to a short grassy connecting bridge. Climb up to the southern grassy area. Run to this small marsh, where there's a crate to destroy. Inside is a Fairy—bottle it! You can also gather water from here. This is only useful for putting out small fires and is not necessary for your current tasks.

Fairy in a Bottle

You got a **Fairy in a Bottle**!

Bottle of Water

You filled your Bottle with **water**!

◄ The reason for the Fairy-containing crate becomes apparent when you walk to the nearby rock wall. A Bomb Rock blocks a hole in the wall. Produce a bomb or Bomb Arrow and destroy the rock, revealing a cave entrance. This leads to a frightening tunnel labyrinth called Lantern Cavern II.

▲

Tip

You return to Lake Hylia and smash open the crate and obtain the Fairy as many times as you wish. Your only limits are your energy and the number of Bottles you have to catch them all in!

Note

You should have a full Lantern and be ready to fill an empty Bottle with oil you gather from Yellow Chus during your upcoming exploration. This is your first chance to explore this area, where you find 15 Chests. One houses a **Piece of Heart** while the rest hold arrows, bombs, seeds, and Rupees!

Lantern Cavern II: First Exploration

Lantern Cavern II

▲ Like the first Lantern Cavern, make sure you've got fuel in your Lantern before venturing into this dangerous network of pitch-black tunnels. Slash through the weeds in the entry passage for a few Hearts, then proceed north into the cavern's first small chamber.

► A torch is in the middle of the first chamber. Light it with a wave of your Lantern, then put your Lantern away to conserve its fuel.

◄ Notice the three large bomb rocks stuck in the chamber's east, west, and north walls. Destroy the west bomb rock to open the way forward; blast through the other two bomb rocks to reveal two small alcoves. Each contains a treasure chest.

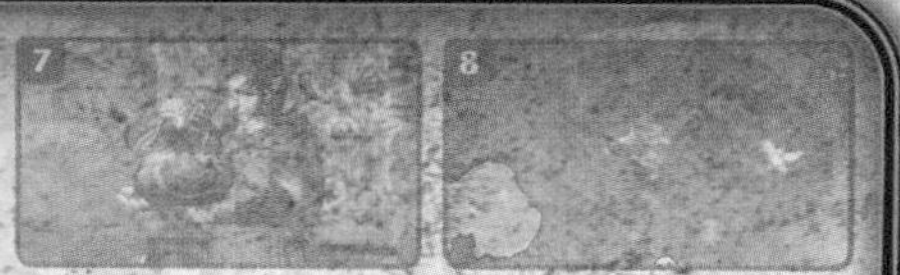

Legend
Poe Soul
Piece of Heart
Bomb
Arrows
Seeds
Red Rupee
Orange Rupee
Purple Rupee
Yellow Rupee
You put yellow Chu Jelly in your bottle!

After raiding the alcoves, continue down the west path. A Yellow Chu guards the next small chamber, a convenient source of free Lantern fuel! Light the chamber's central torch, then put away your Lantern and ready an empty Bottle. Defeat the Yellow Chu and scoop its remains into your Bottle for Yellow Chu Jelly, which you may use to refuel your Lantern if it runs low.

This second chamber features two bomb rocks, one to the east and the other to the west. Destroy the east bomb rock to reveal a small alcove where treasure chest #31 is found, then open the chest for a Red Rupee (20). Blast the west bomb rock to clear the passage to the third chamber.

Treasure Chest #31: Red Rupee (20)

The east alcove holds treasure chest #29, which a few Keeses are guarding. Dispatch the Keeses and open the chest for some Bombs (5).

The north alcove holds treasure chest #30, which contains a Yellow Rupee (10).

Treasure Chest #29: Bombs (5)

Treasure Chest #30: Yellow Rupee (10)

◄ The ceiling of the tunnel that leads to the third chamber is covered with Torch Slugs. Either defeat them from range with the Clawshot or Hero's Bow, or move forward slowly to make them drop, then hack them with your sword.

▲ An Imp Poe haunts the third chamber. If you haven't reached the point in the adventure where you're able to transform into a wolf at will, there's nothing you can do against this little fiend. Light the torch in the middle of the chamber, then retreat into the previous tunnel to make the Imp Poe lose interest in you.

Tip: If you're able to change into wolf form, use your sense view to detect this Imp Poe, then rip it apart it to claim Poe Soul #16.

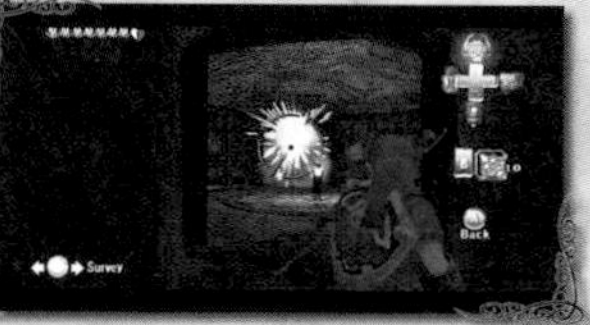

▲ From the safety of the east tunnel, fire a Bomb Arrow at the third chamber's west and north bomb rocks to destroy them. Cross the chamber and open treasure chest #32 in the west alcove for Arrows (10), then dart into the north passage to proceed.

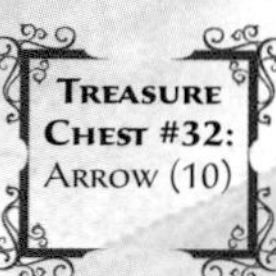

Treasure Chest #32: Arrow (10)

▲ Be careful: there's a pit in the north passage! Cross it via the wooden plank, then defeat the Tektites on the pit's opposite side.

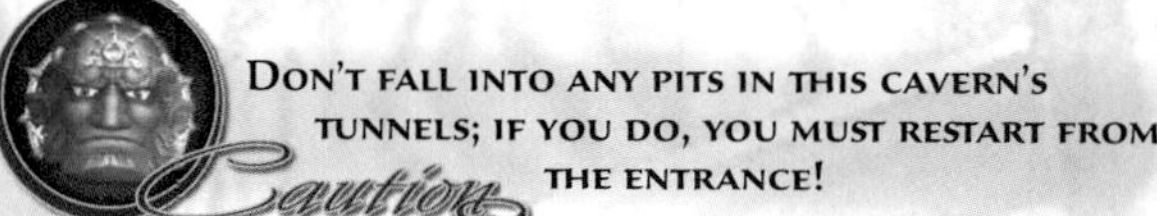

Caution: Don't fall into any pits in this cavern's tunnels; if you do, you must restart from the entrance!

▲ Watch out: a Beamos defends the fourth chamber. Fire an arrow into its laser eye from the safety of the south passage, then enter the chamber and light the torch to the west so you can put away your Lantern.

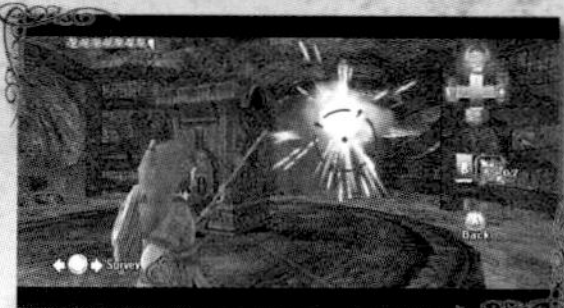

▲ Blast the room's north and east bomb rocks, then search the north alcove to locate treasure chest #33, which holds a Red Rupee (20). Smash the skulls in the alcove for a couple of hearts, then enter the east tunnel to proceed.

Treasure Chest #33: Red Rupee (20)

▲ The cavern's fifth chamber is filled with goodies. Light both its torches to reveal treasure chest #34, which contains an Orange Rupee (100). Squash the Yellow Chu that drops from the ceiling, then scoop its Yellow Chu Jelly into a Bottle to keep your Lantern burning bright.

Treasure Chest #34: Orange Rupee (100)

▲ Destroy the north bomb rock to reveal a small alcove. Defeat the Tektites that spring out of the alcove in ambush, then open treasure chest #35 for a Red Rupee (20). Afterward, blast through the east bomb rock to open the passage to the sixth chamber.

Treasure Chest #35: Red Rupee (20)

◄ You face a fire-breathing Dodongo in the sixth chamber. Circle around the beast and slash at its tail until you defeat it, then destroy the east bomb rock to reveal a small alcove containing a tall shaft of light. It's an exit point! Don't leave yet, though; there's still a lot to do in the cavern.

Enemies Encountered: Keese, Chu, Torch Slug, Imp Poe, Tektite, Beamos, Dodongo

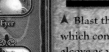

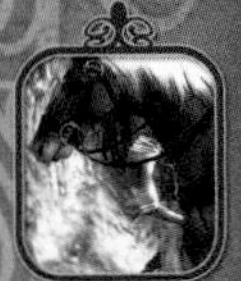

Characters Encountered

Fyer

Epona

▲ Blast the north bomb rock to reveal another small alcove, which contains treasure chest #36. A few Tektites pop out of the alcove as well; dispatch them, then open the chest for Bombs (5), which you need at this point! Cut away the weeds near the chest for a couple of Hearts, then destroy the east bomb rock to open the way forward.

Treasure Chest #36: Bombs (5)

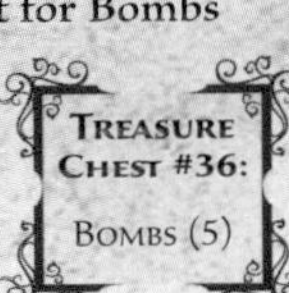

Caution: There are a few more pits in the east passage, but no enemies to worry about. Don't fall in!

▲ Another Beamos defends the cavern's seventh chamber. Fire an arrow into its laser eye from the safety of the previous passage. Enter the room and light its torch so you can stash your Lantern and conserve its oil.

▲ Blow up the three bomb rocks in this chamber to reveal a south alcove, an east alcove, and another passage to the north. Defeat the Keese in the south alcove, then open the treasure chest (#37) for Arrows (10). Lift the lid on treasure chest #38 in the east alcove for a Purple Rupee (50).

Treasure Chest #37: Arrows (10)

Treasure Chest #38: Purple Rupee (50)

➤ Use caution when entering the north passage; more Torch Slugs line its ceiling. Defeat each one in turn, and be careful not to fall into the pits you encounter after the passage bends west.

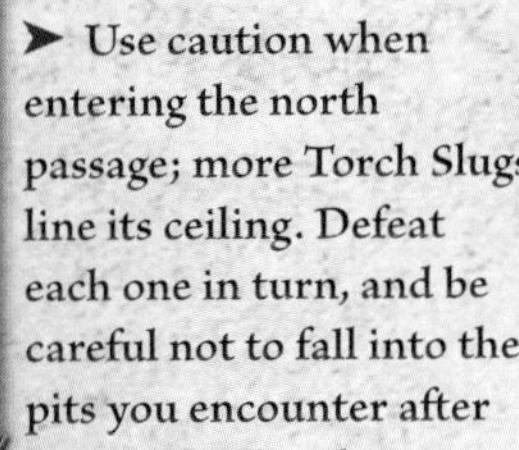

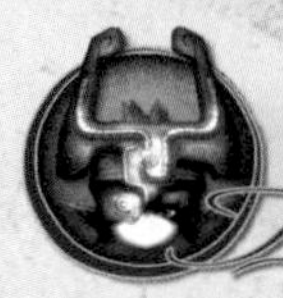

Tip: Make good use of the Spin Attack when Torch Slugs and Keeses surround you; you'll rid yourself of nearby threats, and you're less likely to fall into a pit using this maneuver.

◄ Another Imp Poe floats about in the cavern's eighth chamber. If you're not at the point where you're able to transform into a wolf at will, there's nothing you can do against this enemy. Dart in and light the torch in the middle of the chamber, then retreat into the previous tunnel so the Imp Poe stops chasing you.

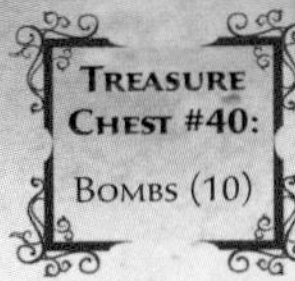

Tip: Change into wolf form if you're able, then tear into this Imp Poe to collect Poe Soul #17.

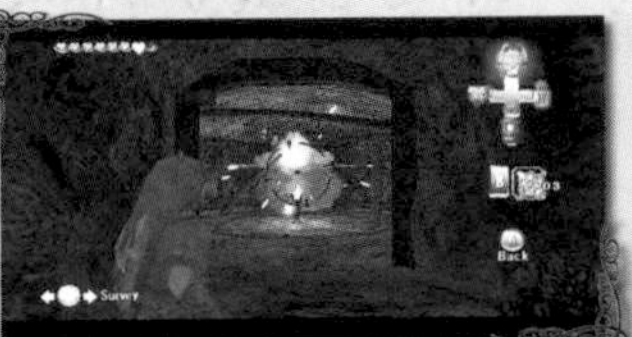

▲ Use Bomb Arrows to destroy the eighth chamber's north, south, and west bomb rocks from range. Tektites hop out of the west alcove; dash forward and cut through them, then open treasure chest #39 in the north alcove for a Purple Rupee (50) before the Imp Poe zeroes in on you.

Treasure Chest #39: Purple Rupee (50)

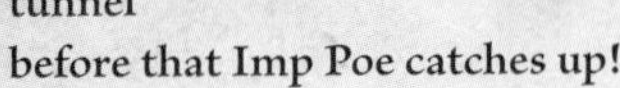

➤ Dart into the west alcove and open treasure chest #40 to obtain Bombs (10). You've pillaged this room, so hurry into the south tunnel before that Imp Poe catches up!

Treasure Chest #40: Bombs (10)

➤ It's an uneventful trip to the cavern's ninth chamber, but the Dodongo duo that guards this room makes up for that. Focus on eliminating one of these nasty creatures before tackling the other to avoid fighting both at once.

▲ After dealing with the Dodongos, destroy the room's two bomb rocks, then open treasure chest #41 in the north alcove for Seeds (50) for your Slingshot. There's a Yellow Chu in the alcove as well; waste it and scoop its remains into a Bottle for more Yellow Chu Jelly to keep light in your Lantern.

Treasure Chest #41:
Seeds (50)

▲ The tenth chamber is quiet; there are no enemies here at first. Take out the room's two bomb rocks and to reveal a Keese-filled alcove to the west and a passage to the south. Slice through the Keeses and open treasure chest #43 for an Orange Rupee (100), then head into the south tunnel.

Treasure Chest #42:
Orange Rupee (100)

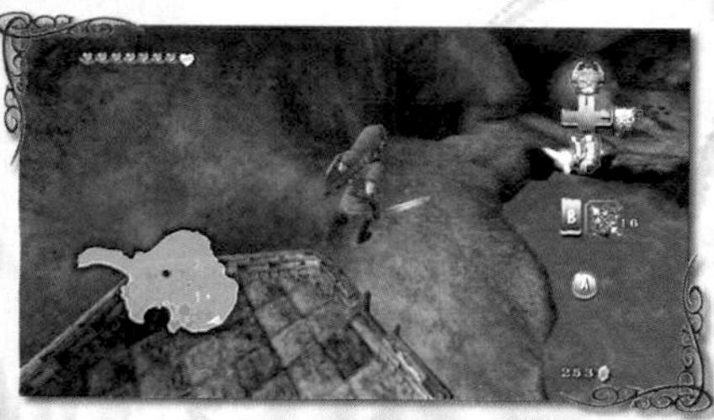

◄ Watch your step through the south passage; pitfalls abound! Navigate the wooden planks that stretch across the pits, eliminating Keeses who ambush you with the Spin Attack.

▲ The passage leads to the cavern's eleventh and final chamber. Another Imp Poe hovers about here; avoid it if you're unable to combat it in wolf form, and focus on lighting the room's two torches instead. Doing so reveals treasure chest #43, which contains Piece of Heart #16!

Treasure Chest #43:
Piece of Heart #16

Piece of Heart
You got **Piece of Heart #16**! Collect **4 more** for another full Heart Container.

Tip: If you're able to transform into a wolf, it's best to defeat this Imp Poe and claim Poe Soul #18.

➤ That's it! You have ransacked Lantern Cavern II. If you couldn't get the three Poe Souls from here during this run, come back for them later. Step into the shaft of light in the final chamber's south alcove to return to the surface with the loot you've gained.

Lake Hylia: Up the Tall Tower

◄ After you've explored Lantern Cavern II and all but the Imp Poes remain, head out and check the sloping ground and large plateau to the east. There's an Imp Poe to avoid here and no real prizes for cutting grass, but there is a huge tower to climb, at the top of which you'll see a great view of the lake. Come back here later to meet someone called Auru, but for now, try an impressive leap off!

Author Note

That tower is tall. How tall is it? Well, we started climbing at night, and when we reached the top, dawn was breaking!

➤ The time has come to explore some of the other areas, so locate Fyer and pay for another cannon flight out of here. Exit via the Flight-by-Fowl building, and head up the fenced entrance to the Hyrule Field area and to the bridge. You don't want to run everywhere, so locate the Horse Grass at the fork in the road and summon your faithful friend Epona.

Enemies Encountered

Tektite

Beamos

Keese

Torch Slug

Imp Poe

Dodongo

Chu

Characters Encountered

Postman

Barnes

White Wolf

Hero's Shade

Before you cross the bridge, though, quickly detour to the large Bomb Rock just to your right. You get four Blue Rupees (5). At night, watch for Stalhounds and Bokoblins roaming about.

Golden Bug: Male Mantis

Collection: 11 (of 24)

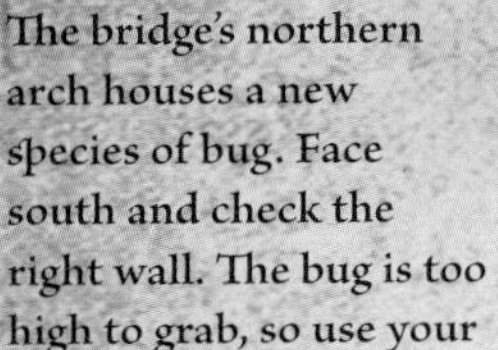

The bridge's northern arch houses a new species of bug. Face south and check the right wall. The bug is too high to grab, so use your **Gale Boomerang** to whisk it to you. Pick up the Male Mantis and add it to your collection, which is now almost half complete! Now cross the bridge.

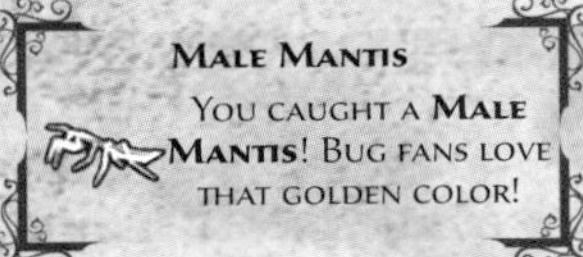

Male Mantis

You caught a **Male Mantis**! Bug fans love that golden color!

As you cross the bridge (or at any other location after you leave Lake Hylia), the Postman comes huffing and puffing toward you with another two missives. One is from Barnes, who says he's perfected the Water Bomb. The other is from the Lanayru Tourist Association letting you know that Iza and Hena's Playground for Grown-ups has opened in the Upper River area, where the carrier dropped you and you met Iza for the first time.

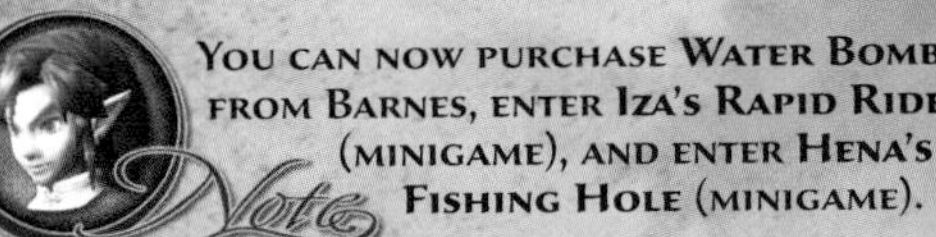

Note: You can now purchase **Water Bombs** from Barnes, enter **Iza's Rapid Ride** (minigame), and enter **Hena's Fishing Hole** (minigame).

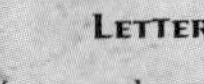

Letter #5

You got Letter #5: "Good stuff inside!" by Barnes.

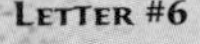

Letter #6

You got Letter #6: "Now open for business" by Lanayru Tourist Association.

➤ As you cross this large bridge, be sure you pause for a moment and begin to attack a swarm of Guays fluttering and swooping about here. When you've defeated your final one, a ring of Rupees falls from the sky! Cash in, then head south.

▲ Gallop south past the bridge and under a gigantic dead tree and rocky walled area. Halt when you encounter a group of Chus dropping from the tree to the ground. Optionally engage them in combat, cutting them into smaller Chus before they finally explode. You can scrape Red, Blue, and Purple Chu into a spare Bottle.

Red Chu Jelly

You put **Red Chu Jelly** in your Bottle. Use this to restore up to **eight Hearts**.

Blue Chu Jelly

You put **Blue Chu Jelly** in your Bottle. Use this to restore **all energy**.

Purple Chu Jelly

You put **Purple Chu Jelly** in your Bottle. Who knows what will happen....

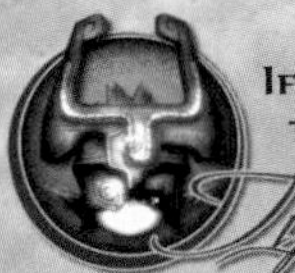

Tip: If you're after Red and Blue Chu Jelly, which acts the same as like-colored potions sold in stores, save the money and simply come back here.

◄ If you approach this area during the evening or at night, expect encounters with Stalhounds. Dismantle those bony fiends before attempting to locate your next Golden Bug!

Golden Bug: Female Mantis

Collection: 12 (of 24)

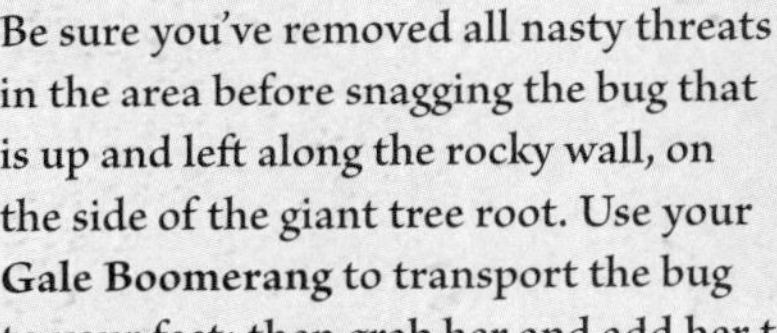

Be sure you've removed all nasty threats in the area before snagging the bug that is up and left along the rocky wall, on the side of the giant tree root. Use your **Gale Boomerang** to transport the bug to your feet; then grab her and add her to your collection.

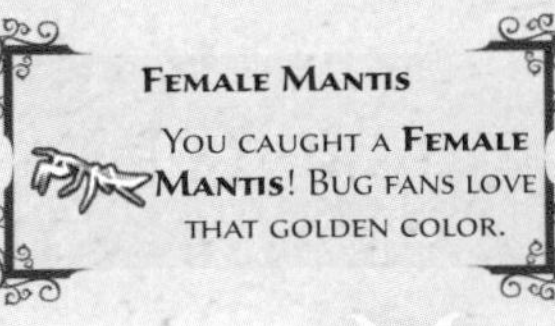

Female Mantis

You caught a **Female Mantis**! Bug fans love that golden color.

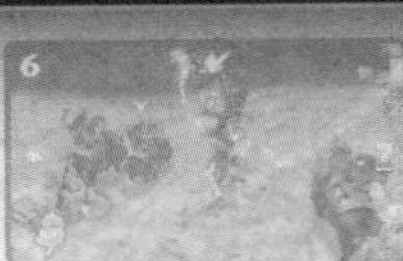

◄ Ride down this trail, over a small wooden bridge, and into a grassy path where Bokoblins are roaming. There are at least three of them to deal with while you're either on horseback or when you reach a Bomb Rock overlooking the lake below. Optionally, during combat with Bokoblins, you can lay a bomb, explode the rock, and then inspect the treasure left behind—two yellow Rupees (10).

► The trail leads to a blocked passage and sealed gate to Hyrule Field (south), so return to the Great Hylian Bridge and inspect the north arch. There's a small piece of vine growing on this span, but you don't have a Clawshot to reach it. Come back here later. For now, head north to the section of Hyrule Field near the Castle Town gate.

Enemies Encountered

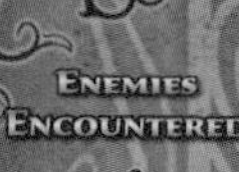

Stalhound

Bokoblin

Guay

Chu (Red, Blue, Purple)

Bulblin Archer

Task 4: Thoroughly Explore the Fields and River

Hyrule Field (East): Bug and Wolf Hunting

Golden Bug: Female Butterfly

Collection: 13 (of 24)

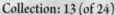

Journey on horseback to the area of Hyrule Field where you entered Castle Town, and prepare for a minor fracas with a Bulblin Archer or two. When you're done, check the rocky outcrop above and left of you, along the north rock wall. In the long grass on the outcrop's edge is a Female Butterfly. Catch it using your **Gale Boomerang.**

Female Butterfly
You caught a **Female Butterfly**! Bug fans love that golden color.

Golden Bug: Male Butterfly

Collection: 14 (of 24)

While you're in this area of Hyrule Field, journey south, to the right of the outcrop where you found the Female Butterfly, to a small clump of tall flowers. The Male Butterfly is here, near the entrance to the amphitheater. Catch that bug!

Male Butterfly
You caught a **Male Butterfly**! Bug fans love that golden color.

Hidden Skill #3: Back Slice

Your exploration of this area shouldn't end with the bug hunt. There's an incredibly important meeting you need to attend with the White Wolf, who's sitting patiently on the plinth in front of the Castle Gate entrance. Head here, slaying a Bulblin along the way, and climb up the short vine wall onto the plinth. The White Wolf waits for you. You awaken in the ghostly ether. The undead Hero's Shade asks if you wish to learn your next skill. The answer is yes!

Your teacher first ensures that you learned the previous Hidden Skill correctly and asks you to show him that you've mastered the **shield attack**. Simply target Ⓩ and move your Nunchuk forward to push the Shade back, then attack with a sword slash.

Satisfied, he will now teach you the **back slice**. This technique is useful to counter a foe that has a shield and armor, preventing a front attack. They frequently expose their backs to attacks, and this technique takes advantage of that. Now you try it.

Back Slice: Target Ⓩ and press Ⓐ while tilting ◄ or ► to jump and roll around your foe; then perform a jumping slice with a Wii Remote slash.

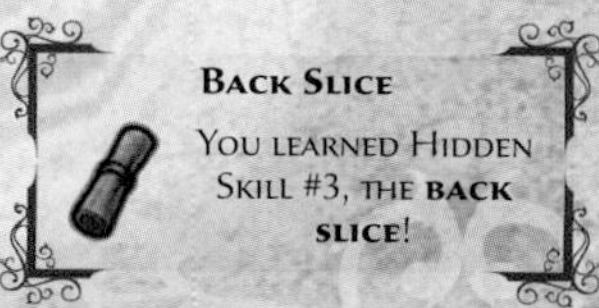

Back Slice
You learned Hidden Skill #3, the **back slice**!

Characters Encountered

Epona

Zora

Postman

➤ After you've mastered your skill, continue on your Bomb Rock quest and find the two in this part of the land. The first is just in front of the castle wall. Fight a couple of Bulblin warriors, then plant the bomb. Expect two yellow (10) and three blue (5) Rupees from this haul. Then head north and plant a second bomb at this rock, also near the castle wall. There are three green (1), one blue (5), one yellow (10), and one red (20) Rupee in this one!

Hyrule Field (North): Breaking through to the Other Side

➤ Ride north to the adjacent field and thoroughly inspect this area. The first rock, at the fork in the path, isn't a Bomb Rock, so ignore it.

Instead, head to the banked road with the wooden fence along the side; the road takes you out of this field to the east but is blocked with this rock barricade. However, after a swift bombing, you clear the path and can freely travel forward. The bombs leave three yellow Rupees (10).

▲ This path winds along a canyon road with towering walls on either side, some of which have an odd **groove pattern** chiseled into them. Perhaps some sort of **spinning device** is needed for their secrets to be revealed? Pass the Bulblin, and you'll reach another rock barricade. Once through, this leads straight to the Great Hylian Bridge.

➤ There's little point in heading to the bridge right now, so double back and journey to the northern Hyrule Field. Begin a search for Bomb Rocks; there's one in the eastern corner just below the elevated path you came from; destroy it for a purple Rupee (50).

◄ Now head northwest, following this area's northern edge, into a rocky path with stone walls on each side. Take the right fork in the road, staying close to the north wall, and bring out your sword to whack a Tektite. At the next junction, where a Bulblin and Tektite fall to your attacks, turn right toward the path heading into the northern wall. Remove the rock barricade with a Bomb Arrow. This way is now open!

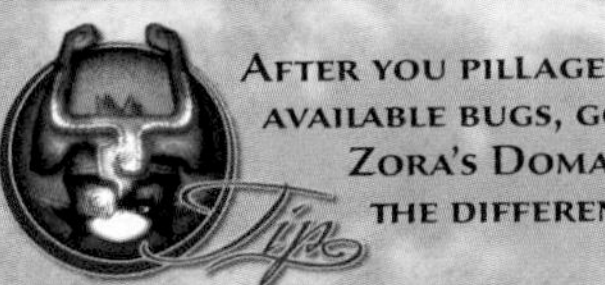

Tip

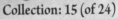

After you pillage Hyrule North of all currently available bugs, goods, and treasure, head north into Zora's Domain and uncover more paths that link the different provinces together.

◄ Turn south and with a great view of Castle Hyrule, ride right, along the fenced path, and then cut in at the next junction to a rocky clearing just south of the exit you just bombed. Slow Epona down, and slice a wayward Tektite before dismounting.

Golden Bug: Female Stag Beetle

Collection: 15 (of 24)

There are a couple of interesting elements to this clearing. First, check out the shining dot above this blocked cave entrance. That's another Golden Bug, and your trusty **Gale Boomerang** is excellent for collecting it. Pick it up and pocket it. That's quite a collection!

Female Stag Beetle

You caught a **Female Stag Beetle**! Bug fans love that golden color.

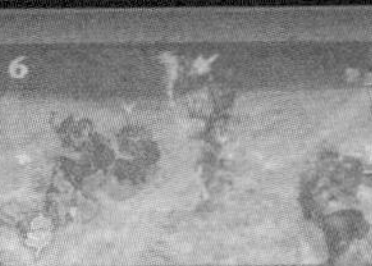

➤ The other area of interest is the blocked cave entrance. Shoot it with your Bomb Arrow and it explodes, leading to a very icy cavern. You can enter only into the first initial chamber, as an icy blockade stops you. Return here with a **ball-and-chain-style** item that can shatter this tough ice. Now look for the other insect in this area.

Golden Bug: Male Stag Beetle

Collection: 16 (of 24)

Finding this next beetle is easy. Maneuver around the eastern part of the plains, crossing the bridge in this direction. Keep straight, and the next tree on your left, at the junction, contains your insect. Gather it with the **Gale Boomerang**.

Male Stag Beetle

You caught a **Male Stag Beetle**! Bug fans love that golden color.

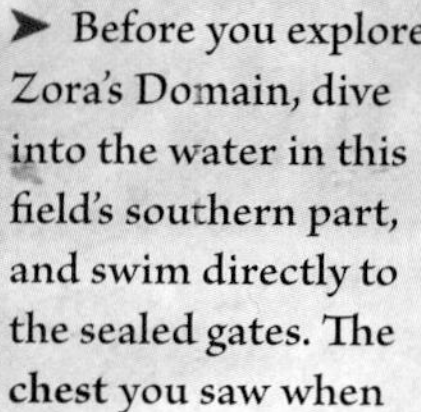

➤ Before you explore Zora's Domain, dive into the water in this field's southern part, and swim directly to the sealed gates. The **chest** you saw when this was dry is still behind a small cage, but you can use your **Iron Boots** and sink to the chest. Open it for a large boost to your Rupee collection!

Overworld Chest #44: Orange Rupee (100)

Bug Hunting in Zora's Domain

➤ The rock wall you destroyed in the north boundary leads directly to Zora's Domain. Head down there and locate a couple of Golden Bugs. As you enter, peer out over the long balcony ledge. There's something flitting around the western ledges. Bring out your **Hawkeye** to see that it's an Imp Poe.

➤ This is where the next Golden Bug is located, but there's some interesting exploration you can do first. Head north, and instead of diving into the waterfall pool, turn right, and run up the tunnel stairs to the rock blocking your path. Place a bomb and explode this Bomb Rock.

➤ Take the two green (1), one blue (5), and one yellow (10) Rupees left behind, and continue up this tunnel to a second Bomb Rock. Bring out the **Hero's Bow** and fire a Bomb Arrow into this rock, clearing the tunnel that leads to the throne room in Zora's Domain. Afterward, grab the green (1), blue (5), and yellow (10) Rupees. There's also a blue Rupee (5) in the water as you reach the top of the waterfall.

Caution

If you place a regular bomb to remove this rock, it rolls down the steps straight at you. If you don't have arrows, find some or plunge into the waterfall pool and get a Zora to take you to the top of the waterfall; then bomb this from the other side.

➤ Sprint north, into the throne room, where the heat from the molten shard makes for a relaxing bath! Unfortunately, the mood is somber after the death of Queen Rutela. The guards you speak to are waiting for the return of Prince Ralis.

It isn't all doom and gloom here, though. Check the wall behind the throne to find the Postman hiding here. He's having trouble finding a "Mr. Zora" to deliver the letter to. It could be any of these fishy folk!

➤ Before heading south, down the waterfall to locate the next Golden Bug, produce your Lantern. There are two unlit torches here, and you must swing the Lantern at both of them. Once lit, they reveal a secret chest that appears just below the water, in the plunge pool area. Sink down with your boots, and open the chest for a Rupee prize. Then head back south.

Overworld Chest #45: Purple Rupee (50)

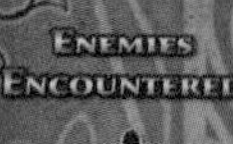

Enemies Encountered

Bulblin

Tektite

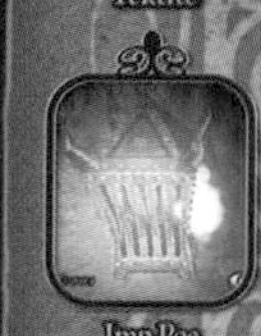

Imp Poe

Characters Encountered

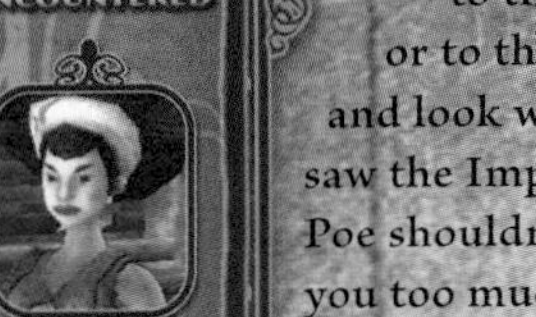

Iza

Zora

Plumm

➤ Head back to the balcony or to the waterfall, and look where you saw the Imp Poe. The Poe shouldn't trouble you too much, but there are a couple of bugs to capture near it. Drop down into the waterfall pool and swim across toward the rock. Clamber onto the ledge behind the rocks and run up the grassy ramped ledge.

Golden Bug: Male Dragonfly

Collection: 17 (of 24)

As the ramped ledge turns, a Male Dragonfly flits about above the patch of grass, near a crate. To catch him, wait for him to descend. If this takes too long, use the **Gale Boomerang**, wait for the bug to fall, and grab him.

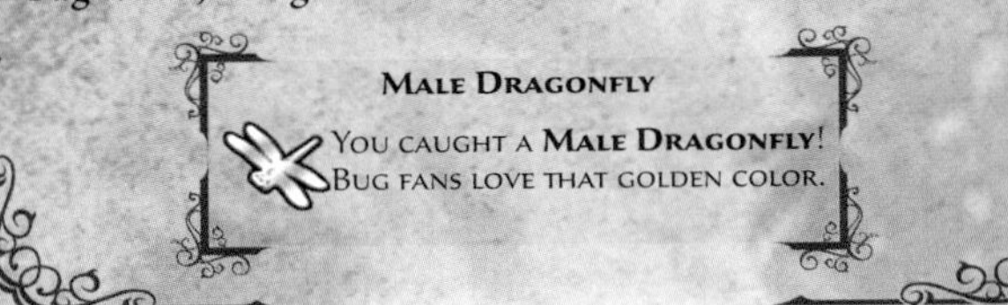

Male Dragonfly

You caught a **Male Dragonfly**! Bug fans love that golden color.

➤ Head south, out of Zora's Domain and into the upper river area, where (if you have any bombs left) you can explode the Bomb Rock on the river's north bank. There's one green (1), four blue (5), and one yellow Rupee (10) inside, adding 31 to your total. Then move to toward Iza's dwelling and wait a moment.

Golden Bug: Female Dragonfly

Collection: 18 (of 24)

Run to the signpost and look for the next insect, which is flying over the rapid river, out of reach. The only way you can currently grab this creature is to target it with your Gale Boomerang. Stand on flatter ground or it flies out of reach again. This takes a little wrangling to grab, but it's worth it!

Female Dragonfly

You caught a **Female Dragonfly**! Bug fans love that golden color!

Warp Portal

As soon as you finish grabbing the 18th Golden Bug, head around the river's northern bank, and a portal activates, bringing Twilit Messengers down to earth and forcing you to dispatch them in the usual manner.

The arena is large, so back away from the group, locate the straggler, dispatch him, and then find the two Messengers lolloping about near each other. Use the spin attack to easily slay both at the same time. When they disappear, you now have a new portal to warp to the Upper River area.

Taming the River Rapids

➤ Head toward Iza. She's impressed enough with your swashbuckling abilities to invite you into her cabin, where she explains that she used to rent boats in this area of the river, but a rockfall dammed the route. She asks if you can help her if she gives you some Bomb Arrows. Agree to this plan and you instantly receive 30 arrows and 30 bombs.

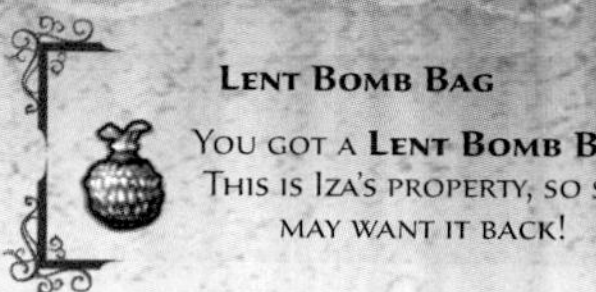

Lent Bomb Bag

You got a **Lent Bomb Bag**! This is Iza's property, so she may want it back!

Head onto the small jetty and climb into the boat. Begin to paddle downstream. There are a few Rupees placed along the route that you can grab.

Tip: If you come back here later with the Clawshot, you can try grabbing these Rupees from the water, but they aren't that valuable and are not necessary to collect.

◄ Your boat can be difficult to control, especially as you head down a massive water-filled tunnel! Time to remember a few boating lessons:

Boating Tips

- Leave your boat completely alone for some of the time. Only use ◎ to steer when you begin to drift off-course.
- Maneuver in the direction opposite than the one you're heading to steer away from walls, debris, or other danger.
- Pressing ⍋ increases your speed and makes your boat very difficult to steer from side to side.
- Pressing ⍒ slows you down, but it's still more difficult than normal to steer; so only press ⍋ and ⍒ when you really need to.
- Practice makes perfect! Small nudges are better than yanks!

➤ The merriment continues as you're buffeted downstream, through waterfalls and near pieces of debris, which you can optionally destroy with your Bomb Arrows. However, it is just as easy to avoid them.

If you get turned around, just steer in the opposite direction without pressing ⍋ or ⍒. There's a final, terrifying waterfall stretch before you reach your blockade.

➤ Iza's Zora helper surfaces at this time and tells you that the rubble up ahead is blocking the river's flow. Produce your Hero's Bow, combine bombs and arrows, and fire twice at this rubble to remove it completely.

▲ Follow the Zora downstream, through a series of winding tunnels where debris is piling up. You can leave be as close as this picture indicates to clear the debris. Keep some control of your boat, and don't worry about banging into the sides.

The river finally exits into Lake Hylia, where the Zora drops you off on the small jetty. The Zora tells you that you can keep the Bomb Bag for helping out. If you want to quickly return to Upper River, warp or ride to North Hyrule Field and take the exit in the north wall.

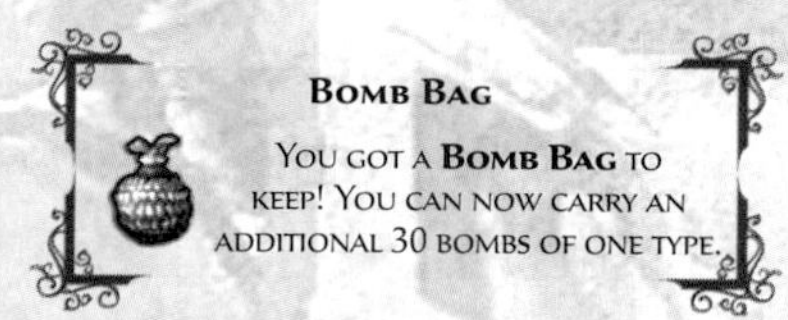

Bomb Bag

You got a **Bomb Bag** to keep! You can now carry an additional 30 bombs of one type.

◄ Now you're in Lake Hylia. You can blow on the grass and talk to Plumm at this location. This and the other small grassy plateau near Fyer's cannon hut is where you should go to play Plumm's minigame. However, you need to be the wolf to do so.

Missing Links

1. Hearts in the Right Place

If you want a couple of Hearts before you go on this river rapids run, smash the pots behind Iza.

2. Fishing Near and in the Spirit Cave

After your run down the rapids fishing on the jetty in front of the spirit cave or inside the cave itself is a great way to unwind!

Enemies Encountered: Imp Poe, Twilit Messenger

7 8

Iza

Hena

Running the Rapids for Fun and Profit

The next time you return to the Upper River area, Iza has affixed two yellow pots to the front of her store. She must have reopened her fun little game! Enter and speak to her, and begin this wild ride once again, taking what you learned about controlling the boat and figuring out what this game is about.

Basically, you must ride down the river, which is slightly calmer than before, and smash the different pots that are hanging from walls or sitting on small islands. The **yellow pots** are worth 1 point.

The **red pots** are worth 2 points. If you strike the sides of the riverbank, you lose a point, so remain in the water at all times!

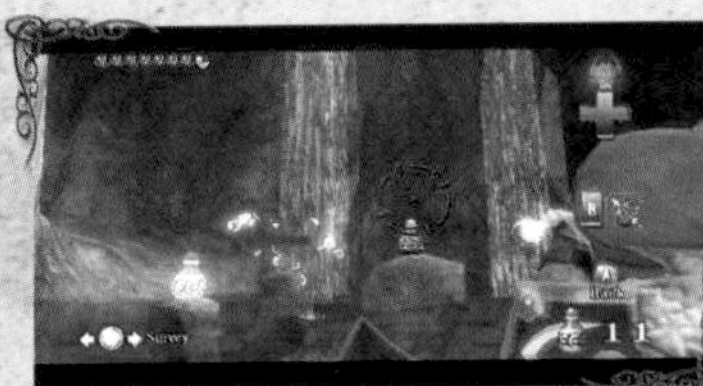

This game takes a fair number of tries to complete, and when you reach this part of the river, try to paddle left, as this section has many more pots to easily aim at.

Always keep an eye out for and fire at every pot, but if you're finding that impossible, be sure you hit every red pot. Also learn that these pots are bigger than you think and are some distance away. Therefore, aim **higher** than the middle of your target, so the bomb arrows fall in a slight arc and strike home. The final rapids section is very difficult, but let off accurate arrows as fast as possible, and then return to paddling.

There are a total of 20 yellow pots and 5 red pots to smash with your arrows. If you score 25 points or more, the Zora gives you a grand prize: the **Giant Bomb Bag**. This allows you to carry twice as many regular bombs (60 compared to 30, for example).

Giant Bomb Bag

You got the **Giant Bomb Bag**!

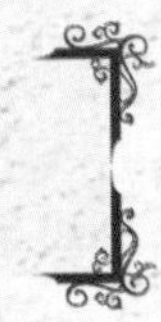

- The maximum you can score in this game is 30 points; you struck all pots and didn't hit the side once.
- The easiest way to receive 25 points is to steer but not worry too much about hitting the sides. However, don't strike the sides more than five times. And aim to destroy all the pots!

Tip

- If you succeed in obtaining the maximum score, you're awarded with an orange Rupee (100). Only the most skillful of paddlers will ever see this!

Gone Fishing: Exploring

The fishing note, also in the Upper River area, is now open for business. Enter it via the door in the north wall of this zone, and you'll be in a self-contained, tranquil place where you can really get relaxed and learn the intricacies of fishing.

Note

There are some items you should try to claim right now, as they will help you on your quest.

A fishing hole for all seasons.

Enter the fishing hole, and you'll be in a wonderful summer glade. However, when you **leave this place** and return (even if you just close the door, then come back in), the season changes. When you've chosen your seasonal mood, head toward the hut that has the sign reading "Bobber fishing open to public. Check in for lure fishing! **Sinking lures prohibited.**"

Bobber fishing is simply you, your fishing rod, and appropriate bait (either a Worm, a Bee Larva, or a special gift the Zoras give you later on).

Lure fishing is in a boat, with a guide if you choose, and a selection of lures. Lure fishing allows you to add fish into a tank inside the fishing hut. Lure fishing, unfortunately, is not recorded in your Fish Journal, so if you're trying to capture a big fish, you can either get it recorded but not visible in the store tank or you can land it from your boat and look at it in the hut, but not in your records.

Note

Enter the fishing hut, and you're greeted warmly by Hena, the shop proprietor and an ace fisherwoman. Here, you can view her large tank, talk to her parrot, view her photos, and play her little minigame.

Hena:

Hena is between 10 and 20 years old and is sister to Iza and Coro. She takes an active and healthy enjoyment in fishing, caring for fish in her tank, keeping a photographic record of the largest past catches, and renting out boats (and her advice) to those who wish to fish!

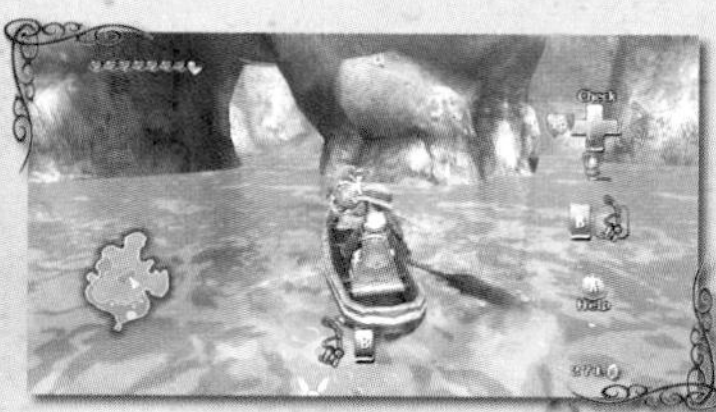

Ah, this is the life! Pay Hena 20 Rupees (or 100 each subsequent time), and paddle out on the lake for a relaxing fishing experience.

➤ When a place is called a Fishing Hole, it's no secret that you can catch lots of fish there! As a matter of fact, you can land each and every type of fish that appears in Hyrule just by fishing along the west bank near the wooden bridge. All except for one, that is... the distinctive Reekfish is only found in Zora's Domain!

Just to be thorough, here's a list of the different types of fish you can catch here while bobber fishing at the Fishing Hole:

- Greengills
- Hylian Loaches
- Hylian Pike
- Hyrule Bass
- Ordon Catfish

Frog Lure

Required to advance?: No.

First chance to get?: After Dungeon 2: Goron Mines. (After saving Spirit Lanayru.)

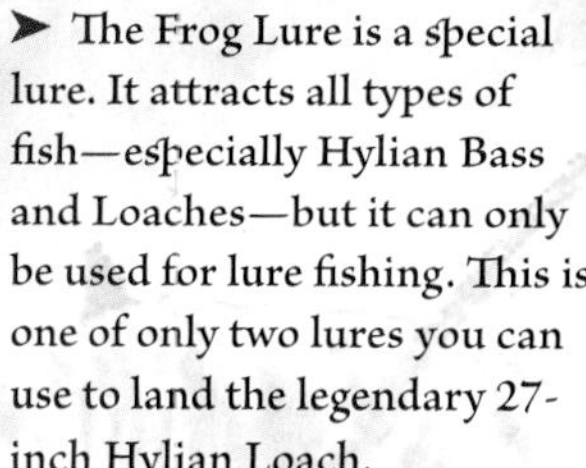

➤ The Frog Lure is a special lure. It attracts all types of fish—especially Hylian Bass and Loaches—but it can only be used for lure fishing. This is one of only two lures you can use to land the legendary 27-inch Hylian Loach.

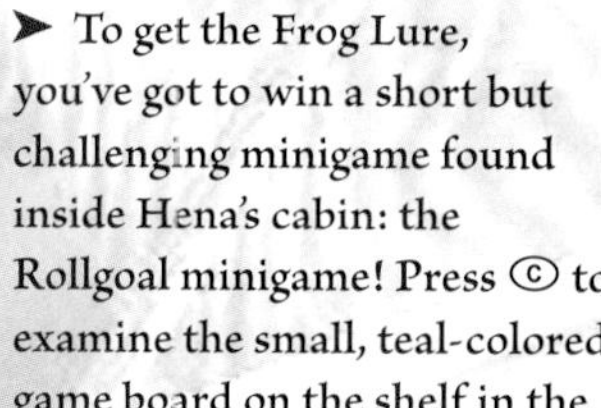

➤ To get the Frog Lure, you've got to win a short but challenging minigame found inside Hena's cabin: the Rollgoal minigame! Press Ⓒ to examine the small, teal-colored game board on the shelf in the cabin's northeast corner. Hena notices your interest in the game, and asks you if you'd like to try it for just 5 Rupees. If you win, you get 10 Rupees as a reward... but there's a much greater prize to be had! See the "Rollgoal Minigame!" sidebar for details.

Rollgoal Minigame!

Hena's Rollgoal minigame is made up of eight different levels, and each level contains the same eight boards. You begin at level 1-1 (level 1, board 1) and work your way up through 1-8 (level 1, board 8). If you beat level 1-8, you win the Frog Lure and begin at level 2-1 the next time you play (level 2, board 1). The eight boards are exactly the same throughout each level; you're just given less time to reach the goal.

The object of the game is to maneuver the small glass ball along the short narrow path and into the finish cup. If the ball drops off the path, you lose and must pay another 5 Rupees to try again. Reach the finish cup within the time limit (which is very generous at first) to clear the board and collect your Rupees.

After winning a board (for example, board 1-1), leave Hena's cabin and then reenter. Hena changes the board when you leave to surprise you with a new one on your next visit (in this case, board 1-2). If you don't leave the cabin, you can continue to play the same board for the 5-Rupee prize you get each time you win... but you've got to play through board 1-8 if you want to win the Frog Lure!

Naturally, the boards become progressively more difficulty to win. Later boards feature more corners, and some even have steep dips that are quite tricky to handle. The worst thing you can encounter is a dip followed by a corner; approach these with caution, as it's easy to overshoot these troublesome spots!

Characters Encountered

Iza

Hena

Rollgoal Minigame! (cont'd)

Keep in mind that Rollgoal—in character with the Fishing Hole itself—is a game of relaxation and enjoyment. Though you're playing under a time limit, you've got three whole minutes to reach each board's finish cup (when playing through the first level). Don't feel like you've got to speed through the boards; stop whenever you feel it necessary and just take your time. Make minor adjustments to avoid mistakes; slow and steady wins the game.

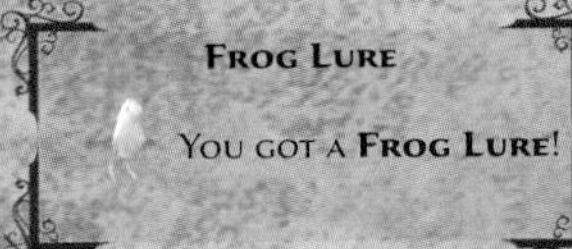

Beat board 1-8 to win the Frog Lure from Hena, and if you're really enjoying yourself, play all the way through board 8-8! If you clear the eighth level, Hena fills your current wallet to the brim, no matter how many Rupees it takes!

Frog Lure

You got a **Frog Lure**!

Here's what each board looks like:

Board 1

Board 2

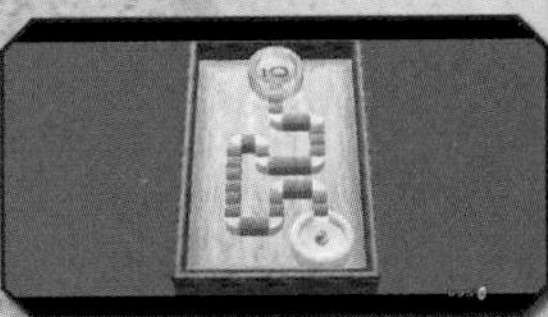
Board 3

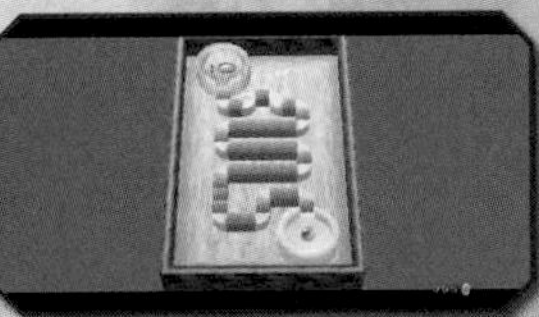
Board 4

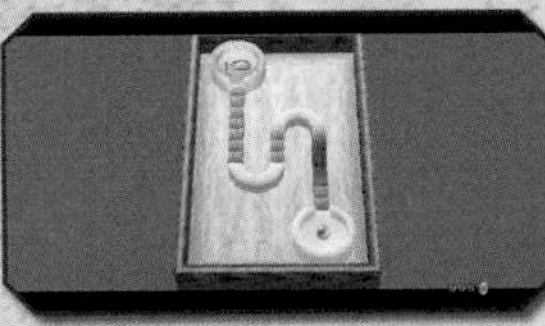
Board 5

Board 6

Board 7

Board 8

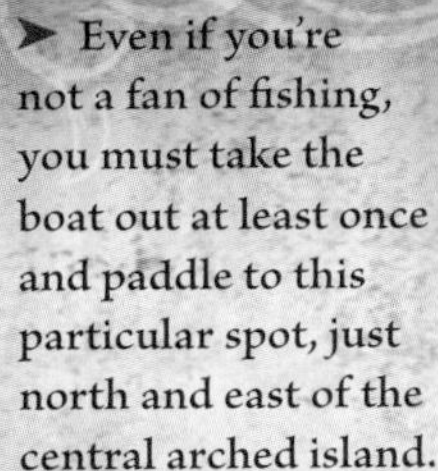

➤ Even if you're not a fan of fishing, you must take the boat out at least once and paddle to this particular spot, just north and east of the central arched island.

➤ Swing your lure (any type is fine) at the **Piece of Heart** that's sitting on the underside of the arched rock, and reel it in. You've grabbed another fifth of a **Heart Container!**

Piece of Heart

You got **Piece of Heart #17**! Collect **3 more** for another full Heart Container.

◄ Now you can experiment with **lures, areas of the lake, and seasons,** and land the three different types of fish (Bass, Catfish, and Pike), and even the legendary 27-inch **Hylian Loach!**

The Legendary Hylian Loach!

Once you've acquired either the Frog or Sinking Lure, you're able to snare the granddaddy of all fishies; the legendary Hylian Loach! This bad boy is unlike any of the loaches you can catch while bobber fishing; it's nearly 30 inches long and by far the most difficult fish to land in the game!

First thing's first; the legendary Hylian Loach only appears during the summer season. Leave the Fishing Hole through the main door and reenter until the place looks like it's summertime (as pictured).

Next, armed with either the Frog or Sinking Lure, rent a canoe from Hena. (Don't have her come with you if you're planning to use the Sinking Lure!) Paddle out to the north-most tip of the Fishing Hole, then cast your lure into the collection of lily pads. This is where the legendary Hylian Loach is found!

The Legendary Hylian Loach! (cont'd)

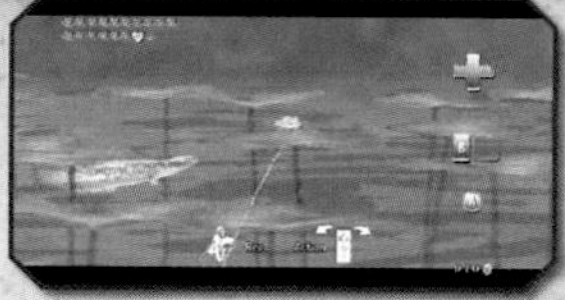

Once you've located the big guy, do everything you can to get him interested in your lure. This isn't hard to do as long as you're using the Frog or Sinking Lure.; the tough part is reeling him in!

Tip: If you're using the Frog Lure, be sure to let your prey take it a few feet underwater before yanking back on the Wii Remote to snare it. The Frog Lure has a tendency to pop out of a fish's mouth when you pull too soon.

Once you've snared the loach, prepare for an epic battle of man against fish. Reel it in as fast as you can, but always be ready to stop reeling and tilt the Wii Remote forward whenever he jumps out of the water. Keep on reeling until you get it near the boat.

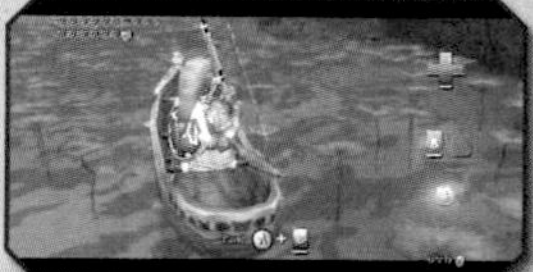

Your opportunity to land the legendary Hylian Loach comes in a window of about a half-second. Watch for the "land" icon to appear at the bottom of the screen and be ready to slap Ⓐ+Ⓑ the instant you see it.

Well done! Even Hena is impressed by your catch; she praises your skill when you return to her cabin. Stop for a moment to admire the legendary Hylian Loach as he swims about her fish tank.

Here's a mug shot of our grand prize in the fishing expedition—the rarest fish in all of Hyrule!

The Empty Bottle

Head to the fishing hole's northern section, to this small rickety bridge. Here you can fish for an Empty Bottle. That means you can store **Fairies, oil, potions, water,** and anything else you might want to keep. This is the second of four Bottles to find.

Empty Bottle

You caught an **Empty Bottle**!

The Sinking Lure

Finally, you can attempt to fish for the completely illegal **Sinking Lure**, which attracts every type of fish without fail! You must meet some objectives before finding this, but here's the place to stand. When you're finished in here, journey to Castle Town via the eastern entrance.

The Sinking Lure is a special lure. Considered unsportsmanlike by Hena (but not so much by her brother, Coro), this shiny, metal lure attracts fish like pins to a magnet!

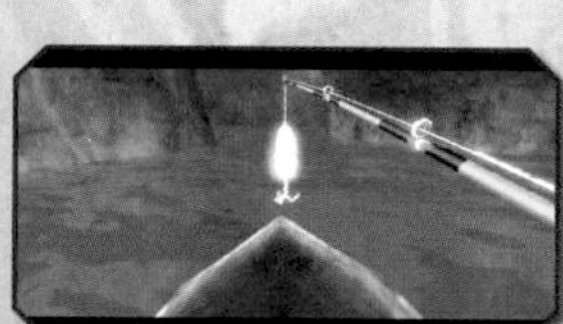

To get the Sinking Lure, pay 20 Rupees to rent Hena's canoe, then catch (and keep!) the following three types of fish while lure fishing:

***Hylian Pike:** Fish the waters north of the pond's arch-shaped rock formation.*

***Hyrule Bass:** Often found in the waters between the pond's arch-shaped rock formation.*

***Ordon Catfish:** Easily caught in the waters south of the pond's arch-shaped rock formation.*

Make sure to keep one of each type of the above fish so they are stored inside the fish tank in Hena's cabin. Once you've done this, leave the Fishing Hole through the main door and then return to change the season. **Do not** warp out of the Fishing Hole or your recent catches won't be recorded!

Characters Encountered

Hena

Charlo

Soal

Chudley

The Sinking Lure (cont'd)

Standing for the Sinking Lure

It's important to stand in just the right location when attempting to secure the sinking lure. You must fish from this exact position; facing north at the far end of the grassy bank, past the bridge where you can catch the Bottle. Cast your regular line a number of times from here, and eventually you'll secure this item. Having problems? Then exit the Fishing Hole, return and try again.

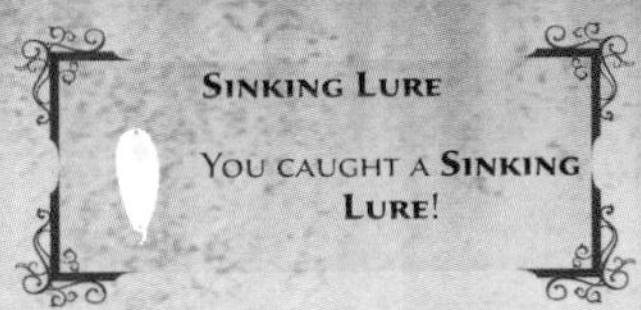

Sinking Lure
You caught a Sinking Lure!

Caution

Don't let Hena catch you using the Sinking Lure! If you bring her along in the canoe with you and then equip this lure, Hena takes it away! You can always get it back by fishing in the same spot to drag it up.

Missing Links

1. Tank Trouble

If you're mischievous, you might want to stir up a little trouble by rolling into that large fish tank. Hena shouts a warning the first time. She asks you to leave the third time you try, and you won't be able to hire a boat until you apologize.

2. Who's a Purdy Boy, Then?

Hena's pet bird is called Purdy, and if you listen closely, he sometimes says strange things. We can't tell you what though—it's a surprise. You can also be asked to leave if you roll into Purdy's cage repeatedly. What were you thinking?!

3. Fascinating Fish Photographs

Hena has assembled a great collection of fishermen and their catches. Check them to find out the local records and fishing legends.

4. Hanging Your Hat

Inspect the hat rack on the fishing hut's wall, and Hena mentions it's polite for everyone to do this! Unfortunately, your head gear is staying where it is.

5. Pot Luck

There's no point in trying to slam into the wall with a roll and knock the pots down so they smash. Hena asks you to leave if you try that caper more than once!

6. Catch of the Day!

When you finally do manage to catch all four types of fish (including the legendary one), return and view them in the fishing tank.

7. The One That Didn't Get Away

Hey! How did *that* picture get on the wall? We're not telling, but if you want legendary photos, you'd better catch a legendary fish!

8. Grass Slashing

The entire area surrounding the fishing hole has patches of grass to trim, trees to run into, and Rupees and Hearts to gather after your mowing is complete!

9. Duck Luck

Finally, don't forget to return here in Wolf form when you can; the two ducks are definitely chatty, and they don't like refuse in their fishing hole, either!

Task 5: Thoroughly Explore Castle Town and Southern Field

Castle Town in the Daylight

Wander into the town's **East Road** and you can talk to the people chatting instead of listening to their spirits. These two are mentioning **Prince Ralis**. He's the next person to visit if you aren't concerned about collections, masses of Rupees, and incredible Heart Container assembling!

◄ Continue to the left, and you'll pass a tall wizened man who's praying for peace in Hyrule. Apparently, this takes Rupees. Although you may be tempted to ignore him, if you're after a special prize, donate 50 Rupees to his cause. Come back here in a moment.

1

2

3

4

5

6

Charlo:

Charlo stands near the goat pens and collects donations and offers devotions for a charge. Some think this is some kind of scam, but to those with deep pockets, he offers a special reward....

◀ You can enter the city fountain area and walk to the **small band of musicians** playing their lilting melodies in the northwest corner of this courtyard.

Head around the fountain in a circle to listen to the old ladies gabbing again; this time, however, they think you're a tourist and urge you to check out the spirit cave!

Visiting Chudley's Emporium

➤ The next place you must visit is the general store in the southwest part of town. The people outside tell you it's very snooty. So snooty, in fact, that the door attendant won't let you in with those disgusting mud-coated boots. You'll need to meet the shoe-shine boy, Soal, who cleans your boots for 10 Rupees. He's just outside, by the steps.

Soal:

A small boy who makes a little cash by polishing shoes in the Castle Town streets. He's making a good living since the celebrated store owner Chudley came to town with his exclusive wares and ludicrous prices!

➤ You enter the newly opened Chudley's, where only the finest and most incredibly expensive goods are on display. You've heard about price gouging, but this is ridiculous. The posh proprietor looks down his nose at you and offers the following wares at incredibly expensive prices.

Store

Chudley's Fine Goods and Fancy Trinkets Emporium

Item Name	Price	Effect
Arrows (10)	2,000 Rupees	Constructed of the lightest materials, these are safe for all skill levels.
Blue Potion	10,000 Rupees	This potion restores health through its aromatherapeutic qualities.
Red Potion	3,000 Rupees	This red drink burns with a fiery color that ignites passion in the hearts of all who see it.
Bombs	3,000 Rupees	A staple Barnes Co. product. It's been a top seller for generations.
Water Bombs	6,000 Rupees	This is a shop original. We've wrapped the explosive in fine leather.
Pocket Bombling	9,000 Rupees	This dangerous pet is popular with the ladies in town.
Magic Armor	100,000 Rupees	Armor for the richest and most precious customers who value their lives over their Rupees.

You can't even find a wallet that holds even half the amount the arrows cost! These prices are truly outlandish, and you can't buy any of the items. Don't bother trying while Chudley is the owner of this place; it needs new management!

Chudley:

About 30 years old, Chudley runs a very swanky store in Castle Town. He looks down on you as if you're simply too common to be coming into an emporium as elegant as his. If you're one of the Hyrule high rollers, though, he's a simpering fool.

◀ Wander back into the fountain area and check out the trio of townsfolk lounging around here. They like your outfit and reckon you're here to check out the new tent that's just been built on the east side of town.

Characters Encountered

Goron

Kili, Hanna, Misha

Purlo

Agitha

The Goron Trading Post

➤ Move to the southeast part of this central area. The large arched door is now open, and a place where three Gorons are hanging out is uncovered. Head through to the base of the stairs, where the small Goron you saw back at Kakariko Village tells you they've been unable to enter the town's inner gate. You can pick up the following goods from this location.

Store

Goron Trading Post

Item Name	Price	Effect
Red Potion	30 Rupees	Adds 8 Hearts to your energy; from the small Goron at the base of the stairs
Lantern oil	30 Rupees	Refills your Lantern; from the small Goron at the top of the stairs
Arrows (30)	40 Rupees	Refills your Quiver; from the large Goron on the observation deck

➤ Head to the top of the stairs, where another small Goron lies around. He mentions he has Lantern oil for sale. His father is on the observation deck, which affords an excellent view of the castle and town beyond. The small Goron's father feels there's something not quite right going on. Purchase arrows from him if necessary, and then leave this establishment.

Missing Links

1. The Crate Escape

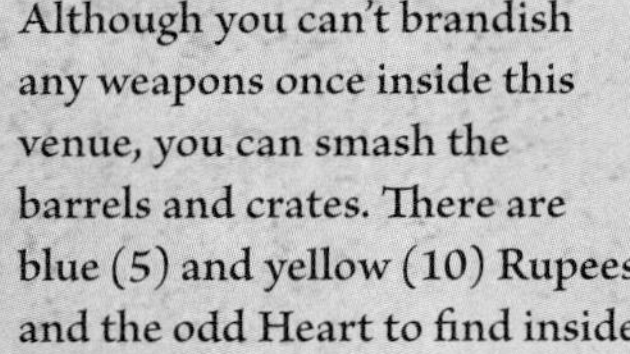

Although you can't brandish any weapons once inside this venue, you can smash the barrels and crates. There are blue (5) and yellow (10) Rupees and the odd Heart to find inside.

A Stroll around the Southern Market Stalls

➤ Exit the Goron's trading post and visit the tea shop next door for a psychological conversation and a mention of the **fortune-teller** in town. After this chat, check the south thoroughfare.

Inspect the line of market stalls. The first one sells **bread**. It's fresh, tasty, straight from the oven, and too expensive!

The grocer at the next store seems to think that although the people hide it well, they're all still very frightened.

➤ Move farther along the market stalls, and a soldier stops you. He asks if you know the whereabouts of Jovani. The guy has been missing so long, he's turned into an urban legend. The fair-haired lady standing with the soldier is his lady friend. Or was.

▲ You move to the flower stall, where you pluck a **pretty flower** and have the Rupees to pay for it this time. However, there's no shopkeeper, so you put it back. Next is a soldier who gives you directions.

➤ Move to the Gorons at this street's southern end. The small Goron mentions his dad can't get any **Hot Springwater**, so he just sits outside the **western gate**. The Goron asks you to speak with the **Goron village elder** about it. You can also check out the apples and speak to the storeowner on the opposite side.

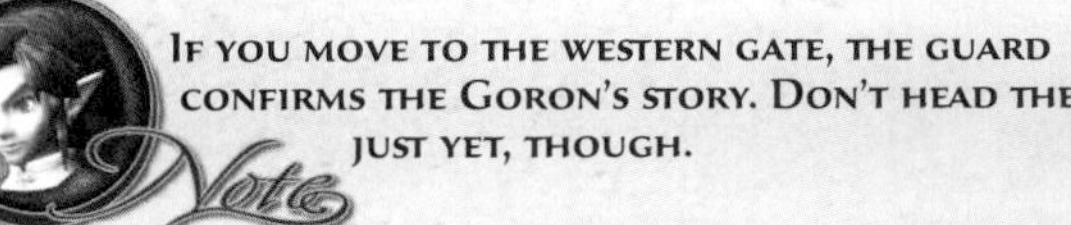

Note

If you move to the western gate, the guard confirms the Goron's story. Don't head there just yet, though.

Missing Links

1. Catnapping

If you wander near Jovani's house, you can pick up any of the cats and play with the ball that's in this area. Nothing happens, except the cats are exceedingly cute!

2. The Dog and Bone Man

Similarly, there are two cute puppies in the east and west alleys. You can pick them up and a nearby bone. Throw the bone so they play fetch. That's just as cute!

3. Shifty Guy Standoff

Over on the western alley is a shifty-looking man looking north. He tells you there's a guy across the way looking right at him! Head north to the medical center (which is locked) and talk to him. He tells you there's a guy across the way looking right at him....

The Tent, the Castle, and the Mansion

◄ Head to the eastern alley and inspect the tent area, where you can play fetch with the cute doggy. Outside, there are three girls waiting for the owner; he's so handsome! Head into the tent if you dare.

Kili, Hanna, and Misha:

These three 10-year-old girls are always out in a group, and they're all in love with the same boy. Whoever can muster the nerve to complete the challenges inside the tent will win a fabulous prize!

◄ Enter the tent and you're greeted by Purlo, who asks you to step right up to play the STAR game for 10 Rupees! Simply leap through all the stars in the cage, and a fabulous prize awaits you! At the moment, the game is impossible. Come back here with a Clawshot and you'll pay him back!

Castle Town South Road

► Exit the tent area, vowing to return to claim victory (there's a special item to win if you do), and head south, turning the corner and stopping at Agitha's castle. Ignore the rude boy outside the door and step inside.

Enter Princess Agitha's castle and step inside her playroom. Well, it's more of an insect zoo. Head over to the window at the room's far end. You can optionally climb a ladder to an upstairs balcony, which is also filled with insect paraphernalia.

Speak with the princess, and she tells you a story: Agitha is the princess of the bug kingdom and has invited 24 Golden Bugs to a formal ball, but none have shown up yet. She's hoping you found some of her friends on your travels. Speak to her again. She asks if you have a bug.

Time to offload those bugs you've found. Pick any of them (ideally one with a partner) and hand it over. The princess adds the bug to her collection (your insect screen now has a butterfly icon next to each bug you've given Agitha) and gives you a prize: the Big Wallet!

Big Wallet

You got the **Big Wallet**! You can now hold up to **600 Rupees**!

Tip: The Big Wallet is an excellent item to have, as it allows you to open more chests before becoming full—perfect for your dungeoneering to come!

You got an orange Rupee (100)!

◄ The prizes don't end there, either. The princess offers happiness if you bring her another bug. This translates to a purple Rupee (50).

CHARACTERS ENCOUNTERED

Agitha

Charlo

Fanadi

Goron

The offer becomes great happiness if you bring her the other partner to each bug. This translates to an orange Rupee (100).

THE PRINCESS IS A GREAT WAY TO GAIN A LOAD OF CASH VERY QUICKLY. BY NOW YOU HAVE GATHERED 18 OF THE 24 GOLDEN BUGS. YOU RECEIVE A BIG WALLET FOR THE FIRST BUG, 150 RUPEES PER PAIR FOR THE REMAINING EIGHT PAIRS, AND ANOTHER 100 RUPEES TO COMPLETE THE FIRST PAIR YOU GAVE AGITHA: THAT'S A TOTAL OF 1,300 RUPEES!

Note

Princess Agitha:

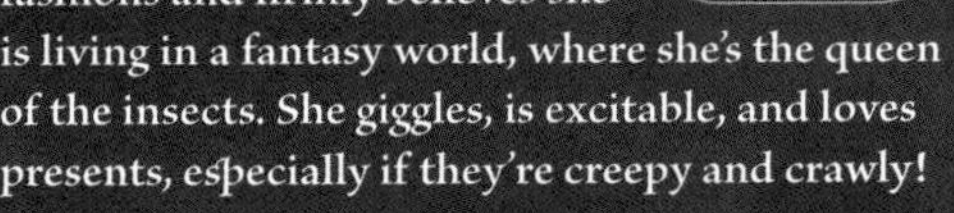

Around 10 years old, Agitha is a princess and lives alone in a tiny castle in town. She is an avid butterfly collector. She dresses in cutesy gothic fashions and firmly believes she is living in a fantasy world, where she's the queen of the insects. She giggles, is excitable, and loves presents, especially if they're creepy and crawly!

➤ You should now speak to Princess Agitha and begin to offload all of the bugs in your collection. Don't worry, you don't need to grab them again and can still read about where you caught them, but there's an **extra special** prize for collecting all 24 bugs and presenting them to her.

▲ When your Big Wallet is filled with Rupees, leave Princess Agitha. Exit and head back to Charlo, the man who is praying for you. Although it may seem strange, we recommend you donate **all 600 Rupees** to him. That's a total of 650 Rupees you've given him now.

Go back to Agitha's Castle, where the party is in full swing, and produce more Golden Bugs from your travels. If you've been following this walkthrough, you can stock your Big Wallet up to 550 Rupees. Then head back to Charlo.

➤ Charlo requires some additional cash, and don't hesitate to donate! After you donate a total of 1,000 Rupees (which you'll have to keep track of in your head or on a piece of paper), he blesses you with the spirit of love—another Piece of Heart!

PIECE OF HEART
YOU GOT **PIECE OF HEART #18**! COLLECT **2 MORE** FOR ANOTHER FULL HEART CONTAINER.

➤ There's no need to visit Charlo anymore, but keep coming back to Agitha. Drop off your remaining Golden Bugs if you need the Rupees, and then run to the house next door; this is Fanadi's mansion, and it's quite a palace!

Cross Fanadi's palm with 10 Rupees and choose to hear the future. You can select either "Career" or "Love." "Career" gives you a clue where to go next (in this case, Telma's Bar). "Love" shows you the location of the nearest Piece of Heart (but you've found all the ones you currently can go for). Leave this place.

Madame Fanadi:

Somewhere between 40 and 50 years old (even Fanadi herself is unsure, despite her supposed powers), Fanadi sits in her mansion, waiting for patrons to cross her palm with Rupees before she recalls some mostly dubious information for them. However, she can sometimes be accurate, if you can understand the doublespeak she mutters!

THERE'S NO NEED TO EVER RETURN TO FANADI FOR A FEW REASONS:

1. YOU'RE CARRYING A WEIGHTY TOME WITH ALL THE ANSWERS TO YOUR QUESTIONS (THIS GUIDE)
2. THE ANSWERS SHE GIVES YOU ARE VAGUE
3. IT'S A WASTE OF YOUR HARD-EARNED MONEY
4. ONLY RETURN IF YOU WANT TO OFFLOAD RUPEES

Tip

EXPLORATION AT THE SOUTHERN CASTLE TOWN HYRULE FIELD

◄ Head south for the first time, out of Castle Town, and into another part of Hyrule Field. Once you're outside the town gate, pass under a pair of stone towers linked by an overhang with a grooved indent. A large chest sits between the two sets of exterior steps. Come back to claim treasure from this area later. For now, run down the steps for another spot of Golden Bug hunting.

1

2

3

4

5

6

Golden Bug: Female Ladybug

Collection: 19 (of 24)

Head down the eastern set of steps. Look closely at the three trees planted in the rectangular formal grass. This particular one has a small clump of grass where a bug is nestling. It usually hops off, so slowly follow, capture it, and keep it in your collection.

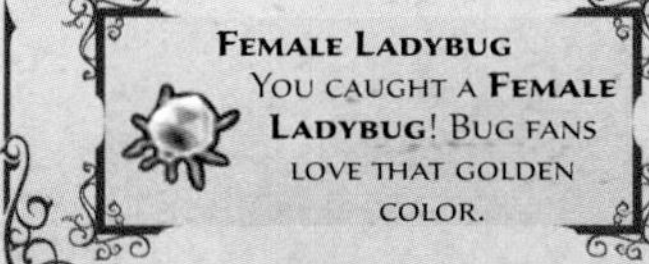

Female Ladybug
You caught a **Female Ladybug**! Bug fans love that golden color.

➤ You should now inspect this entire area of the southern Hyrule Field, as this is your first opportunity to do so. First, exit the Castle Town steps, heading directly south to a blockade that a Goron is standing in front of. Another pesky rockfall is blocking the path from here to the next section of Hyrule Field. If the Goron had **Hot Springwater** to quench his thirst, he'd have the power to bore straight through this rubble!

Note: Keep a mental note to help the Goron out; currently any Hot Springwater you take from Kakariko Village turns into regular water by the time you reach here.

➤ Move away from the Goron and begin inspecting this entire area. The most interesting bit of scenery is the large hole in the ground to the east! Peer over the edge, and you'll see a treasure chest sitting on a tiny alcove. There are Clawshot medallions everywhere! Alas, you can't leap down and land on the alcove ledge, but you can jump into the rapids below.

Tip: If you try leaping into this hole (or off this area's eastern edge), you'll land in the water and end up at the western end of Lake Hyrule. This is an unusual and not often-used shortcut!

➤ Move to the opposite side of the field and investigate a small rock tower encased in vines. Amid the tall grass to the south is a nasty little Deku Baba to slay. Watch for a second Deku Baba close by too. Then prepare to shield block a dive-bombing Guay!

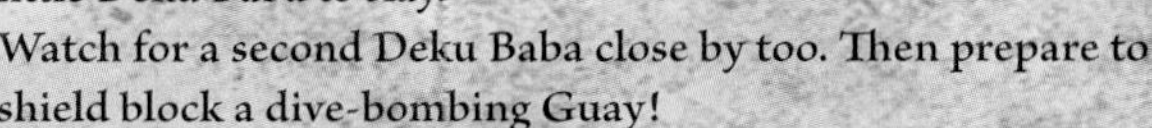

➤ There's an entire flock of these black birds soaring above the rock tower, so deal with any of them that swoop in; then climb to the top of the vines. Stand up, quickly block the bird attacks with your shield, and begin to pick them off one at a time. Your Bow, Slingshot, or Sword are all options, but targeting with Z is the easiest way to slay. With the last Guay gone, a small ring of Rupees rains down from the sky.

▲ There's even more Rupees to seize if you place a bomb at the Bomb Rock to the side of the town steps, just north of the rock tower. Once it explodes, collect three green (1), three blue (5), and two yellow (10) Rupees from the remains.

Golden Bug: Male Ladybug

Collection: 20 (of 24)

Your climb and perhaps your eagle eyes (or the use of your **Hawkeye**) has allowed you to spot another Golden Bug that's buzzing at the top of the rock tower. Use the **Gale Boomerang** to gather the insect from the tower once it flies around on the ground.

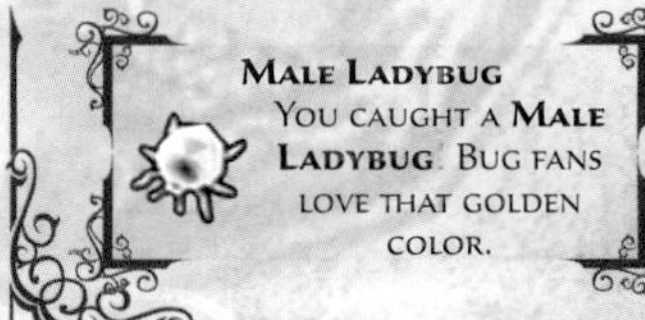

Male Ladybug
You caught a **Male Ladybug**. Bug fans love that golden color.

Enemies Encountered

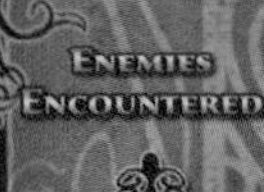

Deku Baba

Guay

Characters Encountered

Goron

Telma

Ilia

Borville

Louise

Missing Links

1. Grass Cutting at the Southern Gate

As always, there's a tiny payoff for slicing through tall grass, and this place is no exception. Try the following places:

Grass: The areas just south of the hole in the ground (Rupees)

Grass: The areas just north of the hole in the ground (Rupees and Heart)

Grass: The area to the south and west of the road (Rupee)

Grass: The area to the west of the road (Rupee)

Grass: The area north of the rock tower (Rupees)

Task 6: Escort Telma, Ilia, and Prince Ralis Safely to Kakariko Village

Let the Wagon Roll: Turmoil at Telma's

You should now head back into town via the southern entrance. Pass the Gorons at the springwater stand (where there's still a shortage) and turn left into the alley leading to Telma's Bar. It's time to rescue the Zora Prince!

A strange, goggle-eyed old man with a doctor's case leaves Telma's Bar, shoving you aside. Ilia pleads with him to help save Prince Ralis's life to no avail.

Telma has heard of a shaman in Kakariko Village who might be able to help. The Soldiers of Hyrule are pleased to accompany such a pretty girl until Telma mentions to Ilia that they must be escorted past dangerous beasts.

Telma knows you know Ilia, but the girl has completely lost her memory. There's no time to worry about that now; the bridge to the east is the only option. Alas, it's guarded by King Bulblin! Now in the wagon, Ilia thanks you. Did she just wink at you?

Borville:

Borville is the town's medical doctor who has excellent credentials and is a regular at Telma's Bar. Where he falters is his bedside manner. He has stormed out of the bar when he was summoned to diagnose a problem with a Zora prince; these aren't his specialty! Some say his rudeness to all his patients is actually a defense mechanism and that he's really a coward.

Louise:

A Persian cat and resident of Telma's Bar, Louise is spoiled by her owner, Telma. But she's always a pleasant kitty and could be a great ally if you could speak to her in an animal tongue.

The wagon is rolling, and Telma isn't messing around. She charges south toward the Great Hylian Bridge, and it's up to you to catch her. Mount Epona and spur her on as quickly as possible. There's a fearsome combat to come, so you can use spurs as much as you need to.

Let the Wagon Roll: Battle on the Bridge II

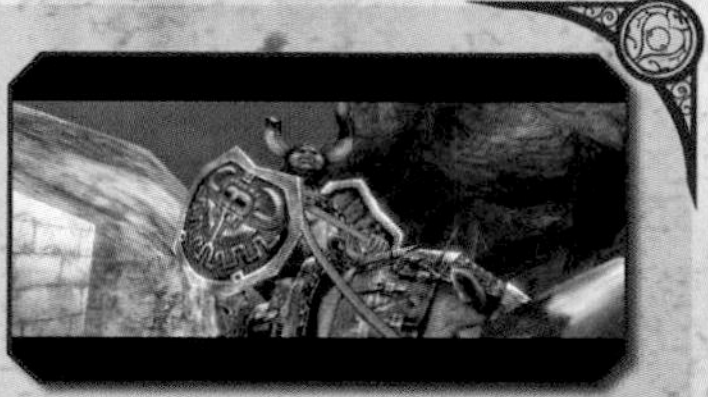

When you reach the bridge, King Bulblin (riding Lord Bullbo) stares you down from the opposite side of the structure. He produces two large shields that he's wearing on each arm—this time he isn't about to be struck from his Bullbo with a simple sword swipe!

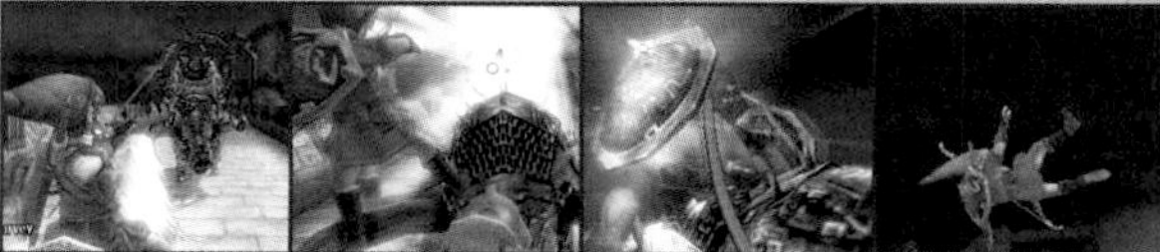

Step 1: This shows the beginning of a fine plan and also what happens when you leave your attack too late. To start with, slow Epona down; there's a disadvantage to speeding up, as you don't have enough time to aim and fire with your **Hero's Bow**, which is the only way to defeat King Bulblin this time. He shrugs off sword swipes as he slams his shields into you, sending you flying over into Lake Hylia!

Wait until you see the evil red glow of King Bulblin's eyes, then fire an arrow into that disgusting face!

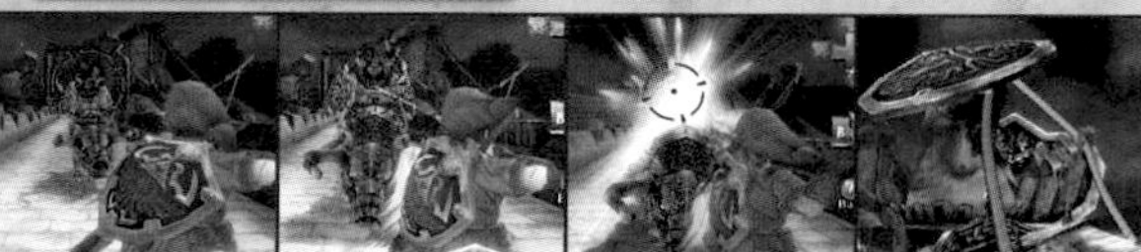

Step 2: Your plan should work if you fire at the point shown in this sequence of screens. Ready your bow as you canter forward, making sure it is aimed squarely at the head of King Bulblin. As he nears, fire when he's about 10 feet away. He veers off around you. The second time you successfully strike him; he's done for!

King Bulblin takes a nasty knock to the helm and temporarily loses control of his mount. It's Lord Bullbo that makes a mistake, ramming the side of the bridge wall and sending King Bulblin flying off into the murky air, for a long plummet down into the lake below.

Let the Wagon Roll: A Fierce and Fiery Fracas!

◄ Telma maneuvers her wagon across the bridge, and the chaperoning continues as you and the wagon (which you should let through first) trundle down the rocky path toward the Hyrule Field plains. However, just after the small wooden bridge, several Bulblin Archers appear on top of the rocky canyon sides and begin raining down fire arrows. If you're incredibly quick, you can target them (they're too far to target with Z) and dispatch them.

➤ However, a wiser plan is to simply ignore these enemies and pass them; they don't give chase. The arrows they fire are flaming, though, and this sets the wagon on fire. A meter at the screen's top shows how tough the sturdy wagon is. When it catches fire, race toward it, bringing out your **Gale Boomerang**, and target the wagon to blow out the fire. Stop when you reach this closed gate.

➤ Dismount and open the gate by pushing its middle; then the overeager Telma races forward into the southern Hyrule Field plains. Quickly mount Epona and follow her in. As you reach a slight bend in the path, a group of Bullbo Riders join in the fray!

◄ These riders are a constant menace, no matter how many you dispatch, so ride through them as they chase the wagon and use your spin attack to defeat each couple of Bulblins. Your real concerns aren't with the Bulblin Riders though; you may not have noticed, but a Kargarok flies overhead and drops a bomb on the road. This *always* causes the wagon to veer off to the left.

Enemies Encountered

King Bulblin

Bulblin Archer

Bulblin Rider

Kargarok

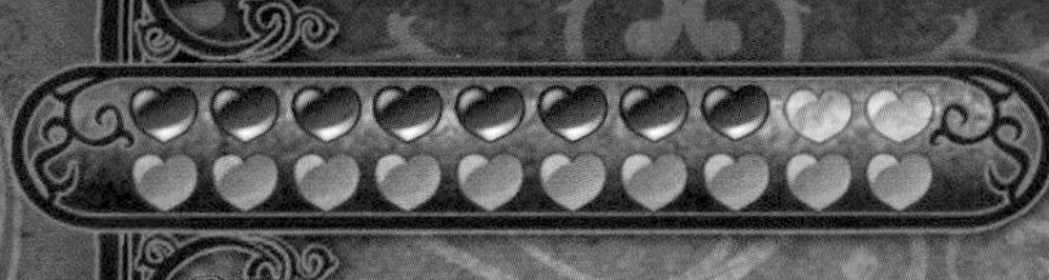

Telma

Renado

Colin

Rutela

Midna

◄ The wagon now takes a long circular path across the plains, and then back onto the path you were just diverted from. This is a real problem, as combat could continue indefinitely if you don't get Telma to stay on the path! For the moment, though, slay any Bulblin Riders that are close to the wagon, and quickly switch to your Boomerang when the fire on the wagon reaches half damage or greater. Another Kargarok drops a bomb when you double back to this point.

▲ If the wagon is struck at this point, it goes off road and across the plains in a lengthy detour before emerging back near the shallow lake area where the combat began. As you reach this point in the road, douse the flames on the wagon and look out for a Kargarok swooping down.

▲ As you reach the road, gallop forward so you're neck and neck with the wagon. You'll be close enough to target Ⓩ the Kargarok with your **Gale Boomerang**. Fire at the creature, and the bomb it was carrying explodes in midair. Now, instead of turning left, Telma trundles along the path and out of this area. You can now keep the wagon fire-free and slay the Bullbo Riders as quickly as possible.

◄ Combat continues into the canyon path between the two plains areas, and the riders become vicious. However, they are easily dispatched with a spin attack or arrows targeted with Ⓩ. Keep the wagon from burning up, and stay about 20 feet behind it as you enter Kakariko Gorge.

► As you reach the bridge to cross the gorge, another Kargarok swoops in to lay an annoying bomb on the path ahead. If you're incredibly fast, you can quickly target Ⓩ and defeat him. More likely, however, Telma takes another detour, careening right into the plains. Fortunately, this area is a lot smaller, and the detour isn't quite as long.

► Bring out your **Hero's Bow** and don't follow the wagon. Instead, stay in the middle of the field, scanning for a Kargarok. When it appears, ignore the wagon and riders, and charge until you're automatically targeting the creature. Fire, and it drops out of the sky with an explosion. You can now keep the wagon on track.

► The wagon arrives at the closed spiked gate to Kakariko Village. Dismount after galloping around the wagon to see if you need to defeat any more riders. You may spot a couple, but spin attacks from the ground or Bomb Arrows are more than a match for them.

Mysterious fires are breaking out on the wagon. Check in front and behind; a couple of Bulblin Archers are the culprits. Tackle them, then open the gate and enter Kakariko Village.

Author Note

This tumultuous battle where wagons, riders, and a flying fiend that wasn't immediately obvious took the longest time to figure out. We just thought Telma was a terrible driver until we finally, after 20 straight minutes of blowing out wagon fires and shouting an increasingly loud series of panicked commands at the lady, managed to work out she was avoiding a bomb.

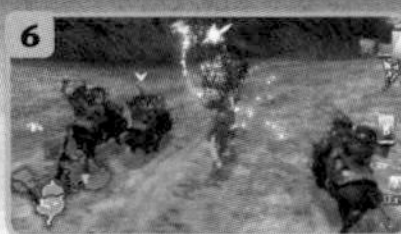

Task 7: Obtain the Zora Armor

Enemies Encountered

Bulblin Rider

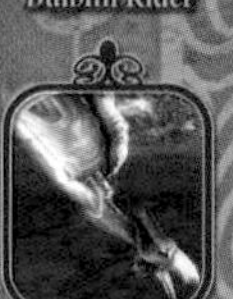
Kargarok

Bulblin Archer

Renado's Healing Hands: The Prince Lives!

▲ You meet Renado outside the Elde Inn. The prince should be okay, as long as he rests. Colin tells Renado he will look after Prince Ralis, no matter how long it takes.

Outside the inn, Colin asks about Ilia's memory loss, and Renado tells him that time should be a factor in healing these scars. Telma asks if you'd be prepared to join the resistance in Castle Town.

◄ Telma says she'll stay a little longer in the village; she's still worried about Ilia and wants to see more of Renado.... She leans over at you, telling there's a **secret passageway** in her bar leading to the castle.

You're about to enter the Elde Inn when you notice a shadow. It's the spirit of the Zora queen Rutela! She floats off down the thoroughfare and flits in and out of your vision.

A Gift from the Zora Queen

◄ The spirit of Queen Rutela is strong, and she beckons you to follow her. Oblige, and she floats south and then west, past the Shaman's sanctuary and into the graveyard. Follow her to the steps and the grassy area beyond. She reveals a small tunnel under a ceremonial stone. Enter the tunnel.

◄ You appear in a small lagoon, which is actually the resting place of Queen Rutela's husband. She hovers above his grave. In return for helping her son receive help, she offers you a special garment—royal armor that enables you to move freely through the water. The grave slides back and the armor is revealed. You've acquired the Zora Armor!

Zora Armor

You got **Zora Armor**! This armor was handed down through the Zora royal family.

Zora Armor

Zora Armor is made from the scales of fallen Zora heroes, and the armor allows you to breathe underwater. Place this on any time you dive into a pool. You can **dive down** by pressing Ⓐ and maneuver much more easily than before. You can wear this on dry land, too, but not in areas where fire and ice appear or when enemies attack with these types of weapons—you'll receive triple the damage if you do!

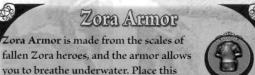

▲ Queen Ruleta disappears after asking you to tell Prince Ralis that he should not grieve his mother's passing; she wanted him to live on and become king of his people. She leaves you, and Midna appears, telling you to get to the lakebed and find the next Fused Shadow!

Task 8: Locate all the Underwater Bomb Rocks, Then Enter the Water Temple

Water Bombs and Underwater Explosions

➤ By now you should be wanting to head directly to Barnes' Bomb Shop and purchase a brand-new explosive device: the Water Bomb. Here's what Barnes currently has for sale:

Store

Store: Barnes' Bomb Shop

Item	Name	Price
	Bombs (10)	30 Rupees
	Bombs (20)	60 Rupees
	Bombs (30)	90 Rupees
	Water Bombs (5)	30 Rupees
	Water Bombs (10)	60 Rupees
	Water Bombs (15)	90 Rupees

Water Bombs
You got **Water Bombs**! These explode rocks and enemies, even underwater.

Note: Barnes now offers a "buyback" plan, where bombs you don't need can be sold back for the same price you paid. That way you can fill up with the more versatile Water Bombs, or gather loads of regular bombs for less expense. The choice is yours. We recommend maxing out one or two Bomb Bags with Water Bombs, and the rest with regular bombs.

Water Bombs

Water Bombs are exceptionally useful in many situations, and if you have enough Rupees, you should buy them exclusively, ignoring regular bombs from now on. Water Bombs have all the functionality of regular bombs (they can explode rocks or foes on land too), but they also work the same way underwater (except you can't combine them with your Bow).

➤ Exit the bomb shop with as many Water Bombs as you can carry (you have two Bomb Bags, so you should have at least 30 bombs), and spend time gathering Rupees and other collectibles from the various chests and crates in the village, if you didn't before. Next, head to the plunge pool behind the spirit of Lanayru's grotto, where you freed the Cuccos.

➤ Dive down into the plunge pool, which is now easily navigated, and look for the Bomb Rock at the pool's bottom. Put on your Iron Boots (and your Zora Armor), and leave a Water Bomb to explode the rock. Grab the purple Rupee (50) from the rubble.

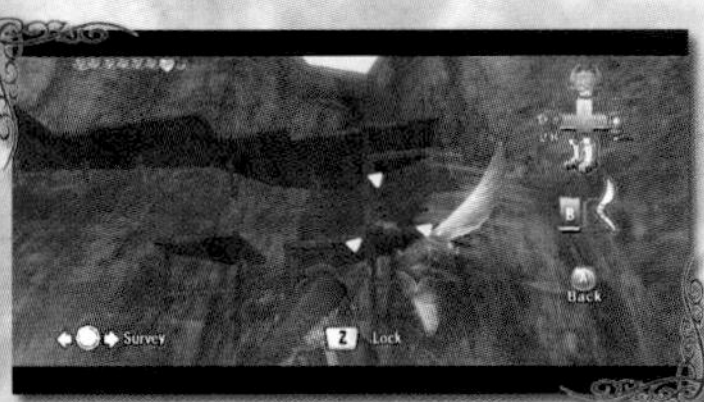

➤ Use the same methods you have previously used to grab goods. For example, the crate on this ledge, which you reached earlier by Cucco, can be destroyed and the red Rupee delivered to your hands if you stand on the roof of the building with the hole in it and double target using the Gale Boomerang.

➤ When you're ready to leave, head toward the graveyard and up the steps. There's another group of Guays flocking around the tree, and there's a Hylian Hornet Nest on the other tree, which you can smash with any of your weapons. Watch the stinging, though!

Enter the Zora king's final resting place through the crawling tunnel, and drop down into the pool in front of the grave. Produce a Water Bomb, and with your Iron Boots on, trudge to the Bomb Rock in the chamber's southern part. There are 20 Rupees inside this one.

➤ Over on the pool's northern side are two rocks blocking what seems to be a channel. Place a single Water Bomb in front of these rocks, and they explode. Sure enough, there's a hole behind there. This is a secret passage you heard the Zora speak of, and if you enter it, you appear in the water at the foot of the waterfall in Lake Hylia. The current is strong—this is a one-way trip!

1 
2 
3 
4 
5 
6 

Tip: Use this to quickly reach Lake Hylia from Kakariko Village, when you don't have the luxury of warping.

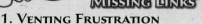

Missing Links

1. Venting Frustration

If you dive and swim toward the waterfall from Lake Hylia, you can see the bubbling vent that leads back to the graveyard. Alas, the current is too strong to enter.

Lake Hylia: Two More Chests to Find

◄ With your Zora Armor and the freedom to look for chests underwater, you can locate another chest that's very difficult to spot without your new gear. Drop into the lake's southern part. Swim to these reeds and locate the chest behind them.

Overworld Chest #46: Orange Rupee (100)

Tip: Technically, it's possible to find this chest before you don the Zora Armor, when you're flying around with the Cuccos for the first time. But grabbing the chest now allows you to locate it much more easily.

► That's the last remaining chest you can open in Lake Hylia. Or is it? We managed to unearth Overworld Chest #22 on top of the platform, which contained an orange Rupee (100), after hours of exploring every underwater nook and cranny of Lake Hylia. The problem was, this chest only appeared once and disappeared completely when we reloaded the game! We later realized this was Overworld Chest #22 (the one you open if you land on the topmost platform on the Isle of Riches after Flight-of-Fowl), and it was located directly below the pole the platform is rotating around. If you chance upon this chest, you know what it is.

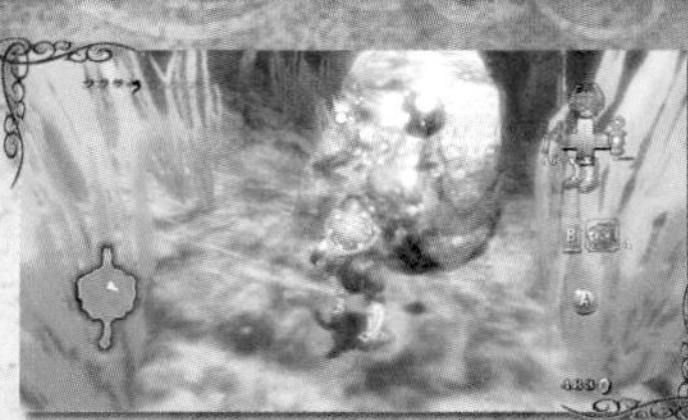

◄ Head into the spirit cave on the south side of Lake Hylia, and take the plunge. You've ransacked both the chests underwater here, but there's a Bomb Rock to blow up. Inside are two green (1), one blue (5), one yellow (10), and one red (20) Rupee. Then head to the pool's southeast area; there's another Bomb Rock on a small ledge. This one contains one green (1), two yellow (10), and one red (20) Rupee.

Tip: This concludes the available Bomb Rocks in Lake Hylia, aside from those at the entrance to Dungeon 3. You now have the earliest opportunity to find the remaining Bomb Rocks underwater throughout previously explored areas. Go for it!

Bomb Rocking All around Hyrule: Hyrule Field (North)

► Hyrule Field (north): Take your horse and travel to the bridge crossing the river that leads back to Upper Zora's River and dismount. Head for the water past the bridge.

► Use the tried-and-true formula of your Iron Boots, Zora Armor, and Water Bombs and drop to this Bomb Rock, just south of the bridge. Inside it are a green (1), two blue (5), and two yellow (10) Rupees.

Swim against the current to the other Bomb Rock, between the steps in the canal section of the river. Place the bomb on the rock's north side, or the current takes it away from you! A yellow (10) and two red (20) Rupees are your reward.

Bomb Rocking All around Hyrule: Zora's Domain

◄ Use the entrance in the northern wall of Hyrule Field (north) to reach the balcony overlooking the waterfall pool; then ascend the stairs before finally reaching the Zora throne room. There are some rocks to tackle in the plunge pool, but first there's some optional Missing Link Rupees to find around the sides.

Enemies Encountered

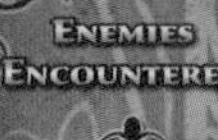

Guay

Hylian Hornets

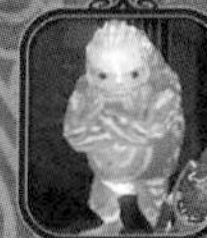

Characters Encountered

Zora

Goron

Missing Links

1. Wall and Small Rock Rupee Hunt

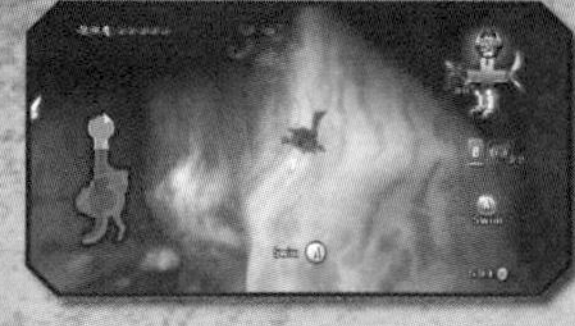

Start by collecting several yellow (10) Rupees stuck on the outer middle ledges. There's one in the southeast area, one above a Bomb Rock in the northeast area, and one almost at the surface in the northern area.

Continue to work your way around, and land on a small ledge with two green stones on it. Lift the tiny rock; there's a blue Rupee (5) underneath. Lift two more rocks on this ledge's narrow left section; there's a blue (5) and yellow (10) Rupee under these.

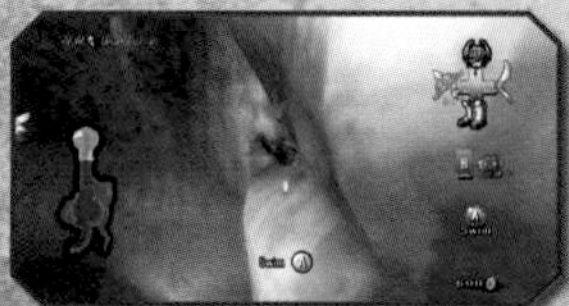

Swim at approximately the same depth to the northwest part of this plunge pool, and scrape a yellow Rupee (10) off the wall.

Swim to the large ledge on the pool's western side, and lift three rocks to find a green (1) and two blue (5) Rupees under each of them.

Don't forget to grab the small rock on this ledge, in the pool's northern part; there's a yellow (10) Rupee for your troubles.

Swim down to the pool's bottom and begin lifting the small rocks surrounding the molten shard. Green Rupees (1) are available here.

After you finish Rupee hunting, optionally float down to the Zora on the southeastern ledge and talk to her. She has a strange feeling about the molten shard; it's like it's alive and looking at her. How strange.

Now you can begin to make some serious rock explosions! Swim to the rock underwater in the pool's northern section, and place a bomb next to it (it rolls but is still effective). This creates some smaller rocks, plus six green (1) and one blue (1) Rupee. The real value is the small rocks; lift them for two yellow (10) and one red (20) Rupee.

Now head to this pool's main section, the molten shard. Stand on one of the small ledges around the impact of the shard, and drop a bomb there. The shard splinters, and out pops a Goron, who was swallowed up in the lava after taking a nap. He's got a gift for freeing you—a **Bag of Bombs**! You now have all three Bomb Bags.

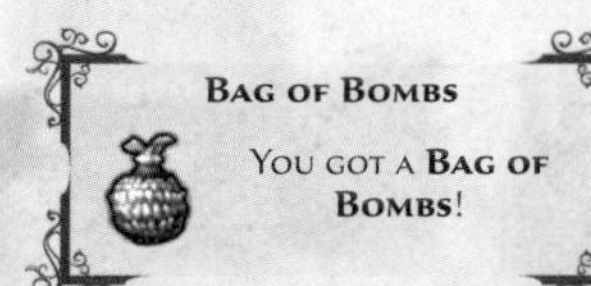

Bag of Bombs

You got a **Bag of Bombs**!

Note: Check out the ⊖ menu screen where your major items are stored. As you can see, there's now space for masses of regular or Water Bombs, or any combination thereof!

◄ Now swim up to the throne room, and exit via the waterfall to the south. Using your Iron Boots and Zora Armor, you might wish to inspect the base of the river just outside the throne room. There are three blue Rupees (5) on the left and right sides of the channel.

Bomb Rocking All around Hyrule: Waterfall Pool

▲ Take the plunge into the waterfall pool below. Talk to the Zora who can transport you back up here, and he explains the wonders of this area. When you're done and have optionally taken the ride back up and then dived down again, search for more Bomb Rocks.

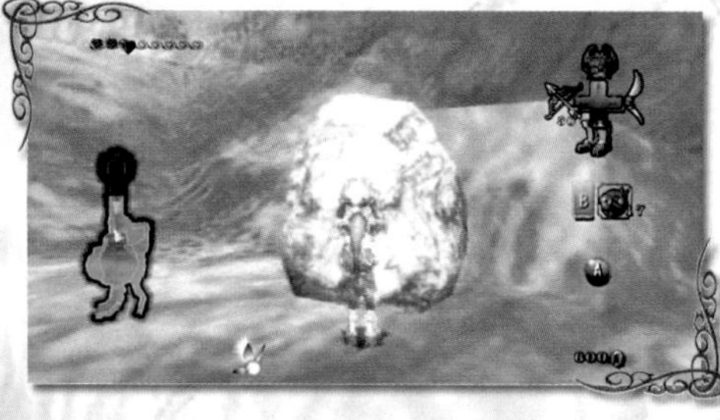

◄ The first Bomb Rock in the northern part of the waterfall pool. Dive deep down, place the bomb, and collect two yellow (10) and two red (20) Rupees from the remains.

Swim to the pool's middle now, and drop to deliver an explosive charge to another rock. It splits apart and delivers two green (1), one blue (5), one yellow (10), and one red (20) Rupee.

▲ During your bombing run, you can emerge from the water and speak to the Zoras on the ledges surrounding you, including those at a new cave entrance, which was blocked by ice before. You can optionally enter this cavern and adventure into Snowpeak!

Snowpeak: Abandon All Hope Ye Who Enter Here

▲ It won't end well, but this is the very first time you can enter the harsh environment of Snowpeak; change your outfit to the heroic clothing and enter the tunnel. You emerge at the top of a series of ledges leading to a cracked and half-frozen lake.

▲ Drop to the lake edge. Don't fall in or you'll be instantly frozen and must restart this area. Make careful jumps, heading in a general northeasterly direction, and you can maneuver across the frozen lake in its entirety.

Zora

Midna

White Wolfos

Threat Meter

Once across the lake, you can trudge into the snow itself, which quickly becomes waist-deep. Strange ghostly wolves appear from the mist and leap upon you. These are White Wolfos and are the guardians of this area. They attack with leaping strikes, and then stalk you, well aware they can outmaneuver you. Currently, the only current way to tackle them (as they attack in pairs) is to shield block the leap, then strike the second one with a single, well-timed blow.

Too fast for you, and too sly to attack without prowling around you, White Wolfos hounds are to be faced later in your adventure.

▲ Once you've tackled the Wolfos, you can begin slowly wading up the snowbank. Midna appears and tries to warn you that you'll freeze if you continue and that you should turn back. Ignore her, and after a few more Wolfos attacks, you fall and expend your energy in the corner of Snowpeak's initial area and must restart this zone. Head back to Zora's Domain right now!

Bomb Rocking All around Hyrule: Upper River

▲ Back in the relative warmth of the river, swim into the Upper River area, near Iza's dwelling, and begin destroying the underwater Bomb Rocks, starting with this one in the southeast area. Expect to collect three green (1), four blue (5), and two yellow (10) Rupees.

◀ This next Bomb Rock, underwater in the middle of the river area, yields one green (1), four blue (5), and one yellow (10) Rupee. In the southern part of the area, near the submerged ramp, is a third Bomb Rock, which is easily missed. Blow it up for two green (1), two blue (5), and two yellow (10) Rupees.

Entering Dungeon 3: The Water Temple

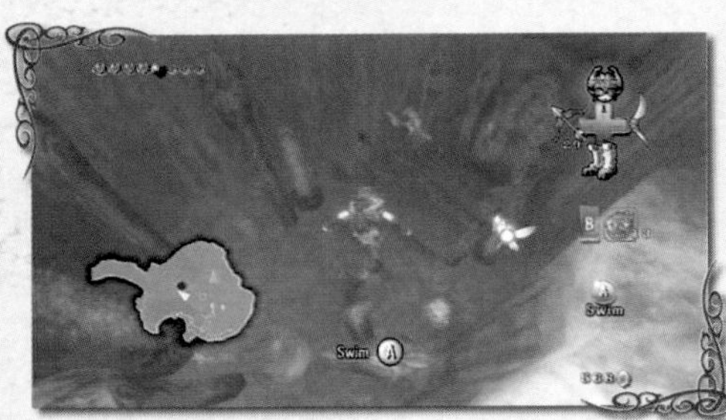

◀ You've exhausted your Overworld expedition, so now you should entertain Midna and finally dive into the depths of Lake Hylia. Swim to the purple dot on your map, and down to a rift at the lake's bottom. The entrance to the dungeon is flanked by Zora ceremonial spires. This is a special place.

1 
2 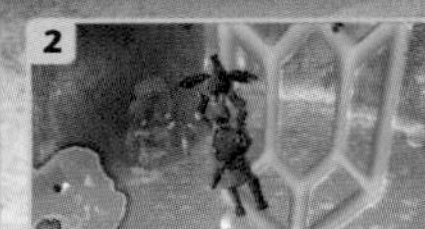
3 
4 
5 
6 

Enemies Encountered

White Wolfos

➤ It's also a place where you can set off a Water Bomb and destroy another Bomb Rock in the area. Search for it, detonate it, and clear two blue (5), one yellow (10), and one red (20) Rupee from the explosion. Over on the opposite side of the rift is a second Bomb Rock. The plan is much the same, although you gain one green (1), one blue (5), and three yellow (10) Rupees.

▲ Swim to the air vent directly below the ornate entrance, and watch it for a moment. It bubbles, then stops. Wear your Iron Boots and wait to produce a **Water Bomb** until the vent starts to bubble. Then place it on the vent. The bomb ascends and explodes as it reaches the rock above. Because the ledge holding the rock is too narrow to place a bomb on, this is the only way into the dungeon. Take a deep breath...and swim inside!

▲ Float across to the stone entrance and speak to the Zora there. He tells you that the place beyond the rock is sacred to his people and was once called the Zora Temple. After being overrun by monsters, the only thing they could do was seal off the place. Time to break that seal!

Missing Links

1. Yellow Rupee Wrangling

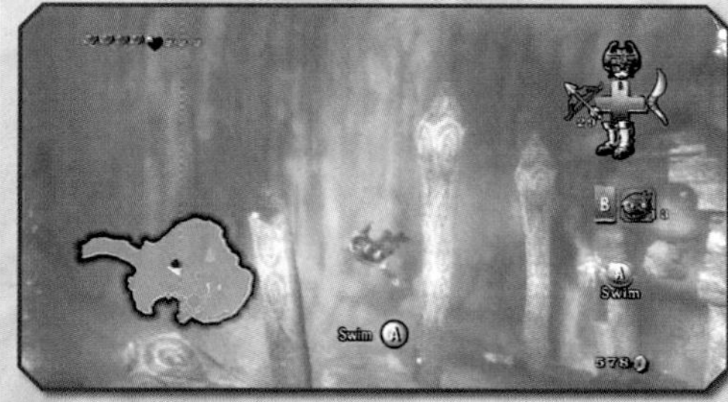

Before you enter the dungeon, check the two broken carved spires in the surrounding rift, as they both contain yellow Rupees (10).

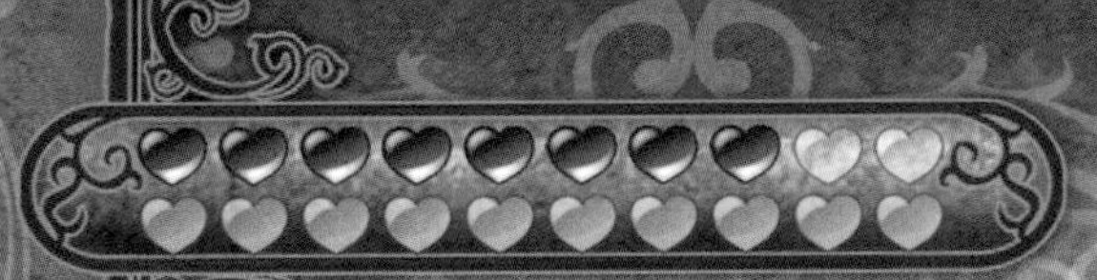

Dungeon 3: Lakebed Temple

1F

3F

2F

4F

Enter Connecting Bridges, Fight Enemy Lizalfos

Open Locked Door in Hub Chamber

Open Floodgate in First Reservoir Tower

Locate Fabled Clawshot from a Bloated Deku Toad

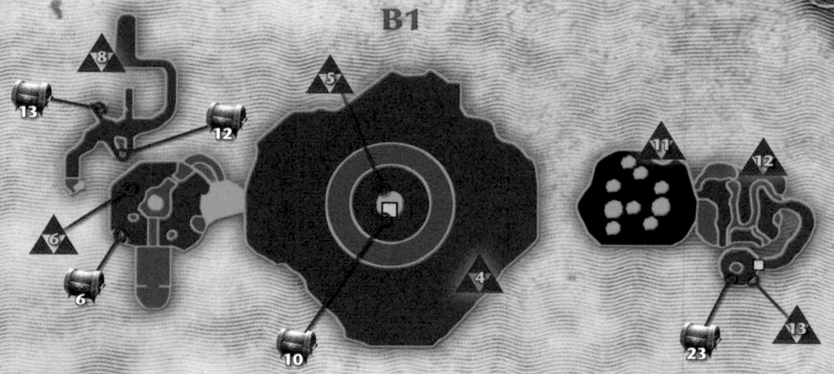

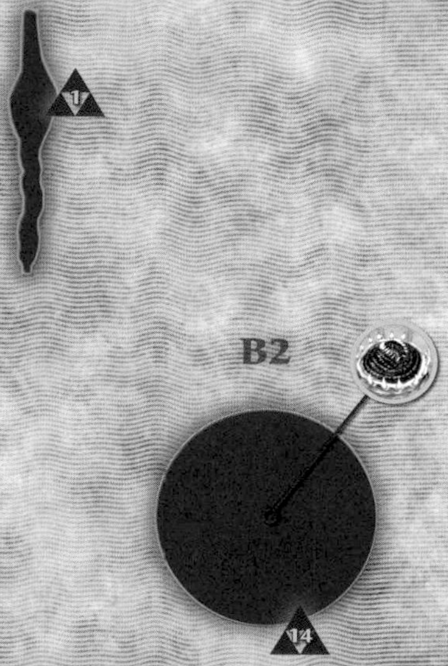

B1

B2

Legend

Room Legend

1. Entrance Tunnel and Grotto
2. Temple Entrance
3. Stalactite Cavern
4. Connecting Bridges
5. Lakebed Column Hub
6. Single Cog Cavern
7. Western Reservoir Tower
8. Crescent Cavern and Snaking Waterway
9. Lair of the Deku Toad
10. Double Cog Cavern
11. Eastern Reservoir Tower
12. The Grotto and Underwater Maze
13. Big Key Plunge Pool
14. Boss Battle! Twilit Aquatic Morpheel

Number of Treasure Chests: 26

1. Arrows (20)
2. Arrows (20)
3. Water Bombs (10)
4. Arrows (20)
5. Dungeon Map
6. Small Key
7. Water Bombs (5)
8. Small Key
9. Bombs (10)
10. Red Rupee (20)
11. Small Key
12. Red Rupee (20)
13. Bombs (5)
14. Clawshot
15. Water Bombs (10)
16. Red Rupee (20)
17. Bombs (10)
18. Compass
19. Red Rupee (20)
20. Bombs (20)
21. Red Rupee (20)
22. Water Bombs (5)
23. Big Key
24. Piece of Heart #19
25. Red Rupee (20)
26. Piece of Heart #20

Items

Fairy in a Bottle

Characters

Deku Toad

Twilit Aquatic Morpheel

5 Open Floodgate in Second Reservoir Tower pg 233

You got the big key!
Use it to gain access to the lair of this dungeon's boss!

6 Locate the Big Key pg 237

7 Find Both Pieces of Heart pg 239

8 Defeat Twilit Aquatic Morpheel pg 241

A Link to the Present

Ordon Sword

Wooden Shield · Hylian Shield

Heart Pieces: 3 (18 Total)

Hero's Clothes · Zora Armor

Big Wallet

Quiver

Golden Bugs: 20 (of 24)

Hidden Skills: 3 (of 7)

Fused Shadow Pieces 2 (of 3)

Ilia's Scent

Fish Journal

Letters 5 (of 16)

Items Already Acquired

Hero's Bow · Heavy Boots · Gale Boomerang · Lantern · Slingshot · Fishing Rod · Hawkeye

Water Bombs · Bombs · Bombs (2) · Bottle #1 · Bottle #2 · Bottle #3

Items to Obtain

Arrows (20) · Water Bombs (10) · Ooccoo · Dungeon Map · Small Key #1 · Small Key #2

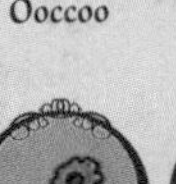

Bombs (10) · Fairy in a Bottle · Small Key #3 · Clawshot · Compass · Big Key

Piece of Heart #19 · Piece of Heart #20 · Fairy in a Bottle · Heart Container · Fused Shadow #3

Dungeon Denizens

Characters

Midna · Ooccoo

Enemies

Shell Blade · Bari · Purple Chu

Red Chu · Yellow Chu · Tektite

Helmasaur · Lizalfos ("Axe-tail") · Skullfish

Chu Worm · Toado · Keese

Lizalfos ("Skull-face") · Bombfish

Bosses

Mid Boss: Deku Toad · Big Boss: Twilit Aquatic Morpheel

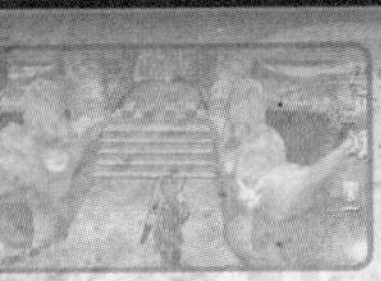
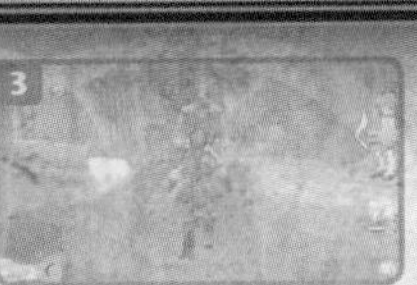

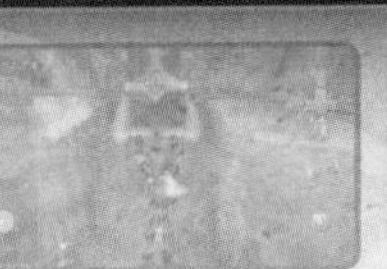

The Lakebed Temple: Overview

This was once a series of wondrous carved chambers where the Zora tribe swam with pride. Now it has been reduced to a dark, dank ruin, an underwater catacomb teeming with monstrous and unhealthy creatures and scavengers. Fortunately, many of the mechanisms the Zora architects placed in this dungeon still work, including the ceremonial floodgates, opened via two reservoir towers at each end of the dungeon. Water used to pour down channels and turn giant cogs, with purposes now lost to time. Only by using this antiquated technology can you thoroughly investigate this lost structure, locating a giant toad and making it cough up a prize. After you collect all items and open all floodgates, a large arena fills with water, and you can call a giant lurking fiend into the light, and eyeball it—literally. Only after these tasks are complete can you collect the last of the Fused Shadows.

Enemies Encountered

Shell Blade

Bari

Task 1: Enter the Connecting Bridges, Fight Enemy "Lizalfos"

Chamber 1: Entrance Tunnel and Grotto (2F)

Before you submerge and swim into this temple, bring along the following:

- Room in your Wallet, so you can collect more from the treasure chests
- Additional arrows and Water Bombs
- Bottles filled with Red Potions or captured Fairies
- Your Iron Boots positioned on the ✚ part of the ✚ so you can slip them on and off quickly
- Arrows and the Gale Boomerang within easy access

Tip

- Water Bombs as your main Ⓑ item
- Also, purchase your additional Water Bombs from Barnes at Kakariko Village

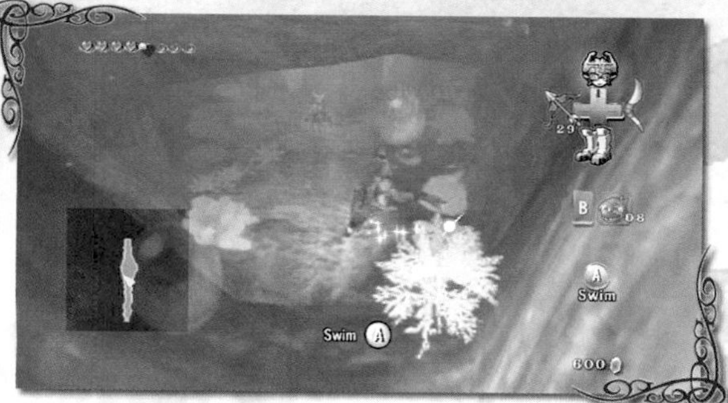

▲ With your Zora Armor on (otherwise you'll drown in seconds!), swim through a water-filled tunnel. This tunnel heads down at an angle, and then bulges out slightly to a grotto with a variety of plant life. Put on your Iron Boots.

Shell Blade

Threat Meter

In this grotto lurks a nasty, clamlike creature known as the Shell Blade. It isn't that threatening, but, its thick shell is impervious to vertical slashing moves. However, you can slice the squashy interior bits with any horizontal slice; the spin attack is excellent for this purpose.

A spray of purple goop indicates that any horizontal swipe has hit home: shell shock for the Shell Blade!

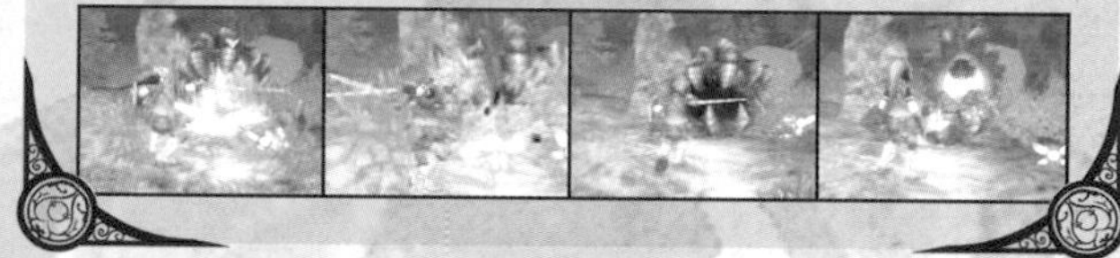

▲ Escape the grotto and swim up a long conduit. Avoid the large, electric, jellylike beings. Currently, you have no way to defeat these Baris, but when you obtain a new weapon, you will prevail!

Characters Encountered

Midna

Chamber 2: Temple Entrance (2F)

Swim to the conduit's top to end up in a circular pool. Clamber out and draw your sword. A giant Purple Chu is about to attack! Use a mixture of shield blocking and sword swiping to cut it down to size, then defeat its smaller offspring. Tackle a Red Chu on the pool's southern rim. Scoop it if you need extra energy in a Bottle.

Treasure Chest: After dealing with the Chus, skirt the perimeter, smashing a couple of pots for the Hearts inside. Find a small chest in the room's eastern part. It contains some arrows.

Treasure Chest #1: Arrows (20)

Arrows

You got **arrows (20)**! Use arrows to shoot far-off foes!

This room hasn't given up all of its goods yet. Run south, and check out a small chest. This one offers Water Bombs.

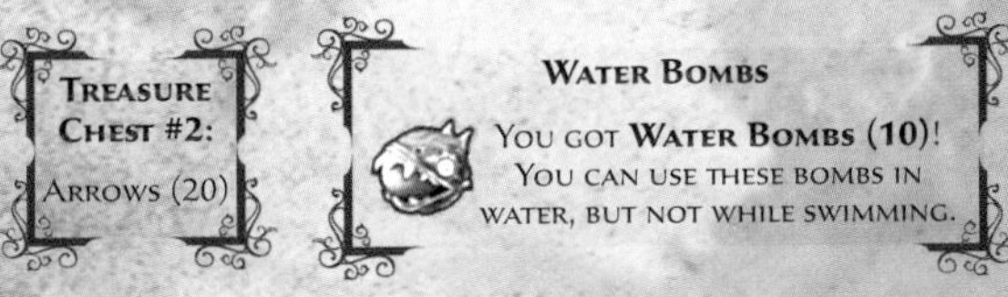

Treasure Chest #2: Arrows (20)

Water Bombs

You got **Water Bombs (10)**! You can use these bombs in water, but not while swimming.

Check the chamber's western part to discover two pots, but more importantly, a Red Chu. This provides another chance to scoop up its remains after combat. Then move to the northern temple entrance, and tackle a Purple Chu.

Run up the steps to the entrance door, which is sealed. That is, until you run from the ledge and leap off, catching the large gold handle and pulling it down. This activates the door, and you can move into the next chamber. However, a couple of Red Chus and a Blue Chu (which gives you an even more potent potion) ooze out of the walls. Tag and bag them!

Missing Links

1. Chus Life

The longer you stay in this chamber, the more chance you have that a Red Chu will fall from the ceiling. Look up to see if any are hanging around (there are five total). There are purple ones too, but they don't give you quite the energy boost.

2. Pottery Pulverizing

Smashing everything you can see works well in this chamber. Steal blue Rupees (5) and green Rupees (1) from pottery you smash.

Chamber 3: Stalactite Cavern (2F)

You appear in a strange cavern with many hanging stalactites and some odd-looking creatures charging about below. Before you leap down, Midna appears and advises you to make sure those rock formations are sturdy so they don't fall on you. Oblige her.

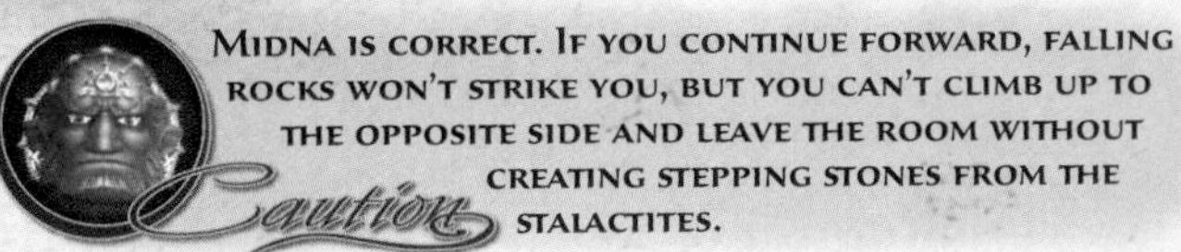

Caution

Midna is correct. If you continue forward, falling rocks won't strike you, but you can't climb up to the opposite side and leave the room without creating stepping stones from the stalactites.

Bring out your Hero's Bow, and combine arrows with bombs. If you have a stash of regular bombs, use these, and keep Water Bombs for later. Aim for the crack in each stalactite, and break apart all four of them; they fall and become platforms. Be sure the room looks like this before you proceed.

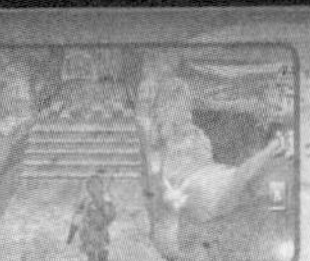

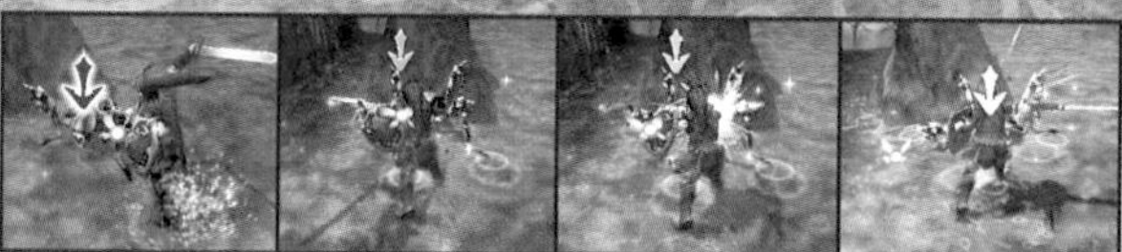

▲ Head down the slope, bring out your sword, and drop off to either side. Ignore the strange enemy with the armored back for the moment, and locate a couple of Tektites skating below. Slice into both of them, until they expire and give you a Heart. Explore the area heading south, back up to the entrance door. There's nothing except a series of ledges to climb to get back up to the sloping platform in the middle. Turn and head north. You have a new creature to tackle.

Helmasaur

Threat Meter

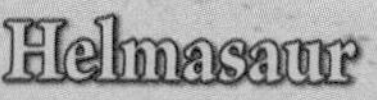

Climb to the first southern ledge, bring up your shield, and Z target a trotting foe with a large armored helm. It will strike and send you flying off the ledge's side. It can push you back even if you're blocking. You cannot hurt the Helmasaur by hitting it from the front or sides. You must target it, then jump or maneuver around until you're facing its rear, then strike (with a spin attack, or Hidden Skill #3, the back slice). Avoid confrontations in rocky spots such as this one, as it's difficult to get behind it. When you receive the Clawshot later in this expedition, the combat options improve immensely!

This creature is plated with an impressive armor that covers most of its body. Find that part that's exposed, and it becomes helmless, and helpless!

Note: The Helmasaur's carapace armor doesn't explode after combat. You can use it like a rock, and throw it as an ineffective weapon! However, there may be a different use for this in a dungeon to come....

◄ Defeat or avoid the two Helmasaurs on this ledge and jump to two of the stepping stones you created earlier, allowing you access up the northern ledges. Smash pottery as you go, and continue until you reach the exit door.

◄ Treasure Chest: Don't leave this chamber yet! In the chamber's northwest corner are a couple more stepping stones and a small waterfall. Climb to a small ledge where two pots and a tiny chest reside. Open and loot everything, then return to the north door and open it.

Treasure Chest #3: Water Bombs (10)

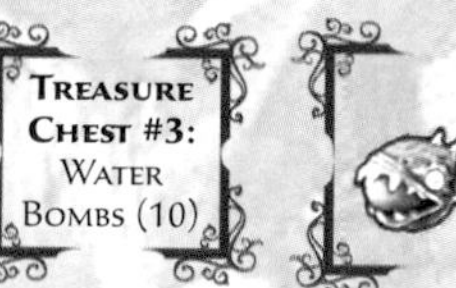

Water Bombs
You got **Water Bombs (10)**! You can use these bombs in water, but not while swimming.

Missing Links

1. Pottery Pulverizing

This chamber holds a number of pots to break:

- Next to the northwestern wall on a large ledge, behind a stepping stone: Heart
- On an unreachable platform in the stalagmite cluster on the eastern wall; use the Gale Boomerang: blue Rupee (5)
- By a stalagmite in the upper ledge, northeast corner: Heart
- In the upper northwest corner, next to Treasure Chest #3: blue Rupee (5) and arrows

Chamber 4: Connecting Bridges (2F)

◄ Enter an impressively large rock chamber with swirling waters below you, and a number of bridges jutting from a central column. Look closely to see a second corridor above you. For the moment, however, peer forward to see a scaly fiend running at you. Bring out the sword!

Enemies Encountered

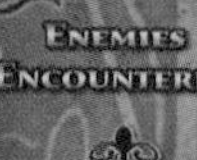

Chu (Purple, Red, Blue)

Tektite

Helmasaur

Task #1
Enter the Connecting Bridges, Fight Enemy "Lizalfos"

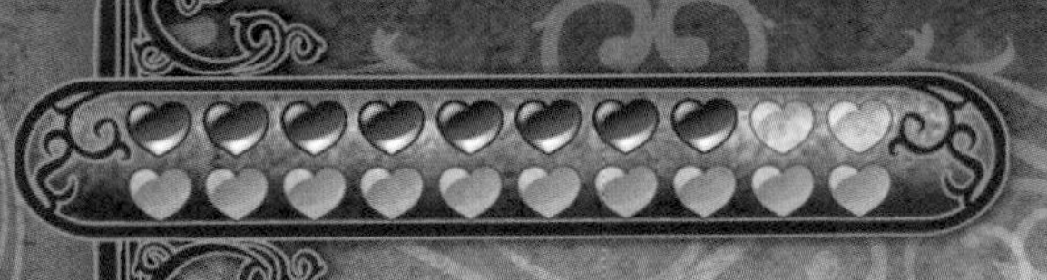

Lizalfos ("Axe-tail")

Threat Meter

Padding down the hallway at you is a species of Lizalfos, a scaly denizen with a mean streak. It has two bladed attacks: a sword it carries and a tail with an axelike blade attached to it. This blade, when whipped around, can knock you off your feet. The Lizalfos is also skilled in defense, meaning you can't simply wade in and defeat it. Multiple simple sword strikes are required to down it. A better plan is to shoot Bomb Arrows from range or use the back slice. Start by Ⓩ targeting, ram it with your shield to stun it, then roll around with Ⓐ and slice its exposed back!

Don't target and leap against a Lizalfos because it can slice faster than you. Regroup, and turn defense into offense.

Task 2: Open the Locked Door in the Hub Chamber

Chamber 5: Lakebed Column Hub (2F to 1F to BF)

◄ After you defeat the Lizalfos, walk to the north door, and enter the interior column. This reveals itself to be a huge circular room, containing handles, doors, a large staircase you can turn with those handles, vine walls, pots, chests, and more! You can spot a chest on a chandelier, above the large staircase.

Caution: Don't run around pressing stuff. Interact methodically with the scenery to avoid getting lost, confused, or worse!

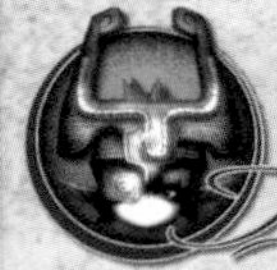

Tip: The purple and blue floor tiles point to gaps you can investigate, handles you can pull, or doors you can enter. Follow these if you get lost.

◄ You can spot a locked door on the west side of the circular balcony you're standing on, but a wall draped in scales and skin doesn't allow you access here. You need a key first anyway, so step forward, and head down the stairs (you can't drag that gold handle yet).

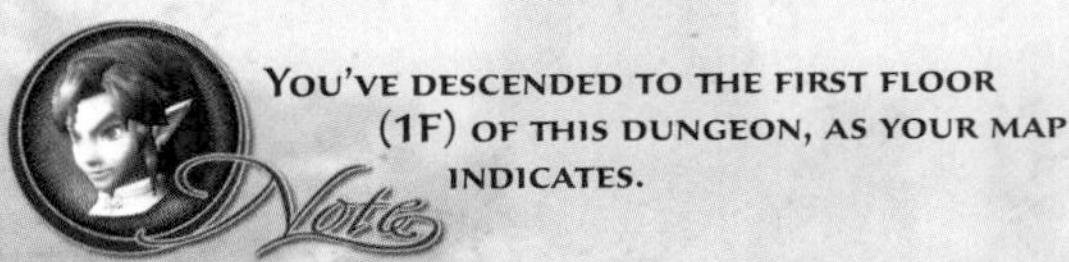

Note: You've descended to the first floor (1F) of this dungeon, as your map indicates.

▲ Down on the first floor, turn left if you feel the need to slice open pottery. Don't worry about the chest on the scaly wall's other side yet. Instead, optionally take a plunge, diving off a gap in the first floor balcony where you see vines.

You'll land in a circular plunge pool that's beneath the staircase. Dive into the murky waters to see the column that's holding up the chamber above. A half-dozen horrible little fish also bite you!

Skullfish

Threat Meter

Skullfish inhabit this temple's central pool. These nasty creatures swim at you to take a nip out of your hide. This only takes a quarter energy, but it's still unpleasant. Simply swim away because you're faster than them. Here are some ways to defeat them:

The least obvious is to get out your Fishing Rod! This isn't a favored fishing hole, but you can catch Skullfish here, although they aren't added to your Fish Journal. You get a Heart of energy for each fish you catch. The problem is you don't dispatch the Skullfish and must throw it back!

A better way to dispatch these Skullfish from dry land is to use your **Gale Boomerang**, targeting up to five fish at once (or auto-targeting), then throwing it. This is very effective. Your Hero's Bow, a new item you're about to claim called the Clawshot, and even dropped bombs also work. Finally, if you're in the water, draw your sword and wear the Iron Boots, and tackle them from the deep (this doesn't work in the plunge pool though, as the Skullfish swim above you).

▲ Ignore the Skullfish, walk to the plunge pool's north side, and face south. Survey (with Ⓒ and ◎) the central column to discover an opening in it! Now that you've uncovered a few secrets you can't reach yet, head onto the narrow ledge surrounding the plunge pool and locate the vine walls: one in the northeast and one in the northwest. You may need to dissuade a Tektite from attacking before you make the climb.

➤ **Treasure Chest:** Either vine wall brings you up to the first floor. Continue around this ledge to the south, bringing out your sword to deflate a leaping blue Tektite along the way. Against a scaly wall in the southwest is a treasure chest holding more arrows. Open this, then return to an eastern door with a channel running below it. Perhaps this needs to be filled with water? For the moment, open this door.

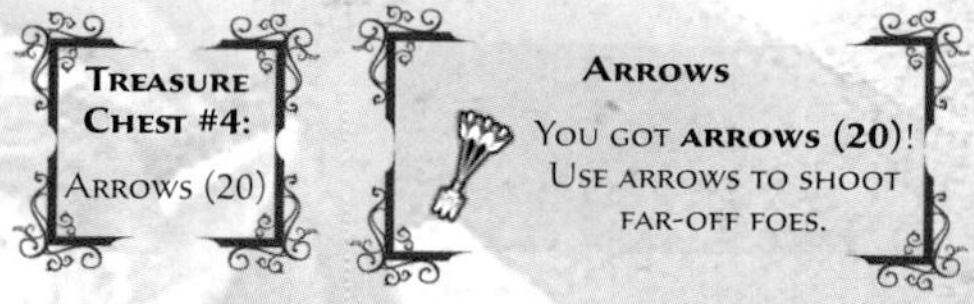

Treasure Chest #4: Arrows (20)

Arrows

You got **arrows (20)**! Use arrows to shoot far-off foes.

Missing Links

1. Pulverizing Pottery

Destroy the ornate pottery for tiny prizes. Here's where to find them:

- 2F: Against the scaly wall, to the entrance's left: Rupee and Heart
- 2F: Against the scaly wall, to the right of the entrance: Rupees
- 1F: Against the scaly wall, northwest area: Rupee and arrows
- BF: On the narrow ledge surrounding the plunge pool, north area: Hearts

Chamber 4: First Return to Connecting Bridges (1F)

◄ Unsheathe your Ordon Blade and prepare to strike a Tektite who's leaping at you as you head east back into the Connecting Bridges area. This time though, you're on the opposite side and one floor down. When you strike the Tektite, you see it was guarding a couple of pots (smash them to grab a Rupee and Heart), and a large waterwheel that you can't move. Head back into the Lakebed Column Hub.

Enemies Encountered

Lizalfos (Axe-tail)

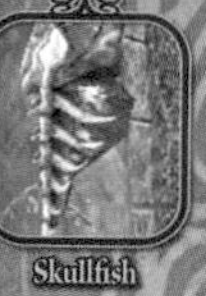

Skullfish

Tektite

Ooccoo

Chamber 5: First Return to Lakebed Column Hub (1F to 2F)

◀ Return to the first floor Lakebed Column Hub, and head to the ledge's southern part. Face north to see a gold handle you didn't pull when you went for the treasure chest. Leap and catch it, and the staircase rotates 180 degrees. This allows you to ascend it. It leads to the north part of the second floor (2F)—the area you haven't explored yet.

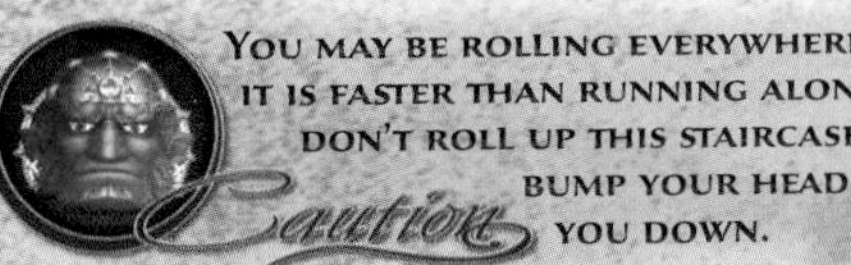

Caution: You may be rolling everywhere (as it is faster than running alone), but don't roll up this staircase or you bump your head, slowing you down.

➤ Make a right at the top of the stairs. You pass a door and encounter some pottery to smash on the other side of a scaly wall (inside are Rupees you can't grab). Instead, turn left, and draw your sword to smite a Tektite hopping about this area. Step across a channel leading to a locked door, and run to the scaly wall where a single pot awaits. It's shaking slightly. Pick it up and you discover your old friend: Ooccoo! You can now meet her son and leave the dungeon whenever you like!

Ooccoo

You are reunited with **Ooccoo**! This kind character can let you out of dungeons and return you to where you were.

◀ There are two doorways, each with a channel under it. The one to the west is locked. The one to the east isn't, so move there. You're about to enter another passage above the one containing the waterwheel you saw before.

Chamber 4: Second Return to Connecting Bridges (2F)

➤ Enter this passage. There's no Tektite, but otherwise this is similar to the one directly below you. It's blocked by a waterwheel that won't budge, and there are a couple of pots to smash for a Rupee and Heart. There's little else to do except memorize this area.

Chamber 5: Second Return to Lakebed Column Hub (2F to 1F)

◀ You've already moved the giant stone stairway 180 degrees, but now it's time to point it east to west. Head out into the Lakebed Column Hub and grab the gold handle straight in front of you. The staircase grinds to this location. You can now head down the stairs, rolling if you wish, and moving directly west to an open door you haven't explored yet.

◀ Before you leave this area, turn right, and locate the chest at the dead end. It's the one you saw earlier, and it contains a useful item! Pick it up before you leave.

Treasure Chest #5: Dungeon Map

Dungeon Map

You got the **Dungeon Map**!

Chamber 4: Third Return to Connecting Bridges (1F)

➤ Enter the first floor passage heading west, and bring out your shield and sword to defend yourself against this nasty Helmasaur. Dodge its charge and poke it where it's armorless, then open the unlocked door.

1

2

3

4

5

6

Chamber 6: Single Cog Cavern (1F and BF)

◄ The Zoras' construction is impressive. Walk into this large cavern containing a giant cog in front of you, with three round platforms hanging from it. It looks like this room continues up to the second floor (2F) and down to the basement (BF). Step forward to the edge.

◄ Your first plan of attack is to drop a stalactite from the northern ceiling with a Bomb Arrow. Then turn left and fire off another Bomb Arrow at the second stalactite (it's in the mist and difficult to spot). These two falling rocks plug (or are caught by) a couple of fountain jets on the basement level, allowing easy access throughout your exploration.

Now inspect this chamber thoroughly. You can drop down to the basement level, which has shallow water everywhere although it's not deep enough to impede your running. To climb back to the first floor, use the large granite steps to the right.

➤ From the entrance, turn right, and run forward to a small tunnel entrance. Jog down this tunnel, and you appear under the circular platforms attached by a chain to the giant cog. You're now in the basement level, and the stalactite you just released has created a path from north to south.

➤ Head south to a vine that's growing on the central column in this lower area, and cling to the vine, shifting around until you're on a ledge facing the southern part of this chamber. Look south to spot a grand archway with a sealed gate. However, the bridge to cross this area is below you; the water needs to be raised. Ignore this for the moment, and face southwest. There's a small chest on an equally tiny ledge. The rock island you leap to is the second stalactite piece you destroyed, and it ascends and descends on a water jet. Stand on it and don't fall off, then leap to the chest when it rises.

Treasure Chest #6: Small Key

Small Key

You got a **Small Key**! This opens a locked door, but only in this area.

◄ You will return to this room in the future, but for the moment, you've got what you came here for. Inspect the waterlogged area's southern part, slicing a Tektite or two with your sword. Climb up the vine wall to the ledge cluster in the middle, or up the granite steps, and exit the way you came in.

Missing Links

1. Gale Force Fun

You can't leap to the ledge on the room's north side, but you can target the pots there with your **Gale Boomerang** and bring the Rupees to you (drop down to collect them if they fall).

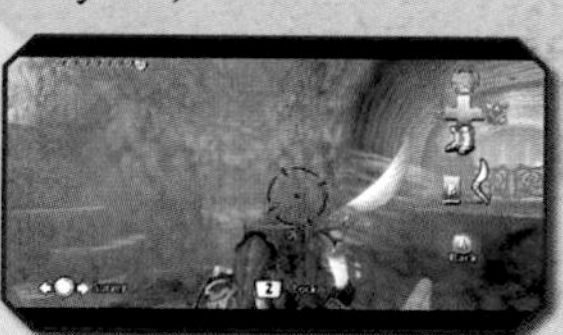

A second place to try your long-range wind power is when you're standing on the rocky center of the basement level. Point your Gale Boomerang to this small plinth with a single pot on it. This contains a yellow Rupee (10).

2. Pulverizing Pottery

There's the regular way to shatter pottery, starting with the two next to the entrance door, near the small tunnel. These hold a Heart and a Rupee.

Chamber 4: Fourth Return to Connecting Bridges (1F)

▲ Back up on the first floor, run across this linking platform to the hub. You're searching for a locked door: the one you found earlier on the second floor.

Enemies Encountered

Tektite

Helmasaur

Task #2

Open the Locked Door in the Hub Chamber

Chamber 5: Third Return to Lakebed Column Hub (1F to 2F)

➤ There's no need to look for a gold handle to wrench; you're heading back the way you came. Run up the large staircase, and make an immediate left. The locked doorway, with pink stone surroundings to differentiate it, is in the second floor west section.

Task 3: Open the Floodgate in the First Reservoir Tower

Chamber 4: Fifth Return to Connecting Bridges (2F)

➤ The locked door leads onto the connecting bridge platforms. This is one you haven't visited before, so ready a sword or prepare to flee from the Helmasaur. You can easily open the door at the far end.

Chamber 6: First Return to Single Cog Cavern (2F)

➤ **Treasure Chest:** It may not be obvious, but you're above the Single Cog Cavern area you just negotiated! Compare your in-game map levels. The difference is that you're currently negotiating the outer passages surrounding the central cog. Turn left to deal with the Tektite. Run to the corner and open an easily overlooked chest.

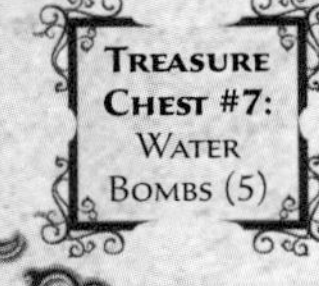

Treasure Chest #7: Water Bombs (5)

Water Bombs

You got **Water Bombs (5)**! You can use these bombs in water, but not while swimming.

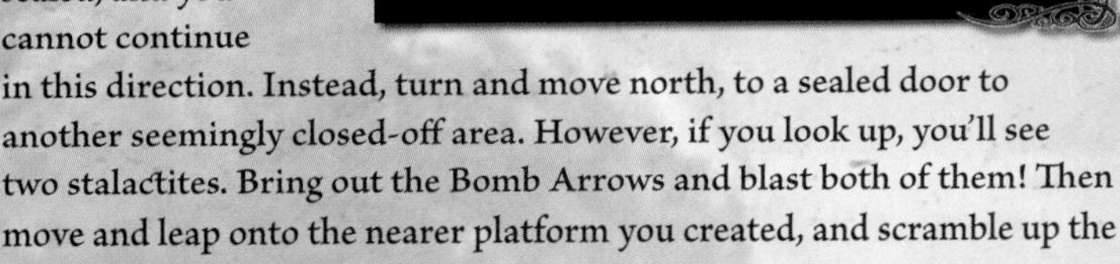

➤ Head across to the opposite side and smash some pots (which contain arrows), and inspect the grating to the south. This is firmly sealed, and you cannot continue in this direction. Instead, turn and move north, to a sealed door to another seemingly closed-off area. However, if you look up, you'll see two stalactites. Bring out the Bomb Arrows and blast both of them! Then move and leap onto the nearer platform you created, and scramble up the vine wall.

➤ As long as you blasted both stalactites, you can access an area of broken wall near the vines, which has a gold handle on the western side. Line yourself up and jump, pulling the handle down. This activates the sealed door below you.

Author Note

Were you stuck on this puzzle for ages, despite having all the clues (the vines, the chest with bombs, and the arrows in the pot) needed to solve it? Don't worry; we had the same problem!

➤ Run westward around the cavern's perimeter, and pass by a door in the south wall that leads to the middle of this chamber. Instead, inspect that large rock blocking your path. A quick Bomb Arrow destroys the rock. Beyond is a short dirt ramp, with two Helmasaurs ready to charge. Back up away from the rubble to deal with them. Head up the dirt ramp to a door, but open it in a moment.

Back up, leap to the side of a charging Helmasaur, and dish out some damage to its rump!

➤ First, backtrack to the south wall door and open it. This leads to the giant cog you saw with the chained circular platforms hanging from it. You're on top of this area, in the chamber's central part. Begin your exploration by heading left.

➤ Smash pottery if you wish, then leap onto the gigantic cog. A Lizalfos guarding a southwest door trots over to deal with you. A swift collection of strikes should knock it down to size. Investigate the southern ledge, then leave via this door.

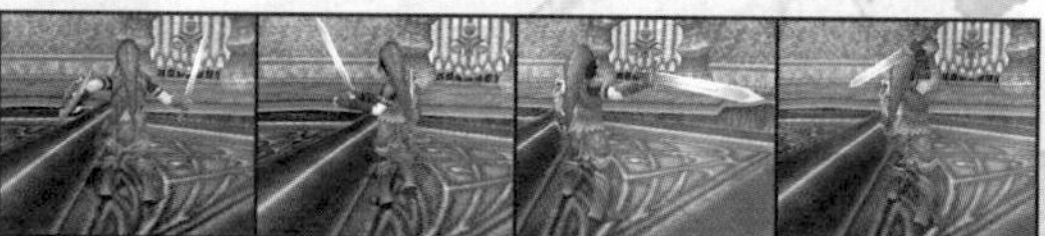

Tip: Are you feeling particularly satisfied with this, or any other takedown? If you defeated a strong enemy, such as this Lizalfos, you can finish your sword-based attack with a flourish! Stand still and press Ⓐ, and you perform a heroic sword sheathing twirl. Impressive!

➤ After you're in this southwest perimeter path, take a left and investigate another gigantic cog, which looks like it's water-powered but stationary. Smash the pots, then inspect the chest on the outer wall. A Keese who flutters in waylays you. The chest contains a Small Key that will be useful in a forthcoming chamber!

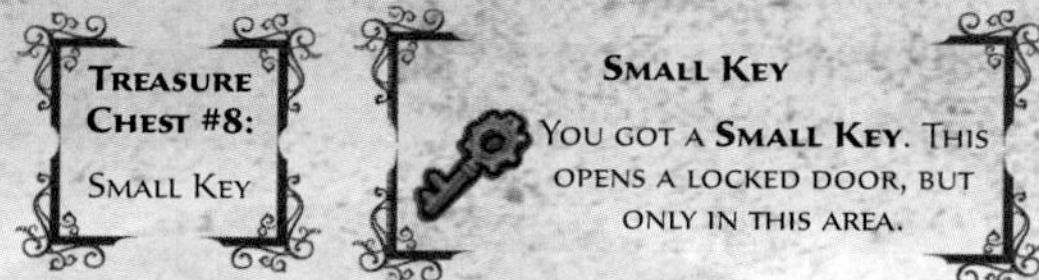

Treasure Chest #8: Small Key

Small Key

You got a **Small Key**. This opens a locked door, but only in this area.

➤ This perimeter corridor's opposite end has a number of pots to smash, plus gloopy Chu enemies to fight. Slice up a couple of Purple Chus and one Red Chu. Aside from the pottery, there's little else to do here. There's a door to the west, but you can't climb the wall with the water channel embedded in it. Instead, run to the dirt ramp and the unlocked door.

Note: The door at the dirt ramp's end is actually right next to the one you couldn't reach when you were fighting the Chus. You can easily access this door now, but only in one direction!

Missing Links

1. Pulverizing Pottery

This general area has a number of pots that need smashing. Here are a few locations to look for:

- The perimeter corridor, next to Treasure Chest #6: arrows
- The northeast ledge in the central cog chamber area: Rupees and Heart
- The south ledge in the central cog chamber area: Rupees and Heart
- The perimeter corridor, next to Treasure Chest #7: blue Rupees (5) and Hearts
- The perimeter corridor, near the Chus in the western dead end: Rupees

Enemies Encountered

Helmasaur

Tektite

Lizalfos (Axe-tail)

Keese

Chu (Purple, Red)

Chamber 7: Western Reservoir Tower (2F to 3F to 4F)

Chu Worm

Threat Meter

Step through into an enclosed chamber, where an odd wormlike fellow hops into a large Chu Jelly bubble and bounces around. The bubble is impervious to your sword strikes, but the Chu Worm isn't safe from Bomb Arrows. Simply Z target the wriggling foe, and launch a Bomb Arrow.

It's a wonder the Chu Worm has survived in the Hylian wilds. It's one of the least aggressive mites around!

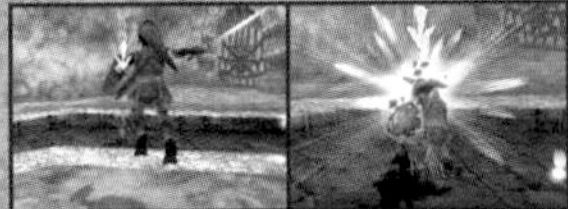

That bubble shield explodes, leaving the creature exposed. You can fire another Bomb Arrow as it weakly hops away, but it's better to finish this foe with a flurry of sword swipes. Don't forget to try the Clawshot against this creature later on; the results are very satisfying!

◄ Step into this small chamber and check it out thoroughly. A water channel leads to a door just to the left of the one you came through. This leads back into the perimeter of chamber 6, where you fought the Chu. Don't head there yet! Instead, move to the only locked door, opposite the one with the channel under it. Use the Small Key you just found.

► You arrive in a tall, circular room with a winding water chute curling up the exterior wall. This is one of two reservoir channels for the entire temple, and releasing water into these channels should activate the waterwheel cogs you've seen elsewhere.

◄ You have to jump into the pit below the ledge you're standing on. Ignore the gold handle you can see (but not reach yet). Climb over the channel wall, and climb the chute. As you climb from the second floor to the third floor, fight a couple of Tektites.

◄ Treasure Chest: Continue to the chute's top, facing another Tektite on the way. As you reach the top, the channel flattens out, and there's a bridge to cross. Before you do so, head straight across the channel, to this small chest, and secure a few more bombs for this operation. These aren't Water Bombs, so use them with your Hero's Bow against enemies on land.

Treasure Chest #9: Bombs (10)

Bombs

You got **bombs (10)**!

► Turn to the chute's top and investigate this area. There's a squared off arch with two ladders embedded in each side. Choose one ladder, scale it, and at the top, peer to the opposite side. A treasure chest is here, but you can't take it yet. Instead, line yourself up with the gold handle and grab it.

A cascade of water tumbles out of the roof gates (siphoned from Lake Hylia), and runs down the chute into the circular reservoir at the chamber's base. Drop down onto the channel, and head to the chute. You can ride the water down (it's slightly uncontrollable, but fun!). But beware: once you start the ride, you can't stop!

Note: You could also run along the chute's outer channel wall, or jump off the chute into the water.

Tip: To return to the chute's top (if you forgot to open Treasure Chest #9, for example), you must jump onto the chute wall, don your Iron Boots, and slowly clump to the top. This takes ages, but it's the only way to ascend after the water starts.

◄ Once at the reservoir, swim to the platform at the central tower's base, clamber on, and then line yourself up with the gold handle and leap to grab it. This opens a floodgate at the opposite end of the chamber, and allows water to flow down the channel you saw along the perimeter of chamber 6. Head back there now.

Missing Links

1. Pulverizing Pottery

Inanimate jars don't stand a chance when you're searching for Rupees and Hearts. Look around the western ledge (second floor) for four pots containing Rupees and Hearts. The eastern pit near the vine wall has three pots. They contain two blue Rupees (5) and one yellow Rupee (10).

Enemies Encountered

Chu Worm

Tektite

Purple Chu

Helmasaur

Task 4: Locate the Fabled Clawshot from a Bloated Deku Toad

Chamber 6: Second Return to Single Cog Cavern (2F)

▲ Run across to the two doors, and choose the one on the right with the rushing water underneath it. Step into the perimeter of the cog cavern, and leap off the end. Fight a couple of Chus if you wish. The pots have also respawned! Head to the waterwheel cog next to the open chest (#7), and pass between the wheel's blades.

► This leads to the final part of this chamber's perimeter and a dead end. The gate you saw when you first entered this perimeter area is the same one you're facing now. Smash both the pots. The one on the right houses a Fairy! Produce one of your three Bottles, and capture it. Attack a Purple Chu that's dropped down, as you retrace your steps under the waterwheel cog.

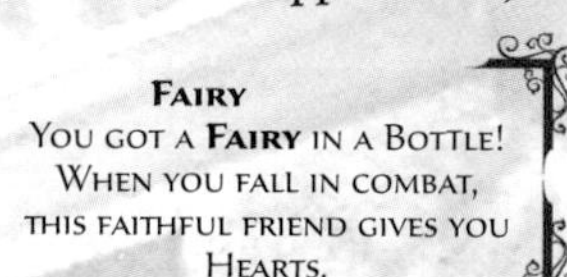

Fairy

You got a **Fairy** in a Bottle! When you fall in combat, this faithful friend gives you Hearts.

◄ Head to the door leading to the middle of this chamber, and open it. The gigantic cog has started to move after the water turned the waterwheel, and the three circular chain platforms below are now rotating. Drop through the cog to get back there, or secure treasure: Exit via the north door and head east, to the main hub.

Chamber 4: Sixth Return to Connecting Bridges (2F)

▲ First though, you must negotiate the connecting bridge platform running west to east, and the fearsome Helmasaur on the way. Exit via the door opposite.

Chamber 5: Fourth Return to Lakebed Column Hub (2F to BF to 1F to 2F to 1F)

➤ **Treasure Chest:** Once across the bridge, you see that the floodgate you opened is flooding this central chamber. Dash forward, and dive off the ledge's edge (dive to one side so you don't hit any steps below) into the plunge pool. Ignore the Skullfish, and swim to the central pillar. You can now open the chest in the pillar alcove you spotted before.

Treasure Chest #10: Red Rupee (20)

➤ Climb back up to the first floor, and run around to the southern side of the ledge. Face north, and leap to pull the gold handle so the stairs trundle and stop in a north-south orientation. Run up to the second floor, jog around to the east side of the ledge, and grab another gold handle, bringing the stairs to an east-west orientation. Run down these stairs, and directly ahead is a door to the west. Slay a Tektite, and head through.

Chamber 4: Seventh Return to Connecting Bridges (1F)

➤ Open the door, and speed across the connecting bridge. Your Helmasaur foe is here, but it's as easy to roll past it as fight it. Open the door at the far end, and you're back at the cog chamber.

Chamber 6: Third Return to Single Cog Cavern (1F)

➤ The rotation of the platforms hanging from the cog by chains allows you to reach a couple of previously impossible-to-reach ledges, each with a door. Begin your expedition by leaping to the door in the north wall, and open it.

Chamber 8: Crescent Cavern and Snaking Waterway (1F)

➤ **Treasure Chest:** This leads to a curved cavern with two sections. The other section is accessed via the other door in chamber 6. Now that you've entered the door in the north wall, don't continue north, as a dead end to your left contains a treasure chest. Inspect this to find a Small Key.

Treasure Chest #11: Small Key

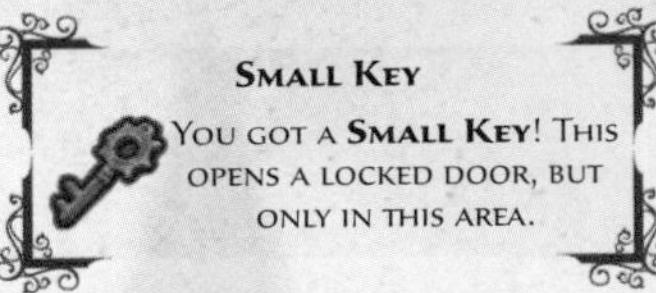

Small Key

You got a **Small Key**! This opens a locked door, but only in this area.

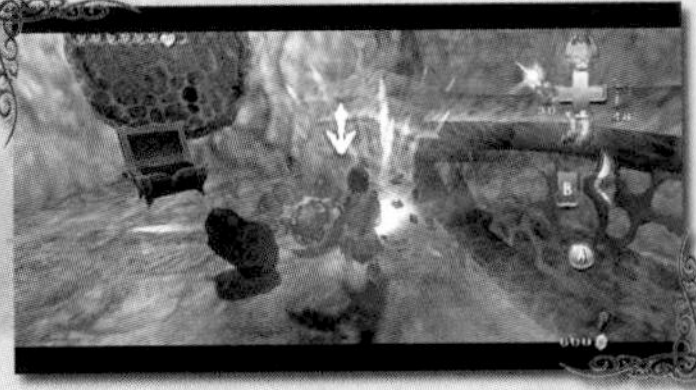

➤ Watch out! When you open the chest, expect to be rained on by a Purple Chu and a Yellow Chu, too! Face them down, optionally scooping the Yellow Chu if you require Lantern fuel. Then check the door to the north.

Chamber 9: Lair of the Deku Toad (1F)

▲ This door leads to a sealed gate, and what looks like a damp, green circular chamber beyond. You can't enter this area yet, so smash the three pots for a blue Rupee (5) each, and return to the Crescent Cavern, then back to the Single Cog Cavern.

1

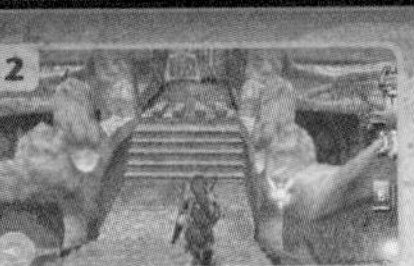
2

3

4

5

6

Chamber 6: Fourth Return to Single Cog Cavern (1F)

◄ Back in the familiar cog room, wait for a rotating platform to arrive, jump and land on it, and journey to the other door; this one in the west side of the room.. It leads to the other part of the Crescent Cavern.

Chamber 8: First Return to Crescent Cavern and Snaking Waterway (1F to BF)

Enter the Crescent Cavern to see a locked door ahead of you. This is the reason you grabbed that Small Key earlier! Before you open the door, head right to a dead end and defeat a Helmasaur. Break open the pots here for some blue Rupees (5) and a Heart.

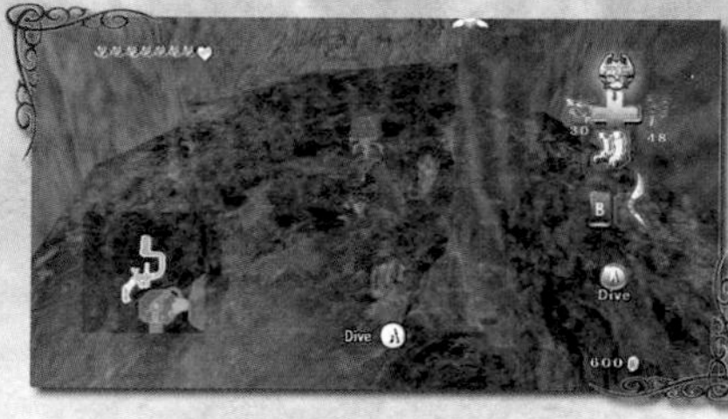

➤ Unlock the door and head through. You can now explore the area below the Crescent Cavern (BF). This is a snaking waterway containing nasties to battle or avoid. Swim through the lagoon, and then wear your Iron Boots and trek along the floor, avoiding the electrical discharge of the Bari.

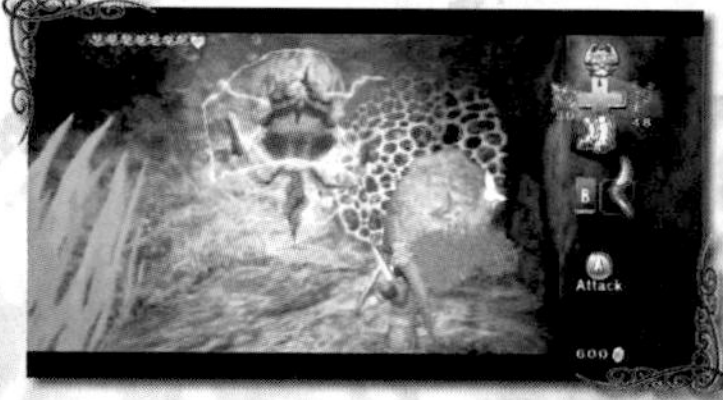

➤ **Treasure Chest:** The middle section contains four small dead-end passages. Trudge along until you reach the openings on each side. Check the opening on the right first, using your Iron Boots so the current doesn't blow you about. Open the chest at the passage's end.

Treasure Chest #12: Red Rupee (20)

◄ **Treasure Chest:** Turn and head north, along the side passage in the opposite direction, and continue forward. A tiny alcove on the side wall hides a chest containing bombs.

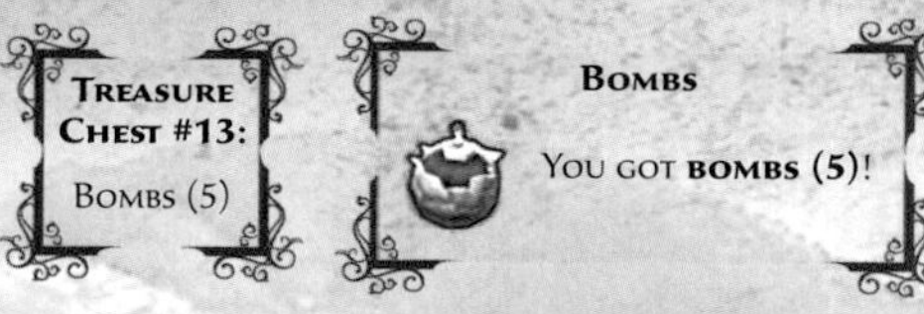

Note: These are regular bombs if you're full of Water Bombs, otherwise, expect to find Water Bombs in these (and other) chests containing this item type.

Treasure Chest #13: Bombs (5)

Bombs

You got **bombs (5)**!

◄ The other two upper passages aren't interesting, so stomp east, until you reach a Bomb Rock. Produce a Water Bomb and drop it at the rock. After it explodes, enter the gap in the scaly membrane, and maneuver into a winding underwater channel. Slay a couple of Shell Blades and swim north. You emerge in an odd, circular chamber.

Chamber 9: Lair of the Deku Toad (BF to 1F)

Toado

Threat Meter

The room is silent, aside from water splashing. That's not coming from you! A couple of fat Toadoes swim up and aim for your ankles, nipping as they go. The Toadoes are easily countered. Just wait with your sword at the ready, then spin attack and defeat the two Toado attackers with a single swipe.

Toado attackers harangue you in twos and threes. One spin attack dispatches all comers at once!

Enemies Encountered: Tektite, Helmasaur, Chu (Purple, Yellow), Bari, Shell Blade, Toado

Task #4
Locate the Fabled Clawshot from a Bloated Deku Toad

You speak to Midna, who has a bad feeling about this. You look out. A gigantic Deku Toad is latched onto the ceiling, and it's dropping spawn from its back! These are the Toadoes you've defeated. The Deku Toad wakes up, belches, falls off its stalactite, and shakes off its brood!

Characters Encountered

Midna

Deku Toad

Threat Meter

With dozens of Toadoes attacking you, there's only one move to try: spin, Link, spin!

Step 1: The first attack isn't from the Deku Toad at all, but the dozens of baby Toadoes swarming you. Optionally back up to the edges (so you can't be attacked from behind), then spin attack, and mop up with slices before and after. Continue with this tactic until the last Toado is defeated.

Step 2: The Deku Toad leaps high into the cavern, leaving you in peace for a second or two. You see its looming shadow as it falls to earth. Flip out of the way so you aren't caught in the disgusting belly flop!

Step 3: The Deku Toad then lies on the ground, exhausted, with its tongue lolling on the ground near its open maw. Draw your sword and immediately dash to this area, Z targeting the snaking organ, and slicing it until the Deku Toad rears up in anger and pain! It then waddles upright and sounds a massive roar! Take this opportunity to lob a bomb (either regular or water) into that maw! You must be close to be successful.

If a bomb strikes the Deku Toad, he will not leap or shake off Toadoes.

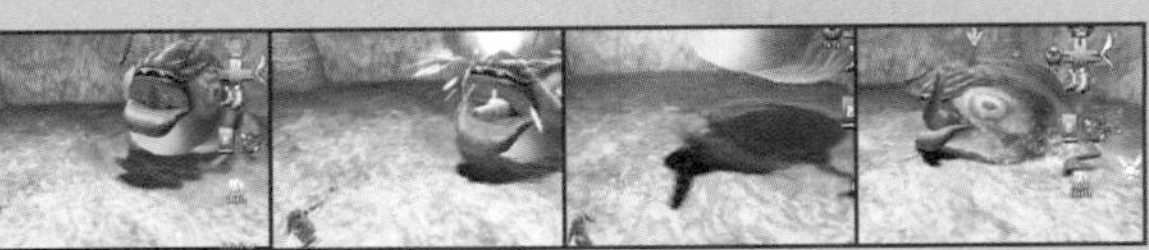

Step 4: Cut onto that giant tongue, but to ensure you strike with your bomb, combine your arrows and Z target the creature as soon as it stands up. Just as it is about to open its mouth, fire. Then wait, and the bomb explodes inside its gullet, and it collapses! Run in, slice that tongue, and when it stands, aim another Bomb Arrow. Complete this twice, and your foe...croaks!

When the Deku Toad ingests two or three bombs, it thrashes in the water, before belching up a dirt bubble and collapsing, deflated. The creature disappears, and the dirt falls away, exposing a chest.

◄ Run over and open the chest. It contains one of the greatest pieces of equipment you'll ever own: the **Clawshot!**

Treasure Chest #14: Clawshot

Clawshot

You got a **Clawshot**! It's a long chain with a claw.

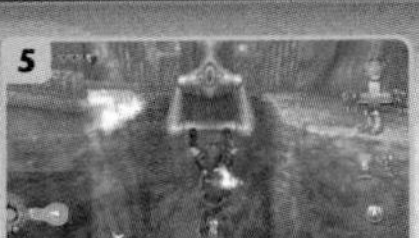

Clawshot

Clawshot: One of the most versatile, useful, and entertaining pieces of equipment you'll own, the Clawshot is unique because it's both a weapon and an item. Aim with the Wii Remote, and fire with Ⓑ. Here's what you can do with it:

- Aim it at Clawshot medallion plates (gold plates with red in the middle), and fire at them. The claw grabs the plate, and pulls you into it, letting you maneuver across massive (and sometimes bottomless) gaps!
- When you reach a medallion plate, as long as it's pointing down, you can either let go (Ⓐ), or use ⇧ and ⇩, respectively, to lower or raise yourself on the chain. This is useful so you can (for example) lower yourself to a platform you couldn't see otherwise.
- You can aim your Clawshot at pots, crates, and barrels, and smash them from a distance.
- You can then fire the Clawshot again, and pick up a dropped item, such as a Heart or Rupee.
- You can also hassle (and sometimes dispatch) enemies by locking on to them and firing the Clawshot.
- Vines work the same as medallions, meaning you never need to climb again. Just aim at the top of every vine, and Clawshot up there!
- You can combine this with a second Clawshot (found much later) to form the legendary Double Clawshot. This device is so incredible, you'll ignore all other items in your inventory!

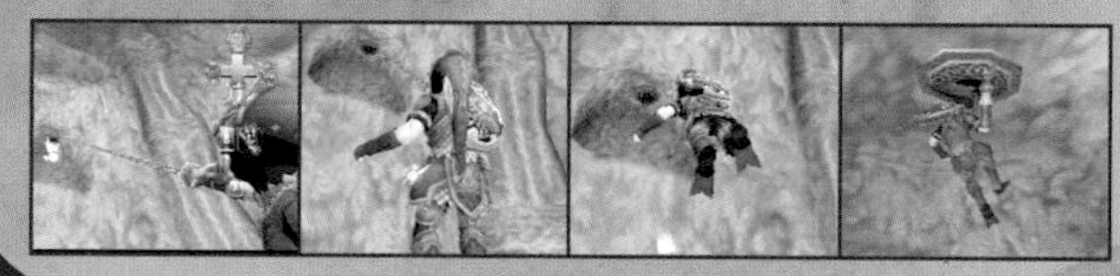

▲ Practice with your new item, making sure you replace your current item on the ⊖ menu with the Clawshot. Aim and move up to the high alcove in the north wall. Drop and smash the pots for a Heart, and blue (5) and yellow Rupees (10). Do the same in the southern wall too. These pots contain blue Rupees (5) and a Heart. Clear the alcove in the west wall for yellow Rupees (10).

▲ The easiest way to exit this chamber is via the south door. Aim at the Clawshot medallion, then hang from it with ⇩. Your weight opens the gate, and you can drop to the steps, smash the pots, and leave.

Enemies Encountered

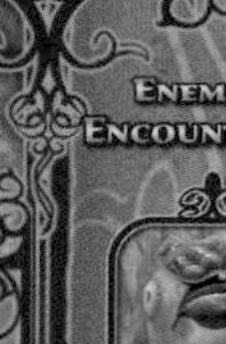

Deku Toad

Helmasaur

Task 5: Open the Floodgate in the Second Reservoir Tower

Chamber 8: Second Return to Crescent Cavern and Snaking Waterway (1F)

◄ Exit into the dirt-floored Crescent Cavern, and prepare for combat with Helmasaurs. However, now that you have the Clawshot, you can easily remove their armor. Ⓩ target the beast, avoiding the charge, and fire the Clawshot. The Clawshot rips the armor off the beast's back. Throw it away or back at the creature, then finish the Helmasaur off, attacking any part of it!

The ultimate in humiliation: rip the armor off a Helmasaur, then throw it at the beast!

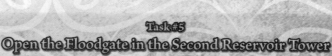

Chamber 6: Fifth Return to Single Cog Cavern (1F)

➤ Head south, back into the Single Cog Cavern, and use the Clawshot after riding the rotating platforms around, to aim at the vines on the ceiling, just above the exit door. Grab the vines, drop down, and exit, without climbing the granite ledges or running through the tunnel.

Chamber 4: Eighth Return to Connecting Bridges (1F to BF)

◄ Enter the connecting bridge area, and defeat the Helmasaur with a hilarious armor-removal attack, then wait before you return to the central hub. A vine wall above and left of the exit door allows you into the large pool below the bridges. You land in the basement level.

◄ Drop into the water, wearing your Iron Boots, and you can search around the rocky pool surrounding the central column. Bring out your sword and slice the Shell Blades.

Farther along the rocky pool (southwest area) is a column with a pot next to it. Smash the pot with your sword, and discover a yellow Rupee (10) inside. There's another in the south area.

Bari

Threat Meter

You can easily defeat the otherwise impenetrable Bari. Target (or Z target) the creature with your Clawshot, and fire! The Clawshot grabs the creature's brain, and brings it to you! Both brain and outer tendrils then explode!

◄ When you've finished fooling around in this dead-end rock pool, locate the stepping stones near the western bridge, and Clawshot up onto some vines, and back down to the first floor bridge platform. Head for the hub now.

Chamber 5: Fifth Return to Lakebed Column Hub (1F)

➤ With the Clawshot, you can activate a medallion in this chamber that was previously impossible to trigger. You begin in the room's western part, so use your Clawshot and launch yourself onto the exterior wall, over the chest that contained the Dungeon Map, and run to the eastern area. Look into the middle, and up. Clawshot and hang from the medallion. This reroutes the water flow, allowing you access to this dungeon's unexplored area. Enter the door behind you.

Chamber 4: Ninth Return to Connecting Bridges (1F)

▲ Move along this passage, with your sword ready to strike the Tektite here, and the pots you already smashed once (for a Heart and Rupee). Now though, the waterwheel is moving, and you can roll through the gap and exit via the eastern door.

Chamber 10: Double Cog Cavern (1F to 2F)

◄ **Treasure Chest:** Enter this large, gray cavern containing Keeses fluttering about, and two gigantic cogs. Jump to the first one, then look up and left, locate a medallion, and Clawshot up and onto it. Descend on the Clawshot until you spot a tiny plinth below. Drop onto it, and inspect the chest.

Treasure Chest #15: Water Bombs (10)

Water Bombs
You got **Water Bombs (10)**! You can use these bombs in water, but not while swimming.

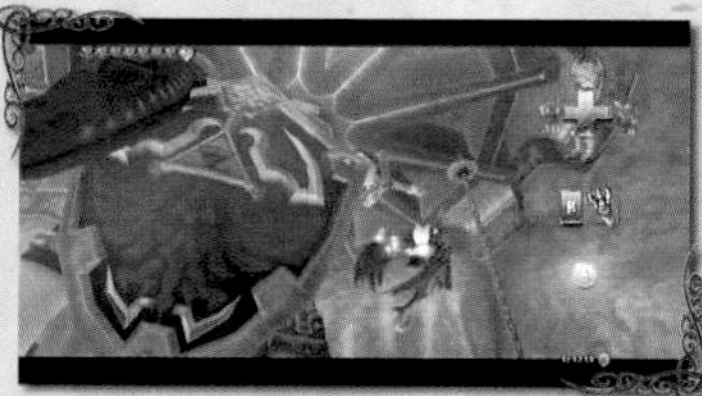

◄ Stand on the plinth, and look up and around. If Keeses are hassling you, Z target with your Clawshot, and punt the Keese across the room, into a wall! This works well with any small flying creature.

➤ Cross this chasm. Unlike the other room containing a rotating cog, if you fall here, the drop is permanent. Look to the north, and you'll spot some vines on the bumpy wall. Aim and fire at them, then propel yourself across. Shimmy around the corner, and drop onto a small ledge. From this ledge, look up at a tall pillar with more vines on it. Propel yourself up here, and drop down onto the next small ledge.

◄ **Treasure Chest:** Continue on your chest hunt by looking to the right of the ledge you're on, around the pillar. From here you can launch to a medallion, which leads to a small chest. The reward is a red Rupee (20).

Treasure Chest #16: Red Rupee (20)

➤ Now to find a way out! Head toward the ledge with the vines from which you launched. Propel yourself there, then look northeast at the door with the ledge in front of it. Fire yourself to the vines, shimmy to the ledge, and leave.

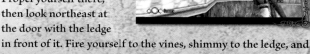

◄ You're still in the Double Cog Cavern, but you're wandering the perimeter, as you did on the other side of the dungeon. Turn left, and you'll encounter another Chu Worm. However, with your Clawshot, you can Z target, fire at the worm, and wrench it out of its bubble: finish it with sword swipes!

➤ Behind the Chu Worm's remains is a waterwheel, without the water to drive it. Turn around and inspect this passage's opposite end. Two waterspouts jet from the ground. Look up and shoot a Bomb Arrow into the stalactite, and you create a floating platform. Wait until the platform descends, climb on it, then jump across the gap in the wall, avoiding the sealed door. Drop into this perimeter area's eastern part, and dish damage on a couple of Tektites. The way is blocked with a channel and a wall, but there's a Clawshot medallion! Use it.

Missing Links

1. Pulverizing Pottery

This cavern has a number of pots to shatter.

- On the right side of the entrance area: arrows and Hearts
- In the northern part of the perimeter, near the Chu Worm, inside alcove: arrows and Rupees
- The western small ledge: yellow Rupees (10)
- One of the small plinths (1F); use the Clawshot: yellow Rupees (10)
- The southern perimeter area, just after the waterwheel (first return): Rupee and Heart
- The northwest perimeter area, after the waterwheel (first return), near Treasure Chest #20: Rupee and Heart

Enemies Encountered

Helmasaur

Bari

Tektite

Keese

Chu Worm

Shell Blade

Chamber 11: Eastern Reservoir Tower (2F to 3F to 4F)

Enter a similarly shaped cavern to the one you were in earlier, complete with two Chu Worms. (Clawshot these hapless invertebrates!) After pottery slaying for a blue Rupee (5) and Heart, look for the way into the tower chamber. There are no doors, so Clawshot to a set of roof vines.

➤ Drop into an almost identical tower area as the one before, except this one has a waterspout. From this position, turn and look for a Clawshot medallion, shoot at it, then launch yourself onto the water chute.

◀ **Treasure Chest:** After attacking a Helmasaur, run to the gap in the chute, and Clawshot to the medallion on the other side. Continue your ascent, tackling three more Helmasaurs on the way to the top. When you reach the flat channel and square arch, head over and open another treasure chest. These contain bombs (if you're full of Water Bombs) or Water Bombs (if you're not).

Treasure Chest #17:	**Bombs**
Bombs (10)	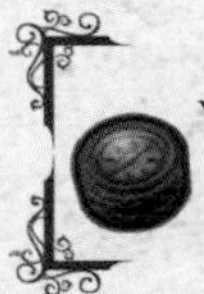 You got **bombs (10)**!

◀ It's time to release the other floodgate, and crank the waterwheel in the Double Cog Cavern. Climb up either ladder of the square arch and leap onto the gold handle, pulling it down. Water streams down from above.

Treasure Chest: Before you leave, definitely check the opposite ledge, where a chest is sitting. Use your Clawshot and propel yourself through the waterfall (if you activated the handle), and then drop down.

Treasure Chest #18:	**Compass**
Compass	You got the **Compass**! This tool shows you where to find objects hidden in this dungeon.

▲ Drop off the ledge, then ride the chute to the hole, drop, and ride it the rest of the way to the lower level (2F). Swim across to the gold handle that opens the floodgate to the rest of the dungeon, and leap to activate it. Skullfish swim in this reservoir pit; use the Clawshot to catch them if you wish.

▲ Exit this chamber by running to the entrance wall, using your Clawshot to reach the ceiling vines on the wall's other side, dropping down (there's no need to hand-over-hand on the vines if you aim farther than the wall), and then check the left exit, which you haven't been through yet.

Missing Links

1. Pulverizing Pottery

The two pots outside the tower room aren't the only pots you can disintegrate. Three pots on the chamber's north side, near the waterspout, contain blue Rupees (5) and a Heart. Three crates in the alcove beyond that are empty. A pot in the reservoir pit yields a blue Rupee (5).

1 
2 
3 
4 
5 
6 

Task 6: Locate the Big Key

Enemies Encountered: Chu Worm, Helmasaur, Bari, Lizalfos (Skull-face), Chu (Purple, and Red)

Chamber 10: First Return to Double Cog Cavern (2F to 1F)

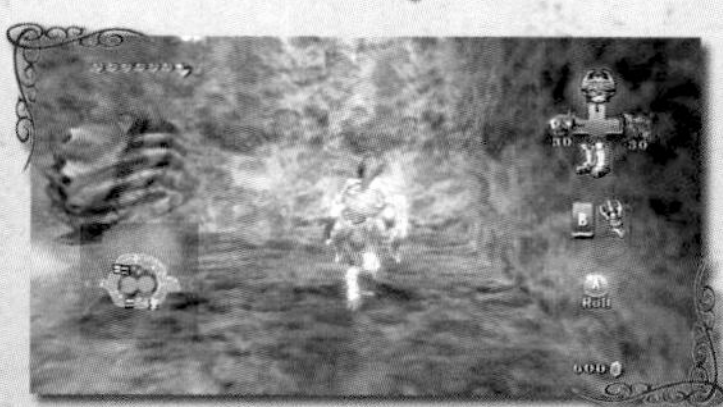

➤ **Treasure Chest:** You're in the Double Cog Cavern's southern perimeter. As the water gushes down the channel, move to the small pool, and swim across the surface of it. Get out, and fire on the Bari from the ground. With that beast cleared, drop down to the western end to open this chest.

Treasure Chest #19: Red Rupee (20)

➤ When you've slain the remaining Bari and Shell Blade in this pool, swim west to the opposite side, and climb up to a waterwheel cog. Run between the blades, defeat some pottery, and enter the south door, back into the middle of the chamber.

Lizalfos ("Skull-face")

Threat Meter

As you enter the inner chamber, a Lizalfos with a skull-shaped head trots into your view. Slay it with the same plan you used on the "axe-tail" Lizalfos: skip around to the back and slice. Then continue to the other cog, where a second Lizalfos engages you. Finish by knocking it off its feet, and skewer it!

The skull-headed Lizalfos is a frightening foe to behold!

➤ **Treasure Chest:** Before you leave via the southwest door, take the northeastern exit you propelled to earlier. This time, turn left when you exit, and you see the waterwheel moving. You can now roll between the blades and enter a previously unexplored area. Defeat a Chu Worm, three Purple Chus, and one Red Chu. The prize is a chest filled with bombs! Head to the two giant floor cogs.

Treasure Chest #20: Bombs (20)

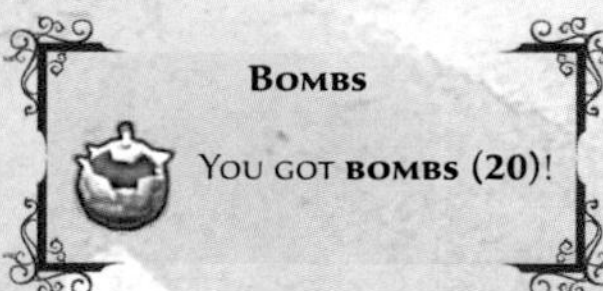

Bombs

You got **bombs (20)**!

➤ **Treasure Chest:** The only exit you haven't been through yet is the one in the southwest corner, so use it, turn left, and inspect another treasure chest in the water channel. When you open the chest, Purple Chus drop from the ceiling. Prepare for battle!

Treasure Chest #21: Red Rupee (20)

➤ With the Chus taken care of, the only way to head is westward. Look in this direction, and upward, to see a Clawshot medallion. Propel yourself, activating the switch that opens the sealed door below.

➤ It isn't time to leave this chamber yet! Return to the middle of the cog room, and locate this vine wall and ledge on the northern wall.

Take careful aim with your **Clawshot** at the medallion on the underside of the rotating cog, and aim at it. This takes some skill, so be patient.

➤ Use [icon] to descend (but don't release the Clawshot!) onto a small plinth for pots, or better yet, the ledge leading to a door on the eastern end of this chamber. Drop down, smash a couple of nearby pots (for Hearts), slay a Keese or two, then exit.

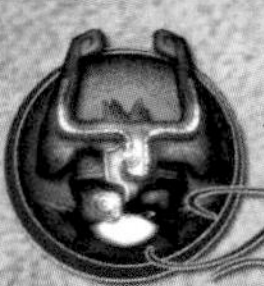

Tip: AIM YOUR CLAWSHOT AT THE TWO POTS ON THE FAR-OFF PLINTH BEFORE YOU LEAVE. THERE ARE TWO YELLOW RUPEES (10) IN IT FOR YOU!

Chamber 12: The Grotto and Underwater Maze (1F to BF)

➤ You appear in an enclosed grotto, with water to your left. Dive in from the ledge you're standing on, and head southward. Swim toward an underwater shelf with a couple of pots and smash them for two blue Rupees (5). Remember your location because it's easy to get lost down here!

Drop to the floor of the underwater grotto, under the shelf you landed on, and prepare to tackle a Shell Blade. Use your **Clawshot** to stun the Shell Blade into opening its mouth, then finish it with a spin. Wear your Iron Boots.

➤ Swim or walk northward, along this grotto's floor, until you reach an arch on your right side. Swim through to this area's middle section, and turn to face south.

Bring out your Clawshot, and pull the insides from a Bari. Swim to the surface. Something is chasing you....

Bombfish

Threat Meter

The Bombfish is a nasty little critter who doesn't care about its own existence. It explodes as a defense mechanism! The only way to fight back is to attack from dry land, or underwater with your Iron Boots on, and [Z] target with your **Clawshot**. Reel the fish in, and it sparks. Use it to explode a nearby rock, or throw it away from you before it detonates!

If you're on dry land, the only way to fish for Bombfish is to use your Clawshot and auto-target. Throw your catch back quickly!

➤ Look southward. Dive in and swim to a shelf halfway between the surface and the floor of the grotto. A Bombfish swims here, and a Bomb Rock is nestled on a platform. Use the Bombfish, or one of your own Water Bombs, and plant it against the Bomb Rock.

Head through the hole the Bomb Rock was covering, into the eastern portion of this maze, and look down. Another Bomb Rock is wedged in a hole below you. Sink down with your Iron Boots, and bomb this.

Tip: NOTICE A TUNNEL ENTRANCE ALONG THE EASTERN WALL OF THE SECTION YOU'RE IN BUT IGNORE THIS FOR THE MOMENT. BOMB THE ROCK FIRST!

➤ **Treasure Chest:** Before you enter through this hole, swim up past the tunnel entrance in the eastern wall, and surface. You must be in this grotto's far eastern part. Open a chest on a small ledge, then return to the bomb hole. This is also useful if you're out of Water Bombs and can't bomb the rock.

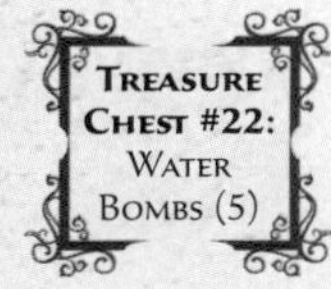

TREASURE CHEST #22: WATER BOMBS (5)

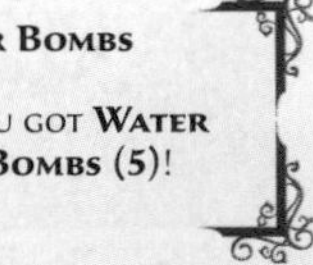

WATER BOMBS

YOU GOT **WATER BOMBS** (5)!

◄ Dive to the bomb hole, and swim through. Put your boots on, and draw your sword because a Shell Blade is just around the corner, to your right. When the coast is clear, swim all the way up to the surface. You're now at the southern end of this grotto and can enter an otherwise impossible-to-reach door.

Chamber 13: Big Key Plunge Pool (1F to BF)

The door leads to a tiny circular chamber where a Chu Worm has made its home. Grab it with the Clawshot, introduce it to your Ordon Sword, and after it's dispatched (giving you arrows), go on a pot-shattering expedition. Find Hearts, a blue Rupee (5), and three yellow Rupees (10) to find.

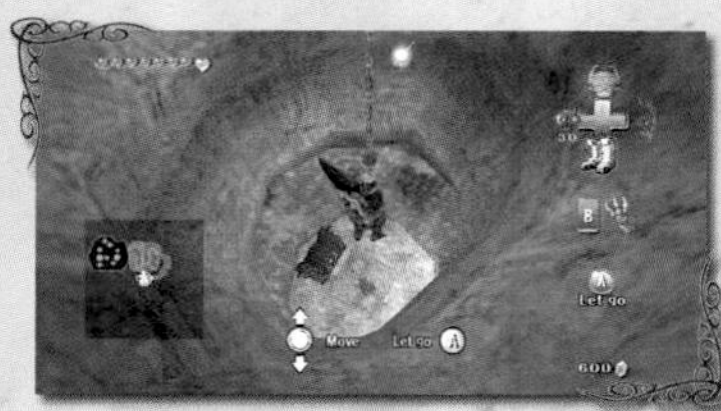

◄ Now for the cunning part. Look up at the ceiling, and notice a Clawshot medallion. Hit it, and lower yourself through a hole in the middle of the floor. Delicately land on a tiny raised plinth, holding an ornate black chest. Inside is the most important key!

Treasure Chest #23: Big Key

Big Key
You got the Big Key! Use it to gain access to the lair of this dungeon's boss!

Note: Bring out your Fishing Rod and rest for a moment, catching some of the many Skullfish in this pool. There are tiny Loaches, too!

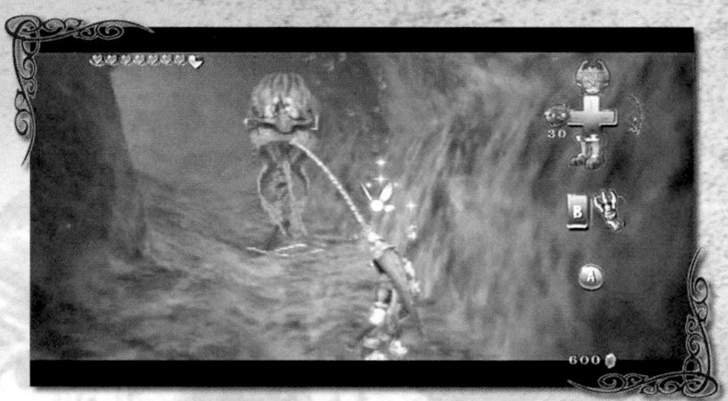

▲ Dive off the plinth holding the chest, and into the plunge pool. Move around the chamber's perimeter, smashing pots for yellow Rupees (10) and Hearts. This is the best moment to fight Skullfish with your blade. Exit via the only door, and trudge down a long, curved tunnel, to the grotto area. On the way, remove the innards from two Baris.

Task 7: Find Both Pieces of Heart

Chamber 12: First Return to The Grotto and Underwater Maze (BF to 1F)

◄ The tunnel snakes around and you appear in the eastern wall, in the grotto. Swim to the surface, locate the northern dry ground, and head west, smashing a couple of pots for blue Rupees (5). Swim and emerge onto the exit ledge where you first arrived.

Chamber 10: Second Return to Double Cog Cavern (1F)

▲ Negotiate this cavern, staying on the same level, by shooting a Clawshot at one of the moving cogs, then dropping to this ledge where you found Treasure Chest #15. From here, use the Clawshot to hit the vines. Climb up and exit via the western door.

Enemies Encountered

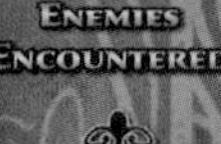

Keese

Shell Blade

Bari

Bombfish

Chu Worm

Chamber 4: Tenth Return to Connecting Bridges (1F)

➤ You must negotiate the connecting bridges to the hub. The waterwheel is rotating against you, so roll from the side, into the space, and back out again. Open the door to the west.

Chamber 5: Sixth Return to Lakebed Column Hub (1F to 2F)

You're in the staircase-rotating chamber, and this time you must ascend the steps that are cascading with water. On the way, tackle two Tektites.

➤ Once atop the steps, turn and face the middle of the chamber. If you remember the chandelier, now is the optimal time to fire your Clawshot at the medallions above it, and land on the light itself. A chest awaits your prying, and the results are well worth it; you've secured your first Piece of Heart.

Treasure Chest #24: Piece of Heart #19

Piece of Heart
You got a **Piece of Heart**! Collect **one more** for another full Heart Container. Piece of Heart #19 of 45.

Chamber 4: Eleventh Return to Connecting Bridges (2F); to Chamber 6: Sixth Return to Single Cog Cavern (2F)

➤ Before you try to use the Big Key, there's the small matter of the chest you couldn't reach, at the Western Reservoir Tower's top. Run to the west exit of chamber 5, then dash around the north perimeter of chamber 6, past the Helmasaurs, and enter chamber 7.

Chamber 7: First Return to Western Reservoir Tower (2F to 3F to 4F)

➤ Enter chamber 7, and run to the water chute. Climb over the chute wall, don your Iron Boots (or you'll be swept into the reservoir), and trudge up the chute. Quicken your pace by climbing on the chute's inside lip and running up, but watch your step! Jump down, after putting the boots on, each time you encounter a Tektite. You could also use your Clawshot, but this isn't as fast as heading up the inside lip.

➤ You reach the chute's top and can bring out your Clawshot. Aim at either medallion, fly through the waterfall, and land by the chest you couldn't reach earlier. The prize you came all this way for? A red Rupee (20).

Treasure Chest #25: Red Rupee (20)

Chamber 4: Twelfth Return to Connecting Bridges (2F); to Chamber 6: Seventh Return to Single Cog Cavern (2F); to Seventh Return to Lakebed Column Hub (2F to 1F)

➤ Head through the dungeon to the Lakebed Column Hub, and drop to the first floor. You're looking for this gold handle, in the western area. Pull down hard on it, and divert the water flow from the dungeon's eastern part, into the west, for the first time.

Chamber 4: Thirteenth Return to Connecting Bridges (1F); to Chamber 6: Eighth Return to Single Cog Cavern (1F)

◀ Backtrack to the Single Cog Cavern, making sure you're on the floor with the rotating circular platforms. Remember that bridge at the bottom of this chamber? Well, the water you just diverted into this chamber has raised the bridge. Head down to it.

Cross the bridge, heading south, to a tiled floor leading to a sealed gate. One of the tiles is pressure-sensitive. Stand on it and the gates swing open, and out charges a Lizalfos! Engage it in decisive combat, rolling and back slicing its rear. Cut down a couple of Tektites, too!

➤ **Treasure Chest:** After the fight, stand on the pressure sensitive tile, but stay on it. The gates are open, but they close when you leave the tile. Aim your Clawshot at the medallion on the south wall, and propel yourself there. You get there before the gates close, and you can open the chest here. The reward is well worth it this time! When you're ready to leave, depart via the Clawshot medallion on the ceiling.

Treasure Chest #26: Piece of Heart #20

Piece of Heart

You got a **Piece of Heart**! You collected **five Pieces** and formed a new Heart Container. Piece of Heart #20 of 45.

Task 8: Defeat Twilit Aquatic Morpheel

Chamber 4: Fourteenth Return to Connecting Bridges (1F); to Eighth Return to Lakebed Column Hub (1F)

➤ With the Big Key in your possession, you can challenge a vicious dungeon boss! Check that you've collected all the treasure chests (especially the two containing **Pieces of Heart**), then return to the Lakebed Column Hub. Dive into the middle and swim to the pillar holding up the stairs. The door requiring the Big Key is here. Once inside, smash some pots and equip an empty Bottle. There's a Fairy to scoop. Descend into the ominous hole!

Fairy

You caught a **Fairy** in a Bottle. When you fall in combat, this faithful friend gives you Hearts.

Chamber 14: Boss Battle! Twilit Aquatic Morpheel

After Midna encourages you to dive down to the depths of a huge circular subterranean temple arena, you don your Iron Boots and land with a heavy thud. A strange tendril flaps from a hole in the ground. Others soon snake out, followed by a gigantic roaring mouth! Behold the Twilit Aquatic Morpheel!

Enemies Encountered

Tektite

Helmasaur

Lizalfos (Skull-face)

Twilit Aquatic Morpheel

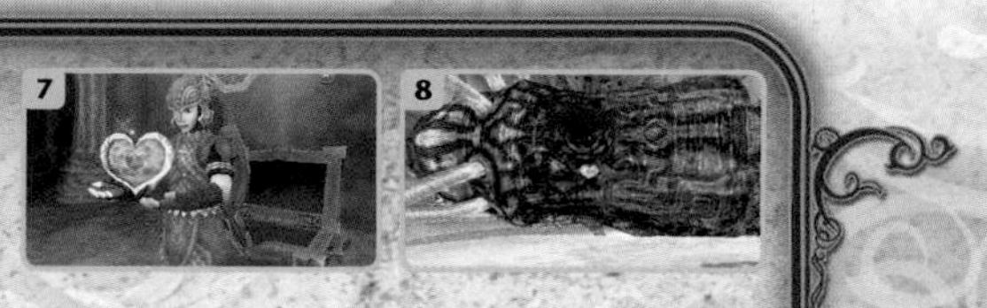

Twilit Aquatic Morpheel

Threat Meter

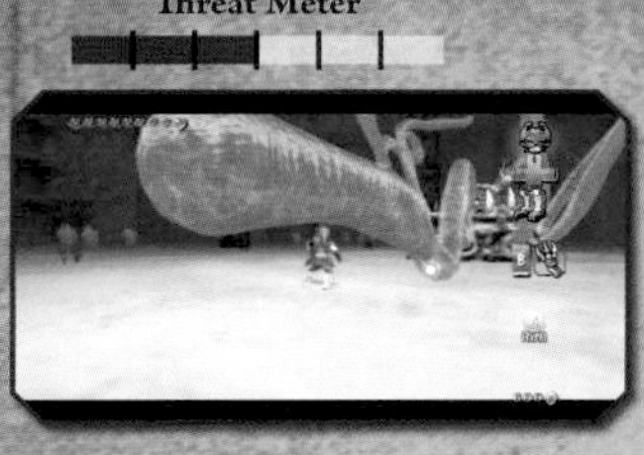

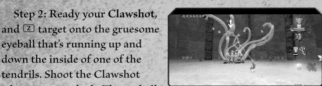

Step 1: You're wearing your Iron Boots, and this makes you a target for the beast's tendrils. Expect to be scooped up by one, then dropped into its giant maw! If this happens, take off your boots, and swim away from the creature.

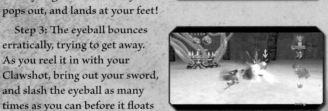

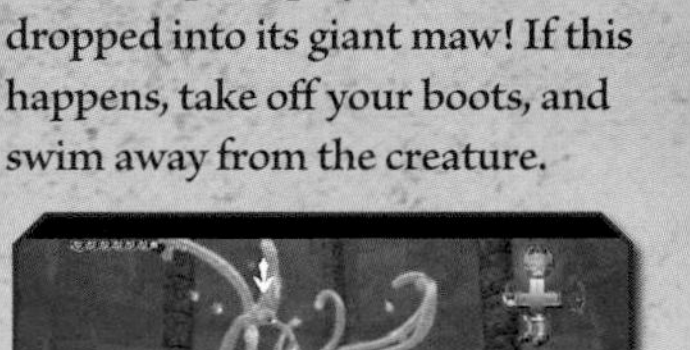

Step 2: Ready your **Clawshot**, and Z target onto the gruesome eyeball that's running up and down the inside of one of the tendrils. Shoot the Clawshot when you get a lock. The eyeball pops out, and lands at your feet!

Step 3: The eyeball bounces erratically, trying to get away. As you reel it in with your Clawshot, bring out your sword, and slash the eyeball as many times as you can before it floats inside the Morpheel's tendril.

Step 4: Beware! As the eyeball is being struck, the Morpheel releases four or five Bombfish, which swim directly toward you! They land at your feet. Spin attack so they flash red, then swim away from them. If you don't, you're caught in the explosion. Repeat all steps until you've struck the eyeball a good 10 or so times.

The tendrils and mouth snake back into the hole. Congratulations! You've...what's that rumbling? The ground shakes as the Twilit Aquatic Morpheel roars out of the hole, revealing itself to be a gigantic snaking creature as fearsome as a thousand charging Ordon goats!

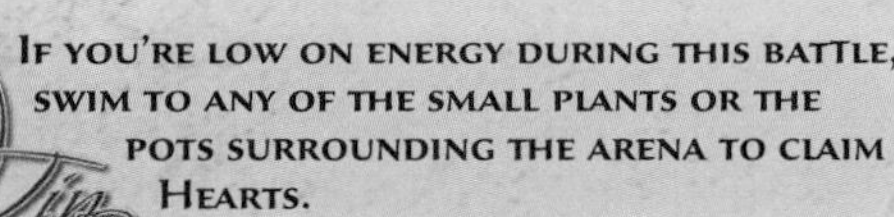

Tip: If you're low on energy during this battle, swim to any of the small plants or the pots surrounding the arena to claim Hearts.

Step 5: The Morpheel swims about this arena in a rage, knocking over the finest Zora columns. Watch for chunks falling near or on you. Swim away from the Morpheel until it finishes ramming the scenery. Talk to Midna and she recommends some tactics.

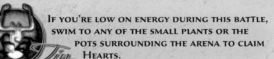

Step 6: Swim alongside the Morpheel, or over the top of it, and attempt to secure a Z target. With your **Clawshot**, aim at the eye, propel yourself onto the beast's back, then take out your sword, and stab it consecutive times into that eyeball!

Repeat Step 6 until the Morpheel gives up the fight, and the eyeball spills the last of its ink.

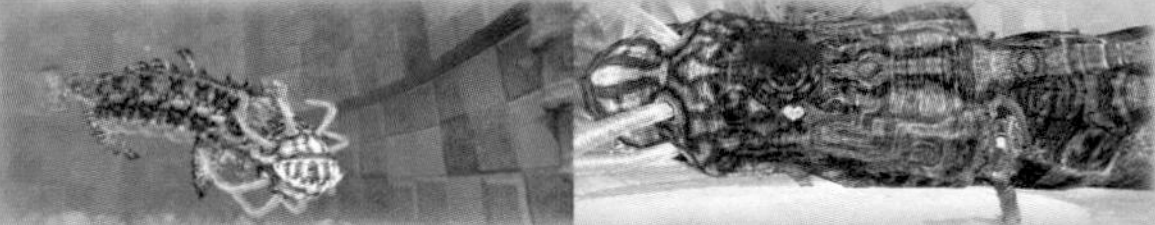

The Twilit Aquatic Morpheel swims erratically, slamming into columns, and thrashing through the water until it falls forward, and rams maw-first into the side of the arena wall. This springs a large leak, and the entire arena drains away in seconds. The eyeball explodes, and the beast disintegrates in a shower of shadows.

Midna appears, as the shadows form the last part of the Fused Shadow she's been after. She's now ready to face **Zant, King of Shadows**. She apologizes for ordering you around Hyrule, and creates a warp portal out of here. She's ready when you are. Walk over to the **Heart Container** and pick it up. Now you're ready to leave!

Heart Container
You got a **Heart Container** (#3 of 8). Your life energy has increased by **one** and been **fully replenished**!

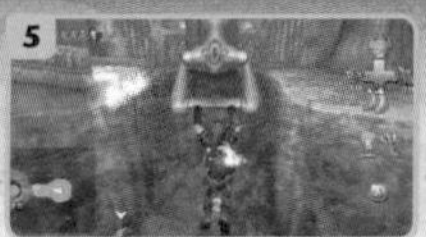

You're transported to the spirit cave near Lake Hylia. You turn around and are shocked to see a giant armored figure behind you! Clad in **ceremonial shadow armor**, *Zant remains motionless as the Spirit Lanayru rises from his lake.*

Zant releases a shockwave of energy that knocks you off your feet and strikes the Spirit Lanayru with the full force of a tyrant magician. Lanayru loses power, and the light sinks into the lake. The cave is bathed in twilight!

"Zant!" Midna appears, clad in Fused Shadow armor, which is promptly disassembled by Zant's power. An ancient and withered power cannot match Zant! He wonders why Midna has become a traitor. She has no alliance to one who abuses his tribe's magic!

Zant's power is different. It has been granted to him by his god. It will be respected! A fireball is summoned. Your wolf form blocks it, and a piece of the magic dissolves into your head. Zant draws Midna near. He needs her, so that sweet darkness will blot out this harsh light!

Midna turns to help you. She will then, says Zant, learn the error of her ways. He summons Spirit Lanayru, who blasts the full force of light at her! She collapses. You are transported to Hyrule Field. The shard of magic embedded in you.... Midna's weakened state.... Princess Zelda will know what to do!

Task#8
Defeat Twilit Aquatic Morpheel

Overworld: The Great Hylian Treasure Hunt

Zora's Domain

Snowpeak (Entry Area)

Fishing Hole

Upper Zora's River

Snowpeak

Hidden Village

Hyrule Field (North)

Death Mountain

Hyrule Field (Bridge of Eldin)

Broken Bridge

Entrance to Arbiter's Grounds

Lantern Cavern 2

Jovani

Hidden Skill #5

Telma's Bar

Hidden Skill #4

Auru

Gerudo Desert

Kakariko Village

Gor Liggs (Hot Springwater)

Gor Ebizo (Donations)

Hidden Skill #5

Gerudo Desert Start

New Warp Portal

Cave of Ordeals & Bridge Section

Faron Woods

Sacred Grove

Hidden Skill #4

Ordon Ranch Farm

Ordon Village

Legend

- Piece of Heart
- Magic Armor
- Rare Chu Jelly
- Great Fairy's Tears
- Master Sword
- Golden Bug

1 Journey to Princess Zelda pg 246

2 Obtain the Master Sword pg 250

3 Begin to Hunt for Treasure & Imp Poes pg 254

4 Repair the Bridge to Castle Town pg 259

Overworld Denizens

Characters

Auru | Shad | Ashei

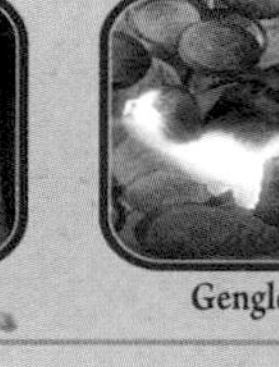

Jovani | Gengle

Enemies

Puppet | Bubble | Moldorm

Midbosses

Skull Kid | King Bulblin

A Link to the Present

Ordon Sword

Heart Pieces: 0 (20 Total)

Wooden Shield | Hylian Shield

Hero's Clothes | Zora Armor

Big Wallet | Quiver | Golden Bugs: 20 (of 24) | Hidden Skills: 3 (of 7)

Ilia's Scent | Fish Journal | Letters 5 (of 16)

Items to Obtain

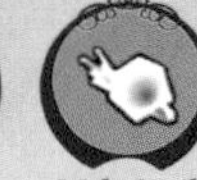
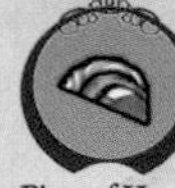

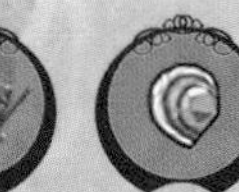

Master Sword | Male Snail | Piece of Heart #21 (of 45) | Rare Chu Jelly | Letter #7 | Bombling | Piece of Heart #22 (of 45) | Hot Springwater

Hidden Skill #4 (of 7) | Piece of Heart #23 (of 45) | Piece of Heart #24 (of 45) | Letter #8 | Magic Armor | Great Fairy's Tears | Big Quiver | Chu Jelly

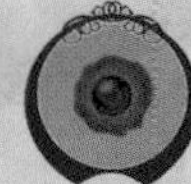

Piece of Heart #25 (of 45) | Auru's Memo | Male Dayfly | Female Dayfly | Hidden Skill #5 (of 7) | Small Key | Piece of Heart #26 (of 45) | Poe Soul #37 (of 60)

5 Continue Hunt for Treasure & Imp Poes pg 262

6 Obtain the Magic Armor pg 268

7 Continue Hunt, Enter the Gerudo Desert pg 270

8 Locate Entrance to Arbiter's Grounds pg 275

Midna

Auru

Shad

Ashei

The Great Hylian Treasure Hunt: Overview

The time has come to explore the grassy plains, rolling hills, and pristine waters of Hyrule! First however, you must travel to Zelda, who is the only one with the knowledge to heal your badly battered companion, Midna. She, in turn, reveals the location of a fabled weapon, the Master Sword, that only a true hero of the goddesses can wield! After an altercation with a strange, horn-playing, skull-faced child, you gain the sword. You can bring it to bear on foes, as you can transform between wolf and human at will!

This allows you to explore the lands for hours at a time, and the optimal path to take is shown here. You'll need to commence a search for evil spirits called Imp Poes who have stolen a man's soul, and more outrageously, frozen his cat to his head! Continue your search while helping the Gorons build a bridge to Castle Town, allowing you to finally purchase the finest armor money can buy (and keep buying, as you'll find out!). Once the Magic Armor is yours, you can finally meet up with a group of like-minded heroes, and journey to the windswept Gerudo Desert, where your next fabled item—the Mirror of Twilight—and dungeon awaits....

Task 1: Journey to Princess Zelda

The Route to Hyrule Castle: To Telma's Bar

➤ You begin your quest to reach Princess Zelda in the field north of the castle. Ignore the enemies for now, and run south to the Hyrule Field east of Castle Town. On the way through this field, dodge a Deku Baba and more Bulblins.

Missing Links

1. Digging for Victory

Even with Midna slumped on your back, you can still locate a couple of good dig spots in this field: in the field's southeastern corner (Hearts and Rupees), in the field's southwestern corner (Hearts), and in the eastern clump of grass (Rupees).

➤ Locate the Castle Town gate, run over the bridge, through the inner doors, and head south along the alley. Talk to a tiny frog, found near the market stalls, who gives you a hint: you must reach Telma's.

➤ Take the frog's advice. Run down the alley and into Telma's Bar...

A moment after you're thrown outside, Telma's cat Louise appears. She lets you in on a secret: the window leads along the attic ledges of the bar, and to the waterway passage you need.

➤ To reach this upper window, get behind and push a large crate to the rest of the crates in the alley's corner. Leap onto them all, and through the window.

The Route to Hyrule Castle: Across the Attic

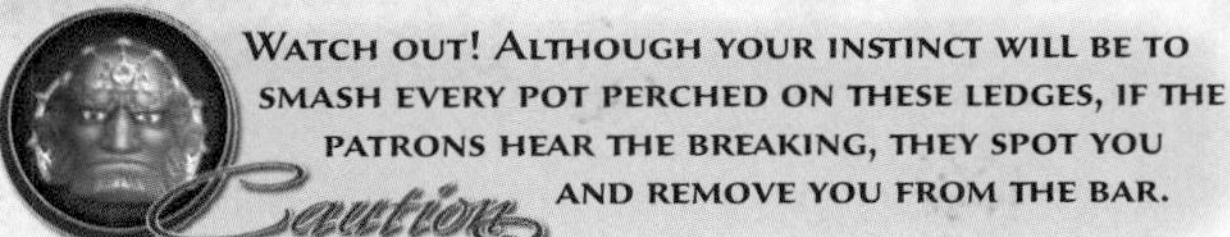

Caution

Watch out! Although your instinct will be to smash every pot perched on these ledges, if the patrons hear the breaking, they spot you and remove you from the bar.

➤ Silently, turn right and walk to the rope at the end of the ledge on which you are. Line yourself up with it, and walk across to a small platform. Turn 90 degrees to another rope, and walk across this, to the western ledge above the bar. During your creeping, you can hear Telma and a Goron's complaints.

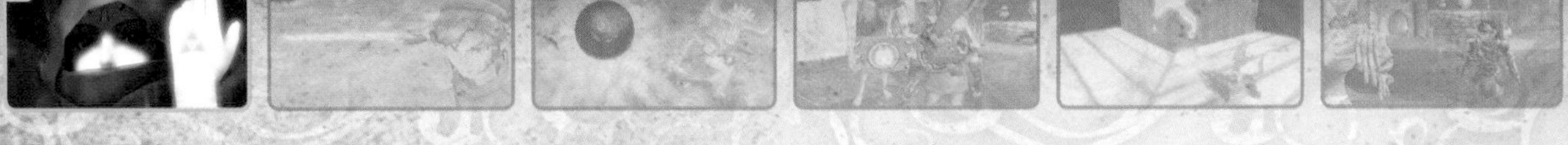

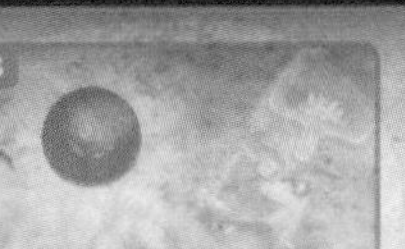

◄ Turn north, and make your next maneuvers as slow and delicate as possible. Gently shift some pots, either by rubbing against them or by picking them up, turning, and placing them back on the left behind you. This allows you to reach the last rope.

► As you cross this rope, listen to a heated discussion at the table below, as three townsfolk discuss the "hero." Exit via the opening in the room's northeast corner.

Auru:

Between 60 and 70, Auru is a senior member of the resistance, a group of people seeking to restore the kingdom. Auru used to be the royal family's tutor, then he retired and kept his distance. He recognized that something unsettling was occurring, so he came back to offer his aid. He knows about the royal family, and their past history with an ultimately evil entity called Ganondorf. Though aged, Auru remains in good physical condition and is a very skillful fellow.

Shad:

Between 18 and 20 years old, Shad is another member of the resistance. He's a handsome city boy, with glasses. When Shad was a child, his father (who was a butler with the royal family) told him a tale about a city floating in the sky. Since this time, Shad has studied about this city, and he realizes that a secret pertaining to its origin is somewhere under the graveyard in Kakariko Village. With the current terrors Hyrule faces, he believes the airborne people (the first Hylians to roam the land) could help the cause.

Ashei:

She is around 24–25 years old, and one of the members of the resistance. Her father was a soldier for the Hyrule royal family, but he left the kingdom due to trouble with a superior. She has learned combat skills from her father, and hearing the gossip that the Hylian soldiers are weak and powerless, she decides to visit the kingdom. Currently, she's studying about a small tribe of Yeti that inhabit Snowpeak mountain. Stronger than most men, with a slender physique, Ashei is a cavalier, but quiet. She favors strong, muscular men as companions.

The Route to Hyrule Castle: Jovani's Curse

◄ The opening leads to a small house bulging with the most treasure you've ever seen! A silent man sits on a throne. Nearby, a strange floating lamp wafts about the room. Speak to the frozen man, then defeat this ghost!

Poe Soul #1

The lamp is the only part of an Imp Poe you can see. Facing one for the first time as a wolf, switch your sense view on to see the ghostly fiend with a sickle ready to fight! Z target this ghoul and strike him twice. He falls onto his back. Target him again to see that his soul is exposed. Dive onto it, and grab that soul!

Congratulations! You've grabbed your first Poe Soul! Your ghostly collection begins now!

Poe Soul
You got the **Poe Soul**! Collect one from each Poe you defeat!
Poe Soul #1 of 60.

Note: Check your Collection menu. The final icon in the cluster of eight under your picture has been filled in. Every time you find another Poe and defeat him, this total increases.

- There are 60 Poes, each with a piece of Jovani's soul, scattered throughout Hyrule.
- To find and fight them, search for them between dusk and dawn; they are invisible during the day, and you cannot find them.

Tip:
- Attack them in wolf form, and use your sense view.
- Strike them so they're prone, then finish with a bite, taking the soul with you.

Enemies Encountered

Deku Baba

Bulblin

Imp Poe

Characters Encountered

Midna

Jovani

Gengle

Princess Zelda

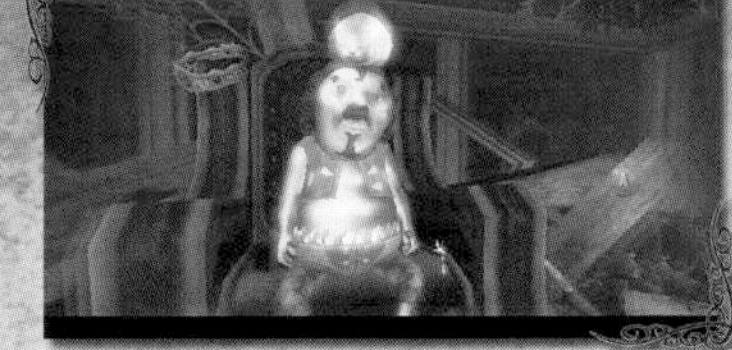

➤ Return to talk to the frozen fellow, Jovani. He sold his soul for gold! He mentions that the Poes have stolen parts of his soul! Collect 20 of them and he might be able to move again. To return, you can use the outside dig spot, near where the cats are. It's raining, so he opens a treasure chest, which is actually a secret entrance to the waterways.

Jovani:

About 40 years old, Jovani made a deal that was shortsighted and greedy, and sold his soul to an evil spirit, which has rendered him (and his cat) immobile. He asks you to reclaim his soul from the Poes. He hopes his girlfriend will still remember him!

Gengle:

Jovani's cat is his best friend, but Jovani's greed has turned the feline into a cat-sized rock of gold, now perched on his head. The other cats in town are worried about where Gengle's got to. Gengle is immobile, but knows he wants to rid himself and his master of all riches as soon as possible!

The Route to Hyrule Castle: The Waterways

➤ This entrance leads to a water conduit that you ride down into a large sewer pool, with multiple barred passages. Swim to the shallow ledge on this area's exterior, and battle a few Rats, staying on the ground so you aren't prone. Then run to the northern part of this sewer and grab the handle that releases the adjacent gate. Ride another chute to a second part of the waterways.

Caution

MIDNA IS SEVERELY WEAKENED, AND BY NOW, YOU SHOULD HAVE REALIZED THAT YOU CANNOT PERFORM HER AREA-ATTACK TECHNIQUE (HOLDING Ⓑ). YOU MUST RELY ON YOUR TEETH, AND Ⓩ TARGETING!

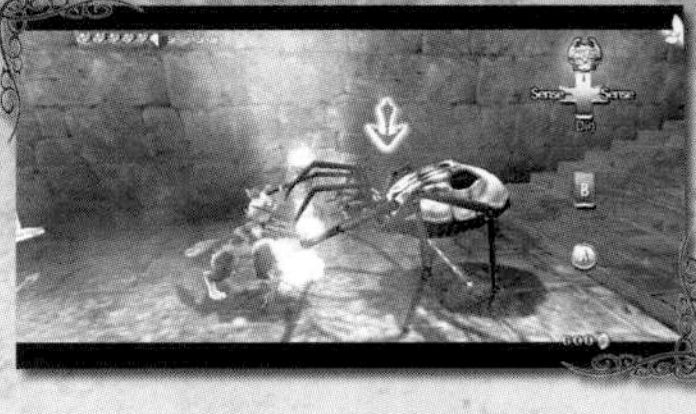

➤ You land in a large pool. Climb the stairs, and a Skulltula attacks you. There's a second at the web, atop the stairs. You can circle each Skulltula, then leap and attack from the side or behind. Or, you can grab a stick, light each end, and charge the Skulltula with it.

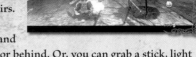

After defeating the arachnids, smash skulls, pick the stick up again, light either or both ends, and burn the web.

➤ Take the stick and head through the web, into a debris-filled castle labyrinth. To the side as you enter is another torch, light it. In a moment you'll see why you need to keep a constant source of flames.

➤ Move to the left and light another torch. Place your stick down, and engage a couple of Keeses, then head north to the massive, blocked-off archway, and light another torch in this vicinity. When this last torch is lit, you can temporarily drop the stick, and finish off any other Keeses. Smash some more skulls for Hearts, and loot a group of crates in one corner for Rupees.

➤ The reason for the torch-lighting is now obvious: turn and face west. There's a web to burn through, so use the torches to lit the stick and burn that web.

➤ Bound through into an area of ruined columns, and fluttering Keeses. Drop the stick and run north (the crates are empty). Amid the Keeses is one Bulblin. Defeat them all. Destroy the final batch of crates for a green (1) and red (20) Rupee, then exit via the archway.

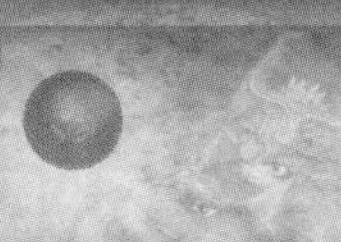

▲ This brings you to a dead end, and a Bulblin Warrior. Defeat him then search the area. The earthen floor in the middle is a clue; there's a dig spot here, so tunnel down. You appear in the catacombs you visited after Midna first found you!

The Route to Hyrule Castle: Sewers and Battlements

◄ The area below you is impassable, so move up the dirt ramp, scavenge Hearts from the skulls, and climb the tower. Bound up the stairs, zigzagging to avoid a Bulblin Archer's flaming arrows. Target and bite into him.

▲ Pad across the rope, to another part of the crumbling spiral staircase, and land on the steps before targeting and dispatching another Bulblin. Climb the staircase, using every rope you come across until you reach another couple of Bulblin warriors on different levels. Dispatch them after you finish your rope-walks.

The ordeal ends with a series of smaller ropes linking the last of the staircase, and a final rope to the fenced top area. A Bulblin is waiting here, but stay on the rope, and then spin attack to avoid this problem.

► You emerge at the tower's base. Leap at and defeat a Bulblin Archer, and finish off a couple of Keeses afterward. The exit is easily spotted. Head out the open door, and onto the castle battlements. Circle the two Bulblins to avoid their arrows, and pounce!

Note: There are a couple of skulls to smash as you exit onto the battlements; one contains a Heart you might need.

◄ You've done this before so progress quickly. Defeat another Bulblin, then turn and clamber onto the wooden structure, and leap across to the next section of crenulations. A Kargarok swoops to attack you: Z target, don't leap off, and jump attack as the Kargarok moves into range.

◄ Continue north, optionally smashing the skulls for Hearts, until you reach the piece of flapping wood that used to be a bridge to a tower. This fearful jump is the only way forward! Wait until the howling wind blows the wood horizontally, then leap on and run to the small tower. The skulls here give you a green (1) and blue (5) Rupee.

► Turn and drop onto the roof of the castle. The remainder of your rooftop ramble is to reach the open doorway to Zelda's tower. The crates, skulls, and other debris you can smash for cash and Hearts are in the same places as before. Ignore the Kargaroks, or else wait for them to swoop in, then dispatch them. Climb to the doorway, and exit.

◄ You appear halfway up the spiral staircase to Zelda's room. Move up to the door that's ajar. Enter it, optionally cracking open a couple of crates to the left with Hearts inside.

You enter Zelda's bedchamber. Midna asks how your curse can be removed. Zelda informs you that you must leave for the sacred grove that is deep within Faron Woods where the Master Sword waits for you! Evil is cloaking you, and only the sword can remove it!

Midna hopes you can continue without her, and find the Mirror of Twilight. Zelda transfers her energy, despite Midna's protests. Midna is healed, but at what cost?

Enemies Encountered

Rat

Skulltula

Keese

Kargarok

Characters Encountered

Midna

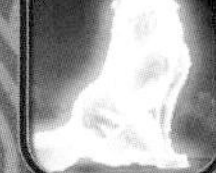

White Wolf

As you gallop out of Castle Town, Hyrule Castle is bathed in an eerie yellow light. It seems the castle is sealed from you. Only the location of the Mirror of Twilight can help!

➤ As soon as you can, follow the princess's advice to the letter, and head directly for North Faron Woods. Don't go there on foot; it would take ages! Instead, warp there using Midna's newly regained power. Select "N. Faron Woods" as your warp point.

Task 2: Obtain the Master Sword

Journey to the Sacred Woods: Entering the Grove

➤ You arrive in north Faron Woods (and if you're trying to cross the mist-filled woodland area, warp again). Head northward, past Trill's Shop, toward the entrance to the Forest Temple. Your monkey chum leaps in but is waylaid by four strange mannequins!

Puppet

Threat Meter

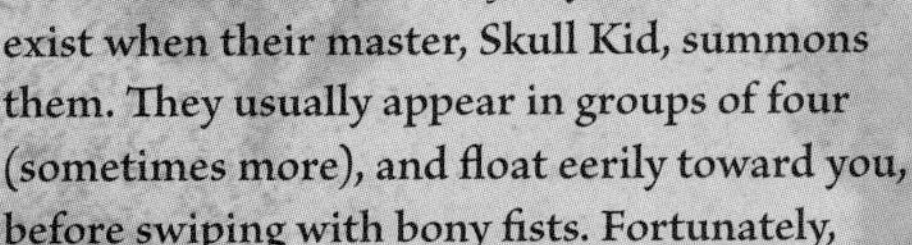

Puppets are strange, jerky creatures that exist when their master, Skull Kid, summons them. They usually appear in groups of four (sometimes more), and float eerily toward you, before swiping with bony fists. Fortunately, they are very weak and one spin attack flattens all of them. Or, you can Z target one, leap and bite, and continue this technique to finish the rest off. Try this out now, and save that monkey! Other moves to try are Midna's area-attack, and if you're Link (and don't have time to change), a spin attack.

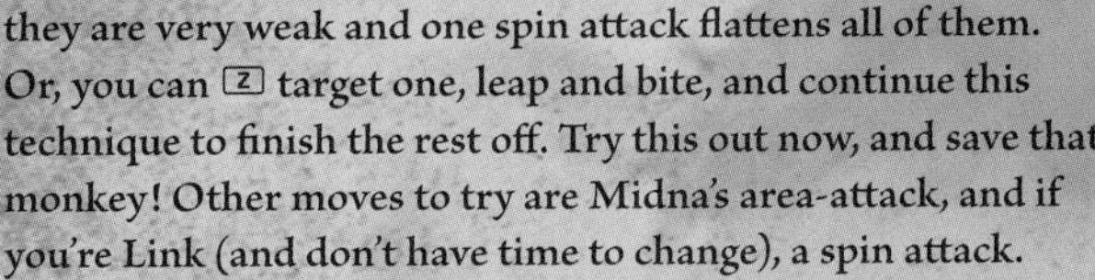

➤ When the monkey has been saved, she points out the way to go. Stand on the flat stump platform, and Midna departs from you to a nearby landing spot. There's another section of forest to explore.

Leap three times to land on the floating platform. Then attempt three more Z targeted leaps, to land on a hidden entrance to the Sacred Grove. Move toward two rotating bridges, and defeat a couple of Keeses.

➤ Wait for the wind to blow the bridge straight in front of you, then leap to it and bound to the second bridge. Wait until this second structure rotates 90 degrees, then run off onto a small grassy platform. Face the rope ahead, and wait for a swinging log to pass. Then quickly walk across the rope to a floating platform. Wait for a second log, and pass by that to a larger grassy ledge. Inspect the Wind Stone, then enter the cave ahead.

Hidden Skill

Howling for the White Wolf

Before you continue, you must investigate that strange ceremonial stone on the grassy ledge you're nearby. Listen and the wind whistles a tune through the hole in the rock. You must now recite the tune. Listen to the tune, then replicate it. The pitch is as follows: High, Low (hold), High, Low, Middle, High (hold). Use ⬆ to howl high and ⬇ to howl low on your ◎. For mid-range howling, don't move the stick.

You appear as a wolf, high in the heavens near a sacred forest. The White Wolf appears at the end of a leafy edge, on the opposite side of the world. You howl the tune again. When you finish, the White Wolf tells you "Let teachings of old pass to you...." The wolf leaps down into the land.

Note

You have summoned the White Wolf! He is currently waiting for you by the wall outside the southern exit of Castle Town. You must head here as Link, and learn your next Hidden Skill! The walkthrough tells you the earliest point that this is possible.

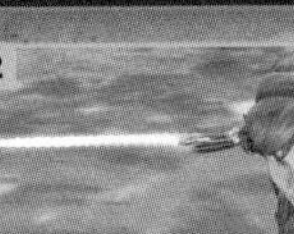
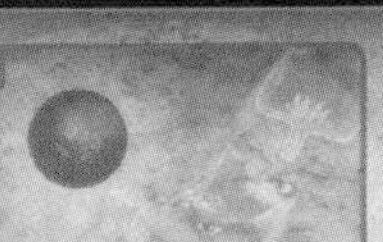

Missing Links

1. Digging for Victory

The entrance to the Sacred Grove has a couple of places to find hidden Rupees and Hearts. Dig at dig spots on the grassy platform after the second rotating bridge for Rupee and Hearts, and just behind the Wind Stone for Hearts. Investigate the grassy ledge where the Wind Stone sits for Rupees and Hearts.

Sacred Grove: Stalking the Skull Kid

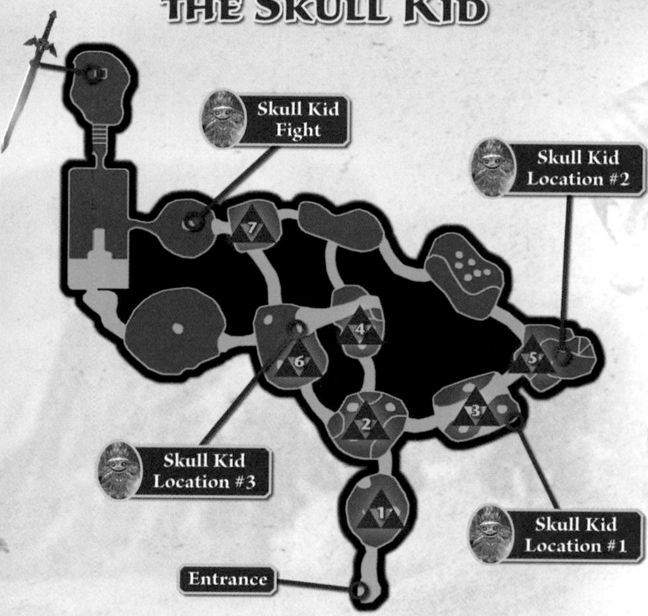

➤ Enter a small grove that's glistening with dew drops, and scamper around. Inspect a Wind Stone, much like the one you just listened to, but with a Triforce symbol carved into it. Howl along with the song: Middle (hold), High, Low (hold), Middle, High, Low (hold).

➤ A strange little man descends from the trees and looks at you with an odd smile. He produces a trumpet and blows, giggles, and opens the sealed tree trunk doorway. Follow him into the Sacred Grove. As you do, four Puppets descend from the treetops and chase you. Stop and execute a spin attack to rid yourself of them.

Tip: The Puppets continuously appear and chase you throughout the Sacred Grove. Simply stop, wait for them to congregate around you, and then launch a spin attack. Rid yourself of them temporarily before you begin any difficult moves too, such as climbing large tree steps.

➤ Scamper into the next linked Sacred Grove area (#2), and launch an area-attack on the Puppets. Or stick with your spin attack. Now try to head through this area without getting lost. Here's how:

➤ Head directly through this exit. You arrive in Area #3, which has butterflies flitting about. Run to the opposite end of this glade.

The Skull Kid is waiting in the raised area inside a giant hollowed out clearing. Defeat all the Puppets, then strike Skull Kid once. He laughs and flees the area!

➤ Backtrack to Area #2 (with the shallow water in it), and find another exit, shown here. Defeat any Puppets, then head up inside a hollowed-out log to Area #4.

Area #4 has a series of large tree trunk steps leading to a fallen tree platform. Drop down from here after securing a load of Rupees and Hearts from the grass, then backtrack to Area #3. The passage near the tree clearing where you first hit Skull Kid is now open.

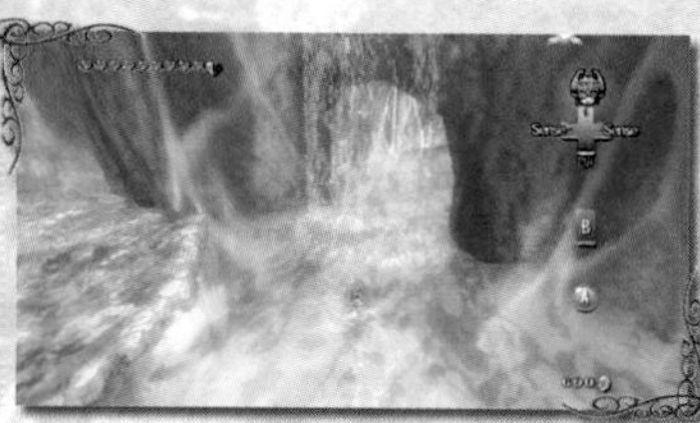

➤ Enter Area #5, which has a small pool to one side. Swim here, to the archway through the small waterfall.

Attack the Puppets on the series of large stairs, and then make a leap for Skull Kid, who's standing on the tree trunk platform overlooking the pool.

Tip: Follow the laughter and the trumpet-playing in your search for Skull Kid. If you can't hear either, wander around until you can; he's nearby!

Enemies Encountered

Puppet

Keese

Skull Kid

Midna

➤ Head back from Area #5, toward Area #3 (which has the long grass and butterflies), and then back to Area #2 (with the shallow water). An all-new opening has appeared! Dart through to Area #6.

◄ Area #6 has two torches and a sealed arch ahead. Look up, and you'll see Skull Kid at the edge of a ledge! Dash to the opening just to one side of the sealed arch.

This leads to a new entrance into Area #4, and the ledge you saw Skull Kid on is up the tree trunk steps and across the fallen tree. Bound forward, target Skull Kid, and bite!

◄ Skull Kid whisks himself away and unseals the arch with the torches either side. Follow him down to a new area, #7. This area has only one exit: into the Sacred Grove arena! Head through the torch-lit archway. You emerge on a high ledge, overlooking the arena. Drop down.

Missing Links

1. Digging for Victory

There are various grass clumps and spots in the Sacred Grove where you can scrabble for Rupees and Hearts. There's no map to follow, so just do this in every area, usually at the foot of trees.

- Area #1: At the foot of a tall tree (Rupees and Hearts).
- Area #3: Grass throughout the area with the butterflies and tall grass (Rupees).
- Area #4: The foot of the tree trunk steps (masses of Rupees and Hearts in the grass, one Rupee from the dig spot).
- Area #5: Two dig spots on the ground next to the pool (Rupees).
- Area #6: The middle of the ground (Rupee).
- Area #7: In the corner, near the stone archway and skulls (Rupees).

Skull Kid

Threat Meter

Step 1: The Skull Kid makes a stand. He drops down to one of the six or so platforms dotted around this arena and summons four Puppets. Use the spin attack to defeat all the Puppets. The area attack is less effective, as you can be stopped by the obstacles all around.

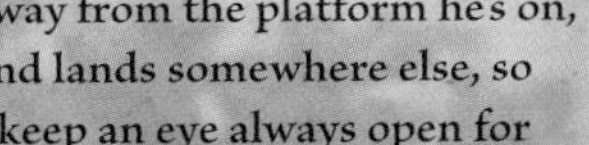

Step 2: The Skull Kid summons five, six, and even seven Puppets, and lets them loose on you! React by defeating them while prowling for Skull Kid, who's randomly landed on one of the platforms. Z target him and pounce with a leaping attack!

Step 3: If you're too slow in finding him, Skull Kid teleports away from the platform he's on, and lands somewhere else, so keep an eye always open for him! Continue to batter his Puppets, then leap and strike him three times.

◄ Skull Kid titters, and waves good-bye before disappearing and opening a doorway for you. Spend a few moments inspecting this arena; there's a large Bomb Rock (with a dig spot under it) that you can't move. However, you can roll small rocks and smash skulls for Rupees and Hearts.

The True Sacred Grove: Obtaining the Master Sword

◄ When you're ready, enter the doorway that leads up to a large grassy clearing. Ignore the two large statues for the moment, and check the southern area out.

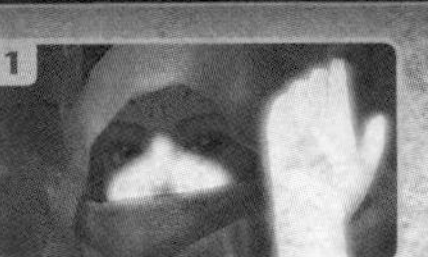
1

2

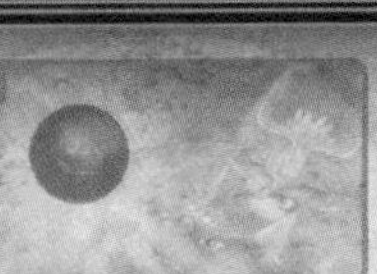
3

4

5

6

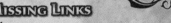

▲ There are two cracks in the southern wall, and the one on the western side leads to a ruined set of steps, and a looted chest. Roll the nearby stones for Rupees and a Heart, then return. A shiny Golden Bug is here, but you can't grab it with your paws!

▲ Once you've explored the area, run to the middle of the grassy area guarded by two statues. Stand on the Triforce carving on the ground between them, and howl the same melody you did to enter the Sacred Grove earlier. A magical incantation commences, and the arena falls away, the statues move, and a puzzle begins! You must guide the statues so they are placed where they once stood!

▲ Guiding the statues back to the marked spots is a convoluted process. You mustn't get stuck yourself or get the statues stuck so only one moves. And remember that each statue moves in the opposite direction from the other! However, there is a solution and here's the quickest way to solve it:

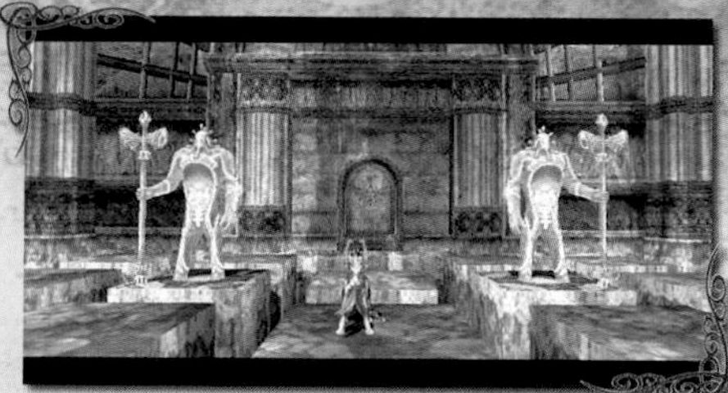

◄ Move yourself: Left, Down, Right, Right, Up, Left, Up, Up, Left, Down, Down, Right, and finally, Up. The door to the true Sacred Grove opens!

Missing Links

1. Splendor in the Grass

The Ruins to the Temple of Time has a number of clumps of grass to chew on, spitting out Rupees and Hearts.

The True Sacred Grove: The Master Sword Returns!

► Bound through the door straight ahead of you, to a mist-shrouded clearing, where dappled sunlight beams down onto the blade of a large, spectacular weapon. Check it out.

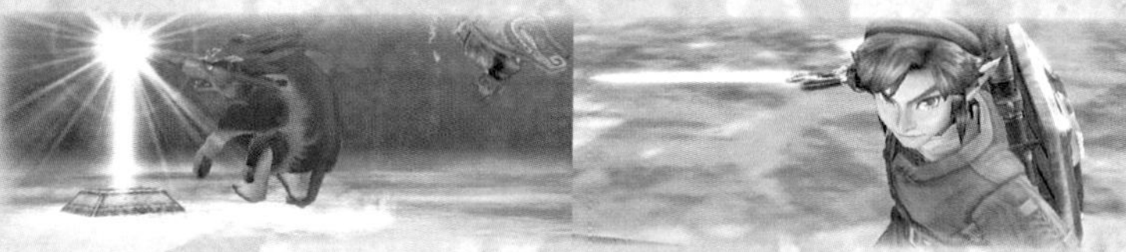

The sword glows a brilliant white and pulsates, enveloping you. Zant's evil magic shard is cast from you. You remove the sword, and claim it! You can now turn from boy to wolf at any time!

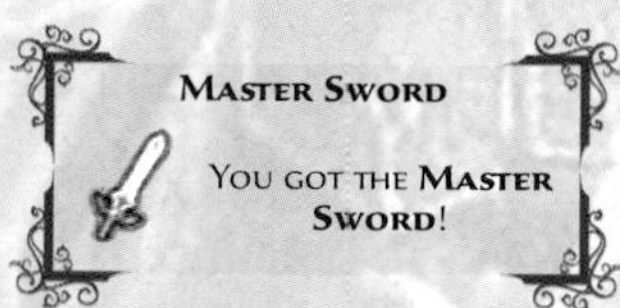

Master Sword

You got the **Master Sword**!

Sacred Grove: Hunting for Items

Note: You can now transform into a wolf and back to Link at any time. Simply press ✚ and you can talk to Midna, transform to and from wolf form, and warp to anywhere you wish! You now have complete freedom to roam about the countryside!

Enemies Encountered

Skull Kid

Puppet

Characters Encountered

Midna

Golden Bug: Male Snail

Collection: 21 (of 24)

First snag the Golden Bug that's nestled in the corner of the ruined passageway to the south. Use the Clawshot to pick the bug off the wall, maneuver to your feet, then sweep it up. The Female Snail is near here, but you can't claim it yet!

Male Snail
You caught a **Male Snail**! Bug fans love that golden color!

◄ Now clear as much of this area as possible. Start with the arena where you fought Skull Kid. Head to the bomb rock in the center of the area, place a bomb next to it, and explode it.

Poe Soul #2

The Bomb Rock is hiding more than just a dig spot; another Poe lantern is here. Quickly transform into your wolf form, switch on your sense view, then leap and attack, or attempt Midna's area-attack.

Poe Soul
You got the **Poe Soul**! Collect one from each Poe you defeat! Poe Soul #2 of 60.

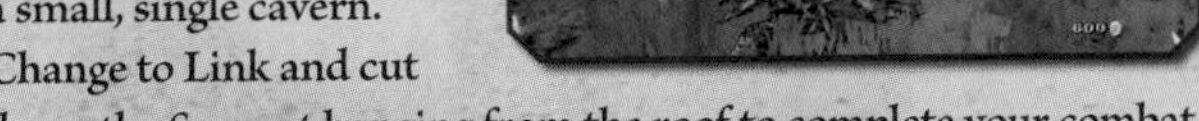

Dig Cavern #1

The Bomb Rock also allows you to enter another dig cavern. Drop down, and defeat every single Baba Serpent in a small, single cavern. Change to Link and cut down the Serpent hanging from the roof to complete your combat.

There are numerous Hearts and Rupees in the long grass, so slice this too! When every Baba Serpent is defeated, a chest mysteriously appears. Run to the ledge and open it; inside is a **Piece of Heart!**. Claim it, then exit via the rock with the light shining on it.

Overworld Chest #47: Piece of Heart #21

Piece of Heart
You got a **Piece of Heart**! Collect **five pieces** to form a new Heart Container. Piece of Heart #21 of 45.

Note: There's another Imp Poe in this area, in the clearing where you found the Master Sword. However, he only comes out at night, and it's easier to return for him later.

Tip: You can now freely explore the wilds of Hyrule! To aid in your progress, we're covering every new area to explore in chronological order, based on when you first arrived. Let's start with Ordona Province. Warp there now.

Task 3: Begin to Hunt for Treasure and Imp Poes, Across the Land

The Great Hyrule (and Poe) Hunt: Ordona Province

◄ Warp back to the Ordon Spring. You can transform into Link, or howl by the Horse Grass to summon Epona. Ride south to your home village, all the way to the pasture where you herded the goats. You can herd them again, and attempt to beat your record.

Step into the goat barn and you'll see that the Postman is hiding out here, inspecting a recently chewed letter. The goats can have it!

Dig Cavern #2

Return to the barn in wolf form, and dig at the ground just behind the Postman. This leads to a dig cavern teeming with Rats. Slay all of them, but as soon as you spot a Chu dropping from the ceiling, transform into Link. This is an ultra-rare **Gold Chu!** Select an Empty Bottle, attack the Gold Chu, then scoop it! You now have Rare Chu Jelly!

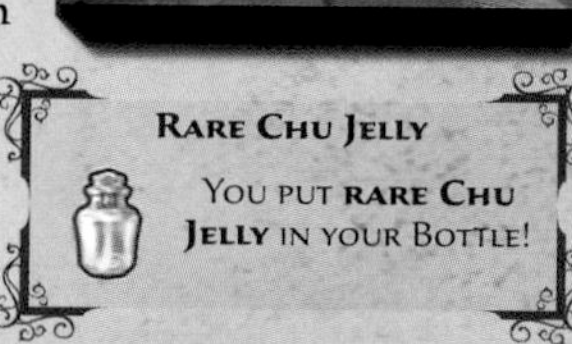

Rare Chu Jelly

You put **rare Chu Jelly** in your Bottle!

Note: Rare Chu Jelly offers the most potent healing combination of any item in Hyrule! It replenishes all Hearts and briefly boosts attack strength! Put this away in your inventory so you don't accidentally swig it! You can return here for more of this stuff, as long as you used the previous one.

Smash some pots and slice grass for minor Rupees and Hearts before inspecting the room a little more closely. Lighting both the unlit torches at the north end of the room to summons a chest with a purple Rupee inside. Now you can leave.

Overworld Chest #48: Purple Rupee (20)

Missing Links

1. Run, Goat, Run!

This is one of the first times you can dismount from your horse, and slice into a goat or two. They seethe red with anger and can knock you off your feet (but you aren't harmed)!

The Great Hyrule (and Poe) Hunt: Faron Province

Poe Soul #3

Your next Poe is deep in Faron Woods. Warp to either side of the murky mist, and then use Midna to leap to the central tree stump in the middle of the woods. Engage the Imp Poe here.

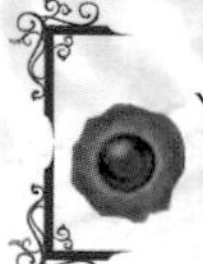

Poe Soul

You got the **Poe Soul**! Collect one from each Poe you defeat! Poe Soul #3 of 60.

➤ Now gallop into the Faron Province area of Hyrule Field, where you found your first Golden Bugs. Race to the area under the bridge, where you spotted that chest earlier. Bring out your Clawshot, fire it at the medallion in the bridge ceiling, then drop down and open the chest. Use the same medallion to escape.

Overworld Chest #49: Orange Rupee (100)

Dig Cavern #3

After obtaining the chest from under the bridge, head to the circle of grass in the northern part of the area, and dig into a quiet and tranquil dig cavern. This hole is completely silent! However, this is a great fishing spot to snag everything other than fish! Boots, bags of Rupees, small wheels, and other flotsam and jetsam can be yours. Here is a complete list:

- Bag of Rupees (amount varies)
- Boot (an old discarded boot with little value)
- Twigs (a bunch of old twigs with little value)
- Wheel (an old wheel with little value)

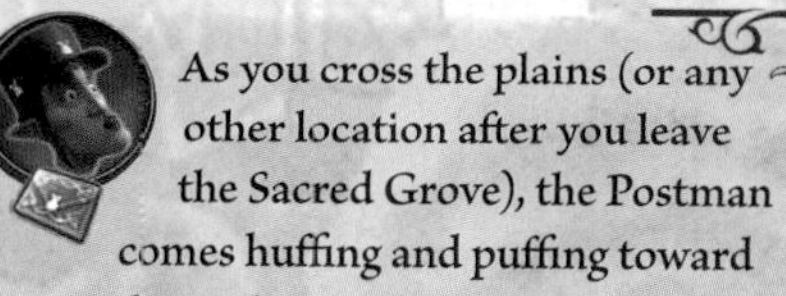

As you cross the plains (or any other location after you leave the Sacred Grove), the Postman comes huffing and puffing toward you with another two missives. The letter is from Telma, concerning a group of faithful heroes who have arrived at the bar and are waiting to meet you. Go there when you wish to continue your quest (Task #7).

Letter #7

You got Letter #7: "They came so quickly!" by Telma.

Enemies Encountered

Baba Serpent

Rat

Imp Poe

Chu

Poe Soul #4

Stay in this field until the sun goes down, and you can race to the middle of this field, to a raised area near a tree, overlooking the path. An Imp Poe waits for you here. Defeat the Bokoblins and Kargaroks first, to make your Poe combat easier. Then strike!

Poe Soul

You got the **Poe Soul**! Collect one from each Poe you defeat! Poe Soul #4 of 60.

The Great Hyrule (and Poe) Hunt: Kakariko Gorge

Poe Soul #5

Continue your travels into the Kakariko Gorge, and head up the sloping hill next to the road, toward the single tree and fenced area. Defeat the Kargaroks flying about before turning your attention to this Imp Poe.

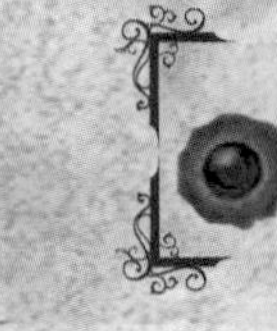

Poe Soul

You got the **Poe Soul**! Collect one from each Poe you defeat! Poe Soul #5 of 60.

◄ After you've defeated the Imp Poe, dig around at the spots you previously found (when you were following the scent). Also locate a group of Guays circling this tree, and chew or slice each one. The tree rains down Rupees after the last is slain.

Caution

You can also attempt to Clawshot to the medallion on the rock in the middle of the bottomless gorge, as there's still a chest to open around here. The problem is that you'll plummet to an inky doom if you do! This area requires a Double Clawshot. Come back when you find one.

➤ By now, a new menace has arrived in Kakariko Gorge: Purple, Blue, Yellow, and Red Chus. They shift about in the northern part of the zone and aren't that aggressive. You can ride over them to easily dispatch them, but you need to dismount and scoop if you want their Jelly!

Poe Soul #6

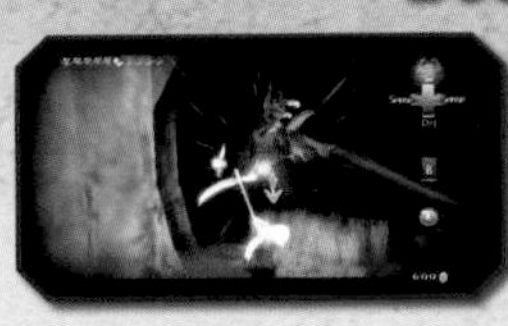

Don't leave the Kakariko Gorge until you enter the Lantern Cavern I, and journey to the dead end in the northwestern corner. Take the right fork and prepare to tackle a Poe in the dead-end area.

Poe Soul

You got the **Poe Soul**! Collect one from each Poe you defeat! Poe Soul #6 of 60.

The Great Hyrule (and Poe) Hunt: Kakariko Village

◄ Head to Kakariko Village (as Link to avoid alarm), and speak to Beth, who's standing near the sanctuary on the thoroughfare. Beth tells you that Prince Ralis is depressed and hanging out at the graveyard. Visit him later.

Tip

Transforming into the wolf can be difficult in populated areas; Midna won't allow you to if there's a possibility of scaring a pedestrian, but everything is based on line-of-sight. You can still transform if you (for example) head around a corner, so no one can see you!

➤ First though, you're cordially invited to talk to Gor Liggs, outside of the Malo Mart! He asks whether you've spoken to his brothers in Castle Town, who are running short of Hot Springwater. They have loads of it, but the bridge needs repairing. Perhaps you could donate?

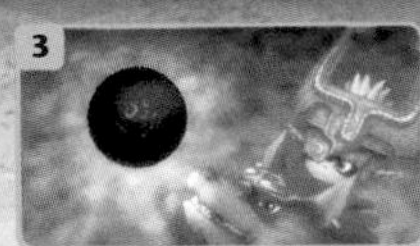

◄ Head into the Malo Mart to see Gor Ebizo, who's jingling a donation box. He tells you the Castle Town shops are price-gouging! Malo Mart is preparing a relief plan: Phase One: Repair the broken bridge to improve traffic. Phase Two: Buy Chudley's Emporium and sell products at reduced prices!

Of course, this doesn't come cheap; the bridge costs 1,000 Rupees to repair! Donate all of this, as soon as possible, because the results are well worth it! Put all your available Rupees into this donation box.

➤ Now find the rest of the donation money, and fast! Give your Golden Bugs to Agitha, or consult the Walkthrough for the nearest 100 Rupee chest. Or ring the sanctuary bell with your Bomb Arrow, run to the wall near the dead tree by the sanctuary building, transform to the wolf, use Midna to bound up to the roof, and claim the Silver Rupee (200) piece that fell from the bell!

◄ You are free to move about Kakariko Village. You can visit the graveyard, and tag the Guays with your Clawshot. The resulting 22 Rupees for defeating them all isn't quite the 200 you need to repair the bridge, but it's a start. Head through the hole to the Zora grave.

◄ Prince Ralis is standing by his father's grave. He realizes who you are. The young prince lacks confidence, though. Remember his location for later, and leave via the graveyard.

Step to Barnes' Bomb Shop, where the proprietor has created a brand new model: a Bombling! Try this remote bomb out. Bomb Arrows are more useful, however.

Store

Store: Barnes' Bomb Store

Item	Name	Price	Effect
	Bombs (10)	30 Rupees	I sell these in packs of ten. You get a slight discount that way.
	Water Bombs (5)	30 Rupees	These bombs even work underwater! I sell 'em in sets of five.
	Bombling (1)	6 Rupees	These cute little bugs walk around and blow up all on their own!

Bombling

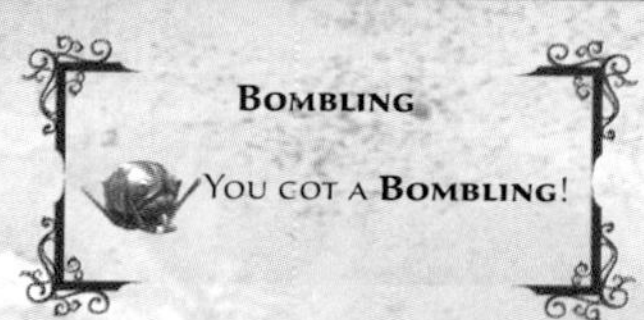

You got a **Bombling**!

The Great Hyrule (and Poe) Hunt: Death Mountain Trail

➤ Head up the Death Mountain Trail next, and when you reach the rocky clearing where the Wind Stone is, turn and locate this alcove with the vine hanging from it. Clawshot to this point, and climb up. Then draw your sword because there's a Chu in here! The type of Chu is random. It could be Yellow, Red, Purple, Blue, or Gold!

Tip: The Chu hides on the alcove's ceiling. If the rare Gold Chu is lurking there, you'll see faint sparkles when you look up from the ground. That way you know you can scoop an impressive elixir!

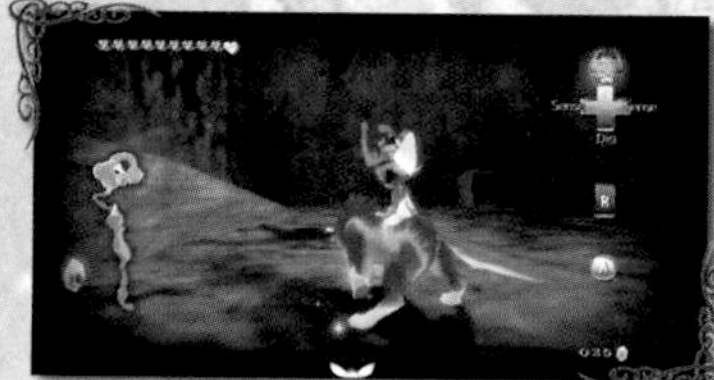

➤ You can now teleport to the base of Death Mountain, and enter the elevator area in wolf form. Explore some dig spots to unearth blue (5) and yellow (10) Rupees, plus Hearts.

➤ Use the elevator to ascend to the Goron Mines (Dungeon 2) entrance. At the sumo wrestling circle, you can meet Gor Coron again. You can also meet Darbus for the first time since you fought his fiery alter ego, Fyrus!

Enemies Encountered

Imp Poe

Bokoblin

Kargarok

Guay

Chu (Purple, Blue, Yellow, and Red)

7

8

Goron

Midna

Gor Ebizo

Gor Liggs

Don't forget to enter Dungeon 2, and work your way to the Mine Loading Dock and claim Treasure Chest #17. This is your earliest opportunity, as you can now use the Clawshot, shoot up to the mesh, and clamber onto the previously inaccessible platform. The prize is a purple Rupee (50).

Leave the mines, either by carefully descending, or leaping down from the entrance. Can you jump from here with a Cucco?

Poe Soul #7

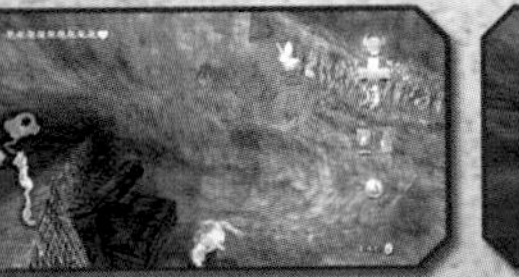

On your way up or down the trail (at night), stop at the Goron by the second barricade, and ask him to launch you to the rocky slope above. Turn and head south, until you see the bobbing light, then face and defeat the Imp Poe up here. Use Midna's area-attack; it's safer than jumping, as you can fall back down to the trail.

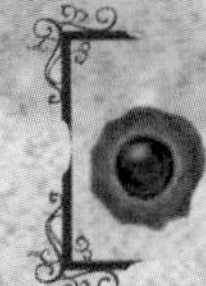

Poe Soul

You got the **Poe Soul**! Collect one from each Poe you defeat! Poe Soul #7 of 60.

Poe Soul #8

Your next Poe is back in Kakariko Village. At night, find him floating above the remains of Barnes' bomb shack. Use the interior, a Goron, or a Cucco to reach this path, then face the fiend and gnash on his stolen soul!

Poe Soul

You got the **Poe Soul**! Collect one from each Poe you defeat! Poe Soul #8 of 60.

Poe Soul #9

Stay in this area, and follow the snaking pathway up the promontory, all the way to the lookout shack at the northern end of the village. The platform the shack is on houses your next ethereal Poe foe. Bring out the bite, and snatch that soul!

Poe Soul

You got the **Poe Soul**! Collect one from each Poe you defeat! Poe Soul #9 of 60.

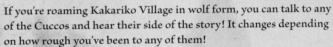

Missing Links

1. Cucco Chatter

If you're roaming Kakariko Village in wolf form, you can talk to any of the Cuccos and hear their side of the story! It changes depending on how rough you've been to any of them!

Poe Soul #10

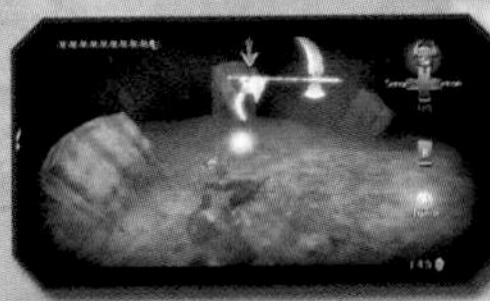

Head down the thoroughfare, around the sanctuary, and into the graveyard. Nighttime is when you'll find this Poe, floating eerily through the gravestones. Sharpen your fangs and have at him! You're halfway to Jovani's target!

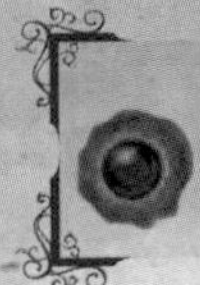

Poe Soul

You got the **Poe Soul**! Collect one from each Poe you defeat! Poe Soul #10 of 60.

Poe Soul #11

Although you can't spot him normally, there's a cunningly hidden Poe. The pushable gravestone on the graveyard's left side houses him! Shove him into the open, then leap and finish him with your fangs.

Poe Soul

You got the **Poe Soul**! Collect one from each Poe you defeat! Poe Soul #11 of 60.

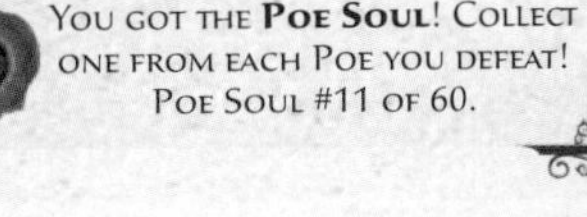

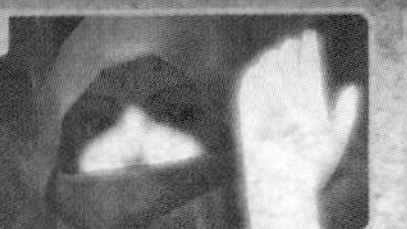

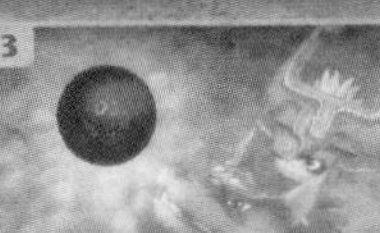

The Great Hyrule (and Poe) Hunt: Hyrule Field (West)

With Kakariko Village completely devoid of additional goods (until you return to finish the donation), head out into the northern passageway linking Kakariko Gorge to the large, flat western Hyrule Field. Produce a Bomb Arrow and remove the blockage.

Ride northward, into the field itself, and then keep to the eastern edge, and you'll soon locate the bridge you're donating to. A Goron sits on the other side. You need to collect funds as soon as possible! Collect 200 Rupees—the rocks near Poe Soul #7 each house a red Rupee (20)—and return to the Malo Mart.

Enemies Encountered

Imp Poe

Bulblin

Task 4: Repair the Bridge to Castle Town

The Great Hyrule (and Poe) Hunt: Repairing the Bridge, Hot Springwater for All!

Enter the Malo Mart and chat with Gor Ebizo. The bridge from Hyrule Field to west Castle Town is now complete! Malo is officially putting that highfalutin' Chudley on notice! There's a new shopkeeper in town! And he's about five years old!

Head outside to speak with Gor Liggs. He asks if you've seen his young one who's sitting near the incomplete bridge. You were just over there (if you've been following this walkthrough!), and Gor Liggs hopes you might look for him. That's the plan!

First, head back into the Malo Mart, and speak with Gor Ebizo. He's decided to start **another** donation scheme to buy out Chudley. The cost is large: 2,000 Rupees! However, if you helped with the bridge, your donation goes down to 200 Rupees!

IT'S WISE TO COMPLETE THIS TASK WHEN YOU CAN. WHEN YOU VISIT AGITHA, OR CLEAN OUT A DUNGEON, BUY ANY EQUIPMENT YOU NEED, THEN DONATE THE REST TO THIS WORTHY CAUSE. THERE'S AN EXCELLENT REWARD!

Note: AS SOON AS YOU CAN DONATE TO THE FINANCING OF A CASTLE TOWN SHOP, YOU CAN RETURN TO CHUDLEY'S AND SEE IT IS CLOSED. IT REMAINS THIS WAY UNTIL THE NEW OWNER CAN FIND FINANCING; YOU'D BETTER RAID SOME TREASURE CHESTS!

Head out to the Hyrule Field area as Gor Liggs requested, and you'll see that the bridge is finished. You can now freely ride to and from the western part of Castle Town. For the moment though, slow down to speak with the lazy Goron.

He's finished the bridge, but he's too tired to move! He needs a dousing with some piping **Hot Springwater**. He's certain there's some back in Kakariko Village! Head back there, speak to Gor Liggs once again, and he prepares a barrel just for this purpose.

You begin in the south part of the Hyrule Field area. Stay by the edge, so you don't attract any attention. Circle the field's perimeter, as you attract fewer enemies this way. The only ones to worry about are a couple of Bulblins, but you can walk around them.

Characters Encountered

Goron

Borville

Agitha

Hero's Shade

White Wolf

Caution

Do not accidentally throw the barrel! Always stop, then place the barrel down, if you're attacked. If the barrel smashes, you'll have to return to Gor Liggs for another!

When you reach the lazy Goron, stand near him, make sure you line up correctly, and throw the barrel at him. The Goron is invigorated and can reopen the market stall in Castle Town! He leaves you a special gift!

Piece of Heart
You got a **Piece of Heart**! Collect **three more** for another full Heart Container.
Piece of Heart #22 of 45.

The Great Hyrule (and Poe) Hunt: Hot Springwater for All

With the bridge repaired and the Goron speeding through into Castle Town, you might wish to use this new thoroughfare. Turn and walk into the opening. You emerge west of Castle Town, at a new gate. Concentrate on rolling around a Bulblin Archer to avoid his arrows, or shield block them. Defeat both Bulblins, then cross the bridge. Turn, and look up, and you'll see another gaggle of Guays flying near the giant diamond force field. Meticulous Bomb Arrows can defeat them all, if you're patient!

In Castle Town visit the Medical Clinic if you wish; this is the first time it is open. Borville is waiting for you. He asks if Ilia mentioned anything about him. Leave this creepy guy to his fermented jars!

Move to the south end of the town, where the Goron stall is, and speak to the little one. His father (who you just helped at the bridge) has a line of customers! He offers to sell you a bottle of Hot Springwater if you can provide the Bottle! Purchase some now.

Store

Goron's Hotwater

Item Name	Price	Effect
Hot Springwater	20 Rupees	Freshly sprung from Kakariko Hot Spring! With the Gor Liggs Seal of Approval!

Hot Springwater
You got some **Hot Springwater**!

Exit via the southern gate, and head into the field. There's a dainty young lass in the circular flower bed, looking for bugs! This must be Agitha. She gives you a running total on the Golden Bugs you caught, and hopes you'll find more for her.

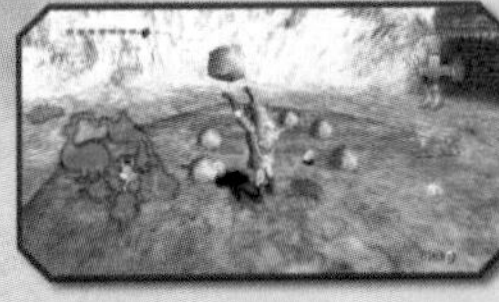

Run along the path heading to the rubble where another Goron stands. He could bash his way through this landslide if he had the **Hot Springwater**. Produce the bottle, and give it to him. Don't accidentally use it yourself! The Goron begins to tunnel the rubble with gusto! Return here after visiting another zone, and the path is open.

Dig Cavern #4

Stay in this area, and investigate the tall rock once again. Ignore the Guays, Clawshot up the vine, and stand atop the rock. Optionally lift the circle of small stones for green Rupees (1), then transform and dig into a cavern. Once down here, transform back, bring out your sword, and quickly spin attack and deal with six or seven nasty Tektites.

Smash some pots and cut some grass too. Finish off the nasty Hylian Hornets with a Bomb Arrow (these drop Larva, which is handy because this cavern doubles as a fishing hole). When you've finished fishing, wrench open the treasure chest, and claim a large denomination Rupee.

Overworld Chest #50:
Orange Rupee (100)

1

2
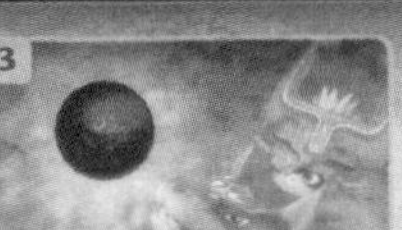
3

4

5

6

Poe Soul #12

When night shrouds the castle steps in this area, turn to your wolf form when no one is looking, and locate the floating Poe here, on the steps. Engage another Poe in ethereal combat, and claim your soul!

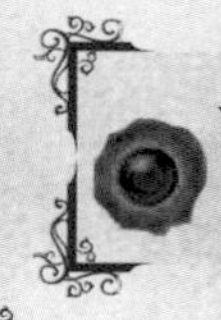

Poe Soul
You got the **Poe Soul**! Collect one from each Poe you defeat!
Poe Soul #12 of 60.

▲ Just by this Poe is the small set of towers that appears in front of the southern gate itself. You can use the Clawshot and your wolf form to claim a chest hidden up here (although it's easier to claim it when you try to reach the chest behind the stone wall, in front of this structure—for that, you need a Spinner).

▲ From this narrow tower top, transform and spin attack the pots (claim the arrows within), and then walk across the rope to the main castle wall. Transform back to Link, then carefully drop and hang from the lip of the ledge. Hand-over-hand across the gate lip to a second ledge and rope. Cross the rope to the opposite tower, where you can claim an orange Rupee (100).

Overworld Chest #51: Orange Rupee (100)

Hidden Skill #4: Helm Splitter

You have an important appointment to keep with the White Wolf, who's sitting patiently on the ground just east of the gate steps. Head here, avoiding the large hole. The White Wolf pounces! You awaken in the ghostly ether. The Hero's Shade forms, and asks you if you wish to learn your next skill. The answer is yes!

First, your teacher ensures that you learned the previous Hidden Skill correctly, and asks you to show him that you've mastered the back slice. Simply use Ⓐ after Ⓩ targeting and leap around and behind him, then slash with your Wii Remote.

"Excellent!" utters the warrior, "let the **helm splitter** be hewn into your mind!" For fully armored enemies that also move fast, the **back slice** isn't that effective. Soften them up with a **shield attack** to stagger them, then quickly leap into the air with Ⓐ to split their helms! Now you try it:

Helm splitter: jab the Nunchuk forward to shield attack, then as the enemy staggers, launch the helm splitter (while still targeting) with Ⓐ.

Hidden Skill
You learned the fourth hidden skill, the **helm splitter**!
Hidden Skill #4 of 7.

◄ Move to the large hole in the eastern part of this area, and peer down. Although there are Clawshot medallions, you need a Double Clawshot to reach the chest down there. If you try it now, you drop into the river to Lake Hylia. This is actually useful, as there are Poes to claim in this region.

Enemies Encountered

Bulblin Archer

Guay

Tektite

Hylian Hornets

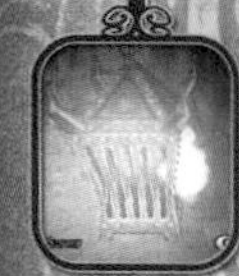

Imp Poe

Task 5: Continue to Hunt for Treasure and Imp Poes, Across the Land

The Great Hyrule (and Poe) Hunt: Lake Hylia and Lantern Cavern 2

Poe Soul #13

Once you're in Lake Hylia, bound along the narrow grassy ledge on the far western side; a floating lamp tells you the location of the next Imp Poe. He's near some previously explored dig spots. Defeat him, and add that soul to your collection.

Poe Soul
You got the **Poe Soul**! Collect one from each Poe you defeat!
Poe Soul #13 of 60.

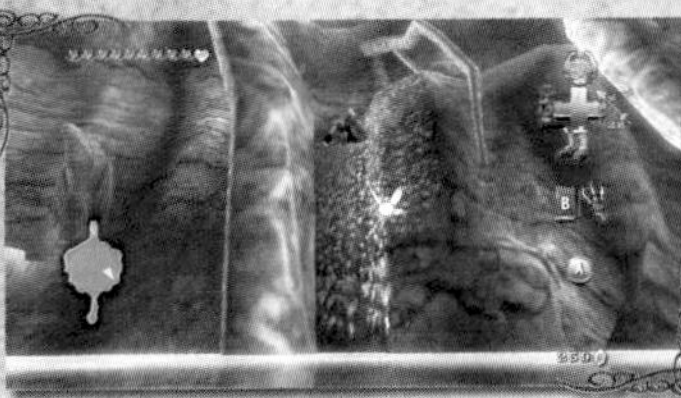

➤ Continue to hunt Poes, but when an opportunity presents itself (as dawn breaks, for example, and you can't hunt any more Poes) head into the Spirit Cave, and swim across to the eastern area. Produce your Clawshot, and propel yourself up to the top of this vine wall. This leads to an unexplored ledge. There's a circular door here; open it.

➤ This leads to a small passage and dead end, but there are a couple of chests. They hold small treasures. Produce your Lantern, and light both the unlit torches here. A chest now magically appears, and this one has the real prize; another Piece of Heart!

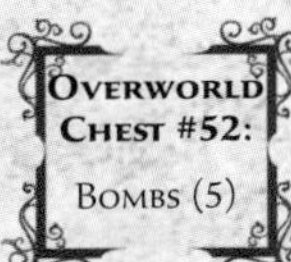

Overworld Chest #52: Bombs (5)

Overworld Chest #53: Blue Rupee (5)

Overworld Chest #54: Piece of Heart #23

Piece of Heart
You got a **Piece of Heart**! Collect **two more** for another full Heart Container.
Piece of Heart #23 of 45.

Poe Soul #14

Continue your Lake Hylia Poe hunt and head to the series of small island platforms in the southern area. Jump across at this point, and then head up and around the rise where you found a Twilit Parasite on a previous search. Engage this Poe and chew on that soul!

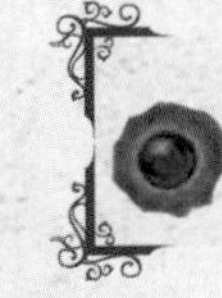

Poe Soul
You got the **Poe Soul**! Collect one from each Poe you defeat!
Poe Soul #14 of 60.

Poe Soul #15

The next ghostly Imp Poe foe is floating around the long tower in the southeastern part of the lake. Head up the ladder, and onto the grass, then fight him for his soul.

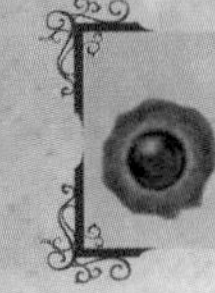

Poe Soul
You got the **Poe Soul**! Collect one from each Poe you defeat!
Poe Soul #15 of 60.

Hidden Skill

Howling for the White Wolf

Before you continue, investigate that strange ceremonial stone on the rocky promontory overlooking Fyer's cannon hut. Listen, and the wind whistles a tune through the hole in the rock. Watch the tune, then replicate it. The pitch is as follows: Low (hold), Middle (hold), High (hold), Low (long hold), Low (hold), High (hold). Use ⬆ to howl high and ⬇ to howl low on your ◎. For mid-range howling, don't move the stick.

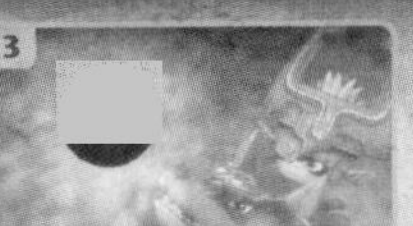

Hidden Skill (cont'd)

The White Wolf appears at the end of a leafy edge, near a huge, sand-filled stadium temple. You howl the tune again, and both of you continue to yelp. When you finish, the White Wolf tells you "Let teachings of old pass to you...."

Note: You have summoned the White Wolf! He is currently waiting for you in a sandy raised area near Arbiter's Grounds, in the Gerudo Mesa (which you haven't explored yet). You must head here as Link and learn your next Hidden Skill! The walkthrough tells you the earliest point that this is possible.

➤ The time has come to revisit the dreaded Lantern Cavern II. This time you're hunting Imp Poes! Optionally catch the Fairy from the crate in the tiny pond near the entrance, then start your search! But first, inspect an area of ground in front of the Lantern Cavern entrance:

Dig Cavern #5

There's a circle of grass near the entrance to Lantern Cavern II, so search around and dig in. Once inside another Dig Cavern, change to Link and shoot the Water Toadpoli in the pool below. Keep this up until you defeat them all; if you don't have Bomb Arrows, bouncing their spittle back at them works almost as well.

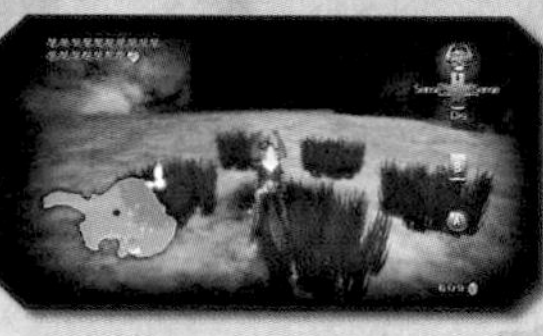

When you finish off your final Toadpoli, a chest appears with an orange Rupee inside. Fish here if you wish (you can catch all manner of junk), then leave after opening the chest.

Overworld Chest #55: Orange Rupee (100)

Poe Soul #16

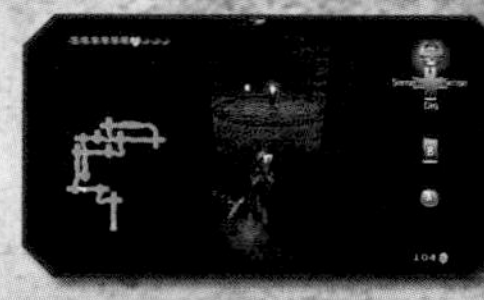

The first Lantern Cavern Poe is floating about in the southwestern junction, just after you battle past the Torch Slugs on the ceiling. Let your senses guide you, and take the Imp Poe out inside the junction itself.

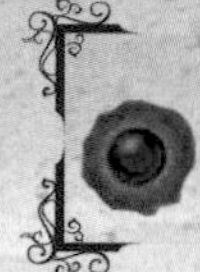

Poe Soul
You got the **Poe Soul**! Collect one from each Poe you defeat! Poe Soul #16 of 60.

Poe Soul #17

The second Lantern Cavern II Imp Poe is lurking in the very northern part of this maze. Simply follow the path and dispatch other beasts as you go before arriving at this junction. Put your Lantern away, then snuff your Poe foe!

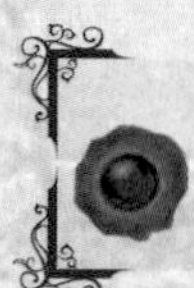

Poe Soul
You got the **Poe Soul**! Collect one from each Poe you defeat! Poe Soul #17 of 60.

Poe Soul #18

The final Imp Poe is, as you'd expect, in the very last chamber of this cavern system! Be incredibly careful negotiating the planks, and then bound into the final junction, defeat the Poe, and leave via the light pouring onto the stone platform.

Poe Soul
You got the **Poe Soul**! Collect one from each Poe you defeat! Poe Soul #18 of 60.

Enemies Encountered: Imp Poe, Water Toadpoli, Torch Slug

Characters Encountered

Plumm

Are you entering the Lantern Cavern II for the first time? Then be sure you:

- Take plenty of oil (at least a full Lantern and a full Bottle).
- Scoop more oil from every Yellow Chu you encounter.
- Follow the tactics presented previously when you could enter this area for the first time as Link.
- Stay methodical and don't rush through any areas.
- Walk, don't run, if you can't see an area in front of you. There are bottomless drops.
- If the Lantern runs out, slow down and switch to your sense view. Then you can see the immediate ground, which helps.

Tip

Author Note

Be very careful when you reach this final chamber in Lantern Cavern II! The sheer drops and inky blackness mean a Lantern and extra oil are a must! We trekked all the way to this location, fell into the bottomless pit (meaning we had to begin from the entrance!), trekked all the way here a second time, fell into the bottomless pit again, and then stopped playing and starting whimpering. Don't let that be you!

Lake Hylia: Plumm's Fruit-Pop-Flight Attraction

◄ Once you've acquired the ability to transform into a wolf at any time, you can play a minigame for valuable prizes! In wolf form, visit Plumm, a small, talking myna bird that hovers above a tiny island just south of Fyer's cannon. Plumm hypes her "Fruit-Pop-Flight" and gives you a quick rundown of the rules.

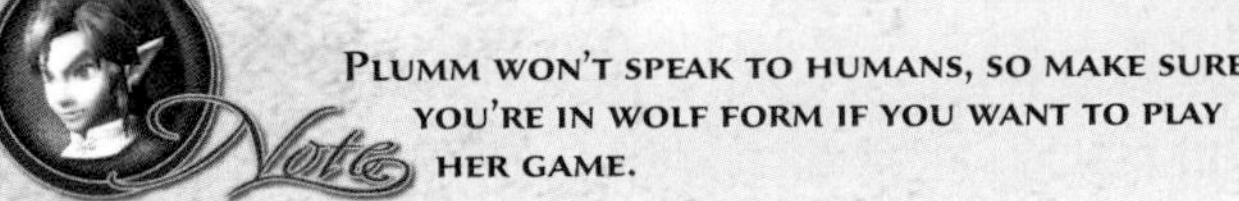

Plumm won't speak to humans, so make sure you're in wolf form if you want to play her game.

Note

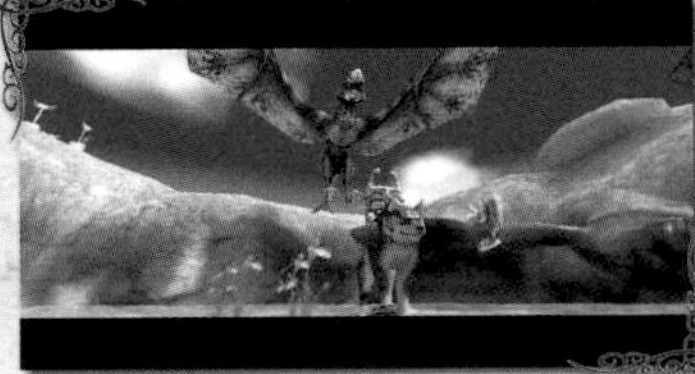

► It's free to play Plumm's game, but you need to call a Carrier Kargarok to begin. Move over to the patch of Hawk Grass that grows from the ground near Plumm, then press Ⓐ to begin howling a tune. Howl four notes in the following pitch sequence: High, Low, High, Low.

A huge Carrier Kargarok swoops down and snatches you up. It carries you off toward Zora's River, where Plumm's "Fruit-Pop-Flight" minigame takes place. Check out the "Fruit-Pop-Flight Minigame" sidebar.

Fruit-Pop-Flight Minigame

This is one of the few minigames you can play for free, so don't fee bad if it takes you awhile to get the hang of it.

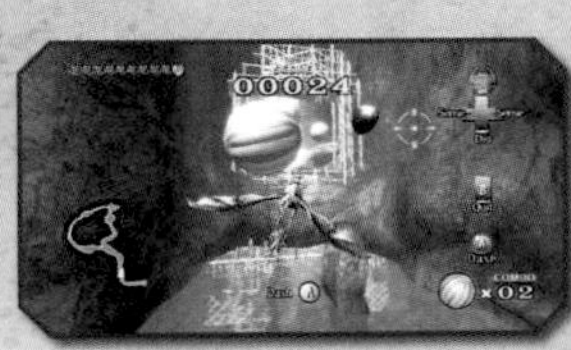

The rules to this minigame are simple: steer the Carrier Kargarok through the chasm along Zora's Riv popping the giant fruit balloons yo by flying into them. Each type of fr worth a certain number of points, a when you pop two of the same type in a row, your score doubles! multiplier is cumulative (to a maximum of 10 times), so when yo keep popping the same type of fruit, your score quickly skyrocket

Watermelons are the largest fruit, but they're each worth only one point.

Oranges are mid-sized balloons, and they're each worth three points.

Strawberries are the smallest, but each one's worth a whoppir points when popped!

The challenge of this minigame lies in adjusting to how slow th Carrier Kargarok is at responding to your commands. This giant bird can't make sharp turns at a moment's notice, so you've got to look ahead and plan out your flight pattern, making each move in preparation for the next. You won't have much luck at this minig until you learn to steer the Carrier Kargarok properly!

If you run into a wall or any other solid objec the Carrier Kargarok drops you and you mu try again.

Caution

If you're unhappy with your performance, pres to start over from the beginning and give another go.

Tip

The secret to attaining high scores from this challenge lies in going after the strawberries. They're worth the most points wh popped, and if you just keep popping them, the score multiplie soon reaches insanely high levels! Pop all the fruit you can until see the first strawberry, then stick with those sweet, sweet berri from that point on.

The Berry Best Route

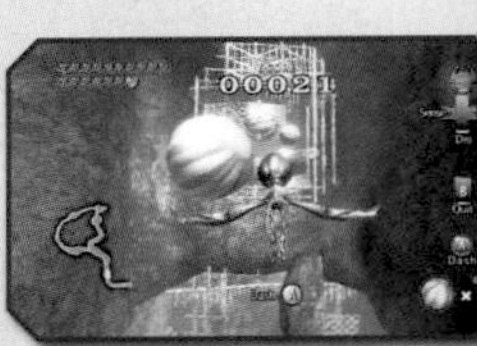

The first strawberry balloon hovers just to the right of the second watermelon. Fly past and pop the strawberry without touching the watermelon.

Fruit-Pop-Flight Minigame (cont'd)

Soar past the wooden scaffolding and then dip downward toward the next string of strawberries. Nab all four strawberries in the row, banking left to grab the final one at the end of the string.

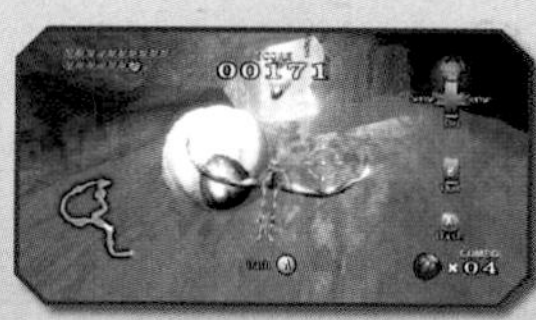

The next strawberry is positioned very near to a giant watermelon. This is a tricky one, because if you pop the watermelon, your strawberry combo is shot! It's not necessary to grab this strawberry, so don't go for it if your approach isn't strong. Instead, focus on nabbing the easier-to-pop strawberry that's just ahead.

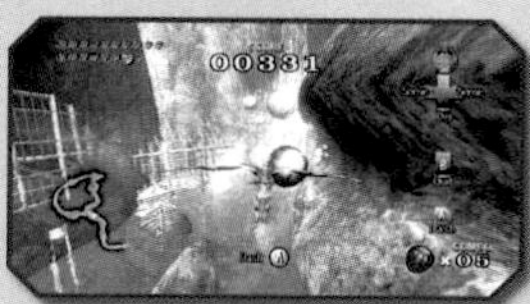

Keep to the right and avoid the giant watermelons as you approach the fork in the river. Pop the strawberry balloon near the right wall, then line up for the next row of strawberries, which hover inside a small tunnel in the right wall.

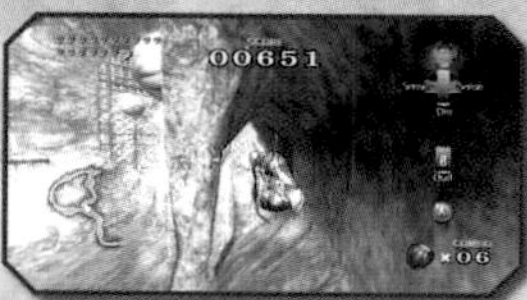

This is a dangerous row of strawberries, but with practice it's possible to get all three. Line up your approach carefully so you're heading straight through the middle of the tunnel, then press Ⓐ at the last second to execute a high-speed dash! Zip through the tunnel, popping all three strawberry balloons in the process.

Pull up as soon as you exit the tunnel and drift toward the left wall. Spy a sneakily positioned strawberry way up high and pop it, then begin a steep descent.

Skim the surface of the water as you go for this strawberry to avoid the giant watermelons that hover just above it. Quickly steer right and then left to avoid the second watermelon, keeping to the center of the river so you don't accidentally hit the rock pillar or the orange balloon to the right.

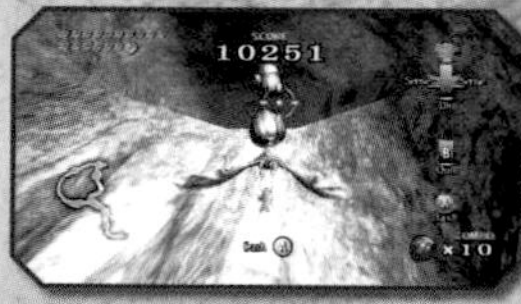

After slipping between the watermelon and the rock pillar, pull up to fly over a massive rock, nabbing four strawberries as you soar above it. Your score should be well over 10,000 points by now!

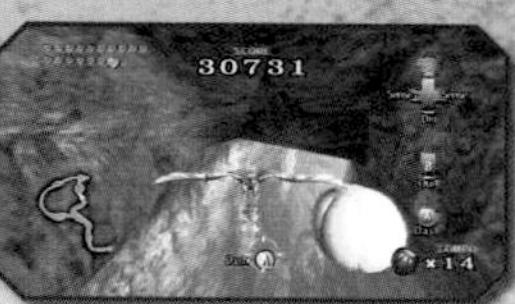

The tunnel narrows drastically after you grab the fourth strawberry in the chain. Make a sharp decent and fly close to the water to enter the mouth of the narrow, keeping to the left to avoid popping the orange balloon to the right.

Tip: If you've got over 10,000 points, don't worry if you pop the orange. Just focus on making it through the narrow without hitting the wall!

Pop the strawberry on the left side of the narrow, then do your best to nab the strawberry that follows without popping the watermelon. Go after the final strawberry that's just ahead to finish with a score to boast about!

If you score 10,000 points or more, Plumm is overwhelmed by your balloon-popping skills. She graciously gives you Piece of Heart #24 as a reward. Nice flying, ace!

Tip: Further impress Plumm by replaying her "Fruit-Pop-Flight" minigame and beating the high score you've set. She gives you an orange Rupee (100) each time you set a new record!

Piece of Heart
You got a **Piece of Heart**! Collect **one more** for another full Heart Container.
Piece of Heart #24 of 45.

Enemies Encountered
Carrier Kargarok

Characters Encountered

Falbi

Auru

Goron

➤ There are still more Poes to face in this area, and one is hidden in a most cunning spot: a ledge directly under Falbi's Flight-by-Fowl building. Use the cannon in Fyer's hut to reach Falbi, pay your 20 Rupees, grab your Cucco, and launch. Turn 180 degrees around so you're facing north, and steer your Cucco to this lonely ledge.

Poe Soul #19

Steer your squirming Cucco onto the ledge and drop to the grass below. Immediately change to your wolf form, flick your sense view on, and defeat the Poe here. Don't leap too enthusiastically; you don't want to drop off the ledge!

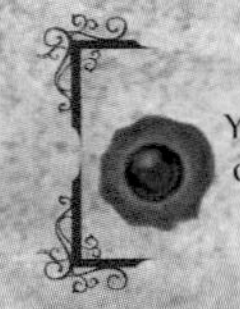

Poe Soul

You got the **Poe Soul**! Collect one from each Poe you defeat! Poe Soul #19 of 60.

Dig Cavern #6

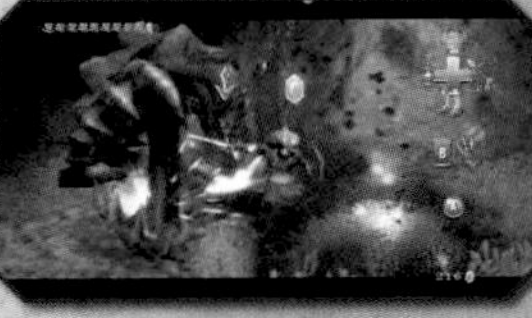

Your crazy ledge antics don't end there, either! Inspect the grassy circle for a dig spot, and scrabble down into a dark dig cavern. Change to human form, put on your Zora Armor, place your Iron Boots on your feet, and dive into the murky water. Four nasty Shell Blades are lurking down here. Defeat them all with **horizontal slices.**

When you've sliced the final Shell Blade, a chest appears on the opposite island. Head up here, optionally smash a few pots and cut grass for Rupees and Hearts, and then open the chest for a real prize! Now head out of the cavern and fly or drop down into Lake Hylia, or warp.

Overworld Chest #56: Orange Rupee (100)

Poe Soul #20

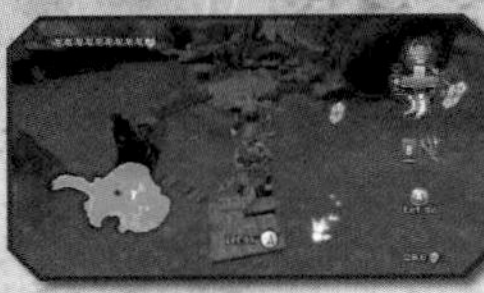

It's time to claim your 20th Poe! This one is floating on the "Isle of Riches" platform. That means you could wait until this moment, and complete the Flight-by-Fowl minigame for all items (including the Poe) on the isle. Whatever your decision, an easy way to reach the Poe is to fly above the isle, then plummet down with your Iron Boots. Defeat the Poe as usual.

Poe Soul

You got the **Poe Soul**! Collect one from each Poe you defeat! Poe Soul #20 of 60.

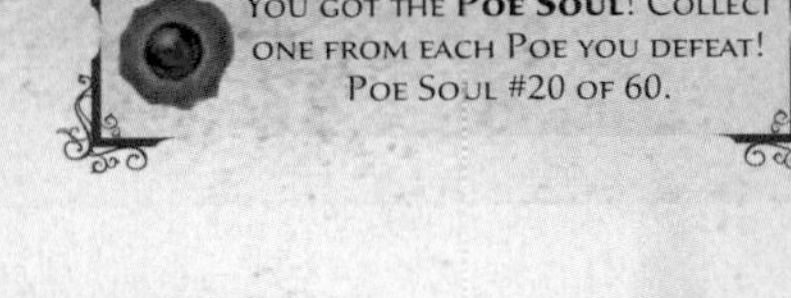

Tip: Congratulations! You've collected the souls of 20 Imp Poes! You can now return to Jovani at any time to claim your prize. The walkthrough mentions the optimal time to try this.

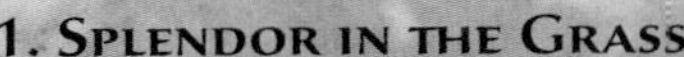

Missing Links

1. Splendor in the Grass

You may not have spotted this tiny island near the jetty to Fyer's hut, but you should cut the grass here for Rupees and Hearts. There's a Rupee dig spot here, too!

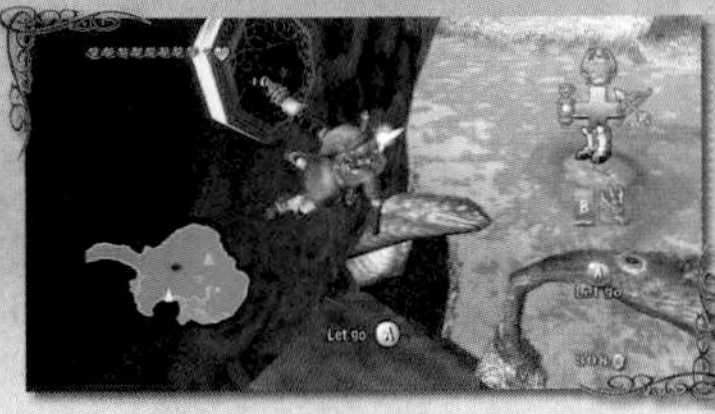

➤ If you haven't already, take the time to Clawshot up to the ledges and ornate overhang of the Spirit Cave, where the two chests (#27 with purple Rupee, and #28 with orange Rupee) can be secured with your new weapon. The real adventurers would have flown here earlier, as the walkthrough mentions!

➤ The final area you can explore again is the massive southeastern tower, which you can optionally climb. You meet an old man named Auru (who you spotted in the bar when you balanced across the rope as a wolf). He reckons this tower is part of the plague of evil, and a visit to the Gerudo Mesa is in order. Don't agree yet; visit Telma first!

The Great Hyrule (and Poe) Hunt: Great Hylian Bridge Area

➤ Now ride south, toward Faron Province, passing under the giant tree roots, and crossing the small wooden bridge. Stop Epona at this point, and scan the left wall, where there's a Bomb Rock to explode. Behind it is a Clawshot medallion. Propel to it, turn and look across the gap in the rock wall, and Bomb Arrow a second rock.

➤ There's a Clawshot medallion here, too. Propel across again, and then once more to another medallion on a small ledge overlooking the wooden bridge.

Poe Soul #21

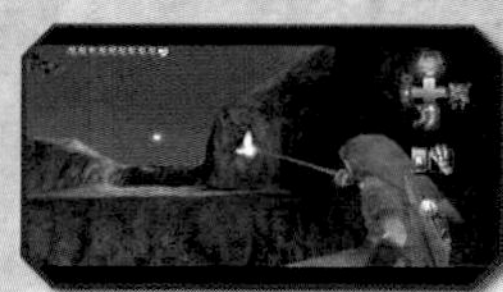

Use the Clawshot to reach this ledge, and then immediately transform into a wolf. Remove a Poe up here and add him to your collection of souls.

Poe Soul
You got the **Poe Soul**! Collect one from each Poe you defeat! Poe Soul #21 of 60.

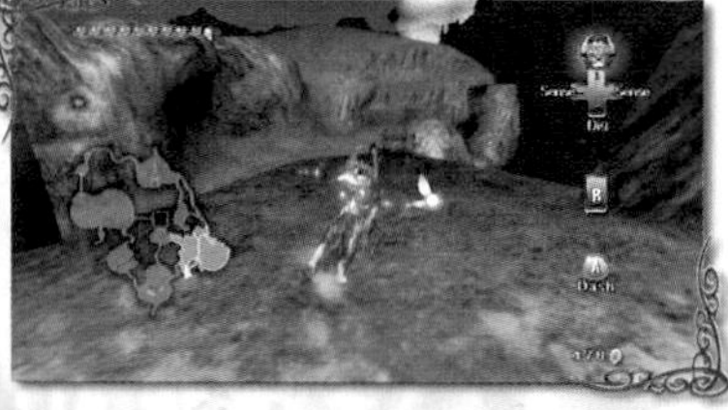

➤ When the Imp Poe is defeated, you can search this area. First open the chest on the ledge edge, and claim the purple Rupee inside.

Overworld Chest #57: Purple Rupee (50)

Dig Cavern #7

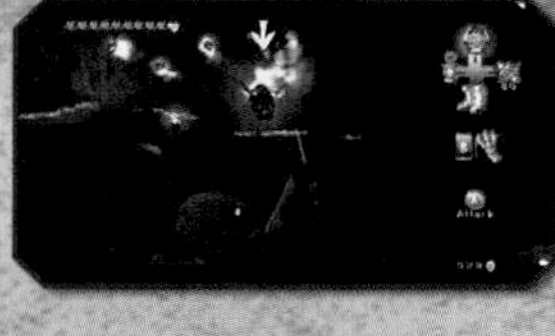

There's a circle of grass (which you can obtain arrows and Hearts from) in the small alcove away from the ledge edge. Inside the circle is a dig spot leading to the most fearsome cavern yet! This is the lair of the Bubbles!

Methodically dispatch the different types of Bubbles. Once the final screaming skull has been defeated, a chest appears on the opposite side of the chamber. Be sure you've smashed the pots, and cut the grass, then open the chest for a rare Rupee!

Overworld Chest #58: Orange Rupee (100)

Bubble, Fire Bubble, Ice Bubble

Threat Meter

These giant skull heads feature flapping wings protruding from each side. You've met these dark denizens on your travels before. Clobber them quickly with a spin attack if you're surrounded. Fight single Bubbles with simple slashes, but watch out for Fire Bubbles (as their damage can destroy wooden shields) and Ice Bubbles, that can freeze you. Attack at range with a Bomb Arrow or regular arrows, and don't try a finishing move on a skull that's been struck and is lying on the floor. They usually hop, and you'll pierce the ground instead.

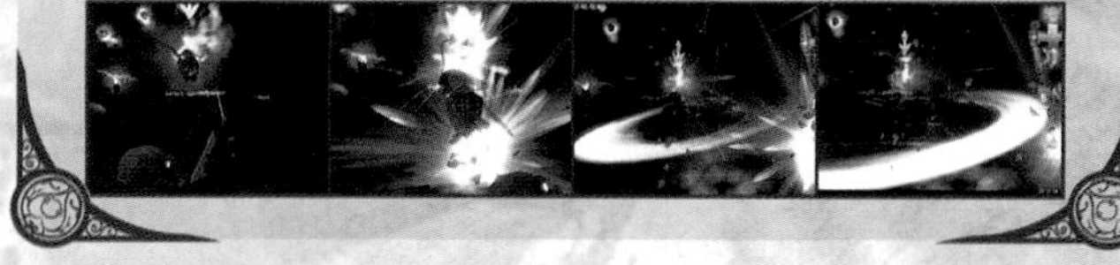

➤ Enough time has passed for you to return to the southern Castle Town gate, and check out the Goron's drilling technique. It is impressive, and you can move easily between here and the Hyrule Field to the south, adjacent to Faron Woods.

Enemies Encountered

Imp Poe

Shell Blade

Bubble

Fire Bubble

Ice Bubble

Gor Ebizo

Malo

Malver

Jovani

Purlo

Task 6: Obtain the Magic Armor

The Great Hyrule (and Poe) Hunt: Making Donations and Magic Armor

◄ Return to the Malo Mart in Kakariko Village, and speak with Gor Ebizo to donate the last of the 2,000 Rupees (or 200 Rupees if you helped build the bridge). Malo tells you to visit the new shop, once he's set up.

You're advised to build the bridge linking Hyrule Field to Castle Town (west) for the following reasons:

- You can easily reach Castle Town now, from Kakariko Village.
- You receive a reward for helping the Gorons out.
- The Magic Armor and other discounted items are not available until you donate to the financing, and this works out cheaper in the long run.

Tip: Your total donation to finance Malo's town store is 200 Rupees, not 2,000. Cost without repairing the bridge: 2,000 Rupees (and a later opening of the store). Cost with repairing the bridge: 1,200 Rupees (1,000 for the bridge, 200 for the store).

When you leave Kakariko Village and head into your next area (either after warping or riding), expect an appearance by The Postman. He has a letter from Malo, who's making you a special offer of Magic Armor in the grand opening special (limit one). That was quick work!

Letter #8
You got Letter #8: "Heroes, come together!" by Malo Mart.

◄ Race to the storefront where Chudley's Emporium once stood. Malo's mug is plastered all over the place, and the previously snooty attendant welcomes you warmly. Step right up!

▲ Once inside, it's like being in one giant party! Groovy music is playing, patrons are excited, and the previously uppity Chudley has been transformed into the wacky costumed Malver, who's more than happy to sell you the same wares as before, but at an incredible discount!

Store

Malver's Marvelous Market—Malo Mart Castle Branch

Item	Name	Old Price	New Price!	Effect
	Arrows (10)	2,000 Rupees	5 Rupees	!Nice Deal! Light, safe, and accurate! Equip these and you will NOT be sorry!
	Blue Potion	10,000 Rupees	50 Rupees	!Act Now! A restorative elixir recommended for those who do not feel 100%. (Requires an empty Bottle.)
	Red Potion	3,000 Rupees	15 Rupees	!Feature! Just one Bottle is the perfect pick-me-up! (Requires an empty Bottle.)
	Bombs	3,000 Rupees	45 Rupees	!Blast Deal! Made by Barnes Co. (set of 30). Only Malo Mart can deliver these savings!
	Water Bombs	6,000 Rupees	45 Rupees	!Big Deal! For aquatic defense (set of 15). No one can beat this price!
	Pocket Bombling	9,000 Rupees	30 Rupees	!Boom Deal! These endangered creatures have been successfully propagated! This is a special 10-Bombling set!
	Magic Armor	100,000 Rupees	598 Rupees	!Special! This is quite a bargain when you think of how valuable your life is. What's a few Rupees to stay alive?

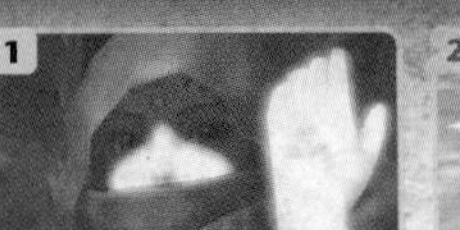

The Magic Armor

The Magic Armor is the finest armor money can buy, but you're going to need a constant supply of Rupees to keep wearing it! The armor basically works like this:

- Put it on, and you're completely invincible!
- However, every second you wear the armor, it magically sucks Rupees from your wallet.
- This means you must have a plentiful supply of Rupees! Why?
- Because when you run out of money, your suit becomes almost immobile. Take it off at once.
- Put this armor away and use it only when facing the fiercest enemies; the walkthrough will recommend when.
- You don't need to worry about maxing out your Wallet when raiding treasure chests any more! Simply put the armor on, reduce the Rupees until the large denomination Rupee you just found can fit, and take the armor off again.

The Magic Armor offers invincibility, but at a price! Head back to Kakariko Village, and you can dance with the Gorons!

Magic Armor

You got the **Magic Armor**!

◄ Purchase whatever you need, and return here as soon as you can with enough funds to purchase that Magic Armor (you also need the Big Wallet from Princess Agitha before you can amass the 598 Rupees it costs to buy it). If you need to scrape together enough funds, head on over to the many other places in town and continue progress at the tent, Agitha, and Jovani's. Head to the western part of the city, and locate the cat-filled alley outside Jovani's house.

◄ Transform into the wolf (in this area—don't scare the townsfolk!), and then burrow in the corner on the other side of the signpost. You appear in the treasure-filled room as you did before and everything is the same. Go over and speak with Jovani.

Jovani before the Poe hunt, and afterward: Gengle is now no longer solid gold, and Jovani is gold, but no longer frozen!

➤ Jovani begins to move! The 20 Poes you've collected have allowed him mobility. However, he's still golden. To help you on your way, he offers you **the most potent healing potion in the land!** Use this to restore **all Hearts and briefly boost attack strength.** Apparently there's more of this if you investigate a **cave** on the eastern edge of Gerudo Desert.

Tip: This cave Jovani speaks of is the Cave of Ordeals, and an adventure into this fearsome place should not be undertaken lightly!

Great Fairy's Tears

You got the **Great Fairy's Tears**! This sacred water contains the Great Fairy's prayers.

▲ Now head toward the tent on the same stretch of road as Agitha and Fanadi's places. Step inside and speak to Purlo. Now that you have the **Clawshot**, you can effectively dominate the "STAR Tent" minigame!

Characters Encountered

Kili, Hanna, Misha

Purlo

STAR Tent Minigame

Level 1: Easy

The trick to winning the first level of the "STAR Tent" minigame lies in using a secret weapon: the Clawshot! Steel mesh encases the entire arena, making the whole place into one giant Clawshot medallion. The moment the buzzer sounds, fire and latch onto the steel mesh above the first platform to quickly reach the top, snagging the first star in the process.

Immediately drop down onto the platform, then run and jump onto the platform to the right to collect your second star.

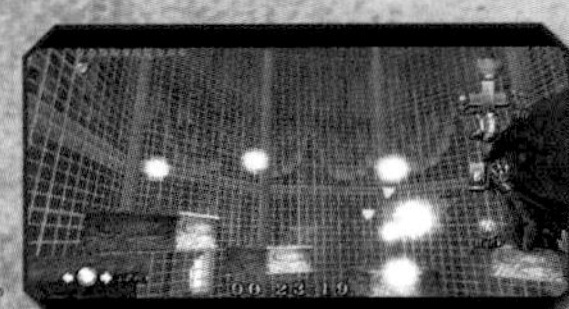

Quickly aim the Clawshot toward the platform that's directly across the arena and then fire to zip across, nabbing a whole row of pink stars in the process. Listen to the ladies cheer!

After landing on the far platform, turn either left or right and jump up the stepped platforms to claim another white star.

You guessed it: aim the Clawshot at the far platform across the arena and then fire to collect a neat row of white and blue stars. The girls can't get enough!

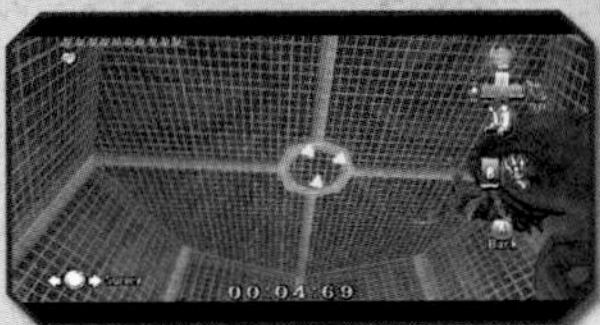

Finally, aim straight up at the ceiling and fire the Clawshot at the central circle. The moment you reach the top, let go to fall straight down the center of the arena, collecting the final line of stars. Well done!

When you finish the first stage within the time limit, Purlo grudgingly congratulates you. It seems he won't be taking you for a ride this time! He's a man of his word, too, and he offers you this excellent prize. Purlo has another level of this game for you to try, but it requires the Double Clawshot! Return here with that when you find it!

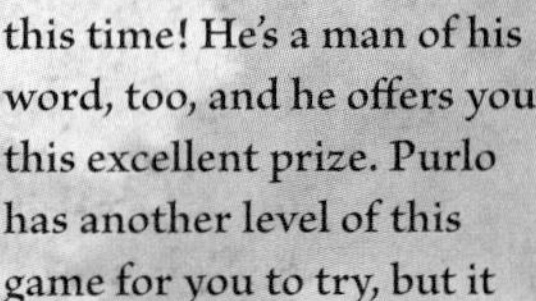

Big Quiver

You got the **Big Quiver**! It can hold up to 60 arrows!

Tip: You can double your available arrows and Bomb Arrows with this handy Big Quiver! Be sure to stock up on bombs and arrows at the Castle Town Malo Mart!

Missing Links

1. A Fan Favorite!

Once you complete this level of the "STAR Tent" minigame, head outside, and watch as Kili, Hanna, and Misha shriek and swoon over you! They drop three Hearts, then skip away, disappearing en route to the fountain.

Task 7: Continue the Hunt, Enter the Gerudo Desert

The Great Hyrule (and Poe) Hunt: North Hyrule Field

Now continue to locate dig caverns across Hyrule, and learn where new monstrous entities are roaming. Begin in the north Hyrule Field, and you'll see that Lizalfoses are patrolling the path here. Use the tactics you tried during Dungeon 3, or bite and hang on if you're in wolf form.

1 

2 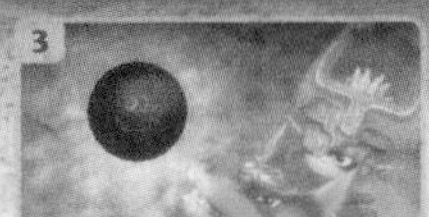

3 

4 

5 

6

Dig Cavern #8

Find the dig spot in this part of the field, and scramble down into another dig cavern. This has a few Baba Serpents to tackle, but remain in wolf form because the real reason for entering this place is to defeat the two Poes hiding here. Slay the Baba Serpents first. Then deal with the two Imp Poes. Then smash any pots and slice any grass you wish, and leave. Your only other prizes are some Deku Nuts!

Poe Soul #22

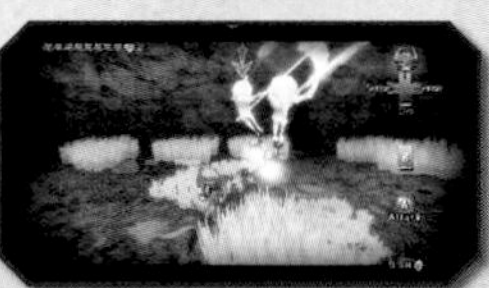

Defeat either Imp Poe by randomly targeting one and leaping, or trying to catch both in Midna's area-attack.

Poe Soul

You got the **Poe Soul**! Collect one from each Poe you defeat! Poe Soul #22 of 60.

Poe Soul #23

Even if one Poe is already prone, finish the other to make grabbing the souls easier.

Poe Soul

You got the **Poe Soul**! Collect one from each Poe you defeat! Poe Soul #23 of 60.

Dig Cavern #9

Your next dig cavern is in the same area, at this circle of grass. Drop down and immediately transform into Link. This chamber is filled with eight Red, and eight Blue Chus! This is a great place to stock up on the Red and Blue Potions you can scoop from them once you dispatch them.

Dig Cavern #9 (cont'd)

If you wait too long, the Blue and Red Chus merge into a giant Purple Chu that takes a very long time to dispatch! Try constantly Z targeting and slicing about to defeat multiple Chus, but don't waste time bottling the Purple Chu, as the health benefits are random, and sometimes harmful. Optionally strike some pottery and grass for Rupees and Hearts, then leave via the lit stone.

Red Chu Jelly

You got some **Red Chu Jelly**!

Blue Chu Jelly

You got some **Blue Chu Jelly**!

Purple Chu Jelly

You got some **Purple Chu Jelly**!

Poe Soul #24

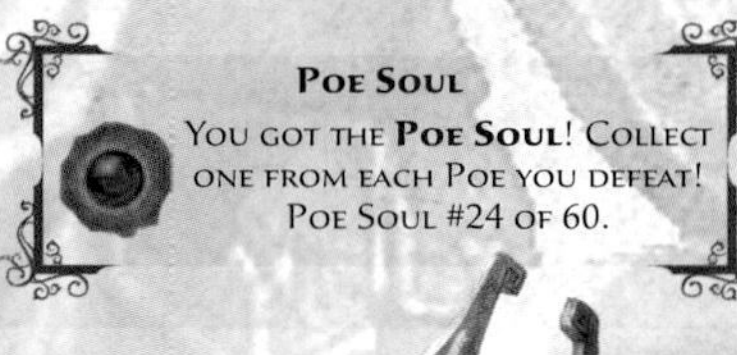

While you're still in the North Hyrule Field, wait at the bridge over the river for night to fall, and target another Poe that wanders the middle of the bridge. Add him to your collection.

Poe Soul

You got the **Poe Soul**! Collect one from each Poe you defeat! Poe Soul #24 of 60.

Enemies Encountered

Lizalfos (Axe-tail)

Baba Serpent

Imp Poe

Chu (Blue, Red, and Purple)

Task #7
Continue the Hunt, Enter the Gerudo Desert

The Great Hyrule (and Poe) Hunt: Western and Eastern Castle Town Gates

Poe Soul #25

Leave the North Hyrule Field, and journey to this gate, either via the large flat field, or through Castle Town. Once the Bulblins at the gate are defeated, watch for an incoming Kargarok, then leap and pounce on the Poe wafting around on the bridge.

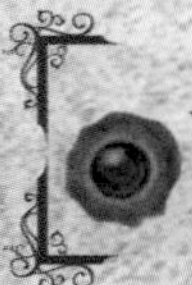

Poe Soul
You got the **Poe Soul**! Collect one from each Poe you defeat!
Poe Soul #25 of 60.

➤ Now warp to eastern Hyrule Field (outside Castle Town) and dash around this area. Helmasaurs are now roaming the landscape. They are difficult prey as a wolf, but not as a human.

Dig Cavern #10

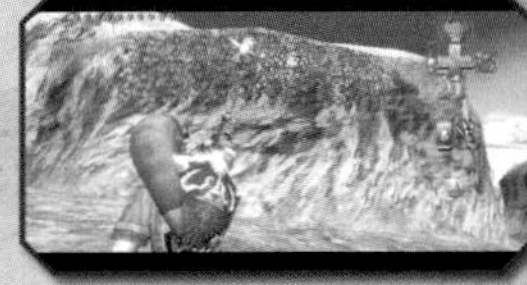

While you're in this part of the field, near the Castle Gate, look up at the vine-covered ledge on the outer rock wall, near where you caught a Golden Bug earlier. Use your Clawshot to propel up to the ledge here. At the end is a ring of stones. These can be thrown for Rupees, but the interesting area is the dig spot the stones surrounded. Drop in.

Immediately change to Link, and defend yourself against four rampaging Helmasaurs! Stand near the wall and scoop the armor off each with your Clawshot, then slay them. Concentrate on one Helmasaur at a time. When the last one keels over, open the chest that appears. Then leave after smashing pots and cutting grass for Rupees and Hearts.

Overworld Chest #59: Orange Rupee (100)

Poe Soul #26

The next Poe on your list should be the fellow floating about the amphitheater in this field, just over the rise. With a view of Lake Hylia in the distance, head down the steps, tackle the Bulblin Warrior, then drag the soul out of the Poe.

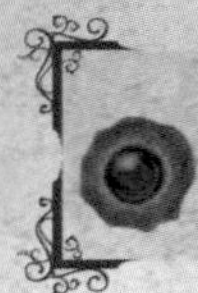

Poe Soul
You got the **Poe Soul**! Collect one from each Poe you defeat!
Poe Soul #26 of 60.

The Great Hyrule (and Poe) Hunt: Zora's Domain and River

Poe Soul #27

Warp to Zora's Domain, and take a plunge down into the waterfall pool, before swimming between the rocks. Trot up the winding grass ramp, and locate another Poe in these parts, near where you found a Twilit Parasite earlier.

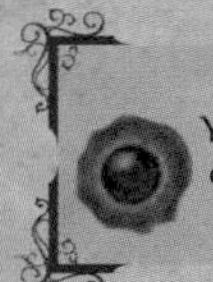

Poe Soul
You got the **Poe Soul**! Collect one from each Poe you defeat!
Poe Soul #27 of 60.

Poe Soul #28

While you're in Zora's Domain, move around to the entrance to Snowpeak, then use Midna to jump to the area behind the waterfall. Another Poe is lurking here, and he's easy to miss. Tackle him, and then dig for a Rupee at his location.

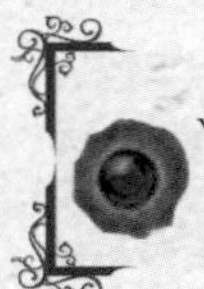

Poe Soul
You got the **Poe Soul**! Collect one from each Poe you defeat!
Poe Soul #28 of 60.

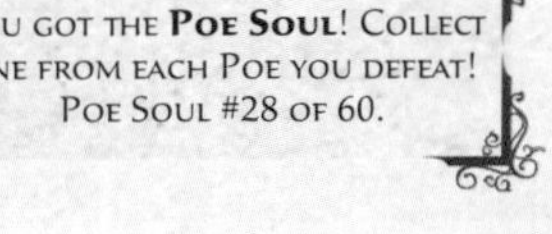

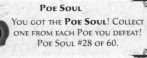

Poe Soul #29

Warp to Upper Zora River, and then find the small area of grass next to the torch-lit tunnel. Fight the current and swim across, then defeat the Poe on the small hill here.

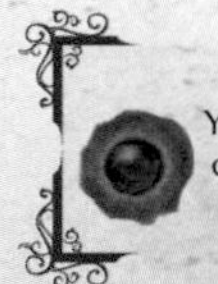

Poe Soul

You got the **Poe Soul**! Collect one from each Poe you defeat! Poe Soul #29 of 60.

The Great Hyrule (and Poe) Hunt: Bridge of Eldin

◀ Now warp up to the Bridge of Eldin near the large flat field. You can now obtain another chest (or save for later if you're full of Rupees). Stand at the north end of the bridge, and face south. Look up at the tiny vine on the north entrance, and Clawshot here. Then hand-over-hand to the opposite end of the entrance, where an impressively well hidden chest can be pillaged!

Overworld Chest #60: Orange Rupee (100)

▲ Now that you've cleared the bridge of goods, it's time to investigate the ledge where you plucked a Golden Bug earlier. Now that you have the Clawshot, shoot it at the medallion on the rock wall, and propel to this ledge. Run to the end, and enter the hole. You're about to step into the Lava Cavern!

Lava Cavern

You can practically feel the heat rolling off of this hostile place the moment you step inside. Smash the crates and barrels near the Lava Cavern's entrance for a Heart and some arrows, the latter of which soon come in handy.

Walk to the end of the metal ledge and have a look around. You're at the top of a tall, cylindrical cavern, and the bottom is filled with lava. Needless to say, you don't want to fall into that stuff!

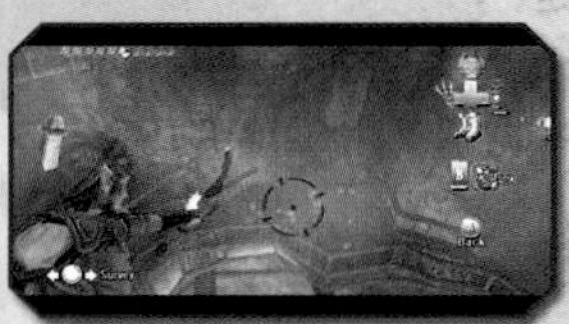

It's time to put those arrows to good use. Spy a collection of Bulblins on a ledge below you and defeat them all from here. Bomb Arrows work best if you've got explosives to spare.

The magnetic beam that's directly beneath you is your ticket to reaching the cavern's next ledge. Face south and line up with the beam, then run and jump off the ledge. Quickly don your Iron Boots as you plummet downward. When you pass through the beam, you're drawn over to the south ledge!

If you wasted the Bulblins from the top ledge, there won't be much for you to worry about here save a few Fire Keeses. If you decided to conserve your arrows, you'll find that the Master Sword makes short work of Bulblins, anyway!

Use the next magnetic beam to reach the east ledge below. Do this just as you did before: line up carefully with the beam, then run and jump toward it, equipping the Iron Boots in midair to avoid splashing into the molten substance below.

Enemies Encountered

Kargarok

Bulblin

Imp Poe

Helmasaur

Fire Keese

Characters Encountered

Midna

Postman

Telma

Auru

Rusl

Shad

Ashei

Fyer

Lava Cavern (cont'd)

En guard! An ill-tempered Dodongo lurks down here. Block its fiery breath with your shield, circle around to its backside and slice into its tail to quickly defeat it. Afterward, open the nearby Overworld chest for a shiny red Rupee (20).

Overworld Chest #61: Red Rupee (20)

Don't bother leaping off of the south portion of this ledge; there's nothing below you but a lake of scorching lava. You're attacked by a couple of Keeses here as well, so there's little point in venturing over here.

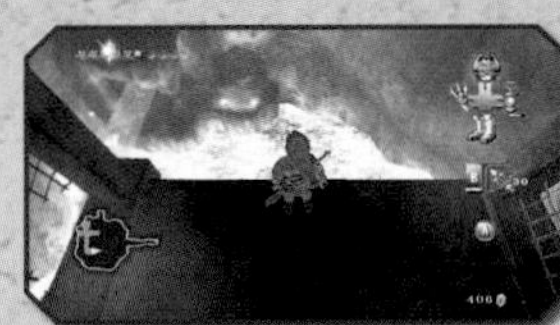

Instead, return to the middle of the ledge and face east to locate yet another magnetic beam below. This one leads to the final ledge, where the real treasure awaits! Make a running jump and slap on those Iron Boots as soon as you're airborne.

Made it! That was quite a ride, but you're not out of danger just yet; another fearsome Dodongo protects the treasure chest down here. Hack away at its tail until the Dodongo is no more, then open the chest to claim Piece of Heart #25.

Overworld Chest #62: Piece of Heart #25

Piece of Heart
You got a **Piece of Heart**! You collected **five pieces** and formed a new Heart Container: Piece of Heart #25 of 45.

But wait, there's more! Did you notice two unlit torches nearby? Use your Lantern to light them both and reveal a chest that contains an orange Rupee (100). Not bad for a day's work!

Overworld Chest #63: Orange Rupee (100)

You've raided this place dry, so it's time to move on. Head through the nearby tunnel to exit the Lava Cavern and return to Hyrule Field (Bridge of Eldin). You've got a bit of climbing to do from here. Clawshot along the line of medallions to return to the surface (or have Midna warp you to a new location).

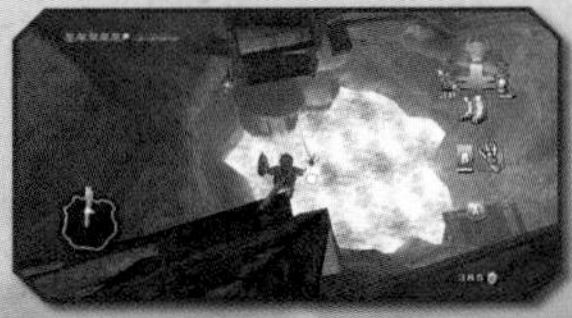

Cut to the Good Part: To significantly shorten your trip through the Lava Cavern, walk halfway out onto the first metal ledge (at the very top of the cavern), then face east and look straight down. From here, you can spot the magnetic beam far below you, near the bottom of the cavern.

Line yourself up with the magnetic beam, then run and jump off ledge. Equip your Iron Boots as you fall; when you pass through the beam, you're automatically sucked over to the cavern's lowest ledge! Pop open Treasure Chest #61 and #62, then exit the cavern through the nearby tunnel. (You miss the red Rupee from Treasure Chest #60 if you take this shortcut.)

Tip

Journey to Gerudo Mesa: An Audience at Telma's

◄ When you're completely finished with your Overworld antics and hunting, follow the clues the Postman gave you, and head to Telma's bar to meet the three adventurers she told you about.

The Postman is here, sitting in a quiet corner, mumbling about ordering some meat! Leave him to it. Where do you think he'll pop up next?

◄ Head over to Telma, she insists you speak to a man named Auru. If you climbed the massive tower in Lake Hylia, you saw him at the top! Run to the

back room, where three adventurous sorts are poring over a map. Speak to each of them.

Author Note

That map looks familiar! Cartographers have recreated a complete version for your adventuring pleasure and attached it to this book!

➤ Who is this masked man? It's Rusl, who says nothing if you speak to him once, but speak again. He takes off his helm and talks about Uli, the fact that the children are safe, and that he's joined the resistance as he wants to help the cause.

➤ Talk to the brown-haired fellow opposite Rusl. This is Shad, and he's formidable—at book reading! He isn't the combative type, but he can give you a quick history lesson. Here goes:

- He's entranced by the sky beings known as Oocca.
- According to legend, Hyrule was made by the Hylians, who, as we all know, are the closest race to the gods.
- But long ago, a fable mentions a race even closer to the gods, and that these creatures made the Hylians.

Note

- They created the people of Hylia, and a new capital, a floating city in the heavens!
- They dwelt there, and some still believe the race lives there still.

➤ The final adventurer is a girl named Ashei, who grew up in the mountains, and was trained as a warrior. She's light on social graces, but handy in a scrap or fracas! She's researching Snowpeak mountains currently.

Journey to Gerudo Mesa: Creating a Cannon

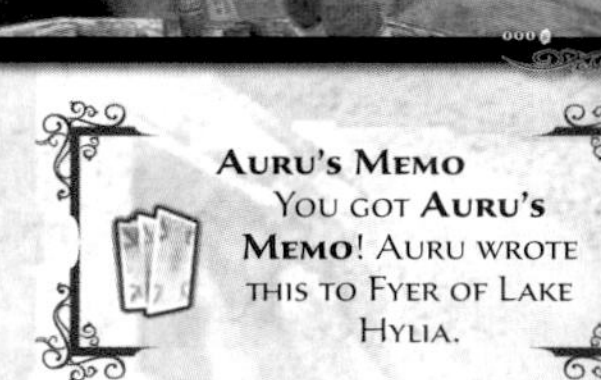

➤ Leave Telma's Bar, and journey to Lake Hylia. Once there, ascend the long tower in the southeast corner, and meet Auru. Agree "yes" that you're going to the desert, and you receive a memo to take to Fyer, at his cannon hut.

Auru's Memo
You got **Auru's Memo**! Auru wrote this to Fyer of Lake Hylia.

➤ Head down to the old coot at the cannon hut (dive from the tower if you dare!), and present him with **Auru's Memo**. Fyer mumbles something about an **Oasis flight**, and asks if you really want to go. Answer "yes" unless you have more hunting to do here.

Enemies Encountered

Dodongo

Moldorm

Task 8: Locate the Entrance to Arbiter's Grounds

Adventuring in Gerudo Desert

*Midna tells you the magic wielders who tried to rule the sacred realm were banished to the Twilight Realm, and she's a descendant of that tribe! The realm was peaceful until Zant arrived and obtained a great power. There is only one **link** left between here and her home, accessed via the Mirror of Twilight. It must be found!*

Caution

The Gerudo Mesa is a featureless landscape, with looming dunes and craggy rocks, but the biggest concern isn't the burrowing Moldorms, but the fissures between the sand. Leap in here, and you won't find the bottom! You're placed back on the sand with an energy Heart missing.

Midna

Moldorm

Threat Meter

The creatures that are constantly burrowing about your feet then leaping out at you for a quick bite are nasty little Moldorms. They shouldn't be a major concern, as you can simply ignore them. Fighting them with a sword is simply impossible; they're too fast to keep track of. Dispatch them by Z targeting, firing your Clawshot and pulling them out of the ground, and then slashing them with your sword.

Begin a methodical search of the Gerudo desert, avoiding the leaping Moldorms and looking for this small rock island in the map's southwestern corner. Aim your Clawshot at the tree, zip up and drop down, then open the small chest.

Overworld Chest #64: Red Rupee (20)

Golden Bug: Male Dayfly

Collection: 22 (of 24)

Your insect collection of Golden Bugs is almost full, but a quick journey almost directly east of your starting position allows you to watch a Male Dayfly fluttering about on the sand. Search this area, then pick him up. No equipment is needed except a steady hand!

Male Dayfly

You caught a **Male Dayfly**! Bug fans love that golden color!

Poe Soul #30

From your starting location, look northward during the night time, and you'll spot a floating lamp. There's a Poe out here in this southwestern edge of the desert! Snag his soul as you reach him.

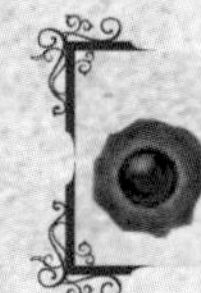

Poe Soul

You got the **Poe Soul**! Collect one from each Poe you defeat! Poe Soul #30 of 60.

Dig Cavern #11

The Imp Poe was floating above three skulls. Smash them and then burrow down into a dig cavern.

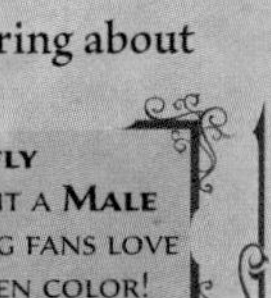

Immediately transform to Link. You need your sword available to cut down a quartet of nasty Skulltulas! Shield attack, and leap to skewer them.

Once every Skulltula is defeated, begin to methodically destroy all the hanging pots (with your Clawshot) and pottery on the ground. Then head over to the chest that appeared, and claim your beautiful Rupee prize.

Overworld Chest #65: Orange Rupee (100)

Head north from the Golden Bug location, and look for a horseshoe-shaped area of rock lying flat on the sand, with a small rock jutting from it. Look closer, and you'll see a chest to pry open for arrows.

Overworld Chest #66: Arrows (10)

Arrows

You got **arrows (10)**! Use arrows to shoot far-off foes!

Skirt the fissure, just east of your starting location, and notice a small piece of solid flat ground. Follow the fissure around to a small chest, and claim your prize!

Overworld Chest #67: Red Rupee (20)

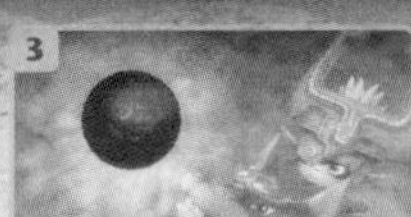

Golden Bug: Female Dayfly

Collection: 23 (of 24)

Continue eastward until you locate this trench, and peer along the southern wall, where your penultimate Golden Bug is nestled. Transform into Link, and wait for the Moldorms to leap at you. Defeat them with your Clawshot, then aim at the bug, and bring it down to your feet. You may need to follow it slowly because it likes to fly off and up for a little while.

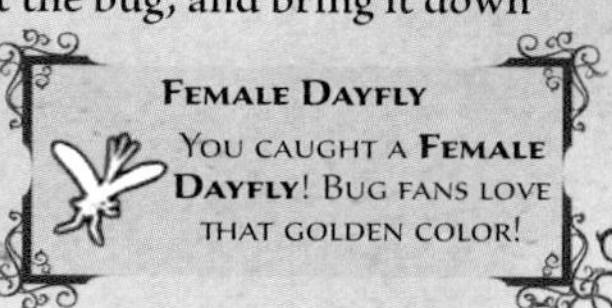

Female Dayfly

You caught a **Female Dayfly**! Bug fans love that golden color!

Continue to progress to the southeastern corner of the desert. You can begin to explore the other areas, but it's better to reach this spot, as it will soon be a warp portal. Run to the strange flat rock with the stone bridge section sticking up from it!

Step to the lowest part of the flat rock plateau, and gaze up at the gnarled tree. Clawshot up to it, and then wait and listen for a fluttering noise. This is the sound of a Peahat, a floating creature that's completely harmless. It's used exclusively for ferrying yourself to and from difficult-to-reach places. Clawshot onto it, then drop down to the plateau.

Warp Portal

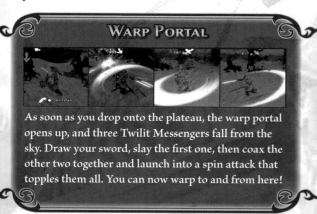

As soon as you drop onto the plateau, the warp portal opens up, and three Twilit Messengers fall from the sky. Draw your sword, slay the first one, then coax the other two together and launch into a spin attack that topples them all. You can now warp to and from here!

Poe Soul #31

Once the warp portal exists, move to the far end of the plateau, and climb the small ledges to the upper plateau area. At the top, transform to a wolf, and defeat the Poe waiting up here.

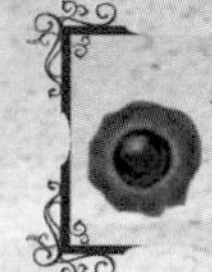

Poe Soul

You got the **Poe Soul**! Collect one from each Poe you defeat! Poe Soul #31 of 60.

As the sun rises over the Gerudo Mesa, you can take in the spectacular view, and odd stone protuberance. Midna asks you what it is and where you should warp it to. This is the missing portion of the **Bridge of Eldin**, so choose that area of your map.

Midna departs from you, and summons her giant orange arm to lift the gigantic piece of stonework, and you both warp to the Bridge of Eldin. Midna lowers the piece, and the bridge is repaired! You can now cross easily between the Hyrule Field (west) and the northern rocky paths.

Missing Links

1. Skull Smashing in the Desert

The Gerudo Mesa is littered with skulls, like the ones you've smashed before. If you're after a Rupee or Heart, search these out; they're usually near a rock or an alcove. If you see three in a group, chances are there's a dig spot here.

Enemies Encountered

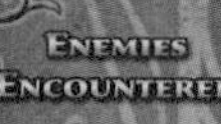

Moldorm

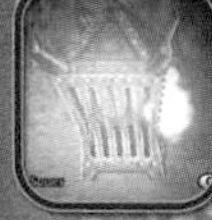

Imp Poe

Skulltula

Twilit Messenger

Missing Links (cont'd)

When you Warp back to the desert, you'll notice an indent where the bridge was protruding. Look closer, and you'll see these are steps leading down to the dreaded **Cave of Ordeals**! Refer to the walkthrough for more details, but for now, don't enter the cave. You need more specialized equipment to complete it!

Drop down from the warp portal area, but stay on the higher ground, and search the eastern side of the desert. Notice a bottomless fissure with a chest on the other side. Stand precisely at this point, and wait for a Peahat to hover over you. Then Clawshot onto it.

Ride the Peahat over the fissure, and then drop down to the sand below. Run to the chest on the solid rock bed, and open it. Return to the main desert using the same Peahat-riding technique.

Overworld Chest #68: Purple Rupee (50)

Dig Cavern #12

Run around the rock that's semicircled by a low rock wall north of the warp portal point, and dig between the three skulls. You discover a dig cavern here. Change immediately to Link, and engage three Chus in battle! Fight a Red, Blue, and Purple Chu. Chu Jelly is this cavern's prize; there's no chest. If you want Red or Blue Chu Jelly, don't just run around madly. Instead, stop as you drop, keep to one side, and coax one Chu at a time toward you. Don't let them merge, or all your Chu Jelly will be purple! When you're ready to leave, smash pots, cut grass, and lift small rocks for Rupees and Hearts, then stand in the light.

Advancing on the Arbiter's Grounds: Bulblin Encampment

◄ It's time to head north, and investigate the last part of the Gerudo Desert. As you head north, a small encampment of Bulblins spot you, and two Bullbos rear up as their riders head in to intercept your path.

▲ These Bulblin Riders are a real menace, as they charge you on their horned steeds and toss you onto the sand. They also shoot at you with flaming arrows. Fight fire with fire! Immediately switch to Bomb Arrows and Z target each foe as they charge. Quickly let rip, and they crumple with a single strike! No Bomb Arrows? Then use quick dodging and your sword's spin attack.

▲ When one or both of the Bulblin Riders have been removed from their mounts, you can inspect the encampment. There's still a trio of lookouts on the tall towers, so either shoot them from extreme range (using the Hawkeye and arrows), or better yet, ignore their arrows and clamber aboard a Bullbo! Control him just as you would Epona. However, when you want a burst of speed, be sure you're ready for a slightly uncontrollable gallop! The good news is that this extra speed smashes any defenses in the encampment! Try charging through all six of the lookout towers.

◄ Your plan isn't subtle, but it's simple: Use your Bullbo and charge every single wooden structure in the desert! This includes wooden barricades, blockades, and of course, lookout towers. This way, you can access the chests that the towers were built on top of. Single Bulblin Riders appear from time to time during your rampage. Stop, and fire at them from Bullbo-back, or get off for a better aim.

◄ Complete your destruction with this wooden barricade, between the two stone towers. This marks the entrance to the Arbiter's Grounds, and it is your next area to investigate—after you ransack the chests outside, of course!

Advancing on the Arbiter's Grounds: Encampment Search

► Begin your search by smashing this small barricade on either side of a rock, in the northern wall of the encampment area, west of the stone pillars. Secure the Rupee from the chest inside.

Overworld Chest #69: Red Rupee (20)

◄ Now do the same at the small barricade on either side of a rock on the northern wall to the east of the stone pillars. There's another red Rupee (20) in this chest.

Overworld Chest #70: Red Rupee (20)

◄ Now return to the completely devastated encampment, and pry open three chests around the campfire. The left, middle, and right all give you different goods:

Overworld Chest #71: Purple Rupee (50)

Overworld Chest #72: Red Rupee (20)

Overworld Chest #73: Arrows (10)

▲ Your final exploration of Gerudo Mesa begins now! As evening falls, search the remaining area for any outstanding Poes, chests, and Peahat access points. Start by smashing the barricade to the south, allowing you back up into the upper two-thirds of the desert. Check the following information for available Poes and chests, and when you're done, head north through the two stone pillars.

Poe Soul #32

Now that the encampment is clear of Bulblins, take a Bullbo to the far western edge of the lower part of the desert (don't enter the southern exit), and up a large, shallow sand ramp. At the top is a gnarled tree. Clawshot up here, then run along a thin strip of sand to a wayward Poe. Tackle him!

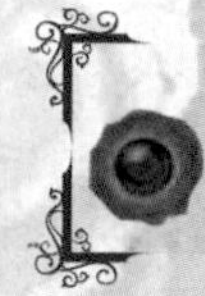

Poe Soul

You got the **Poe Soul**! Collect one from each Poe you defeat! Poe Soul #32 of 60.

Dig Cavern #13

The Imp Poe (#32) that you just defeated was guarding a dig cavern flanked by three skulls. Smash them, then burrow down into a cavern surrounded by Bomb Rocks! Watch out; there are two more Imp Poes down here!

Enemies Encountered

Chu (Red, Blue, and Purple)

Bulblin Rider

Bullbo

Imp Poe

Characters Encountered

Hero's Shade

Poes #33 and #34

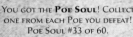

Stay in wolf form, and back up to a wall, with your sense view on. As the Imp Poes float your way, target one and jump to attack, or perform the area-attack courtesy of Midna. If the Poes disappear behind the rocks, wait for them to reappear, or change to Link, and destroy a few of the rocks, then transform back.

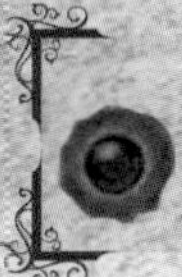

Poe Soul

You got the **Poe Soul**! Collect one from each Poe you defeat! Poe Soul #33 of 60.

Poe Soul

You got the **Poe Soul**! Collect one from each Poe you defeat! Poe Soul #34 of 60.

As well as the pottery to pulverize and small rocks to lift, there is a chest to uncover, too! Destroy all the remaining Bomb Rocks, then bring out your Lantern. Light the three unlit torches. They are hidden in the shadows, and the last one is on the raised rock where the chest appears.

Overworld Chest #74: Orange Rupee (100)

Note: During your romp through the desert, you may notice a small structure with platforms, and an odd owl statue. Ignore this for the moment because you can't claim this chest yet.

Advancing on the Arbiter's Grounds: Outer Keep and Dungeon Entrance

When you've exhausted your search for items in the Gerudo Desert, head north past the two stone pillars, and up the four small ledge steps. Take a left.

Run around to a dead end where crates, barrels, pots, and a small chest are found. There are Rupees in everything, except the chest! The arrows are perhaps an indication of what's ahead.

Overworld Chest #75: Arrows (10)

Poe Soul #35

Now head right. Providing you summoned the White Wolf, he's waiting patiently for you, although you won't access his knowledge until you're in human form. Instead, run to the right, to a second dead end, and fight an Imp Poe. Watch for Leevers emerging and surrounding you! Stop, wait until they merge, then spin attack or use Midna's area-attack. Now defeat the Poe. There are three dig spots to unearth here, too, for a Rupee and Hearts. Find more Rupees in the crates.

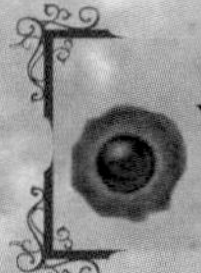

Poe Soul

You got the **Poe Soul**! Collect one from each Poe you defeat! Poe Soul #35 of 60.

Hidden Skill #5: Mortal Draw

Your exploration of this area shouldn't end with the Poe hunt. The White Wolf waits for you to come, sword in hand! He growls at you, and you draw your sword. He pounces! You awaken in the ghostly ether. The Hero's Shade forms, and asks you if you wish to learn your next skill. The answer is yes!

First, your teacher ensures that you learned the previous Hidden Skill correctly, and he asks you to show him you've mastered the **helm splitter.** Simply Ⓩ target and move your Nunchuk forward for a shield attack, then tap Ⓐ to perform the helm splitter, when indicated.

"Very well!" utters the warrior, "let the **mortal draw** be hewn into your mind!" This technique is used to counter creatures who have already learned to guard against shield attacks and back slices. Sheathe your sword so you're unguarded, then look at, but **do not** Ⓩ-target the enemy. As they draw near, press Ⓐ and execute the mortal draw! Now you try it:

Hidden Skill #5: Mortal Draw (cont'd)

Mortal Draw: Wait for an enemy without your sword drawn, and without targeting it. Wait for a foe to near you, then quickly press Ⓐ.

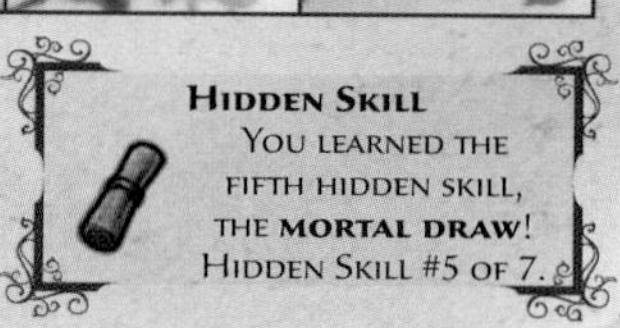

Hidden Skill
You learned the fifth hidden skill, the **Mortal Draw**! Hidden Skill #5 of 7.

◀ With your Hidden Skill learned, head up the middle passage, and you arrive at the keep outside the Arbiter's Grounds. Up ahead, you can see the glow of a campfire. For the moment though, skirt the initial sandy area. There are crates to smash for Hearts.

➤ Step through the first defensive wall, but stay alert. You can see a tower behind the main gate, and it has Bulblin Archers atop them. Not for long! Bring out your **Hero's Bow** and tag the lookout. Then run to the next wall and smash more crates for Rupees.

➤ Enter the gate and turn left. Inspect the area under the tower, where there's multiple scenery items to break. Check the corner for a small chest containing arrows.

Overworld Chest #76:
Arrows (10)

◀ Turn right, and stand near the arched entrance. Ahead by the torch, you can see a Bulblin guard. Either run in and attack, or bring out your bow. A Bomb Arrow provides an impressive takedown! Now run forward, trudge up the thick sand, and turn left. Try your new Hidden Skill out on this Bulblin!

➤ As you step forward into the encampment, you hear a Bulblin yell. Another lookout has spotted you, so bring out the Hero's Bow again, and hide behind the wall. Press Ⓩ so you can move and fire while manually aiming, and then sidestep out, fire, and duck back before his arrows strike you. Then clear the area. A barrel in the corner contains arrows, and crates in the opposite corner contain Rupees.

◀ Head past both the small tents, into the back walled area of the keep. Multiple Bulblins now attack you, so ignore your new Hidden Skill technique and begin to spin attack as if your life depended on it—because it does! After around six Bulblins fall, check this back area for crates. Some in the corner have Rupees inside.

Run down the sandy ramp to the middle of this exterior area, looking for lit torches, and a Bulblin standing guard at a large but rickety gate. He's guarding a lock. Bring out your sword and attack. Another lookout spots you and sounds the alarm.

◀ You can step back, and aim at the lookout on the opposite side of this area with your arrows, or just retreat to the sandy ramp and defeat another six or so Bulblins in combat. Prioritize the one or two archers on the ground. As the battle rages on, more Bulblins appear, but keep your shield up and tackle them one at a time. Finally, return to the locked gate, remove any more Bulblins from the ground, then shoot the lookout archer.

◀ Move to the western side of this keep, and ransack the crates and barrels to the south for Hearts and Rupees. Then turn north, and run to a Bulblin who's happily roasting a Bullbo on a spit. Wipe the smile off his face with some dazzling swordplay! He's joined by another four Bulblins with an archer, so tackle them all with your weapon of choice. Afterward, locate the Small Key that the first Bulblin was carrying.

Small Key
You got a **Small Key**! This opens a locked door, but only in this area.

Enemies Encountered

Imp Poe

Leever

White Wolfos

Bulblin Archer

Task #8
Locate the Entrance to Arbiter's Grounds

➤ After combat, inspect this area for crates and other scenery you can destroy for Rupees and Hearts. Check the southeastern corner for a chest there. More interesting is the roasting Bullbo, which looks succulent enough to eat! Target and whack the carcass with your sword, and a Piece of Heart spins out!

Overworld Chest #77: Purple Rupee (50)

Piece of Heart
You got a **Piece of Heart**! Collect **five pieces** to form a new Heart Container. Piece of Heart #26 of 45.

◄ You've now defeated most of the Bulblins and ransacked the entire area except for the central tent beyond the rickety gate. Head there now, using the Small Key you found on the Bullbo-roasting Bulblin, and enter this tent. As you spot a Bullbo in the corner, a pair of red eyes appear out of the darkness. King Bulblin is back again, and this time he's carrying a giant axe!

King Bulblin

Threat Meter

Step 1: The King of the Bulblins carries an axe that's three times the size you are, so avoiding that is a high priority. To begin with, try some test sword slashing, and you'll discover King Bulblin use the axe to guard, too. All frontal attacks are useless.

The massive King Bulblin is incredibly strong, but you're incredibly nimble! Get behind him and hack!

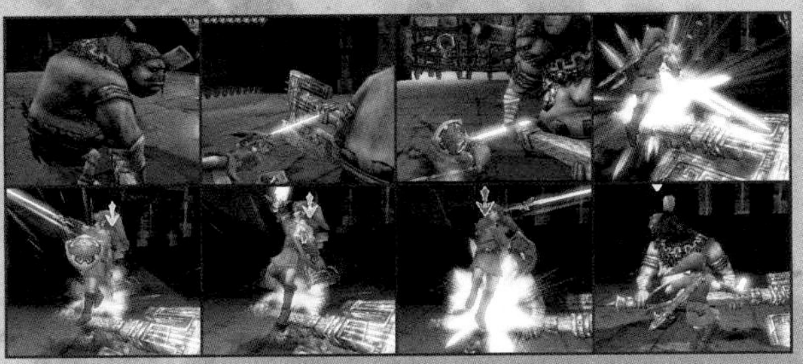

Step 2: The only way you'll take down King Bulblin this time is to Z-target him, and roll around behind him to his exposed back. Make a 180-degree roll around, and then begin to slash, or better yet (as shown), execute the back slice Hidden Skill. Do this continuously. You could roll then spin attack if you haven't mastered the back slice yet.

After three or four good back strikes, King Bulblin drops his axe, and dejectedly shuffles away from you. You win this time! He closes a gate behind him, and you suddenly realize it's a trap! The tent has caught fire! Quickly race to the waiting Bullbo, steer him toward the rickety gate, and ram your way out of here!

Poe Soul #36

The Bullbo takes you to the steps of Arbiter's Grounds, but don't venture forth just yet. Turn around, and backtrack through the walled corridor you just smashed through, back to King Bulblin's tent. There's a cunningly hidden Poe here.

Poe Soul
You got the **Poe Soul**! Collect one from each Poe you defeat! Poe Soul #36 of 60.

➤ You can enter the Arbiter's Grounds now, as the area is almost completely free of foes. Move to the base of the ornate steps and run up them. The large and imposing entrance to **Dungeon 4: Arbiter's Grounds** is just ahead!

1 2 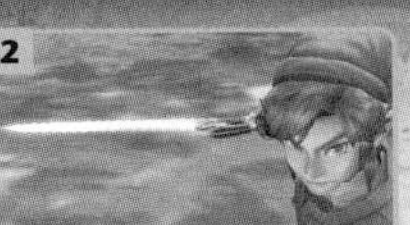 3 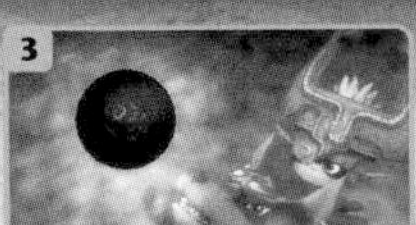 4  5  6 

Poe Soul #37

The area is almost completely free of foes, but not Poes! Climb up the steps, and then look to your right. In the fenced stone courtyard is another Poe. Grab him before you enter the dungeon.

Poe Soul
You got the **Poe Soul**! Collect one from each Poe you defeat! Poe Soul #37 of 60.

➤ Do one last investigation. Move to the opposite courtyard from the Poe (you can smash the skulls for Hearts), and check the two unlit torches. Bring out your Lantern, and light them both. A chest forms between them. Ransack this, then it's finally time for the Arbiter's Grounds!

Overworld Chest #78:
Purple Rupee (50)

Enemies Encountered

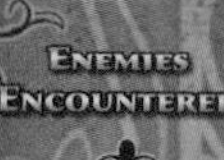

Bulblin Warrior

Bulblin Archer

Lord Bullbo

King Bulblin

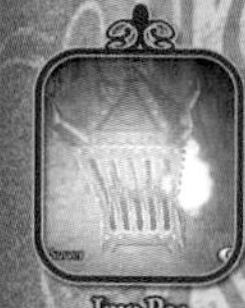
Imp Poe

The Great Hylian Fish Hunt

Now that you've spent some time exploring, you might wish to know where the best spots to catch fish are throughout the Kingdom. Well, you've come to the right chart!

Greengills

Location	Item(s) Required	First Chance to Get	Notes
Ordona Province; Ordon Village	Fishing Rod	Before Dungeon 1: Forest Temple	In deep water
Lanayru Province; Fishing Hole	Fishing Rod	After Dungeon 2: Goron Mines (After saving Lanayru)	All over the place
Lanayru Province; Lake Hylia	Fishing Rod	After Dungeon 2: Goron Mines (After saving Lanayru)	Outside Lanayru Spring
Lanayru Province; Lake Hylia (Lanayru Shrine)	Fishing Rod	After Dungeon 2: Goron Mines (After saving Lanayru)	In main pool
Lanayru Province; Upper Zora's River	Fishing Rod	After Dungeon 2: Goron Mines (After saving Lanayru)	In deep water (rough current)
Eldin Province; Kakariko Village (Graveyard)	Fishing Rod	After Dungeon 2: Goron Mines (After escorting Prince Ralis to Kakariko Village)	West pool

Hylian Loaches

Location	Item(s) Required	First Chance to Get	Notes
Lanayru Province; Fishing Hole	Fishing Rod	After Dungeon 2: Goron Mines (After saving Lanayru)	North-most alcove, in lilypads
Lanayru Province; Lake Hylia (Lanayru Shrine)	Fishing Rod	After Dungeon 2: Goron Mines (After saving Lanayru)	In main pool
Eldin Province; Kakariko Village (Graveyard)	Fishing Rod	After Dungeon 2: Goron Mines (After escorting Prince Ralis to Kakariko Village)	West pool

Hylian Pike

Location	Item(s) Required	First Chance to Get	Notes
Lanayru Province; Fishing Hole	Fishing Rod	After Dungeon 2: Goron Mines (After saving Lanayru)	Near arch-shaped rock formation
Lanayru Province; Hyrule Field (North)	Fishing Rod	After Dungeon 2: Goron Mines (After saving Lanayru)	Southeast corner of central pool
Lanayru Province; Lake Hylia	Fishing Rod	After Dungeon 2: Goron Mines (After saving Lanayru)	Outside Lanayru Spring
Lanayru Province; Upper Zora's River	Fishing Rod	After Dungeon 2: Goron Mines (After saving Lanayru)	In deep water (rough current)

Hyrule Bass

Location	Item(s) Required	First Chance to Get	Notes
Lanayru Province; Fishing Hole	Fishing Rod	After Dungeon 2: Goron Mines (After saving Lanayru)	North of west wooden bridge

Ordona Catfish

Location	Item(s) Required	First Chance to Get	Notes
Ordona Province; Ordon Village	Fishing Rod	Before Dungeon 1: Forest Temple	In deep water
Lanayru Province; Fishing Hole	Fishing Rod	After Dungeon 2: Goron Mines (After saving Lanayru)	Near west wooden bridge

Dungeon 4: Arbiter's Grounds

1F

2F

3F

4F

1 Pg 287
Gain Entrance to Grand Ceremonial Hallway

2 Pg 290
Locate and Defeat the Second Poe

3 Pg 291
Locate and Defeat the Third Poe

4 Pg 293
Locate and Defeat Fourth and Final Poe

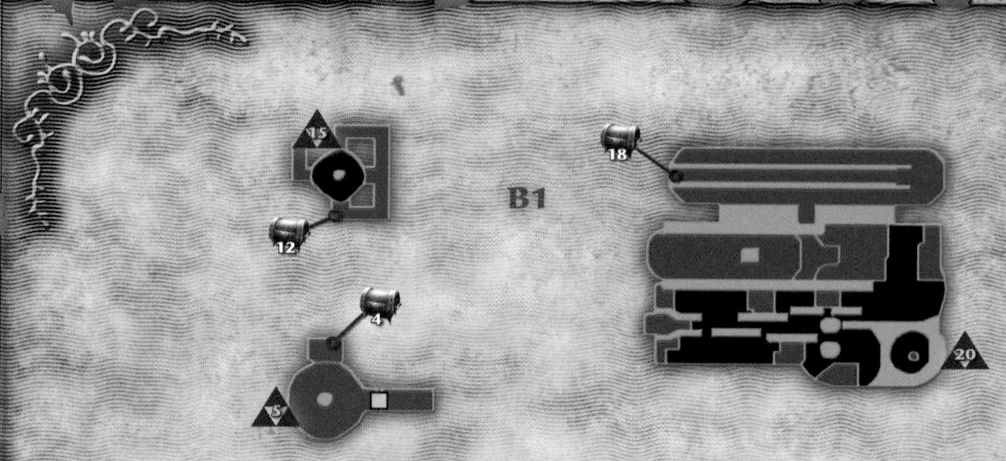

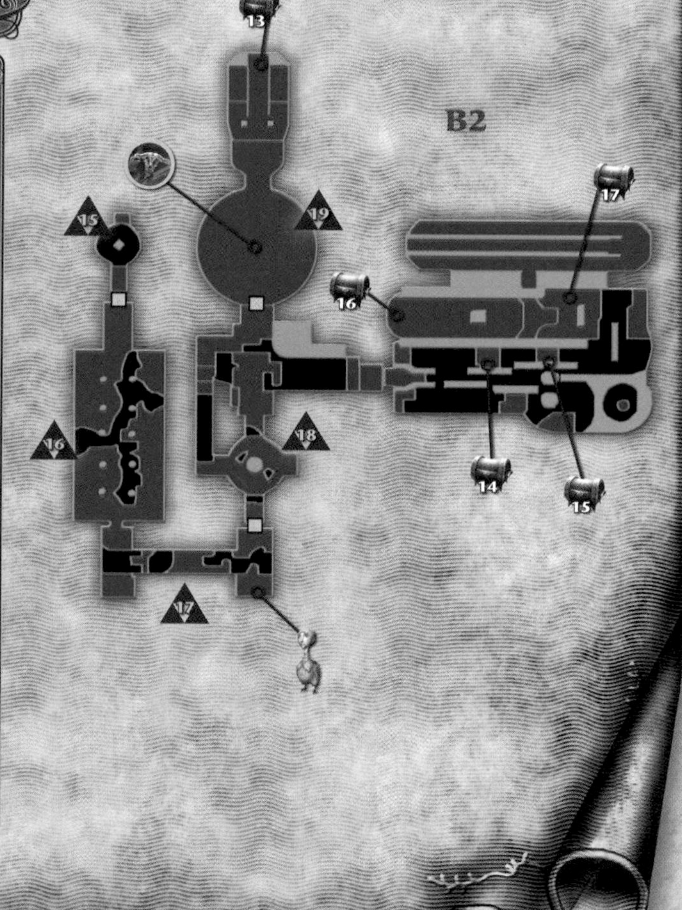

Legend

Room Legend

1. Entrance and Sand Traps
2. Entry Crossroads
3. Stalkin Ambush Room
4. Grand Ceremonial Hallway
5. Circular Rotation Chamber
6. Lantern Chamber
7. Chandelier Chamber and Statue Room
8. The Ruined Corridor
9. Lair of the Ghoul Rat
10. Chandelier Chamber II
11. Star Chamber of the Stalfos
12. Shrine to the Snake Deity
13. Chamber of the Fourth Poe
14. Spinner Cog Room
15. Circular Pit
16. Spike and Sand Trap
17. Poison Mite Alley
18. Chamber of Traps
19. The Domain of Death Sword
20. Spinner's Paradise
21. Big Key Passage
22. The Great Spiral Shaft
23. Boss Battle! Twilit Fossil Stallord

Number of Treasure Chests: 19

1. Small Key (1st)
2. Piece of Heart #27 (of 45)
3. Dungeon Map
4. Small Key (2nd)
5. Compass
6. Small Key (3rd)
7. Small Key (4th)
8. Red Rupee (20)
9. Red Rupee (20)
10. Bombs (5)
11. Bombs (5)
12. Small Key (5th)
13. Spinner
14. Bombs (10)
15. Red Rupee (20)
16. Piece of Heart #28 (of 45)
17. Yellow Rupee (10)
18. Yellow Rupee (10)
19. Big Key

Items

- Fairy in a Bottle
- Poe Scent
- Ooccoo
- Lantern Oil Bowl

Characters

- Death Sword
- Twilit Fossil Stallord

5 — Defeat Death Sword; Obtain Spinner — Pg 295

6 — Obtain the Big Key — Pg 298

7 — Ascend the Great Spiral Shaft — Pg 300

8 — Defeat Twilit Fossil Stallord — Pg 300

CHARACTERS ENCOUNTERED

Midna

A Link to the Present

Ordon Sword, Master Sword

Heart Pieces: 1 (26 Total)

Wooden Shield, Hylian Shield

Hero's Clothes, Zora Armor, Magic Armor

Big Wallet, Big Quiver

Golden Bugs: 23 (of 24), Hidden Skills: 5 (of 7)

Ilia's Scent, Poe Souls 37 (of 60)

Fish Journal, Letters 8 (of 16)

Dungeon Denizens

Characters

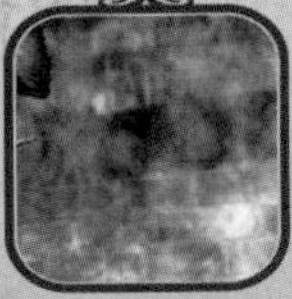

Midna

Ooccoo

Enemies

Bubble, Fire Bubble, Stalkin

Poison Mite

Poe

Redead

Ghoul Rat

Stalfos

Staltroop

Zant

Bosses

Mid Boss: Death Sword

Big Boss: Twilit Fossil Stallord

Items to Obtain

Small Key (1st)

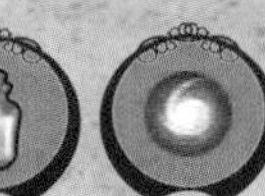
Lantern Oil

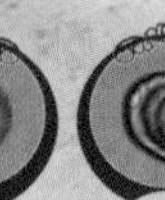
Poe's Scent

Piece of Heart #27 (of 45)

Dungeon Map, Small Key (2nd)

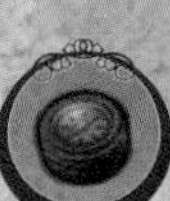
Compass

Small Key (3rd)

Small Key (4th)

Small Key (5th)

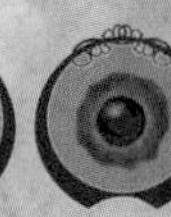
Poe Soul #41 (of 60)

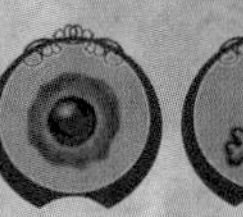

Small Key (6th)

Ooccoo

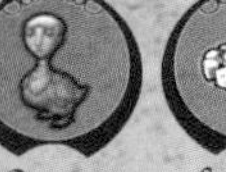
Spinner

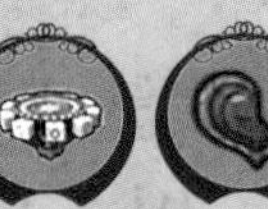
Piece of Heart #28 (of 45)

Big Key

Fairy in a Bottle

Heart Container #4

Items Already Acquired

Clawshot

Hero's Bow

Iron boots

Gale Boomerang

Lantern

Slingshot

Fishing Rod

Hawkeye

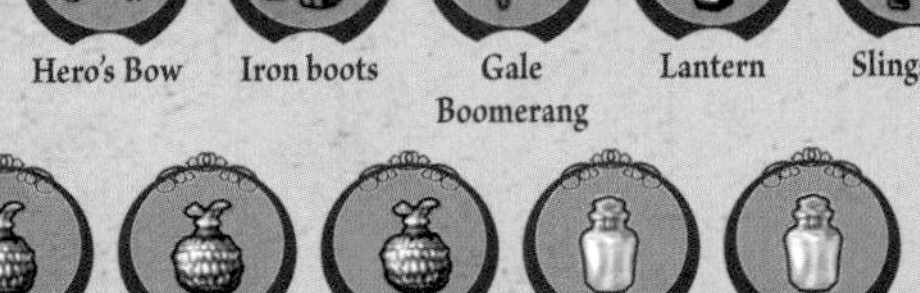

Bombs (Bag #1)

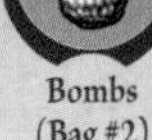
Bombs (Bag #2)

Bombs (Bag #3)

Bottle #1, Bottle #2

Bottle #3, Bottle #4

The Arbiter's Grounds: Overview

A dungeon half sunk into the Gerudo Desert holds the key to righting the wrongs of the twilight world, and Midna is determined to locate the Mirror of Twilight that's supposedly hidden inside. You should be more concerned with the sinking sands that suck you down. This dungeon is the home to four Poes. These priest-like ghoulish foes get added to your Jovani soul collection, but they also light the way to the second part of these catacombs. Then you must negotiate some fearsome new enemies, including the horrific Redead and Stalfos. Only after you defeat them, and a giant ethereal spirit carrying the biggest sword you've ever seen, can you obtain your next major item: the Spinner. Once you've figured out how to travel on this device, you'll use it to gain access to the final chamber: a gigantic pit, where the remains of a Stallord lies. Let's hope Zant doesn't arrive and hinder your progress....

Enemies Encountered

Moldorm

Task 1: Gain Entrance to the Grand Ceremonial Hallway

Chamber 1: Entrance and Sand Traps

Before you enter these decrepit catacombs, you might wish to bring along the following:

- A Bottle filled with a Blue Potion
- Your Hero's Bow positioned on ✚ so you can click it on and off quickly
- A Lantern and Gale Boomerang within easy access
- The Clawshot set as your main Ⓑ item
- The Hylian Shield bought from Kakariko Village
- The Magic Armor for rare occasions you may need it (buy it in Castle Town)

Tip

➤ Enter the massive squared-off entrance and head north down some steps. You appear in an ornate chamber. The ground has already given way, and two Moldorms are burrowing through the sand.

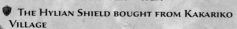

➤ Your best plan is to ignore these critters, but if you must defeat them, launch a Ⓩ targeted Clawshot to hook them and then slash away. Don't try this on the edge of a sand trap (as shown) or your slashes cause you to fall into the trap!

The whirling sand in the middle of this chamber is deadly! Wade in here, and you're sucked in to your doom. Then you must retry the room with one energy less.

Caution

Your movement is also impeded whenever you step on sand, and you'll slowly be sucked down into the sand. Keep moving, and use Link's form because he isn't as low to the ground as the wolf is. Head to flagstone areas as soon as you can!

➤ When you've finished looking over this entrance chamber scan the walls. Over on the right side is a Clawshot medallion. Use it and drop down.

You land on a jutting stone platform that's positioned above the sinking floor. If you fall off this platform, you can't make it back to the stone floor safely, so make every step count! Begin by smashing a few skulls; there's a Heart in it for you.

➤ Now turn and face the room's interior, and position the camera so you're facing the next floating platform directly and leap. Don't rush, or you might land right in the sand trap! From here, there are two other platforms. You can turn right, leap across, and ignore the platform in front of you, or take the long way around and jump to the outer platform. Smash the skull on the outer platform if you wish, then leap over to the section of firmer ground with the skulls on it.

Tip: You can transform into a wolf at any point during this dungeon exploration. You walk through the sand faster, but unfortunately you sink faster too!

From your stone floor with skulls, smash a few (for a Heart), then look across to the north. There's a gate ahead, so wade across the sand to it, and up onto the safer ground. But the gate is firmly sealed.

Turn and check out the chamber's northwestern corner. There's a chain to pull to open this gate, so wade past the skull stakes to another stone floor. Smash pots and skulls for Rupees and Hearts. Then watch as the earth stirs!

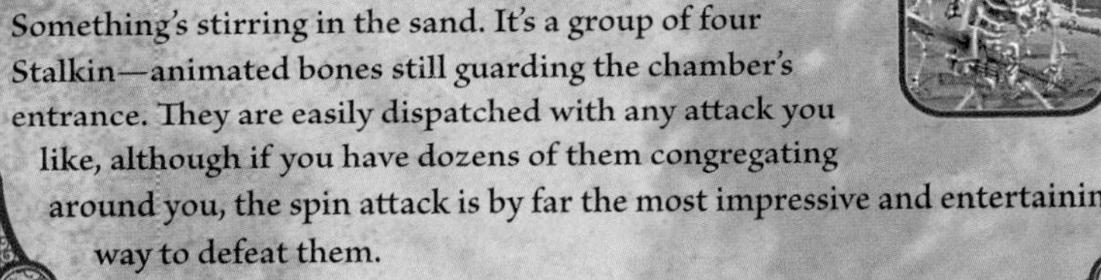

Stalkin

Threat Meter

Something's stirring in the sand. It's a group of four Stalkin—animated bones still guarding the chamber's entrance. They are easily dispatched with any attack you like, although if you have dozens of them congregating around you, the spin attack is by far the most impressive and entertaining way to defeat them.

Missing Links

1. Skull Smashing, and Pottery Pulverizing

Skulls and pots are scattered about the floor. Skulls usually give you green Rupees (1) and Hearts. The pots here reveal a blue Rupee (5).

Look at the chain tethered to the north wall. This opens the gate. Aim at it with your Clawshot, pull it in, then grab it and heave southward. The gate creaks open!

Chamber 2: Entry Crossroads

Pass through the open gate, climb up some steps, and stop at a crossroads junction. The door ahead is firmly locked. There's a small chamber to your right with a chest at the end.

Treasure Chest: Bring out your sword, and quickly destroy the wooden planks blocking the doorway, step into the chamber. Run along the right side onto a stone platform, then quickly cross the sand. Head up to the chest, clearing the skulls (and grabbing a Heart), and open it.

Treasure Chest #1: Small Key

Small Key

You got a **Small Key**! This opens a locked door, but only in this area.

Poison Mite

Threat Meter

As you reach the sand you're attacked by a swarm of disgusting Poison Mites. There are dozens of them! They don't harm you, but they slow you down, and if you're wading through sand, this can spell doom! Don't stop and fight or you'll sink! Struggle to solid ground then bring out your sword and execute a spin attack.

Or, you can shine a Lantern and the Mites retreat in fear, leaving you alone.

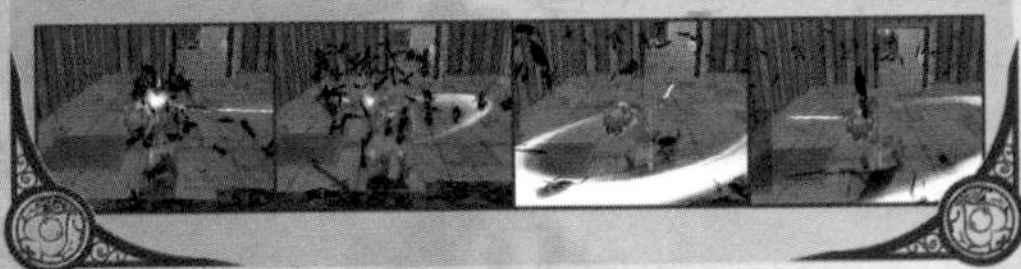

Run across from the chest chamber and check out the small alcove. Smash a couple of pots for Rupees, and inside you'll find a ceremonial bowl of lantern oil. You can return here at any time to refill your Lantern, and any empty Bottles. Only a Lantern's worth of oil is needed however. Now move to the door and unlock it.

Oil

You got **oil** in your Lantern!

Chamber 3: Stalkin Ambush Room

◄ The Lantern is necessary in this chamber, as portions of the floor are covered in sand to suck you down. Bring out the Lantern, and as you progress, you'll see disturbances in the sand. A whole squad of Stalkins rises up!

▲ This calls for a spectacular retaliation! Run around the stone floor areas of this room, coaxing Stalkins from the sand in the four different areas, and when all of them are almost upon you, execute a vicious spin attack. The entire room is filled with explosions and flying bones as you disintegrate them all!

▲ When the Stalkins explode, gather the Rupees and Hearts they expel, and look for skulls to smash for Hearts. Then follow the narrow stone floor paths and light torches on either side of the north door. Then enter the grand chamber to the north.

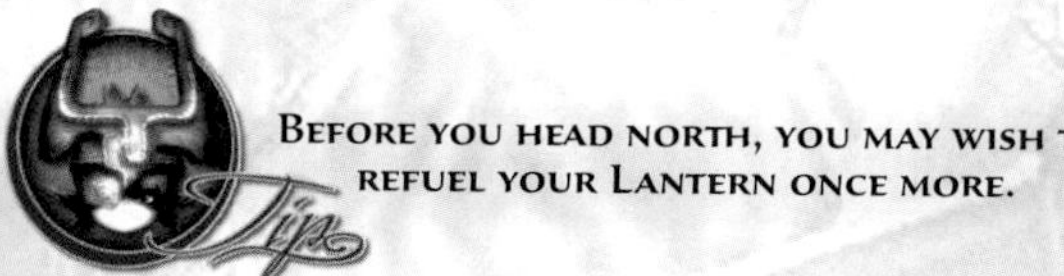

Tip: Before you head north, you may wish to refuel your Lantern once more.

Chamber 4: Grand Ceremonial Hallway

◄ You enter a grand hallway with doors to the left, right, and straight ahead. Flanked by statues, four large torches with the Hylian crest carved beneath them stand on either side of the exit door. Four lamps appear, the door closes, and the lamps circle you menacingly!

Poe

Threat Meter

Poes inhabit the same ghostly plane as Imp Poes, but these cowled figures are far more imposing! Defeat them using your wolf's biting attack, Z targeting, and then leaping on the Poe and biting it until the specter throws you off. Remember, you can only strike a Poe when they are glowing. Do this twice, and the Poe completely deflates, and you can claim another soul for Jovani.

Four fearsome fiends can be seen and attacked only with your keen senses. Grab these gruesome ghouls, and add their souls to your collection!

Poe Soul #38

Your next Poe is in this chamber, and he attacks you immediately! Retaliate and take his soul quickly, after some biting tactics instead of the regular leaping attacks or area-effect takedowns.

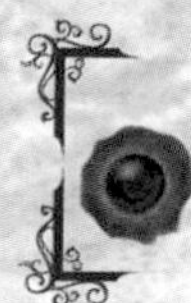

Poe Soul

You got the **Poe Soul**! Collect one from each Poe you defeat! Poe Soul #38 of 60.

Enemies Encountered

Stalkin

Poison Mite

Poe

Task #1

Gain Entrance to Grand Ceremonial Hallway

Poe's Scent

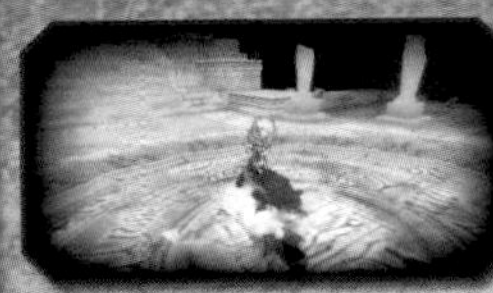

Once you've vanquished the first Poe the light of its lamp drifts and settles on one of the four ceremonial torches. However, if you sniff the area where the Poe departed, you'll discover a new scent.

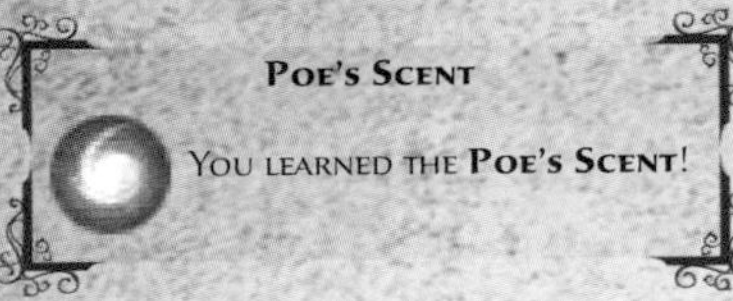

POE'S SCENT
YOU LEARNED THE POE'S SCENT!

Missing Links

1. Pottery Pulverizing

This chamber has three pots in the southern corners, with Rupees, Hearts, and arrows inside. There are also some skulls here; the ones in the western and northwestern parts hold a Heart.

➤ **Treasure Chest:** Before you sniff the air for more Poe trails, thoroughly inspect this area. Step to the western side, next to the main stairs, and peer into the gloom. There's a chest ahead, it's easiest to Clawshot there.

PIECE OF HEART
YOU GOT A **PIECE OF HEART**! COLLECT **THREE MORE** FOR ANOTHER FULL HEART CONTAINER. PIECE OF HEART #27 OF 45.

➤ Now that you're by the treasure chest, check the room out. Look at the sand falling from the upper level, and the large chandelier above you. Don't try wading back through the sand; aim at the medallion on the outer wall, and propel to this point instead.

➤ **Treasure Chest:** Move over to the opposite side of the staircase and draw your sword. Two Bubbles are flapping around so swipe them or bring them in with your Clawshot. Then walk north, onto the stone floor that sinks into the sand. Keep moving forward and you reach another chest. This contains the useful **Dungeon Map**. As before, use the Clawshot on an exterior wall medallion to avoid the sinking sand.

TREASURE CHEST #3:
DUNGEON MAP
DUNGEON MAP
YOU GOT THE DUNGEON MAP!

➤ Now follow the Poe's Scent trail around the chamber. It disappears into a small sandy opening in the stone floor. Dig at this point to uncover a buried handle with a chain attached. Pull the handle back, and a staircase appears in the floor! Although you can choose to open either the east or west door, the scent path is visible at this lower level. Descend.

Task 2: Locate and Defeat the Second Poe

Chamber 5: Circular Rotation Chamber (BF to 1F)

➤ Head down into the basement level of the Circular Rotation Chamber. In sense view, you can see that the Poe's Scent trail disappears up into a square hole in the ceiling. First, savage a Bubble. Then smash all pots and skulls for a few arrows and Rupees.

MAKE SURE YOU KNOW WHICH FLOOR YOU'RE ON, AS THIS CHAMBER LOOKS THE SAME ON MULTIPLE FLOORS!

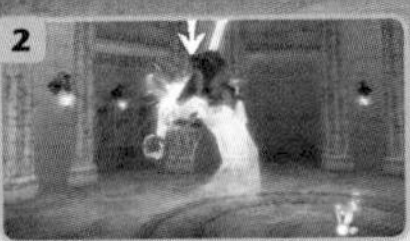

◄ Check the room thoroughly and you'll find a large stone lever on the central pillar. Shove this clockwise, and the entire room shifts, exposing a small antechamber in the north. Uh-oh! What's that?!

Redead

Threat Meter

The Redead, a mummified foe brought back to life, is a terrifying entity to behold. He attacks with a paralyzing scream, which stops you in your tracks. Then he cuts you down with a nasty sword pound. Step back, Ⓩ target, and then fire two Bomb Arrows into the monster. If you don't have any of Bomb Arrows, leap onto the corpse in wolf form, and bite it until it yields.

◄ **Treasure Chest:** The Redead was guarding a tiny chest. Inside is a **Small Key**, which you need to continue. Now look up through the gap in the ceiling. This has revolved too, and there's a Clawshot medallion up here. That way, you don't have to shift the entire room to leave. Propel yourself up into the first floor of this chamber, slice some Rats, and switch your sense view on.

Treasure Chest #4:
Small Key

Small Key
You got a **Small Key**! This opens a locked door, but only in this area.

Chamber 6: Lantern Chamber

Poe Soul #39

From this chamber, head north, and open an unlocked door while in wolf form. This leads to a Lantern Chamber with a few Bubbles to fight and some debris to smash for Hearts. Your larger concern, as the scent has led you straight here, is a Poe that's hiding. Look for the lamp in the east wall that's not attached and is bobbing slightly. Turn on your sense view, and bite!

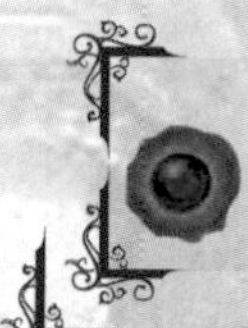

Poe Soul
You got the **Poe Soul**! Collect one from each Poe you defeat! Poe Soul #39 of 60.

Enemies Encountered

Poe

Bubble

Redead

Rat

Task 3: Locate and Defeat the Third Poe

Chamber 6: First Return to Circular Rotation Chamber (1F to BF), to First Return to Grand Ceremonial Hallway

◄ You must return to the Grand Ceremonial Hallway so the light can float into the ceremonial torch. Head south, back to the rotation chamber, and drop down to the basement level. Rotate the pillar and head up the stairs. Two torches of the four are now lit!

Chamber 5: Second Return to Circular Rotation Chamber (1F)

◄ Look around the hallway, and you'll see scent from the last two torches. Follow the trail that leads westward, back to the Circular Rotation Chamber. Dash around the pillar and then use the Small Key you found to open the locked door.

Chamber 7: Chandelier Chamber and Statue Room (1F to 2F)

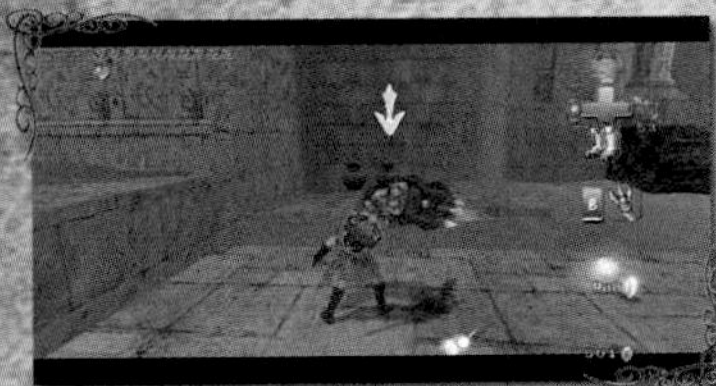

➤ Enter the large chamber and switch on your sense view. The Poe's Scent trails off to the south, through the entrance. Step forward and make a sweep of the area, smashing pots and skulls. Then use your Clawshot to extract the Moldorm from the sand so he won't bother you during the objective to come.

➤ Head north, to the series of small stone tile pieces, and proceed westward toward the low stone platform ahead. As you reach a gap in the sand, four spikes spring up. Stop and turn, and maneuver around these spikes as they lead you in an erratic course to the edge of the platform.

➤ Once on the platform, head to the cube-shaped cellblock blocking your path. Pull it back, then slot it into the gap between the upper stone platforms to the side. This reveals a Clawshot medallion, which you can use if you decide to return here.

➤ Now head up the steps, and your path is blocked by a giant chandelier. Turn right and climb up onto the upper stone platform. Ignore the nasty-looking spike log and locate the chain handle. Wrench the chain back until the chandelier has risen off the ground. You need to stand on the cube you just pushed to fully extend the chain.

➤ Make sure the chain is fully extended before you let go, or you won't have time to exit this chamber! As soon as you drop the chain, sprint up the steps and then run south and reach the stairs. Or better yet, stop in the middle of the walkway, in the lit circle, and let the chandelier drop around you. Then climb over it, and drop off. Battle up the stairs to the second floor.

➤ **Treasure Chest**: Battle to the top of the stairs, into a small chamber with a statue on a pedestal. Check the tiny southern alcove for a treasure chest. Open it to discover the Compass.

Treasure Chest #5: Compass

Compass
You got the **Compass**! This handy tool shows you where to find objects hidden in this dungeon.

➤ Head north, back to the statue and pedestal, and rotate it 90 degrees. The whole room moves, and a passageway to the east and west is revealed! The Poe's Scent drifts off to the east but don't follow it yet. Check the small dead end—or should that be Redead end? One of these feared foes shambles to life, attack with biting grapples as the wolf.

➤ **Treasure Chest**: Inspect the room thoroughly. Redeads usually drop a red Rupee (20), so steal that, then the arrows, Rupees, and Hearts from nearby pots. Finally, pry open the chest for another Small Key!

Treasure Chest #6: Small Key

Small Key
You got a **Small Key**! This opens a locked door, but only in this area.

Chamber 8: The Ruined Corridor (2F)

➤ Head back to the pedestal statue, and go around to the locked door in the opposite wall. Use the key and step through into a corridor with ruined floors. The scent wafts through here. Follow the corridor around, using your sword to defeat the Stalkins wobbling toward you. Turn the corner to face north, and you see a Redead behind these Stalkins, so keep your distance, retreating a little until all the Stalkins have come to you. Then aim and fire two Bomb Arrows at the Redead, or attack in wolf form. Continue around the next corner, and repeat the plan on a second Redead!

▲ When the tattered foes have fallen, smash pottery for items, and then stop for a moment. Keep your sense view on, and you'll see the Poe's Scent disappears into the floor. Dig to discover a handle. Pull that chain, and the entire adjacent wall slides back!

Poe Soul #40

This reveals the third Poe's hiding spot, which doesn't even appear on the map! Bare your fangs and attack! Once you defeat the Poe, he deflates, and the torch light returns to the Grand Ceremonial Hallway. Check this secret room for a pot with a Heart in it.

Poe Soul

You got the **Poe Soul**! Collect one from each Poe you defeat! Poe Soul #40 of 60.

Enemies Encountered

Moldorm

Redead

Stalkin

Poe

Ghoul Rat

Task 4: Locate and Defeat the Fourth and Final Poe

Chamber 9: Lair of the Ghoul Rat

◄ **Treasure Chest:** After that fraught fight, you need a breather, so head northward to the end of the corridor, and open the door. This leads to a circular room with a stepped area. Everything is eerily (and suspiciously) quiet! Smash a few skulls and pots then look south. There's a chest in the southern alcove.

Treasure Chest #7: Small Key

Small Key

You got a **Small Key**! This opens a locked door, but only in this area.

Ghoul Rat

Threat Meter

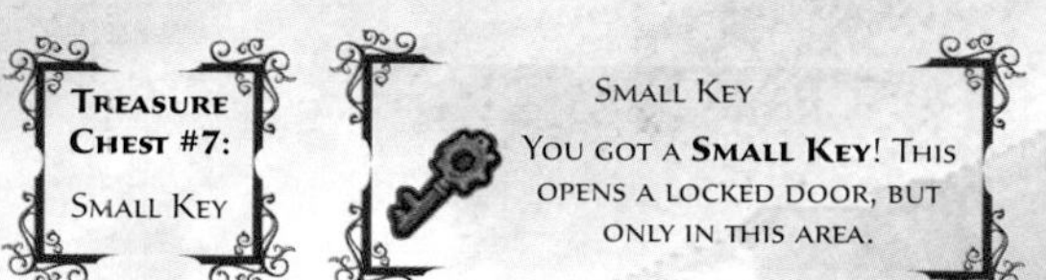

Step back into the center of the chamber, and you realize you're covered with gruesome Ghoul Rats. They don't actually harm you. They just slow you down, leaving you open to other creatures! Transform to the wolf, turn Senses on, and spin attack to shake them all off. Then pounce or bite to finish the stragglers.

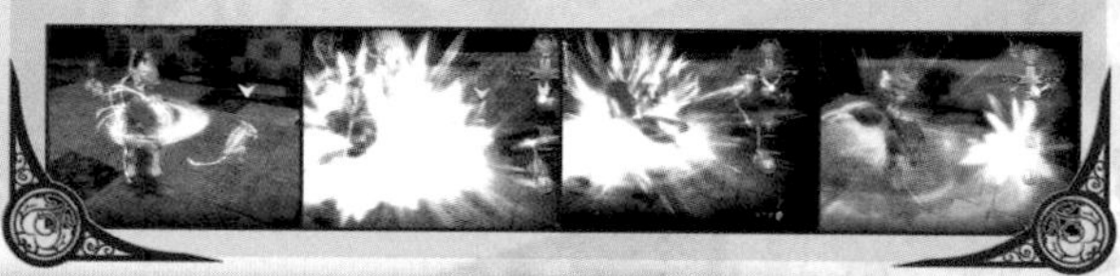

Chamber 4: Second Return to Grand Ceremonial Hallway (2F)

➤ After the Ghoul Rats exit via the door in the opposite wall. The **Small Key** you just acquired lets you through. You return to the Grand Ceremonial Hallway, only this time you're looking out on the second floor. The third torch is lit! Now leap across to the chandelier, as the Poe's Scent shows that the Poe passed through the door opposite. Leap again, and leave via this eastern door.

Chamber 10: Chandelier Chamber II (2F to 1F)

➤ You appear on a balcony overlooking another large chandelier and sand. The scent is wafting south, through an opening on the far side. To get to it, turn and head down the steps, and then leap to another gated cube with a stone top. Drop down and push it eastward until it slots into place.

➤ Treasure Chest: This allows you to scrabble up and onto the cube and yank a chain, but don't attempt this yet. Moving the cube allowed you to enter a small passageway with a chest just inside. The passageway leads back to a couple of Bubbles, and some scenery to smash, and then to the Grand Ceremonial Hallway. You could have opened this chest earlier, but this is the most optimal path, so open it now.

Treasure Chest #8: Red Rupee (20)

➤ Now return to pulling the chain out from the wall to lift the chandelier. However, when you're halfway through this maneuver, you're attacked by some leaping Moldorms from the sand below! Drop down to the small stone floor on the other side of the cube, and Clawshot all the Moldorms. Once all the enemies are defeated, try the chain once more!

➤ **Treasure Chest:** The chandelier slowly ascends from the stone platform, and once you've pulled as far as you can, release the chain and run south to the edge of the room, where you can break open a chest for more Rupee prizes! To return to the chain (because you're stuck—the chandelier has blocked your path), aim at the Clawshot medallion on the western wall, drop down, head up the passage, and climb back onto the cube.

Treasure Chest #9: Red Rupee (20)

Tip: Have you filled even the Big Wallet with your Rupee hunting? Then put your Magic Armor on, lessen the burden on your Wallet, then open the chest again, if you must open and successfully store every item in this dungeon!

➤ When the chandelier is fully extended, run and stand in the middle of it (the lower stone square indicates where this is), and let the chandelier drop around you. Then climb on it, face east, and move to the edge. Leap across the gap, and exit via the unlocked door where the Poe's Scent is drifting through.

Note: If you look carefully, you see an additional Clawshot medallion on the north wall. This is for adventurers who are returning through this chamber. You're not about to get lost, so don't worry about retracing your steps!

Chamber 11: Star Chamber of the Stalfos (1F to 2F)

Stalfos

Threat Meter

Hack the wooden planks aside, and step into a star-shaped chamber with many alcoves. As you investigate this chamber, what appears to be a fallen foe rises up from the ground, bony hand gripping a large and vicious-looking blade! This is the fabled Stalfos, and he's invincible! Well, nearly. Just Z target him, fire a bomb arrow, and he drops in a second! Simple, effective, and the only way to stop him from reanimating: defeat with bombs only!

This fearsome warrior keeps coming back for more! That is, until you explode him!

Tip: If you don't have bombs, search the alcoves for them, then shield attack, knock the Stalfos down with a barrage of sword strikes, and lay a bomb on his remains. This is the long way to defeating him!

➤ With the Stalfos defeated, you can inspect the room. There are two chests in this area, and both house bombs in case you didn't have any when you arrived. Spend a few moments smashing pots and skulls for the usual items, and then open both chests. The bars on the exit door were removed when Stalfos fell, so exit.

Treasure Chest #10: Bombs (5)

Treasure Chest #11: Bombs (5)

Small Key
You got a Small Key! This opens a locked door, but only in this area.

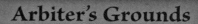

Chamber 12: Shrine to the Snake Deity (2F)

➤ Head south up the stairs, following the scent trail, which floats right, and disappears into a wall in the western part of this shrine. A giant statue sits with a snake wrapped around her. In front are five unlit torches in a line, and one in front of you. Light any of the back torches, except the one on the far right, and a dozen Stalkins rise from the sand, and advance!

➤ There's some sort of order to this torch-lighting business, so switch to your sense view, and you'll see the Poe's Scent wafted against the front torch, and the back right one. Light these two torches only, and the wall rumbles open.

Chamber 13: Chamber of the Fourth Poe (2F)

Poe Soul #41

Head into the chamber where the last Poe's Scent took you, and look at the four lanterns. One is swaying a little differently, so face southwest and challenge this entity to battle! He splits into four identical forms, who circle and attack! Fortunately, the real Poe shines brighter than his three clones, so Z target him, and launch into a bite. Do this again until the Poe deflates. Then smash some scenery and leave by the north door.

Poe Soul

You got the **Poe Soul**! Collect one from each Poe you defeat! Poe Soul #41 of 60.

Task 5: Defeat Death Sword in Battle; Obtain the Spinner

Chamber 10: First Return to Chandelier Chamber II (2F to 1F), to Third Return to Grand Ceremonial Hallway, to Chamber 14: Spinner Cog Room

➤ With the last Poe defeated, you can use the Clawshot medallion in Chandelier Chamber II and propel yourself back to the door leading to the Grand Ceremonial Hallway. The north door opens, and you can bound through, into a strange, circular chamber. Attack the Fire Bubbles and regular Bubbles, then inspect the ground. There's a strange circular groove in here....

➤ There are two exits, but the one to the right leads to a small thin room with a giant chest at the end. But you can't reach it yet because a sand trap prevents you. Instead, turn and exit via the doorway opposite.

Chamber 15: Circular Pit (1F, BF, B2)

➤ Enter a circular pit with a long drop to the bottom of this dungeon. However, check the small corridors dotted throughout the drop. Look over the edge, and fire your Clawshot at the medallion you can see on the south alcove. Crack a skull for a blue Rupee (5), but otherwise, spikes prevent you from continuing. Continue down to the B2 level, either dropping or using the Clawshot. Only Rupees from scenery can be stolen at the moment. Fight the Bubble when you reach the bottom.

Enemies Encountered

Bubble

Moldorm

Stalfos

Stalkin

Poe

Fire Bubble

Ooccoo

➤ To retrieve the real treasure behind the spikes in these alcoves, raise the central pillar by turning the giant handle at the base of this pit. Turn it and raise the platform one level. Then enter the alcove in the eastern wall, run round, and open the chest cunningly hidden here. You can now raise the platform another level, and enter another alcove, but you find only pots and skulls to smash. Now return to the handle, and push the platform all the way to the bottom, unlock the door, and exit via the south.

Treasure Chest #12: Small Key

Small Key
You got a **Small Key**! This opens a locked door, but only in this area.

Chamber 16: Spike and Sand Trap (B2)

➤ Exit through the southern door, and run into a long room with columns stretching throughout the middle. Change to your wolf form, as Ghoul Rats are about! Canter forward, and move along the right wall until spikes appear, preventing your progress. Turn left, move across, and around more spikes, across the sand to the opposite wall. Turn to face south.

Tip: Turn your sense view on. That way you can see when Ghoul Rats head your way, and shake them off. Also, every time a spike rises, a ghostly residual image remains if you keep your sense view on, so you can see the path more easily.

➤ Proceed south until spikes block your route once more, then turn, shake off some Ghoul Rats, and work your way across to the right wall again. Turn south, and pass over the sand—the only gap without spikes. Then turn left, and head to the other side once more. Stop and defeat all the Ghoul Rats you can see!

➤ Turn and charge southward, so you're in the southeastern corner of this chamber. Then Z target a Redead and clamp yourself to it, biting it twice until it falls. Now shake off the final Ghoul Rats. This is much more difficult if you're not in wolf form!

➤ With the Redead defeated, turn and head north, then west, all the way across, then south to the opposite corner, where you need to pull a chain. Then retrace your steps to where the Redead was, and head for the middle of the southern wall, which is closing rapidly! Squeeze through before it closes, or you'll have to pull the chain again.

Chamber 17: Poison Mite Alley (B2)

➤ Head into a connecting chamber, stepping on and off some sinking tiles, and then turn east, and run onto a stone path flanked with two spiked Spinners. These traps hurt you and push you into the sand if you're not careful. On the way, you're attacked by Poison Mites. Produce your sword and spin, or light your Lantern and run!

➤ Continue to the end of this alley, and check the door to the north, then swing around and head to the skulls and pot. This one contains more than just Rupees: Ooccoo is here!

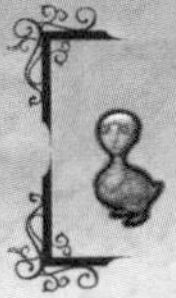

Ooccoo
You are reunited with **Ooccoo**! This kind character can let you out of dungeons and return you to where you were.

Chamber 18: Chamber of Traps

➤ Head north through this door, and roll to increase your speed as you pass by a rotating spike log. There's a gate to your left, and an alcove opposite that you can roll to and smash some scenery.

Tip: If you want to remain in cover, but still bash some skulls for the items inside, stay in this alcove, and aim with your Clawshot. Shoot it once to smash the skull, and twice to pick the item up!

▲ Enter the next chamber, and ready yourself for some fraught combat. A true adventurer would be armed with Bomb Arrows, and as soon as the two Stalfos awaken, shoot them both twice to finish them off. Or, use the back slice and when they collapse, drop a bomb. Make sure both are defeated before you continue because when you turn west, there's a third Stalfos hidden in the alcove area! Bring out a Bomb Arrow for this guy, but first run over to him so he rises up.

▲ When the third Stalfos falls, the gate near the spiked log trap opens. Backtrack here, and head around to a long, thin passage filled with small tiles of stone and lots of sand. You can actually run up here, wade through the sand, and climb up on the other side, despite the Poison Mites. Or, use your Lantern to fend them off. Or, use the Clawshot medallions. Or, use your spin attack!

▲ The passage leads to a gap where the third Stalfos was slumped. Leap over it, then run around the upper stone floor toward an exit door with pots and skulls nearby. Open this, and enter a massive circular chamber, with a huge and ominous sword in the middle.

Chamber 19: The Domain of Death Sword

Death Sword

Threat Meter

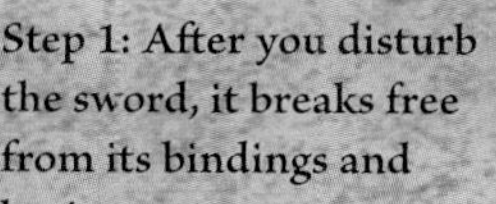

Step 1: After you disturb the sword, it breaks free from its bindings and begins to swipe at you. This sword is gigantic, and there doesn't seem to be any way to defeat it! Or does there? Change to your wolf form, and with your sense view, you can see that an entity is wielding this weapon!

It's a massive skeletal being with a huge sword. Although truly terrifying, he's surprisingly easy to tackle!

Step 2: The entity is a giant horned skeletal figure who's intent on ending your days of adventuring! Ⓩ target this large foe, and when he swings the blade, dodge it, and then leap on him as he flashes white. Keep gnawing on his bony form until he throws you off.

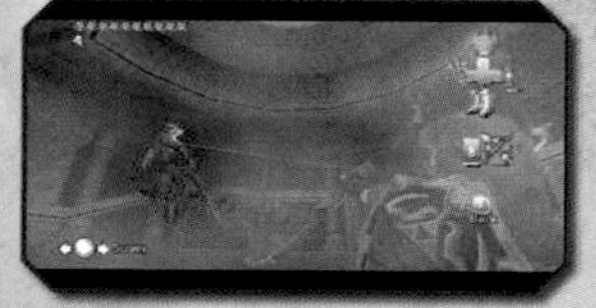

Step 3: He now becomes partially solid, aside from the cloud of vapor he trails. Now transform into Link, and begin a specific takedown technique. As he floats about, bring out your **Hero's Bow**. Manually target the enemy's head or body, and fire. It is recommended you aim at the body as it is a bigger target. Strike him with a single shot. Bomb Arrows work well, too.

Step 4: As soon as you strike him with your bow, put it away, bring out your sword, and Ⓩ target Death Sword as he circles around you. He stops immediately if you strike him using the bow, so you don't need to constantly watch him. If you don't fire an arrow, he continuously circles, and then brings his sword down. When he stops, he also brings his sword down. Dodge this and then begin a barrage of sword slices, spin attacks, and slashes! He collapses to his knees. Continue the punishment!

Enemies Encountered

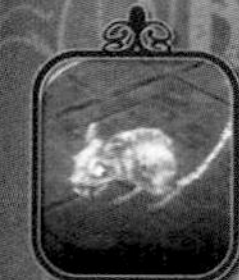

Ghoul Rat

Redead

Poison Mite

Stalfos

Death Sword

Task #5
Defeat Death Sword in Battle; Obtain the Spinner

Death Sword (cont'd)

Step 5: He soon rises and circles you again. At this point, fire an arrow directly into Death Sword's head or torso. Now repeat Step 4 three more times until Death Sword yields. If Death Sword produces these purple poison balls, simply shield attack them, pushing them away, and return the favor with an arrow. If you aren't quick enough with an arrow, Death Sword turns invisible, and you must complete the combat from Step 1. Act fast, and be accurate with that bow!

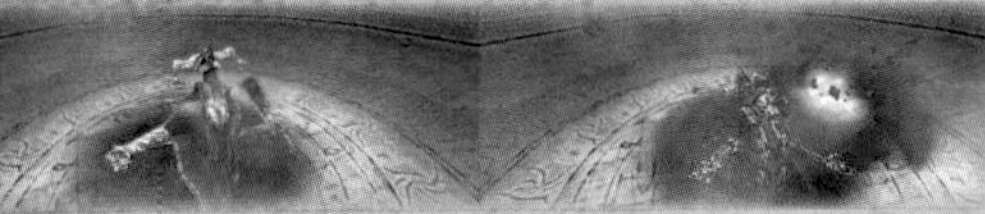

After you deal your final blow to Death Sword, he lets out an inhuman shriek and falls back. The sword explodes, and the entity dissolves into dust. The Arbiter's Grounds is a slightly safer place for future adventurers!

◄ **Treasure Chest**: Once Death Sword has been defeated, head north, into the long hall beyond his arena. Here you find a chest with one of the most impressive devices ever constructed by ancient boffins! Behold, the **Spinner**!

Treasure Chest #13: Spinner

Spinner

You got the **Spinner**! It's an ancient machine designed to float over land.

Spinner

The Spinner is an exciting device that allows you to journey across the sand traps and along the grooves of walls you may have seen during your travels across Hyrule. It keeps its speed up if it's connected to the grooves on walls, and when it slows down, it disappears. You can also attack enemies by pressing Ⓑ, although this isn't an impressive offensive power. The Spinner's uses are limited and you can't (for example) ride it for extended periods. Stay in this chamber and practice riding the Spinner.

When using the Spinner, heed the following advice:

- Always look for grooves, as they speed you up.
- Press Ⓑ when on a groove to leave it, ideally heading toward another groove.
- Place the Spinner on ✚ so you can easily activate and deactivate it, like the Iron Boots.
- Pressing Ⓑ gives you a short burst of speed, but don't rely on it!

Tip

- You can still get caught in a sand trap if you're traveling too slowly!
- Make sure you're traveling in the correct direction as you join a groove, or you'll ride the opposite way.

Task 6: Obtain the Big Key

Chamber 18: First Return to Chamber of Traps

◄ Exit the domain of Death Sword, and inspect the previous chamber. Look carefully, and you'll see a groove in the left wall, so produce your Spinner and ride it around. As you reach the eastern sandy part you haven't explored before, press Ⓑ to jump off the groove, and steer it to the opposite wall. Ride this up the slope, to the exit door.

Chamber 20: Spinner's Paradise (B2 to BF to 1F)

◄ Enter this giant chamber and you can uncover the Spinner's full potential! Here's the quickest route out of here: Begin by speeding east on your Spinner, using the low grooves to bounce between.

◄ Stop here, on the lower ground, climb over the low groove wall, and open this chest.

Treasure Chest #14: Bombs (10)

➤ Spin across the sand to the next chest, on the second stone tile area. Open this too.

Treasure Chest #15: Red Rupee (20)

◄ Now get back on the Spinner, and head between these two low groove walls. Continue in an easterly direction.

◄ Then follow the sloping wall with the groove in a semicircle until you're traveling west. Drop off the end and land in the second part of the floor below.

➤ Continue to stand on the Spinner until you reach this upper area, and optionally knock into the Stalfos. Get off the Spinner, then engage the Stalfos in combat, ideally with Bomb Arrows. Then pry open this chest. This one's a keeper!

Treasure Chest #16: Piece of Heart #28

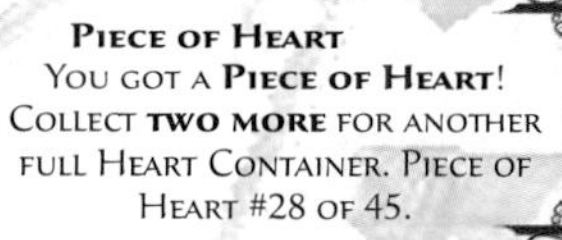

Piece of Heart

You got a **Piece of Heart**! Collect **two more** for another full Heart Container. Piece of Heart #28 of 45.

◄ Turn and stand on the Spinner, then face east and ride along the left groove wall, timing the move so you aren't struck by the rotating spike trap. When you reach this point, as the wall runs out, press Ⓑ and hop across to the other wall, then back again. This leads to another leap across to a circular groove track.

◄ Before you make this jump, drop off the left wall at this point. A chest is cunningly hidden below you.

Treasure Chest #17: Yellow Rupee (10)

➤ Stop the Spinner, and land on the small slightly domed island in the chamber's southeast corner. Stand on the Spinner again, and this time ride in the opposite direction, clockwise around the chamber's outer perimeter. At the end of the groove, drop to the northern section of this area.

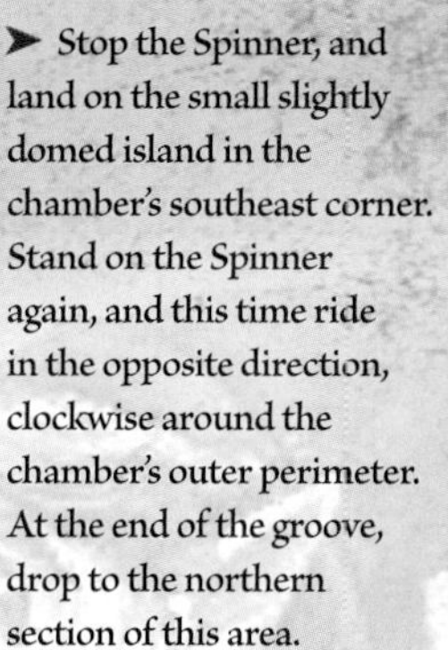

➤ Land in this northern area, which is one long grooved chamber, and ride the Spinner to the west, locating this chest. Drop down, then engage two Stalfos in battle. Fire off two Bomb Arrows to defeat each one, then pry open this chest.

Treasure Chest #18: Yellow Rupee (10)

◄ Travel to the far eastern end of this grooved section, to a ramp in the middle. Ride the Spinner westward now, staying on each groove until you're about to be struck by a spiked Spinner, then leaping across with Ⓑ. Dodge the Spinners until you reach the exit door.

Chamber 21: Big Key Passage

◄ The exit from Spinner's Paradise dumps you back in the midst of the dungeon, in the small thin chamber where you saw the Big Key chest so you can claim this most important item. Then use the Spinner to head back to Chamber #14.

Treasure Chest #19: Big Key

Big Key

You got a **Big Key**! Use it to gain access to the lair of this dungeon's boss!

Enemies Encountered

Stalfos

7 8

Task #6

Obtain the Big Key

Task 7: Ascend the Great Spiral Shaft

Chamber 14: First Return to Spinner Cog Room

◄ It now becomes clear what the circular groove in the floor was for; insert the Spinner by standing on the groove, and then begin to tap Ⓑ quickly to activate a series of cogs under the stone floor. This eventually causes the entire room to shift. Head north, into the chamber that's been revealed.

Chamber 22: The Great Spiral Shaft (1F to 2F to 3F to 4F)

▲ Enter this chamber by Spinner, and locate the groove on the outer wall. Ride this to the very top, to a small crumbling ledge with iron bars protruding from it. Drop down, and smash the pots. One has a Fairy in it. If you don't have one already, grab it and place it in a Bottle.

Fairy in a Bottle

You got a **Fairy in a Bottle**!

◄ Now ride down the perimeter groove until you reach this jagged stone ledge on the third floor, and stop. Walk out to the edge, and you'll see a central platform that's cut off from the surrounding area. Line yourself up, jump from this ledge, and grab the edge of the central platform.

▲ Pull yourself up onto the platform, and bring out the Spinner. Slot it into the circular groove, and begin to rapidly tap Ⓑ to spin the device. A massive grinding noise signifies a giant spiral groove appearing from the sand below!

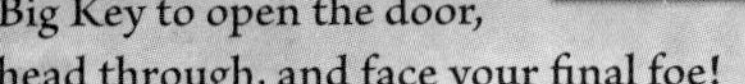

► Hop on the groove at any point, and ride it up to the fourth floor. The spiral groove leads you to a short ramp with a door at the end. Use the Big Key to open the door, head through, and face your final foe!

Task 8: Defeat Twilit Fossil Stallord in Combat

Chamber 23: Boss Battle! Lair of Twilit Fossil Stallord

◄ You're in a giant circular arena, with a rim of stone around the circumference, and a large sinking dip in the middle. In the sand is a gigantic skeletal beast.

Twilit Fossil Stallord

As you run down to inspect the bones, Zant appears! He is surprised that you are still living, but the reunion is bittersweet! He summons a shard of twilight and stabs it through the skull of the giant beast. The eye sockets flicker! It rises up and roars!

Form 1: Giant Stallord Half-Skeleton

Threat Meter

Step 1: The Stallord is still emerging from the sand, and he seems to be sealed in the dirt. This means he can turn but is otherwise stationary. Take your Spinner, and race around the groove in the outer ledge. Jump with Ⓑ when a spiked Spinner closes in on you, or you'll be struck by it. Two are zipping around this groove with you.

Tip: There are plenty of Hearts; just move to the outer rim of this room and search the small pots.

Step 2: The Stallord searches the room, turning around on the spot, and then rearing up to belch a disgusting concoction of purple spew. Run in either direction if this happens, or steer your Spinner away from the jet. It stops in a few seconds.

Step 3: The Stallord summons Staltroops to block your path to him, but don't let that dissuade you from leaping on the Spinner. Use the rim of the arena as a groove to accelerate, and then jump off the groove and steer directly into the Stallord's spine. As you head into the middle of the arena, dodge the Staltroops and then press Ⓑ just as you reach the spine. It cracks, and the beast roars!

Staltroop

Threat Meter

The Staltroop are the Stallord's minions: resurrected warriors with no intelligence. They are simply obstacles to your goal, which is striking the Stallord's weak spine. Avoid them, and if you're standing on the sand (because your Spinner slowed down too much) roll back up to the groove, and avoid the Staltroops.

The Staltroops are simply automatons, with no aggressive tendencies. Simply avoid them, or you'll slow down and sink!

Keep steering down to the Stallord's spin, executing Step 3 two more times, until the Stallord collapses under his own weight! He sinks slowly into the sand that begins to fall into a large pit below. You drop down. Run around the perimeter of this pit, smashing pots and collecting Hearts.

Enemies Encountered

Twilit Fossil Stallord

Zant

Staltroop

7

8

Task #8

Defeat Twilit Fossil Stallord in Combat

Characters Encountered

Twilit Fossil Stallord (cont'd)

Form 2: Giant Stallord Floating Fireball Skull

Once you've finished your energy collection, inspect the giant skull. It seems lifeless, so head to the very center of the chamber, and slot your Spinner into the circular groove. Begin to spin, and you raise a giant cylinder in the middle of the pit. What's that sound?

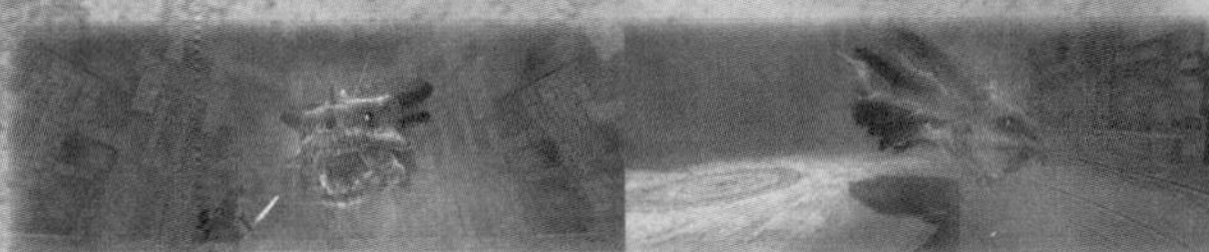

As the cylinder rises, the giant head's eye sockets flicker into life! The giant skull head floats up, opens its disgusting mouth, then swoops in and knocks you off the cylinder!

Step 4: You must now reach the top of the cylinder by riding along the spiraling groove. The outer wall also has grooves, but they remain at the same level. As you reach the top, the Stallord head appears and summons a huge fireball! If this strikes you, you fall back to the ground, so leap as the fireball emerges from its mouth. You land on an outer groove. Wait for a second fireball to emerge, and leap back.

Step 5: The next step is to continue ascending the middle cylinder. As the skull turns to look at you and closes in, leap off with Ⓑ, and strike the skull right in the jaw! It tumbles to earth and lies motionless. Run over to it immediately, with your sword drawn!

Step 6: Ⓩ target the shard embedded in the skull, and begin to slash it rapidly with your sword. Quick slicing techniques and (of course) the spin attack are mandatory. Keep on slashing! The skull floats up again. Repeat Steps 4, 5, and 6, but bounce away from a spiked Spinner when you encounter it.

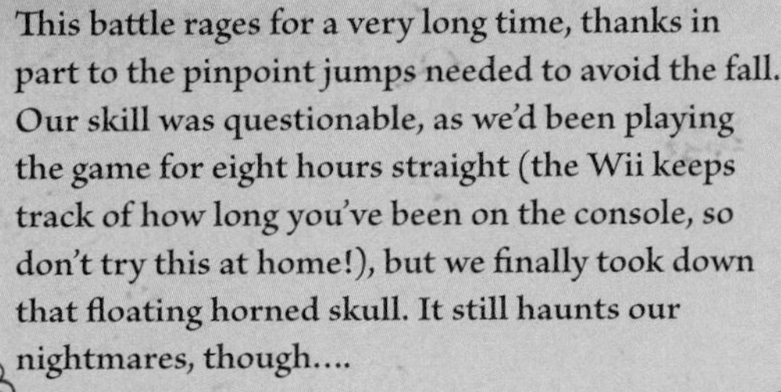

Author Note

This battle rages for a very long time, thanks in part to the pinpoint jumps needed to avoid the fall. Our skill was questionable, as we'd been playing the game for eight hours straight (the Wii keeps track of how long you've been on the console, so don't try this at home!), but we finally took down that floating horned skull. It still haunts our nightmares, though....

As you strike the twilit shard in the skull for the second or third series of blows, the shard finally ruptures and sends the skull flying up into the arena roof, before it tumbles down to the ground, rolls away, and explodes. The shard lands at the top of the cylinder and explodes. A Heart Container appears, and a bridge extends to your exit.

◄ Midna is impatient for you to leave, but first head over to the **Heart Container** and claim it. Your energy is now at impressive levels! Now exit this place.

Heart Container
You got a **Heart Container**! Your life energy has increased by **one** and been **fully replenished**! Heart Container #4 (of 8).

Task #8
Defeat Twilit Fossil Stallord in Combat

Characters Encountered

Midna

Overworld: Climbing Snowpeak Mountain

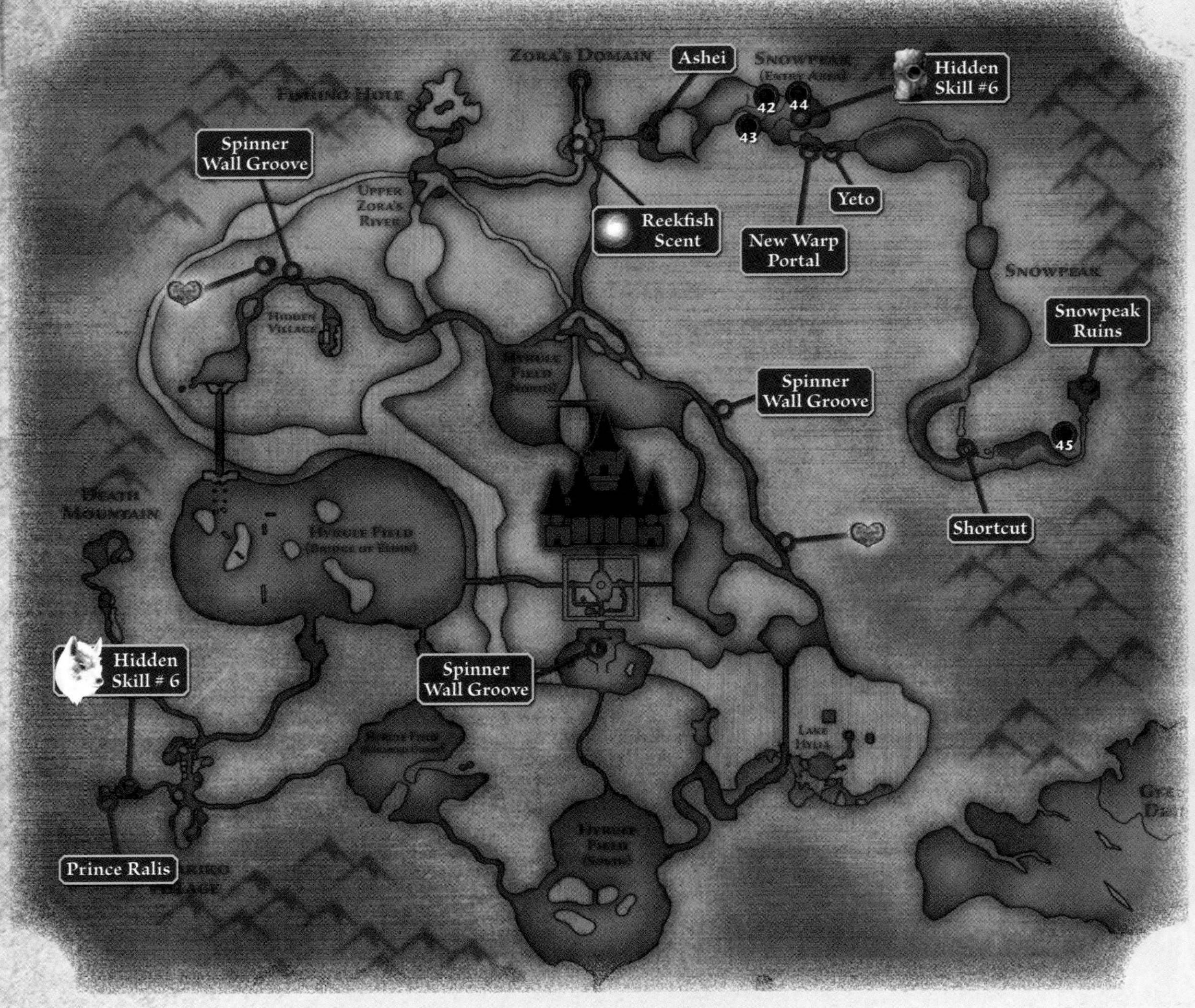

Zora's Domain
Ashei
Snowpeak (Entry Area)
Hidden Skill #6
42
44
43
Fishing Hole
Spinner Wall Groove
Upper Zora's River
Yeto
Reekfish Scent
New Warp Portal
Snowpeak
Hidden Village
Snowpeak Ruins
Hyrule Field (North)
Spinner Wall Groove
45
Death Mountain
Hyrule Field (Bridge of Eldin)
Shortcut
Hidden Skill # 6
Spinner Wall Groove
Lake Hylia
Prince Ralis
Hyrule Field (South)

Climbing Snowpeak Mountain: Overview

After the trekking you've done so far, the preparations for your next dungeon are not as intense, but the knowledge you learn from the Sages at the Mirror Chamber is shocking! It seems that Ganondorf, the leader of a band of thieves and using powers only two others possess, has influenced the evil King of Shadows, Zant. While you ponder these ramifications, tour Hyrule searching for Spinner tracks; there are a couple of Pieces of Heart in it for you. Check in with the resistance. Telma informs you that you must climb Snowpeak, providing you can sniff out a path. On the way, howl with the White Wolf, and chase a Yeti down a treacherous mountain slide!

1 Locate All Available Items with Spinner Pg 305

2 Learn the Scent of the Reekfish Pg 307

3 Climb to Summit of Snowpeak Mountain Pg 308

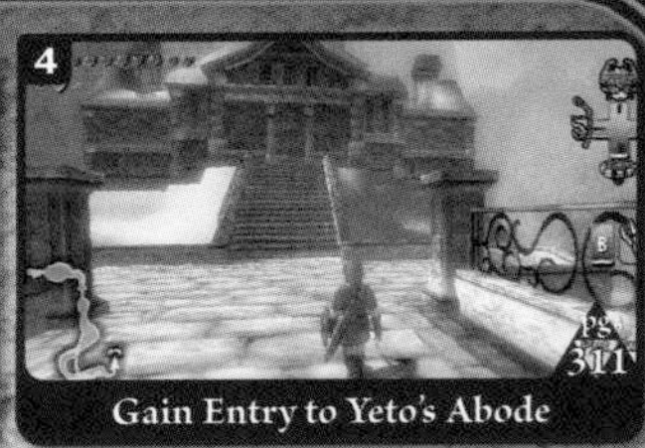

4 Gain Entry to Yeto's Abode Pg 311

Overworld Denizens

Characters

Sage

Yeto

Enemies

Ice Keese

A Link to the Present

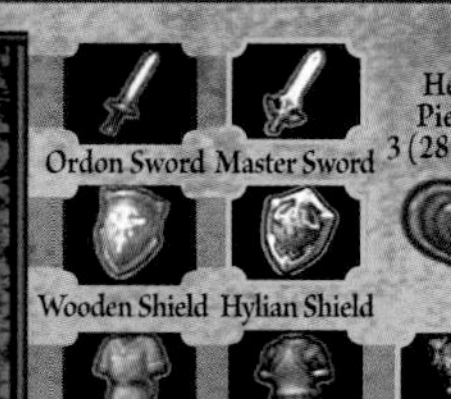

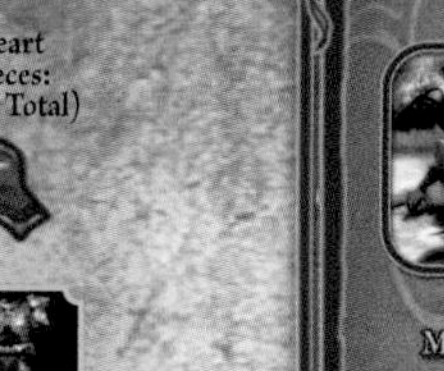

Ordon Sword Master Sword

Heart Pieces: 3 (28 Total)

Wooden Shield Hylian Shield

Hero's Clothes Zora Armor Magic Armor

Big Wallet Big Quiver Golden Bugs: 23 (of 24) Hidden Skills: 5 (of 7)

Poe's Scent Poe Souls 41 (of 60) Fish Journal Letters 8 (of 16)

Items to Obtain

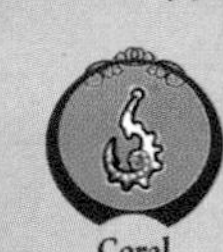

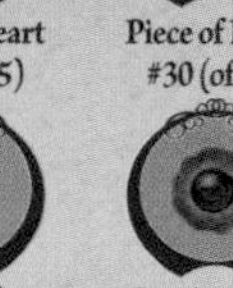

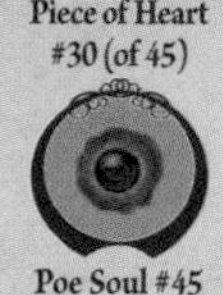

Letter #9 (of 16)

Bombs (5)

Piece of Heart #29 (of 45)

Piece of Heart #30 (of 45)

Ashei's Sketch

Coral Earring

Reekfish Scent

Poe Soul #45

Enemies Encountered

Twilit Messenger

Task 1: Locate All Available Items with the Spinner

Past Terror at the Mirror of Twilight

Leave the Arbiter's Grounds, and you appear at the base of some stone steps. Leap up them, avoiding the gaps, until you reach a curved corridor with arched alcoves along each side. Follow this until you reach the impressive Mirror Chamber. Walk forward.

Warp Portal

Five Twilit Messengers descend on you. The wide combat area allows you to coax the last two together easily—let rip!

Five Twilit Messengers drop out of the sky, and you can attack them in either form, although wolf is preferable, because the area attack has the widest range. Defeat the initial two Messengers, then turn left and bite the third, before finding the last two and dispatching both together.

Move to the central statue in this Mirror Chamber, and inspect it. It doesn't take long to figure out that you can ride up that grooved channel using your Spinner. At the top, stop, reposition yourself in the massive statue's center, and tap Ⓑ.

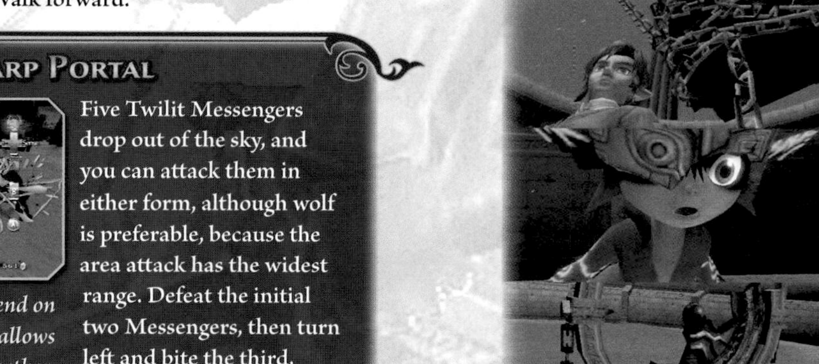

Your spinning in the circular groove creates a small seismic disturbance as a giant rock, harnessed by the chamber, rises from the ground. Steps appear too, and the Mirror of Twilight is at the top of them. Midna floats over to look and is shocked. The Mirror of Twilight is cracked!

Midna is startled as ghostly figures form at the top of the chamber's spires. These are Sages, who have guarded the Mirror of Twilight since ancient times. The Mirror has been fragmented by mighty magic, dark magic that only one possesses—Ganondorf!

A leader (and demon thief) of a band of thieves who invaded Hyrule to hold dominion over the Sacred Grove, Ganondorf was a powerful magician who used his powers to thwart and terrify. But he was blind to danger, so he was subdued and brought to justice.

By some divine prank, he too had been blessed with the chosen power of the gods, his hand glowing with a symbol few had seen, and of which fewer had knowledge. Ripping free, he cast aside the ceremonial sword and was quickly banished into the twilight world.

Perhaps that malice and power has been passed to Zant! But Midna thinks it's too late. However, only the true leader of the Twili can destroy the Mirror. Zant has simply broken it into pieces. One is in the snowy mountain heights. One is in an ancient grove. And one is in the heavens.

Sage:

Approximately 50 years old, but with a strange ethereal power masking their true age, there are seven Sages of ancient times who succeeded in capturing the mad warrior magician known as Ganondorf. Executing him with a ceremonial blade, they attempt to keep the world of Hyrule at peace. They don't possess physical bodies, and they have graceful, poetic movements.

Warp from the Gerudo Desert area. Your task is clear: you must search for the Mirror of Twilight's second piece (the first is in the frame). Warp to the Hyrule Field; ideally the Bridge of Eldin.

Characters Encountered

Midna

Sages

Postman

Telma

Shad

Auru

Preparation for Snowpeak: The Spinner Hunt

As soon as you warp to a place with a pathway, expect a letter delivery from the constantly breathless Postman. It's from Barnes, who is letting you know he's got a rare type of bomb in stock. However, this is only the Bombling, which you've already inspected. This letter arrives to prompt you if you haven't checked the Bombling out yet.

Letter #9

You got **Letter #9**: "Rare item in stock!" by Barnes.

➤ Head to the winding rocky path that runs from the Bridge of Eldin to the north Hyrule Field. When you reach the small wooden bridge holding the Bulblin Archers, halt and defeat all the foes you wish to. Look for the Spinner track groove in the rock wall here.

Dig Cavern #14

Ride along the Spinner track until you land on a remote and rocky ledge. Don't jump from the Spinner or you'll plummet into the gorge! Inspect the ring of grass (there are Rupees and Hearts), then dig in the middle. You land in a dig cavern. Change to Link and arm yourself with Bomb Arrows. Three Stalfoses are advancing on you! Defeat them with a Bomb Arrow (or a bomb if you have no arrows).

1 2 3 4

Dig Cavern #14 (cont'd)

If you have no bombs, don't despair. There's a small chest partially obscured by grass in the eastern part of the chamber. Kick it open to find five bombs. Once the Stalfoses are defeated, you can smash pots, cut grass, and then open the chest that's appeared. The reward is worth the fraught combat! Once you claim it, exit and ride the Spinner back to the path.

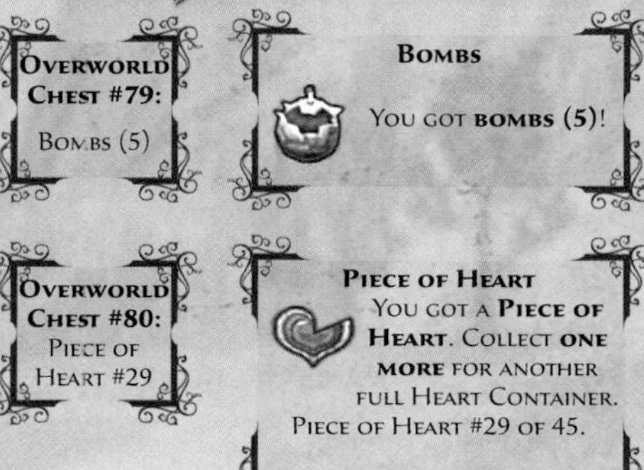

Tip: The easiest way to beat the Stalfoses is simply to run up to the group of them before they split up, and launch a Bomb Arrow. You'll lose half an energy Heart, but combat is over in seconds!

Overworld Chest #79: Bombs (5)

Bombs

You got **bombs (5)**!

Overworld Chest #80: Piece of Heart #29

Piece of Heart

You got a **Piece of Heart**. Collect **one more** for another full Heart Container. Piece of Heart #29 of 45.

◄ Head eastward now, over the north Hyrule Field, to the far eastern road that leads to the Great Hylian Bridge. As you reach this part of the path, stop and ride the Spinner on the track of the outer wall. Ride it up.

◄ Ricochet left and right along the broken sections of marked wall, high above the path! A Lizalfos prowls the path below, but ignore him, and press Ⓑ as you reach the end of the wall section you're on, and bounce to the opposite side. You reach a high ledge with a lone chest. Open it!

Overworld Chest #81: Piece of Heart #30

Piece of Heart

You got a **Piece of Heart**. You collected **five pieces** and formed a new Heart Container! Piece of Heart #30 of 45.

◄ Move to southern Hyrule Field just outside Castle Town, where Agitha was sitting in the flower bed, and the Goron smashed a rockfall for you. Propel up to the left tower outside the main gate, where you previously opened Overworld Chest #51.

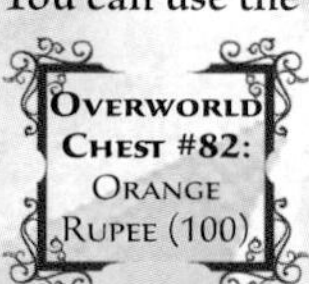

► This time though, you're not going to be walking the tightrope or moving hand-over-hand to the other tower. You can use the Spinner track here. When the Spinner reaches the middle of the track, jump with Ⓑ and steer yourself over the stone wall to the chest above the pool. Open the chest.

Overworld Chest #82: Orange Rupee (100)

Task 2: Learn the Scent of the Reekfish

Preparation for Snowpeak: Heading to the Tundra

◄ If you're unsure of your next actions, visit Telma's Bar in Castle Town and speak to her. She explains that Renado is a talented man, and Ilia's memory will return. She mentions that Ashei is checking out Hyrule's northern mountain. You can now visit the heroes in the back room. Shad isn't much help, but Auru tells you that the Sages served by royal appointment, and tutored Princess Zelda.

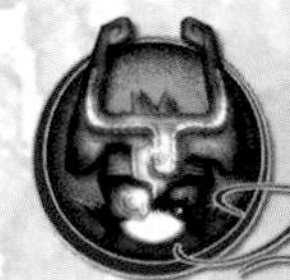

Tip: You can mark Ashei's location on your map by looking at the parchment map on the table.

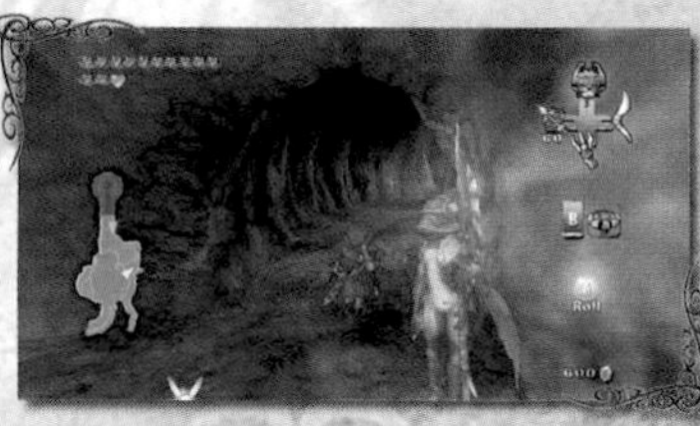

► After you discover where you must go, you can warp to Zora's Domain, and tumble into the waterfall pool. Look for the eastern wall's cave entrance, and head through, into the icy wilds of Peak Province.

Enemies Encountered

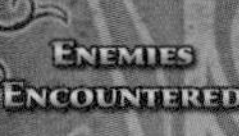

Ganondorf

Bulblin Archer

Stalfos

Lizalfos (Axe-tail)

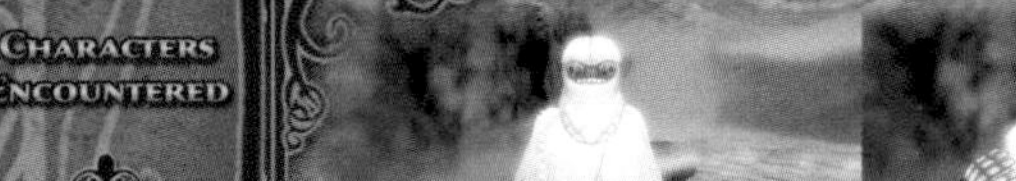

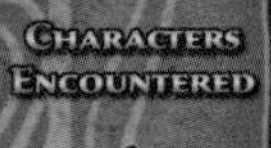

Ashei

Zora

Prince Ralis

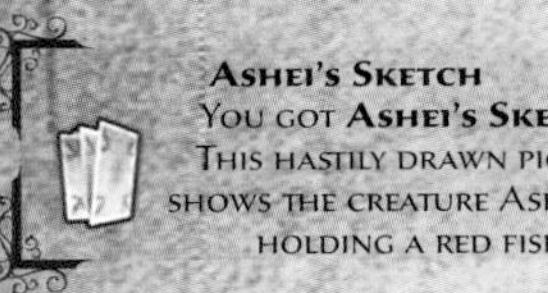

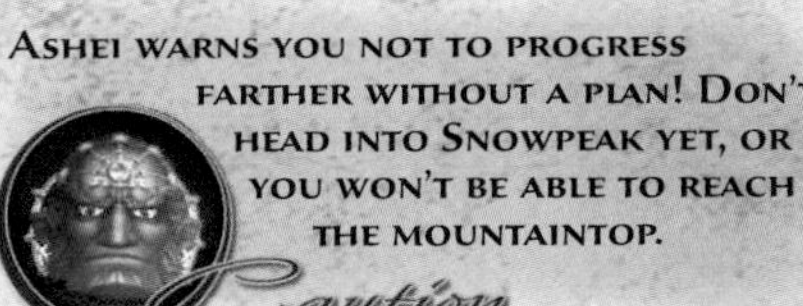

Once at the ice flow, you're startled by a frightening visage! Actually, it's just Ashei, wearing her Yeti mask. Apparently, the beast who lives somewhere on the mountain has been seen frequently in Zora's Domain. She gives you a sketch. The beast is holding a red fish.

Ashei's Sketch

You got **Ashei's Sketch**! This hastily drawn picture shows the creature Ashei saw holding a red fish.

Caution

Ashei warns you not to progress farther without a plan! Don't head into Snowpeak yet, or you won't be able to reach the mountaintop.

➤ In Zora's Domain, talk to the first Zora you see, and show him **Ashei's Sketch**. He instantly recognizes the beast, and the fish is a **Reekfish**. It's called that because of the smell! Nobody besides Prince Ralis was able to catch this type of fish, the Zora tells you.

▲ Warp to Zora's Domain, and take another plunge into the waterfall pool. Follow the prince's advice, and select the Fishing Rod. The coral lure is on it, but you must find the correct place to fish. It is directly across from the entrance to Snowpeak, near the large and small Mother-and-Child Rocks. Cast your rod, and in moments, reel in the Reekfish. Phew! That smells!

▲ Warp to Kakariko Village, and journey across the graveyard to the Zora pool of remembrance. Prince Ralis is still standing by his father's tombstone. Show him **Ashei's Sketch** and he tells you the Reekfish only feeds on coral, and that's the only way to catch it. The prince has an earring made from the stuff, and he gladly gives it to you. He is now ready to return to his village, too. His final advice is where to fish: near the **Mother-and-Child Rocks** in the waterfall basin.

Coral Earring

You got the **Coral Earring**! It's made of precious coral from Zora's Domain. It's in the shape of a fishhook.

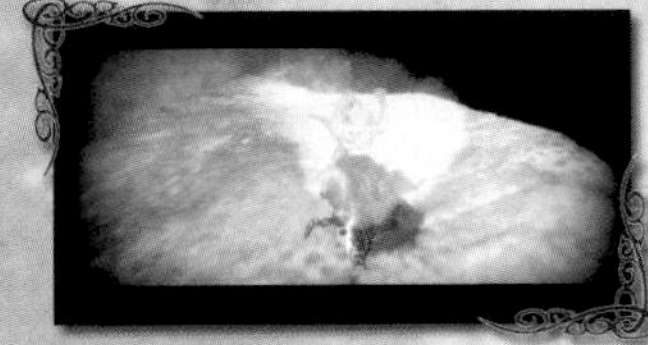

◀ Change to your wolf form, and learn this new scent. Dive into the water, and swim to Snowpeak's entrance, and head through.

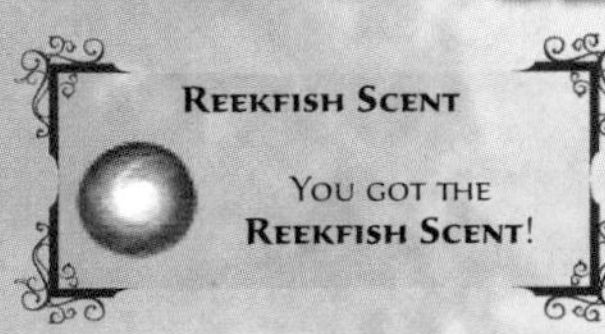

Reekfish Scent

You got the **Reekfish Scent**!

Task 3: Climb to the Summit of Snowpeak Mountain

Snowpeak Climb: Following the Reekfish Scent

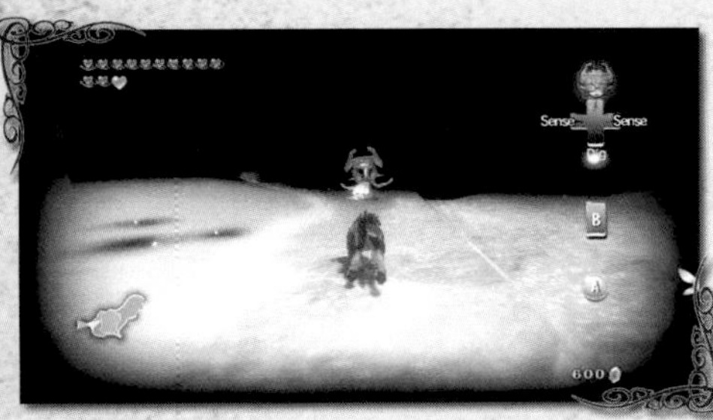

◀ Bound up to the edge, then off the side into the snowy ground ahead. Use your sense view in wolf form to check the Reekfish trail, and begin to carefully maneuver across the broken ice platforms of a half-frozen lake. Keep flicking back and forth to check where the scent is going, and look for easy jumps rather than directly following the scent.

◀ When you finish crossing the ice, you begin a treacherous journey up Snowpeak mountain. This is the area you were unable to reach previously. You encounter two White Wolfos, and they attack you. React by striking them twice with a leaping attack.

1 

2 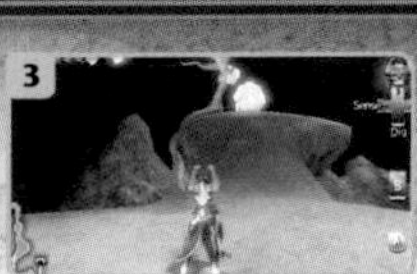

3 

4

▲ Move east through the blizzard, while more White Wolfos leap at you. Stop and execute a spin attack if they're being aggressive, and Z target and leap at them, or ignore them if they're not. You eventually reach a small gap between two icy rocks.

Poe #42

As you emerge from between the rocks, have your sense view on, as an Imp Poe floats about in this weather. He's to the right side of the trail as you emerge from between the icy rocks.

Poe Soul

You got the **Poe Soul**! Collect one from each Poe you defeat. Poe #42 of 60.

Poe #43

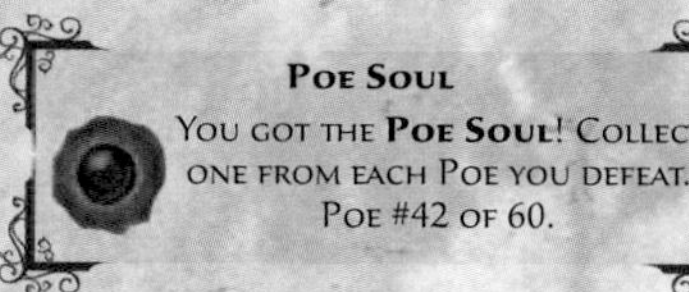

Break away from the trail and investigate this blizzard's southern edge. You're looking for a lone pine tree on a small hill half-buried in snow. There's an Imp Poe waiting here; defeat him!

Poe Soul

You got the **Poe Soul**. Collect one from each Poe you defeat! Poe #43 of 60.

Dig Cavern #15

The Imp Poe is also guarding a dig spot by the tree itself. Scrabble down to a small, cold cavern, where an Ice Keese (which attacks and can be defeated in the same way as a regular Keese) flaps about. The chamber is filled with icy boulders, which you can't destroy. Remember to come back here later, after your visit to Snowpeak is over!

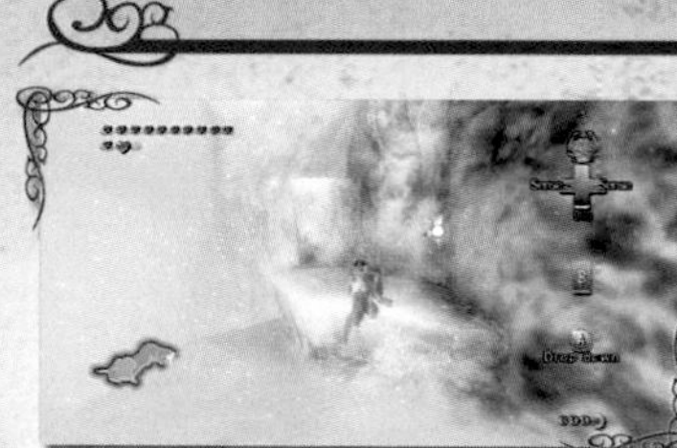

◄ Head back onto the path. The blizzard is clearing slightly as you climb farther up to the top of the mountain. You're looking for these icy ledges to scramble up.

Dig Cavern #16

Continue up the mountainside, following the path of the Reekfish scent, then veer off to a large, sloping plateau area with a great view of the surrounding mountains. Head to this tree, which has a view of the Reekfish trail in the distance. There's a dig spot at the tree's base. Inside, fight off a few Ice Keeses, then destroy the Bomb Rocks against one wall. A Red Chu is hiding here, and you can claim the Jelly if you wish. Leave after smashing more pots for Rupees; you've uncovered everything in here.

Poe #44

Wait until sundown when the sunlight glistening off the snow creates outstanding colors! Wait by the pine tree where you dug down just now, and an Imp Poe appears at dusk. Defeat him, and add his soul to your collection.

Poe Soul

You got the **Poe Soul**! Collect one from each Poe you defeat. Poe #44 of 60.

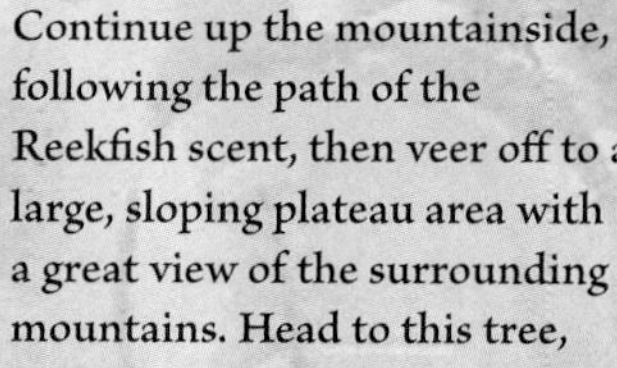

Enemies Encountered

White Wolfos

Imp Poe

Ice Keese

Chu (Red)

Characters Encountered

White Wolf

Hero's Shade

Yeto

The trail continues to the summit. You shouldn't get lost if you keep flicking back between your sense view and the environment. Climb up a ledge and a snowbank, and you reach the mountaintop.

Howling for the White Wolf

Before you continue, it's important that you investigate that strange ceremonial stone on the snowy promontory you're nearby. Listen to the wind whistling a tune through the hole in the rock. You must now recite the tune. Watch the tune, then replicate it. The pitch is as follows: high, middle (hold), low, middle (long hold), low, high, middle, low (hold). Use ⭘ to howl high and ⭘ to howl low on your ⭘. Mid-range howling, don't move the stick.

You appear as a wolf, in the heavens atop snowy peaks. The White Wolf appears at a leafy edge's end, on the world's opposite side. You howl the tune, and both of you continue to yelp. When you finish, the White Wolf tells you "Let teachings of old pass to you...." The wolf leaps down into the land.

Note

You have summoned the White Wolf! He is currently waiting for you in the graveyard area of Kakariko Village. Head here as Link and learn your next Hidden Skill! The walkthrough tells you the earliest point that this is possible.

Hidden Skill #6: Jump Strike

You can either continue on to the summit, or (as this is the first opportunity to) return to the White Wolf, who's sitting patiently at the far end of the Kakariko Village Graveyard, near the small tunnel entrance. The White Wolf waits for you to come, sword in hand! He growls at you, and you draw your sword. He pounces! You awaken in the ghostly ether. The Hero's Shade forms, and asks you if you wish to learn your next skill. The answer is yes!

First, your teacher ensures that you learned the previous Hidden Skill correctly and asks you to show him that you've mastered the mortal draw. Put away your weapon, don't Ⓩ target, wait for the Hero's Shade to advance, then quickly press Ⓐ.

"Very well!" utters the Shade, "let the **jump strike** be hewn into your mind!" The Shade notes that the jump attack is effective against multiple foes, but surrounding enemies that are hit lose less energy. For the jump strike, focus power in your blade. The surge that you release can hit enemies all around you! Now you try it:

Jump strike: Lock on with Ⓩ target and hold Ⓐ until just the right time to release your strength: after the blade finishes shining.

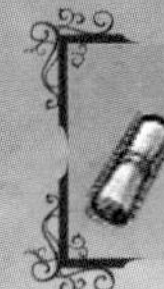

Hidden Skill

You learned the sixth Hidden Skill, the **jump slice**! Hidden Skill #6 of 7.

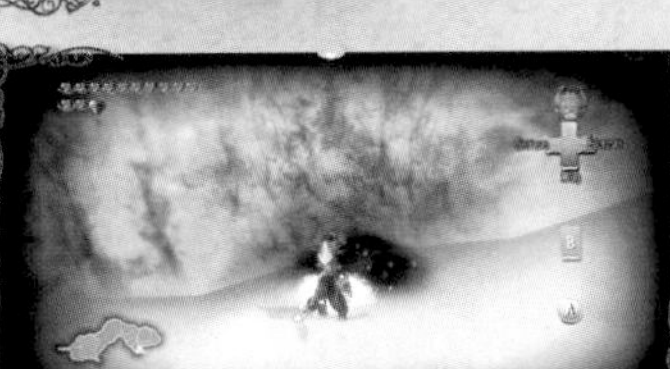

Return, and progress to the mountain peak. Follow the trail through tree-lined hills, following the Reekfish scent to a dig spot in the rock wall.

Missing Links

1. Digging for victory

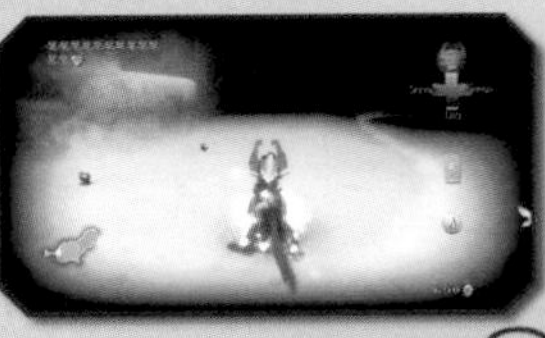

The Snowpeak has a few dig spots, where you can find Hearts and Rupees. Try digging to the side of the Reekfish scent trail, west of the icy lake.

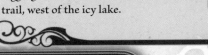

Task 4: Gain Entry to Yeto's Abode

Enemies Encountered

Ice Keese

Twilit Messenger

Snowpeak Summit: Descent to a Yeti's House

➤ Enter a cavern thick with cool air. The Reekfish trail continues to a ladder. If you're in wolf form, dig for Hearts and Rupees at the multiple dig spots, then transform. Watch the icy boulders at your sides; they can freeze you. Clawshot to the vine ceiling.

▲ This takes you to a long stepped cavern heading upward. Defeat an Ice Keese along the way, then smash the crates, skulls, and pottery for the usual prizes. There are dig spots up here, too. At the vine wall atop the steps, watch for another Ice Keese, then use the Clawshot to reach the top passage, leading to a door. Exit.

Warp Portal

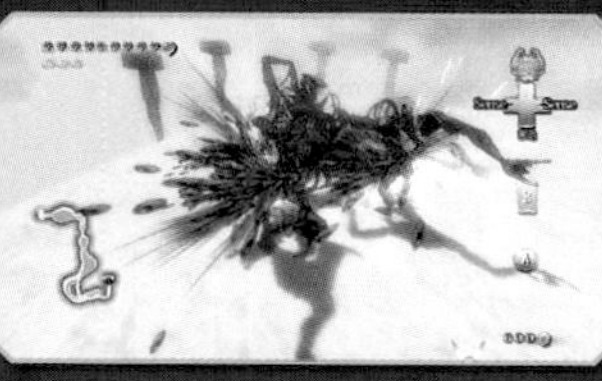

As you reach the summit, you see a dozen Ice Keeses flittering about. Run to them, and then watch as a portal opens, and three Twilit Messengers descend. As you may strike Keese during this combat, huddle all the Messengers together and then defeat them all with a spin attack or Midna's area strike. You can now warp back here whenever you please!

Tip: Once the Warp Portal forms, this is the optimal time to visit the White Wolf in the Graveyard and learn Hidden Skill #6.

◄ With the Twilit Messengers dispatched, night falls, and you can see a large hunched fellow standing next to a tree with some giant frozen leaves attached to it. This is where the Reekfish trail leads you, so head up to this small platform.

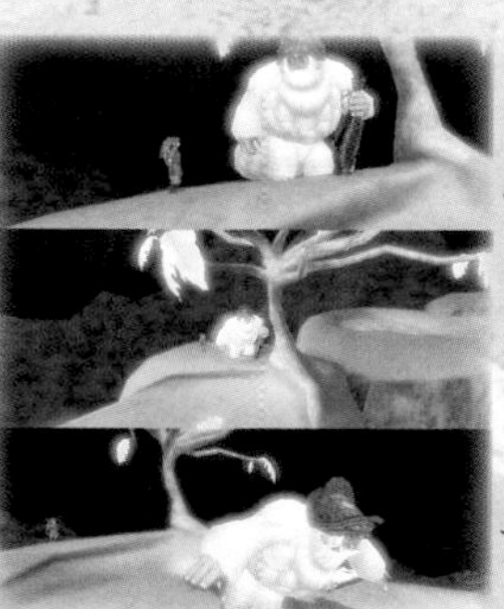

You meet Yeto the Yeti and he tells you a hilarious joke. He mentions that he has seen a shard of the Mirror for which you're looking. He invites you to his house, then bashes the nearby tree, leaps on a fallen leaf, and slides down the mountain!

Missing Links

1. Rare Color of Wolf! Tasty!

If you approach Yeto as a wolf and listen to him, he looks at you and waggles his fish. Although you're tasty, he's having Reekfish tonight!

Yeto:

About 40 years old, Yeto is a male Yeti, with a massive frame. He's cheerful and happy, and Yeta's husband. They live in an old mansion on a remote and snowy clifftop. Yeto was out hiking one day and found a shard of Mirror. He didn't know it was cursed, and he gave it to Yeta, who has been feeling ill ever since. When you meet Yeto, he's carrying a fish home, hoping his cooking will improve Yeta's health.

Characters Encountered

Yeto

Slip-Sliding to Yeto's House

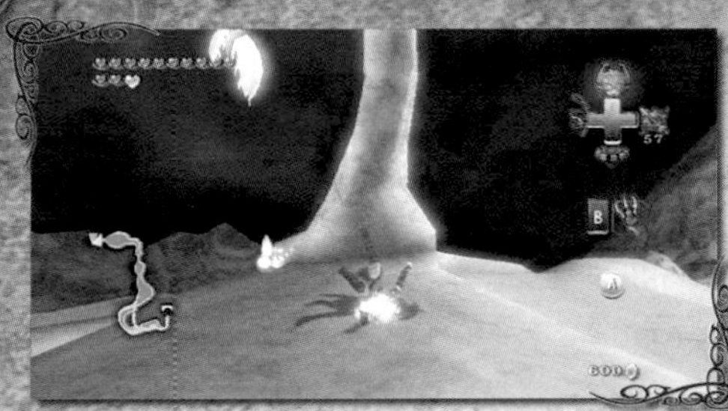

➤ You must follow Yeto to his home, and the only way to reach it is via an icy leaf slide. Roll into the tree to dislodge a leaf, then stand on it. You're about to slide down a mountain on this leaf, so prepare yourself! Step on, draw your sword, and let's go.

Sliding down on this leaf is easier if you know the following techniques:

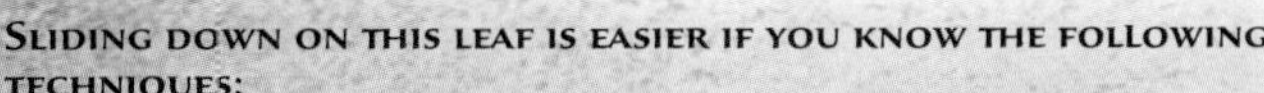

- Draw your sword. If you execute a spin attack near Yeto and hit him, he will slow down.
- Like river boating, if you press ◎ you go faster, but can't turn as quickly.
- Turn ◎ and ◎ to change direction, and ◎ to slow down. You can't stop, though!
- You can jump with Ⓐ, and this can speed you up, too.

Tip

- Follow the main route of the mountain the first time through.
- There are shortcuts, and these are revealed when you race Yeto after completing Dungeon 5. Look for those tactics then!

➤ Speed down the slope, and you automatically launch over the precipice that stopped your journey on foot.

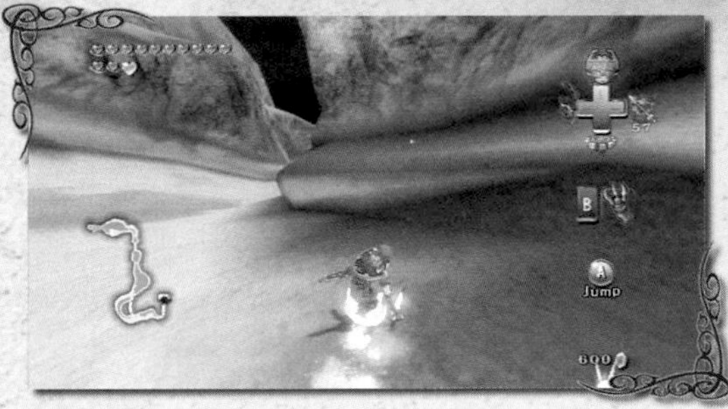

➤ When you reach this point, you can leap onto either snowbank on the side and collect the Rupees. This isn't necessary though.

▲ When you reach the bridge with the gaps in it, don't jump! You may land in a gap and have to race again. When you pass the Keeses, try a spin attack to defeat them.

▲ When you launch off this hill ramp, keep straight, and land on three tiny platforms on three trees. Each has a valuable Rupee on it: blue (5), red (20), and purple (50). Hit all three and keep your speed up.

▲ Watch out for icy shards! They stop you in your tracks, so slide to the side of them, then spin attack to destroy them.

▲ Leap at this point, on the right side of the course, if you want to take a frightening shortcut!

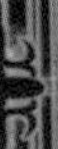

1 2 3 4

It leads up a bridge holding Rupees, and off onto a series of thin ledges with a bottomless cliff on each side! Slow down and take each ledge straight on, or go the slow route, which is less dangerous.

If you stay on the slow route, go under the bridge, then smash this ice shard, and slowly glide around the course, staying away from the drop on your left.

Stay straight as you reach this gap in the course. With Yeto's house in the distance, coast along.

After winding around a long, flat, ledged rock, you arrive at the bridge to Yeto's house. Get off your leaf, run up the steps, smash the pottery, and explore Dungeon 5!

Enemies Encountered

Ice Keese

Poe #45

Before you enter Yeto's house, transform into the wolf, and run over the bridge to check out the plateau rock. Climb up the ledges to the top, and engage an Imp Poe in combat. It appears here no matter the weather. Defeat it, then scrabble for Rupees and Hearts in the dig spots.

Poe Soul

You got the **Poe Soul**! Collect one from each Poe you defeat. Poe #45 of 60.

Dungeon 5: Snowpeak Ruins

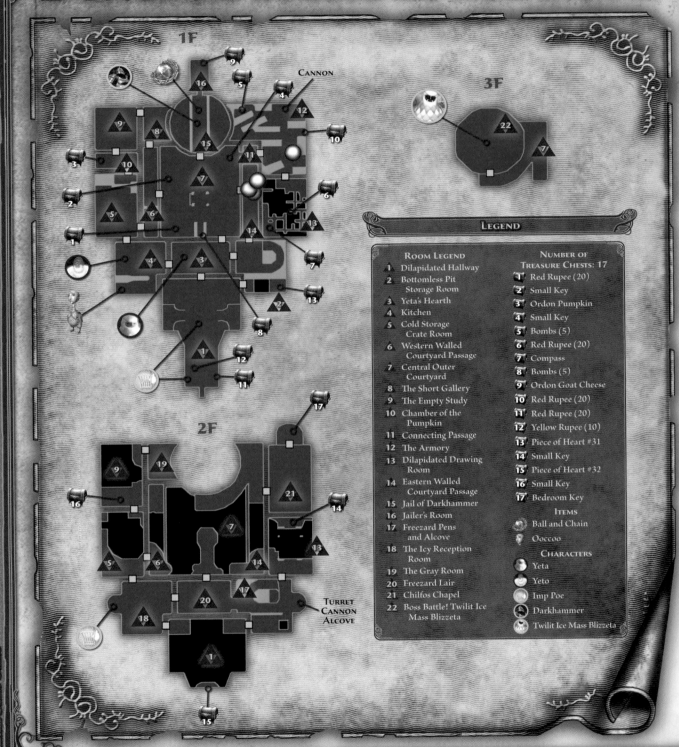

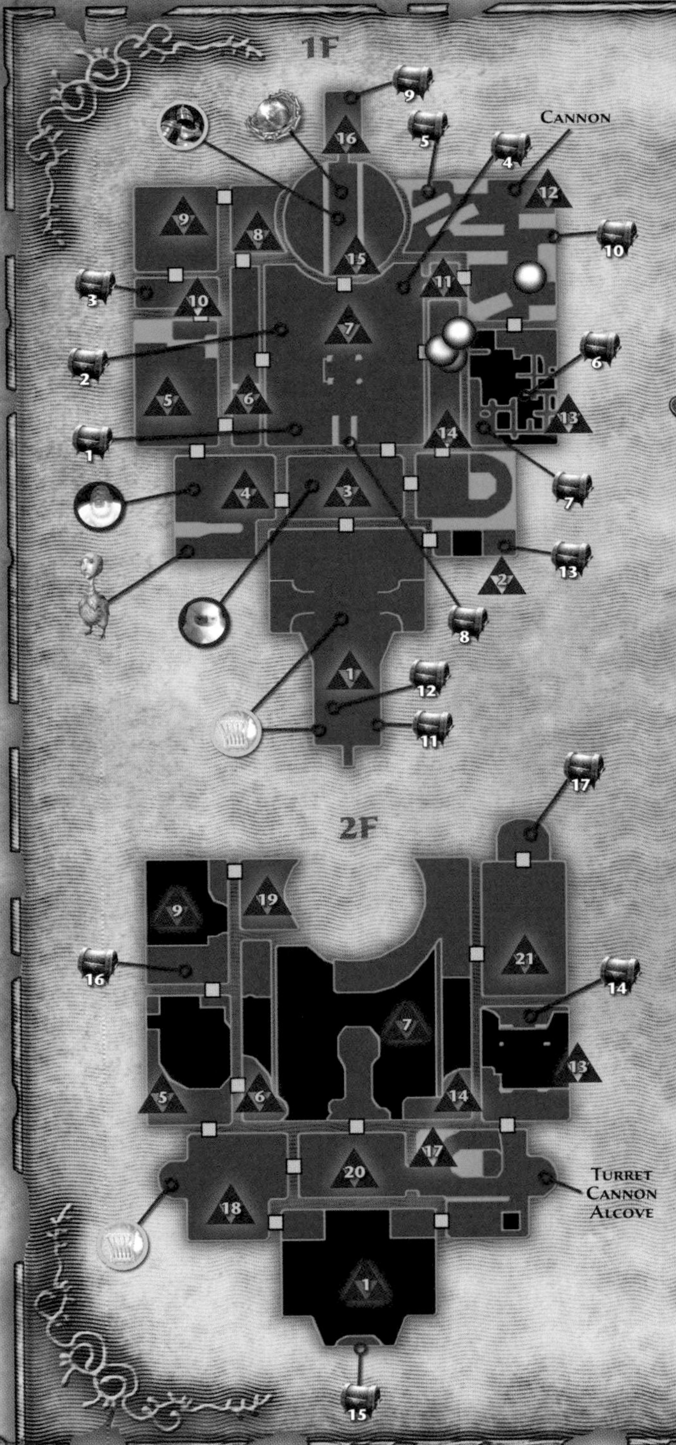

1F

Cannon

3F

2F

Turret Cannon Alcove

Legend

Room Legend

1. Dilapidated Hallway
2. Bottomless Pit Storage Room
3. Yeta's Hearth
4. Kitchen
5. Cold Storage Crate Room
6. Western Walled Courtyard Passage
7. Central Outer Courtyard
8. The Short Gallery
9. The Empty Study
10. Chamber of the Pumpkin
11. Connecting Passage
12. The Armory
13. Dilapidated Drawing Room
14. Eastern Walled Courtyard Passage
15. Jail of Darkhammer
16. Jailer's Room
17. Freezard Pens and Alcove
18. The Icy Reception Room
19. The Gray Room
20. Freezard Lair
21. Chilfos Chapel
22. Boss Battle! Twilit Ice Mass Blizzeta

Number of Treasure Chests: 17

1. Red Rupee (20)
2. Small Key
3. Ordon Pumpkin
4. Small Key
5. Bombs (5)
6. Red Rupee (20)
7. Compass
8. Bombs (5)
9. Ordon Goat Cheese
10. Red Rupee (20)
11. Red Rupee (20)
12. Yellow Rupee (10)
13. Piece of Heart #31
14. Small Key
15. Piece of Heart #32
16. Small Key
17. Bedroom Key

Items

- Ball and Chain
- Ooccoo

Characters

- Yeta
- Yeto
- Imp Poe
- Darkhammer
- Twilit Ice Mass Blizzeta

1 Try Yeto's Simple Soup pg 316

2 Locate Bedroom Key (First Attempt) pg 317

3 Defeat Darkhammer, Claim Ball & Chain pg 320

4 Sample the Superb Soup pg 324

Dungeon Denizens

Characters

Midna

Ooccoo

Yeto

Yeta

Enemies

Imp Poe

Purple Chu

Yellow Chu

Ice Keese

Bubble

Mini Freezard

Chilfos

Freezard

Bosses

Mid Boss: Darkhammer

Big Boss: Twilit Ice Mass Blizzeta

A Link to the Present

Ordon Sword · Master Sword

Heart Pieces: 0 (30 Total)

Wooden Shield · Hylian Shield

Hero's Clothes · Zora Armor · Magic Armor

Big Wallet · Big Quiver

Golden Bugs: 23 (of 24) · Hidden Skills: 6 (of 7)

Reekfish Scent · Poe Souls 45 (of 60) · Fish Journal · Letters 9 (of 16)

Mirror of Twilight: 1 (of 3)

Items to Obtain

Map of the Mansion

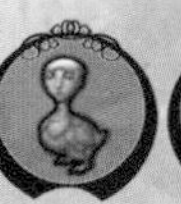
Ooccoo

Simple Soup

Small Key

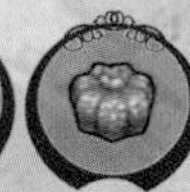
Ordon Pumpkin

Good Soup

Small Key

Bombs (5)

Compass

Bombs (5)

Ball and Chain

Ordon Goat Cheese

Superb Soup

Piece of Heart #31 (of 45)

Small Key

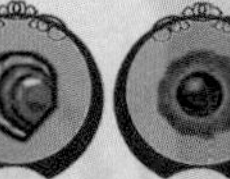
Piece of Heart #32 (of 45)

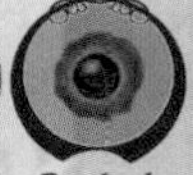
Poe Soul #48 (of 60)

Small Key

Bedroom Key

Twilight Mirror Shard

Heart Container

Items Already Acquired

Spinner

Clawshot

Hero's Bow

Iron Boots

Gale Boomerang

Lantern

Slingshot

Fishing Rod

Hawkeye

Bombs (Bag #1)

Bombs (Bag #2)

Bombs (Bag #3)

Bottle #1

Bottle #2

Bottle #3

Bottle #4

5 Defeat All Imp Poes Pg 326

6 Remove Freezard from Bedroom Ledge Pg 328

7 Locate Bedroom Key (Final Attempt) Pg 330

8 Battle Twilit Ice Mass Blizzeta Pg 331

Characters Encountered

Yeto

Yeta

Midna

Ooccoo

Snowpeak Ruins: Overview

With a crumbling mansion and a forgetful and strange Yeti wife, old Yeto has his problems, but he manages to concoct numerous broths to help heal his wife's malaise, which suspiciously started when she received a shard of the Twilight Mirror as a gift. She happily points out where her bedroom key is, so you can see the mirror for yourself. However, she is quite forgetful and sends you all over the mansion, where you face several new foes, most of which can freeze you in seconds! The real challenge comes during a battle with Darkhammer, a fully armored Lizalfos with a vicious ball and chain. Perhaps if you can beat this beast and claim the weapon for yourself, you can finally reach Yeta's bedroom, see the source of her illness, and take the mirror on behalf of Midna—but expect a little resistance.

Task 1: Try Yeto's Simple Soup

Chamber 1: Dilapidated Hallway

Before you enter this dilapidated mansion, consider doing the following:

- Have a Bottle filled with Blue Potion, Fairy Tears, or a Fairy.
- Have the Hero's Bow within easy access.
- Carry the Clawshot as your main B item.
- Purchase the Hylian Shield from Kakariko Village.
- For rare occasions, purchase the Magic Armor from Castle Town.

Tip

➤ The initial hallway has fallen into disrepair. There's a massive hole in the roof, and ice is coating the floor. Check the alcoves near you; there's some armor that wobbles when you strike it. Perhaps it will shatter with stronger force....

Poe Soul #46

Transform into your wolf form, and trot to the chamber's middle. A waving lantern announces the arrival of an Imp Poe. Switch on your sense view and leap at it, or use Midna's area attack. Then claim its soul.

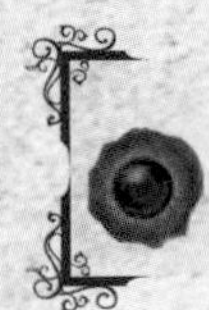

Poe Soul

You got the **Poe's Soul**! Collect one from each Poe you defeat! Poe Soul #46 of 60.

Chamber 2: Bottomless Pit Storage Room

◄ After you deliver the final blow to the Imp Poe, explore the hallway. It's preferable to be Link at this point, as there's a Purple and Yellow Chu (one is under the stairs; the other is on the middle of the steps). You can't move any farther up a floor, so check the door to your right. It leads to a bottomless pit! On the other side is a chest, but you can't reach it yet.

Chamber 3: Yeta's Hearth

◄ You enter a once-grand chamber with a female Yeti sitting by the fire. Go over and talk to her; this is Yeta, wife of Yeto. She knows you want to look at the mirror. After she obtained it, monsters have appeared, so they keep it locked on the third floor. She gives you a marked map to help you find it. She also unlocks the door to the kitchen.

Yeta:

Yeta is about 30 years old in Yeti years and is Yeto's wife. They both live in an old house, surrounded by snow. She recently received a present from her husband—a piece of an ornate mirror—and ever since she's felt strange. Sometimes angry. Sometimes tired. She isn't her old self. She spends her time resting near the fire and eating comfort food prepared by Yeto.

1

2

3

4

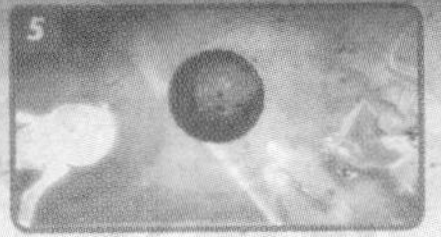
5

6

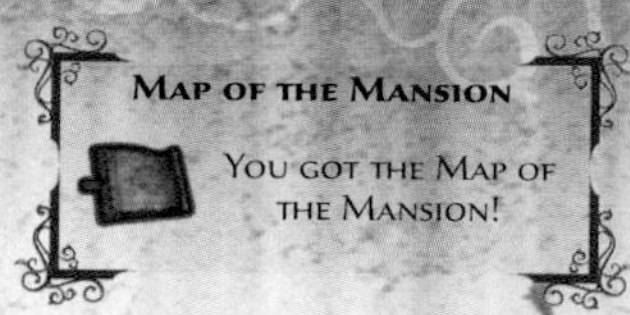
Map of the Mansion
You got the Map of the Mansion!

Chamber 4: Kitchen

➤ Exit through this door to enter the mansion's expansive kitchen. Yeto is busily preparing a giant cauldron full of fish and other ingredients. He tells you the soup's for Yeta, but you can have a taste. Head there and check out the room.

◄ There is a pantry area to the south. Run around the shelving and locate the pottery at the far end. One of the pots is shaking, and you know what that means! Your friend from the skies has arrived. Pick up Ooccoo.

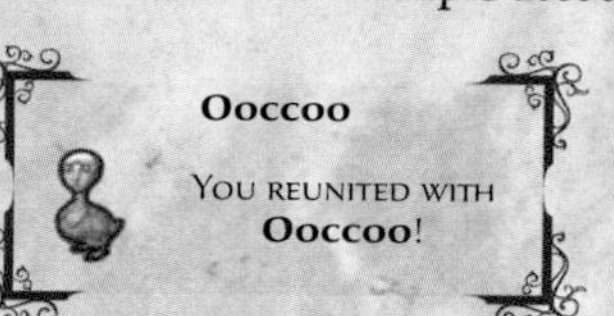
Ooccoo
You reunited with Ooccoo!

Missing Links

1. Pottery Pulverizing

Yeto doesn't allow sharp blades other than the ones he yields in his kitchen, so you must smash any pottery by picking it up. The few Rupees aren't worth your time.

◄ With Ooccoo in your inventory, check out the chef's concoction. Climb the crates in front of the cauldron and dip an empty Bottle into the bubbling broth. The broth restores only two Hearts! Of course, Yeto is still working on the ingredients and consistency.

Simple Soup
You put Simple Soup in your Bottle! It smells like fish broth.

Tip: Although this soup is low on energizing properties, there's an infinite amount to drink. If you need energy, come back here, dip your Bottle, and swig. Repeat until you're full!

Caution: There's another reason for bottling some soup—there are no Hearts in this mansion to refill your energy. Those Yetis need to rekindle their love!

Enemies Encountered

Imp Poe

Chu (Purple, Yellow)

Task 2: Locate the Bedroom Key (First Attempt)

Chamber 5: Cold Storage Crate Room

➤ Exit the kitchen via the north door, and enter a cold storage room, complete with a gate that's sealed you in. To move the gate, you must place a heavy object on the floor switch to keep the gate open.

Caution: Don't touch the crate or the middle floor switch, which are encased in ice, as you'll be frozen for a couple of seconds. Thaw them out later in your adventure.

▲ You must shove a crate over the floor switch to unlock the gate and door. Start by pushing this crate in the southeast corner, across to the southwest area.

Then push the crate in the northwest corner across so it touches the ice-encased crate. Stand behind the same crate and push it south. Then run and push the crate west one space so it hits the first crate. Now you can push the crate one more time south, onto the floor switch. Exit via the door in the southeast corner.

Chamber 6: Western Walled Courtyard Passage

Step out into a confined passage with an ice block in front of you. The only area of interest is a low arch to your side. Transform into the wolf so you can dig under this wall.

Chamber 7: Central Outer Courtyard

On the other side of this dig spot is a three-level outer courtyard. For now, stay in wolf form and tackle two White Wolfoses. Then, another appears; target and defeat them, and don't touch the wall of ice blocks on the right side.

Caution

There's deep snow in this chamber's south and north. Avoid trudging through here and attacking from here if possible, as your movement is severely slowed.

Treasure Chest: With all the White Wolfoses defeated, check the southern area, near the wall, to find a small chest. Open it to claim your Rupee prize.

Treasure Chest #1: Red Rupee (20)

Treasure Chest: There's another treasure chest in this area; it's half-buried and not immediately visible, so dig around it until you uncover it. The reward is worth your time. Then exit via the door you can unlock, into the next part of the courtyard passage.

Treasure Chest #2: Small Key

Small Key

You got a **Small Key**! This opens a locked door, but only in this area.

Chamber 6: 1st Return to Western Walled Courtyard Passage

Mini Freezard

Threat Meter

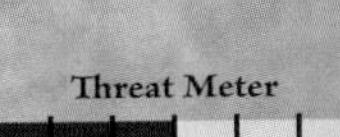

As you enter this long passage, watch the icy ground; you can't make agile moves here. Be sure to block with your shield, and then try to engage two Mini Freezards who bounce around and can encase you in ice when they strike you. This isn't very damaging (you lose less than one Heart energy), but you are exposed during this time.

Without a Ball and Chain, defeating the slippery Mini Freezards is a mixture of shield-blocking and quick sword strikes.

It's best to crush them with a Ball and Chain, but unfortunately, you don't have this weapon yet, so make do with a sword strike, then block, and a second to finish. Multiple Mini Freezards are a problem, as they can bounce around and behind you, so stick to defeating one at a time, and strike them so they ricochet into a wall that's far from you; if you don't, you'll be frozen after a quick bounce back, as shown!

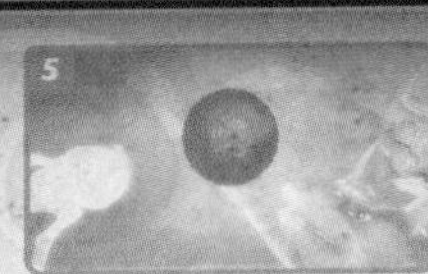

Chamber 8: The Short Gallery

➤ Head through the passage's north door, into a frozen chamber containing three Mini Freezards. Block them and strike one at a time so you aren't overwhelmed. After you defeat them all, a gate sealing the door in the northwest corner slides open. Enter it.

Chamber 9: The Empty Study

➤ You enter a square-shaped chamber with a window in the south wall. You can see the chest Yeta was talking about! Race to the door, but be warned: it shuts tight with a barred gate, and two icy threats materialize. These are the terrifying Chilfoses, whose spears have shattered many an adventurer's destiny!

Chilfos

Threat Meter

Before you obtain the Ball and Chain, chill the Chilfos out by battering his spear into pieces; then finish with a spin.

The deadly Chilfoses are a real problem to overcome, as they throw an icy spear that knocks you off your feet (and allows you to be struck by other attacks). Even worse, the spear regenerates in their hands. You have several combat options. The first is to fire two Bomb Arrows, one after the other, as quickly as possible. The first arrow staggers a Chilfos, but he soon recovers and regenerates his energy, so you must strike again when he's just been hit. This works well—from range!

The other technique is for when you're close to a Chilfos (however, be aware of others in the vicinity that can throw spears and stop this technique). You want to batter the Chilfos back until he's stunned. Start with a thorough series of slashes from your sword, which weakens and finally shatters his spear. When this occurs, finish with a spin attack, then follow up (as the Chilfos is stunned again) with more slices until it finally falls.

Chamber 10: Chamber of the Pumpkin

▲ **Treasure Chest:** With all the Chilfos threats abated, the gate opens, and you can move south, to the room that contains the key to the Twilight Mirror. Open the chest there. The key is distinctly different than your usual opening devices—it's orange and pumpkin-shaped!

Treasure Chest #3: Ordon Pumpkin

Ordon Pumpkin
You got the **Ordon Pumpkin**! This pumpkin was grown in your hometown of Ordon.

Enemies Encountered

White Wolfos

Mini Freezard

Chilfos

Midna

Yeto

Yeta

Task 3: Defeat Darkhammer, Claim the Ball and Chain

Chamber 5: 1st Return to Cold Storage Crate Room

➤ Midna appears and isn't very happy! Yeta must have gotten her treasure chests mixed up. You must now return to Yeta, so exit via the door to the south, back to the Cold Storage Crate Room. There's another entrance in the chamber's northwest corner, on the second floor, but you can't reach it yet; a crate is blocking your way on the upper ledge. Drop down and exit via the unlocked door to the south.

Chamber 4: 1st Return to Kitchen

Yeto is still preparing his soup, so head over to him. He sees you have a pumpkin and gladly grabs it from you to add to his broth!

➤ Before you leave, pumpkinless, you might as well taste the new soup. Climb onto the boxes near the cauldron, then dip your Bottle in. This is the **Good Soup**, which restores **four Hearts.**

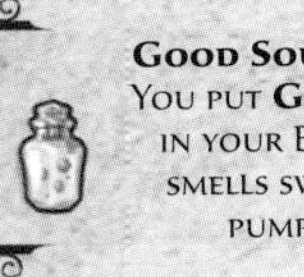

Good Soup
You put **Good Soup** in your Bottle! It smells sweet, like pumpkins.

Chamber 3: 1st Return to Yeta's Hearth

➤ Leave the kitchen and return to Yeta. Since you haven't found the key, she marks another chamber, in the northernmost part of the mansion, for you to explore. Exit via the door in the room's northeast corner.

Chamber 7: 1st Return to Central Outer Courtyard

➤ You appear on the side of the outer courtyard opposite the one you were on during your first foray here. However, the enemies are still the same; there are two White Wolfoses that jump at you, and another then appears. Take your time defeating them all, and stay on the shallow snowy areas so you aren't bogged down.

Freezard

Threat Meter

After you dispatch the White Wolfoses, head to the courtyard's northern section. A large Freezard stands in front of a door. He shoots out a freezing breath that saps energy and freezes you. Defeating this monster requires quick targeting with the Ball and Chain or some other thick round object to smash into him. Retreat from him for the moment.

The bigger Freezards are thankfully immobile. However, they're aggressive with their freezing breath, allowing others to strike you while you're immobile.

➤ **Treasure Chest:** Thoroughly check the ground in this area, as there's a chest hidden in the snow in the courtyard's northeast area. Dig it out. It contains a Small Key you can use to open the door to your right. However, resist the temptation for the moment.

Treasure Chest #4:
Small Key

Small Key
You got a **Small Key**! This will open a locked door, but only in this area.

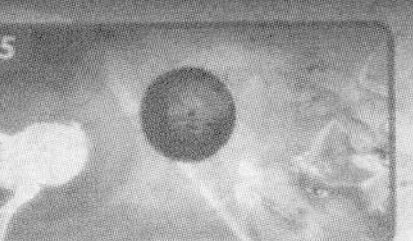

Inspect the rest of the chamber. In the middle of the chamber is a cannon, but it's useless without a projectile. To the right is a locked door with an iron holder next to it. You can use the Small Key to unlock it, but for the moment, hop through the open window in this chamber's northeast corner.

Chamber 11: Connecting Passage

Clamber over the windowsill to enter a tiny, square-shaped chamber with only one exit—the door ahead of you. Open it and enter the mansion's armory.

Chamber 12: The Armory

The armory is a treacherous place to roam, as there's around seven Mini Freezards you must dispatch one at a time. Also, the entire floor is icy, so keep your running to a minimum. Defeat the bouncing Mini Freezards in the initial icy portion of this room, and then carefully walk forward, avoiding the ice blocks, which can freeze you.

In front of you is a heavy iron cannonball. Pick it up; you'll need it momentarily. Turn and head north, around the shelves of weapons, and face left. Another Mini Freezard is heading your way, so drop the cannonball, bring out your sword, and defeat him and the others in this vicinity.

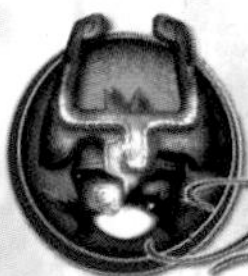

Tip: Instead of placing the cannonball down, you can throw it (if you're moving). If your aim is true, it can smash a Mini Freezard.

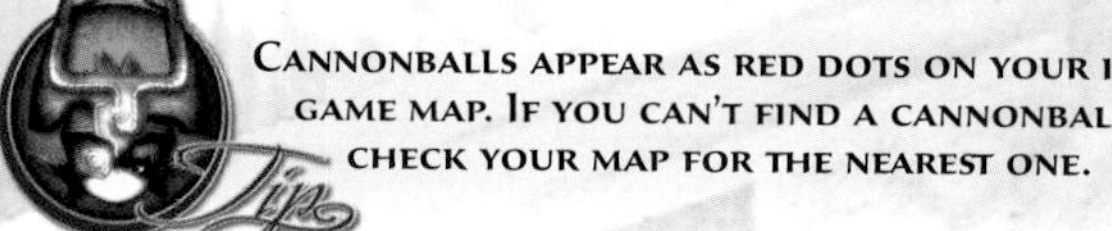

Tip: Cannonballs appear as red dots on your in-game map. If you can't find a cannonball, check your map for the nearest one.

Continue winding around this armory until you reach the room's northeast corner. There's a cannon here. Ensure you've defeated all nearby Mini Freezards, and inspect the faded parchment on the wall. It reads: "Insert...iron...continue...put in...explosion...launch."

This clue is easily understandable; you need explosives to fire the cannon, so try it out! Leave the cannon where it is, and place the cannonball inside. Step onto the wooden plate and then place (don't throw) a single bomb (or Water Bomb) into the cannon's hole.

Treasure Chest: The cannon blasts the ball across the armory, and an icy block in the northwest corner explodes. Check out this newly accessible area to find a treasure chest next to the cannonball. Break open the chest, then carry the ball back to the cannon.

Treasure Chest #5: Bombs (5)

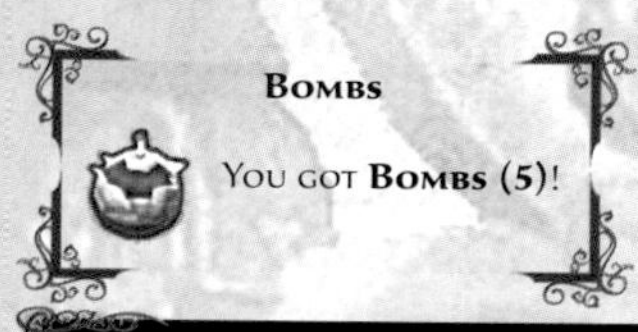

Bombs

You got **Bombs (5)**!

Place the cannonball inside the cannon, then turn the cannon to face south. There's a line of ice blocks you can shatter. This creates a pathway leading south, all the way to the exit door.

Note: There are additional ice blocks that are still intact in the armory. Don't worry about them or the items behind them; you can return to shatter these later.

Enemies Encountered

White Wolfos

Freezard

Mini Freezard

Chamber 13: Dilapidated Drawing Room

➤ Enter the next chamber. This is a tricky room to negotiate, so carefully step to the left, and onto this wooden piece. Stop at the edge, and deliver a blow to two Ice Keeses.

➤ Stay facing south, and you'll see a Mini Freezard blocking your path. Knock the Mini Freezard back with your Clawshot; he slides off into a second Mini Freezard, and both drop into the murkiness below. Now run and jump over to where the Mini Freezard was, and slide between these two pillars. Then stop!

Caution

There are numerous slides, slopes, and icy patches in this room, and all of them cause you to plummet down into the darkness below. Move slowly and on an exact path to avoid this embarrassing temporary end to your adventuring!

◄ Be *incredibly* careful now. Turn and face west. Position yourself and jump to this jutting wooden beam. Then turn west again and leap to another beam. These beams don't have ice and aren't sloping.

➤ **Treasure Chests:** Now turn right and walk toward the small treasure chest at the edge of the beam you're on. Ransack the chest for a red Rupee (20), then turn left and walk carefully to the sturdier floor in the room's southwest corner. Inspect this second chest for the Compass.

Treasure Chest #6: Red Rupee (20)

Treasure Chest #7: Compass

Compass
You got the **Compass**! This handy tool will show you where to find objects hidden in this dungeon.

➤ Now turn north and locate the Clawshot medallion next to the exit door. Propel yourself back here, and enter the armory, and head back to the Outer Courtyard.

Chamber 12: 1st Return to Armory, to Chamber 11 (1st Return to Connecting Passage) to Chamber 7 (2nd Return to Central Outer Courtyard)

◄ With the Compass and the knowledge of how to fire a cannon, you can now unlock the door to the Eastern Walled Courtyard Passage.

Chamber 14: Eastern Walled Courtyard Passage

◄ Once inside this chamber, grab one of the three cannonballs lying here and placing it on the iron scooped holder. Before placing the cannonball, you must tug the lever so the holder is down.

Chamber 7: 4th Return to Central Outer Courtyard

➤ Exit via the same door you came in from, and inspect the lever next to it. Tug on it so the ball holder descends, and the cannonball rolls out and stops in the holder. Grab the ball, and ferry it over to the cannon in the middle of this chamber. It's time to crack some ice!

▲ Keep the cannon facing south, and drop the cannonball into the cannon. Drop a bomb into the cannon and watch as the ball blasts through an ice block to the south. Behind it is a chest, with more bombs inside. Claim them, then take the ball and put it back into the cannon.

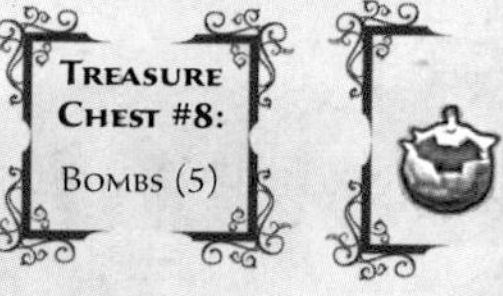

Treasure Chest #8:
Bombs (5)

Bombs

You got **Bombs (5)**!

▲ Slot the ball back into the cannon, then rotate the entire device so that it's pointing north. Drop the bomb into the cannon, and watch as the ball flies across the courtyard and straight into the Freezard! It shatters, leaving only a Mini Freezard to contend with. Now head north and open the door. You're hopefully near the key!

Chamber 15: Jail of Darkhammer

You run to the chamber's north end, and suddenly the door ahead shuts and seals! You listen as the clanking of chains announces the arrival of a huge armored knight swinging a deadly Ball and Chain. He smashes a suit of armor and aims for you next!

Enemies Encountered

Ice Keese

Freezard

Mini Freezard

Darkhammer

Darkhammer

Threat Meter

Step 1: Darkhammer isn't carrying a hammer, but he is incredibly dangerous. You have two different options to try. The first is to immediately switch to your Clawshot, and aim at one of the medallions behind and above Darkhammer before he strikes you. Be sure to aim at a medallion, or you won't be able to hang off the ceiling. When you achieve this, drop down when Darkhammer's back is to you, or after he throws the Ball and Chain, and slash him.

Step 2: If you can't use the Clawshot, step inside Darkhammer's Ball and Chain whirls for the moment. Here you'll see he's almost completely armored except for an exposed tail. Use this knowledge to your advantage.

Step 3: Be patient, as rushing in only saps your energy completely. As Darkhammer advances, roll under his rotating Ball and Chain, and when he's close to you, he attempts to throw the Ball and Chain. Roll out of the way. It is at this point that he's prone to your sword.

Step 4: Run around behind him, and Z target his tail. Then bring the full force of your sword down onto that exposed scaly hide. Try a spin and two slashes, then back up before the Ball and Chain strikes you again. Then repeat either Step 1 or Step 2, and then Steps 3 and 4 two more times until Darkhammer loses all his energy.

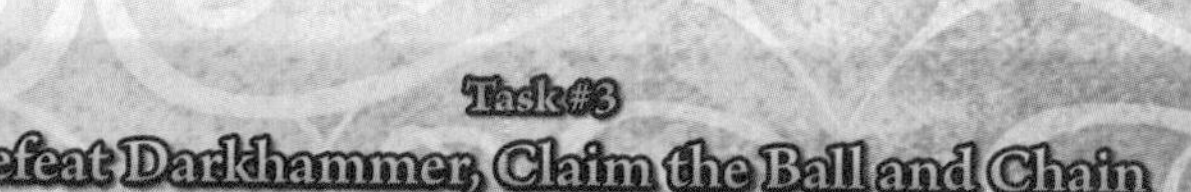

Characters Encountered

Midna

Yeto

Yeta

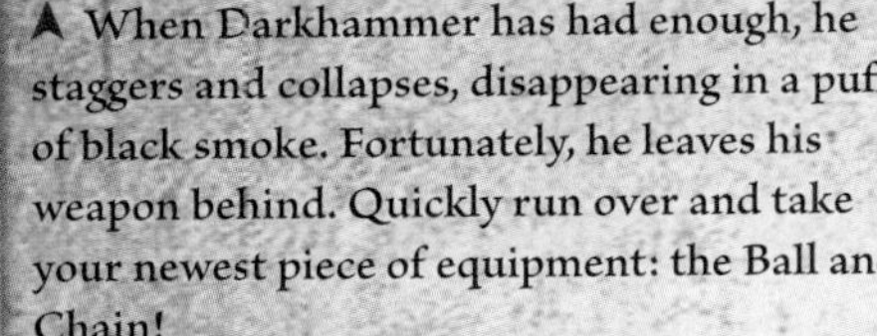

▲ When Darkhammer has had enough, he staggers and collapses, disappearing in a puff of black smoke. Fortunately, he leaves his weapon behind. Quickly run over and take your newest piece of equipment: the Ball and Chain!

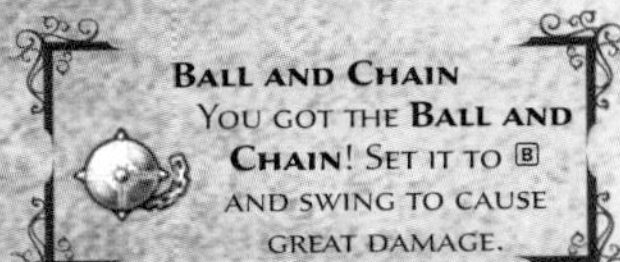

Ball and Chain
You got the **Ball and Chain**! Set it to B and swing to cause great damage.

Ball and Chain

The Ball and Chain is one of the most useful (but slow) weapons you'll add to your repertoire. There are two methods of attack with this weapon, and both are used to smash objects and enemies that are in your way. The first is whirling it around your head. Hold Z so you can move in this viewpoint. The way you tip the Wii Remote indicates where the Ball and Chain will strike (usually keep it at mid or ground level when rotating). You can move with the whirl and are almost invincible.

The second attack is a throw. This strikes twice, once on the way out and once on the way back. When you throw, use your red target to aim at where you want the ball to land. Watch out; you're prone after the throw, before you gather the Ball and Chain back up again. This technique is great for hitting enemies at range and smashing ice blocks.

Tip: Utilize the Ball and Chain in your ✥ setup. Place the Ball and Chain at ✥, and the Hero's Bow (with Bomb Arrows) plus the Clawshot at ✥ and ✥ respectively. You're now ready for anything.

Task 4: Sample the Superb Soup

Chamber 16: Jailer's Room

◄ **Treasure Chest:** Enter the room to the north via the now-unsealed door. Inside is a wall of ice, two suits of armor, and a bookcase. Bash the armor, then whirl and smack a Bubble that appears from the armor. Then disintegrate the ice wall, the table, and all other scenery, until only the chest survives. Open it up. The key is certain to be...

➤ ...not in here! Yeta has stored some Ordon Goat Cheese in here instead. Midna appears and takes the news well. Time to retrace your steps.

Treasure Chest #9: Ordon Goat Cheese

Ordon Goat Cheese
You got the **Ordon Goat Cheese**! This cheese is made from milk from Ordon goats.

Chamber 7: 4th Return to Outer Central Courtyard

◄ Head south, back through the jail to the Central Outer Courtyard. You can now begin destroying the ice barricades throughout this area, giving you easy access between the mansion's west and east wings.

➤ **Treasure Chest:** Before you head back to Yeta, you can visit the armory again and smash the ice block along the east wall. There's a chest behind here that contains a red Rupee (20).

Treasure Chest #10: Red Rupee (20)

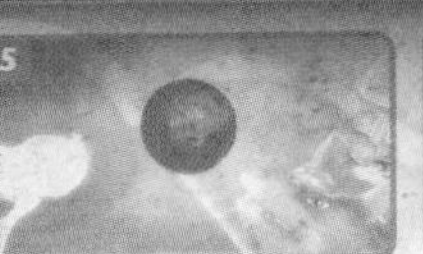

1 2 3 4 5 6

Chamber 3: 2nd Return to Yeta's Hearth

➤ Return to Yeta's Hearth. She is puzzled that you received Ordon Goat Cheese instead of a key. Perhaps her husband moved it? Whatever the case, return to the kitchen in a moment; first there's some searching to do in the entrance chamber. Head south.

Chamber 1: 1st Return to Dilapidated Hallway

◄ Return to the mansion's entrance, and search the southern passage, where the eight suits of armor stand. They can now be destroyed, so begin demolition with your Ball and Chain. The northeastern suit has a Bubble behind it; smash it! There's an orange Rupee (100) in the debris.

◄ **Treasure Chest:** One of the eastern suits of armor, when struck twice, crumples away to reveal a chest. Inside is a red Rupee (20). Grab it and continue your smashing.

Treasure Chest #11: Red Rupee (20)

Poe Soul #47

Now turn and smash the armor on the corridor's eastern side, and keep pummeling the pile of remains until an Imp Poe appears from the debris. Transform into a wolf and defeat this Imp Poe now.

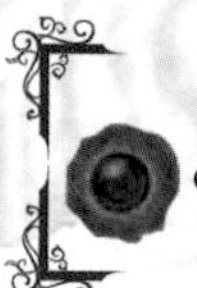

Poe Soul
You got the **Poe's Soul**! Collect one from each Poe you defeat. Poe Soul #47 of 60.

▲ **Treasure Chest:** You should be almost cleared up here, so smash the northwest suit of armor twice, and locate the chest behind here. Inside is a small reward.

Treasure Chest #12: Yellow Rupee (10)

Tip: Smash each suit of armor with your Ball and Chain until it disintegrates, as there is an orange Rupee (100) in one of the suits. This is more enticing than the chests!

Chamber 3: 3rd Return to Yeta's Hearth to Chamber 4 (2nd Return to Kitchen)

▲ You must discover where this key is, and Yeta suggests you meet Yeto. He takes the Ordon Goat Cheese from you and adds this to the bubbling brew and lets you scoop as many Bottles of it as you wish. This is **Superb Soup**, which acts in the same way as a Red Potion, restoring **eight Hearts**. Return to claim more whenever necessary.

Superb Soup
You put **Superb Soup** in your Bottle! It smells deliciously cheesy!

Enemies Encountered

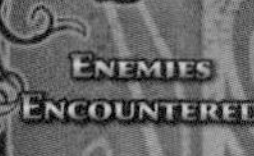

Bubble

Imp Poe

Task #4
Sample the Superb Soup

Characters Encountered

Yeta

Task 5: Defeat all Imp Poes

Chamber 3: 4th Return to Yeta's Hearth

➤ Head back from the kitchen and into Yeta's Hearth. She suddenly remembers that the key must be in the northeastern chamber, on the second floor. She opens the door in the eastern wall to let you through.

Chamber 17: (1F) Freezard Pens and Alcove

➤ Open the door to the east and enter the first floor of the Freezard Pens. Ahead, you can see a Freezard in a large circular pen, unable to escape. Ignore him for now and face north. There's a door with a cannonball holder. Open the door.

Chamber 14: 1st Return to Eastern Walled Courtyard Passage

◄ Enter the walled courtyard area where you picked up a cannonball. Ahead is the crate you couldn't shift earlier. Push it so it drops into the sloping ground below. Then run north, pick up the nearest cannonball, and bring it back to the door. Pull the lever, place the cannonball on the holder, and head back into the Freezard Pens. Turn and press the lever again, and grab the cannonball. Place it on the floor.

Chamber 17: (1F to 2F) 1st Return to Freezard Pens and Alcove

➤ Carry the cannonball to the edge of a sloping floor that spirals up to the second floor. Ahead of you is a large cage, and inside is a Freezard. Watch as the Freezard breathes an icy blast left and right. When he is turning away from you, quickly run up, turn westward, aim through the gap in the cage, and smash him twice with your Ball and Chain.

➤ Run to this chamber's second floor, and you'll encounter another Freezard breathing his freezing plume. Wait until he turns completely to the right, then run onto the small ledge opposite the open part of the cage. Back up so you aren't caught by the blast as he turns right to left; then run to the opening and smash him twice before he turns back toward you.

◄ With only Mini Freezards bouncing about in the cage now, you can smash them up for Rupees (use the Clawshot to grab the Rupees), or leave them be. Return down the slope for the cannonball, and bring it up to the second floor. Deposit it next to a wall of ice, then smash the ice with your Ball and Chain, revealing a cannon in a turret alcove.

▲ Quickly switch to your sword and slash the two Ice Keeses that swoop in from the alcove. Pick up the cannonball, place it in the cannon, and turn the cannon to face west. Don't fire it yet; a couple of metal crates block the trajectory path.

▲ Instead, move into the adjacent room, which has a red carpet and a locked door. Check the floor. The section in the southeast corner looks unstable. Place a bomb on the cracked floor and it splinters, creating a hole.

Chamber 2: (2F to 1F) 1st Return to Bottomless Pit Storage Room

➤ Treasure Chest: Drop through this hole; it leads back to the second chamber you encountered in this mansion. You're on the other side and can easily walk to the chest. Open it, take the Piece of Heart, and then use your Clawshot to return to the second floor.

Treasure Chest #13: Piece of Heart #31

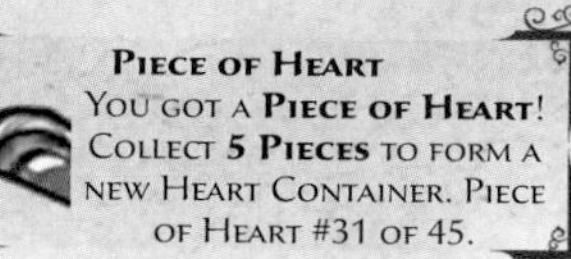

Piece of Heart
You got a **Piece of Heart**! Collect **5 Pieces** to form a new Heart Container. Piece of Heart #31 of 45.

Chamber 17: (2F) 2nd Return to Freezard Pens and Alcove

➤ Return to the alcove area and the red carpet. There's still no way to open the locked door yet, so move north, past the cannon, and open the door in the north wall.

Chamber 13: (2F) 1st Return to Dilapidated Drawing Room

➤ Open the door and step into the upper floor overlooking the dilapidated drawing room downstairs, where you found the Compass. Immediately run across the wooden floor and slice into a Chilfos. You can use your sword and spin attack, sending it flying off the side into the bottomless pit below. Or, you can smash it with your Ball and Chain.

Missing Links

1. Ball and Chain Bashing

Now that you have the Ball and Chain, you can smash almost any piece of scenery, such as tables, chairs, sofas, and barrels. Although fun, only barrels ever contain anything, usually Rupees (like the yellow Rupee [10] in this barrel). Bash through every room in the mansion if you must destroy everything in sight!

➤ Look across the room to see a chest on the north ledge. In the middle of the ceiling is a metal chandelier; use this to reach the ledge. Bring out your Ball and Chain, and smash the ice block on the left wall; this reveals a Clawshot medallion. Now strike the chandelier. As soon as it begins to swing quickly, put your Ball and Chain away, and wait for it to swing near you. Then leap onto the chandelier, and hop off onto the ledge.

Tip: If you don't have enough momentum, the chandelier slows and you miss the jump. Make sure this is swinging vigorously before you leap on, and leap off as quickly as possible. If you're stuck, Clawshot to the medallion you just uncovered.

Treasure Chest #14: Small Key

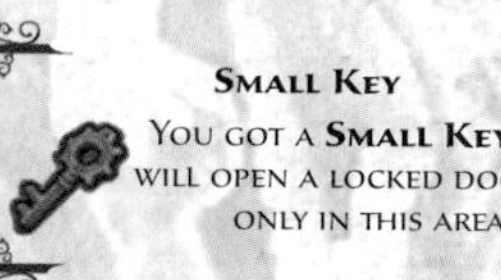

Small Key
You got a **Small Key**! This will open a locked door, but only in this area.

Chamber 17: (2F) 3rd Return to Freezard Pens and Alcove, to Chamber 1 ([2F] 2nd Return to Dilapidated Hallway)

➤ Use the Clawshot medallion to reach the wooden ledge on the opposite side, and exit back to the Freezard Pens and Alcove. Now run to the area with the locked door and the hole you just made in the floor. Open the locked door, and step back into the first chamber you visited. This time, you're on the second floor. Smash the ice block to your right to reveal a Clawshot medallion. Then fire a Bomb Arrow at the Chilfos across the way.

Enemies Encountered

Freezard

Mini Freezard

Ice Keese

Chilfos

Task #5
Defeat all Imp Poes

SMASH THE ICE BLOCK TO REVEAL THE MEDALLION, AS THIS ALLOWS YOU TO HEAD BACK UP HERE EASILY IF YOU FALL DOWN TO THE FIRST FLOOR.

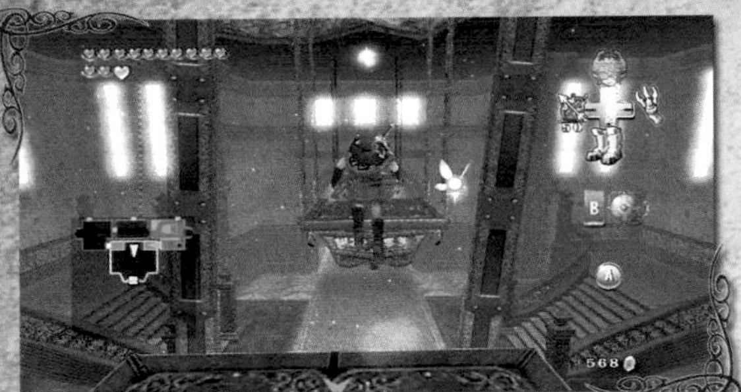

Treasure Chest: Although you can smash a Ball and Chain into the chandelier and cross to where the Chilfos was standing, you should instead leap to the first swinging chandelier and face south. There's a second and third chandelier, with a chest on a high ledge at the opposite end. Bash the first chandelier twice, leap on quickly, then bash the second twice, leap onto that, then off it and grab the ledge the chest is on. The prize is worth effort!

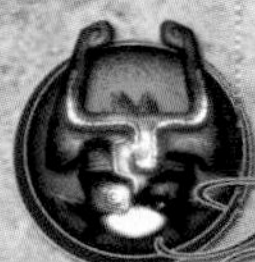

REMEMBER TO Z TARGET EACH CHANDELIER AND MAKE QUICK BALL-AND-CHAIN THROWS AFTER ONE ROTATION. BE QUICK!

TREASURE CHEST #15: PIECE OF HEART #32

PIECE OF HEART
YOU GOT A **PIECE OF HEART**! COLLECT **4 PIECES** TO FORM A NEW HEART CONTAINER. PIECE OF HEART #32 OF 45.

Chamber 18: The Icy Reception Room

Use the Clawshot to return to the second floor, then cross to the door the Chilfos was guarding. It leads to a room completely encased in ice. Immediately bring out your Ball and Chain, as there are eight Mini Freezards heading your way. Whirl attack, keeping your weapon twirling close to you, then advance slowly while holding Z. Keep this up until you shatter all the Mini Freezards.

Poe Soul #48

Move toward the ice wall on the room's west side. An Imp Poe floats out before you can smash the ice, so transform into the wolf and snag his soul before he floats back behind the ice.

POE SOUL
YOU GOT THE **POE'S SOUL**! COLLECT ONE FROM EACH POE YOU DEFEAT! POE SOUL #48 OF 60.

THERE'S A LOCKED DOOR IN THE EAST WALL OF THIS ROOM. REMEMBER THIS FOR LATER!

Task 6: Remove the Freezard from the Bedroom Ledge

Chamber 5: (2F to 1F) 2nd Return to Cold Storage Crate Room

While in the reception room, you can smash the rest of the ice at the alcove, but there's only Ice Keese to defeat. Instead, turn and exit via the north door, back into the Cold Storage Crate Room. Now you can shove the metal crate along the ledge and down to the ground. This allows you access into the room from all floors.

Descend to the first floor, and smash the ice from the metal crate and middle floor switch.

Time to solve another sliding puzzle! You need move only two crates: Start by pushing this crate from the north to the south.

▲ Now run to the south, face north, and shove this crate up the middle of the puzzle so it passes over the middle floor switch.

▲ Now shove the first crate west and then north, so it's sitting adjacent to the middle floor switch.

▲ Run to the crate that's the farthest north, in the middle, and push it clockwise around the rim of the puzzle so it hits the crate you haven't moved yet.

▲ Finally, face north and push the crate against the one adjacent to the floor switch. It lands on the switch, unlocking a door on the second floor. Climb onto the crate you pushed off the second floor ledge, and exit through this newly unlocked door.

Chamber 6: 1st Return to (2F) Western Walled Courtyard Passage

◄ You emerge on the battlements outside and above the courtyard passage. Quickly aim your Hero's Bow at a Chilfos, striking it twice with Bomb Arrows. Do the same with two more Chilfos in the chamber's northwestern corner.

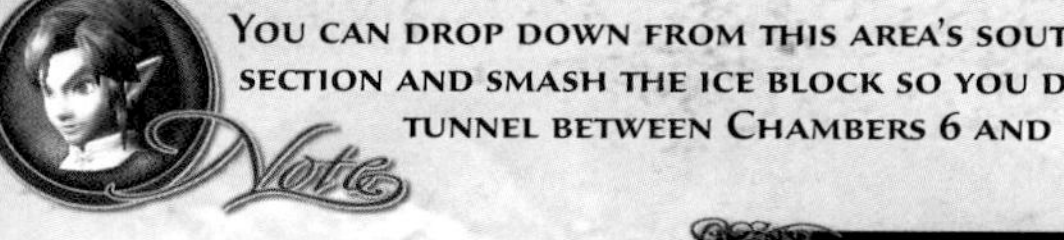

Note: You can drop down from this area's southwestern section and smash the ice block so you don't have to tunnel between Chambers 6 and 7.

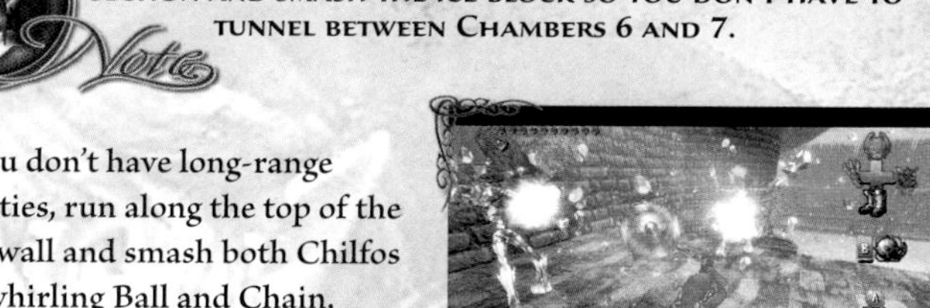

► If you don't have long-range capabilities, run along the top of the broken wall and smash both Chilfos with a whirling Ball and Chain.

► There's a cannon overlooking the courtyard, above the cannon you used to reach Darkhammer's jail, but you can't reach it yet. Instead, walk to the top of the broken wall to where the two Chilfos were standing. Your way onward is tricky to find; look north through the ruined wall, into the room beyond: there's a Clawshot medallion you can aim at!

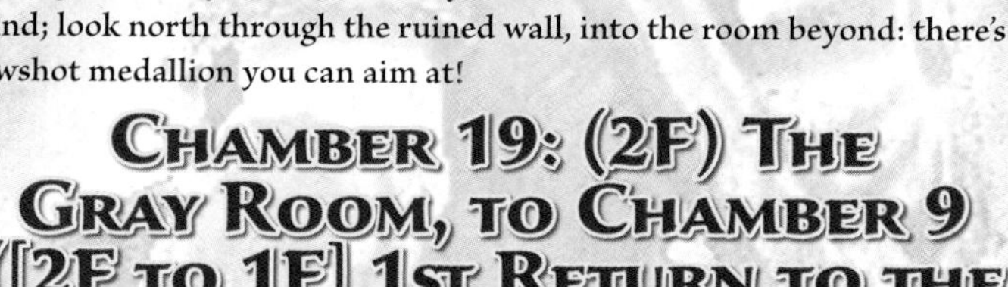

Chamber 19: (2F) The Gray Room, to Chamber 9 ([2F to 1F] 1st Return to the Empty Study)

◄ **Treasure Chest:** You land in a stone chamber. Leave immediately via the only door. This leads you into the room where you first fought two Chilfos, shortly before you discovered your Pumpkin prize. Begin by smashing the ice on the wall to reveal a Clawshot medallion (so you can return here if you fall). Then smash some barrels for Rupees. When you're finished, bash a chandelier, leap onto it, and turn south. Bash a second chandelier, leap to that, and across to the ledge opposite. This holds some destructible furniture and a small chest.

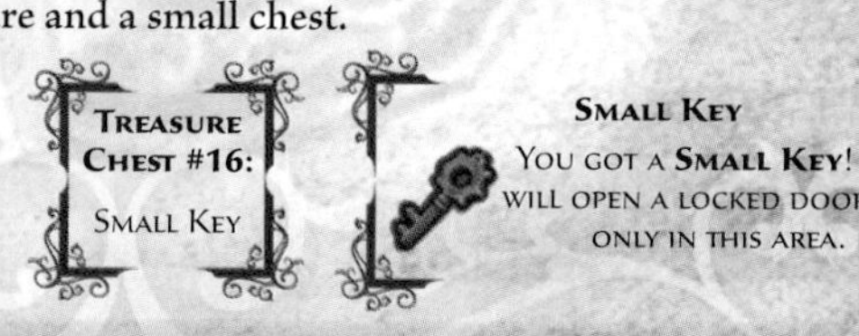

Treasure Chest #16: Small Key

Small Key

You got a **Small Key**! This will open a locked door, but only in this area.

Enemies Encountered

Mini Freezard

Imp Poe

Freezard

Ice Keese

Chilfos

Task #6

Remove the Freezard from the Bedroom Ledge

Characters Encountered

Yeta

Chamber 5: (2F) 3rd Return to Cold Storage Crate Room, to Chamber 18 (Icy Reception Room)

➤ Take the door on the south wall back to this Cold Storage Crate Room. Climb the crates in the southeast corner, and run across the icy ledge, back to the Icy Reception Room.

◀ The gaggle of Mini Freezards have returned. Break out the Ball and Chain again and defeat them all. When you're done, slide to the eastern wall and unlock the door.

Chamber 20: Freezard Lair to Chamber 17 (2F 4th Return to Freezard Pens and Alcove)

➤ The next room houses two large Freezards. Run toward them until they begin spraying their icy breath, then back up. The Freezards spray in a circular motion, so dash in when they turn away from you, and bash them with two Ball-and-Chain strikes. Tackle them one at a time, as Mini Freezards are created after you shatter each Freezard. Then bash any barrels for some Rupees.

➤ Move to the chamber's eastern section and inspect the two metal crates. Push them from this direction, and they fall into the Freezard Pens! You can now easily access the pens and the Freezard Lair, which is perfect, as you require a cannonball and can easily carry the cannonball up to the second floor without being frozen. Head to the alcove where you placed a cannonball earlier, turn it to face west, and fire!

Tip: If you haven't prepped this cannon yet, head to Chamber 14 on the first floor and grab a cannonball, then ferry it to this cannon.

Chamber 7: (2F) 5th Return to Central Outer Courtyard

◀ Pick up the cannonball from where it landed, and slot it into the holder next to the north door. Open the door, and head onto the ledge above the Central Outer Courtyard. You're now in the same place as the cannon. Turn and pull the lever so the cannonball rolls out. Also, smash the ice on the wall to expose a Clawshot medallion (useful if you wish to return here from the lower ground).

➤ Run with the cannonball to the cannon on the circular ledge, and deposit the ball into it. Place a bomb into the cannon, and watch as the ball smashes the Freezard, allowing you to continue on your way. Now drop down, enter over the windowsill or through the door to Chamber 14, and climb the steps. At the top, block with your shield, then use the Ball and Chain to crush the remaining Mini Freezards. Open the door on the east wall.

Task 7: Locate the Bedroom Key (Final Attempt)

Chamber 21: (2F) Chilfos Chapel

Now you know why this chamber is known as Chilfos Chapel. Just pray you can emerge victorious!

▲ As you enter the chapel, the doors seal, and a total of six Chilfos welcome you. Draw your sword and begin to advance; there's some

1

2

3

4

5

6

frantic combat in your future. You can also try staying at extremely long range and quickly blasting Bomb Arrows twice in a row. If you're having trouble with this technique, switch to your shield, and block the incoming ice spears. Then try a leaping strike followed by a spin attack; the spin is excellent for damaging multiple foes. Concentrate on one Chilfos at a time, and eventually, with some rolling, shielding, and a little luck, you'll prevail.

◄ Once you've smashed the final Chilfos into pieces, the doors unlock and you're free to move about the chapel. The pews can be hit, but nothing is in them. Enter the chapel's north section and open the chest. That's the key you've been trying to find!

Treasure Chest #17: Bedroom Key

Bedroom Key
You got the **Bedroom Key**! This will let you access the bedroom that houses the Mirror Shard.

Chamber 7: (2F to 3F) 6th Return to Central Outer Courtyard

▲ Finally! This metal key is designed to unlock Yeta's tower bedroom. In fact, she meets you on the curved stone balcony that leads to her room. Follow her here, and unlock the door.

Enemies Encountered

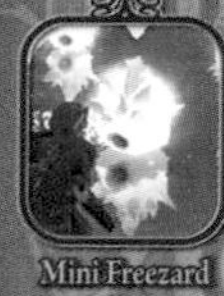

Mini Freezard

Freezard

Chilfos

Twilit Ice Mass Blizzeta

Task 8: Battle Twilit Ice Mass Blizzeta

Chamber 22: (3F) Boss Battle! Twilit Ice Mass Blizzeta

Twilit Ice Mass Blizzeta

Threat Meter

Yeta leads you into her bedroom and waddles over to the Mirror Shard. She looks at the mirror lovingly. The room darkens. "NOT TAKE MIRROR!" she growls, and transforms into a terrifying ice mass; behold Blizzeta!

Step 1: Blizzeta can control the element of ice. She encases herself in a giant ice-doll sculpture. She slides toward you; bash her back with the Ball and Chain.

Step 2: As you strike her, her ice casing gets progressively smaller, and she sheds a load of Mini Freezards; whirl your Ball and Chain to deflect them. Continue this style of attack until all the ice layers fall away and you see Blizzeta.

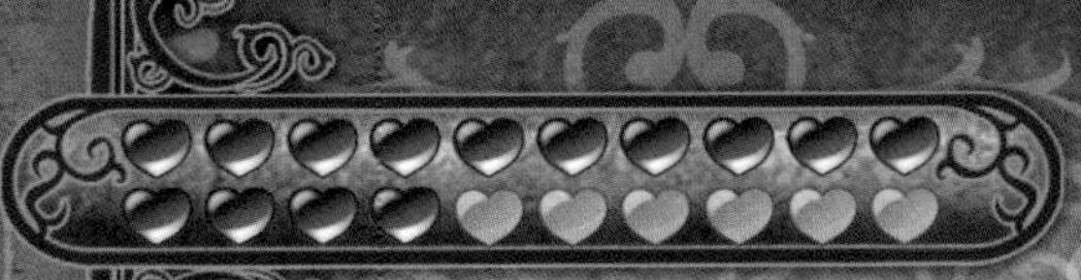

Characters Encountered

Midna

Yeto

Yeta

Twilit Ice Mass Blizzeta (cont'd)

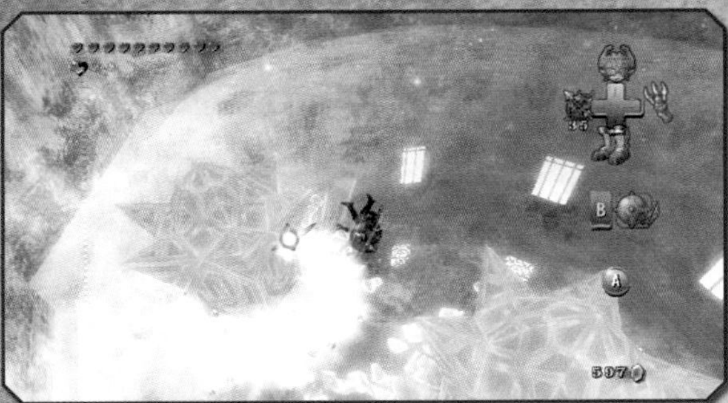

Step 3: Blizzeta wiggles and floats upward, creating an ice palanquin to sit in and surrounding herself with ornate shards. They follow you around the room. Look at their reflections, and when they start to descend, roll out of the way multiple times.

Step 5: The remaining shards form a circle, as shown, and descend, pinning you in the middle. This is when your smashing skills used in Step 4 come in handy; the gaps you made by bashing shards should be used to escape, or you're flattened by Blizzeta's falling palanquin!

Step 4: As soon as the shards finish falling, quickly bring out your Ball and Chain and smash as many of them as possible. Try to split at least two apart.

Step 6: The final step is to turn while you're out of the circle (ideally when there's only three or four shards left), and bash Blizzeta's palanquin after it drops. Repeat Steps 3–6 twice more, and Blizzeta yields to your amazing ice-bashing prowess!

Tip: A Heart is left behind after each Mini Freezard (Steps 1 and 2) and ice shard (Steps 3 - 4), so grab any hearts that are available without ignoring the raining ice above you!

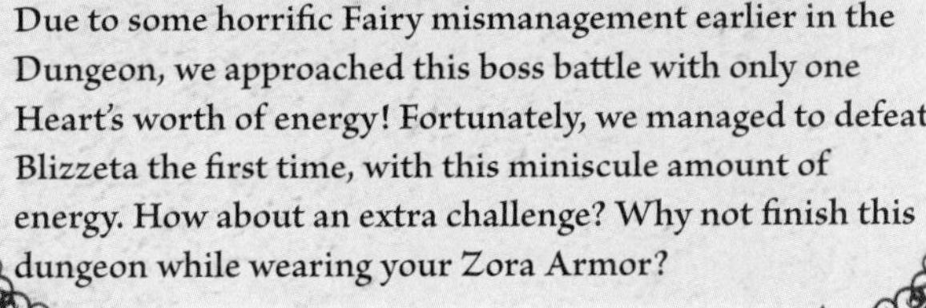

Author Note

Due to some horrific Fairy mismanagement earlier in the Dungeon, we approached this boss battle with only one Heart's worth of energy! Fortunately, we managed to defeat Blizzeta the first time, with this miniscule amount of energy. How about an extra challenge? Why not finish this dungeon while wearing your Zora Armor?

1

2

3

4

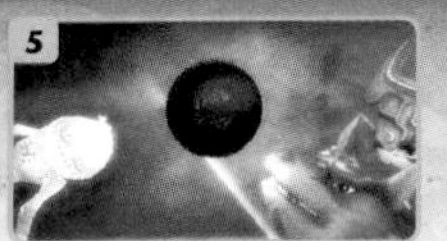
5

6

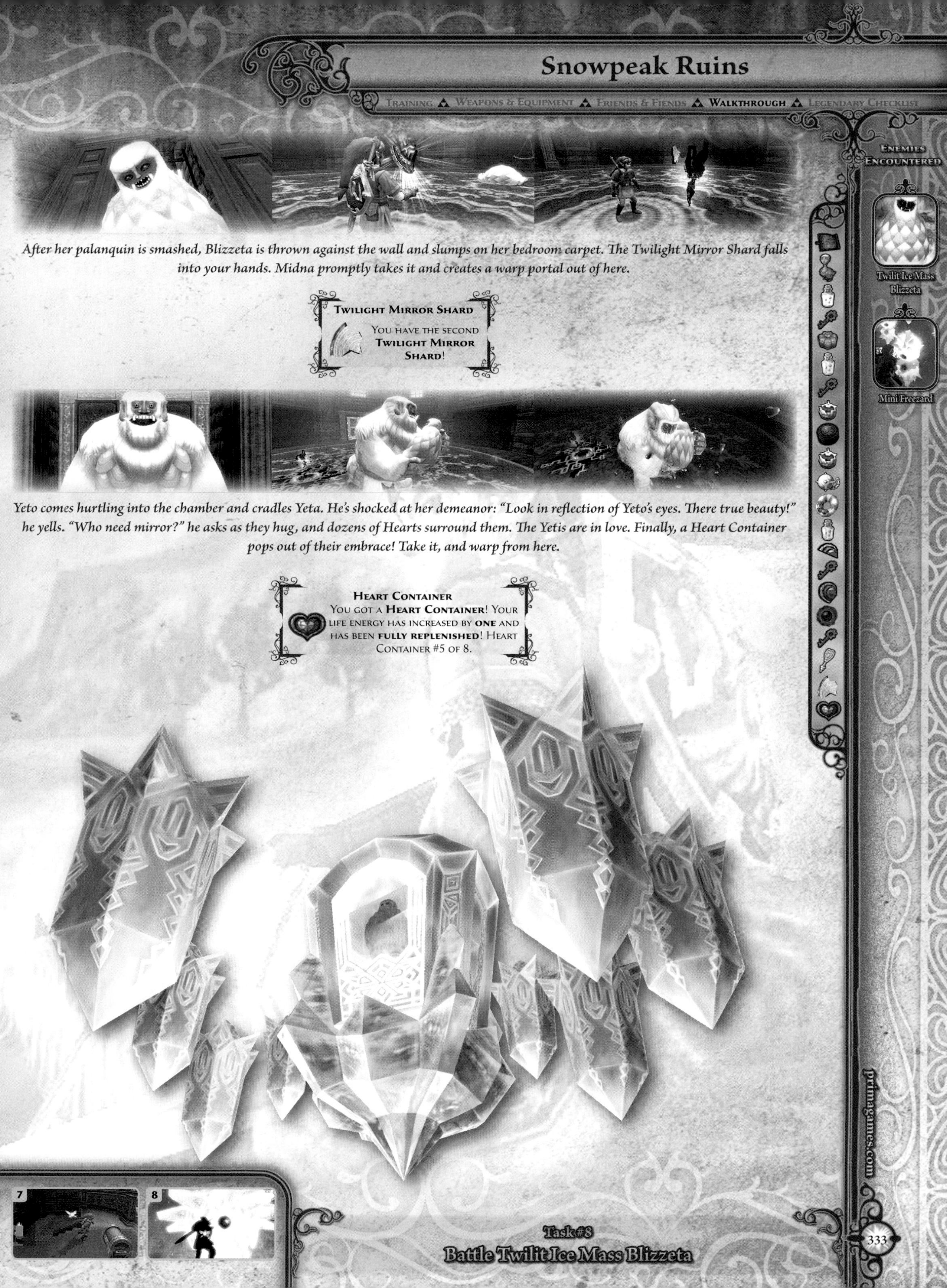

After her palanquin is smashed, Blizzeta is thrown against the wall and slumps on her bedroom carpet. The Twilight Mirror Shard falls into your hands. Midna promptly takes it and creates a warp portal out of here.

Twilight Mirror Shard

You have the second **Twilight Mirror Shard**!

Yeto comes hurtling into the chamber and cradles Yeta. He's shocked at her demeanor: "Look in reflection of Yeto's eyes. There true beauty!" he yells. "Who need mirror?" he asks as they hug, and dozens of Hearts surround them. The Yetis are in love. Finally, a Heart Container pops out of their embrace! Take it, and warp from here.

Heart Container

You got a **Heart Container**! Your life energy has increased by **one** and has been **fully replenished**! Heart Container #5 of 8.

Characters Encountered

Yeto

Yeta

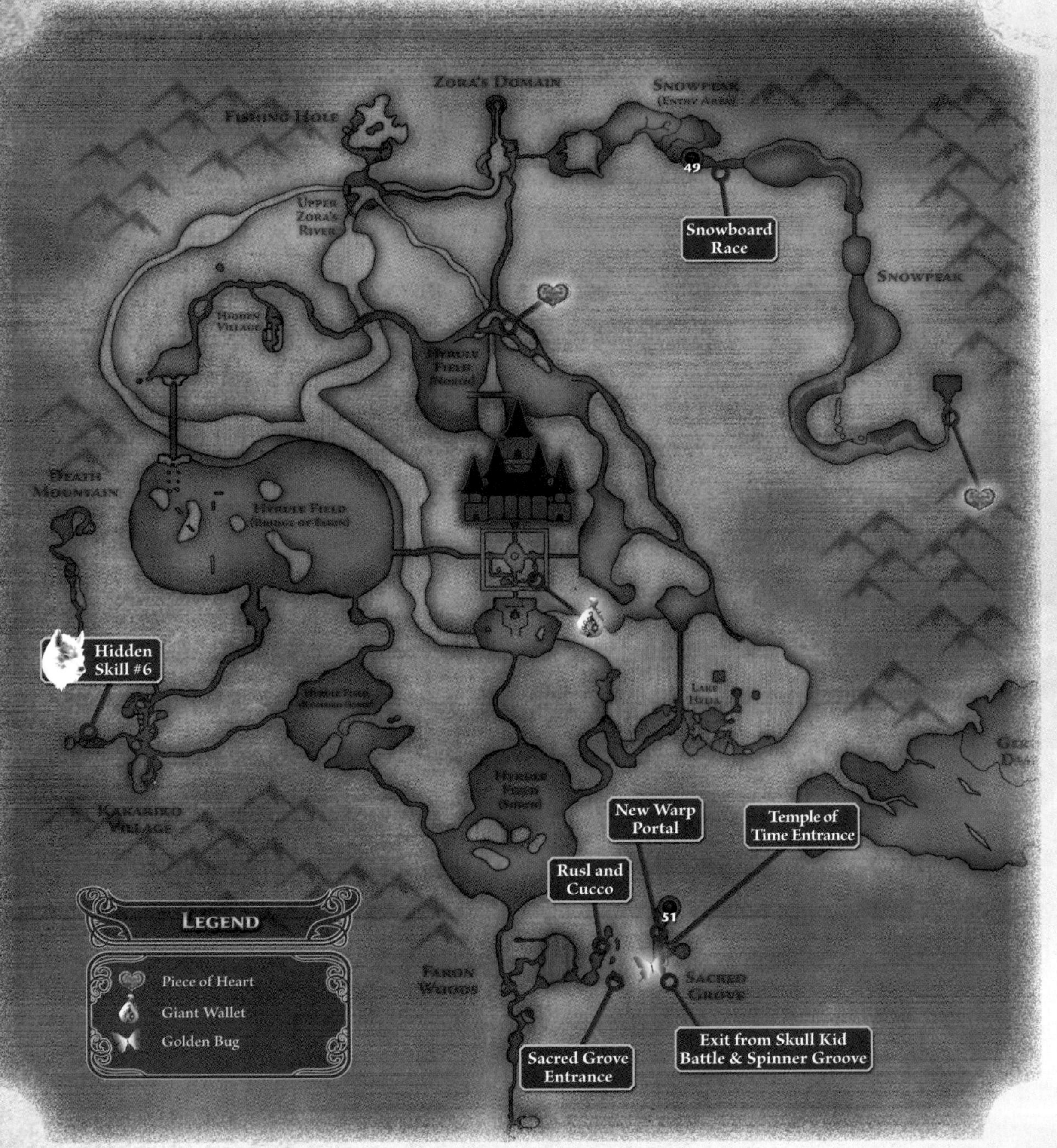

Overworld: Return to the Sacred Grove

Zora's Domain

Snowpeak (Entry Area)

Fishing Hole

Upper Zora's River

49

Snowboard Race

Snowpeak

Hidden Village

Hyrule Field (North)

Death Mountain

Hyrule Field (Bridge of Eldin)

Hidden Skill #6

Lake Hylia

Hyrule Field (South)

Kakariko Village

New Warp Portal

Temple of Time Entrance

Rusl and Cucco

51

Faron Woods

Sacred Grove

Sacred Grove Entrance

Exit from Skull Kid Battle & Spinner Groove

Legend

- Piece of Heart
- Giant Wallet
- Golden Bug

Pg 335

Hunt for Items Around Snowpeak

Pg 340

Find the Golden Cucco

Pg 340

Follow and Fight the Strange Skull Kid

Pg 342

Obtain the Giant Wallet

Return to the Sacred Grove: Overview

With your fifth dungeon completed, and providing you're attempting to obtain everything at the earliest possible juncture, you can cross some major accomplishments off your "to do" list during this part of your Overworld adventuring. For a start, you can clear your final dig cavern and collect your last Golden Bug to claim the grand prize from Princess Agitha. But your main objective is to rendezvous with Rusl, who is convinced an old temple lies somewhere within the Sacred Grove. Journey there, find a novel way to enter the grove, and head back in time...with Ooccoo!

A Link to the Present

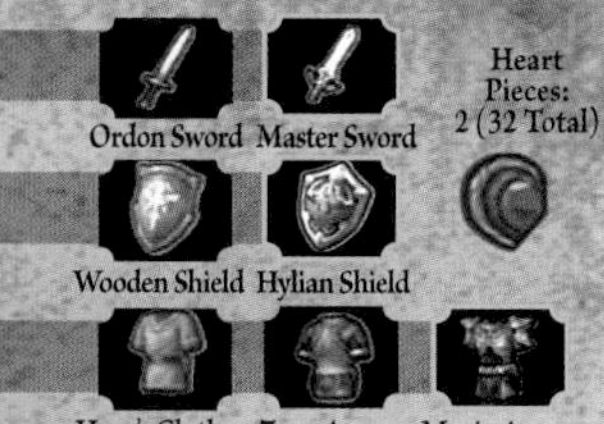

Big Wallet, Big Quiver, Golden Bugs: 23 (of 24), Hidden Skills: 6 (of 7), Reekfish Scent, Poe Souls 48 (of 60), Fish Journal, Letters 9 (of 16)

Mirror of Twilight: 2 (of 4)

Items to Obtain

Piece of Heart #33 (of 45)

Piece of Heart #34 (of 45)

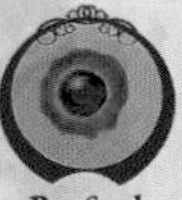

Poe Soul #51 (of 60)

Female Snail

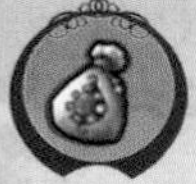

Giant Wallet

Task 1: Thoroughly Hunt for Items around Snowpeak Mountain

After Snowpeak Ruins: Minigame: Sledding to Victory

▲ After you leave Snowpeak Ruins, don't immediately warp away to the Hyrule Fields. Instead, climb to the top of the mountain and talk to Yeto, who asks if you want to race him. Agree to this challenge.

▲ Begin your race, and follow the route as you did when you slid down here previously. Learn the shortcuts, and how best to take them, or even take the regular way around. You should easily beat him if you don't fall! When you win, speak to Yeta, and she'll tell you the best time.

Return to the top of the mountain, and speak to Yeta this time. She wants to race you too, and she's incredibly skilled! Learn the following route to beat her:

5
Pg 343
Enter the Temple of Time

Characters Encountered

Yeta

Perform a spin attack as you both meet after the first jump.

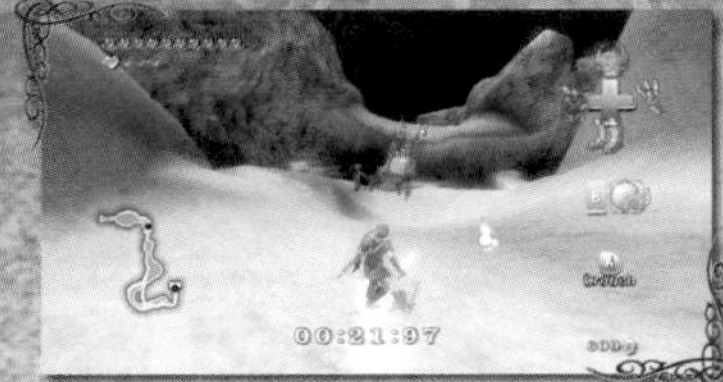

Press ◯ and make smooth, subtle turns through the first snowbank, heading to the broken bridge.

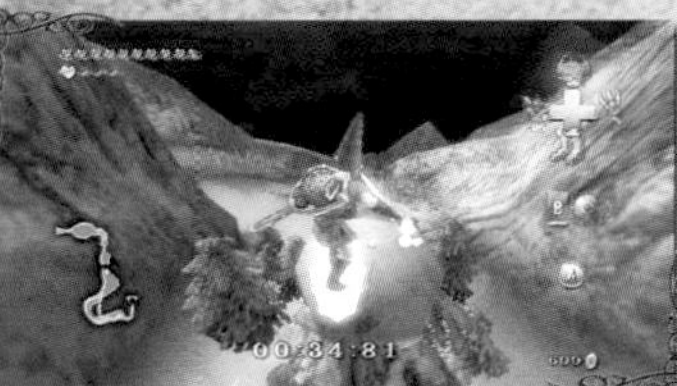

Launch off the middle of the ramp, and hit all three tree ledges.

Crouch and leap onto this right snowbank here, preparing for the shortcut.

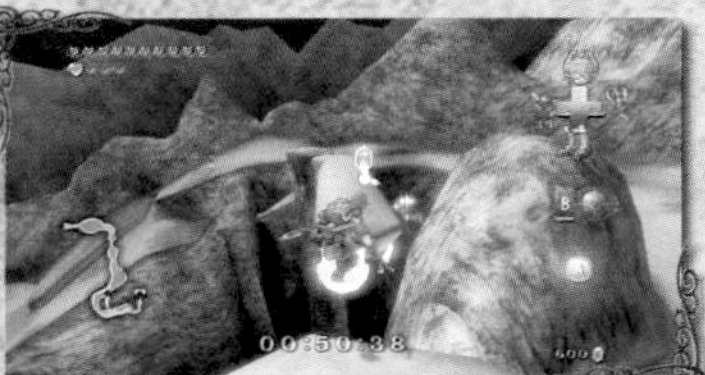

Jump off the edge, onto the shortcut, and stay on course!

Stay on the right, high snowbank as you spot the mansion in the distance.

Stay crouched and press ◯, but don't strike the sides on the last bend. Perform a spin as you finish, so you don't get beaten at the post!

◄ Providing you beat Yeta, she tells you how impressive you are and gives you a gift: a **Piece of Heart**! Add it to your collection, and wave good-bye to the Yetis!

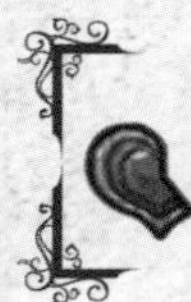

Piece of Heart
You got a **Piece of Heart**! Collect **two more** for another full Heart Container. Piece of Heart #33 of 45.

Author Note

We managed a reasonably respectable time of 1:16 to beat Yeta, but we've heard tales of skilled sledders managing a time of 1:12! Can you beat that?

After Snowpeak Ruins: The Final Reconnoiter

Poe Soul #49

Backtrack into the cavern with the ladder that you climbed to reach the top of the mountain. Open the round door with the hand prints on it, head down to this point, where a couple of ice blocks remain, and smash them. One contains a Poe, and the other an unlit torch. Change to wolf form and bring that Poe down!

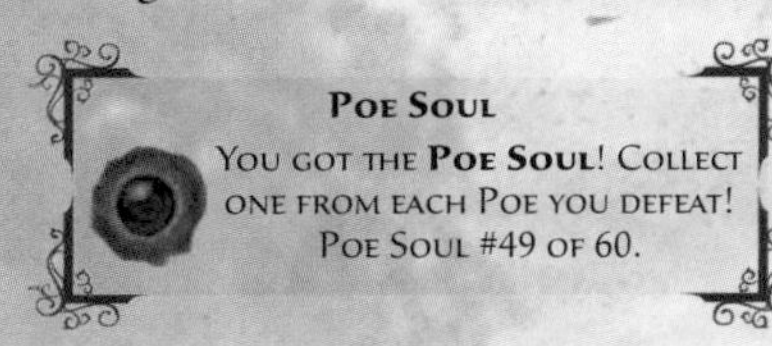

Poe Soul
You got the **Poe Soul**! Collect one from each Poe you defeat! Poe Soul #49 of 60.

▲ Now inspect the unlit torches. There are two, and as you'd expect, lighting both of them produces a reward in the shape of a treasure chest. Look inside for an orange Rupee.

Overworld Chest #83: Orange Rupee (100)

Dig Cavern #15

Now return to this dig cavern, on the way up Snowpeak Mountain (follow the Reekfish trail to a snowy plateau), looking for the lone pine tree and dig spot nearby. Once you drop in, smash the Ice Keese and then destroy one of the ice blocks making up the wall ahead of you. There are four Freezards here, and if you had bashed all the ice blocks, you wouldn't be able to use them as cover! After some freezing fun, bash the last Freezard into pieces and open the chest he was sitting on.

Overworld Chest #84: Orange Rupee (100)

Note: Congratulations! You've ransacked all 16 dig caverns in Hyrule!

Enemies Encountered

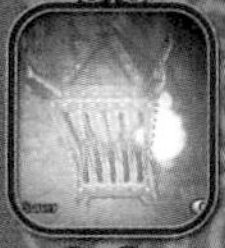

Imp Poe

Ice Keese

Freezard

Mini Freezard

After Snowpeak Ruins: The Crate Escape—Ice Block Puzzle Cavern

◄ Next warp back to Hyrule, and head to the north field, and the north section of the field. Enter the cave whose Bomb Rock you destroyed a while ago. Now that you have the Ball and Chain, you can enter this area.

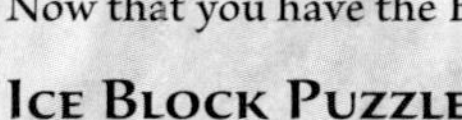

Ice Block Puzzle

You must smash through a giant block of ice to reach the Ice Block Puzzle Cavern's first room, and the only way to do that is with a little help from the Ball and Chain. Smash through the ice, then enter the first room and prepare to use your noodle.

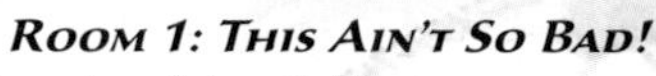

Room 1: This Ain't So Bad!

Here are the steps to solving the first room:

1. Push the southwest block to the north.

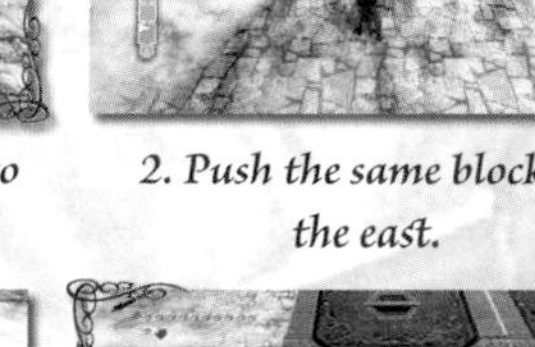

2. Push the same block to the east.

3. Slide the southeast block to the west.

4. Shove the northeast block to the south.

5. Shove the same block to the west.

6. Push the same block to the north.

7. Slide the northernmost block to the east.

8. Slide the same block to the south.

9. Push the same block to the west.

10. Finally, shove the same block to the north.

The block lands on the room's pressure switch, opening the north gate.

Room 2: Okay, This Is Tough

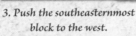

The second room's far more challenging. Here's one way to solve it:

1. Push the southwest block to the north.

2. Slide the northeast block to the south.

3. Push the southeasternmost block to the west.

4. Shove the east block to the north.

5. Slide the same block to the west.

6. Push the middle west block to the east.

7. Push the same block to the south.

8. Shove the same block to the west.

9. Slide the same block to the north. The room's northernmost pressure switch is now depressed.

10. Push the northernmost block to the east.

11. Slide the southwest block to the east.

12. Shove the northeast block to the south.

13. Slide the southernmost block to the west.

14. Push the northernmost block to the south. This releases the northernmost pressure switch.

15. Slide the southwest block to the north.

16. Shove the southernmost block to the west.

17. Shove the same block to the north.

18. Push the same block to the east. The room's southernmost pressure switch is now depressed.

19. Slide the easternmost block to the north.

20. Oops! Slide the same block to the south.

21. Shove the same block to the west.

22. Push the northwest block to the south.

23. Push the same block to the east.

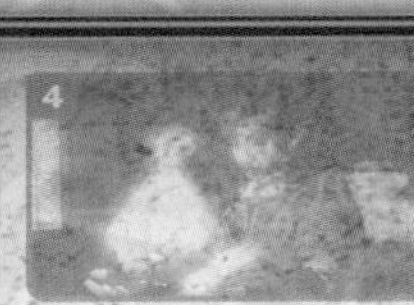

24. Slide the southwest block to the east.

25. Slide the same block to the north.

26. Shove the same block to the west.

27. Finally, push the southwesternmost block to the north.

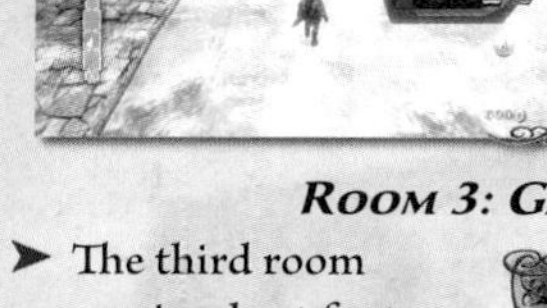
28. The room's two pressure switches are now depressed. The north gate swings open.

Room 3: Gaaah! My Brain!

➤ The third room seems simple at first, with only one pressure switch to activate. Yet it's surprisingly tricky! Here's one solution:

1. Push the northeast block to the south.

2. Shove the southwest block to the north.

3. Shove the same block to the east.

4. Push the same block to the south.

5. Slide the middle block to the west.

6. Shove the southeast block to the north.

7. Shove the same block to the west.

8. Push the east block to the north.

9. Push the southwest block to the north.

10. Slide the northeast block to the west.

11. Slide the same block to the south.

12. Shove the northwest block to the east.

13. Slide the southernmost block to the east.

14. Push the northeast block to the south.

15. Finally, slide the northeast block to the west.

16. The room's central pressure switch is now depressed. The north gate opens up.

➤ Excellent work! Now hurry into the north chamber and crack open that Overworld chest to claim Piece of Heart #34!

Overworld Chest #85: Piece of Heart #34

Piece of Heart
You got a **Piece of Heart**! Collect **one more** for another full Heart Container. Piece of Heart #34 of 45.

Characters Encountered

Rusl

Cucco

Task 2: Find the Golden Cucco

Return to the Sacred Grove: Rusl's New Partner

➤ Warp to the North Faron Woods, near Trill's Shop, and run northward, to the area where you first took Midna and bounded across to the Sacred Grove. Rusl is waiting to tell you there's an ancient **temple deep in the woods** that guards a sacred power. To reach the Sacred Grove, he offers you his flying companion: a golden Cucco!

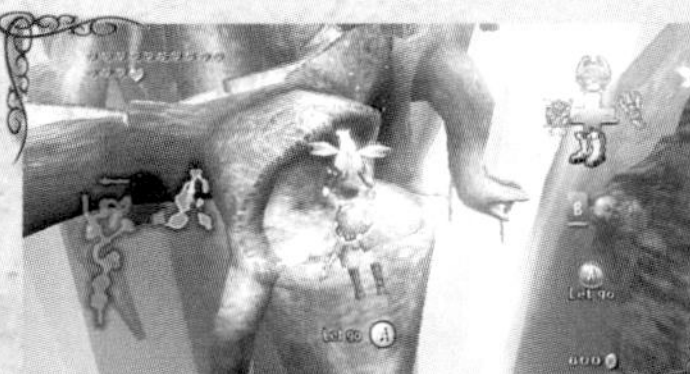

➤ Grab the Cucco, and launch yourself off the ledge you're standing on. Fly across to the tree root in the sky, and the next, before swooping in on the entrance to the Sacred Grove. Run to the edge, and use your **Gale Boomerang** to flip the bridge so it faces north-south.

➤ Float down to this bridge, then drop the Cucco, and spin the bridge onto the next ledge. Grab the Cucco, then position yourself southward, facing the swinging logs. Soar past them to the tiny platform, and again onto the ledge leading to the main Sacred Grove entrance.

Missing Links

1. Golden Cucco Chat

Remember that you can transform into your wolf form and chat with the Cucco. What does he say? We're not telling!

Task 3: Follow and Fight the Strange Skull Kid

Return to the Sacred Grove: Skull Kid's Lantern Game

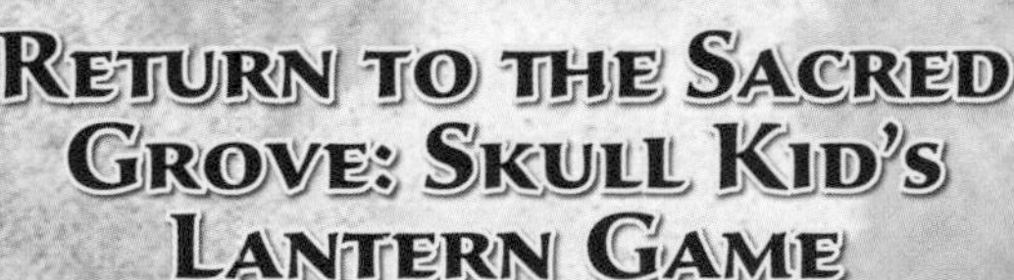

Tip: As you enter the Sacred Grove once more, use the map provided in this tome so you don't get lost, as there's no in-game map!

➤ **Chamber 1:** Enter the initial chamber of the Sacred Grove. You'll find that the Skull Kid is back, and he's brought his Puppets! Spin attack the four that arrive, and exit via the opening to the north that Skull Kid created.

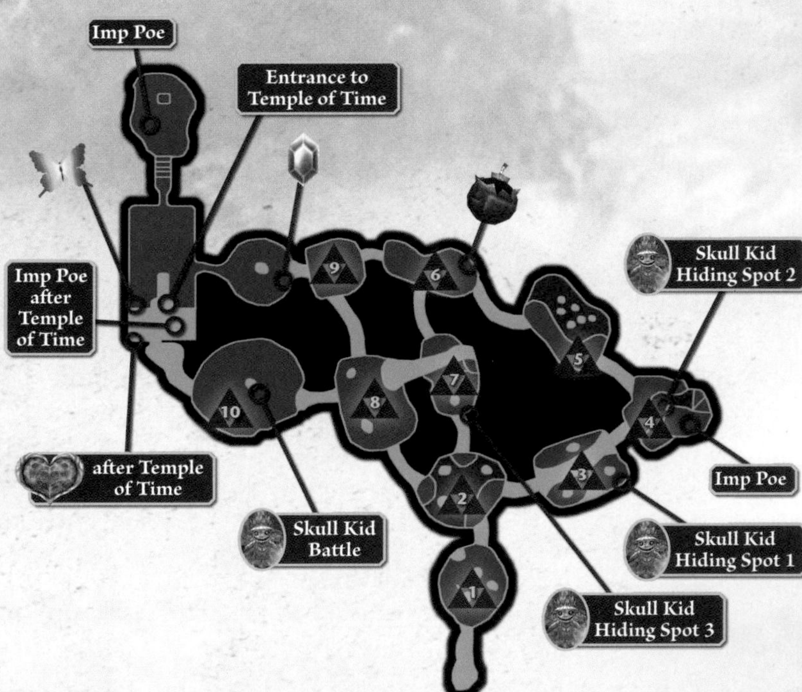

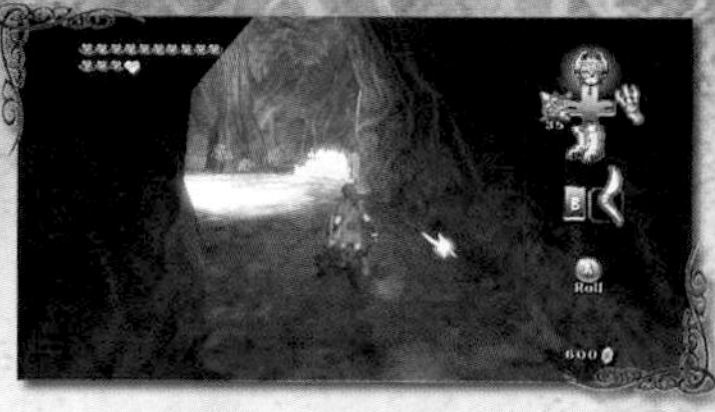

➤ **Chamber 2–3:** The Skull Kid leaves a trail of light in this gloomy grove, so follow him into the second chamber, and make a right. Check the tunnel in this direction as there's light coming from Chamber 3. Follow it up there.

Tip: IF YOU GET LOST DURING THIS HUNT, BACKTRACK AND CHECK EVERY TUNNEL ENTRANCE. THE ONE WITH LIGHT GLOWING IN THE CHAMBER BEYOND IS THE WAY TO HEAD.

◄ **Chamber 3:** Skull Kid is hiding in this chamber, behind the tree on the upper area. Bring your sword out, and give him a friendly thwack. He opens up a tunnel and moves into Chamber 4. Follow him there.

Poe Soul #50

Chamber 4: Skull Kid takes a left and runs up the tunnel to Chamber 5. Meanwhile, explore this area, heading through the archway on the pond, and around and up the tree platforms to the stump overlooking the tunnel. There's a Poe up here to add to your soul collection.

POE SOUL

YOU GOT THE **POE SOUL**! COLLECT ONE FROM EACH POE YOU DEFEAT! POE SOUL #50 OF 60.

◄ **Chamber 5–6:** Head to Chamber 5 now, with the posts coming out of the water, and ignore the Skull Kid for the moment. Head to the next chamber (Chamber 6), and light both the torches in here. A chest appears. Grab the bombs and continue your hunt back in Chamber 5.

OVERWORLD CHEST #86: BOMBS (30)

◄ **Chamber 5:** Move back to Chamber 5, where the Skull Kid is amusing himself. Aim a Bomb Arrow at him, and he flees the scene!

➤ **Chamber 5–2, then 7:** The Skull Kid takes a romp all the way back through the chambers you've previously visited, to Chamber 2, and then opens a tunnel northward, to Chamber 7, with the tree trunk platform and bridge. Take the shortcut via Chamber 6 if you wish.

➤ **Chamber 8:** Skull Kid heads under the tree bridge, to Chamber 8, and then passes through a tunnel to Chamber 9. Optionally light the torches if you wish (nothing happens), deal with a few more Puppets, and continue onward.

◄ **Chamber 9 to 6 to 7:** The Skull Kid now flees toward Chamber 7, via Chamber 6. Follow him and then climb the steps and go around to the tree bridge. That's where he's hiding! Climb onto the middle of the bridge and look left. Deal with any Puppets, then fire a Bomb Arrow at Skull Kid.

▲ **Chamber 7 to 8 to 10:** The Skull Kid now opens the tunnel on the bridge that leads to the balcony overlooking Chamber 8. Head here, drop down, and then run to the ruined arena for another fracas with this fellow!

ENEMIES ENCOUNTERED

Skull Kid

Puppet

Imp Poe

Characters Encountered

Agitha

Ooccoo

Return to the Sacred Grove: Skull Kid Battle!

➤ Chamber 10: You can now face Skull Kid in a battle you may already be familiar with, except this time you're fighting in human form. Begin by defeating the Puppets that Skull Kid sends to waylay you. Look for Skull Kid's location (he's standing on one of the many ledges). When all of the Puppets are defeated, fire a Bomb Arrow at him.

Tip: If you're missing arrows, try smashing skulls on the ground. If you don't want to use Bomb Arrows, use the Clawshot or Slingshot, but they aren't nearly as effective.

➤ Continue this attack strategy two more times. Wait for Skull Kid to land and summon more Puppets (his last attack summons around nine!) and defeat them all with spin attacks and slashes. Then quickly find and manually aim at the Skull Kid. When he's taken enough punishment, he titters and leaves, then reveals a secret exit to the west.

Task 4: Obtain the Giant Wallet

Return to the Sacred Grove: The Wayward Poe

◄ This hidden exit is a ramped path leading to an upper balcony overlooking the Sacred Grove square where you acquired the Master Sword. The temple entrance must be around here somewhere. Head across the grass, optionally smashing skulls (for Hearts). You can even creep up on the birds as a wolf and try to speak with them. Then head to the large block with the Hyrule crest on it, and push it off the ledge.

➤ Before you enter the temple, there are a couple of outstanding treasure-hunting matters to attend to! Run off the ledge, past the ancient open chest, and down to the first arena where you fought Skull Kid, long ago. Move to this vine wall and Clawshoot to the top.

➤ At the top is a ledge, but of more interest is a Spinner track running the circumference of this glade. Step on your Spinner and ride it to a ledge. Get off and inspect the chest. There's a large-value Rupee in here for your trouble.

Overworld Chest #87: Orange Rupee (100)

Note: Did you notice the Hylian Hornet nest as you were spinning around the grooved track? You can fire at it from this chamber, and pick up the larvae in the previous chamber (Chamber 10).

Poe Soul #51

Now head into the glade where you found the Master Sword, and wait until the sun sets. This is where a Poe resides, and it's easy to forget about him. Brandish your fangs and leap at the Imp Poe, grabbing his soul. Only nine more to go!

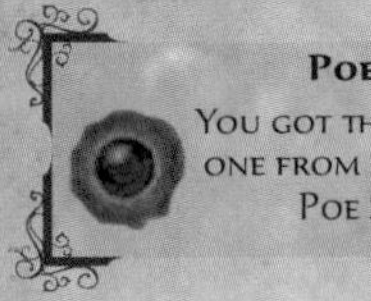

Poe Soul

You got the **Poe Soul**! Collect one from each Poe you defeat! Poe Soul #51 of 60.

Arriving at the Temple of Time

◄ Now stride to the place where you drew the Master Sword, and insert it into the grooved holder. The statue that was standing at the entrance to the temple vanishes. Draw back your blade, and head toward the entrance.

Note: The block you pushed down now allows you to enter and exit the Temple of Time easily.

Warp Portal

As you head past the two statues, a portal rips into existence, and five Twilit Messengers descend. However, a flock of Keeses also descends on you! Spin attack as they all close in for a vicious takedown! Defeat all the Keeses first, as they play havoc when you're trying to keep two final Twilit Messengers from falling. When only two Messengers are left, try a couple of short swipes and herd them together. Then finish them with a spin attack. Another portal is now available. You need not return through the Sacred Grove to reach here!

▲ Now run around through the gap in the wall, past the broken chest, and up and over the block you pushed. You're now at the entrance to the Temple of Time itself. Open the doors! Ahead is a bleary view into the past, when this Sacred Grove was a mighty temple! Step inside.

◀ You emerge in an entrance chamber, exactly as this grove looked many centuries ago. Head down the steps and you can see the two statues you moved earlier, still guarding this place. Head down the steps and make a left turn.

Golden Bug: Female Snail

Collection: 24 (of 24)

You can spend a few moments smashing some pottery, collecting the Hearts and arrows that you find, and looking at another owl statue (have you noticed that they're all around Hyrule?). Now look for your final Golden Bug: the Female Snail on the staircase. Grab it with your **Gale Boomerang**. You've done it! All 24 are yours!

Female Snail

You caught a **Female Snail**! Bug fans love that golden color!

Congratulations! This is the earliest possible time you could have collected all 24 Golden Bugs! Remember to claim your reward!

➤ Technically, you can warp out of the Temple of Time, and head back to Castle Town, either before or after you complete the next dungeon, and visit Princess Agitha. Present all the Golden Bugs to her. You may wish to purchase the Magic Armor if you haven't already. When you give her the 24th Golden Bug, her bug ball is deemed a success and she thanks you with an even more copious Wallet!

Giant Wallet

You got the **Giant Wallet**! It's a symbol of a distinguished citizen in the insect kingdom. It can hold up to 1,000 Rupees!

Enemies Encountered

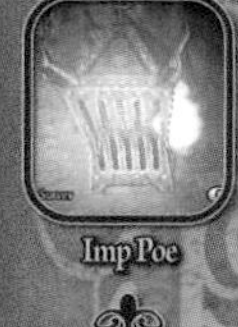

Imp Poe

Twilit Messenger

Keese

Hylian Hornets

Task 5: Enter the Temple of Time

All that remains is for you to enter the Temple of Time now. Head north, into the next chamber, which is a past view of the Master Sword glade. Plunge your sword into the slit, and a magical staircase appears. Ooccoo trots up the steps. Follow her, into the Temple of Time!

Dungeon 6: Temple of Time

1F

2F

3F

4F

5F

Defeat First Armos, Mechanical Guardian

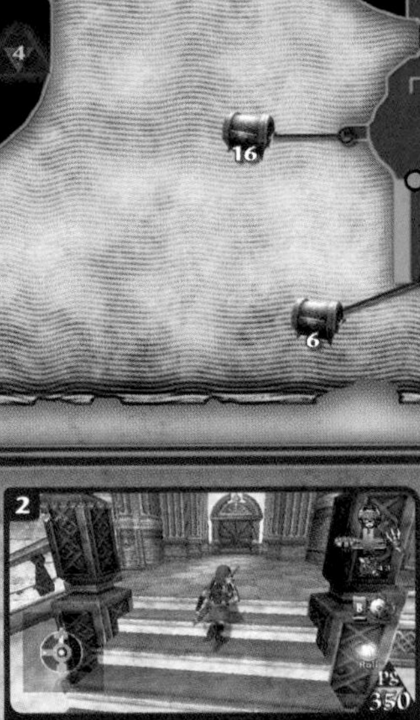

Unlock Door

Locate the Big Key

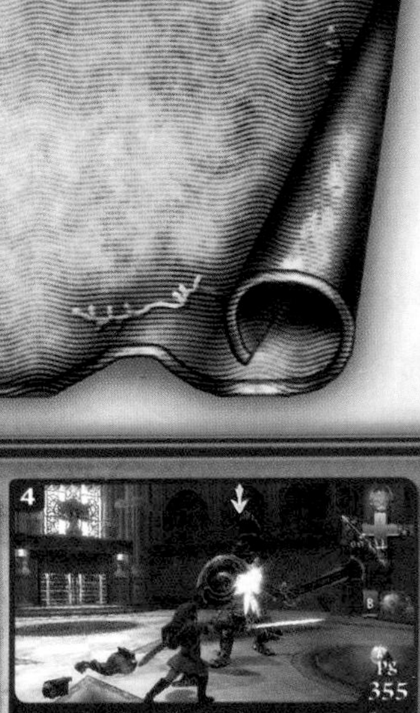

Face the Deadly Darknut in Combat

6F

7F

8F

Mechanical Statue

Legend

Room Legend

1. Grand Entrance (1F to 2F)
2. Connecting Corridors (2F to 3F)
3. Hexagonal Junction (3F)
4. Central Mechanical Platform (3F to 4F to 5F)
5. Armos Antechamber (5F)
6. Moving Wall Hallways (5F)
7. The Scales of Time (6F to 7F)
8. Four Floor Switch Puzzle Room
9. Upper Spiketrap Corridors (7F to 8F)
10. Armos Guardian Room (8F)
11. The Arena of Darknut
12. The Crumbling Corridor (1F)
13. Boss Battle! Twilit Arachnid Armogohma (1F)

Characters

- Darknut
- Twilit Arachnid Armogohma

Number of Treasure Chests: 16

1. Small Key
2. Arrows (30)
3. Dungeon Map
4. Red Rupee (20)
5. Small Key
6. Red Rupee (20)
7. Compass
8. Purple Rupee (50)
9. Red Rupee (20)
10. Red Rupee (20)
11. Big Key
12. Small Key
13. Purple Rupee (50)
14. Dominion Rod
15. Piece of Heart #35 (of 45)
16. Piece of Heart #36 (of 45)

Items

- Poe Soul
- Ooccoo
- Fairy
- Horned Statuette

Temple of Time: Overview

Back in time, the Sacred Grove was a far more splendid place. It was a multi-floor dungeon with machinery built by the people Ooccoo is from, complete with a variety of mechanical devices and machinery. It is somewhere in here that you can locate the third Mirror Shard, and you must travel methodically, up to an arena high atop the Temple of Time, to secure the necessary equipment to help you gain access to this shard. Along the way, you need to figure out how to deal with enemies that are getting tougher, and puzzles that require a steady hand and a thoughtful brain. Even the combat is more mentally taxing, when you encounter a knight clad in onyx armor—a fiend known as Darknut! Once you've obtained his gift, and used it to power some archaic statuary, you're finally granted entrance to the chamber of the biggest arachnid Hyrule has ever seen, in this time or any!

Maneuver Statue over Scales of Time

Collect Both Heart Pieces

Reach End of Crumbling Corridor

Defeat Twilit Arachnid Armogohma!

Characters Encountered

Occoo

A Link to the Present

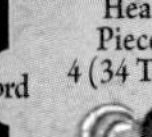

Ordon Sword Master Sword

Heart Pieces: 4 (34 Total)

Wooden Shield Hylian Shield

Hero's Clothes Zora Armor Magic Armor

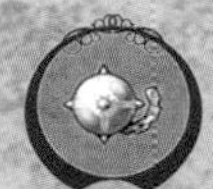

Giant Wallet, Big Quiver, Golden Bugs: 24 (of 24), Hidden Skills: 6 (of 7)

Reekfish Scent, Poe Souls 51 (of 60), Fish Journal, Letters 9 (of 16)

Mirror of Twilight: 2 (of 4)

Items Already Acquired

Ball and Chain, Spinner, Clawshot, Hero's Bow, Iron Boots, Gale Boomerang

Lantern, Slingshot, Fishing Rod, Hawkeye, Bombs (Bag #1), Bombs (Bag #2)

Bombs (Bag #3), Bottle #1, Bottle #2, Bottle #3, Bottle #4

Items to Obtain

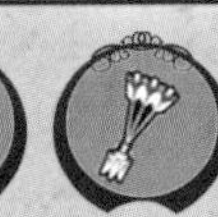

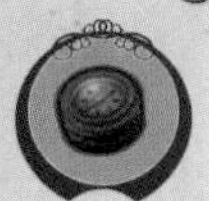

Occoo, Small Key #1, Arrows (30), Dungeon Map, Small Key #2, Compass

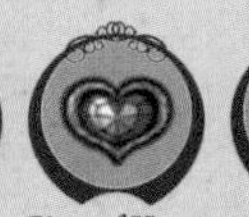
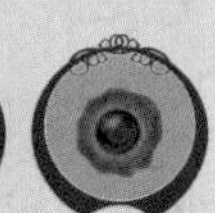

Big Key, Small Key #3, Fairy in a Bottle, Dominion Rod, Piece of Heart #35 (of 45), Poe Soul #53 (of 60)

Fairy in a Bottle, Piece of Heart #36 (of 45), Fairy in a Bottle, Mirror Shard #3 (of 4), Heart Container #6

Dungeon Denizens

Characters

Midna, Occoo

Enemies

Young Gohma, Armos, Keese

Lizalfos, Beamos (White), Baby Gohma

Dynafols

Bosses

Mid Boss: Darknut

Big Boss: Twilit Arachnid Armogohma

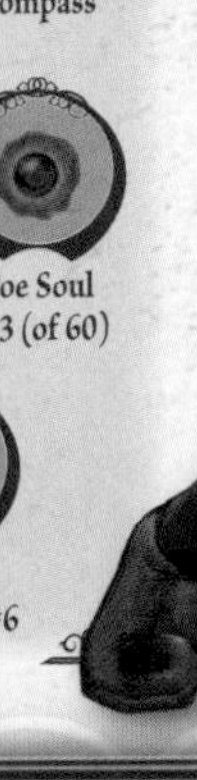

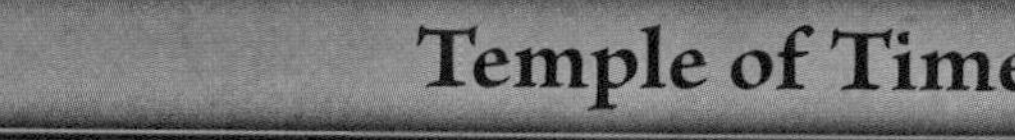

Task 1: Defeat your First Armos, the Mechanical Guardian

Enemies Encountered

Chamber 1: Grand Entrance (1F to 2F)

Before you go back into time, you might wish to bring along the following:

- Multiple Bottles filled with a Blue Potion, Fairy Tears, or a Fairy
- Your Hero's Bow positioned on ✚ so you can activate it on and off quickly
- The Clawshot within easy access
- The Spinner within easy access
- The Hylian Shield, purchased from Kakariko Village
- The Magic Armor for rare occasions you may need it; purchase it from Castle Town
- Completely filled Big Quiver and all Bomb Bags; you don't want to run out!

Tip

◄ Run down the stairs to the first chamber, an impressive entrance with two sets of stairs flanking you, and a bell house with a giant bell hanging from it. You can't currently ring the bell, so pass it by and head toward the north end of the chamber.

► When you move up to the door to the north it is firmly sealed. On the left side of the doorway is a small alcove with a mechanical statue holding a large axe. Use your wolf form's sense view. You see another statue forming on the opposite side. This is residue of a statue that used to stand here. You must find the statue and complete this puzzle!

◄ You can't reach the stairs from your current area, but if you look closely, you'll see a section of flooring you could raise into a step. Head to the square raised plinths either side of the shallow steps, and you see that one has a small metal horned statuette, and the other has a pressure switch. Take the horned statuette and place it on the switch. The floor section rises, and you can climb the staircase surrounding you.

Author Note

We played a little dexterity game by throwing the horned statuette onto the floor switch instead of placing it. This requires skill and timing as the distance is tricky to figure out. Can you manage to land the statuette on the switch first time?

▲ When you reach the top of the stairs, you spot Ooccoo (and her strange floating head of a son, if you used him in a previous dungeon). She tells you that this is the place she's been searching for.

Ooccoo

You are reunited with **Ooccoo**! This kind character can let you out of dungeons and return you to where you were.

Missing Links

1. Pottery Pulverizing

This chamber has many pots to smash, for Hearts, Rupees, and arrows. Take care of the pottery between the torches where you find Ooccoo, and near the floor switch.

Treasure Chest: The way northward is sealed, and the way up the stairs to the south is locked. It looks like you're stuck until you bring out your Lantern and run down to the two unlit ceremonial torches at the edge of the left staircase. Light both torches and a chest appears. Inside is the Small Key you require to head south.

Treasure Chest #1:

Small Key

Small Key

You got a **Small Key**! This opens a locked door, but only in this area.

Chamber 2: Connecting Corridors (2F to 3F)

Head up the stairs to the south, to the second floor, and use the Small Key you just found to open the locked door. Step through into a small crossroads chamber with gates, pottery, and a strange hairy creature scuttling about.

Young Gohma

Threat Meter

Young Gohma is a scuttling creature a little like a Skulltula, but with a giant all-seeing eye. It likes to bound and strike a foe with its front pincers. Fortunately, it is rather ineffective. Defeat it easily with two sweeping sword strikes.

Young Gohma doesn't have a cunning method of disposing of its foes; it just leaps at you. Simple swordplay counters this!

With the Gohma threat dispatched, look around. The gates to the west and south are firmly closed. A central floor switch opens the gates, but you require an item to set on it. So, for the first time ever, you must not smash the pottery! Make sure one pot survives and place it on the floor switch. When the switch is pressed, the gates open, and another one closes at the top of the western staircase. Head this way for a moment, and slash the Young Gohma scuttling around. You could even try your new Hidden Skill: the jump strike.

Note: If you accidentally smash all the pottery, don't despair. Head back to Chamber 1 and then return here, and the pottery is back and intact.

Now explore the crossroads chamber thoroughly. Begin by checking the alcove to the east. A giant bell hangs from the top of the alcove here, and you can ring it with your Ball and Chain. All your other weapons have no effect. A red Rupee falls from this bell. Pick it up!

Treasure Chest: Don't forget that the gate to the south opened too. This leads to a tiny alcove with a window at the end, and two jars to smash for Rupees. Open the small chest in the middle for arrows, which you'll need in a moment.

Treasure Chest #2:

Arrows (30)

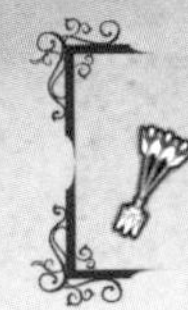

Arrows

You got **Arrows (30)**! Use arrows to shoot far-off foes!

Note: While looking around the room, you may notice a Clawshot medallion above the west gate. Don't worry about this now; this is used when you return here later.

Now head up the staircase to the west. Unfortunately, it's blocked by a gate! Turn around, and once you're behind the open first gate, shoot the pot (with Bow, Boomerang, or Clawshot) you placed on the middle floor switch. The gate closes behind you, but the one above you opens!

◄ Turn and run up the steps, turning north and continuing up. On your ascent, bring out your weapon and counter an incoming Lizalfos's attack. Slice him with your jump strike, or another preferred technique. Continue to the top of the steps.

Chamber 3: Hexagonal Junction (3F)

▲ At the top of the stairs, the corridor expands into the Hexagonal Junction. Three Lizalfoses prowl the area, and there's a strange statue with a giant hammer in the alcove opposite. Don't venture too far into the room. You want to tackle the Lizalfos first, and the statue later. This is the perfect spot for a jump strike (as shown), coax all three Lizalfoses and slash them all! Otherwise, spin attacks work almost as well.

Armos

Threat Meter

The Armos is a jerky mechanical beast that is impervious to your strikes until you discover that rear weak spot!

Approach the Armos with caution, as it shrugs off all your attacks, but fortunately it moves very slowly once you step around 20 feet away from it, and it starts to jump slowly toward you. The trick here is to strike the blue weak spot on its rear. Simple slashes cause it to jump more quickly, and it brings down a hammer with considerable force.

Simply roll around and spin attack, stab, or try one of your Hidden Skill strikes, and with one or two hits, the Armos begins to shine with a bright intensity and malfunction. This is your cue to run away from it, because it's about to explode!

Tip: Another great way to defeat an Armos is to run behind him without targeting or having your sword drawn, and execute Hidden Skill #5, the Mortal Draw. You'll defeat the Armos just as it wakes up!

▲ **Treasure Chest:** Once the Armos has been destroyed, a previously invisible treasure chest appears in the southwest alcove in this chamber. Open it and grab the Dungeon Map, so you can see the climb to the eighth floor you're going to make.

◄ **Treasure Chest:** Your hunt for chests doesn't end here either. There's already a small chest in this chamber, flanked by two horned statuettes near a window, with a lowly Keese guarding it. Dispatch the Keese quickly, then open the chest for a red Rupee.

◄ Now you must find a way to open the gate to the north. Take the horned statuette to one side of the treasure chest, and carry it to one of the two floor switches on either side of the gate. Then repeat this plan (remember, you can try throwing the horned statuettes for fun and to show off your skill). The gate swings open. Ignore the bell in the alcove and continue northward.

Missing Links

1. Keeping Keese at Bay

Every alcove and small hidden area near a window is likely to have an easily dispatched Keese or two. Smash the pottery here for a Heart, then continue.

Enemies Encountered

Young Gohma

Lizalfos (Axe-tail)

Armos

Keese

Task #1

Task 2: Unlock the Door in the Central Mechanical Platform Chamber

Chamber 4: Central Mechanical Platform (3F to 4F to 5F)

➤ Head north up the steps to a corner with a Keese to dispatch, then turn right and run toward the door at the end. Open it and step forward into a giant, cylindrical chamber with a circular and ornate fence in the middle. Dozens of tiny Gohmas scuttle around here. Don't venture too close to this area, or you'll be zapped by an electrified fence.

➤ Turn right, and begin to secure this third floor (the floor you're currently on). Run around to locate three Lizalfoses, and engage them in combat. The most entertaining way to defeat them is by shield attacking so they're stunned, and then jump striking them to deliver a dispatching blow in a single attack!

➤ Continue around to the north side of this chamber. As you reach a gate to the east, you see two pots to smash, and a small alcove you can't reach. Return here later. For the moment, run north, and avoid the pink laser fire from a Beamos. Back up, then finish any remaining Lizalfoses.

Beamos (White)

Threat Meter

The Ceremonial Beamos, or White Beamos, is stationary, activates when you move too close, and sends out a short-range laser that can cut into your energy. Simply step back, and fire an arrow (no need for Bomb Arrows) out of its laser range. To utterly destroy a Beamos, you may need a giant hammer carried by a robotic servant to finish the job!

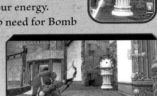

The White Beamos has a pink laser. Otherwise, it reacts the same way as the previous Beamoses you've faced. Deactivate it with an arrow in the eye!

Tip: Don't shoot a White Beamos with an arrow until it activates, as the machine is impervious to any weapon (bar a giant hammering) prior to the eye switching on.

Missing Links

1. Hearts Aplenty

Thoroughly inspect the pots in this room, as they contain arrows, Rupees, and in the case of the pot behind the Beamos, three Hearts! Grab them if you're feeling low on energy. Inspect every pot in the rest of this dungeon.

2. Ring My Bell

Don't forget you can ring a bell in almost every chamber! There's one on the top floor of this chamber, for example, and almost all give you a red Rupee. Use a Ball and Chain to strike the bell.

➤ Head up to the fourth floor of this chamber now. Climb up the stairs to the point where they've given way. You can use the Spinner, so catch the groove in the wall, and ride up to a locked door in the north area.

➤ You need to get a key to open this door. Turn and face south, and run down to a large ornate circular platform. Two spiked Spinners are rotating around in different directions. Avoid them by dodging between them, and move to the western ledge, where a lone horned statuette stands. Take this.

➤ Run around to the platform's south side, to a ledge leading to another similar-looking doorway in the south wall. This one appears unlocked but has two pressure switches on the floor. You can't climb up to reach the door yet. Walk over and place the horned statuette on one of the plates. You now need to find the other.

Caution: Previously, you may have been fooling around, throwing these statuettes at the floor switches instead of placing them. Don't do it this time because the horned statuettes may land on the upper stone area, or fall off to the third floor below, and delay your exploration!

➤ Now head to the middle of this elaborate platform, to a large handle and cog system. Push the handle clockwise and the platform descends. Push it in the opposite direction and it ascends. Descend the platform back to the third floor, where you started. Head off and you see a horned statuette ahead. However, you're in the circular fenced area with the Gohmas. Fight!

Baby Gohma

Threat Meter

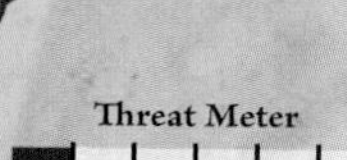

Baby Gohmas look disgusting, as they haven't formed into their hairy, one-eyed brethren yet, but they aren't aggressive. However, they are tricky to quickly dispatch as they run directly away from you. You can fire off Bomb Arrows, or quickly tag them with a Clawshot, but an easier plan is to just run forward and slash from side to side, as if you were cutting grass. Keep this up until all Baby Gohmas are defeated.

➤ When you've dispatched all the Baby Gohmas, the electrical charge on the fence dissipates, and you can easily get from the outer ring to the inner platform on the third floor. This is useful if you dropped a horned statuette, but for now take the statuette at the top of the shallow ramp and place it on the platform. Turn the handle and rise to the fourth floor. Then place (don't throw!) the statuette on the other pressure switch.

Caution: If you accidentally drop a horned statuette, or throw it onto the ledge you want to climb onto, find a couple more by the east gate you can't open. Use the Clawshot to ricochet the statuettes off the tiny ledge they're on to pick them up.

Another way to grab a horned statuette you accidentally threw beyond the floor switch is to bring out the Ball and Chain, and bash the statuette back down to your level.

Chamber 5: Armos Antechamber

➤ Step into a long stone chamber guarded by two Armos machines ahead of you. Bring out a weapon (try the Ball and Chain for a one-hit dispatch if you're quick enough), and defeat both of them. Either before or after you fight with the Armos machines, break the pottery between the two sets of steps for arrows.

▲ **Treasure Chest:** As soon as the fight is over, a chest materializes in a tiny alcove over on the eastern side of the chamber. Open it to discover a Small Key.

Treasure Chest #5: Small Key

Small Key
You got a **Small Key**! This opens a locked door, but only in this area.

Enemies Encountered

Beamos (White)

Lizalfos (Axe-tail)

Young Gohma

Baby Gohma

Keese

➤ Treasure Chest: The hunt for treasure chests doesn't end here. Head south, to the area of the chamber you haven't yet investigated, and check the raised channel between the two sets of stairs. At the far end is a small chest that's easily overlooked. Open that for a red Rupee.

Treasure Chest #6: Red Rupee (20)

➤ There's another secret part to this area, but you can't activate it yet. Practice your throwing by lobbing one of the two horned statuettes you can pick up (the third is behind the low metal fence on a narrow ledge you can't reach) into the narrow ledge on the right. Remember to come back here later, then leave.

Chamber 4: First Return to Central Mechanical Platform (5F)

▲ Now that you have the Small Key, return to the Central Mechanical Platform chamber, and run across the platform itself. There's no need to activate it. Simply head north, across to the locked door, and open it.

Task 3: Locate the Big Key

Chamber 6: Moving Wall Hallways (5F)

➤ Enter a hallway with a fence to your right and a diamond switch to your left. Ahead is a Beamos. Bring out your Hero's Bow, and dispatch it. Clear the curved ledge with the diamond switch of pottery (there's a Heart inside one). There are arrows in one of the brown pots near the Beamos, too.

➤ Slash the diamond switch, as this activates a wall piece that slides apart, allowing you to run around and into the chamber's central part. Inspect another giant bell, and crack a few pots underneath for a Heart and arrows. Produce your Ball and Chain, and thwack a red Rupee from the bell.

➤ By now, you've realized there's no way out of this chamber because the wall that's moved is blocking your path. To exit, you must strike the diamond switch again, but you can't stand next to it. Instead, position yourself near the stone circle on the ground, and aim an arrow at the switch. Hit the switch, and the wall moves, allowing you to exit.

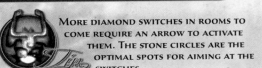

Tip: More diamond switches in rooms to come require an arrow to activate them. The stone circles are the optimal spots for aiming at the switches.

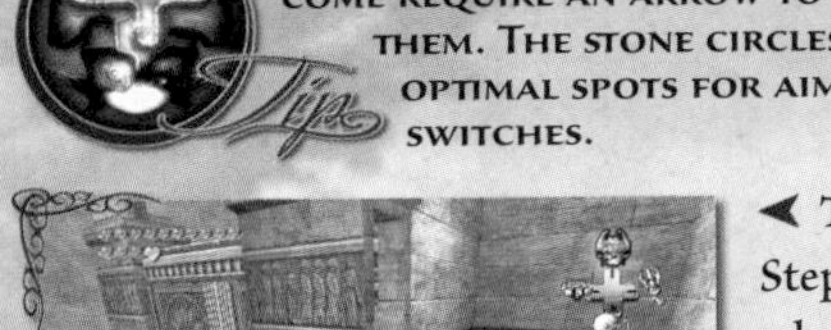

➤ Treasure Chest: Step forward and when the next White Beamos activates, shoot it in the eye. Turn the corner, and run to the three pots at the chamber's far end. Find arrows and a Heart inside. Then look east, to see a small stone alcove with a chest inside. Open it to obtain the Compass.

Treasure Chest #7: Compass

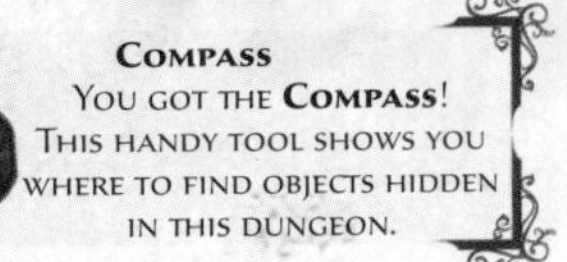

Compass
You got the **Compass**! This handy tool shows you where to find objects hidden in this dungeon.

➤ Spin around to face the diamond switch, which is through two circular openings with spikes protruding from them. Stand on the stone circle to ease your aim, and fire an arrow into the switch. The wall slides back to cover the alcove with the chest you just robbed, and you can climb the steps. Tackle two Lizalfoses along the way. The one at the top is wearing a skull mask.

1

2

3

4

5

6

➤ Head down the ramp and stand on this circle. Look across this part of the chamber and spot a diamond switch high on a ledge. Ahead is a fence with a chest behind. You can grab this on the way out so don't worry about it now. Fire an arrow at the switch, and watch as the wall recedes. Advance with your sword and shield at the ready.

Dynafols

Threat Meter

Notice how a Lizalfos is unable to withstand a shield bash and spin attack? Not so with the armored Dynafols, the meanest armored beast in this dungeon! Defeat him with counter strikes.

As vicious as he is armored, the Dynafols is one of the most difficult ground troops to tackle, as none of the strikes you're used to inflicting actually saps his energy. He attacks with an axe, blocks using a shield, and even has an axe on his tail to slice onto the ground! The trick here is to counterattack the Dynafols. Wait for him to make a sword swing, then (for example) shield block, and immediately retaliate with a helm splitter or spin attack. Block a barrage of his moves, roll around, and back strike his tail. Do this three or four times before combat ends. But most of all, let the Dynafols strike first...and you strike last!

➤ Once the Lizalfos and Dynafols are downed, step to another stone circle, in the middle of this chamber, and fire at the diamond switch again. Don't accidentally electrocute yourself on the gap in the fence! A second wall slides open, leading to another large alcove where you must fight a second Dynafols. After an exhausting battle, smash the two pots for arrows and a Rupee.

➤ Move to the stone circle in the last, curved alcove, and get a steady aim on the diamond switch for one more arrow shot. This moves the last wall to the south out of your way. Exit the chamber by passing the bell behind the fence, and turn the corner, heading upstairs. First smash a couple more pots for Hearts you might need after that Dynafols battle!

Chamber 7: The Scales of Time (6F to 7F)

▲ **Treasure Chest:** At the top of the stairs is a thin corridor leading to a door. Open the door, and enter a chamber of pillars. Two Young Gohmas and dozens of Baby Gohmas scurry about the floor. Begin a run across this courtyard, slashing the Baby Gohmas. Continue to defeat these arachnids until every one is gone, including the Young Gohmas on the stairs. A chest then appears. Open it.

Treasure Chest #8: Purple Rupee (50)

➤ Run up the stairs to a giant pair of golden scales. These are as impressive as they are ornate, and you need to negotiate the scales in order to proceed. In fact, the scales weigh down when you stand on them. The first scale must be lighter for you to continue.

Note: There are seven horned statuettes in this chamber. Two are on the scales, three are on an upper alcove in the northeast, and the other two are detailed below:

➤ To raise the right scale tray, you must weigh the other one down with those horned ceremonial statuettes you've been seeing all about. Some are scattered about this chamber. Climb past the scales to the exit area, and to this ledge. Clawshot across, pick up the statuette, and bring it back. Deposit it on the left scale tray.

Enemies Encountered

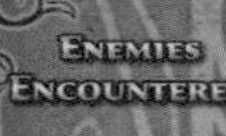

Beamos (White)

Lizalfos (Axe-tail)

Lizalfos (Skull-face)

Dynafols

Young Gohma

Baby Gohma

➤ The other horned statuette is perched atop this column in the main courtyard area. Rolling into the column is easier than knocking the statuette off with a Ball and Chain.

➤ Place three horned statuettes on the left scale to counterbalance the weights and push the other tray up, even with you standing on it. This allows you to reach this tiny ledge—the key to reaching the upper ledges in this chamber. Look to the middle of the room now.

◄ Bring out your Clawshot. Aim at the medallion on the ceiling's center, and then drop down. Ahead is a narrow platform. Run to the end of that, and then jump on your Spinner, and take the groove in the wall all the way around to the left. Don't head the other way, as the groove is broken.

Poe Soul #52

Drop off the Spinner onto an upper ledge overlooking the chamber below. You're on the seventh floor of this dungeon. Quickly change to your wolf form, as a Poe is floating about up here. Dispatch him in the usual manner. Only eight Poe to go!

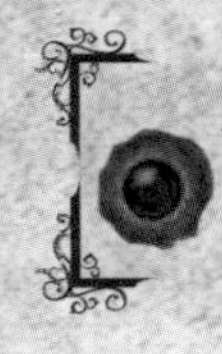

Poe Soul

You got the **Poe Soul**! Collect one from each Poe you defeat! Poe Soul #52 of 60.

➤ **Treasure Chest:** You can now freely roam this upper platform, and to start with, head south to the very end of the area and open a small chest that's next to the door you'll eventually exit. Claim the red Rupee inside. Then stay on this platform, and run to the door in the western area.

Treasure Chest #9: Red Rupee (20)

Chamber 8: Four Floor Switch Puzzle Room

◄ This room contains an Armos and two scuttling Helmasaurs. Immediately bring out your Clawshot, and remove the carapace from the Helmasaur before finishing each. Then run to the Armos to activate him, and defeat him. As usual, smash pottery for Hearts and Rupees. Then look at the large chest on the opposite side of the room.

Tip: If you're quick, you can aim at the Clawshot medallion on the ceiling before you're struck by the Helmasaurs, and then defeat them (and the Armos) from complete safety on the upper ledge!

◄ **Treasure Chest:** The chest has a gate that's sealed in front of you, but there's a Clawshot medallion above you. Use the medallion, and drop down onto the upper ledge of this chamber. Four floor switches are visible, but don't fiddle with them yet. Move to the small alcove and open up the small chest.

Treasure Chest #10: Red Rupee (20)

➤ Now that you're up here, opening the gate below is pretty straightforward: Take the two horned statuettes that are up here, and place one on each floor switch. That's two pressed in, but two more to go! Turn and look at the lower area, and aim your Clawshot to grab a Helmasaur carapace. Fire at it, bring it back, and place that on the third switch. Do this one more time, and the gate opens!

Treasure Chest: Drop down and open the chest for the Big Key. You now have access to the lair of this dungeon's boss! Now return to the Scales of Time.

Treasure Chest #11: Big Key

Big Key

You got the **Big Key**! Use it to gain access to the lair of this dungeon's boss!

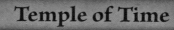

Task 4: Face the Deadly Darknut in Combat

Chamber 7: First Return to the Scales of Time (7F), to Chamber 9: Upper Spiketrap Corridors (7F to 8F)

◄ Return to the chamber with the giant scales, and turn south. Run past the chest you opened, to the exit door in the south wall. Notice the bell in the alcove? You'll need to use that later on, but ignore it for the moment. Open the door, bring out your **Hero's Bow**, and shoot the White Beamos in the corridor junction ahead.

➤ Run into this circular junction chamber, and stay on the outer rim, as you won't be hit by any of the spiked Spinners rotating around the now-defunct Beamos. Head to the south alcove, where there's another bell. Ring it with a Ball and Chain for another red Rupee. Ignore the horned statuettes for the moment, and head west.

◄ The staircase to the west has a Lizalfos waiting for you, and two more (one with a skull face) at the top of the stairs. Bring them down with whatever combat techniques you're happy with (long-range sniping with Bomb Arrows, or shield pushes to stagger them, then sword slashes or your jump strike are all viable options).

◄ Treasure Chest: Now negotiate some sharp and spiky traps. Move to the floor-rolling spike pole, and when it rolls to the right, run after it, then south, and roll under the swinging axe pendulum, into a small alcove with a couple of horned statuettes. Open a chest here and take the Small Key inside.

Treasure Chest #12:
Small Key

Small Key
You got a **Small Key**! This opens a locked door, but only in this area.

◄ Smash the pots on either side of the chest (one has a Heart in it), and then run under the pendulum, stop, and when the rolling spike trap moves away, run to this point, between the two rolling traps. Then run past the second rolling trap, directly north.

➤ Move to the small alcove where you can pick up a horned statuette, but only after you smash a couple more pots (one has three Hearts inside). Then take the statuette, wait for a gap as the rolling trap moves to the western wall, then run 180 degrees around so you're facing north. Drop the statuette on the floor switch. This deactivates an electrical fence.

Chamber 10: Armos Guardian Room (8F)

◄ You're now at the highest point in your dungeon exploration, a shallow, level chamber with two Armos at the far end, and a dozen or so Baby Gohmas. Leap right in, and defeat all of the scuttling sacks, and optionally refill your Hearts and arrows afterward by smashing the 11 pots along the left wall.

➤ **Treasure Chest**: Once all the Baby Gohmas are gone, a chest appears in a flash of brilliant light. Ignore this for the moment, and instead concentrate on activating one of the two Armos; fighting one at a time is much easier! Slice the rear of each Armos, and once they both explode, a gate along the right wall opens. Claim the purple Rupee inside the chest, and smash any remaining pots you wish.

Treasure Chest #13:
Purple Rupee (50)

Enemies Encountered

Imp Poe

Armos

Helmasaur

Beamos (White)

Lizalfos (Axe-tail)

Lizalfos (Skull-face)

Baby Gohma

Scour the room for more pots to smash, and raise your energy to full if it's low; you're going to need it! Then run about the area that was immediately behind the gate, smashing more pots. Head for the locked door, and step through. Prepare for battle!

Before you begin your battle, stop at the entrance door, and look up. Ring the bell here with your Ball and Chain and a Fairy floats out. Use your Clawshot to retrieve it from inside the bell, and scoop it into a Bottle. You may need it!

Fairy

You caught a **Fairy** in a Bottle! When you fall in combat, this faithful friend gives you Hearts.

Chamber 11: The Arena of Darknut

You open the door, and it closes behind you. You step into a large circular arena, with light streaming in from the windows. On a high shelf rests an armored mechanical contraption like the one guarding the first room. A large, black knight clad in onyx armor turns and faces you. This is the domain of Darknut!

Darknut

Threat Meter

A simple dodge, and your trusty Master Sword can whittle down Darknut's armor in moments. Patience and timing lead to victory!

Step 1: Fighting Darknut is almost impossible if you don't follow this excellent technique. If you do though, you can defeat him without being hit at all! First, Ⓩ target him and wait until Darknut raises his massive sword like this.

Step 2: At this precise moment, or as quickly as you can when he steps back with his sword raised, execute a backflip (◯ and Ⓐ). You then flip out of the way as Darknut's sword comes crashing down where you were standing!

Step 3: Immediately after performing the back flip, press Ⓐ without pressing a direction and you leap in with a massive sword slash that rocks Darknut, and pieces of armor fly off everywhere. Combo this move two more times until he raises his shield.

Step 4: Now repeat this technique around five or six additional times. Each time you strike back, more of Darknut's armor peels away and flies off around you. Continue until Darknut looks like this. He's about to change weapons. Get ready for round two!

Step 5: Darknut sheds his sword and throws it at you. You automatically dodge it, but if you fight Darknut again, roll out of the path of the sword. Now Darknut is faster, and a different technique is called for. When Darknut thrusts forward, roll around him using ◯ or ◯ and Ⓐ. Do this until you're at his back.

Darknut (cont'd)

Step 6: Then try to inflict damage with a back slice or a spin attack. Even if Darknut blocks (as he does here), the follow-up slashes can strike him two or three times. Then back up quickly so you aren't struck when Darknut begins to block your strikes. Repeat Steps 5 and 6 until Darknut falls!

Tip: As always, smash and grab the pots around the arena for hearty sustenance.

◄ Treasure Chest: Now move to the far end of the arena, to the chest that Darknut was guarding, and pry it open. Inside is another exceptional weapon. This one is the Dominion Rod!

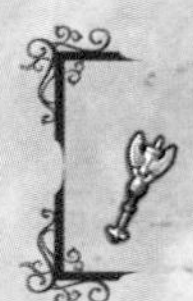

Treasure Chest #14: Dominion Rod

Dominion Rod
You got the **Dominion Rod**! This mystical artifact breathes life into ancient statues.

Dominion Rod

The Dominion Rod is an arcane device that isn't strictly a weapon, but it does allow you to control a few ancient statues and pieces of machinery. It imbues them with a green glow when you target the statue and swing with Ⓑ. Place this weapon on your Ⓑ immediately, and aim at the mechanical statue on the ledge above you. It pulses with green energy and follows your movements. If you head north, it heads north, until it hits a wall, and then stops. If you hit a wall, it keeps going until it hits a wall (this is important when controlling the statue in tight areas). When you swing your Dominion Rod, it swings its weapon, which can crush stone and a few enemies you're unable to bash! Watch out though, because it can strike you, too!

◄ Coax the controlled statue to the arena entrance, and all the way to this bell. When the statue bounces onto the platform under the bell, everything glows green, the bell descends, and the statue is sucked up into the bell area. Remember to bash the bell with a Ball and Chain before the battle to secure your Fairy (or you can grab it now).

Enemies Encountered

Darknut

Armos

Task 5: Maneuver the Statue over the Scales of Time

Back to Chamber 10: First Return to Armos Guardian Room (8F)

Return to the Armos Guardian Room, and you see another bell descend and deposit the statue in this chamber! The bell is using an ancient teleporting technology! Aim at the statue with your Dominion Rod, and activate it, then bounce along to the gate ahead. Raise your Dominion Rod, and bring it down. The statue does the same with its huge hammer, and the gate is smashed. Hop down with your new doppelganger, and head to the two Armoses. Position the statue between them, and drop the hammer twice. The Armoses explode, and you didn't even get close to the combat!

Note: Be very careful with your new power! Don't stand close in front of your statue friend and wave your Dominion Rod about! The statue brings down its hammer, and you'll lose one whole energy each time!

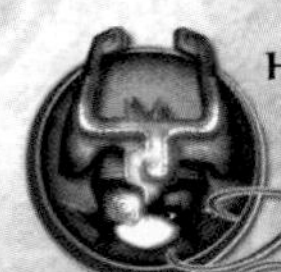

Tip: Have you lost your statue? Don't worry; it appears on your in-game map as a red dot.

Chamber 5: First Return to Armos Antechamber (5F)

Before you return to the initial chamber, go back to the fifth floor, using two statuettes and placing them on the ledge just as you did before. Remember to stand on the ledge before you raise it! Head to the south door and enter the Armos Antechamber.

The Armoses have been replaced by a dozen Baby Gohmas and a couple of Young Gohmas. Run around slashing until they're all defeated, as this makes the next tactic easier. Run to the far end of this chamber, near the open chest, and produce your Dominion Rod. Look for the statuette on the other side of the fence, and maneuver it down the channel to a floor switch. Now grab another statuette (there are two lying about), and throw it over the black fence on the opposite side.

Treasure Chest: Once the statuette is behind the fence, coax it down a similar channel to a second switch opposite the first. When both statuettes land on the switch, a chest appears in the western alcove. There's a Piece of Heart inside. Only nine more Pieces of Heart are left to find!

Treasure Chest #16: Piece of Heart

Piece of Heart

You got a **Piece of Heart**! Collect **five pieces** to form a new Heart Container! Piece of Heart #36 of 45.

Chamber 4: Second Return to Central Mechanical Platform (5F to 4F to 3F), to Chamber 3: First Return to Hexagonal Junction (3F)

Now it's time to return to the initial chamber, so head back to the entrance to the Hexagonal Junction stairs, and descend. At the closed gate, Clawshot over, and then defeat an Armos at the junction itself. Try the mortal draw! Then coax the statue from under the bell and down the stairs.

Task 7: Reach the End of the Crumbling Corridor

Chamber 2: First Return to Connecting Corridors (3F to 2F)

Continue maneuvering downstairs to the Connecting Corridors area, where you first opened the gate via a floor switch. You can afford to be a little less subtle this time; bash the gate with your statue's hammer, and then move the statue into the bell at the end.

Chamber 1: First Return to Grand Entrance (2F to 1F)

Move all the way back to the entrance chamber and run down the stairs. Control the statue out from the last teleport bell, and up the shallow steps to the side of the door, opposite the original statue. The door glows green and slides open!

Chamber 12: The Crumbling Corridor (1F)

The door slides back, and you can enter a narrow and dangerous corridor. Run forward and optionally pause to smash some skulls for arrows, Hearts, and Rupees. Then aim at a White Beamos, destroy it, then leap across the gap after avoiding the spiked Spinner, cling to the edge of the ledge in front, and pull yourself up.

Walk forward, and carry your Hero's Bow, avoiding the ground spikes as they roll back and forth. When you reach this point, and you're half hidden by a pillar, bring the bow out to shoot another two White Beamoses, then avoid the swinging axe pendulum.

1 
2 
3 
4 
5 
6 

Now for some careful maneuvering! Pick up the statuette near the swinging pendulums, and carefully carry it to the floor switch near the chasm at the corridor's north end. Place it on there, and the gate ahead swings open. Line yourself up and leap the gap, and move past the open gate, down some steps, and slay a Young Gohma. Spin around, and from within the staircase, use your Dominion Rod, zap the statuette, and move it off the switch. The gate closes to the south, but the one to the north—and the final chamber—opens!

Step to the door leading to a large arena (according to your map), and stop for a moment. Take down the Young Gohma, and then smash all the pots. The large one on the right wall houses a Fairy! Grab it if you need it!

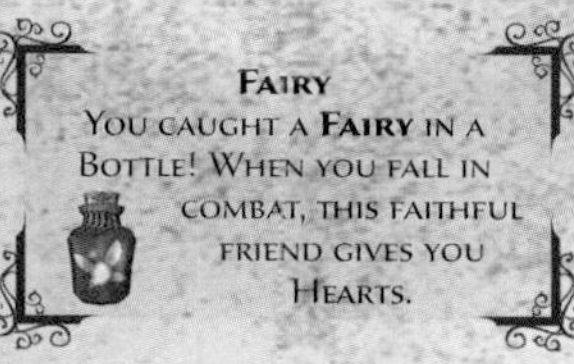

Fairy

You caught a **Fairy** in a Bottle! When you fall in combat, this faithful friend gives you Hearts.

Enemies Encountered

Baby Gohma

Young Gohma

Beamos (White)

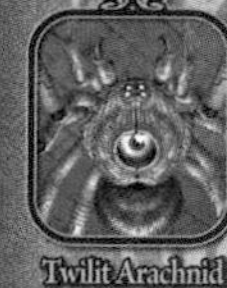

Twilit Arachnid Armogohma

Task 8: Defeat Twilit Arachnid Armogohma!

Chamber 13: Boss Battle! Twilit Arachnid Armogohma

You enter a large and imposing arena. In each of the corners stand a giant statue, with a huge hammer, dormant and waiting. Something is scuttling on the ceiling. Look up to see the gigantic Armogohma. Her huge eye has spotted you! Engage!

Twilit Arachnid Armogohma

Threat Meter

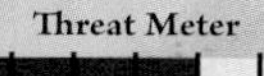

Tip: **Before you begin combat, be sure you have a good fill of energy, your Hero's Bow equipped, and your Dominion Rod within easy reach.**

Step 1: Armogohma is a fearsome furry arachnid with additional abilities her young don't have, and she starts with a nasty bolt of fire that streams forth onto the stone arena below. It can really sting (picture 1)! As you can see where the stream is going, roll away from it quickly, so she traces a tight circle in the ground (picture 2); you definitely won't be struck like this.

Step 2: After two jets of fire, Armogohma scuttles about the ceiling, and comes to rest randomly in one of four corners. As soon as she stops her fire, stand in the middle of the chamber, and bring out your **Hero's Bow**. As soon as she stops, fire an arrow directly into the eye in the middle of her back. This can be done as shown; even when she begins to fire her next jet of fire!

Step 3: As soon as she begins her fall, run directly to the corner, and around the twitching arachnid, bringing out your Dominion Rod as you go. Target the giant statue and possess it, and then make an attack gesture so the statue brings its heavy fist down into the middle of Armogohma. Repeat Steps 1–3.

Step 4: When you've inflicted a nasty knock on her a couple of times, she lays a couple of dozen Baby Gohmas to waylay you during the next battle. Quickly run around, slashing at them, and make sure all of them are dispatched. Then dodge the jet again, and repeat Steps 1–4.

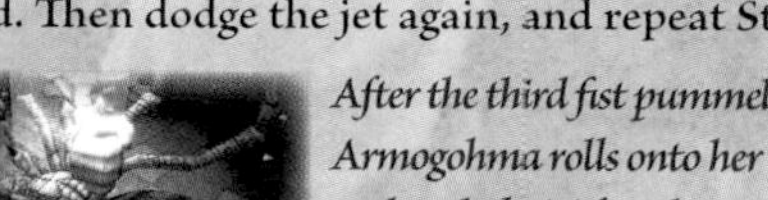

After the third fist pummeling by giant statue, Armogohma rolls onto her back, turns an inky black, and explodes! After the explosion has dissipated, you can see that only the eye is left, and it's actually a Gohma, surrounded by Baby Gohmas! The mass tries to escape, scuttling away from you.

Step 5: There's nowhere to run for this feeble arachnid! Bring out your Hero's Bow and launch a couple of manually aimed shots at the eyeball from a distance, and they all explode!

Out of the mass of twilight descends the third Mirror Shard! Midna takes it, and tells you that you need to reach the sky, as that's where the last shard is supposed to be. She creates a warp portal for you. Collect your **Heart Container**, and depart.

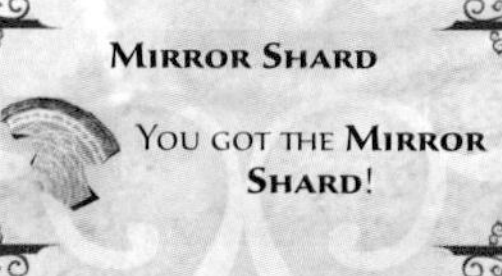

Mirror Shard

You got the **Mirror Shard**!

Heart Container

You got a **Heart Container**! Your life energy has increased by **one** and been **fully replenished**! Heart Container #6 of 8.

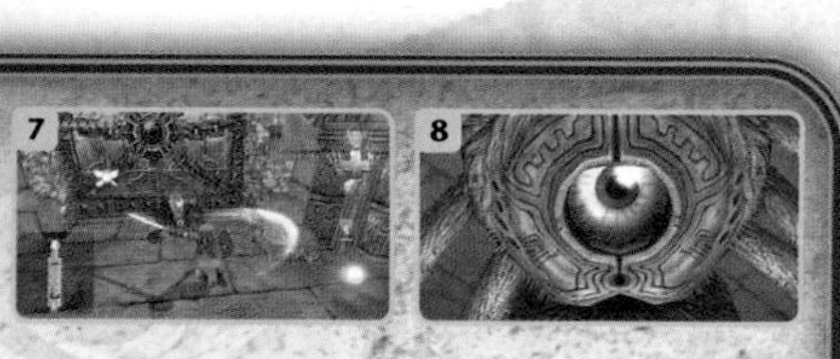

7 8

Task #8

Defeat Twilit Arachnid Armoghoma!

Overworld: Ascension to the City in the Sky

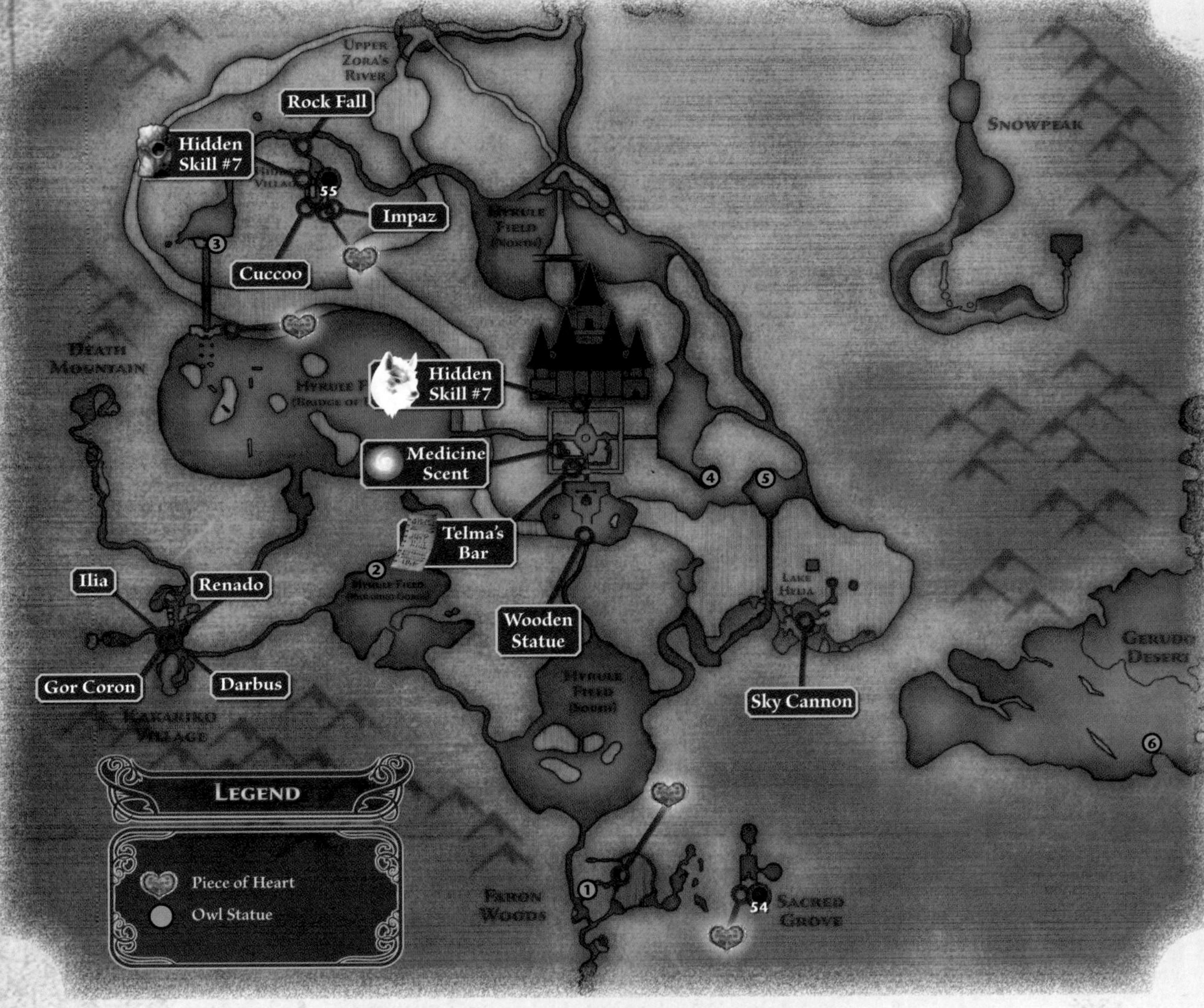

Ascension to the City in the Sky: Overview

As you exit the Temple of Time, your latest item loses power, much to your and Ooccoo's consternation. With no way of journeying skyward, you must rely on your friends, in particular your oldest chum Ilia, whose memory is gradually getting better. She must have some objects presented to her to aid her in remembering you, Ordon Spring, and the life you both used to lead. Achieve this by locating a Wooden Statue she held when she was imprisoned.

The Gorons know this artifact is from an ancient race, and the last survivor still lives in the Hidden Village. After you meet her, she realizes who you are, and with the help of Shad, you learn the secrets of the owl statues. Once the Ancient Sky Book has been assembled and an antiquated cannon rebuilt by Hyrule's finest tinker, you are ready to journey to the heavens for the final Mirror Shard.

1 — Jog Ilia's Memory with Wooden Statue (pg 363)

2 — Assault Hidden Village; Rescue Impaz (pg 366)

3 — Restore Power to the Dominion Rod (pg 370)

4 — Locate All Six Sky Book Characters (pg 371)

Items to Obtain

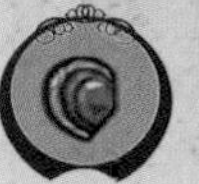

Piece of Heart #37 (of 45) | Letter #10 | Letter #11 | Letter #12 | Letter #13

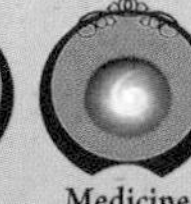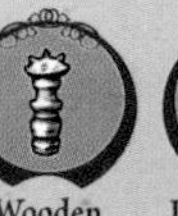

Renado's Letter | Telma's Invoice | Medicine Scent | Wooden Statue | Ilia's Charm

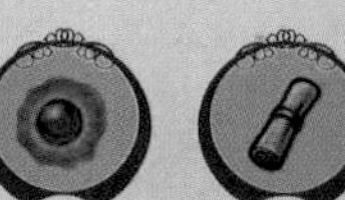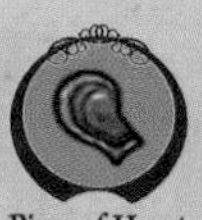

Poe Soul #55 (of 60) | Hidden Skill #7 (of 7) | Piece of Heart #38 (of 45) | Horse Call | Ancient Sky Book

Dominion Rod (Restored) | Sky Character #1 | Piece of Heart #39 (of 45) | Sky Character #2 | Sky Character #3

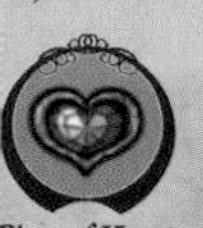

Piece of Heart #40 (of 45) | Sky Character #4 | Sky Character #5 | Ancient Sky Book (Filled)

A Link to the Present

Ordon Sword | Master Sword | Heart Pieces: 1 (36 Total)

Wooden Shield | Hylian Shield

Hero's Clothes | Zora Armor | Magic Armor

Giant Wallet | Big Quiver | Golden Bugs: 24 (of 24) | Hidden Skills: 6 (of 7)

Reekfish Scent | Poe Souls 53 (of 60) | Fish Journal | Letters 9 (of 16)

Mirror of Twilight: 3 (of 4)

Enemies Encountered

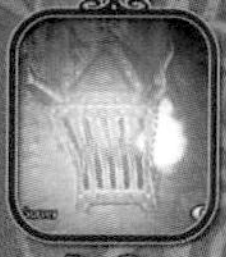

Imp Poe

Overworld Denizen

Impaz

Task 1: Jog Ilia's Memory with a Wooden Statue

The Dominion Rod Loses Power

After completing the sixth dungeon, depart from the Temple of Time and head back to this area immediately; there's some unfinished business to attend to. Head to the entrance steps and around to the west, and look for the owl statue. Aim your Dominion Rod at the statue. It activates! Shift the statue out of the way; it's blocking a door leading to a chest. Inside is a Piece of Heart!

Overworld Chest #88: Piece of Heart #37

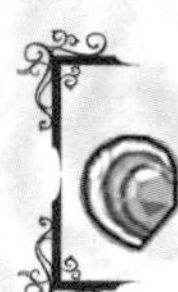

Piece of Heart
You got a **Piece of Heart**! Collect **three more** for another full Heart Container. Piece of Heart #37 of 45.

Head to the Heavens
Pg 375

Missing Links

1. Chest in Time

Do you remember the open, rusty chest back in Sacred Grove? If you pour over your maps, you'll realize this chest you just opened is actually the one outside, in another time!

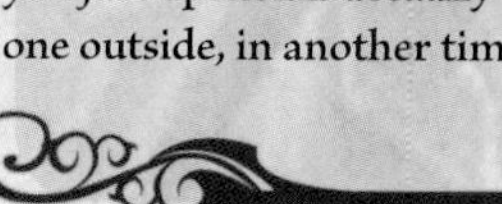

Poe Soul #54

Now head to the staircase's other side and activate this owl statue with your Dominion Rod. As you move it away from a thin alcove, a Lantern floats toward you. It's an Imp Poe! Clobber it and steal that soul: only six more to go!

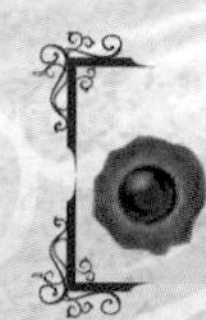

Poe Soul
You got the **Poe's Soul**! Collect one from each Poe you defeat! Poe Soul #54 of 60.

Characters Encountered

Ooccoo

Postman

Agitha

Telma

Ashei

Rusl

Renado

Ilia

Borville

⮝ Head into the Sacred Grove to meet Ooccoo. "Goodness, yes! It's the **Dominion Rod** you found!" she says. However, this device, which can help her return to her people, has lost its power now that you're removed from the time period of the temple. She sets off to figure a way to restore it. You should warp to Castle Town.

The Postman arrives when you next enter a bridge or junction somewhere in Hyrule. He's been busy collecting quite an assortment of letters in your absence. If you took a more indirect path through your adventure, you may have received these letters before or after this point. There are four letters to open:

- Letter #10 is from Renado, telling you to meet him **back at the Sanctuary.**
- Letter #11 is from Ooccoo, telling you how happy she is to reunite with her son. You receive this as soon as you use Ooccoo to exit, then enter a Dungeon.
- Letter #12 is from Princess Agitha, telling you of a strange dream of flying in the sky. This is a subtle reminder to hand over more Golden Bugs!
- Letter #13 is from Yeta, thanking you for your visit and asking you to join them at Snowpeak. This is a reminder for you to play the sledding minigame.

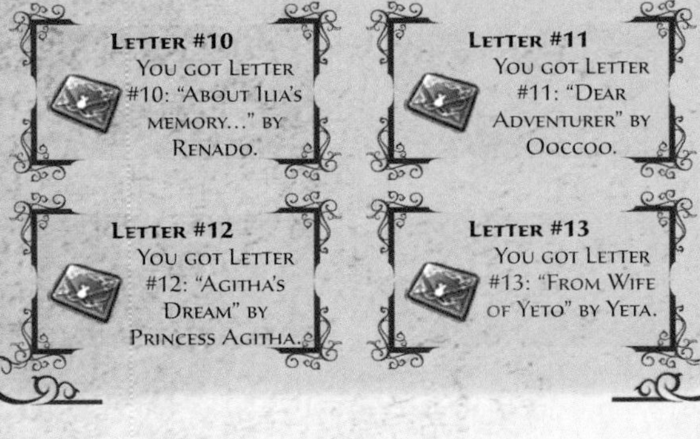

Letter #10
You got Letter #10: "About Ilia's memory..." by Renado.

Letter #11
You got Letter #11: "Dear Adventurer" by Ooccoo.

Letter #12
You got Letter #12: "Agitha's Dream" by Princess Agitha.

Letter #13
You got Letter #13: "From Wife of Yeto" by Yeta.

Inside Castle Town: Outstanding Objectives

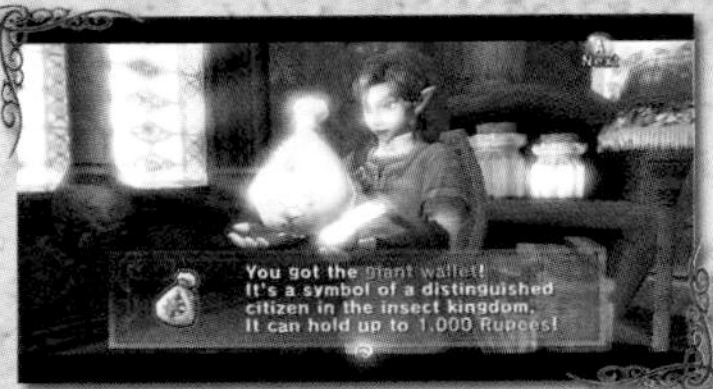

⮜ You should have collected all the Golden Bugs by now, so give them to Princess Agitha. You receive the **Giant Wallet** for your troubles.

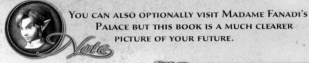

Note: You can also optionally visit Madame Fanadi's Palace but this book is a much clearer picture of your future.

⮞ Visit Telma's Bar, as this is the source of most gossip in the realm. Say hello to Louise, then talk to Telma. She tells you that Shad is in Kakariko Village, looking for something he deemed important. Head over to the table of adventurers.

⮜ Ashei tells you the beast of Snowpeak hasn't reappeared.... Speak to Rusl, and he wonders if you've found anything Shad might be interested in. The Oocca are supposed to be the ancestors of the Hylians, you know! Check your table map for Shad's location.

Powering the Dominion Rod: Kakariko Village

⮞ Warp directly to Kakariko Village, change to Link, and enter Renado's Sanctuary. Gor Coron tells you that an acquaintance of yours has lost her memory and is in some trouble. You know this; Ilia is the person you're here to see!

⮞ Next, speak to Renado. He's heard that when Ilia was saved, she overheard someone talking about the **rod of the heavens.** He needs to trace back Ilia's locations during her memory loss to figure out what this means. Instructions for Telma to think back on who may have come into contact with Ilia are contained in **Renado's Letter.**

Renado's Letter
You got **Renado's Letter**! It carefully details how to treat Ilia to get her memory back.

▲ Ilia remains confused, remembering she was saved by someone who told her about the rod. Then she calls you a **complete stranger!** Ilia's recovery is not complete yet.

Powering the Dominion Rod: Back to Castle Town

◄ Head back to Castle Town and to Telma's Bar. Present **Renado's Letter** to Telma. She tells you that Doctor Borville was the first to bring Ilia in. He won't talk to you until he's paid, so Telma hands you the **Invoice**; the doctor has been seriously boozing in this bar!

Invoice
You got the **Invoice**! This invoice is for the town doctor's running tab, which is an astronomical sum.

◄ Enter Doctor Borville's medical house, and present the invoice to him. He says he can't pay this off right now. If he'd been able to sell the **Wooden Statue** that **young lady** had, he'd have the money. He spilt medicine on the statue, put it outside to dry, and someone stole it. Until he gets the statue back, he can't repay you.

◄ It's time to look for that statue. There's a crate at the back of the doctor's clinic. Push it out of the way to see a green stain emanating from the back wall. This looks like a medicine spill!

➤ Turn into wolf form and activate your senses, and you'll see the cloud of green scent in the air. Forget the Reekfish Scent, and learn the Medicine Scent!

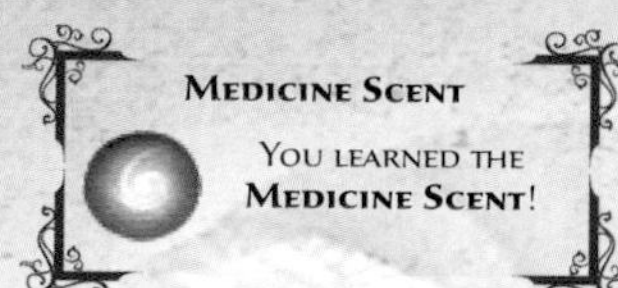

Medicine Scent
You learned the **Medicine Scent**!

Powering the Dominion Rod: Hunting for the Statue

➤ With your scent learned, you can bound onto the crate, leap to the shelving's top, across the ledge (smashing pots for Rupees), and out onto the clinic's upper balcony. The scent trail leads down to the street, but don't jump there yet; check the right alcove for a chest with a red Rupee (20) and some pottery with a blue (5) and green (1) Rupee.

Overworld Chest #89: Red Rupee (20)

◄ Follow the scent trail south, around the alley past Jovani's, then south down the market street, before turning and ending up at Telma's. Louise is waiting and admits she stole the statue! Alas, she was attacked by some skeletal dog beasts who took it from her. The fiends lurk just outside the **southern gate**, and they only come out at night. Mostly. Leave Louise, and head directly out the south gate.

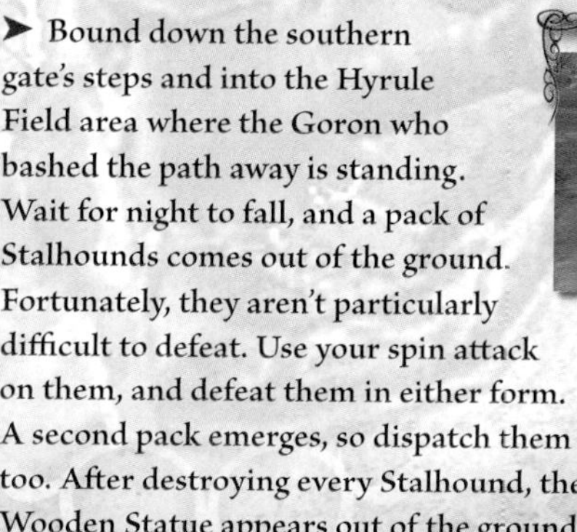

➤ Bound down the southern gate's steps and into the Hyrule Field area where the Goron who bashed the path away is standing. Wait for night to fall, and a pack of Stalhounds comes out of the ground. Fortunately, they aren't particularly difficult to defeat. Use your spin attack on them, and defeat them in either form. A second pack emerges, so dispatch them too. After destroying every Stalhound, the Wooden Statue appears out of the ground.

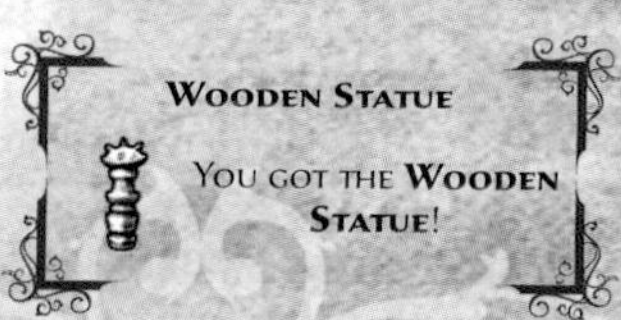

Wooden Statue
You got the **Wooden Statue**!

Enemies Encountered
Stalhound

Characters Encountered

Ilia

Gor Coron

Darbus

Epona

Impaz

Powering the Dominion Rod: Jogging Ilia's Memory

▲ Give the statue to Ilia, and she begins to remember. Gor Coron recognizes the statue as belonging to a tribe that protected the Hylian royal family long ago. The tribe's remaining members live in the **hidden village** on the path to Lanayru Province. Darbus will clear the path!

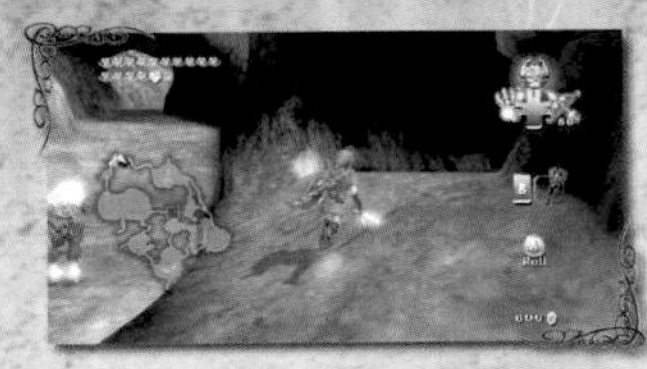

◄ Check your map for the location of the Hidden Village; it's past the Bridge of Eldin, on the rocky path near the wooden bridge and spinner track. Gallop here on Epona, and halt when you see the gap in the right rock wall. Defeat any Bulblins here, then race into the opening.

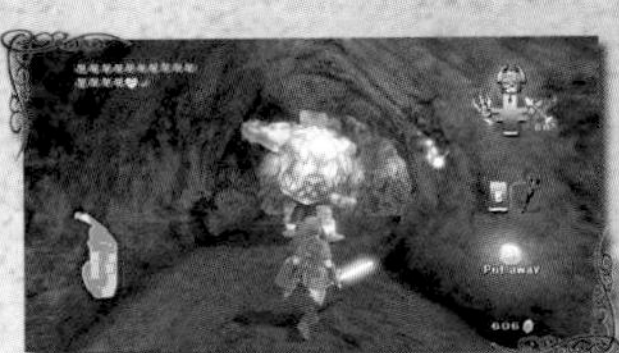

◄ Inside the tunnel, Darbus bashes the rockfall until it disintegrates. He informs you that there are 20 presences you must purge from this place—remnants of a warring tribe you should defeat one at a time, and from range. Head through into the Hidden Village.

Task 2: Assault the Hidden Village; Rescue Impaz

Powering the Dominion Rod: Hidden Village Assault

Note: The following strategy shows you the optimal method of defeating the 20 remaining Bulblins in this village. You may wish to use more aggressive tactics, but don't expect to remain unscathed!

▲ Stride to the entrance to Hidden Village. Ahead you see that 20 Bulblins, both warriors and archers, are holding their ground in this area. Bring out your **Hero's Bow**: this place ain't big enough for the 21 of you!

Note: Once you begin your Bulblin takedown, the new icon in your screen's bottom-right corner shows how many Bulblins you have left to tackle.

◄ **Bulblins 20 and 19:** Step just inside the village limit, and sidestep right with your bow drawn. Target Z and move to the point shown in this screen, and aim at this upper balcony. There's an explosive barrel here; shoot it, and two Bulblins bite the dust!

◄ **Bulblin 18:** Sidestep left with your bow drawn, and shoot the explosive barrel on the ground ahead. A Bulblin investigates the disturbance; drop him from this distance!

► **Bulblins 17 and 16:** Continue sidestepping so you're almost behind these crates, then aim up at the right building balcony, and tag another Bulblin here. Then drop your aim slightly, under the balcony, and shoot a Bulblin under here.

Tip: If you're having trouble aiming at any of these Bulblins, combine the Hawkeye (bought at the Malo Mart in Kakariko Village) with the Hero's Bow. You can now snipe easily!

► **Bulblin 15:** Edge forward until you're standing next to the stacked crates at the village entrance. Aim along the right balcony. Shoot the Bulblin here; he topples to the ground.

1 2 3 4 5

Enemies Encountered

Bulblin Archer

Bulblin Warrior

➤ **Bulblin 14:** Now aim down to the street's end, and take out the explosive barrel; this rocks another Bulblin.

◄ **Bulblin 13:** Continue your hawkeyed shooting; with your bow, take out the Bulblin standing midway down the left upper balconies.

◄ **Bulblin 12:** Slowly move down the street, and wait here, before the end of the first set of buildings. Use your Hawkeye and aim down, then left at the end balcony. Drop this Bulblin before he even sees you!

➤ **Bulblins 11 and 10:** For two more easy takedowns, zoom to the street's far end. One Bulblin is behind a short wall and another is behind some explosive crates. Take them both down!

◄ **Bulblin 9:** Your next Bulblin requires some closer combat; make an immediate right into the building you're standing next to, and run quickly up the steps, avoiding incoming arrows (keep moving). Bring out your sword, and slash the Bulblin Archer here.

Tip

If you're running short on arrows, use the Clawshot to hook onto this mesh above the cattle trough, and climb onto the upper balcony. Run right, around the back of the next building. There are two barrels at the end, one of which contains arrows.

➤ **Bulblin 8:** Use the Clawshot, propel up to the balcony on the street's left side, and move to this point. There's a Bulblin on a lookout tower. Aim at the barrel and blow it up!

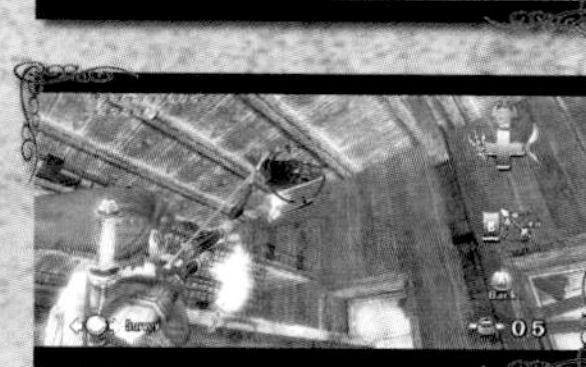

▲ **Bulblins 7, 6, and 5:** Drop to the ground, and move to the second building on the right. Smash the first window you come to, with the barrel next to it, and enter with your sword drawn. Immediately run and defeat the Bulblin on the ground. Sidestep left, behind the crates, and fire at the Bulblin standing on the balcony above, to the south. Now move to the left end of the wooden desk. There's a hole in the roof and another Bulblin here; fire at him before he strikes you with a fiery arrow.

▲ **Bulblin 4:** Head back into the main street, and look for this alley, to the left of the middle building. Bash the barrels, and run around to the alley behind the building. Dash to the archer at the end, Z target him, block his arrows, and defeat him.

▲ **Bulblins 3, 2, and 1:** The final three Bulblins are in the last building on the left, at the street's end. The first is on the ground floor. Shoot him from the street or run in with a sword. The other two are on balconies above. From the street, shoot the first through the window; then enter and defeat the final Bulblin with arrows.

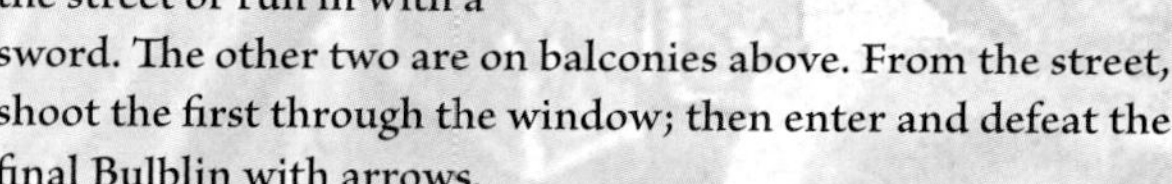

◄ As soon as you defeat the last Bulblin, the door to the hut by the small wall opens. An old lady shuffles out. This is Impaz, and she thanks you for your help.

She has a gift for Ilia—the charm Ilia gave Impaz to protect her. She happily gives you the pendant that kept her safe for so long. Head south.

Characters Encountered

Impaz

White Wolf

Hero's Shade

Impaz:

About 70 years old, Impaz is an aged woman living in fear in a hidden village, where Ilia was locked away. Impaz plays a part in freeing Ilia. Impaz is the last of her tribe, which used to live in this village. She is kind and speaks with a thin but firm voice. She thanks you profusely for saving her.

Ilia's Charm

You got **Ilia's Charm**!

Before you warp back to Kakariko Village, head to the western row of houses, and enter the place where you defeated Bulblins 7, 6, and 5. The smashed outer windows lead to a grassy back garden; there's a Windstone here!

Powering the Dominion Rod: Hidden Village Return

Poe Soul #55

After you complete the cat hunt minigame, return to Hidden Village, ideally at night, as there's an Imp Poe to secure around here. Head to the balcony of the building in the northeast corner. Access the balcony via a Clawshot and climb up the mesh. Change to your wolf form, run around the balcony's corner, and face down your Poe foe! Only five more to go!

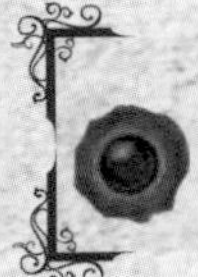

Poe Soul

You got the **Poe's Soul**! Collect one from each Poe you defeat! Poe Soul #55 of 60.

Hidden Skill #7

Howling for the White Wolf

Immediately return in wolf form, and head back to this garden. A Cucco here tells you there are several dig spots to uncover here (search the grass for Rupees and Hearts). Then listen to the Windstone as the wind whistles a tune through the hole in the rock. Watch the tune, then replicate it. The pitch is as follows: Middle, Low (hold), Middle, High, Low (hold), High, Middle, High, Middle. Use ⇧ to howl high and ⇩ to howl low on your ○. For midrange howling, don't move the stick.

You appear as a wolf, high in the heavens with Death Mountain in the background. The White Wolf appears at the end of a leafy edge, above the spires of Castle Hyrule. You howl the tune again. The White Wolf tells you, "Let teachings of old pass to you…" The wolf leaps down into the land.

Note: You have summoned the White Wolf! He is currently waiting for you at the entrance to Hyrule Castle in Castle Town. Immediately head to Castle Town as Link to learn your last Hidden Skill.

Great Spin

The White Wolf is sitting patiently at the entrance to Castle Hyrule. Head north from the fountain in Castle Town to reach him. The White Wolf waits for you to come, sword in hand! He growls at you, and pounces. The Hero's Shade forms and tells you that this is a forgotten skill and the ultimate secret technique, testing the true courage of the one who wields it.

To ensure you learned the previous Hidden Skill correctly, your teacher asks that you show him you've mastered the **jump strike**. Simply Z target and hold Ⓐ until just as the blade finishes shining; then release your strength. "Excellent!" utters the warrior. "Let the **great spin** be hewn into your mind!" Because of your past techniques, you can now magnify the power of your spin attack, but only when your life **energy** is full. Try it!

Hidden Skill #7 (cont'd)

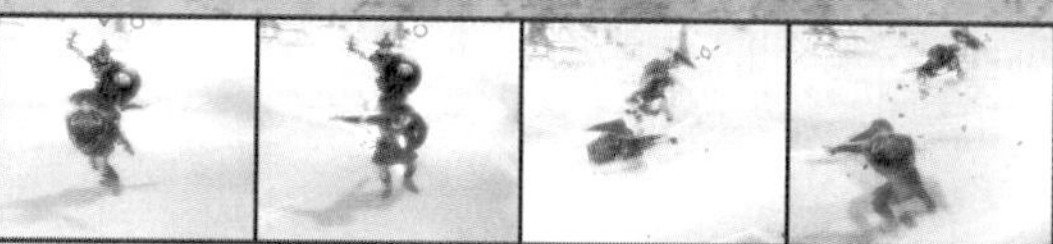

Great Spin: Simply execute a spin attack when you have full energy. This hits more targets and for more damage, at greater range.

The Hero's Shade congratulates you. "Go and do not falter, my child!"

Hidden Skill
You learned the seventh and final Hidden Skill, the **great spin**! Hidden Skill 7 of 7.

Return to Hidden Village in wolf form, and head to the back garden where you spoke to the Cucco and howled at the Windstone. The Cucco has a game for you; there's a special prize if you can locate the 20 cats that are hiding in the village.

The cats have returned from Castle Town, and parts unknown, and are waiting for you to talk to them all. Conduct a thorough search of the area to ensure you find them all! When the 20th cat is found, your mini-game is over.

Enemies Encountered

Imp Poe

Cat Hunt Minigame!

The goal is to speak with all 20 cats who have recently taken up residence within the Hidden Village. There's no time limit, so work methodically.

The kitties move around the village, but they mostly stick to their favorite "turf." Working north to south, here's the location of each Hidden Village cat:

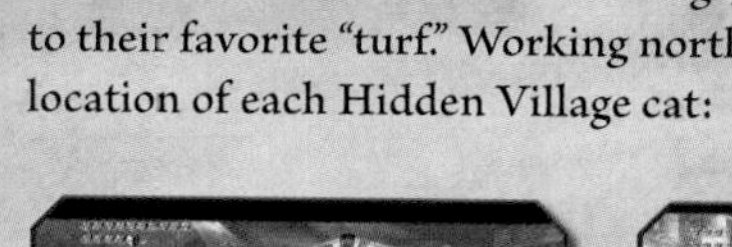

#1: Atop the north stack of wooden crates (target with Z).

#2: In the street near the north stack of wooden crates.

#3: Also in the street near the north stack of wooden crates.

#4: In the street between the village's two northernmost buildings.

#5: Inside the northwesternmost building; second-floor balcony.

#6: On the northwesternmost building's outside balcony.

#7: On the northeasternmost building's outside balcony (use Clawshot to reach).

#8: On the east building's outside balcony.

#9: In the village's east alley.

#10: In the alley between the west and northwesternmost buildings.

#11: Inside the west building; first floor.

#12: Inside the west building, also on the first floor.

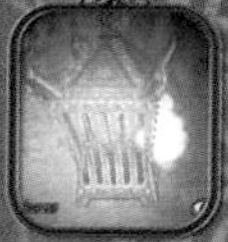

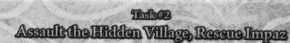

Characters Encountered

Ilia

Shad

Impaz

Midna

Cat Hunt Minigame! (cont'd)

#13: Inside the west building; second floor (use Clawshot to reach).

#14: On the west building's outside balcony.

#15: In the street between the village's east and west buildings.

#16: In the lot just south of the village's west building.

#17: At the south end of the village, near Impaz's house.

#18: In the village's southernmost nook.

#19: Inside the barrels in the southeasternmost building (smash the barrels).

#20: Inside the southeasternmost building, on upper balcony (jump through second-floor window to reach).

For finding all the cats, you win a prize. Outside of Impaz's house is a Piece of Heart! Collect it, and then return to Kakariko Village to try and jog Ilia's memory.

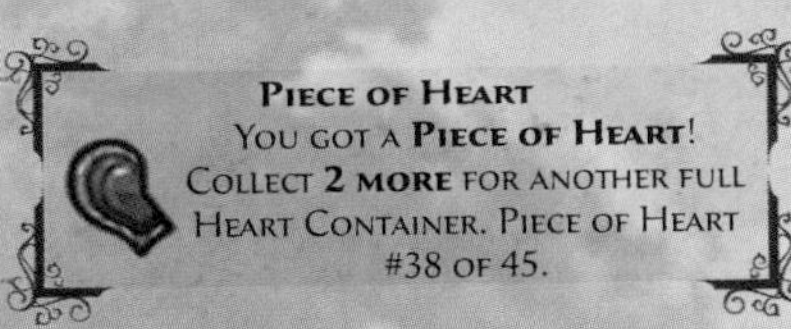
Piece of Heart
You got a **Piece of Heart**! Collect **2 more** for another full Heart Container. Piece of Heart #38 of 45.

Task 3: Restore Power to the Dominion Rod

Powering the Dominion Rod: Success!

◄ Now that you have **Ilia's Charm**, you can show it to Ilia inside the Sanctuary. The scent of hay...she remembers you! Ilia's Charm was meant for you for your journey. She thinks back to the Ordon Spring.

◄ The gift isn't a charm at all; it's actually a **Horse Call**! It allows you to summon Epona from wherever you are in Hyrule (except for Snowpeak and the Desert). Ilia says she'll be waiting for you when you return. Her memory is coming back!

Horse Call
You got the **Horse Call**! Ilia made this just for Epona.

▲ Ilia now informs you that the **rod of the heavens** story was actually about a **messenger**. In the Hidden Village lies a gift for this **heavenly messenger**. They await his return, when he comes bearing a rod....

1 2 3 4 5

➤ Head into the cellar and speak with Shad, who's staring at an owl statue. He asks if you remember the legend of the Oocca. He's seen statues like this, which appear to be related to the Oocca, all over Hyrule. This one is different, though; there's something written on it. It is sky writing, and says, **"Awaken us with the word that breaks the seal."**

➤ Shad hasn't figured out what to do, but you have! Journey back to Hidden Village once more, and enter Impaz's hut. Produce the Dominion Rod, and she is startled. This is the sign that the messenger has arrived! A book, guarded by her ancestors, is to be given to the messenger.

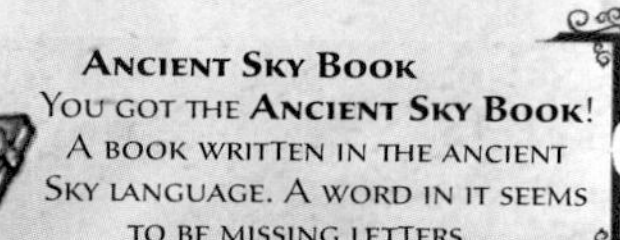

Ancient Sky Book
You got the **Ancient Sky Book**! A book written in the ancient Sky language. A word in it seems to be missing letters....

➤ Shad is shocked when you return to the Sanctuary cellar and present him with the Ancient Sky Book! He takes the book and heads off to try and activate the rest of the owl statues that are scattered about Hyrule. He's marked their locations on your map.

➤ When he departs, you can examine your **Dominion Rod**. Its power has been restored! Now check your in-game map, where all the locations of the owl statues are shown. Perhaps these statues have the hidden missing word....

Dominion Rod
Power has returned to the **Dominion Rod**! This mystical rod breathes life into ancient statues.

Task 4: Locate all Six Sky Book Characters

Owl Statue Hunt #1: South Faron Woods

Note: Begin hunting across Hyrule for the owl statues you've been seeing throughout your adventure. Only search for the ones on your in-game map; you don't need to activate the two at the entrance to the Temple of Time.

➤ Warp to South Faron Woods and run past Coro's hut. Head right into the small glade hidden from view by the Bomb Rock you destroyed earlier. Head behind a tree, where you find the owl statue. Activate it with your Dominion Rod and move it from its alcove.

➤ Maneuver around the statue, and head into the alcove it was resting on. A glowing green character is visible on the ground. Retrieve your first Sky Character. This is a missing part of the word in the Ancient Sky Book and has now been restored to the book.

One Sky Character
You found **one Sky Character**!

➤ After you find the first Sky Character, move the owl statue out again and place it in the round slot between the tree and the stone. Then change into wolf form, and run up the stone ramp. Midna can transport you onto the top of the statue and across the branch.

➤ This leads to a pair of thin rock columns that Midna coaxes you over (Z target constantly) and to a ledge. A mist descends as you reach a high alcove overlooking Faron Woods. Remember the chest you saw but couldn't reach at the start of your adventure? Now you can claim the Piece of Heart inside!

Overworld Chest #90: Piece of Heart #39

Piece of Heart
You got a **Piece of Heart**! Collect **1 more** for another full Heart Container. Piece of Heart #39 of 45.

Owl Statue Hunt #2: Kakariko Gorge

➤ Warp to Kakariko Gorge, and run to the northern part of the field, up onto the ground surrounded by a grassy ledge, and activate your next owl statue. When it is out from its alcove, run in to claim your second Sky Character.

One Sky Character
You found **one Sky Character**!

➤ Investigate the grassy ledge a little more closely now. Activate the owl statue again, and move it to the left gap between the two ledges. Then run up the ledge and leap across, onto the top of the owl statue and to the ledge on the other side.

➤ From the ledge on the other side, activate the owl statue once more. Drag it across to the opposite side and deactivate it. On the way, you'll jump over the alcove where the statue initially sat.

➤ Now place the owl statue carefully an equal distance between the ledge on the opposite side, and then leap onto it and to the other side. You can now reach this treasure chest and claim the orange Rupee (100) inside.

Overworld Chest #91: Orange Rupee (100)

Owl Statue Hunt #3: Bridge of Eldin

➤ Warp to the Bridge of Eldin and change to Link. Run north and bring out your bow. Fire at the Bulblin Archer on the parapet, making sure you Z target and manually shift left and right to avoid his arrows. Then look for the owl statue on the opposite parapet. Step on the circle it was sitting on, and claim your next Sky Character.

One Sky Character
You found **one Sky Character**!

➤ You're not done yet! Activate the owl statue once more, and drop it down onto the bridge. Turn and run south with the owl statue next to you. You're heading for the bridge gate at the bridge's opposite end. When you near, stop and produce your bow. Shoot the archer and two riders ahead of you, right and behind the arch.

➤ Move to the gate and turn left. There's a crumbling hole here that prevents access into the bridge tower beyond. Carefully place the owl statue into this hole, then climb to the bridge road and leap across the gap. You may need to shift the owl statue a few times to line it up so you can make both jumps.

➤ Leap the gap, onto the owl statue, and into the bridge tower. This is the only tower you can get inside, so climb the ladder to the top and immediately block with your shield.

Turn right and advance on a Bulblin Archer. Smack him with your sword, and he falls over the edge. Then run to the chest and open it. You've filled another Heart Container!

Overworld Chest #92: Piece of Heart #40

Piece of Heart
You got a **Piece of Heart**! You collected 5 pieces and formed a new Heart Container! Piece of Heart #40 of 45.

Enemies Encountered

Bulblin Archer

Owl Statue Hunt #4: Eastern Hyrule Field

▲ Warp to Castle Town, and stand in the Hyrule Field. Turn east and run up the path toward the amphitheater. Jump to the structure's base and engage a Bulblin in combat. Make sure you defeat all enemies; then check out the owl statue on the pedestal.

▲ Activate the owl statue and drop it off the pedestal. You can see the Sky Character glowing from the pedestal's platform, but you can't reach it. You must place the owl statue between the amphitheater steps and the pedestal. Then leap from the steps, onto the owl statue, then the pedestal, and claim your next Sky Character.

One Sky Character

You found **one Sky Character**!

▲ Now activate the owl statue and bring it with you as you cross the broken stones to the pedestal containing the chest. Position the owl statue as shown, allowing you to leap across, as you did previously. Land on the pedestal and ransack the chest for an orange Rupee (100).

Overworld Chest #93: Orange Rupee (100)

Owl Statue Hunt #5: Great Hylian Bridge

◄ From the previous owl statue, run along the path that leads to the Great Hylian Bridge. Search the northern grassy area for this alcove in the rock face. This next owl statue must be placed exactly to allow you to access both the Sky Character and the chest on the adjacent alcove. Drop the owl statue, then bring it out approximately six feet from the wall.

➤ Clawshot up to the vines directly above the statue, then drop down. You must land on the owl statue, not the ground! If you miss the statue's top, reactivate it and place it under the vines; then leap across to claim the Sky Character.

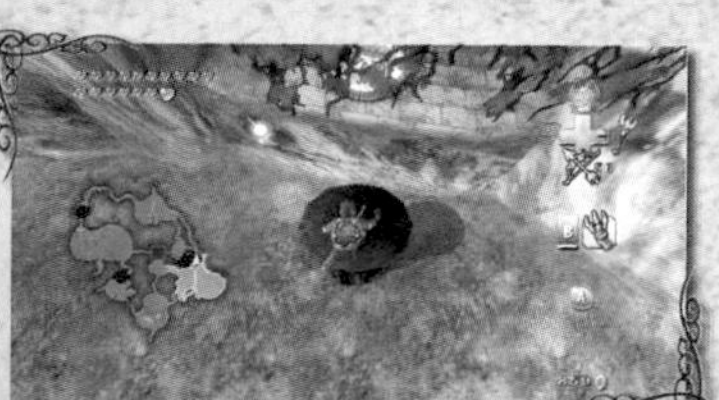

One Sky Character

You found **one Sky Character**!

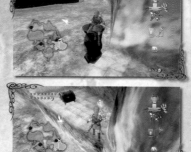

◄ This next part is tricky, so take your time. In order to reach the alcove containing the chest, you must activate the statue and move it to this specific point (picture 1). Place the statue so you can jump and land on it, then turn and jump and land on the second alcove (picture 2). This is the only way to reach this chest, which contains an orange Rupee (100).

Overworld Chest #94: Orange Rupee (100)

Owl Statue Hunt #6: Gerudo Desert

➤ The final owl statue you must use to uncover a Sky Character is located along the Gerudo Desert's southern edge. Warp here, then run to this collection of blocks; the owl statue sits atop one. Transform to Link, bring out your Dominion Rod, and pull the statue onto the ground.

CHARACTERS ENCOUNTERED

Renado

Shad

Midna

Fyer

Ooccoo

With the owl statue still activated, run to this corner of the block area, then walk to this part of the desert, making sure the owl statue rubs up against the lip of the edge of this blocky area. Move to the low block and climb up. Your owl statue should now be equidistant between this set of blocks and the one with the Sky Character. Leap to the owl, then to the glowing circle.

ANCIENT SKY BOOK
THE **ANCIENT SKY BOOK** IS FILLED WITH THE MISSING CHARACTERS! IT'S A CLUE TO FINDING A PATH TO THE SKY.

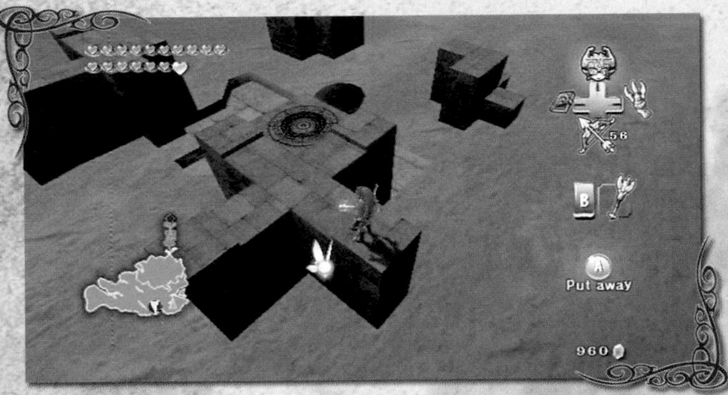

Congratulations! You've found all the pieces of the missing word. Before you head back to Shad in Kakariko Village, solve this puzzle by opening this chest. Stand here, facing south. Activate the owl, and walk across to the opposite side of the plinth.

Deactivate the statue, then run to the edge of your cross-shaped plinth. Turn and activate the owl statue again, and walk to the plinth's opposite edge. Switch off the statue again. You should have maneuvered the statue so you can use it as a step to the cross-shaped plinth opposite. Leap across to it now.

Stand at this cross-shaped plinth's far end and face west. Activate the owl statue, and walk to the opposite edge. Deactivate, move to the inside edge of the other part of this plinth, activate the statue, and drag it south to the lip. Then stop.

Deactivate the owl statue for the last time, turn and face west, and leap to the statue, which should be positioned so you can claim the chest on the tiny plinth in the far corner of this area of blocks. Open it, then drop to the sand.

1 2 3 4 5

Task 5: Head to the Heavens

Owl Statue Hunt #7: Kakariko Village Sanctuary Cellar

◄ With all six Sky Characters assembled, head back to Renado's Sanctuary and drop into the cellar, where you meet Shad. He reads the completed incantation, and the seal on the owl disappears. When Shad leaves whip out the Dominion Rod and move that final owl statue. Enter the owl statue–shaped hole behind the figure and run down the dirt ramp.

▲ You enter a hidden chamber and look at a rusting and crumbling cannon in the cavernous gloom. Shad runs down. This must be the Sky cannon he's read about in his father's notes!

Missing Links

1. Digging for Victory

Check the dirt ramp and the cannon chamber for dig spots; there are many, and they grant you Rupees of different denominations, as well as Hearts.

Speak to Shad again, and he realizes he's in your way and leaves. This allows you to talk to Midna, who asks what you plan to do with this cannon. It must be transported, but where? Remembering what Auru said, choose Lake Hylia on the map, and the cannon is dropped on the round grassy island near Fyer's hut.

► Head over to visit Fyer, who asks if he can get a tour. As he looks over the broken cannon, he offers to mend it for you for the princely sum of 300 Rupees. Do this as soon as possible. Fyer fixes the cannon, and although it may look like junk, this is a powerful propulsion device designed to send you sky-high!

◄ When you're ready to fly to the City in the Sky, step to the cannon's rear and search for the Clawshot medallion. Target and propel yourself into the cannon, and it struts about on its claw legs, adjusting trajectory. It waits for a running Ooccoo to catch you, and then fires you both into the heavens....

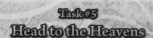

Dungeon 7: City in the Sky

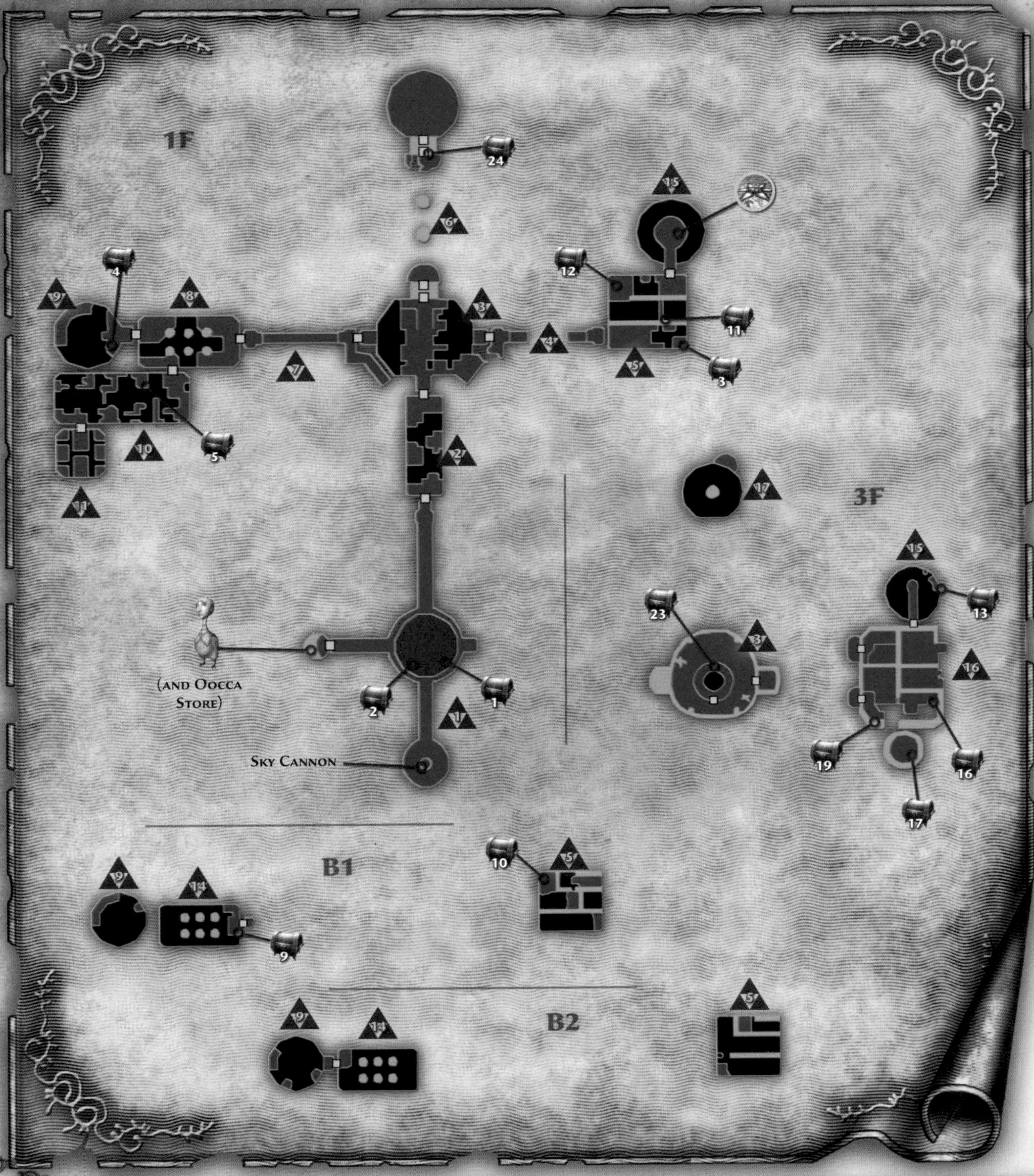

1F
3F
B1
B2
(and Oocca Store)
Sky Cannon

1
Pg 379

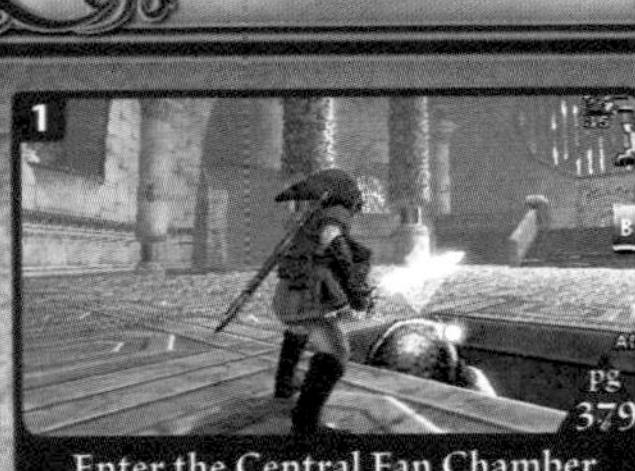

Enter the Central Fan Chamber

2
Pg 381

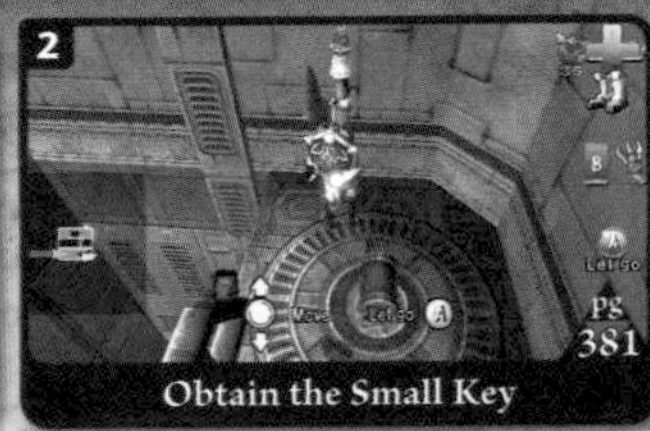

Obtain the Small Key

3
Pg 382

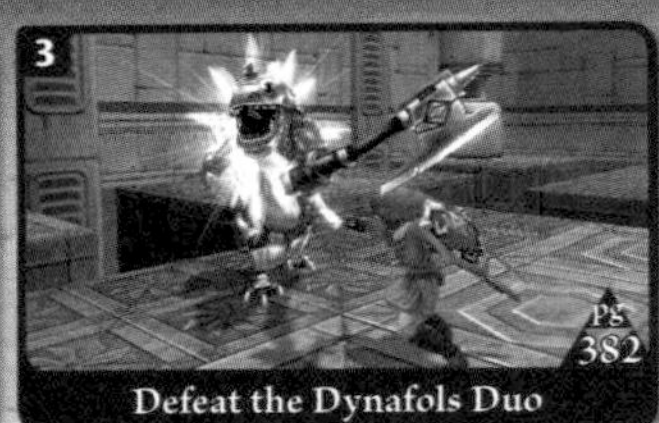

Defeat the Dynafols Duo

4
Pg 384

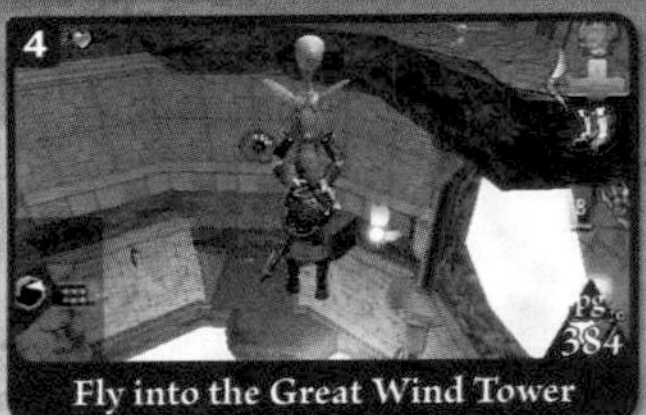

Fly into the Great Wind Tower

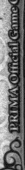

Legend

Room Legend

1. Outer Ledges and Shop (1F)
2. Cannon Bay (1F)
3. Central Fan Chamber (1F to 4F)
4. Peahat Wind Gorge (East) (1F)
5. Eastern Sky Tower (B2 to 3F)
6. Rotating Fan Gorge (1F)
7. Central Sky Bridge (1F)
8. Wind Room (1F)
9. The Great Wind Tower (West) (B3 to 2F)
10. The Floor Maze (1F)
11. Domain of the Dynafols (1F to 2F)
12. Oocca Flying Room (2F)
13. Basement Fan and Battle Chamber (B3)
14. Clawshot Ricochet Room (B2 to B1)
15. Big Baba's Tower (1F to 3F)
16. Peahat Gardens (1F to 3F)
17. Northern Fan Tower (1F to 5F)

Items

- Ooccoo
- Fairy

Number of Treasure Chests: 24

1. Water Bombs (15)!
2. Red Rupee (20)
3. Small Key
4. Dungeon Map
5. Yellow Rupee (10)
6. Red Rupee (20)
7. Purple Rupee (50)
8. Double Clawshot
9. Compass
10. Arrows (20)
11. Red Rupee (20)
12. Bombs (10)
13. Yellow Rupee (10)
14. Arrows (20)
15. Piece of Heart #41
16. Red Rupee (20)
17. Purple Rupee (50)
18. Bombs (5)
19. Piece of Heart #42
20. Red Rupee (20)
21. Purple Rupee (50)
22. Big Key
23. Red Rupee (20)
24. Red Rupee (20)

Characters

- Big Baba
- Aeralfos
- Twilit Dragon Argorok

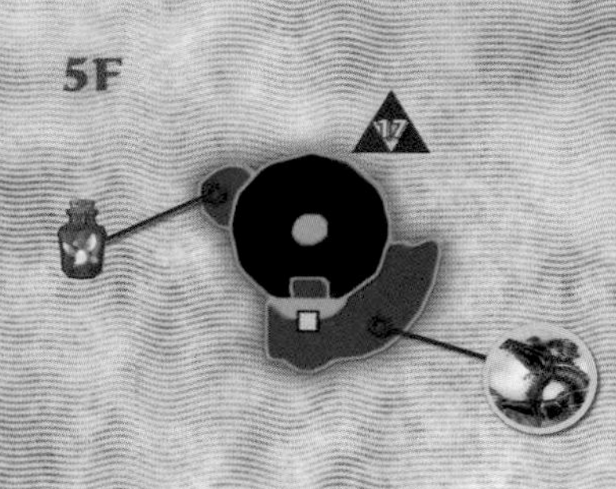

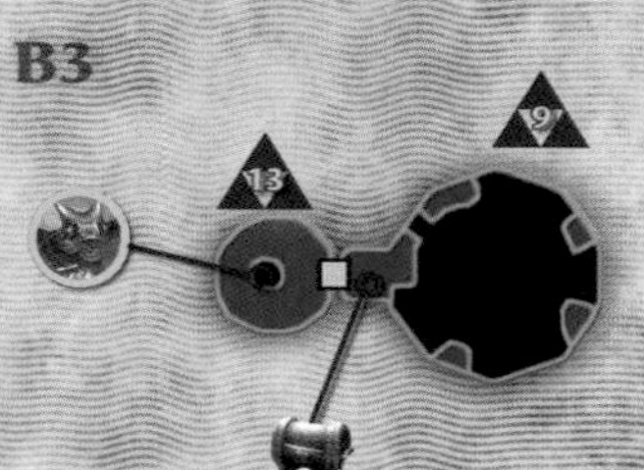

Battle the Aeralfos

Locate and Enter the Peahat Gardens

Activate Fan Turbine in Central Chamber

Defeat Twilit Dragon Argorok

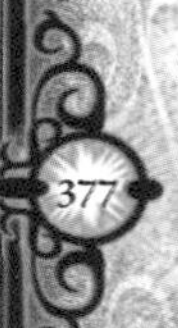

Characters Encountered

Midna

Ooccoo

Ooccoo Jr.

Oocca

A Link to the Present

Ordon Sword Master Sword

Heart Pieces: 0 (40 Total)

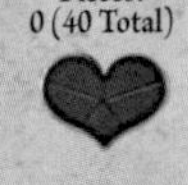

Wooden Shield Hylian Shield

Hero's Clothes Zora Armor Magic Armor

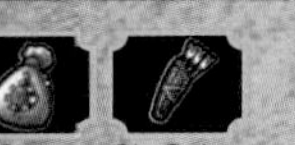

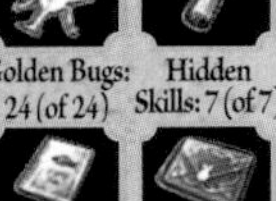

Giant Wallet | Big Quiver | Golden Bugs: 24 (of 24) | Hidden Skills: 7 (of 7)

Medicine Scent | Poe Souls 55 (of 60) | Fish Journal | Letters 13 (of 16)

Mirror of Twilight: 3 (of 4)

Items Already Acquired

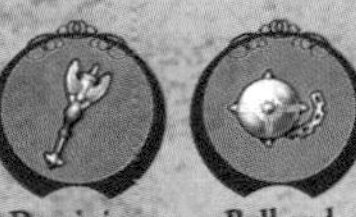

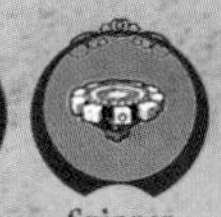

Dominion Rod | Ball and Chain | Spinner | Clawshot | Hero's Bow | Iron Boots

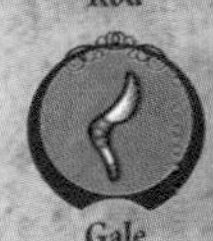

Gale Boomerang | Lantern | Slingshot | Fishing Rod | Hawkeye | Bombs (Bag #1)

Bombs (Bag #2) | Bombs (Bag #3) | Bottle #1 | Bottle #2 | Bottle #3 | Bottle #4

Items to Obtain

Water Bombs | Ooccoo | Fairy in a Bottle | Small Key | Dungeon Map | Double Clawshot

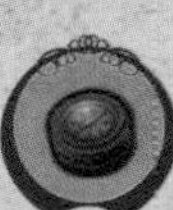
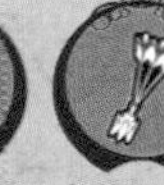

Compass | Arrows (20) | Bombs (10) | Arrows (20) | Piece of Heart #41 (of 45) | Bombs (5)

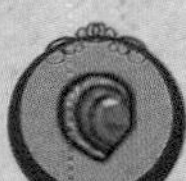

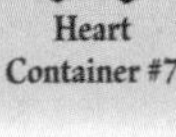

Piece of Heart #42 (of 45) | Poe Soul #57 (of 60) | Big Key | Fairy in a Bottle | Heart Container #7

Dungeon Denizens

Characters

Midna

Ooccoo

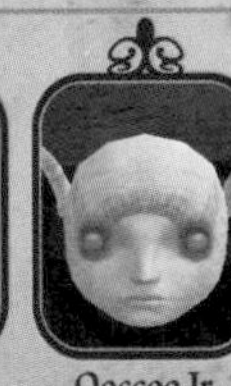
Ooccoo Jr.

The Oocca

Enemies

Baba Serpent

Helmasaur

Helmasaurus

Kargorok

Keese

Tile Worm

Deku Baba

Aeralfos

Dynafols

Purple Chu

Red Chu

Walltulas

Bosses

Mid Boss: Aeralfos

Mid Boss: Big Baba

Big Boss: Twilit Dragon Argorok

City in the Sky: Overview

You're witnessing what Shad could only dream about and research in musty tomes: a hidden city in the heavens, where the Oocca—the ancestors of the Hylian people—live! However, their world is under threat from the twilight too; a massive dragon called Argorok is soaring about the place, destroying the sky bridges and ruining the Oocca's architecture. You must venture into this place, learning to control any fear of heights you may have, and navigate an air maze of towers, fans, rotating platforms, and vents, until you reach a battle with an airborne Aeralfos. He's guarding another Clawshot, and with two of these trusty items, you can scale previously unimaginable heights, activating a series of fans and turbines that allow you to reach the top of the city, and a battle with the dragon himself!

Enemies Encountered

Baba Serpent

Twilit Dragon Argorok

Task 1: Enter the Central Fan Chamber

Chamber 1: Outer Ledges and Shop (1F)

You might wish to bring along the following:

- Multiple Bottles filled with a Blue Potion, Fairy Tears, or a Fairy.
- Your Iron Boots positioned on ✚ so you can activate them on and off quickly.
- The Clawshot within easy access.
- The Hero's Bow within easy access.
- The Hylian Shield; purchase it from Kakariko Village.
- The Magic Armor for rare occasions you may need it; purchase it from Castle Town.
- Fill your Giant Quiver and all Bomb Bags; you don't want to run out!

Tip

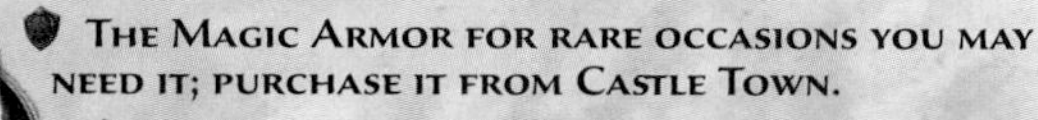

◀ Ooccoo and her son meet another Oocca and flee to the shop. Meanwhile, you should head south and check the location of the cannon. This is your method of leaving the dungeon. There's a Baba Serpent to test your new great spin attack on, resting on the ledge.

➤ **Treasure Chests**: Head to the water pool, and inspect the area underwater. A chest in the southeast houses Water Bombs. Pack them in your bag if you need them, and swim to the southwestern side. A second chest here contains a red Rupee (20).

Treasure Chest #1: Water Bombs (15)!

Water Bombs

You got **Water Bombs**! You can use these bombs in water, but not while swimming.

Treasure Chest #2: Red Rupee (20)

◀ Turn west, and run along the windy ledge. As you reach the pod-shaped building at the end, slice the Baba Serpent and watch that the wind doesn't push you off the gaps between the low walls!

Having problems with your footing? If you're about to be blown off a ledge and into the sky, put on your Iron Boots. You remain stationary, but your movement is slowed.

Tip

◀ Enter the Ooccoo shop. The prices are reasonable, though the proprietor is selling items you don't need (like the Lantern fuel) or have a preferred elixir of (like the Red Potion).

Store

Oocca Pod Shop

Item Name	Price	Effect
Bombs (30)	90 Rupees	Why did I invest in stock that the Oocca can't use?
Arrows (30)	30 Rupees	I figured out that Oocca don't have bows AFTER I ordered these....
Lantern Oil	20 Rupees	If you have an empty Bottle, you should buy some.
Blue Potion	100 Rupees	When you're out of strength, drink this and you'll be fine.
Red Potion	30 Rupees	This makes 8 Hearts beat healthily.

Oocco

Oocco Jr.

Oocca

➤ Ooccoo and Ooccoo Jr. wait for you. Ooccoo says she can't whisk you to Hyrule, only to this shop. Take her with you, and leave the premises.

Ooccoo
You are reunited with **Ooccoo**! This kind character can let you out of dungeons and return you to where you were.

Ooccoo Jr.:

Available after the first time you use Ooccoo to remove yourself from a dungeon, Ooccoo Jr. makes his first appearance in the City in the Sky. He's three years old, sits on his mother's back, and has a limited vocabulary (and no body). He can provide transportation to the store if you wish.

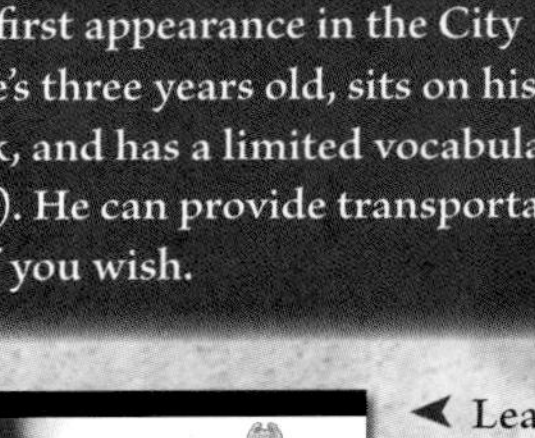

➤ Leave the store and head to the pool, then go north to reach this ledge's end. A Baba Serpent rises to strike as you near some steps, so react with a spin, and slash it. Place your Iron Boots on if you slip in the wind. After the coast is clear, bring out your **Hero's Bow** and aim at the diamond switch above the entrance gate. Shoot it, and the gate opens, allowing you into the first main building.

Missing Links

1. Cutting the Grass

The outer sections of this windswept city have a few thickets of grass growing around, particularly near Baba Serpents and the cannon. Slice them for Rupees and Hearts.

Chamber 2: Cannon Bay (1F)

➤ Walk forward, into a room with blocks of blue and gray stone flooring, and cannons racked up to the side. After smashing a couple of pots in the southwest corner (one contains a Heart), grab an Oocca and float down to the central part of the room. They fly in the same way as Cuccos—under protest!

➤ Land on one of the blue cubes, and it shudders, then drops out of the sky! You have a couple of seconds to move before you fall too, so use these to reach the gray-floored area adjacent. A Helmasaur charged you when you landed, but it fell into that falling cube!

Missing Links

1. Clawshot Crockery

While you spot a pot on a blue section of floor, don't head over to smash it and let the floor give way. Instead, produce your Clawshot and smash each pot, then use the Clawshot again to grab the item and transport it to you. The Gale Boomerang achieves the same effect, but it isn't as exact.

➤ It's time to reach this chamber's northern exit, so aim at the pillar with the vines growing on it, above and to the east. Clawshot to it, shimmy to the outer wall area, and drop. Grab a nearby Oocca and float to this chamber's final part. Land, avoid the Helmasaur or grab its armor with the Clawshot, and leave. You can fight the Helmasaur, but this is dangerous because it could charge and bounce you off the edge! Exit via the door. One of the pots in the corner contains a Heart.

Chamber 3: Central Fan Chamber (1F)

Helmasaurus

Threat Meter

Enter the Central Fan Chamber, and a larger beast with hardened armor charges you. This is the Helmasaurus, the larger cousin to the Helmasaur, and it can withstand a Clawshot on its carapace without being parted from it! Use the same tactics you employed on Helmasaurs before you got the Clawshot: jump around the beast and attack its exposed rear. You can also stand with a blue floor tile between it and you. The beast thunders in, you block or leap away, and it falls out of the sky!

1

2
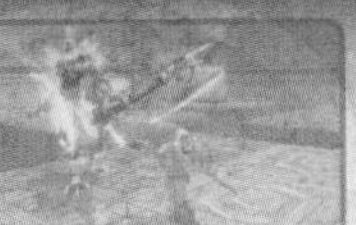
3

4

5

6

➤ Run into this chamber and explore it. It has an extremely high ceiling with a fan in the center. Is that a vine wall growing down? No matter; it's too high to reach. There are pillars with vines growing on them, and falling floor tiles to avoid. Head up the northern steps and Clawshot to this grated window. There's a yellow Rupee (10) in a pot for you. Leap down onto this blue tile, and roll onto firmer ground. Do the same in the southwest corner. The pot here holds arrows.

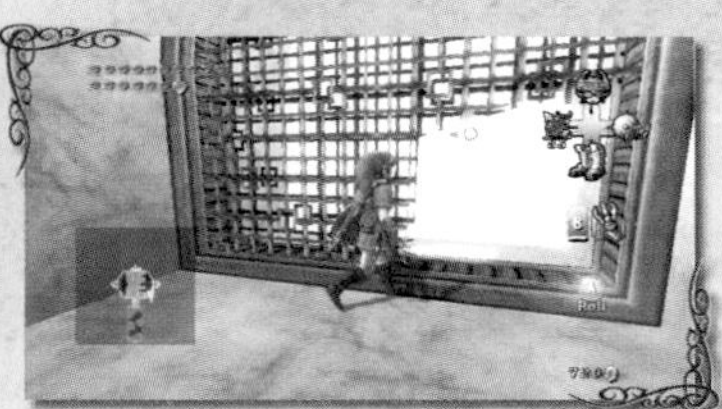

➤ Run to the southeastern window and Clawshot up to it; the Rupee in the pot there is green (1). There's an opening in the grating you can walk through. This is one of two ways to reach Chamber 4.

➤ The last of the four window ledges in the northeast is of particular interest. Clawshot to this ledge, and inspect the pot here. Inside is a Fairy whom you can scoop and place in an empty Bottle. If you don't need this now, remember it for later.

Fairy

You caught a **Fairy** in a Bottle! When you fall in combat, this faithful friend gives you Hearts.

Tip

To return to this chamber's center at any time, Clawshot to any pillar with vines on it within reach, shimmy to solid ground, and drop.

▲ The final part of this initial exploration is to head into Chamber 4. You've found one way (through the open corner of the southeast window's grating), but you can also grab an Oocca from the northern door area and float across to the eastern exit.

Task 2: Obtain the Small Key

Chamber 4: Peahat Wind Gorge (East) (1F)

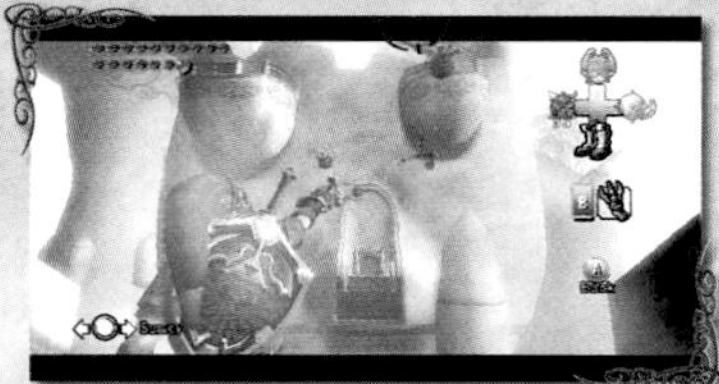

➤ Exit the door and head to a short flight of steps leading...nowhere! There's a gap with fierce gusts of wind blowing, stopping, and blowing again. Above are stationary Peahats, but don't Clawshot to them, as there's nowhere to go except down!

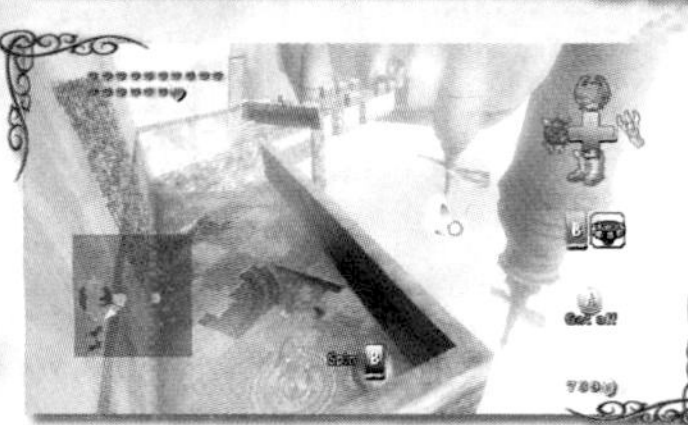

➤ Clawshot from the doorway, or drop from the grated window's open corner, and land in this small ledge. There are two pots (open them for a Heart), and a Spinner circular groove in the ground. Produce your Spinner, and spin on the spot while connected to this groove. A bridge gradually spans from the gorge's east and west sides.

➤ Clawshot to a vine wall, climb up, and maneuver toward the newly formed bridge. Be careful as you cross. Gusts of wind can sweep you off into the clouds, so stop next to each wall section to prevent this. Move quickly, then turn and engage a Kargorok on the steps. Don't fight it on the bridge.

Chamber 5: Eastern Sky Tower (B1 to 3F)

▲ You're on the first floor of a large and multilevel Sky Tower, but your progress is limited. Enter the door and strike out the pots on the side for a Heart and blue Rupees (5). Pass the wall's grating, and run to the far end. Stand at this point. You can look down or across.

If you drop to the B1 floor, you can crack a couple of pots for a green Rupee (1) and a Heart, but the way onward is blocked. Don't Clawshot to the stone tube, it'll fall! For now, Clawshot to the vines on the ledge above you.

Caution

Enemies Encountered

Baba Serpent

Helmasaur

Helmasaurus

Kargarok

Peahat

Oocca

➤ **Treasure Chest:** Remain on the first floor, and move to the right side, gazing at the chamber's corner. Launch onto the Clawshot medallion, then lower yourself to a small ledge holding a chest. This houses a Small Key. Head to the Wind Gorge.

Treasure Chest #3:

Small Key

Small Key

You got a **Small Key**! This opens a locked door, but only in this area.

Task 3: Defeat the Dynafols Duo

Chamber 4: First Return to Peahat Wind Gorge (East) (1F)

➤ Cross the Wind Gorge bridge, rolling to quicken your pace so you don't fall off. As you reach the opposite side, the great dragon you saw earlier swoops down, and collides with the bridge, sending pieces of stone flying!

Chamber 3: First Return to Central Fan Chamber (1F)

➤ Enter the Central Fan Chamber, point your Clawshot up at the vine pillar, and propel there. Shimmy to the safe ground, drop, then plan your next move. You might as well peek at what's outside of the north door. Run past the Oocca and look.

Chamber 6: Rotating Fan Gorge (1F)

➤ This door leads to the Rotating Fan Gorge, which is inactive. Above and across from you are massive floating fans, and the blades look like they can take a Clawshot. For the moment, ignore this area, save for a quick smash of nearby pots (for a Heart and arrows), and combat with a Kargorok. You'll return here later.

Chamber 3: Second Return to Central Fan Chamber (1F)

➤ The only other possible way forward is to run west. Head down the steps, turn, and dash over the falling floor to the door in this side of the Central Fan Chamber, and open it.

Chamber 7: Central Sky Bridge (1F)

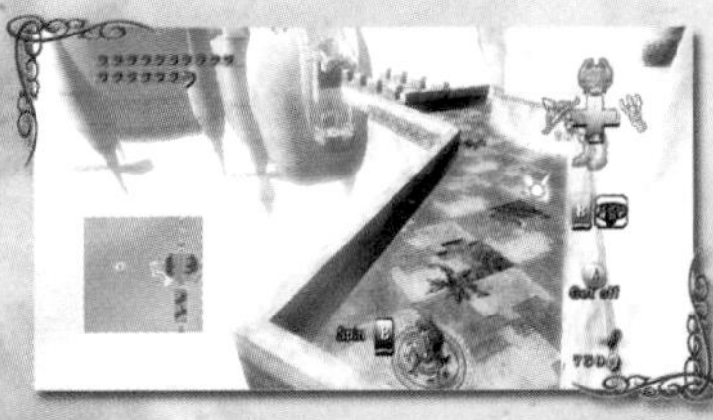

➤ Step into a windy zone, with a large gap stretching ahead of you. Turn left, draw your sword, hack at Baba Serpents along a walled ledge until you reach the structure's southern end. Clawshot up to smash the pots at the grated window, then use your Spinner, slot it into the groove, and press Ⓑ until a sky bridge extends to the western side.

➤ Run along the ledge, and cross this newly formed bridge, rolling quickly after a jet of wind has subsided. As always, if the wind catches you, don the Iron Boots. At the far side, watch for a Kargorok or two sneaking up behind you. Shield bash them so they're stunned, then finish them! Smash the two pots (there are Heart and arrows in them), and open the door.

Chamber 8: Wind Room (1F)

➤ Enter a large, long corridor, and sidestep a couple of Helmasaurs that trot in toward you. Dispatch them with the usual vigor. Then head around to the room's south side, and dispatch some pottery.

1

2

3

4

5

6

Move to the edge of the floor and look north. Two large fans are blowing a gale, but it's the diamond switch that's of real interest. Bring out your Clawshot and tag it. The far fan on the south wall, blowing wind north, shuts down.

▲ Now run to the north side and face west. You must negotiate the two remaining wind fans. Start by running along the north wall. When you're hit by the wind, switch to your Iron Boots, and plod through the gust.

Running into the gust far from the dangerous floor edge, then putting boots on as you're caught, is the fastest way to negotiate this. Otherwise, you'll be cautiously treading forward until you're struck.

➤ Once you're past the first fan's gusting breezes, take off your Iron Boots. This time bring out your Clawshot, aim at the vines on the pillar ahead, and land on them. Shimmy around to the right, and drop. Defeat the Helmasaur, then open the door to the west

Chamber 9: The Great Wind Tower (West) (1F)

◄ Enter the door into an enclosed ledge. Whack the pots to your right, collecting blue (5) and yellow (10) Rupees, then turn and open the chest in the opposite area. It contains your Dungeon Map.

Treasure Chest #4: Dungeon Map

Dungeon Map

You got the Dungeon Map!

Chamber 8: First Return to Wind Room (1F)

◄ Now return to the Wind Room, and run south, across the falling floor pieces, and turn left to reach the exit door. If the fan isn't stopped, retrace your steps and activate the diamond switch. Smash the pots and leave via the south door.

Chamber 10: The Floor Maze (1F)

◄ You enter a long chamber with numerous small floor sections interspersed with frightening drops into the clouds! Turn left and smash the pots with your Clawshot, then run and grab the Heart and arrows, so you don't drop through the floor. Then run to the southeast corner, and turn to face west. Run to the edge of the jutting area of floor. Use your Hero's Bow or Clawshot on a couple of Keeses so they don't bother you during this next maneuver. Wait for an updraft to subside, then leap the gap.

➤ Ignore the chest on the chamber's north side for the moment, and instead continue to face west and look across at this area of floor. Wait for the updraft to stop, and leap across to the gray, not the blue, floor!

➤ Head toward a dangerous **Tile Worm** at the end of the narrow floor tiles after you smash the pot on the south wall. This critter, coupled with the updraft, can spell doom if you don't get rid of it. Bring out your Gale Boomerang and throw it, and the Tile Worm is bounced off and into the clouds. Wait for the updraft to stop, then run and leap across.

◄ Smash the pots under the Clawshot medallion (used when you approach this room from the opposite direction). Now leap to the small, thin floor area running north to south. Turn and line yourself up exactly. You must land on the tiles opposite, and there's little room for error!

➤ Once across, shoot, Clawshot, or slash a couple of Keeses. Then turn west and look for the Tile Worm nudging the floor. Don't step on it! Instead, use the Gale Boomerang. If the Tile Worm lands on the floor, slash it until it falls or is dispatched.

Enemies Encountered

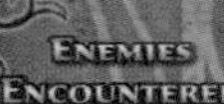

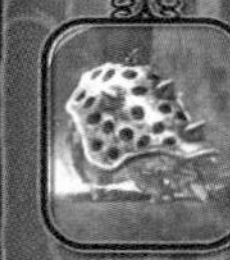

Helmasaur

Kargarok

Peahat

Keese

Tile Worm

Characters Encountered

Oocca

➤ **Treasure Chest**: Run to the north wall, and turn east. Dash along the floor, and jump to the small chest. Then turn and face west. Despite appearances, you can leap to the narrow ledge. Now move to where you last fought a Tile Worm.

Treasure Chest #5: Yellow Rupee (10)

➤ Leap westward to the last dangerous part of this chamber, and target another Tile Worm on the ledge across from an updraft. Defeat it, then leap when the air is clear before turning left at the west wall, and jumping south, to the exit door.

Chamber 11: Domain of the Dynafols

➤ Be very wary as you enter this square chamber. It contains two well-armored Dynafolses, like the ones you encountered during your excursion through the Temple of Time. You want to defeat them one at a time, so coax the first forward by striking it on the helmet from long range with your Clawshot. Then either counter it's axe with a sword strike and spin or, even easier, take them down long range with Bomb Arrows!

➤ Now that the chamber is free from armored Dynafolses, a door opens in the south wall, above you. Optionally smash the pots in the corners for Hearts, then move to the southern floor section, look up, and launch a Clawshot to this vine. Clamber up.

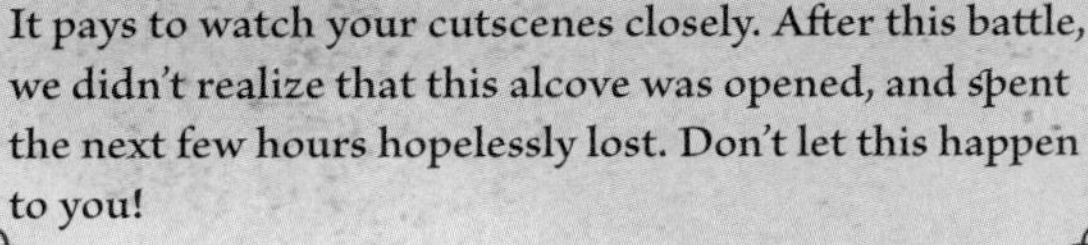

Author Note

It pays to watch your cutscenes closely. After this battle, we didn't realize that this alcove was opened, and spent the next few hours hopelessly lost. Don't let this happen to you!

➤ Climb up to this ornate ledge, and smash some more Oocca pottery, then look up. There's a bulb-like ornate handle, and you must shoot your Clawshot at it. Your weight activates an updraft in the room.

➤ Take an Oocca, and walk to the edge of the ledge. The updraft turns on and off. Just as it turns on, run off and float directly to the wind. It causes you to rise up, and land on a ledge that you couldn't reach before. Exit this chamber, now on the second floor.

Task 4: Fly to the Great Wind Tower

Chamber 12: Oocca Flying Room (2F)

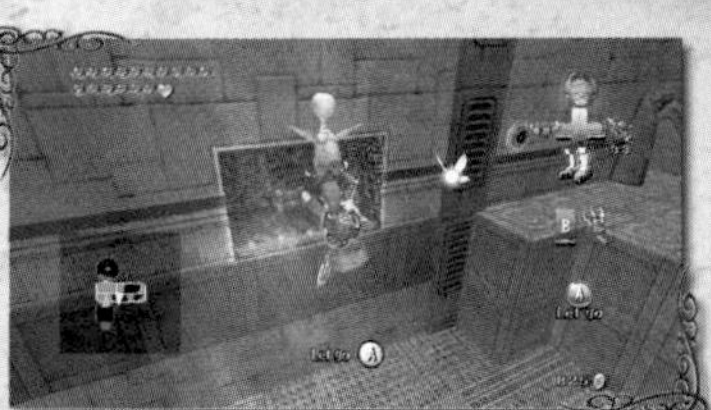

➤ **Treasure Chest**: Head north into a chamber directly above Chamber 10, but with no access to it. Put down the Oocca, and look up. There's a handle to Clawshot to and activate. This unlocks a gate in the south wall, with a chest behind it. Grab another Oocca, run into the gap above the lower middle floor section, and aim for the updraft. Turn around, fly into the ledge, and open the chest.

Treasure Chest #6: Red Rupee (20)

➤ **Treasure Chest**: Drop down to the middle area, and ride the updraft to the upper floor area opposite. There's a broken wall to the north, and a Clawshot medallion on the south. Ignore them both, stand on the updraft vent, and ride the Oocca to the far end of the chamber where another chest resides.

Treasure Chest #7: Purple Rupee (50)

Note: The Clawshot medallion is necessary only if you fall down into the lower floor area near Treasure Chest #7. Fight the Helmasaur down here, then propel yourself back up.

➤ Time to fly again! Pick up an Oocca, stand on the vent near the broken wall, and fly northward, turning west in an arch, and landing on another vent with three pots on it. Each pot holds a blue Rupee (5).

◄ The updraft vent isn't working, so turn and face east with Oocca in hand, and fly to the central vent. Ride it up, then aim for the floor under the ornate handle. Clawshot up to it, which releases the air in the vent. Head back there, and use this new blast of air to ascend through the hole in the west wall. The last part of this chamber holds nothing of interest (the pots are empty). Head through the door to the north.

Chamber 9: The Great Wind Tower (West) (2F to 1F to B1 to B2 to B3)

➤ You emerge in the Great Wind Tower. This is actually the second time you've been here—the first time was when you obtained the Dungeon Map. Now you're on the other side and must methodically descend. Start by smashing the pots to your right for a yellow Rupee (10) and Hearts. Then optionally fly to these pots on the central pillar. Drop and grab the ledge. The usual prizes are inside: a blue (5) and yellow (10) Rupee.

◄ Now that you're on the central pillar, on this tiny ledge, look east to another ledge. Fly here, grabbing the ledge and pulling yourself up. Tug the ornate handle, which opens a gate below. Grab an Oocca, and run off the ledge.

➤ Drop to the ledge opposite, on the tower's first floor. There's a Deku Baba growing here. Stun it with a Clawshot.

From your current vantage point, turn and point yourself and an Oocca friend east, and fly to the small ledge with the two pots. You're now on the B1 level of this structure. Fall and land on the ledge, crack both pots for a yellow (10) and blue (5) Rupee, and turn to look west.

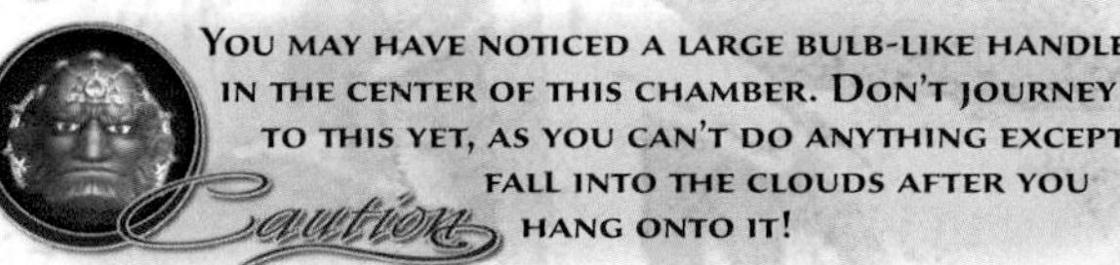

Caution: You may have noticed a large bulb-like handle in the center of this chamber. Don't journey to this yet, as you can't do anything except fall into the clouds after you hang onto it!

➤ Scour the remaining ledges. The one opposite looks good enough, so float down to the B2 level of the tower, and land on this ledge. There's a Clawshot medallion above it. Land and deal with a Deku Baba, and smash the two pots for a Heart and blue Rupee (5).

➤ Your final descent leaves you at the very bottom of the tower, on floor B3. Look over the ledge's left edge and Clawshot to the small ledge underneath. Then turn and run south, to the door in the tower's western part. You're out!

Task 5: Battle the Aeralfos

Chamber 13: Basement Fan and Battle Chamber (B3)

➤ Enter a small circular room. The pottery around the perimeter provides the regular items: Hearts, arrows, and a blue Rupee (5). Of more interest is the bulb handle above a roaring fan. Clawshot to the handle, and give a tug to shut the fan off. Then lower yourself down!

Enemies Encountered

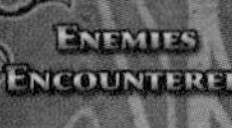

Tile Worm

Dynafols

Helmasaur

Deku Baba

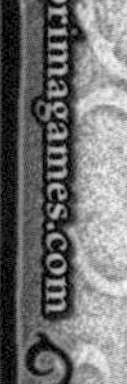

Characters Encountered

Oocca

Aeralfos

Threat Meter

Watch out! Some of the perimeter floor is unsafe, so stay in the middle and constantly Z target for best results.
Caution

Step 1: The Aeralfos is an airborne creature with great speed and nasty attack patterns. However, he is incredibly susceptible to the following strategy. First, Z target the creature. When he's flying like this, wait.

Step 2: As soon as he changes his pose to this, flapping his wings quickly and shielding himself, he's preparing for a nasty swooping charge!

Step 3: As soon as you see him change pose, launch a Clawshot straight at the shield. You're already Z targeting, so just press B. You pull the Aeralfos down and expose his belly. Quickly unsheathe your sword and really bash and slash the foe, getting at least four good strikes on him. He flies up to the ceiling, and Step 1 begins again.

Although there are other tactics to try—like putting your Iron Boots on, Clawshotting toward him, then slashing him—none work as well as this technique!
Note

After four or five collections of slashing, the Aeralfos flies off! He soon comes back and tries a huge airborne charge. Roll out of the way or shield block, and then repeat Steps 1–3. If you get the Aeralfos on the ground and he's blocking, continue a barrage of slashes because some are likely to break through. Keep this up until he falls.

Missing Links

1. Pot Luck

After (or during) the combat, there's a load of pottery to smash around the arena sides. However, there's some on the holes in the walls too, and the best way to bring these items—usually yellow (10) or blue (5) Rupees or Hearts—is to aim with the Gale Boomerang.

Treasure Chest Once you've destroyed all pottery look east, as a gate has opened. Clawshot up to the medallion, and run to the chest. Inside is what you've been waiting for: a second Clawshot, which doubles your shooting prowess!

The Double Clawshot is possibly the finest pair of items ever seen in the land of Hyrule!

Treasure Chest #8: Double Clawshot

Double Clawshot
You got another **Clawshot**! Now you're holding a pair! They're **Double Clawshots**!

The Double Clawshot allows you to hang from a medallion or other vertical grating or vine and raise or lower yourself with ▲ and ▼. However, in addition, you can aim (either manually or with Z-targeting) to a second medallion, grating, or vine, and propel yourself around rooms without touching the ground. You can do the same (except for raising or lowering) from horizontal vines, gratings, and medallions. This is an excellent new toy; equip it now!

- Remember that you can be hanging from a medallion and raising (○) or lowering (○) yourself while you're manually looking at the next Clawshot target!
- Also note that you can hang from any Clawshot-friendly surface and use the second Clawshot as a weapon (to rid yourself of Chus or Keeses, for example).
- Be sure to look for new ways of solving puzzles using both Clawshots. You can't separate them now.

Tip

➤ Use your Double Clawshot and fire it at one of the ceiling medallions, then face east and shoot at the vine in the fan hole. Propel yourself up and out, then return to the tower.

Enemies Encountered

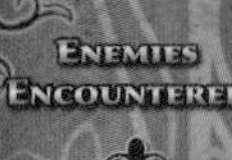

Aeralfos

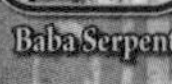

Baba Serpent

Task 6: Locate and Enter the Peahat Gardens

Chamber 9: First Return to The Great Wind Tower (West) (B3 to B2)

◄ Back in the tower chamber, use the Double Clawshot to move around the series of medallions to this ledge, on the B2 floor, eastern wall. Don't drop off (although you can head across to the lower ledges to break a few pots). Instead, look up and Clawshot to the ornate handle above you.

➤ This opens a gate on the B2 level. With the Double Clawshot, you can lower yourself to the open gate, and aim at either medallion above the exit door. Propel yourself to the door, and the gate closes (as you let go of the handle and it retracts). Enter the door.

Chamber 14: Clawshot Ricochet Room

◄ Enter this room, which has no floor, and Z target the nearest Clawshot medallion, on the metal pole suspended from the ceiling. Propel yourself to this pole, and it begins to slide down with your weight. This isn't a problem if you constantly Z target and ricochet all the way up the series of poles.

◄ **Treasure Chest**: Land on this exit ledge. Behind you are two pots housing arrows and a Heart. A treasure chest with the Compass, and two more pots are on a sinking floor in front of you. Grab everything, and leave via the adjacent door.

Treasure Chest #9:

Compass

Compass

You got the **Compass**! This handy tool shows you where to find objects hidden in this dungeon.

Chamber 7: First Return to Central Sky Bridge (Underside) (B1 to 1F)

◄ You appear on a small ledge underneath the Central Sky Bridge. Clawshot to the first grating, then **very carefully** aim and smack the Clawshot into the Baba Serpent's head. While it's stunned, **even more carefully** aim at the stalk and cut it. If you miss, you'll target the grating, propel yourself into the Serpent, and fall! When you've crossed the bridge, climb the vine wall, and head to the central chamber.

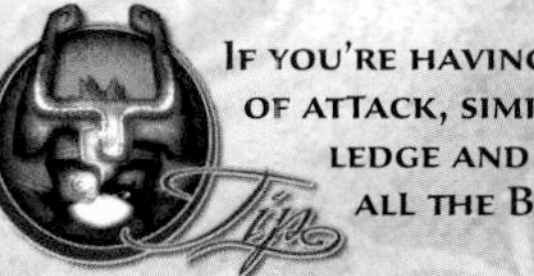

If you're having trouble with this plan of attack, simply stand at the initial ledge and shoot Bomb Arrows at all the Baba Serpents.

Characters Encountered

Oocca

Chamber 3: Third Return to Central Fan Chamber (1F)

➤ Now that you have the Double Clawshot, you can easily explore the western tower you couldn't reach earlier. Move to the doorway by shooting up at the medallion, and the second one above the door, and head west

Chamber 4: Second Return to Peahat Wind Gorge (East) (1F)

➤ The bridge may still be out permanently, but you can cross easily thanks to a combination of your Double Clawshot and the floating Peahats. Always automatically Z target and you'll shoot from Peahat to Peahat in seconds, then drop down at the far end, watching the wind. Exit to Chamber 5.

Chamber 5: First Return to Eastern Sky Tower (B1 to 3F)

➤ Run into this chamber, and begin a very long climb using mostly your Double Clawshot skills. Run to the edge of the vine wall, and peer down. Z target, shuffle forward in this viewpoint, and target the medallion on the pipe below.

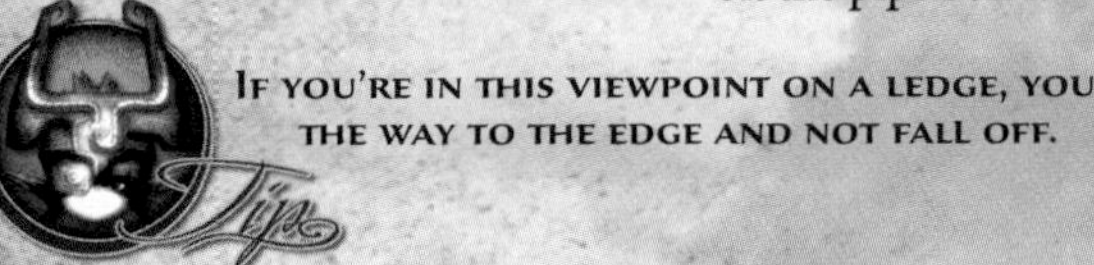

IF YOU'RE IN THIS VIEWPOINT ON A LEDGE, YOU CAN MOVE ALL THE WAY TO THE EDGE AND NOT FALL OFF.

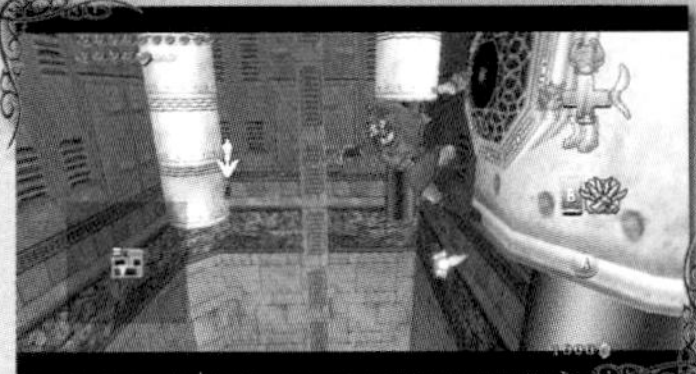

➤ Now quickly Z target and swing around to shoot to the medallions along this series of falling pipes. Fall down and drop from the end one to a very low ledge.

➤ Turn, face north, and propel to this medallion, which is easy to miss.

➤ Turn, look up and south, and aim at this specific medallion, near a ledge. Propel up. You're now on floor B1.

➤ Hang from this medallion, and look to your right. You can propel to a grated archway.

➤ **Treasure Chest:** Or, you can shoot to the grating on the wall to your left, above this large ledge to the north. Look down a floor; there's another grating on the right wall. Shoot yourself down here, deal with the Baba Serpents before opening the chest. Exit via the same medallion. Shoot yourself to the grating, drop onto the stone floor ledge, run through the hole in the north wall, and leap the gap.

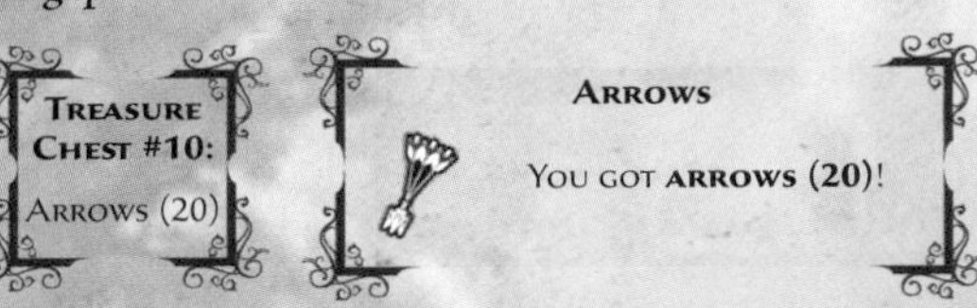

TREASURE CHEST #10: ARROWS (20)

ARROWS

YOU GOT **ARROWS (20)**!

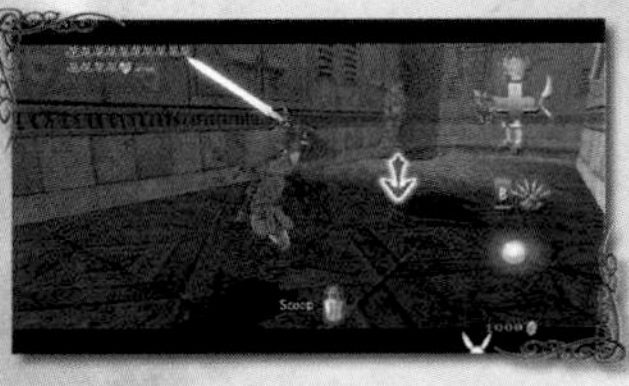

➤ Turn right, and secure this ledge. A couple of Purple Chu and a Red Chu are about to descend from the ceiling. Attack the Red Chu first if you don't want them to combine. Find blue Rupees (5) and arrows inside the pots.

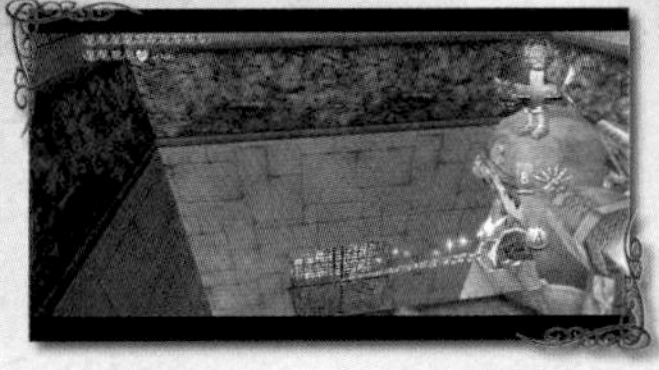

➤ Propel to the west now, down and onto this grating, which is difficult to find. You're back down to floor B2.

➤ Drop off onto the ledge and look east. Two Babas writhe here, so shoot them with Bomb Arrows, or snip them with your Clawshot.

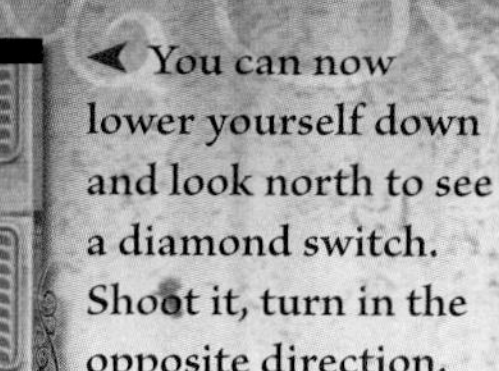

➤ You can now lower yourself down and look north to see a diamond switch. Shoot it, turn in the opposite direction, and a gate opens. Shoot at the medallion, look up, and Clawshot all the way up (via gratings and medallions above you) to 1F.

➤ **Treasure Chest:** There's a chest here, but don't drop from the grating or you'll miss the ledge! Instead, turn and look at the medallion on the ceiling, past the hole in the wall, and shoot there. Then turn back again, carefully jump to the tiny ledge, and open the chest.

Treasure Chest #11:
Red Rupee (20)

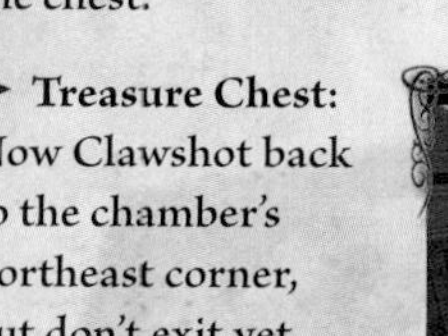

➤ **Treasure Chest:** Now Clawshot back to the chamber's northeast corner, but don't exit yet. There's another chest to locate. Head west along the ledge, use your Gale Boomerang to remove a Tile Worm from your jumping spot, then leap there. Leap, cling on, pull yourself up, and inspect this next chest. Defeat a Purple Chu and a Tile Worm on the south ledge.

Treasure Chest #12:
Bombs (10)

Bombs

You got **bombs (10)**!

Chamber 15: Big Baba's Tower (1F to 3F to 2F)

➤ Enter a circular chamber with a giant Baba plant in the middle. It's the return of Big Baba! He's not alone; there are a few Baba Serpents, too! Fortunately, defeating him is easy!

➤ Step 1: Launch a strike at Big Baba's head, Z targeting him and trying a leaping strike or a spin attack. Continue this, defeating Baba Serpents too, until the head explodes!

➤ Step 2: When the Baba base begins to pulsate, produce a bomb or fire a Bomb Arrow, and let the maw consume the explosive. If you don't have any bombs, either return to the store via Ooccoo, or return to the tower you came from, and open Treasure Chest #12.

➤ Now you can climb this tower, provided you don't receive a mauling from the nearby Baba Serpent. Defeat it, then look up and around at a sliding tube with a medallion on it. Hit it, then quickly swing your Clawshot around to the right and look up; target this vine before you fall!

➤ Treasure Chest: Climb up the vine pillar and onto the top of it. Draw your Hero's Bow, and blast a Baba Serpent with a Bomb Arrow, or use your Gale Boomerang, then leap to its ledge and open a chest.

Treasure Chest #13:
Yellow Rupee (10)

➤ Treasure Chest: Turn back and leap to the vine pillar, and drop down. Work your way around the 2F part of this tower until you reach this very narrow ledge. Stop and shoot any Keeses so they don't attack you. Walk to the small chest, and claim your small prize.

Treasure Chest #14:
Arrows (20)

Arrows

You got **arrows (20)**!

Enemies Encountered

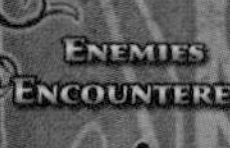

Peahat

Kargarok

Chu (Purple, Red)

Baba Serpent

Tile Worm

Big Baba

Keese

Characters Encountered

Oocca

◄ Edge forward, produce an arrow, and defeat the Deku Baba from range, as it can knock you off the ledge. Then drop down, and run to this chamber's southwestern part, and aim at the Keeses under the floor above, nestling in this alcove. Make sure they're dispatched.

➤ **Treasure Chest:** With the Keeses defeated, turn right, and shimmy hand-over-hand along the lip of the broken ledge until you're under the floor above. Bring out the Bomb Arrows or sword, and tackle a Baba Serpent hanging from the ceiling before you open this next chest. The prize is worth the detour!

Treasure Chest #15: Piece of Heart #41

Piece of Heart
You got a Piece of Heart! Collect **five pieces** to form a new Heart Container! Piece of Heart #41 of 45.

◄ Retrace your steps to where you fought your last Deku Baba, and turn to look up at the exit bridge. Aim your Clawshot at the tube, and fire! Once you're on the tube, a nasty-looking Dynafols comes running along the bridge. Ignore him, and Clawshot across to the second falling tube, then to the vine wall. Remember to Z target! Bomb Arrows will also work a treat.

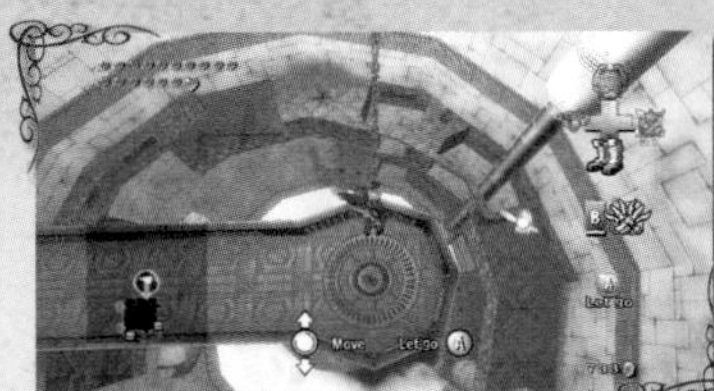

◄ With the Dynafols foiled, aim your Clawshot at the medallion directly above the end of the bridge, and drop to this section. Turn and run to the south exit.

Task 7: Activate the Fan Turbine in the Central Chamber

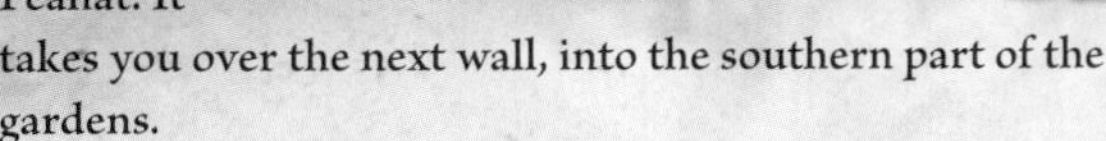

Chamber 16: Peahat Gardens (3F to 2F to 3F)

◄ Enter a large, flat area of overgrown paving, and begin a little weeding with your blade, slicing some Baba Serpents. There's even a blue Rupee (5) in the Deku Baba to the southwest, and two more blue Rupees (5) inside the pots on the promontory.

Tip: Have you tried juggle combos? Cut the Deku Baba's stalk, and with a second slice, hit the head before it touches the ground!

➤ Stand on the eastern side of the garden and look south. Soon you see a slow-moving Peahat gliding through the air, over a broken high wall you couldn't otherwise reach. Head under the Peahat, Clawshot up to it, hang down and travel south to the next part of the gardens.

➤ Optionally drop down to this section of gardens for some items. Then wait for another Peahat. It takes you over the next wall, into the southern part of the gardens.

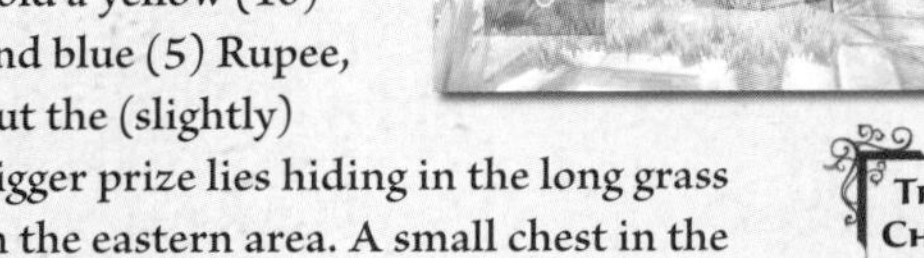

➤ **Treasure Chest:** Investigate the large ledge you're on; the pots to the south hold a yellow (10) and blue (5) Rupee, but the (slightly) bigger prize lies hiding in the long grass in the eastern area. A small chest in the corner contains a red Rupee (20).

Treasure Chest #16: Red Rupee (20)

➤ **Treasure Chest**: Turn and look to the west. There's a chest across from you that you can't reach, and a grassy area down below. But first, look up at the Peahat traveling from north to south. Clawshot up to it, and ride southward to a strange little tree island. Another Peahat is waiting here. Shoot yourself at it, and drop onto the island. When you've dealt with the Imp Poe, open the chest and collect that purple Rupee.

Treasure Chest #17: Purple Rupee (50)

Poe Soul #56

This island is also home to an Imp Poe. The daylight doesn't bother him, so there's no need to wait for the night. Bring out your fangs or Midna's area-attack, and fight! Only four more to go!

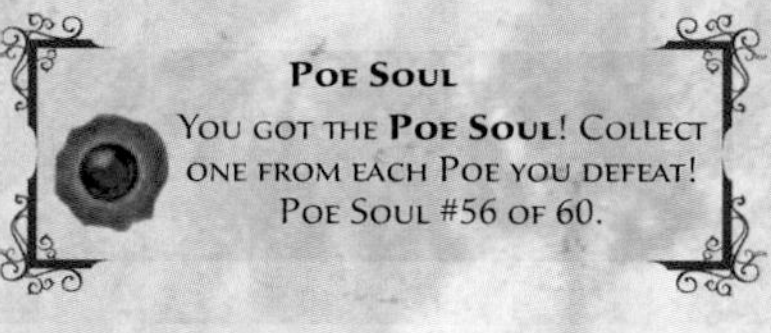

Poe Soul
You got the **Poe Soul**! Collect one from each Poe you defeat! Poe Soul #56 of 60.

➤ Clawshot back up to the Peahat, wait for the moving Peahat to return, then travel north and drop onto the lower grassy area. Draw your sword, dodge around each Helmasaur and Helmasaurus, and slice its rear! Then turn and fire arrows (or aim carefully with your Clawshot) at the Walltulas on the large vine wall.

➤ This lower area doesn't hold anything of value, so Clawshot to the top of the vine wall. Wait for the north-south Peahat to arrive, then journey northward, lowering yourself so you pass under the vertical crack in the wall.

As soon as you pass through this crack, turn left and target another Peahat, then lower yourself immediately, because it's moving north through another crack!

➤ **Treasure Chest**: You arrive in the northwestern part of the garden, and you can drop down into the grassy area. Attack a couple of Baba Serpents, but don't leave before you uncover a partially hidden chest in the southeast corner! Now use the Peahat to ascend to the ledge on the upper floor, and exit to the west.

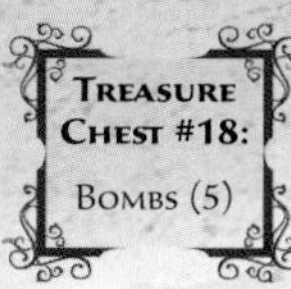

Treasure Chest #18: Bombs (5)

Bombs
You got **bombs** (5)!

➤ You emerge on a tiny ledge with pots and a series of Peahats in a semicircle. Smash the pot for a Heart, ignore the gliding Kargorok, and Clawshot up to the Peahat. Continue Z targeting and maneuver all the way around. Turn left to continue around to the ledge to the south.

➤ **Treasure Chest**: Land on the ledge and open the door. You're back in the garden, but this time you're on the ledge with the chest you couldn't reach earlier. Stride over and take your awesome prize! Then return to the Peahats, and journey across the skies to the central tower.

Treasure Chest #19: Piece of Heart #42

Piece of Heart
You got a **Piece of Heart**! Collect **three more** for another full Heart Container! Piece of Heart #42 of 45.

Chamber 3: Fourth Return to Central Fan Chamber (Exterior) (4F to 1F)

➤ You're now atop the Central Fan Chamber, which is the domed building in front of you. Execute a tour of the exterior, running around clockwise. Two Dynafols prowl around here. Introduce them to your Bomb Arrows.

Enemies Encountered
Deku Baba
Keese
Dynafols
Baba Serpent
Peahat
Imp Poe
Helmasaur
Helmasaurus
Walltula

Oocca

Missing Links

1. A Slash in the Grass

For a large expanse of grass, only limited numbers of Hearts and Rupees appear. This shouldn't be your focus at the moment, although there's a green Rupee (1) to the north.

➤ Now attempt to climb to the top of this domed structure. The long way up is shown below, and it allows you to reach some chests and a Poe. The short way lets you skip all that, but it's tricky to pull off. Stand here, just to one side of the south door, and aim your Clawshot at the vines (you can't see exactly where you're aiming). Shoot upward, and land on the ledge.

➤ The other route is more straightforward. Run to this area of grass on the east exterior wall, with the vine wall growing on it, and Clawshot, then climb to the ledge at the top. Bring out your Clawshot again and bounce it off the head of a Kargorok. It usually flaps back to its perch, to the north.

➤ Bring out your Hero's Bow and shoot the Kargorok, and a second one on a perch in the distance. Now these flapping foes won't swoop at you in this area. Transform to the wolf, and walk along the rope spanning the ledge to the domed building.

➤ **Treasure Chest**: Turn left and walk around the narrow ledge to the vine wall (this is where you could use the shortcut). Aim up and shunt a couple of Walltulas off the vines, and then carefully aim as high and far across as you can, and clamp yourself to the vines. Shimmy left, and then drop as soon as the vines are vertical. At the bottom is a ledge with a chest. Open it!

Treasure Chest #20: Red Rupee (20)

➤ From this ledge, look west to see a rope stretching out to a ledge. There may be a Kargorok to shoot. After the area is clear, change to wolf form and walk across the rope to this ledge, and again to a high section of outer wall with grass on top.

Poe Soul #57

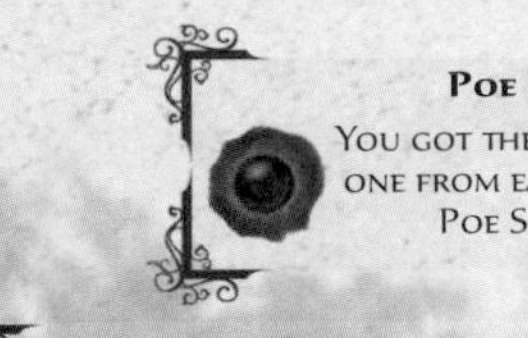

As you cross the rope, look to the sky above the grassy wall section ahead; an Imp Poe floats up here, and he descends to attack as you reach the grass. Bring him down, and finish your Poe hunt in this dungeon!

Poe Soul
You got the **Poe Soul**! Collect one from each Poe you defeat! Poe Soul #57 of 60.

Note: This marks the end of your Poe search in dungeons. The last three Imp Poes are in the Cave of Ordeals, and in Gerudo Desert! Refer to the next chapter for details.

➤ **Treasure Chest**: Now open the chest and take the purple Rupee. Once you're done, drop to the grassy ground below.

Treasure Chest #21: Purple Rupee (50)

➤ Head back to the initial ledge and rope and walk across. Turn right as you reach the ledge around the domed building, and walk to another rope. This leads to the perch the Kargorok was on. Step onto another rope, walk to the second perch, and then to another rope and a ledge on the dome's west side. Enter the door you see here.

➤ You enter an area of the Fan Chamber above the main floor, with a rotating fan and two Helmasauruses to battle! Keep to one side, away

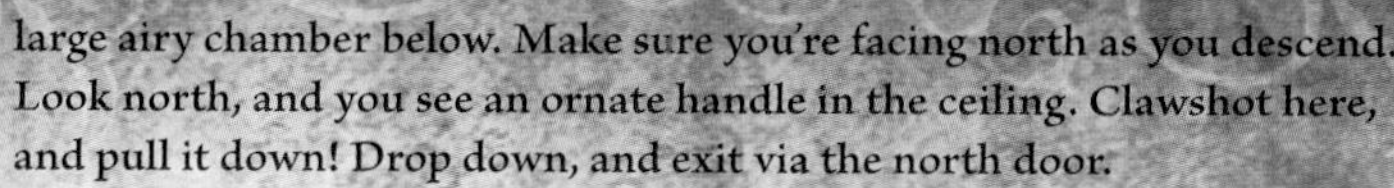

from the blowing air, and tackle each one at a time, stepping around as they charge, and slicing their rumps!

➤ When you move to the room's south side, don't fall down the hole! Engage the other Helmasaurus, and then look up at the ceiling. Between the gap as the fan rotates is an ornate handle. Clawshot and hang from it, and the fan below stops spinning.

◄ **Treasure Chest:** Drop down from the handle, and inspect the ornate chest between the two pots. The pots contain a green (1) and yellow (10) Rupee, but the big prize lies inside the big chest: it's the Big Key!

Treasure Chest #22:
Big Key

Big Key
You got the **Big Key**! Use it to access the lair of this dungeon's boss!

◄ **Treasure Chest:** Drop down the hole to the fan room directly below you, where a second fan has stopped, thanks to your handle-pulling. There's a drop so stay on the outer edge and defeat the two Helmasaurs. Don't let them shunt you down below! The easiest way is to use Bomb Arrows from a distance. When you're done, inspect the chest here.

Treasure Chest #23:
Red Rupee (20)

Tip: If you do fall down to the first floor, use the Clawshot and bound up the vine pillars, then shoot at the vines hanging down from the fan hole to return here.

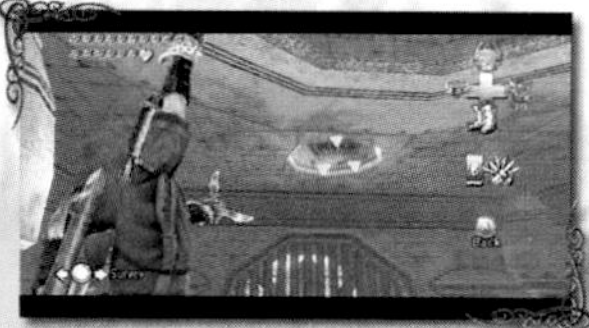

◄ The time has come to activate the fans to the north, allowing you access to the lair of the massive dragon that frightened the Oocca earlier. Fire your Clawshot up at the grated ceiling from the room you're in, and lower yourself through the stopped fan, into the large airy chamber below. Make sure you're facing north as you descend. Look north, and you see an ornate handle in the ceiling. Clawshot here, and pull it down! Drop down, and exit via the north door.

Chamber 6: First Return to Rotating Fan Gorge (1F)

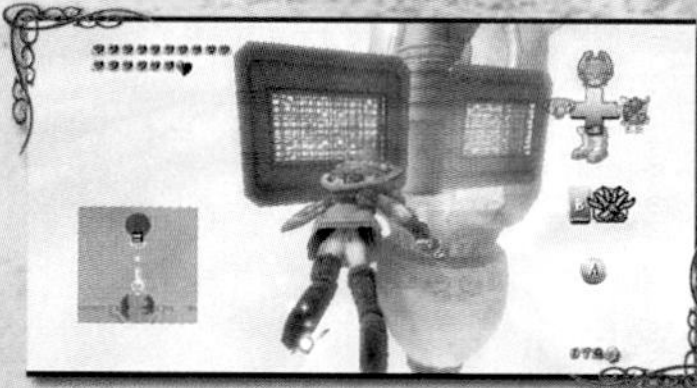

◄ A giant fan turbine is now blowing air against the larger square-ended fans in the gorge to the north. Enter this chamber, and Clawshot up to the first fan blade with the grated surface. Stay on here, make sure the fan rotates to the north, then Clawshot to the next fan. Repeat this all the way to the other side.

➤ **Treasure Chest:** As you finish your fan-hopping, land on the stopped fan turbine ledge above the exit door. Inspect a chest behind here. Then drop down, smash the two pots with your Clawshot, then Clawshot the items—a Heart and a green Rupee (1)—and exit.

Treasure Chest #24:
Red Rupee (20)

Chamber 17: Northern Fan Tower (1F to 5F)

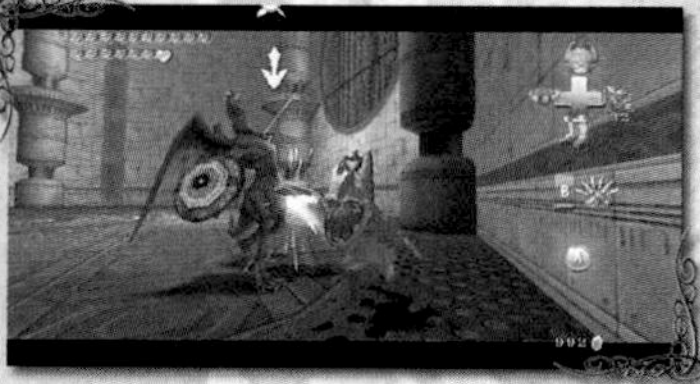

➤ Enter a gigantic tower with fans rotating all the way up the inside. Ignore them for the moment, as you have a nasty Aeralfos to tackle! Remember your combat tactics from the previous battle: wait for him to hover, Clawshot his shield (you should be constantly Z targeting him), and then bring him to the ground before striking him with your sword. Then run around the perimeter, smashing pots for Hearts.

◄ Look above the entrance door to the south, and you'll see a huge fan grating. Clawshot up here as high as you can, and turn to look up. Clawshot to the fan blade grating, and then look above the grating you just shot from. Fire at the diamond switch above it, and the fan you're on begins to move.

◄ Stay on the moving fan as it rotates, and carefully aim at the next fan above you, which is to the north. Fire and land on the grated blade, then drop off into the alcove on the north side of the 2F part of the tower if you want a few Rupees. Most adventurers stay on the fan, or shoot the pots from up here.

Enemies Encountered

Kargarok

Imp Poe

Walltula

Helmasaurus

Helmasaur

Aeralfos

Characters Encountered

Midna

Keep your cool, and accurately predict where a fan will be turning, and fire at that point, to ensure a quick ascent up here. The fans are difficult to Clawshot up through, and you must take careful aim! Don't worry if it takes multiple rotations to leave your current hanging spot.

➤ Look up, propel yourself to the central pillar and the fan up a level, and sit on it for a moment or two. You can now choose to propel to this fan (pictured) in the southeastern area of the tower, and break open the three pots. They contain a yellow (10) and two blue Rupees (5), so ignore this if you wish.

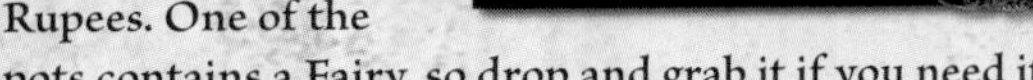

➤ Instead, stay on the central fan and aim up and to the northwest. There's a fan above you in an alcove with more pottery with blue (5) and yellow (10) Rupees. One of the pots contains a Fairy, so drop and grab it if you need it.

Fairy

You caught a **Fairy** in a Bottle! When you fall in combat, this faithful friend gives you Hearts.

◄ Continue up to the next fan at the top of the central pillar, then look for a small alcove with a diamond switch in it (as shown). The fan you're on isn't moving, and this switch activates it. Now rotate all the way around to aim at the medallion above the exit door. Shoot at that, drop down, smash the pots, then use your **Big Key** to unlock the door.

➤ This brings you out and onto the top of the highest tower. Turn right, and look for a support pillar (shown) with a grating on it. Clawshot to here, then turn and look up. You're searching for another pillar with vines growing on it. Shoot to it, then climb to the tower's apex.

Task 8: Defeat Twilit Dragon Argorok

Boss Battle! Twilit Dragon Argorok

Twilit Dragon Argorok

You walk onto the windy tower. From the skies a massive dragon glides in, with huge, powerful wings and a set of fangs with teeth bigger than a Goron! This is the Twilit Dragon Argorok, and you must defeat it!

Step 1: Ascend the spires to the very top to gain a height advantage over Argorok. Do this by Clawshotting to the spire, then alternating between spires until you reach the top. The choice of spires is **important**. Propel yourself to the spires that are close together, as you'll ascend quickly.

Step 2: This attracts Argorok's attention, and it launches a blast of fire at you. Drop down before you're struck, or simply fall (but make sure you land on the grass and roll). Smash some skulls for Hearts near the base of the spires.

Threat Meter

Step 3: When Argorok descends to inspect you, it leaves its tail exposed: Z target it, and propel yourself onto it with your Clawshot. Pull down, and the dragon is unceremoniously dragged out of the air! It falls to the ground, some of its armor shatters, and then it flaps away.

Step 4: Argorok then swoops in and scrapes the ground with its talons. The wind caused by its wings pushes you along. Quickly put on your **Iron Boots** so you aren't blown off the tower.

1

2

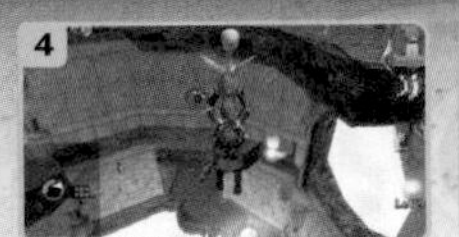
3

4

5

6

Twilit Dragon Argorok (cont'd)

Step 5: Argorok now stops and sits on a spire for a moment. Then it tries to take you down with a talon scrape and wind blow once again. If you're on the flight path, roll so you aren't struck, and immediately put those boots on!

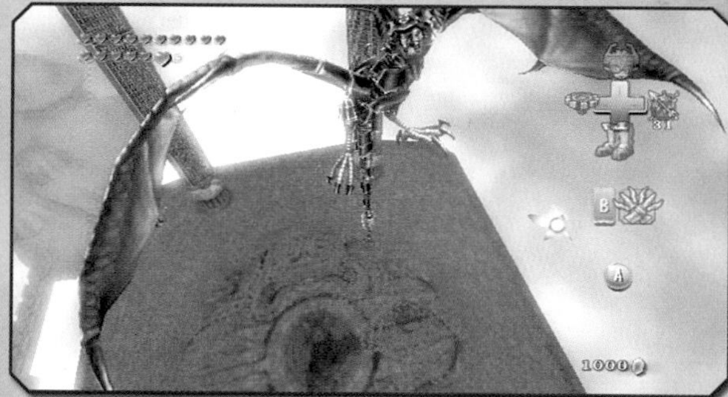

Step 6: Now Argorok circles at a higher elevation, forcing you to climb the spires again. Continue up to the middle of the spire, and continuously try to Z target Argorok's tail. Clawshot to it, and pull the beast down again. The creature flails and the last of its armor falls off, exposing a weak spot. It rises, draws thunder claps, and the final combat begins!

Step 7: Peahats have risen from the ground, and are floating in a large circle above the top of the spires. Clawshot all the way to the top, and Z target your closest Peahat. Then automatically Clawshot from Peahat to Peahat using Z, as Argorok flaps in the middle.

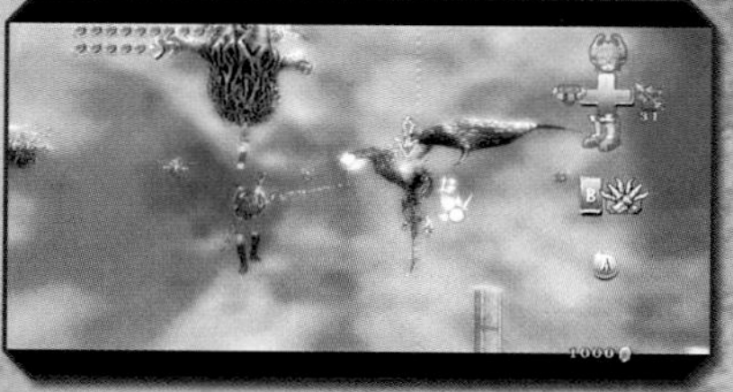

Step 8: Continue to circle around Argorok as it breathes fire; you must quickly reach a Peahat that gives you a view of Argorok's back. Stop here and Z target the weak spot on the back. Be quick!

Step 9: Propel yourself onto Argorok's back, and plunge your sword into that weak spot, as the dragon thrashes around. Keep the swipes and slashes going until you both plummet to the ground. The dragon slowly rises up again.

Step 10: Repeat Steps 7–9 twice more. On the third occasion, as the lightning storm intensifies, stop and wait for Argorok to start breathing fire. Maneuver from Peahat to Peahat, and when the dragon changes direction, you must too. Change direction again (you may need to do this a couple of times), then navigate around so you're facing the dragon's back. Then dish the final damage!

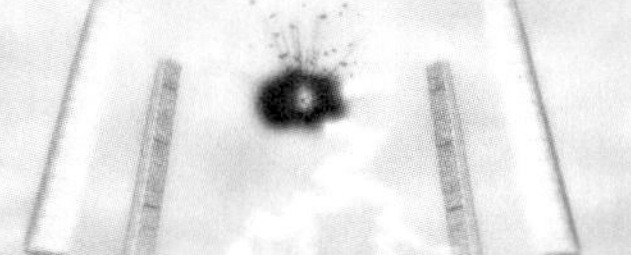

*Midna appears. She says that only the **true ruler** of the Twilit can destroy the Mirror. Zant must be a false king! She opens a portal and asks you to head immediately to the **Mirror Chamber**. All in good time! First, pick up the Heart Container. Then, head back to Lake Hylia via a Clawshot into the back of the Sky Cannon.*

Piece of Heart
You got a **Heart Container**! Your life energy has increased by **one** and been **fully replenished**! Heart Container #7 of 8.

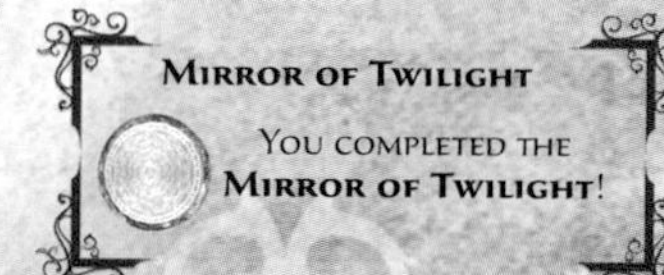

Mirror of Twilight
You completed the **Mirror of Twilight**!

7

8

Enemies Encountered
Twilit Dragon Argorok

Overworld: Assembling the Mirror of Twilight

Entrance to Twilit Palace

Jovani

Sky Cannon

Cave of Ordeals

60 59 58

Death Mountain

Kakariko Village

Faron Woods

Sacred Grove

Ordon Village

Lake Hylia

Gerudo Desert

Legend

Piece of Heart

Giant Quiver

Double Clawshot

Great Fairy Tears

Assembling the Mirror of Twilight: Overview

You have but a few remaining tasks in the Overworld to complete. After that, all your tasks are related to the remaining dungeons. Now that you have gathered all the major items, you can open the kingdom's remaining chests, and defeat all the remaining Poes in the furious battlegrounds of the Cave of Ordeals. Then prepare yourself for a journey to the Twilit world itself. Only when you're ready to go, with a Giant Quiver and a healthy collection of Fairies, Rare Chu Jelly, and a full Giant Wallet, should you venture to the Mirror Chamber, and fit the Mirror Shards together.

1 Obtain all Remaining Chests Pg 397

2 Obtain the Giant Quiver Pg 398

3 Collect Remaining Poe Souls Pg 399

4 Assemble the Mirror Shards Pg 407

Items to Obtain

Piece of Heart #43 (of 45)

Letter #14 (of 16)

Letter #15 (of 16)

Letter #16 (of 16)

Giant Quiver

Great Fairy's Tears

Poe Soul #60

A Link to the Present

Ordon Sword, Master Sword, Heart Pieces: 2 (42 Total)

Wooden Shield, Hylian Shield

Hero's Clothes, Zora Armor, Magic Armor

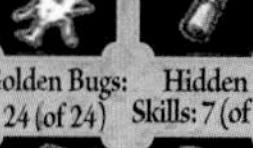

Giant Wallet, Big Quiver, Golden Bugs: 24 (of 24), Hidden Skills: 7 (of 7)

Medicine Scent, Poe Souls 57 (of 60), Fish Journal, Letters 13 (of 16)

Mirror of Twilight: 4 (of 4)

Enemies Encountered

Bokoblin

Task 1: Obtain All Remaining Chests Using Double Clawshot

◄ If you wish, you can return to the City in the Sky by entering the nearby cannon. Just Clawshot into the back of it, and ride it up to the heavens! Do this only if you forgot to capture one of the two Imp Poes. For now, you should set about claiming the last of Hyrule's chests!

Double Clawshot Hunt: Lanayru Spirit Cave

► Enter the the Lanayru Spirit Cave, and stop. Turn and look north and up. Shoot and propel up to a Clawshot medallion.

Double Clawshot around the ceiling of this cavern, until you reach this medallion (stuck to a tree root), which allows you to dangle down. Move and then Clawshot across to two more medallions, then land on an upper ledge you haven't been able to reach, yet.

◄ Turn and run along the western ledge first, which slopes down to a chest. Ease the chest open to uncover an orange Rupee (100).

Overworld Chest #96: Orange Rupee (100)

◄ Now do the exact opposite. Turn and run along the eastern ledge, which slopes down to a second chest. Ease the chest open, and you uncover another orange Rupee (100)!

Overworld Chest #97: Orange Rupee (100)

Double Clawshot Hunt: Kakariko Gorge

◄ When you've finished in the Lake Hylia area, warp as close to the Kakariko Gorge as you can. Gallop here, defeat the nearby Bokoblin, and then aim your Clawshot out to the long rock in the middle of the gorge.

► Turn and hang from the medallion, and look down. There's a second medallion on the outer wall, so Clawshot down to that, then turn and look across at the vine wall. Clawshot over here, and clamber onto the ledge. As always, aim at the top of the vine wall so you don't slip off!

► Once on the ledge, look for a vine wall to climb. Don't Clawshot, as there's nowhere to land. Shimmy around, and then drop to a remote ledge on the inside of the gorge rock with a chest on it.

Overworld Chest #98: Piece of Heart #43

Piece of Heart
You got a **Piece of Heart**! Collect **two more** for another full Heart Container. Piece of Heart #43 of 45.

Characters Encountered

Postman

Purlo

Double Clawshot Hunt: Hyrule Field (South)

➤ The last medallions to leap to and from are in the hole in the southern part of Hyrule Field just outside the gates. Stand on the edge of the hole and look down, aiming for this medallion.

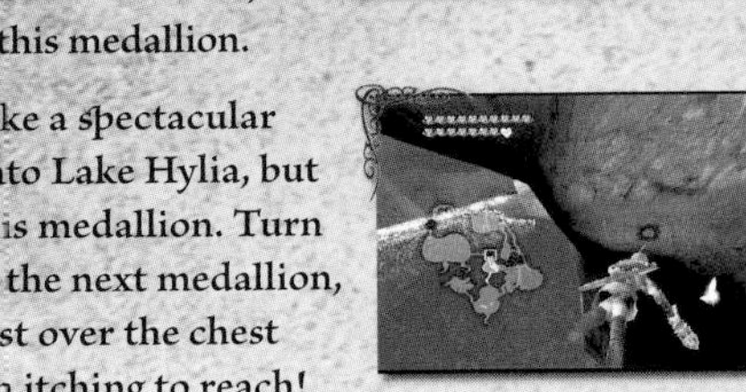

➤ Then take a spectacular dive, not into Lake Hylia, but down to this medallion. Turn and aim at the next medallion, which is just over the chest you've been itching to reach! Land on the tiny ledge, pry the chest open, grab the orange Rupee (100), then Clawshot back up using the same medallions, or drop into Lake Hylia.

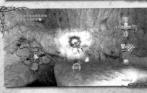

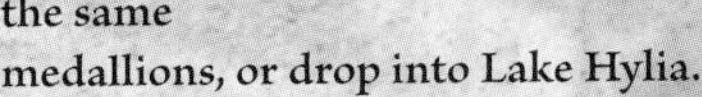

Overworld Chest #99: Orange Rupee (100)

Catching the Final Post

The Postman arrives when you next enter a bridge or junction somewhere in Hyrule. Note that you may have received these letters before or after this point, if you took a more indirect path through your adventure. There are three letters to open:

- Letter #14 is from Purlo, and it's sent once you have the Double Clawshot, telling you of the new challenge awaiting you!
- Letter #15 is from Occoo Jr., and it's a fantastic response! You get this after receiving Letter #11.
- Letter #16 is from Shad, giving you an update on his search for the heavens.

Letter #14
You got Letter #14: "Challenge for you!" by Purlo.

Letter #15
You got Letter #15: "Hey, kidd!!!" by Jr.

Letter #16
You got Letter #16: "Update" by Shad.

Postman:

The Postman is around 20 years old, and he delivers letters all over the kingdom. Whenever he has a letter for you, he yells at you and delivers it by hand, and he's usually out of breath! When he runs, he hums to himself, and speaks with a strange foreign accent. He has a weird and unpleasant laugh. Although always breathless and smelly with sweat, he's a happy-go-lucky fellow!

Task 2: Obtain the Giant Quiver

Purloining from Purlo: The Final STAR Game

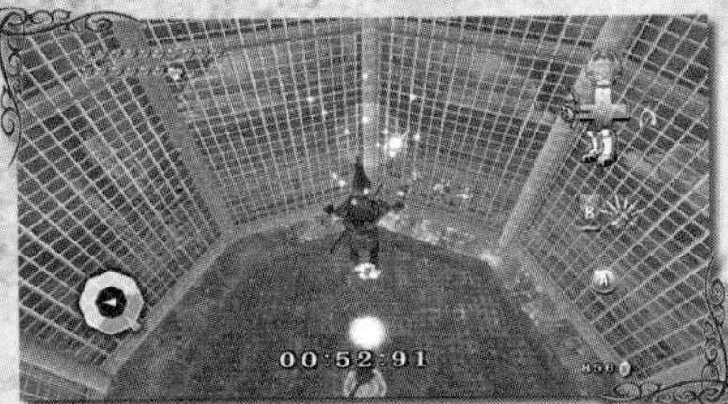

▲ Your next stop should be inside Castle Town, at Purlo's "STAR" minigame! Now that you have the Double Clawshot, he's introduced a final, ultra-difficult level that will tax you. Or will it? Below are the tactics for the quickest route though this game, plus tips on obtaining a near-infinite number of orange Rupees (100)!

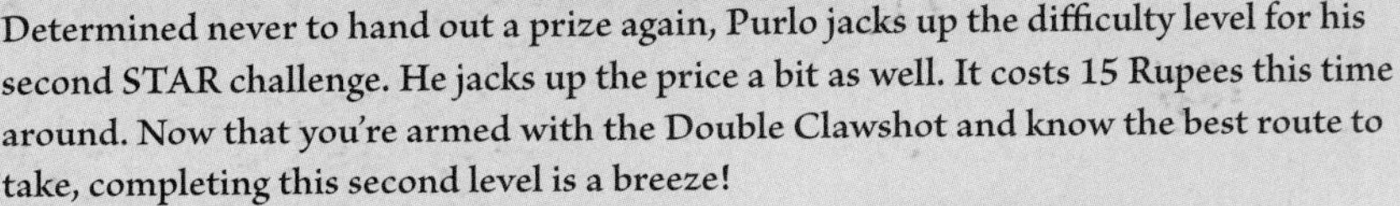

Level 2: Hard

Determined never to hand out a prize again, Purlo jacks up the difficulty level for his second STAR challenge. He jacks up the price a bit as well. It costs 15 Rupees this time around. Now that you're armed with the Double Clawshot and know the best route to take, completing this second level is a breeze!

From the buzzer, aim the Double Clawshot at the lowest white star ahead and zip across to nab it. Don't drop from the cage or you'll land in the spikes below!

Turn and aim the Double Clawshot at the row of white stars to the left. Fire to zip across, nabbing some stars.

1 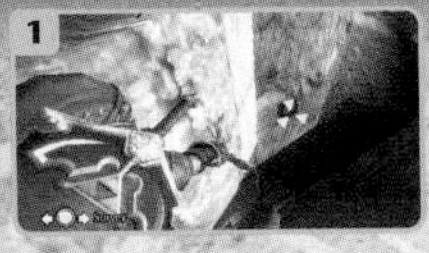 2  3 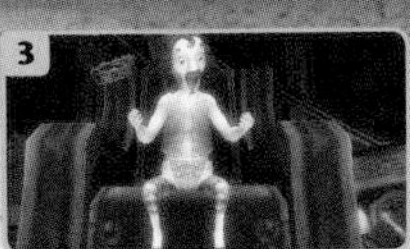 4 

Level 2: Hard (cont'd)

Next, aim at the row of pink stars just to your left and then fire to sail across, collecting them all at once.

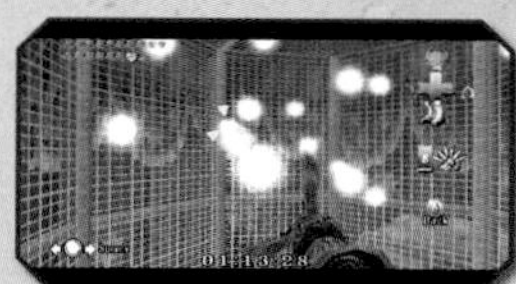

You're doing great! Now target the line of yellow stars, which again are just to your left. Fly out to grab them all in one pass.

When you reach the other side, turn to aim at the long line of blue stars farther to your left. Collect the entire row by zipping straight across the arena.

Next, look for a row of white stars above and to the left. Catch 'em all in one swift pass!

Aim just to your left again, lining up the row of pink stars ahead. Sail across the arena and grab the whole row.

Upon reaching the other side, look for a line of yellow stars below you to the left. Unleash the Double Clawshot to zip through and grab each one.

You're getting there! Now find a string of blue stars just below you. Line up so you catch them all in one go.

Working your way back up now, find a row of white stars above and to the left. Fire away and nab the whole string

Only two moves remain! Look high above and notice a string of pink stars leading toward the ceiling. Aim at the circle in the center of the roof and release to grab all of the pink stars on your way up.

Excellent work! The final column of stars now lies directly beneath you. Simply drop from the ceiling to grab them all and complete the second level of the "STAR" minigame in record time.

Tip: Before letting go and completing the minigame, hang around and let the timer tick away. Drop and win the game just before time runs out so you don't set an unbeatable record time. This comes in handy later!

Flabbergasted, Purlo simply can't believe you've managed to win his STAR challenge *again*. But he has no choice but to present you with a valuable prize: the Giant Quiver! Combine it with bombs for a considerable arsenal!

Note: From this point onward, you can replay the second level of the STAR minigame whenever you wish. If you beat your previous record time, you win an orange Rupee (100)! For this reason, it's best not to finish the game until the very last second. This lets you beat your record over and over for a nearly endless supply of Rupees!

Giant Quiver
You got the **Giant Quiver**! It can hold up to **100 arrows**!

Task 3: Collect All Remaining Poe Souls, Meet Jovani and Gengle

An Epic Quest: Complete the Cave of Ordeals!

◀ Your next task is a brutal one, but it's worth it if you want to test your mettle against the most difficult side dungeon in Hyrule! The Cave of Ordeals is now available to play all the way through. Journey to the Gerudo Desert and head to this entrance, where the piece of the bridge was protruding from.

You need the Double Clawshot to get past some of the later levels in this dungeon. This is also where you'll meet the final three **Imp Poes**, and complete your collection of 60 Poe Souls!

Characters Encountered

Great Fairy

It is advantageous (but not vital) to have the following before you enter the Cave of Ordeals:

- Magic Armor (so you can receive no damage against the harder enemies).
- The Giant Wallet (so you can keep your Magic Armor on for longer periods).
- The Giant Quiver (so you have enough arrows to last you the entire outing).
- The Bomb Bags (all three so you can carry enough Bomb Arrows).
- All special equipment (so you can complete the entire dungeon).
- 18 Heart Containers (so you can survive for longer).
- All four Bottles filled with Rare Chu Jelly, Fairies, or Great Fairy's Tears.
- All Hidden Skills (so you can launch the great spin attack, which is devastating!)
- A good knowledge of what to expect (read on for more information!).

Tip

◄ For every 10 levels you complete of the Cave of Ordeals, Fairies are released into a particular spring in Hyrule. Complete the dungeon, and the Great Fairy blesses you with an amazing gift: the Great Fairy's Tears! This acts just like the Rare Chu Jelly, granting you all your energy back and a temporary boost of attack strength (you can easily strike enemies for around a minute).

The Cave of Ordeals

Room 1: Bokoblin Sentry

The Cave of Ordeals starts off easily enough. Run and jump off the narrow entry ledge to land in the first chamber, where you encounter a lone, blue-skinned Bokoblin. Defeat the creature to open the passage to the next room.

Room 2: Keeses and Rats

The second chamber houses a handful of Keeses and Rats. Leap down from the entry ledge and have at them, using the spin attack to wipe them out fast.

Room 3: Hanging Baba Serpents

Four Baba Serpents hang from the third chamber's ceiling. Before leaving the entry ledge, use the Clawshot or Hero's Bow to sever their heads from their stalks. Then leap down into the room and quickly dispatch them with a spin attack.

The Cave of Ordeals (cont'd)

Room 4: Skulltula Den

Three hungry Skulltulas patrol the next chamber. Jump down and begin your assault with a spin attack to stagger them, then target one and finish it off with the ending blow maneuver. Repeat this tactic to quickly eliminate the other two.

Room 5: Bulblin Archers

Three Bulblin Archers are spread out near this chamber's walls. Quickly roll to each one, using spin attacks to dispatch them. The spin attack is ideal, as it deflects incoming arrows.

Tip

It's tough to get through this room without being hit. If you're attempting to preserve your great spin, you might want to don the Magic Armor.

Room 6: Torch Slug Lair

Before leaping into this chamber, use the Clawshot or Hero's Bow to defeat all of the Torch Slugs on the ceiling. Then jump down and finish off the ones on the ground.

Room 7: Dodongos and Fire Keese

The Dodongos are the real threat in the cave's seventh chamber, but they're not fast enough to track you. Run about and use the spin attack to defeat the Fire Keese in the room, then start hacking away at the Dodongos' tails.

Room 8: Tektite Trouble

This room's packed full of Tektites. Leap down and use the spin attack as often as possible to thin them out. Keep moving and try not to stay in one place for too long.

Room 9: Lizalfoses and Bulblin Archers

Two Lizalfoses stand in plain sight in this second chamber, but watch out: two Bulblin Archers are hiding beneath the entry ledge as well! Leap down and quickly defeat the Bulblin Archers, then turn your attention to the Lizalfoses.

Room 10: Great Fairy

The Great Fairy awaits you in the cave's 10th chamber. She welcomes you to the Cave of Ordeals, and rewards you: Fairies will now appear at the Ordon Spring in Ordona Province! This gives you a place to go and fill your Bottles with Fairies whenever you need them.

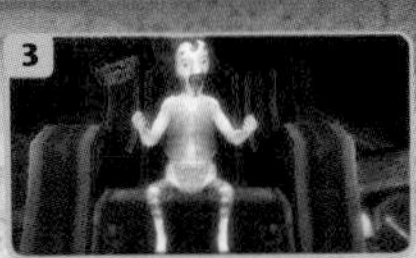

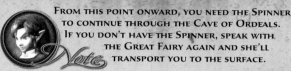

The Cave of Ordeals (cont'd)

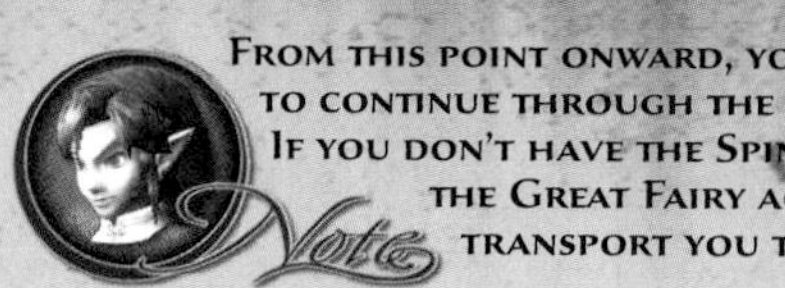

Note: From this point onward, you need the Spinner to continue through the Cave of Ordeals. If you don't have the Spinner, speak with the Great Fairy again and she'll transport you to the surface.

Room 11: Helmasaurs and Rat Horde

The 11th chamber features some Helmasaurs and a large pack of Rats. The Rats chase after you the moment you drop into the room; use the spin attack. Afterward, ready the Clawshot and begin assaulting the Helmasaurs. Stay mobile in this chamber or the Helmasaurs will track you down.

After securing the room, use the Spinner to travel along the Spinner track and reach the door to the next chamber.

Room 12: Giant Purple Chu

One enormous Purple Chu defends the cave's 12th chamber. Keep your distance and use the Clawshot to whittle the Chu down, eventually separating it into tiny Purple Chus that you can defeat with the Clawshot from range.

Room 13: Angry Chu Worms

You face a group of Chu Worms in this chamber. Use the Clawshot to rip them from their bubbles, then slice them up. Defeat each Chu Worm in turn.

Room 14: Bubble Surprise

After you drop into this chamber, the many skulls on the ground sprout wings and attack! Run around and let these Bubbles come to you, then wipe them all out with a well-timed spin attack. Round up any stragglers.

Room 15: Bulblin Brute Squad

The 15th chamber is filled with Bulblins. Drop down and have at them, using the spin attack to create breathing space whenever they swarm in.

Room 16: More Keeses and Rats

You face another large group of Keeses and Rats in this room. Drop in and dispatch them quickly, using the spin attack as often as possible.

Room 17: Stalhound Gang

The 17th chamber is loaded with Stalhounds. An Imp Poe also lurks down here. Run around to round up the Stalhounds, then unleash a spin attack to defeat the majority. Finish off any survivors, then change into wolf form and attack the Imp Poe.

Poe Soul #58

This Poe is technically available after you complete Dungeon 4: Arbiter's Grounds, but you can't finish the entire dungeon if you do it this way. You need a Spinner to reach this level. Attack the Stalhounds with spin attacks, and afterward, deal with the Poe. Only two more to go!

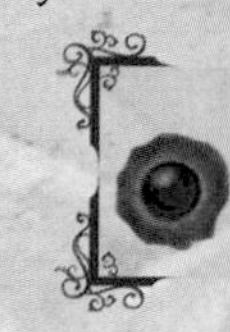

Poe Soul
You got the **Poe Soul**! Collect one from each Poe you defeat!
Poe Soul #58 of 60.

Room 18: Jeepers Leevers!

This chamber seems empty until you leap from the entry ledge, then multiple Leevers emerge from the ground and attack! Allow the Leevers to circle you for a moment, then unleash a spin attack as they begin to close in. Time it just right to defeat them all in one shot!

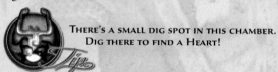

Tip: There's a small dig spot in this chamber. Dig there to find a Heart!

Room 19: Chu Horde

If you're carrying empty Bottles, now's the time to fill them! A ton of Chus drop from the ceiling after you drop into this chamber, including a Blue Chu and a few Red Chus. The Blue Chu is the one to get. Run straight over and defeat it, then scoop up its remains. Run away from the horde afterward and begin methodically defeating the remaining Chus with your Clawshot.

Room 20: Great Fairy

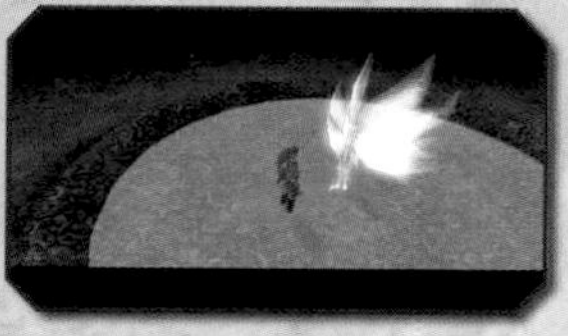

You encounter the Great Fairy again in the cave's 20th chamber. She praises your valor and says she'll now release Fairies into Faron Spring in Faron Province! This gives you another convenient place to go and fill your Bottles with Fairies.

Enemies Encountered
Multiple Fearsome Beasts!

Great Fairy

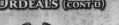

The Cave of Ordeals (cont'd)

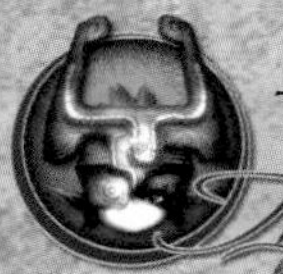
Note: From this point onward, you need the Ball and Chain to continue through the Cave of Ordeals. If you don't have this item, speak with the Great Fairy to return to the surface.

Room 21: Bokoblins and Ice Keese

This chamber's easy enough, featuring some blue-skinned Bokoblins and a handful of Ice Keeses. Use the spin attack to pulverize these fiends, then use the Ball and Chain to smash through the giant block of ice that's covering the door to the next room.

Room 22: Keeses, Rats, and Ghoul Rats

Here's another room full of Keeses and Rats, but the real fiends here are the invisible Ghoul Rats who slow your movements. Use the spin attack to defeat the visible foes, then change into wolf form to eliminate the Ghoul Rats.

Tip: There's another small dig spot in this chamber. Dig there to uncover three Hearts!

Room 23: Stalkin Crypt

The moment you touch down in this chamber, a vast number of Stalkins pop up from the ground and swarm you. Let them draw near, then use the spin attack to wipe out most of them. Run away from any that remain and repeat this tactic.

Room 24: Redead Tomb

A group of Redeads slumber in this chamber. Slowly walk off one side of entry ledge so that you grab onto it as you fall, then drop straight down. This way you don't wake all the Redeads at once. Inch toward one of the Redeads until it rises up, then drill it with the Ball and Chain. The first hit stuns the Redead, and when you yank the ball back toward you, it strikes the Redead a second time, defeating it! Use this tactic against the remaining Redeads.

Room 25: Bulblin Battleground

Be careful when stepping onto this room's entry ledge; a Bulblin Archer fires arrows at you from the room's watchtower! Deflect its arrows with your shield, then quickly dispatch it with an arrow of your own. Leap down into the room afterward and roll about, defeating the remaining Bulblins and Bulblin Archers with spin attacks.

Tip: This is anther tough room to survive without being hit. Put on the Magic Armor to preserve your great spin.

Room 26: Stalfos Vault

A trio of Stalfoses lurk in this chamber. Ready the Bomb Arrows, then leap down and quickly roll away from them. Get the Stalfoses together into a group, then launch a few Bomb Arrows to defeat them all at once. If the Stalfoses keep closing in, execute a few quick backflips to create some breathing room.

Room 27: Skulltulas and Bubbles

Three Skulltulas hang from this chamber's ceiling. Sever their webs with the Gale Boomerang or Clawshot, then drop into the room and combat them, using the ending blow to finish off each one. A handful of Bubbles occupy the room as well; employ the spin attack to quickly eliminate these foes.

Tip: Use your wolf senses to detect a small dig spot in this chamber. Dig there to find a Heart!

Room 28: Red Bokoblins and Lizalfoses

This chamber involves a frantic melee. A pack of red-skinned Bokoblins backed by two Lizalfoses attack you here! The spin attack is the obvious choice for this chamber, but if you'd like to thin the enemy ranks before diving into the fray, fire a few Bomb Arrows from the safety of the entry ledge.

Room 29: Stalfoses and Stalkins

This chamber is filled with skeletal fiends. Leap in and use the spin attack to wipe out the majority of the Stalkins, and once the little guys are no more, finish off the larger Stalfoses with Bomb Arrows. Or simply eliminate the Stalfoses with Bomb Arrows from the entry ledge!

Room 30: Great Fairy

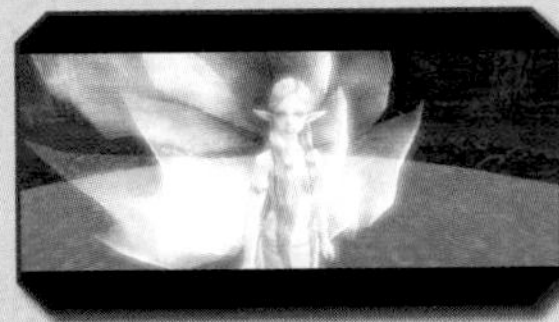

You encounter the Great Fairy again in the cave's 30th chamber. She praises your heroic display, and as a reward, releases Fairies to the Eldin Spring in Eldin Province! Now you can easily collect Fairies from three different places in the Overworld.

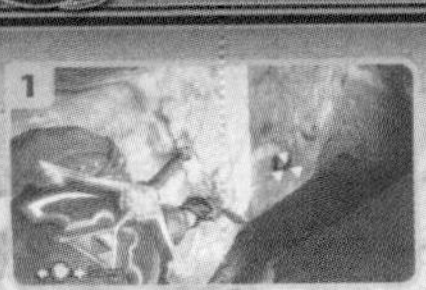

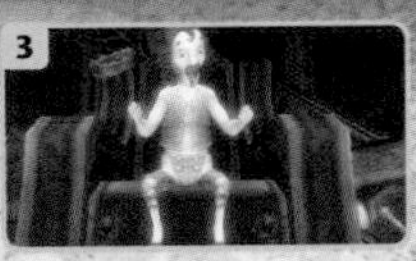

The Cave of Ordeals (cont'd)

Note: From this point onward, you need the Dominion Rod to continue through the Cave of Ordeals. If you don't have this item, speak with the Great Fairy to return to the surface.

Room 31: Beamoses and Keeses

Five Beamoses stand in this chamber. It's best to fire arrows at them from the safety of the entry ledge, but if you leap into the chamber beforehand, find safe spots from which to fire near the room's walls.

After clearing the room, use the Dominion Rod to move the two owl statues off the pressure plates they stand on. This opens the way to the next chamber.

Room 32: Trial by Fire

Fire-based enemies abound in this room. Defeat the Torch Slugs on the ceiling with the Hero's Bow or Clawshot, then leap forward and slice through the Fire Bubbles and Fire Keeses with a few well-timed spin attacks. There are a few Dodongos down here as well; stay mobile and attack them last.

Room 33: Redeads' Revenge

Here's another chamber full of Redeads. One is hidden beneath the entry ledge, so have the Ball and Chain ready to go before you hang and drop into the room. Pound the Redead below as soon as you land, then defeat the others in turn. Stay close to the room's walls to avoid drawing the attention of the Imp Poe that hovers in the center of the room; it's best to deal with it last.

Poe Soul #59

This Imp Poe is technically available after you complete Dungeon 6: Temple of Time, but you can't finish the entire dungeon if you do it this way. You need the Dominion Rod to reach this level. Attack each Redead with the Ball and Chain, then go for the Poe. Just one more to go!

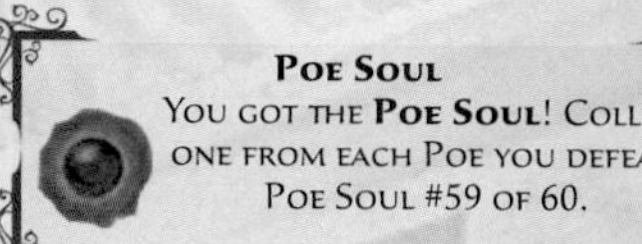

Poe Soul
You got the **Poe Soul**! Collect one from each Poe you defeat!
Poe Soul #59 of 60.

Room 34: Chu and Ghost Rat Lair

Ready an empty Bottle before diving into this chamber. Try to grab the jelly of a Red or Blue Chu for a free Heart-restoring potion, but move fast or they'll merge with the Purple Chus and become diluted. Also watch out for the Ghost Rats in this chamber; they slow you down, making it tough to avoid the Chus' leaping attacks!

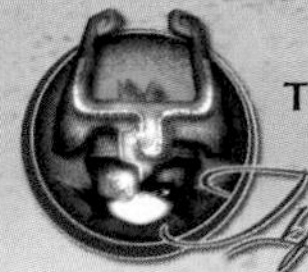

Tip: There's a small dig spot in this chamber. Dig there for a Heart before you move on!

Room 35: Frightening Freezard

This tricky chamber features a central Freezard surrounded by a number of Ice Keeses. From the entry ledge, run and leap to one side of the room, stay close to the walls and run circles around the Freezard, defeating the Ice Keeses as you go. Then use the Ball and Chain to smash the Freezard during the short intervals when it isn't spewing out frost.

Caution: The Freezard shatters into a handful of Mini Freezards after you smash it. Use the Ball and Chain to quickly defeat them.

Room 36: Chilfos Chamber

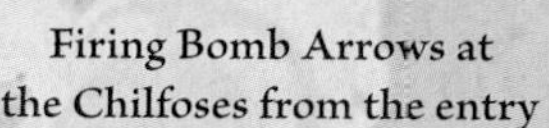

A group of Chilfos warriors defend this room, the Ball and Chain can rip through them in short order.

Firing Bomb Arrows at the Chilfoses from the entry ledge is also effective. Two hits are required to defeat each Chilfos. The second Bomb Arrow must land before the Chilfos brings out another ice spear, however, and it only takes them a few seconds to do this.

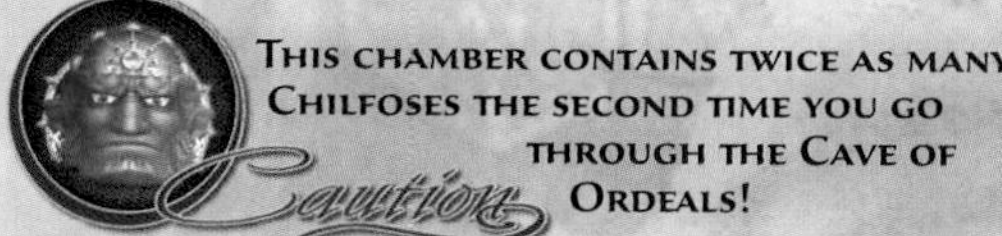

Caution: This chamber contains twice as many Chilfoses the second time you go through the Cave of Ordeals!

Room 37: Leevers and Ice Bubbles

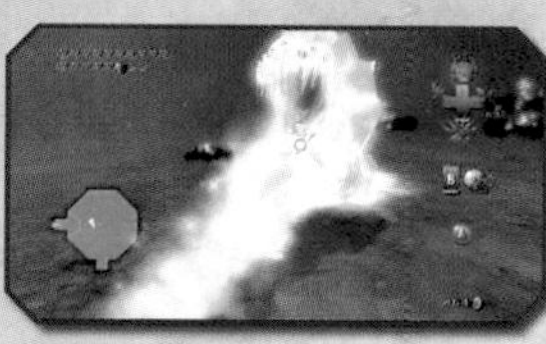

This chamber is a breath of fresh air after challenge of the previous one. Leap into the center of the room, and you're quickly surrounded by Leevers and Ice Bubbles. A few spin attacks later, you're moving on to the next room.

Enemies Encountered

! Multiple Fearsome Beasts!

Great Fairy

The Cave of Ordeals (cont'd)

Room 38: Chamber of Ice

This room is filled with all sorts of ice-based enemies. Two Freezards stand at either side of the chamber, backed by groups of Chilfoses, Ice Bubbles, and Ice Keeses. It's best to fire Bomb Arrows at the Chilfoses from the entry ledge; try to destroy them all before leaping into the room.

Keep away from both Freezards as you take out the Ice Keeses and Ice Bubbles. Afterward, slam each Freezard twice with the Ball and Chain during the brief periods when they're not spewing out frost. Also use the Ball and Chain to smash the Mini Freezards that appear after you shatter the large ones.

Room 39: Darknut Duo

The last chamber was tough, but this one's even worse! Here, two fearsome Darknuts stand ready for battle. You don't want to draw the attention of both at once, so hang and drop off one side of the entry ledge, then inch toward one of the Darknuts until it begins stomping toward you.

Caution: If this is your second trip through the Cave of Ordeals, watch out: a third Darknut is hiding directly beneath the entry ledge!

Back up and let the Darknut come to you. Keep your back close to the wall, leaving just a bit of room behind you. When the Darknut prepares to strike, perform a backflip to escape, then immediately follow up with a jump attack. The jump attack stuns the Darknut; unleash a fast combo to slice off some of its armor. Remember to keep your distance from the second Darknut at all times!

Once you've destroyed the Darknut's armor, it draws a sword and becomes more aggressive. Change tactics and begin using the back slice maneuver to circle around the Darknut and stun it from behind, then follow up with a fast combo to inflict damage. Don't worry if you attract the other Darknut, just keep repeating this tactic until the first one falls. Then repeat this entire strategy for the second Darknut.

Room 40: Great Fairy

The Great Fairy visits you once again in the cave's 40th chamber. Impressed that you've made it this far, she releases Fairies into the Lanayru Spring in Lanayru Province! You may now collect and bottle Fairies at any spring in the Overworld!

Note: You need the Double Clawshot to continue to the end of the Cave of Ordeals. If you don't have this item, speak with the Great Fairy to return to the surface.

Room 41: Army of Armoses

Look before you leap into this dangerous chamber. Three rows of three Armoses stand silently, taking up most of the space. Do *not* leap into the center of the room! Instead, carefully hang and drop from one side of the entry ledge, then target one of the corner Armoses and inch toward it. Watch the Armos carefully and back away when it begins to awaken.

Press your back to the wall and let the Armos come to you. Carefully circle around it and attack the crystal on its back, which is its only weak spot. Take your time defeating this one, and whatever you do, don't move close to the others in the room!

After defeating the first Armos, go after another. Repeat the same procedure, defeating each Armos in turn. You create more breathing room as you defeat each of these enemies. After clearing the room, use the Double Clawshot to navigate the Clawshot medallions on the walls and reach the next chamber.

Room 42: Red Bokoblins and Baba Serpents

This chamber is a refreshing change of pace after the slow, methodical approach you employed in the previous room. Here, a gang of red-skinned Bokoblins and a bunch of Baba Serpents swarm you the minute you enter. Use the spin attack as often as you can, then finish off the Bokoblins with the ending blow. To simplify this room, fire some Bomb Arrows at the Bokoblins from the entry ledge before leaping into the fray.

Room 43: More Lizalfoses and Bulblin Archers

Lots of Bulblin Archers line the walls of this chamber, and a group of Lizalfoses stand near the center. It's best to soften up these foes with Bomb Arrows from the entry ledge, but be careful of the Bulblin Archers' return fire! When you finally leap into the room, roll to each Bulblin Archer in turn, defeating it with spin attacks. Then take out the Lizalfoses.

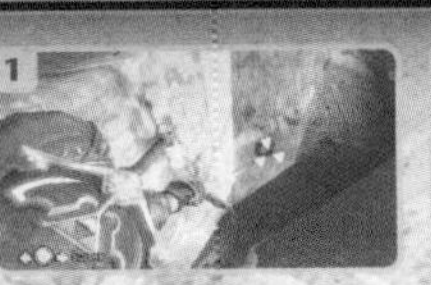

1

2

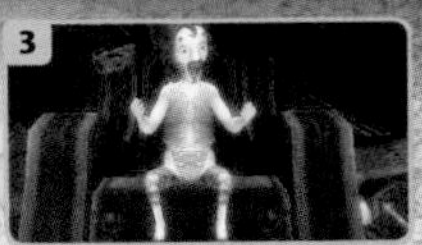

3

4

The Cave of Ordeals (cont'd)

Tip: If you're trying to preserve your great spin, equip the Magic Armor before entering this dangerous chamber.

Room 44: Dangerous Dynafolses

Four hulking Dynafolses patrol this chamber, along with a troublesome Imp Poe! Leap into the center of the room and wail the Dynafolses with a spin attack. If you have access to the great spin, you can defeat most of them in one shot! Finish off any survivors in turn. The back slice is a sound maneuver against these armored fiends. After dealing with the Dynafolses, transform into a wolf and defeat the Imp Poe.

Poe Soul #60

After you defeat the Lizalfoses and Dynofolses, deal with this final Imp Poe.

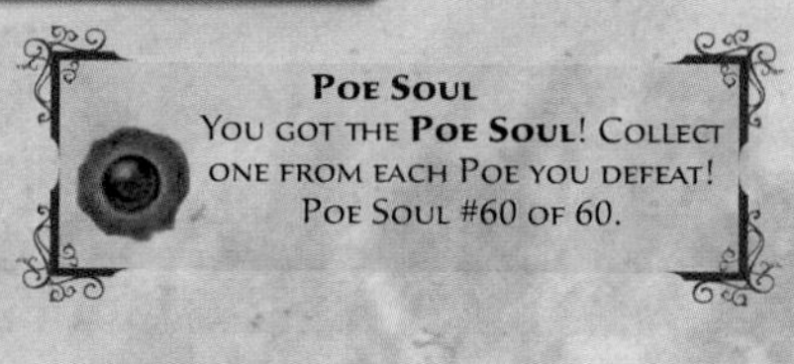

Poe Soul
You got the **Poe Soul**! Collect one from each Poe you defeat!
Poe Soul #60 of 60.

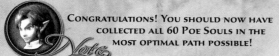

Note: Congratulations! You should now have collected all 60 Poe Souls in the most optimal path possible!

Room 45: Redeads, Bulblin Archers, and Chus

Bring your shield out as you move toward this chamber's entry ledge; two Bulblin Archers fire arrows at you from tall watchtowers! Keep to one side of the tunnel that leads to the entry ledge so that only one Bulblin Archer can fire at you, and defeat them both in turn with the Hero's Bow. Then step onto the entry ledge and launch Bomb Arrows at each Redead inside the room to eliminate them.

Ready an empty Bottle and leap into the room. A bunch of Chus drop from the ceiling, including a golden Rare Chu! Defeat it and quickly scoop its remains into your Bottle This will come in handy very soon!

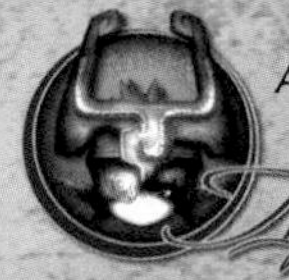

Tip: After the fight, search to find a small dig spot in this chamber. Dig there to find three Hearts!

Room 46: Freezards, Chilfoses, and Ghoul Rats

Four Chilfoses patrol this chamber, backed by two large Freezards. (One of the Freezards is hidden beneath the entry ledge.) Shatter all four Chilfoses with Bomb Arrows, then change into wolf form and leap to one side of the room. Turn on your sense view to find a swarm of Ghoul Rats down here. Keep out of range of the Freezards as you defeat them. Then return to human form and smash apart the Freezards (and the Mini Freezards they spawn) with the Ball and Chain when it's safe to do so.

Room 47: Little Guys

This chamber must have been designed to lull you into a false sense of security, because you face nothing more than a blue-skinned Bokoblin, a group of Stalkins, and a pack of Rats. Drop into the room and tear through these enemies, making good use of the spin attack.

Room 48: Darknut and Aeralfos

This challenging chamber features two Aeralfos and a big, scary Darknut. They all seem to notice you as soon as you drop into the room. Therefore, the best approach is to target one of the Aeralfoses and focus on grounding it with the Clawshot, then punish it with fast attacks. Defeat each Aeralfos in turn in this manner while striving to avoid the Darknut at all times. With the Aeralfoses gone so just hang in there the Darknut is a breeze; use the old tactics against him to defeat him.

Tip: The Aeralfoses beat their wings rapidly before they dive bomb you. When one of them is out of view, listen for the sound of its wings. If you hear them speed up, roll about to avoid the ensuing attack.

Room 49: Terrible Trio

Naturally, the final enemy-filled room of the Cave of Ordeals is one of its toughest. Here stand three Darknuts, ready to thrash any intruders. One of the Darknuts is hiding beneath the entry ledge; make it your first target. Jump off one side of the ledge, keeping as close to the wall as possible. Quickly turn around and face the Darknut beneath the ledge.

Enemies Encountered

Multiple Fearsome Beasts!

Great Fairy

Postman

Jovani

Gengle

Midna

The Cave of Ordeals (cont'd)

Caution: If this is your second trip through the Cave of Ordeals, prepare for the ultimate challenge: four Darknuts guard this chamber instead of three!

Remain as far away from the other two Darknuts as possible while combating the first. You'll probably end up drawing their attention at some point, but at least try to remove the first one's armor before that occurs. Backflip away from the first Darknut's attacks, then jump attack and follow up with sword combos. After removing its armor, use the back slice to open its defenses and finish it off.

Because the back slice is such a chaotic (yet effective) maneuver, it's common to draw the attention of the other Darknuts at this point. If this occurs, focus on defeating the one you've already weakened. Target it and circle around the Darknuts to keep the unarmored one at the front of the pack. Backflip a few times to create some breathing room, then charge and unleash a jump strike. With the Darknuts in a tight group, this move often staggers them all at once, allowing you to sneak in a few quick attacks before they recover.

Caution: Darknuts become extremely aggressive once they lose their armor. It's unwise to remove the armor of more than one Darknut at a time!

Room 50: Great Fairy

The Great Fairy awaits you in the Cave of Ordeals' final chamber. Impressed by your bravery, she awards you with some Great Fairy's Tears! Also, from this point onward, you may visit the Great Fairy by journeying to any province's spring. Speak with her to receive more Great Fairy's Tears whenever you run out!

Great Fairy Tears
You got the **Great Fairy's Tears**! This sacred water contains the Great Fairy's prayers.

▲ Once the Cave of Ordeals is complete, you have **unlimited Great Fairy Tears** (but you can carry only one at a time)! Visit any spring throughout Hyrule with an empty Bottle, and providing you don't already have some, you're automatically given the tears from the spirit of the Great Fairy. You can also Bottle Fairies at any spring.

The Cave of Ordeals: Second Completion

◄ Think you've mastered everything the Cave of Ordeals has to offer? Think again! Once you've finished the Cave of Ordeals, you can re-enter the 50-floor side dungeon again, and battle through a second time! On this occasion, certain enemies multiply. For example, the last dungeon room (shown here) has four Darknuts! Four!

Not only that, but if you complete the Cave of Ordeals for a second time, you'll see the Postman reading a letter on the edge of the last ledge before you meet the Great Fairy. What is he reading? What does he say? We don't know! We ran straight past him and couldn't get back to talk to him! Don't make the same mistake!

Saving Jovani's Soul: 60 Poe Completion

◄ If you've finished the Cave of Ordeals (or at least, reached Floor 44 and captured the final Poe Soul), you can return to the dig spot outside of Jovani's house. Gengle the cat meets you. He wants to go outside and play with his cat friends.

1
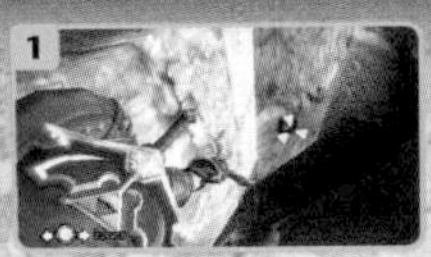

2

3
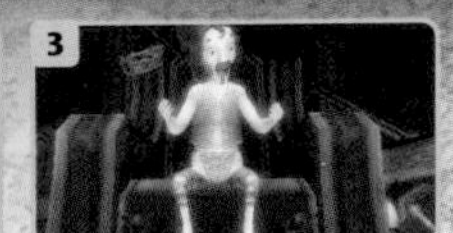

4

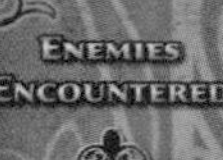

Multiple Fearsome Beasts!

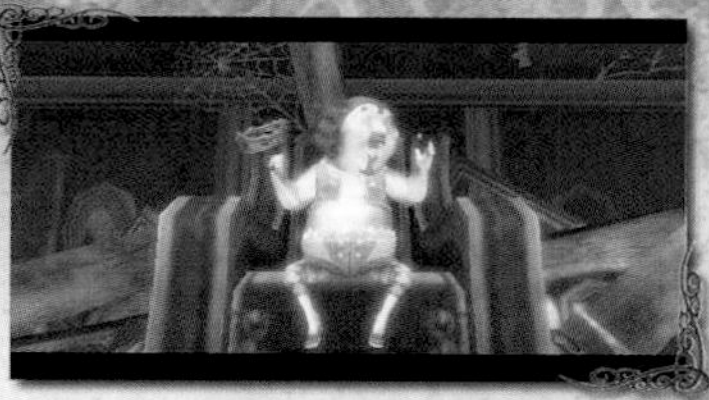

➤ Run up to Jovani, and speak with him. Now that his soul is completely purged of Poes, he's feeling fantastic! He may be a shadow of his former portly self, but that's great news for him! He thanks you with a generous prize: a silver Rupee (200).

◄ Leave Jovani's house and return, and Jovani has vanished! Gengle tells you he's left, and hints that he doesn't know what to do with all the money. You find Jovani in Telma's bar, sobbing uncontrollably. His girlfriend hadn't seen him for so long, she started dating another man!

Saving Jovani's Soul: Saving Infinite Rupees!

◄ If you leave Castle Town and return, you can enter Jovani's hut again and receive a different message from Gengle. Jovani has no one to impress any more, so Gengle is giving their money away! He gives you another silver Rupee (200).

Tip: Leave Castle Town (via walking, not warping) and head to any field. Then return, enter Jovani's house, and you'll receive another silver Rupee (200). This never stops, and it's useful when you're preparing for the Cave of Ordeals second attempt, and need Rupee power for your Magic Armor.

Task 4: Assemble the Mirror Shards

Heading to Dungeon 8: Entering the Mirror Chamber

◄ When you've finished adventuring in Hyrule, and found everything the Overworld has to offer (or not; you can come back at any time to complete these optional tasks), warp straight to the Mirror Chamber in Gerudo Desert.

*The shards of the **Mirror of Twilight** combine, and an astral beam projects through the chained monolith. Zant strikes down a tall, slender female, down in the Palace of Twilight. Midna only cared about turning her world to normal and ridding it of Zant. That's why she used you. But now that she's seen all your sacrifices, she wants to save your world, too.*

➤ A staircase projects toward the portal leading to the Twilight Realm. Step onto these stairs, and at the top, you're transported into Midna's world, where the King of Shadows must finally be stopped. Ganondorf's underling must pay!

Dungeon 8: Palace of Twilight

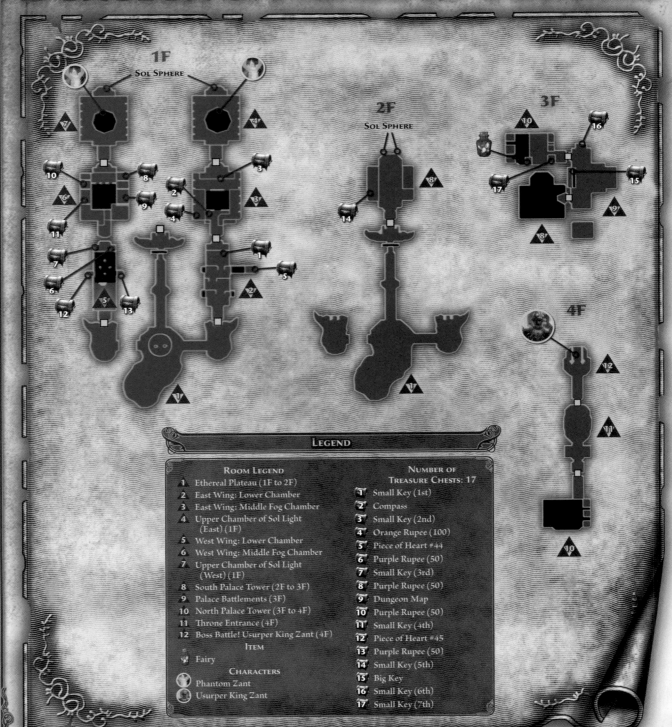

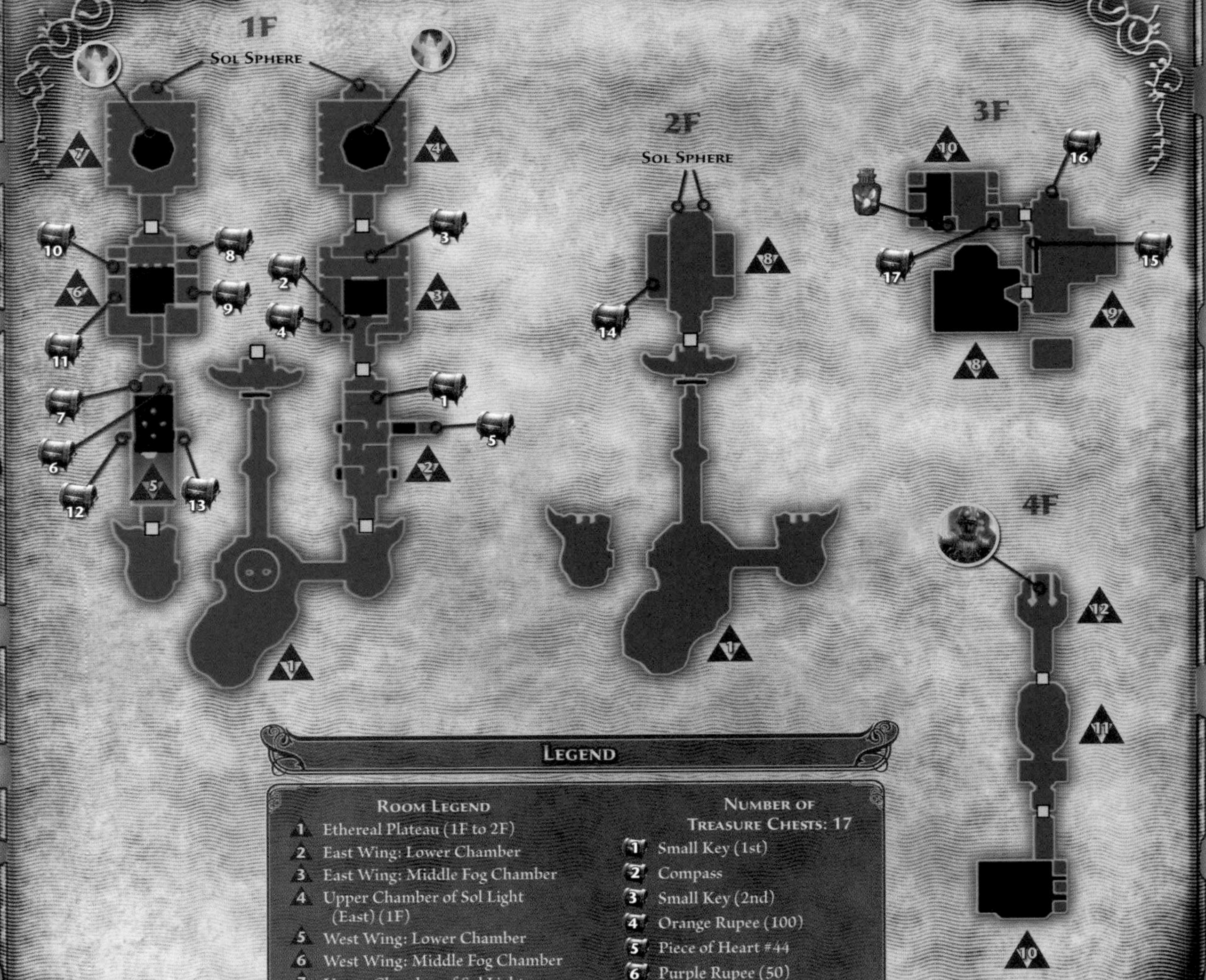

1F

Sol Sphere

2F

Sol Sphere

3F

4F

Legend

Room Legend	
1	Ethereal Plateau (1F to 2F)
2	East Wing: Lower Chamber
3	East Wing: Middle Fog Chamber
4	Upper Chamber of Sol Light (East) (1F)
5	West Wing: Lower Chamber
6	West Wing: Middle Fog Chamber
7	Upper Chamber of Sol Light (West) (1F)
8	South Palace Tower (2F to 3F)
9	Palace Battlements (3F)
10	North Palace Tower (3F to 4F)
11	Throne Entrance (4F)
12	Boss Battle! Usurper King Zant (4F)

Item

Fairy

Characters

Phantom Zant

Usurper King Zant

Number of Treasure Chests: 17	
1	Small Key (1st)
2	Compass
3	Small Key (2nd)
4	Orange Rupee (100)
5	Piece of Heart #44
6	Purple Rupee (50)
7	Small Key (3rd)
8	Purple Rupee (50)
9	Dungeon Map
10	Purple Rupee (50)
11	Small Key (4th)
12	Piece of Heart #45
13	Purple Rupee (50)
14	Small Key (5th)
15	Big Key
16	Small Key (6th)
17	Small Key (7th)

1 Obtain the First Sol Sphere Pg 410

2 Return First Sol Sphere to the Plateau Pg 413

3 Obtain the Second Sol Sphere Pg 414

4 Return Second Sol Sphere to the Plateau Pg 416

Palace of Twilight: Overview

The world of Midna's people is strange but eerily beautiful, but the same cannot be said of her people; transformed into shadow beasts by the hateful King Zant, who rules from this formidable fortress palace. You must bring light back to this land of darkness by moving through each wing of the palace to a ceremonial pedestal and taking a sacred globe known as a Sol Sphere, which shines light and restores balance. Along the way, Twilit forces are out to stop you, but the light's brightness is your savior, and combining two Spheres allows the Master Sword to be imbued with this powerful magic. Only then can you cut through the shadow clouds, scale the palace tower, and face the Usurper King to stop his evil machinations once and for all!

A Link to the Present

Ordon Sword, Master Sword
Heart Pieces: 3 (43 Total)

Wooden Shield, Hylian Shield
Hero's Clothes, Zora Armor, Magic Armor

Giant Wallet, Giant Quiver, Golden Bugs: 24 (of 24), Hidden Skills: 7 (of 7)

Medicine Scent, Poe Souls 60 (of 60), Fish Journal, Letters 16 (of 16)

Dungeon Denizens

Characters

Midna

Twili People

Enemies

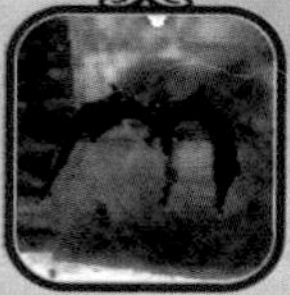

Twilit Keese, Twilit Vermin

Twilit Messenger

Twilit Kargarok, Twilit Baba

Zant Mask

Zant's Hand

Bosses

Mid Boss: Phantom Zant, Big Boss: Usurper King Zant

Items Already Acquired

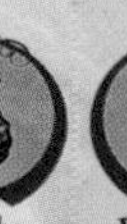

Double Clawshot, Dominion Rod, Ball and Chain, Spinner, Hero's Bow, Iron Boots

Gale Boomerang, Lantern, Slingshot, Fishing Rod, Hawkeye, Bombs (Bag #1)

Bombs (Bag #2), Bombs (Bag #3), Bottle #1, Bottle #2, Bottle #3, Bottle #4

Items to Obtain

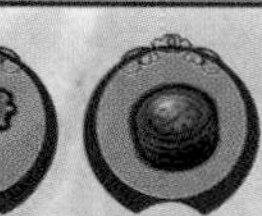

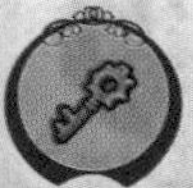
Small Key (1st), Compass, Small Key (2nd), Piece of Heart #44 (of 45), Small Key (3rd)

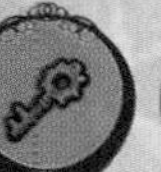
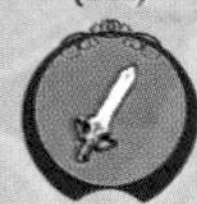

Dungeon Map, Small Key (4th), Master Sword (Light), Piece of Heart #45 (of 45), Small Key (5th)

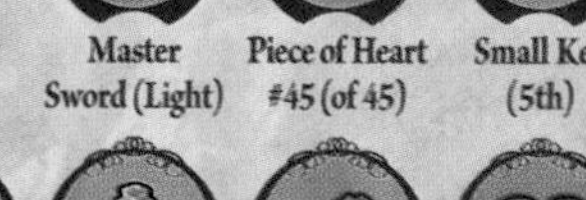

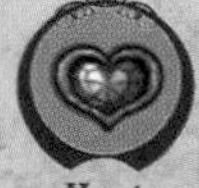
Big Key, Small Key (6th), Fairy in a Bottle, Small Key (7th), Heart Container #8

5 Gain Access to the Battlements Pg 416

6 Obtain the Big Key Pg 417

7 Gain Access to Zant's Throne Entrance Pg 418

8 Battle Usurper King Zant Pg 419

Characters Encountered

Midna

Twili People

Task 1: Obtain the First Sol Sphere

Chamber 1: Ethereal Plateau (1F)

Consider doing the following when you visit the twilight world:

- Bring multiple Bottles filled with a Blue Potion, Fairy Tears, or a Fairy.
- Position your Double Clawshot on ✚ so you can quickly activate it on and off.
- Have the Hero's Bow within easy access.
- Have the Magic Armor for the rare occasions you may need it; purchase it from Castle Town, if you haven't already.
- Completely fill your Giant Quiver and all Bomb Bags; you don't want to run out!

Tip

▲ Turn and face west to see a large gap between this plateau and the one at the area's far side. Return to this point later. There's a ramp ahead, but the door at the end is closed. For now, investigate the ramp to the east; this descends to a door, with a tall Twili standing alone. He flinches if you attack. Smash the pot to the door's left for arrows. Now open the door.

Chamber 2: East Wing: Lower Chamber

◄ Enter into a long lower chamber, and brandish your sword; there's a Twilit Baba and a Twilit Keese to fight in the entry area. Cut them down, head north to a second Twilit Baba, and hack into him. Defeat another Twilit Baba and Keese, then face a new foe!

Zant Mask

Threat Meter

Zant Masks roam the palace, guarding their master with a ranged ball of twilight energy. They have the ability to teleport short distances to flummox the unprepared. React by either blocking the energy and sending it back into the Zant Mask and stunning it, or dodging it completely and running in to slash and bash with your Master Sword. It only takes four or five good hits for the Zant Mask to implode.

A fearsome helm, floating in the twilight and firing energy balls at you. Fortunately, it can be countered and defeated easily.

◄ **Treasure Chest:** Stride down the ramp and engage the Zant Mask in combat. Don't stop until the Mask explodes, giving you a Rupee. If the Zant Mask disappears, it likely reappears and ambushes you. When you defeat the Mask, a chest appears in the alcove ahead. Open it to find a Small Key.

Treasure Chest #1: Small Key

Small Key
You got a **Small Key**! This opens a locked door, but only in this area.

Missing Links

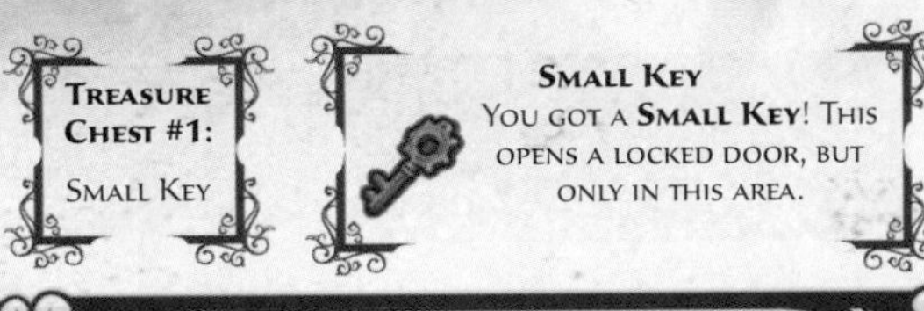

1. Pulverizing Pottery

There are some pots to destroy in this chamber's upper northern section; one contains a blue Rupee (5). Use the Clawshot medallions and land up here, then begin the shattering!

◄ Inspect the room; parts of the walls are made of a fog that contains shadow crystals. The power of Zant transforms you into a wolf if you leap through these walls. There are pots behind the southwest and southeast fog wall; one contains a blue Rupee (5), the other a yellow Rupee (10).

➤ The fog wall in the northeast is also of some interest; there's a Clawshot medallion at the far end above the upper ledge. However, you can't target it yet. Instead, leave the room via the locked door at the north end; open it with your Small Key.

Chamber 3: East Wing: Middle Fog Chamber

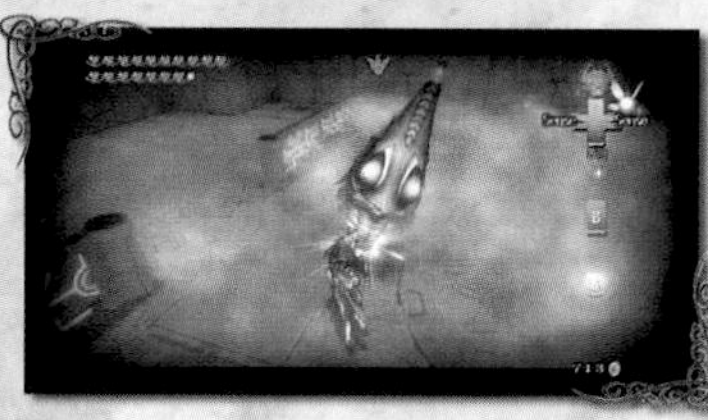

➤ Enter the next chamber and run directly into the fog. Turn on your sense view so you can see through the mist, and begin to attack the Zant Mask. Be ready to strike it a couple of times, and watch for it teleporting and reappearing. Also check the east side of the foggy area for pots; there's a yellow Rupee (10) in one.

➤ **Treasure Chest:** As soon as you defeat the Zant Mask, two chests appear in this room. Smash another pot in the southwest foggy area for arrows, and then move to the chest in the chamber's southwest corner. Execute a spin attack and stop the Twilit Vermin that fall from the ceiling. Open the chest and take the Compass.

Treasure Chest #2: Compass

Compass
You got the **Compass**! This handy tool will show you where to find objects hidden in this dungeon.

▲ **Treasure Chest:** Now that you have the Compass, you see that there are a few chests left to find. Two of them are in this room! Journey north through the fog, and open the second chest that appeared. There's another Small Key inside. Then use the medallion on the northwest corner wall to reach the exit door. Unlock it, and leave after you claim your final chest in this room.

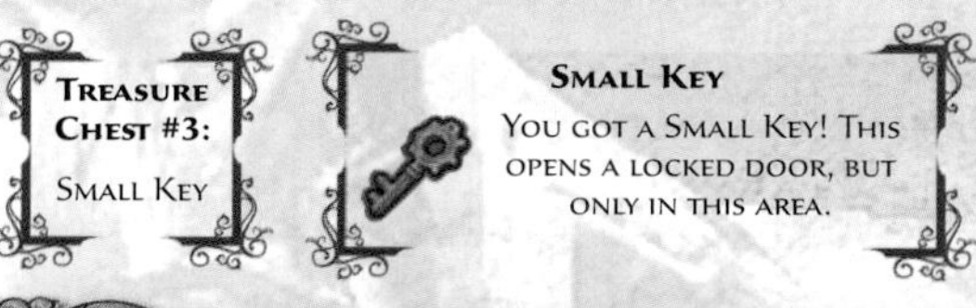

Treasure Chest #3: Small Key

Small Key
You got a Small Key! This opens a locked door, but only in this area.

▲ **Treasure Chest:** The final chest requires some cunning Clawshot maneuvers. First, shoot to the northwest medallion, and turn to look south. There's another medallion on the outer wall. Shoot to it, then to the ceiling, and drop down on the western ledge. Open the chest to find an orange Rupee (100). There is a yellow Rupee (10) plus Hearts in the pots on either side. Now exit this chamber.

Treasure Chest #4: Orange Rupee (100)

Chamber 4: Upper Chamber of Sol Light (East) (1F)

You enter a flat chamber with a strange hand clasping a white shining orb at the room's far end. As you step forward, an energy wall appears and an image of Zant blinks into existence, conjuring a ball of twilit energy and warping in dozens of Twilit Keese!

Enemies Encountered

Twilit Baba

Twilit Keese

Zant Mask

Twilit Vermin

Midna

Twili People

Phantom Zant

Threat Meter

Step 1: A spin takes too long to muster, so quickly back up or run into the cloud of Twilit Keese and begin to rapidly Z target, slice, and target the next, until you defeat them all. This is the first of Phantom Zant's summonings.

Step 2: As soon as you defeat the last Twilit Keese, quickly check the arena's edges, as Phantom Zant appears randomly. Stay in the middle, and as soon as he teleports a couple of times, try to Z target (turning using this lock-on works well), run in, and slice him. It takes three great spins to completely defeat him.

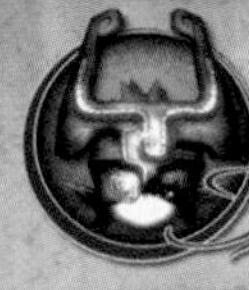

There are several pots on the sides of the arena, and they each contain a Heart if you need it.

Step 3: Phantom Zant will probably conjure the next swarm; this time they're Twilit Vermin. A spin attack rids you of most of them; then tackle the remaining ones quickly.

Step 4: Finally, Phantom Zant teleports around the chamber but always lands in the center at some point. Target with Z and tap the button constantly while rolling to cover the ground quickly, then roll in and attack Phantom Zant with a barrage of slices until he finally yields.

◄ When Phantom Zant is dispersed, avoid the cloud of shadow he leaves behind. Run to the chamber's north end. Midna appears and tells you that the shining Sphere is called a **Sol**. It is a true source of power, and Midna hopes you can take it to the entrance.

▲ Take a couple of swings at the pottery on either side of the hand holding the Sol. Then slice at the hand until it releases the Sol. Pick up the Sol and turn south; carry it toward the cloud of shadow. As the light reaches the cloud, the cloud disperses and the hand starts to glow....

Zant's Hand

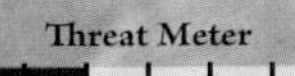
Threat Meter

Zant's Hand holds each of the Sol Spheres in this dungeon and they aren't that aggressive. They float toward the Sol incessantly and will attempt to steal it back, taking it to the pedestal you stole it from. Otherwise, stay away from the Zant's Hand while carrying the Sol, or you'll have to repeat your journey.

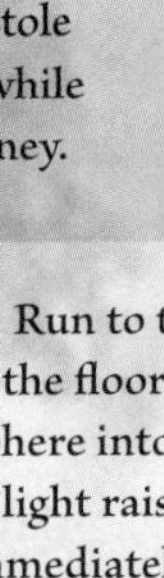

◄ Run to the circular groove in the floor and place the Sol Sphere into it. The power of light raises a set of steps; immediately run up them and execute a quick spin attack to defeat a small group of Twilit Vermin that appear to intercept you. Turn at the top of the steps, making sure you're on the solid ground, and Clawshot the Sphere out of the groove, before Zant's Hand can reach it. Exit back to Chamber 3.

If you're too slow, Zant's Hand grabs the Sol Sphere and deactivates the steps, floating back to the pedestal with the Sphere in its clutches. Bring out your Clawshot and grab it back! You must keep the Sphere in a groove or on your person at all times.

1

2

3

4

5
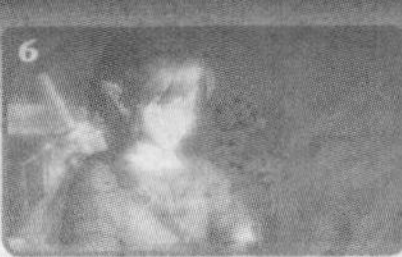
6

Task 2: Return the First Sol Sphere to the Plateau

Chamber 3: First Return to East Wing: Middle Fog Chamber

◄ Carrying the Sol Sphere, run into the middle of the next chamber. Zant's Hand is still chasing you and has warped into the room behind you. Ignore the Twilit Vermin on the ground and slot the Sphere into the floor. Then spend a couple of seconds slicing any Vermin that are attacking you.

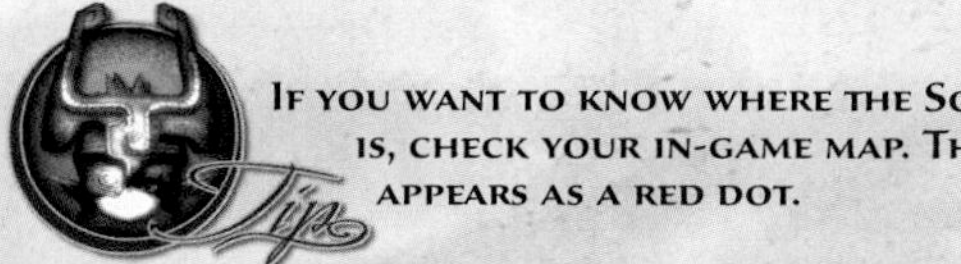

Tip: If you want to know where the Sol Sphere is, check your in-game map. The ball appears as a red dot.

▲ Run quickly up the L-shaped stairs the Sol has created until you're standing on the firm ground to the west. Even if Zant's Hand floats down and takes the Sphere, you can still grab it (as shown), but don't let it float too far north!

► Face south and run up the large stepped area. Throw the Sphere past the step that's too high to run up. At the high ledge, stop and drop the Sphere, and slice at the Vermin that have appeared. There's a red Rupee (20) in the corner pot. Then drop off the ledge, at the exit door, and head through to Chamber 2.

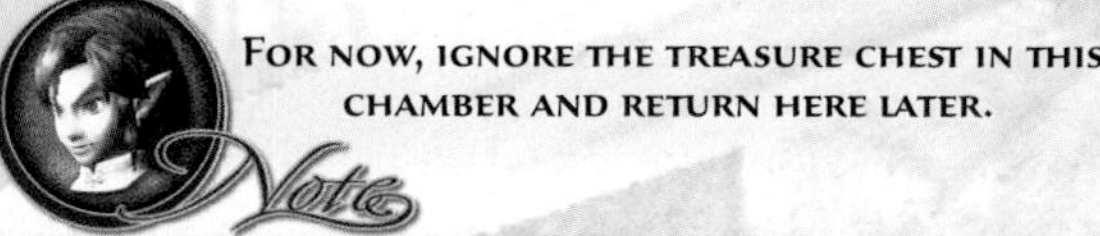

Note: For now, ignore the treasure chest in this chamber and return here later.

Chamber 2: First Return to East Wing: Lower Chamber

► **Treasure Chest**: Zant's Hand is still coming! Run around the Twilit Babas and Keese, ignore the Vermin, and head up the ramped area until you reach the northeast corner where the shadow fog plumes. The Sol Sphere parts the cloud. Once you're through the cloud, drop the Sphere and quickly Clawshot to the ledge containing the chest. Open the chest. The prize is worth the detour!

Treasure Chest #5: Piece of Heart #44

Piece of Heart
You got a **Piece of Heart**! Collect **one more** for another full Heart Container. Piece of Heart #44 of 45.

Now, head south, up the sloping ramp to the exit door. Although there are enemies to tackle, avoiding them is easier; if they waylay you while fighting them, Zant's Hand can take the Sol Sphere. Exit back to Chamber 1.

Chamber 1: First Return to Ethereal Plateau

► Pass the Long Twili on the way back to the central plateau, and an amazing transformation occurs! The Twili loses height and reverts back to his normal state. Move to the circular groove in the plateau's middle and place the Sol Sphere. A light platform is conjured to the west.

Twili:

One of the Twilit Realm's inhabitants is this long fellow. Once you return with the first Sol Sphere, he shrinks to a third of his shadow size and becomes a normal inhabitant of the palace.

◄ Move to the light platform, and ride it across the gap to the western area you couldn't reach earlier. Once the platform lands, run past the long Twili and open the door.

Enemies Encountered

Phantom Zant

Twilit Keese

Twilit Vermin

Zant's Hand

Characters Encountered

Midna

Twili People

Task 3: Obtain the Second Sol Sphere

Chamber 5: West Wing: Lower Chamber

➤ Enter another long lower chamber, this time on the palace's opposite side. Deal with the Twilit Keeses and then drop to the lower ground. Look up to the sides of the chamber, and aim a Clawshot at the medallion and another at the medallion on the ceiling. Lower yourself down to a light platform you can ride.

➤ Be sure you land on the platform, as it begins to move before you're standing on it. Ride the platform to this platform with two dark Spheres on either side. They don't light up when you strike them, so concentrate on bouncing an energy ball back at a Zant Mask up ahead. He disappears. Now quickly leap across the light platforms.

➤ **Treasure Chest**: The Zant Mask will likely appear again, so dodge his attacks and attempt to land on the ledge opposite the light platforms. Slash the Mask so it departs temporarily, and then inspect the chest it was guarding. There's a purple Rupee (50) in it for you.

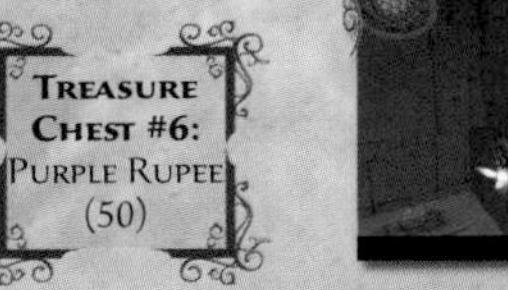

Treasure Chest #6: Purple Rupee (50)

➤ **Treasure Chest**: Now wait for the Zant Mask to appear on this upper ledge, and defeat it. You'll know when you succeed because another chest appears, in the corner opposite the one where you found the previous chest. Grab the Small Key in here. Now leave via the door to the north, using the Small Key to unlock the door.

Treasure Chest #7: Small Key

Small Key
You got a Small Key! This opens a locked door, but only in this area.

Note: There are two more chests in this chamber, but wait until you have a more powerful way to part the clouds of shadow before attempting to open them.

Chamber 6: West Wing: Middle Fog Chamber

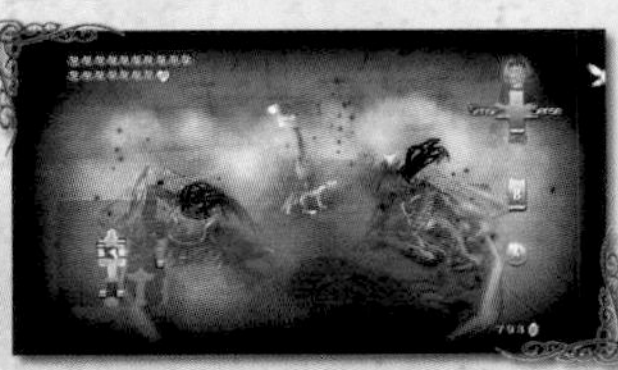

➤ Enter this fog-filled chamber, and you're immediately attacked by two Twilit Messengers. If you defeat them, they rise again, indicating there's a third to destroy. Run into the shadow cloud so you turn into wolf form, then defeat one of the three Messengers. Finally, use Midna's area attack to catch the second and third Messengers (and a Twilit Keese if he gets in your way).

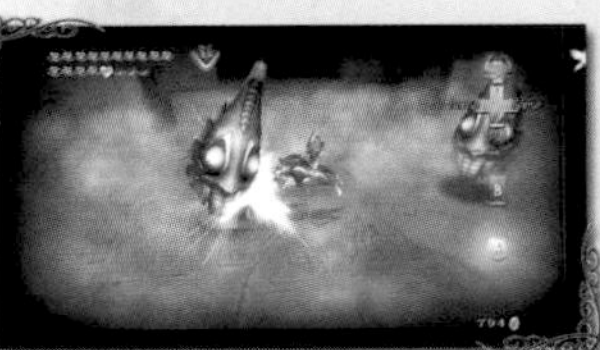

➤ Stay in wolf form and begin a long combat with three Zant Masks. Stay in the fog with your sense view on, and leap to bash each of the Masks, dodging their energy balls easily.

➤ **Treasure Chest**: After you defeat all the Zant Masks, a chest appears, but don't head for it just yet. Instead, transform into Link, and aim at the medallion in the chamber's northwest corner. Then shoot another Clawshot to the medallion on the ceiling. Finally, look east to this alcove, and Clawshot to this small chest. A purple Rupee (50) awaits. You can optionally Clawshot to the alcove directly opposite, but there's only an empty pot here.

Treasure Chest #8: Purple Rupee (50)

➤ **Treasure Chest**: Continue your high-flying plans by Clawshooting to the middle of the ceiling and looking east. The large ledge contains a chest. Propel yourself above it, drop down, smash the pot for arrows, slay the Twilit Keese, and then take the Dungeon Map from the chest.

Treasure Chest #9: Dungeon Map

Dungeon Map
You got the **Dungeon Map**!

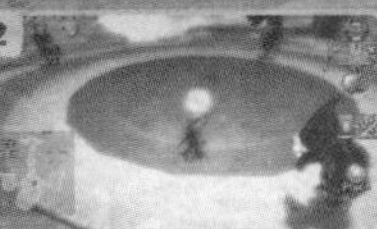
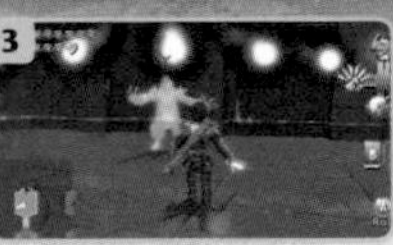

➤ **Treasure Chest:** Keep the Clawshot on hand, and propel yourself back to the middle of the ceiling. Search for the alcove in the chamber's western section. A small chest awaits you here. Drop in and open it.

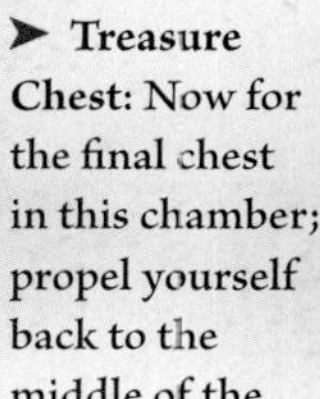

Treasure Chest #10: Purple Rupee (50)

➤ **Treasure Chest:** Now for the final chest in this chamber; propel yourself back to the middle of the ceiling, spin around to face west, and Clawshoot again, dropping to the ledge to get your final chest. The pots don't hold anything, but the chest gets you into the next chamber.

Treasure Chest #11: Small Key

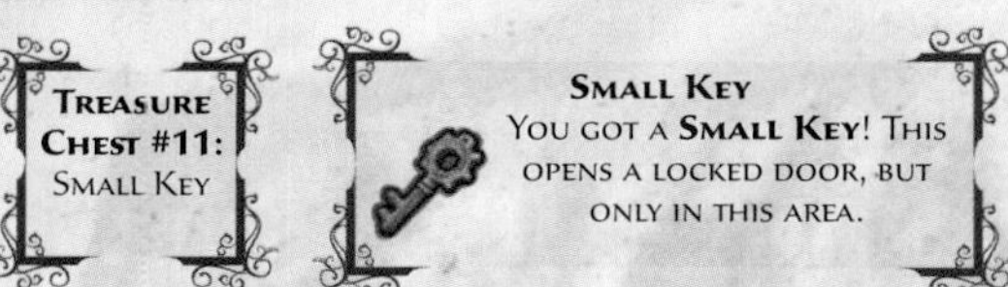

Small Key
You got a **Small Key**! This opens a locked door, but only in this area.

Missing Links

1. Pulverizing Pottery

You may be striking the pots near the chests, but there are certain alcoves that contain pots that have something special for you; smash the one in the southeast alcove for a red Rupee (20).

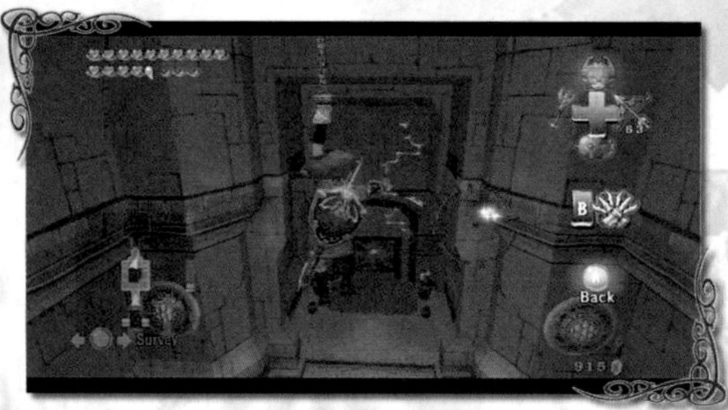

▲ Time to leave! To avoid touching the fog below, swing from the medallions: Aim at the ceiling and head north, dropping down via medallions to the ledge. Before unlocking the door and leaving, get another red Rupee (20) from a pot near the door.

Chamber 7: Upper Chamber of Sol Light (West) (1F)

You walk into another chamber with a glowing Sol Sphere at the far end. As you walk to the Sphere, an energy wall forms. You approach cautiously and realize at the last moment that Phantom Zant has appeared behind you! You thrust but miss, and dark denizens are summoned....

Phantom Zant

Threat Meter

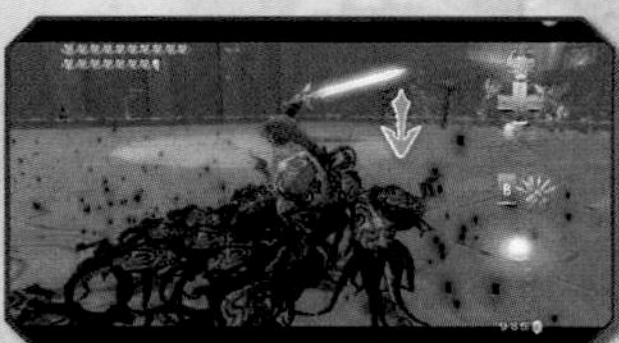

Step 1: Phantom Zant has appeared again, and this time he's summoned a dozen Twilit Babas to stop you. Begin to spin attack all the ones near you as Phantom Zant teleports around the arena. Don't chase him; simply slash him if he appears near you. Stay in the middle and you can strike him a couple of times.

Step 2: Phantom Zant removes the Twilit Babas you don't defeat, so don't bother defeating them all; instead, run to the perimeter and collect Hearts from the pots, and then return to the arena's middle. Wait for a dozen Twilit Vermin to descend, and immediately execute a spin attack before mopping up the rest.

Step 3: Repeat Step 1 again, dealing with another load of Twilit Babas. After these have disappeared, Phantom Zant begins his own attack pattern. Keep looking for him and stay in the middle. When he stops for longer than a second and summons a large energy ball that begins to split into a group of energy balls, roll or run under the attack. Then hit him with a spin or a constant barrage of swipes. He may vanish and attempt the energy-ball attack again; repeat the takedown tactic, and Phantom Zant is vanquished again!

➤ Avoid the remaining shadow cloud and smash the pots on either side of the Sol Sphere at the chamber's north end. There are Hearts and a blue Rupee (5) to bag. Slap the hand with your sword, and take the Sphere to the room's middle. Drop it into the groove as you're attacked by Twilit Vermin and a Messenger. Then run up the stairs, grab the Sphere with your Clawshot, and flee to the southern door.

Enemies Encountered

Twilit Keese

Zant Mask

Twilit Messenger

Phantom Zant

Twilit Baba

Twilit Vermin

Task #3
Obtain the Second Sol Sphere

Midna

Twili People

Task 4: Return the Second Sol Sphere to the Plateau

Chamber 6: First Return to West Wing: Middle Fog Chamber

➤ Head back into this foggy chamber and run to the middle of the room with the Sphere. Place it on the ground, and deliver some slashes to the Twilit Keese and Messenger. Don't bother finishing them off; that Hand is on its way! Drop the Sphere in the groove again, then run and stand on the steps before they ascend too high for you to reach, and climb to the top. As soon as you're on the high southern ledge, Clawshot the Sphere and leave via the southern door.

Chamber 5: First Return to West Wing: Lower Chamber

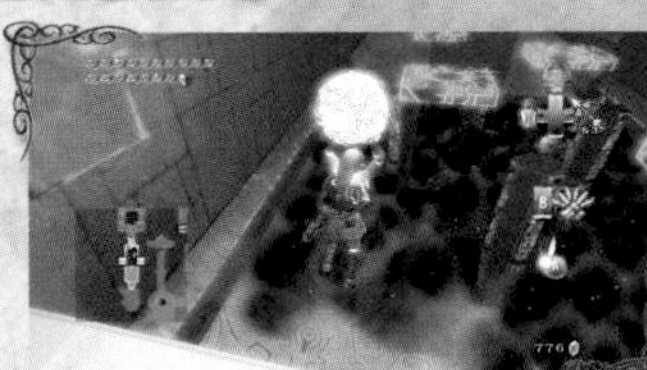

➤ You appear at the lower chamber's northern ledge, but there's no way to reach the floating light platforms ahead. Instead, you must jump into the shadow cloud, ignoring the pots for the moment, and then turn around. Look for the dark globe at the base of the north wall, and stand by it. The light from the Sphere brightens the globe into a white beacon, and two more light platforms appear on either side of it. Ride them up, face south, and carefully leap to the light platforms to escape.

➤ At the south end of the light platform route, don't drop by the two globes, as you'll have to retrace your steps. Instead, wait until the globes shine, creating a new light platform, and ride this to the exit.

Chamber 1: Second Return to Ethereal Plateau

➤ Stand on the light platform. Ride it to the circular plateau, and run around the circumference. You can now change the remaining Twili to their normal forms, as both the Spheres give off considerable light. Then place the second Sphere into the circular groove. Light floods into the blade of the Master Sword. Now inspect the Twili you saved from the shadows!

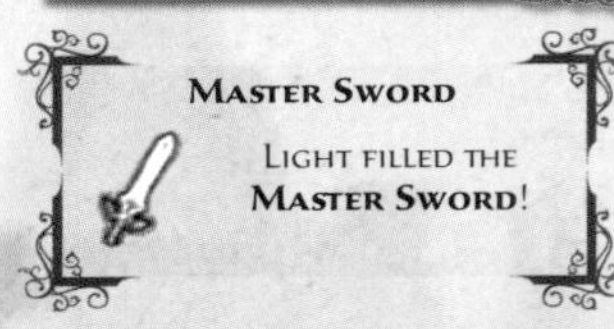

Master Sword

Light filled the Master Sword!

Master Sword of Light

The goddesses have smiled upon you, young Link! The power of the Sol is now imbued into your weapon. This means you can strike any of the globes so they shine brightly, and any shadow clouds will disperse with your slashes.

Task 5: Gain Access to the Battlements

Chamber 5: Second Return to West Wing: Lower Chamber, to Chamber 6

➤ **Treasure Chest**: Now that the Master Sword is filled with light, you can return to the palace's west wing and claim the last two chests on this floor. When you've finished slashing the shadow clouds and picking up Rupees and Hearts from the pottery, stand on this light platform after clearing the fog.

➤ As the platform reaches a small alcove containing a clearly visible chest, run and leap onto the ledge before the platform moves south. Open the chest immediately, as you've reached the climax to your Heart Piece collection!

Note: You've now collected every Piece of Heart in Hyrule and beyond! The only remaining Heart-related item is the Container you'll receive at the end of this dungeon. Congratulations!

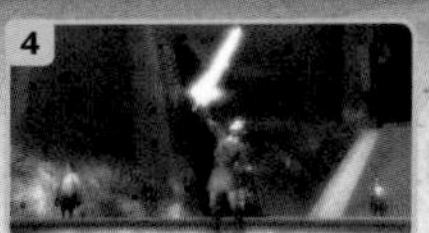

Treasure Chest #12: Piece of Heart #45

Piece of Heart
You got a **Piece of Heart**! You collected **five pieces** and formed a new Heart Container! Piece of Heart #45 of 45

Treasure Chest: Now stand on the platform on the opposite side of the foggy lower ground, and rise to another alcove on the east side. Leap to the chest, and acquire a purple Rupee (50). When you're ready to return, use a Clawshot and summon a platform using the two dark globes.

Treasure Chest #13: Purple Rupee (50)

Chamber 1: Third Return to Ethereal Plateau (1F to 2F)

➤ You're now ready to ascend the palace tower, so head north up the central ramp. Ignore the two pots and the Twili, and concentrate on slicing at three waiting Twilit Kargaroks before they take flight. After you defeat them, part the vertical cloud with your sword and leap across to the door. There's another Kargarok sitting to your right; smash him and the pots near the door (there are arrows inside one of them).

Tip: Spin attacks with your sword temporarily push back the clouds of shadow, allowing you to pass them without transforming into a wolf. Be warned, though: they reappear, so keep swinging!

Chamber 8: South Palace Tower (2F to 3F)

◄ Enter the large chamber and immediately use your sword to sweep the shadow cloud back. Take down the Twilit Keese and Vermin that head out to meet you. Clear the room of pots and reach the steps at the north side. There are two Sol Spheres here, so slay the Twilit Baba, take the first one to the cloud's edge, part the cloud with your sword, pick up the Sphere, and place it in the circular groove. Fend off the Vermin attack, then repeat this on the other side with the second Sphere. Climb the steps that form.

◄ At the top of the steps, smash some pots, then whack the dark globe until a light platform appears just behind it. Ride this to the ledge on the chamber's west side, tackling the Twilit Keese on the way; then drop down and slash the Twilit Baba. You now have a difficult battle with four Zant Masks! Stay on this ledge, block the energy balls they spit, run back and forth to summon them, and spin attack; the light from your sword helps defeat them.

➤ **Treasure Chest:** Make sure all four Zant Masks fall, as only then will a chest appear. Open it for a Small Key, then strike the three dark globes with a spin attack, and ride the appearing light platform to the exit door. As you travel, optionally target incoming Twilit Keese with arrows, then spin as six ambush you from above when you step off. You're showered with Hearts!

Treasure Chest #14: Small Key

Small Key
You got a **Small Key**! This opens a locked door, but only in this area.

Task 6: Obtain the Big Key

Chamber 9: Palace Battlements (3F)

◄ Step onto the palace battlements, where you meet a flock of Twilit Kargaroks. Run east to the balcony, and slash with your sword; bring down a Messenger (you don't need to defeat more than one), and then work on the Twilit Kargaroks. The pottery contains only arrows, no Hearts. Run the battlements, looking for them resting on the parapets; then Z target and slash them. Be patient, and you'll eventually slice all six of them.

◄ Treasure Chest: Now to find the treasure chest that's hidden at the top of a series of medallion hooks. Turn west, and run directly at the wall of shadow cloud, parting it with your sword and leaping into the narrow ledge behind. Defeat the sitting Twilit Kargaroks, then look up for a medallion. Use your Clawshot and work your way from north to south, bounding up the wall until you reach this ledge.

Treasure Chest #15: Big Key

Big Key
You got the **Big Key**! Use it to gain access to the lair of this dungeon's boss.

Midna

➤ You must now attempt to leave the battlements, but a locked door that requires a Small Key blocks your way. Run east, to the battlement platform's edge, and whack the dark globes. Ride the light platform to this southern ledge, leaping off to defeat the Zant Mask. This summons more Masks back on the battlements.

➤ **Treasure Chest:** Use the globes on the ledge to summon the light platform back to the main battlements, where three other Zant Masks have arrived. Engage them all. When the last one tastes the light, a treasure chest appears to the north. Open it up and take the Small Key. Use it to open the door in the room's northwest corner.

Treasure Chest #16: Small Key

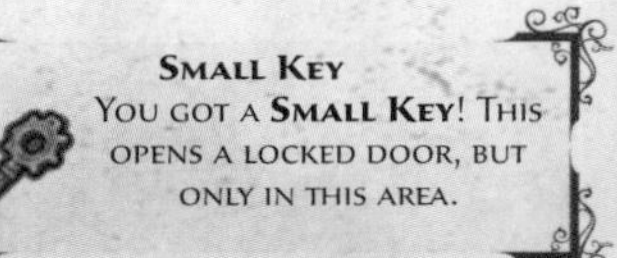
Small Key
You got a **Small Key**! This opens a locked door, but only in this area.

Task 7: Gain Access to Zant's Throne Entrance

Chamber 10: North Palace Tower (3F to 4F)

➤ Enter the North Palace Tower, into a large and flat-floored chamber. Some pottery here rewards green Rupees (1) and Hearts. Walk toward the shadow cloud, and an energy wall forms, trapping you with four Twilit Messengers. Let them surround you, then bring out the sword in a large spin attack. You can defeat them in seconds. Slash back the cloud, summon the light platform from the four globes, and ride it up. Now comes a puzzle....

➤ Ride this platform up, facing east as you do. When you pass above this next platform, leap onto it. Ride it east, then leap to the right platform waiting for you. This travels to a small ledge where a single pot houses a Fairy. Grab this if you need it. Take the left platform if you don't.

Note: This fairy should be caught in a Bottle and only appears if you don't already have a Fairy or other major energy-increasing items. Don't be surprised if this pot is empty!

Fairy
You caught a **Fairy** in a Bottle! When you fall in combat, this faithful friend gives you Hearts.

➤ Take the left platform, and it rises up to a small ledge containing a Twilit Baba. Jump off and defeat it, then leap to the adjacent light platform and ride it up, then west toward three solid platforms and an appearing Zant Mask. As you pass from right to left, Clawshot to the medallion on the wall behind the Mask, drop down and swipe it, then leap to the corner pot for a load of Hearts.

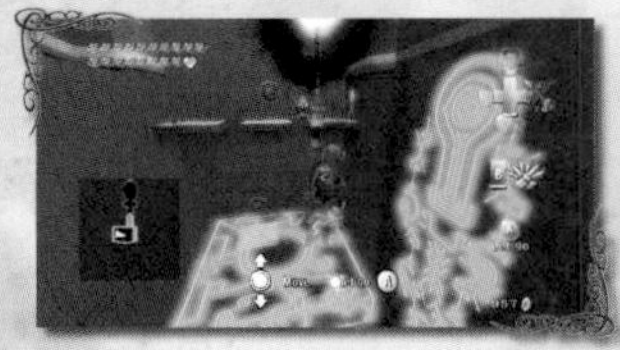

➤ **Treasure Chest:** You're almost at the top, so look for a medallion on the south wall and shoot it; then shoot the medallion on the ceiling and hang from it, avoiding a Zant Mask's energy ball. Move down with ⚲ and dodge, then drop onto the moving light platform. Ride it to the opposite side, and Clawshot to the medallion in the middle of the wall.

A simple slice deals with the Mask, after which a chest appears. Secure the Small Key from it, then move back to the previous stone ledge. A new light platform has appeared; it takes you to the fourth floor and to the locked door you now have a key for.

Treasure Chest #17: Small Key

Small Key
You got a **Small Key**! This opens a locked door, but only in this area.

Chamber 11: Throne Entrance (4F)

➤ Enter the long entrance to the throne room, and use your sword on three Twilit Messengers. The pottery to this side yields green Rupees (1). Enter the cloudy section and an energy wall descends. Two waves of four Twilit Messengers appear; spin attack to defeat each wave, until the wall recedes. Smash the pottery on each side of the door (one has a green Rupee [1], the other a red Rupee [20]), then unlock it with the Big Key; you're about to face the King of Shadows!

1 
2 
3 
4 
5 
6 

Task 8: Battle Usurper King Zant

Chamber 12: Boss Battle! Usurper King Zant (4F)

Zant:

Once in the Twili king's entourage, Zant was furious that Midna's father (the king) didn't appoint him to succeed. This resentment against the royal clan of the Twilit Kingdom grew until a malevolent spirit bestowed a magical power to Zant. He transformed Midna into an impish figure and began to force the kingdom to bend to his—and Ganondorf's—will.

Enemies Encountered

Zant Mask

Twilit Messenger

Zant

Zant

Threat Meter

Step 1: Zant begins combat immediately, transporting you back to the Forest Temple and beginning to rain energy bolts down on you. There are Hearts in the pottery behind you. The takedown is similar to Twilit Diababa's: sidestep or block the bolts, bring out your **Gale Boomerang**, and Z target Zant, then throw it. Zant bounces across to the grass. Run to him, and slice him with your sword. Repeat this.

Step 2: Zant transports you both to the Goron Mines and places you on the metallic platform where you fought Dangoro. Block or sidestep the energy bolts, and place the **Iron Boots** on when Zant pounds the floor. Just after he finishes, take off the boots, and charge him; Z target and stay in the middle. He may disappear several times; wait until he slumps with exhaustion, then run and strike.

Step 3: Quickly don the **Zora Armor** as you appear deep in Lakebed Temple. Place your **Iron Boots** on so you can attack, block the energy bolts, then **Clawshot** Zant out of his giant stone head and into a barrage of your sword strikes. He disappears, and four giant Zant Masks rumble out of the ground. Zant randomly appears in one, so stay between two Masks and wait until the mouth opens from either of them. Then Clawshot him into close combat and slice!

Step 4: Your next encounter is in the Forest Temple, where you fought Ook the Baboon. Zant fires off yet more energy bolts. Change to your **Hero's Clothes.** This is a good time to stock up on Hearts from pots around the sides of this cavern. Wait until Zant stands on a totem pole for a moment, then roll into it twice, knocking him off. Slice him.

Step 5: Your fifth confrontation takes place in Yeta's bedroom, which is encased in ice. Zant is in a gigantic form, so watch his reflection in the ice, roll as he descends, and quickly bring out the **Ball and Chain** and Z target either foot as he attempts to stamp on it. A hit causes him to hop around clutching his stubbed toe, and he shrinks to the size of a Bomskit! Target Z and slice him with your sword. Repeat this.

Step 6: Zant now transports you to a final fight outside the Castle Town south entrance. He begins by transforming his arms into large blades and waddles forward, slicing at you. Block this with your shield, and try to push him back; then roll away while Z targeting, and slash and spin attack as he teleports around you.

Step 7: Once you've dished enough punishment, Zant begins a really nasty spin attack that saps energy and knocks you off your feet. Retaliate by placing your **Iron Boots** on so he can't push you back, and block the entire spin. As Zant slows, or stops completely, he'll either teleport or stop for a second. This is the time to execute a vicious spin attack of your own! Keep this technique going until you deliver Zant a final blow!

Midna thinks she can harness this power to aid you and restore Princess Zelda after what she gave to help Midna. Midna opens a warp portal out of the throne room. Take your **final Heart Container**, and then leave this place. Hyrule Castle must be breached!

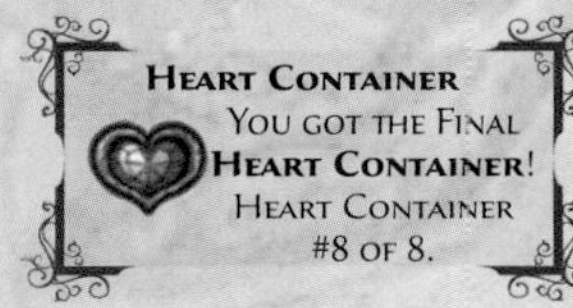

Heart Container
You got the final Heart Container! Heart Container #8 of 8.

Fused Shadows
You got the Fused Shadows! Midna's power is now incredible!

7

8

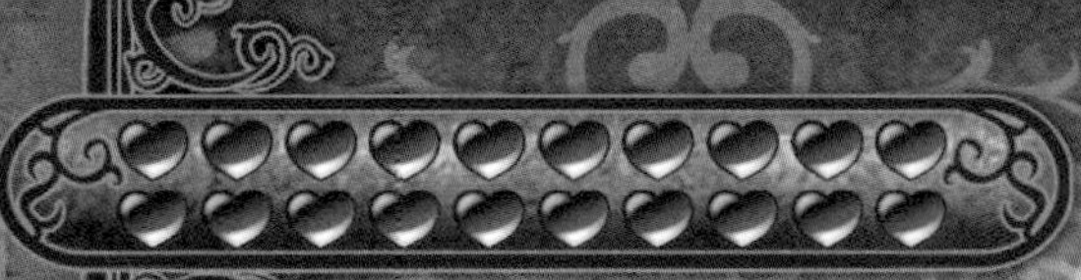

Dungeon 9: Hyrule Castle

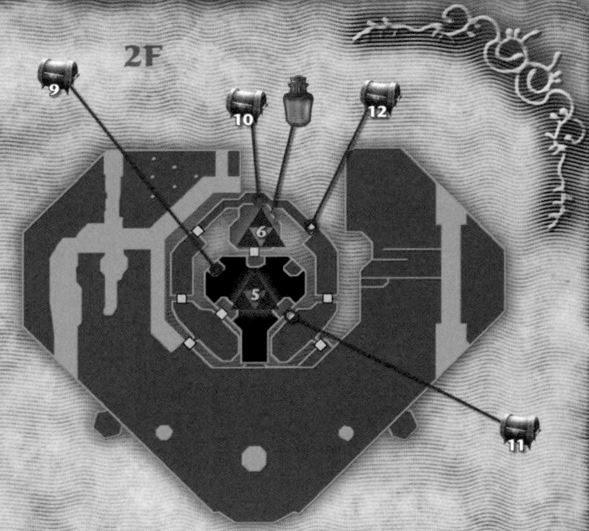

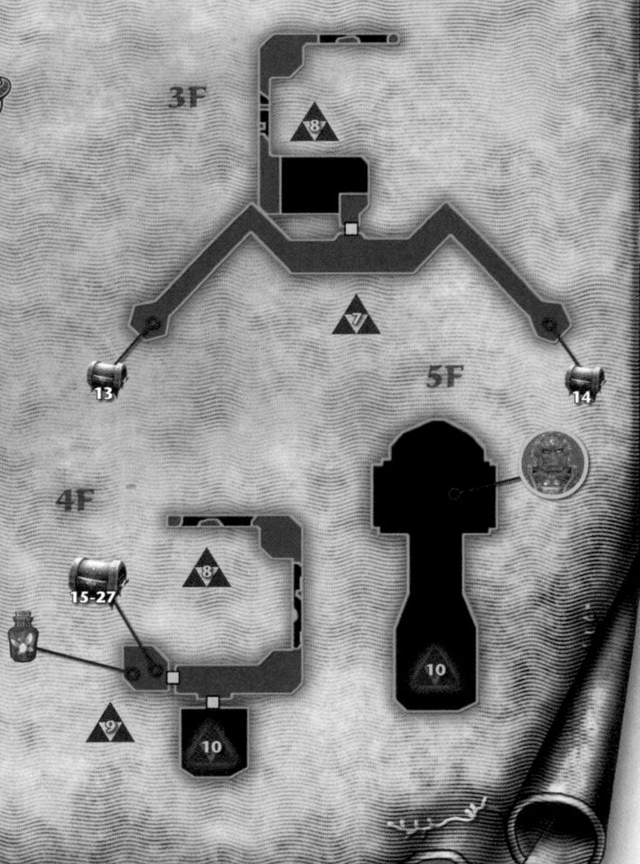

Legend

Room Legend

1 Southern Grounds (1F)
2 Western Grounds (1F)
3 Hyrule Castle Graveyard (1F)
4 Eastern Grounds (1F)
5 Grand Chandelier Hallway (1F to 2F)
6 Connecting Corridors (2F)
7 Castle Battlements (3F)
8 Collapsing Chamber and Staircases (3F to 4F)
9 Castle Hyrule Treasure Room
10 Ganon's Inner Sanctum (4F to 5F)

Number of Treasure Chests: 27

1 Dungeon Map
2 Yellow Rupee (10)
3 Orange Rupee (100)
4 Red Rupee (20)
5 Green Rupee (1)
6 Small Key (1st)
7 Red Rupee (20)
8 Red Rupee (20)
9 Compass
10 Purple Rupee (50)
11 Purple Rupee (50)
12 Silver Rupee (200)
13 Small Key (3rd)
14 Big Key
15 Purple Rupee (50)
16 Bomblings (10)
17 Silver Rupee (200)
18 Seeds (50)
19 Orange Rupee (100)
20 Blue Rupee (5)
21 Yellow Rupee (10)
22 Red Rupee (20)
23 Water Bombs (15)
24 Arrows (20)
25 Bombs (20)
26 Green Rupee (1)
27 Arrows (30)

Items

Lantern Oil Bowl
Fairy

Characters

King Bulbin
Gannondorf

1 Solve the Riddle of the Graveyard

2 Defeat King Bulblin in Final Combat

3 Exit to the Battlements

4 Traverse Collapsing Chamber & Staircases

Dungeon Denizens

Characters

Midna

Rusl

Auru

Ashei

Shad

Zelda

Enemies

Kargarok

Bokoblin

Bulblin Archer

Bullbo

Stalkin

Stalfos

Keese

Rat

Lizalfos

Lizalfos ("Skull-face")

Dynafols

Aeralfos

Darknut

Bosses

Mid Boss: King Bulblin

Big Boss: Ganondorf

A Link to the Present

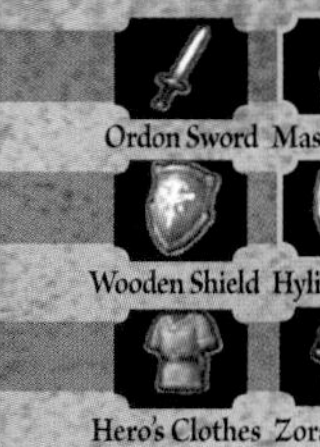
Ordon Sword, Master Sword

Wooden Shield, Hylian Shield

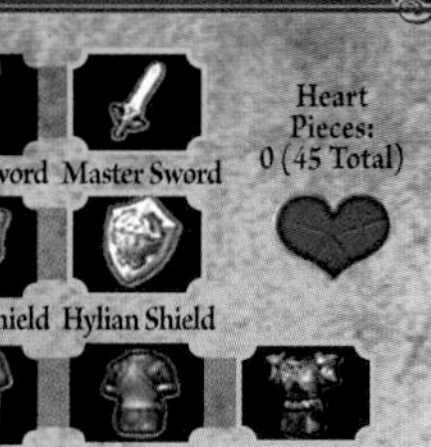
Heart Pieces: 0 (45 Total)

Hero's Clothes, Zora Armor, Magic Armor

Giant Wallet, Giant Quiver

Golden Bugs: 24 (of 24), Hidden Skills: 7 (of 7)

Medicine Scent, Poe Souls 60 (of 60)

Fish Journal, Letters 16 (of 16)

Fused Shadows

Items Already Acquired

Master Sword (Light)

Double Clawshot

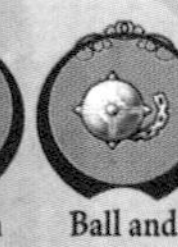
Dominion Rod

Ball and Chain

Spinner

Hero's Bow

Iron Boots

Gale Boomerang

Lantern

Slingshot

Fishing Rod

Hawkeye

Bombs (Bag #1)

Bombs (Bag #2)

Bombs (Bag #3)

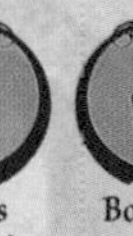
Bottle #1

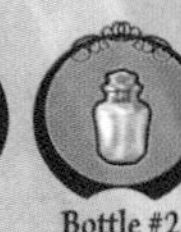
Bottle #2

Bottle #3

Bottle #4

Items to Obtain

Dungeon Map

Lantern Oil

Small Key (1st)

Small Key (2nd)

Compass

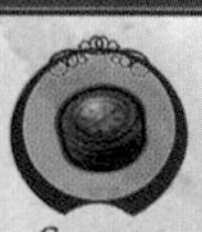

Lantern Oil

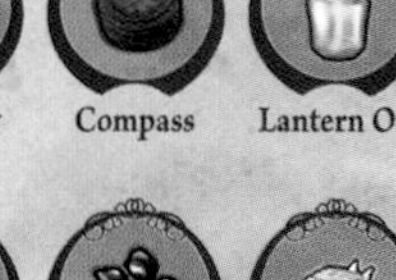

Small Key (3rd)

Big Key

Fairy in a Bottle

Bomblings (10)

Seeds (50)

Water Bombs (15)

Arrows (20)

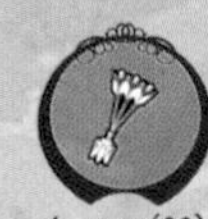
Bombs (20)

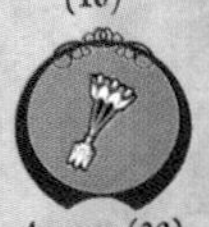
Arrows (30)

Fairy in a Bottle

5 — Ransack the Castle's Treasure Trove pg 428

6 — Prepare for Final Combat! pg 428

Characters Encountered

Midna

Hyrule Castle: Overview

The time has come to halt the evil thief, puppet master, and tyrant known as Ganondorf once and for all! He holds the sway of power from an upper chamber—Zelda's throne room in fact—and you must journey to this tightly guarded area. Once Midna reveals the true power of her ancestors, you can finally enter Hyrule Castle of your own free will, and wander the massive grounds locating chests, puzzles, keys, and an old fiend for one more Bulblin battle! Once you've gathered all the Small Keys outside, head into the castle, where the toughest foes you've faced in your journeys have been summoned by Ganondorf to do battle in arenas. In between your swordplay, raid the castle's many chests before heading up the central tower, optionally opening a treasure trove, and finally facing your final foe for the ultimate confrontation!

Task 1: Solve the Riddle of the Graveyard

Before you visit Hyrule Castle, make sure you have:

- Brought multiple Bottles filled with a Blue Potion, Fairy Tears, or a Fairy.
- Placed your Double Clawshot on ✚ so you can activate it on and off quickly.
- The Hero's Bow within easy access.
- The Magic Armor for rare occasions you may need it; purchase it from Castle Town.
- Completely filled your Giant Quiver, and all Bomb Bags; you don't want to run out!
- Completed every single optional quest contained in the previous chapters (there's no turning back now).

Tip

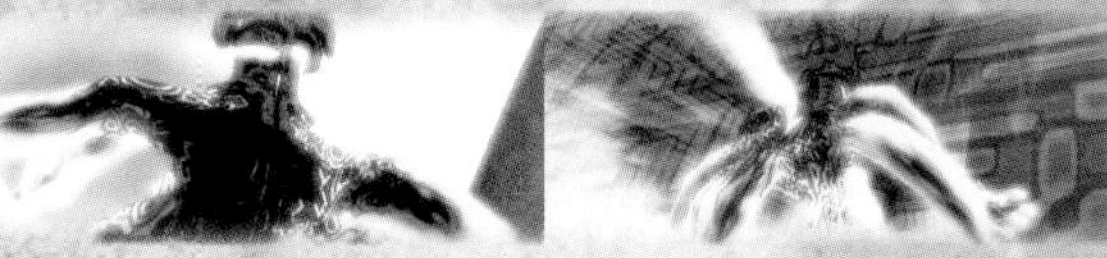

You arrive at the castle gates. The force field is present. Midna floats away, and reappears as a gigantic force of destruction, plunging a shard of light into the field! You see a brilliant flash of white light, and Midna falls into your arms. The castle is accessible!

Chamber 1: Southern Grounds (1F)

➤ Enter the huge southern courtyard of the castle grounds, and quickly investigate the area. Of particular interest are some Bokoblins standing at the far northwestern end. Fend off a Kargarok or two, and head to the Bokoblins. An energy field appears, and you must face four waves of Bokoblins. Fortunately, you can easily tackle them with sword strikes and your faithful spin attack. After the fight, investigate a couple of the nearby barrels for Hearts if you need them.

◀ Proceed eastward, checking the imposing front steps and north door (which is locked), and smashing some crates and barrels for arrows and Hearts. Then move to the far northeastern part of the courtyard, where a similar battle occurs. Defeat more Bokoblins and a couple of wayward Kargaroks in an energy wall. When you're finished, inspect a few more barrels for arrows and a Heart, then depart via the northwest door.

Chamber 2: Western Grounds (1F)

➤ This leads to a second, just-as-imposing courtyard. Stand at the door, wait for a Bokoblin to saunter in to attack you, and drop it with your sword. Remain where you are, and peer toward the cluster of barricades and three rickety towers ahead. Bring out the **Hero's Bow** and shoot each of the three Bulblin Archers standing atop them. Then draw your sword, walk forward, and finish a second Bokoblin near the first tower. Blast some explosive barrels at the foot of this tower to clear the area.

➤ Once the Bulblin and Bokoblin welcoming committee is defeated, search this area thoroughly. Shoot the explosive barrels from a distance, and optionally destroy barricades with your Ball and Chain. However, at the north end of this section of grounds are a couple of Bullbos, standing near the inner wall, and one of them is perfect for a bit of demolition.

◀ Begin a rampage through this area, smashing as many wooden structures as you wish, but be sure you turn west, and ram through to the outer corridor, shown here. Head north, to this rickety tower, and bash through it. Ahead are two more Bulblin Archers standing atop towers. Either ram them, or shoot them from afar. Then gallop forward until you reach the northern inner courtyard in these grounds.

➤ You're looking for a gap in the wall leading to a grassy area with six pillars, each with a wind fan atop it. They seem to be positioned in a triangular pattern. Ignore them for the moment, and instead run through them to this gate. Unfortunately, it is sealed. However, there's something on the ground obscured by leaves. Bring out your Gale Boomerang and blow the leaves away; there's the symbol of the Triforce, with a green "Z" through it!

➤ Back up, face the gate, and target the front, middle left, middle right, and back middle pillars, in that order, with your Gale Boomerang. Launch it, the fans spin, and the gate opens!

➤ Treasure Chest: Run forward, through the wooden barred gate that rumbles open, and step into a relatively small stone room. In front of you is a chest. Pry it open, and take the Dungeon Map inside! Then smash the nearby barrels for a blue Rupee (5), and climb the ladder in this room.

Note: If you sniffed around outside, you'd find a dig spot with leaves near the wind pillars. Ignore it for the moment and come back to it later.

Treasure Chest #1: Dungeon Map

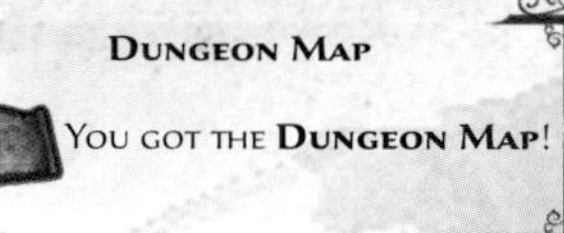

Dungeon Map

You got the **Dungeon Map**!

➤ **Treasure Chest**: At the top of the ladder, you find yourself on the top of the inner wall. You can look out at the grounds where you rampaged with the Bullbo, then run south, following the wall to the end, where another chest awaits your pilfering! The reward is less than impressive!

Treasure Chest #2: Yellow Rupee (10)

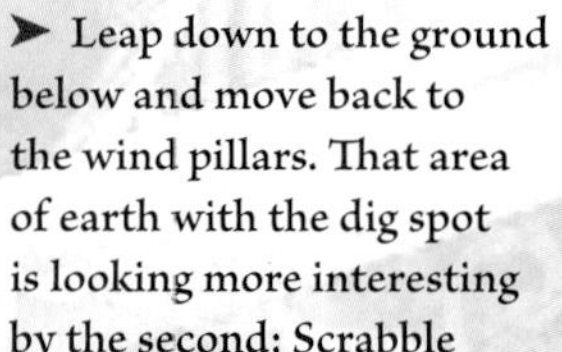

➤ Leap down to the ground below and move back to the wind pillars. That area of earth with the dig spot is looking more interesting by the second: Scrabble down there, and you appear in the adjacent cemetery.

Chamber 3: Hyrule Castle Graveyard (1F)

Enemies Encountered

Bokoblin

Bulblin Archer

Kargarok

Stalkin

Stalfos

➤ The spirits are restless in this place! Once you've emerged from your dig spot, you can begin to run around this eerie place, but stop and look east as soon as you enter the area. You're startled as you sense three ghostly soldier spirits standing on this hallowed ground. Watch them closely; they're pointing to the south wall.

➤ Progress a little farther north, and you're accosted by a small group of Stalkins who emerge from the earth to thwart you. Spin attacks crumple them in seconds. Your progression north is stopped as a Stalfos rises from the ground, and you cannot defeat it in wolf form, so change into Link. Bring the Bomb Arrows out, and blast it! It seemed to be guarding a small chamber with an unlit torch on either side.

➤ If you bring out your Lantern and attempt to light the torches, the rain that's falling in this area snuffs the fire out. Curses! There must be another way to open this gate, and there is; head to the northwestern area of this graveyard, and battle three Stalfos foes. Z target, then flip backward and launch a Bomb Arrow for an acrobatic and impressive takedown!

➤ Then inspect the large gravestones scattered around. This one, in the corner, reads "the cursed swordsman...sleeps before...the sacred tree." The adjacent one reads "in the land...where the rain stops...the statue of time...moves." There's another gate to a stone chamber with pottery in it near here, too.

➤ The clues from the gravestones should lead you here, to the only tree in the graveyard, near the north wall. Change to wolf form, stand here, and you notice a circle of spirits all looking at the tree! Upon closer inspection, there appears to be a small rock half-embedded in the soil at the foot of the tree. Bring out a bomb, and place it here, then retreat. The rock explodes, exposing a floor switch!

Task #1
Solve the Riddle of the Graveyard

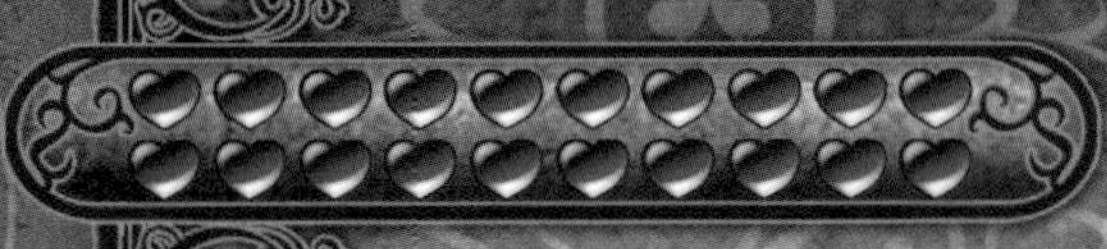

➤ **Treasure Chest**: Stand on the floor switch, and the gate in the west wall where the three Stalfos appeared rumbles open. Inside is a bowl of Lantern oil, an unlit torch, some pottery you can smash for a blue Rupee (5), and three chests! The largest of the three holds an orange Rupee (100), and the others hold a red Rupee (20), and your least-impressive treasure chest prize ever: a green Rupee (1). Refill your Lantern using the oil in the bowl.

Treasure Chest #3:
Orange Rupee (100)
Treasure Chest #4:
Red Rupee (20)
Treasure Chest #5:
Green Rupee (1)
Oil
You got oil in your Lantern!

➤ With the oil in your Lantern, light the torch inside the stone room you're in. Amazingly, the rain stops (but only for a short time, so hurry!). Quickly run to the other gate with the two torches outside, and light both of them before the rain returns. Inside are two owl statues. Bring out your **Dominion Rod** and maneuver one statue southward.

➤ The parchment note on the wall behind the owls gives you a clue to where to place these statues. Bring the first and second statues over to the south wall, near the dig spot, and where the spirits are pointing to. Create two stepping stones and then bound up the left stone steps, and leap across, accessing the upper part of this chamber.

➤ **Treasure Chest**: Run up the steps and head inside a small stone antechamber with a barred gate and a chest behind it. Grab the nearby chain and pull it to access the chest. Inside is a Small Key. You've completed your search of the graveyard, so return to Chamber 2.

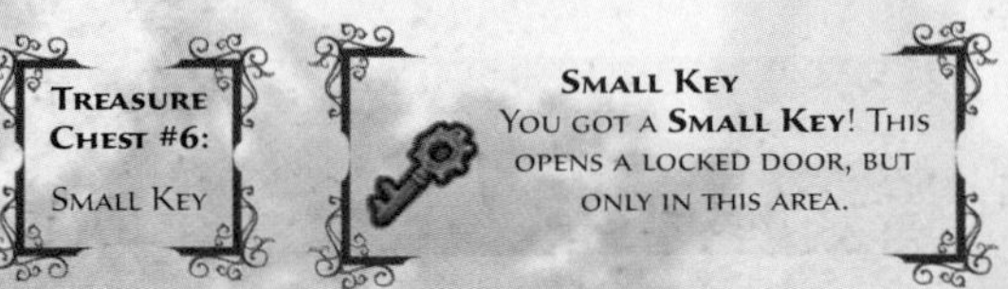

Treasure Chest #6:
Small Key
Small Key
You got a Small Key! This opens a locked door, but only in this area.

Task 2: Defeat King Bulblin in Final Combat

Chamber 2: First Return to Western Grounds (1F)

➤ Return to the wind fan pillars, and head west, through the gap in the wall. The Bulblin towers have been rebuilt, so turn north and secure a new Bullbo mount near the two barrels you can smash for a blue Rupee (5) and a Heart, and careen through all the barricades, all the way back to the Southern Grounds.

Chamber 1: First Return to Southern Grounds (1F), to Chamber 4: Eastern Grounds (1F)

➤ Once in the Southern Grounds, you may be tempted to enter the main castle door. Don't! You can attempt some optional exploration if you head across the grounds to the northeast door. Open it, and enter the Eastern Grounds. Run past the wooden barricades, and into a grassy field. An energy wall closes around you, and out trot eight Bokoblins. Draw your sword and spin! Once the wall recedes, inspect this area; some grass to the east gives you a Heart.

▲ Continue your progress by heading east through the gap in the wall the Bokoblin horde came through. This leads to a pleasant and small formal garden, with some grass to slash for a Heart and to uncover a chain! Grab and pull this chain and a portcullis grinds open, allowing you to enter the north section of this chamber. Turn right after you pass under the portcullis; there's a blue Rupee (5) in the grass near the wall. Stride into the open, and an energy wall forms. Who's there? An old friend...!

King Bulblin

Threat Meter

Step 1: If you recall the battle you had with King Bulblin in his tent outside Arbiter's Grounds, you know how to defeat this hulking brute. First, dodge his giant axe by backing up when he raises the weapon. Fortunately, he swings it so slowly that it's difficult to actually get hit by it! Then roll around to his rear, and strike with three quick slicing moves, or spin attacks, or finish with a back slice. Continue this technique five or six times, and the brute finally yields!

"I have come to play!" says King Bulblin. End the game quickly by attacking his exposed back, and hack!

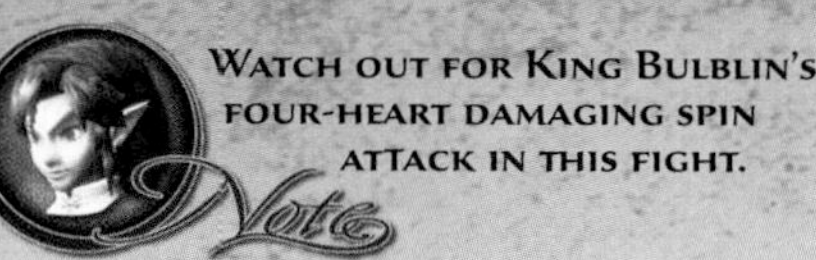
Watch out for King Bulblin's four-heart damaging spin attack in this fight.
Note

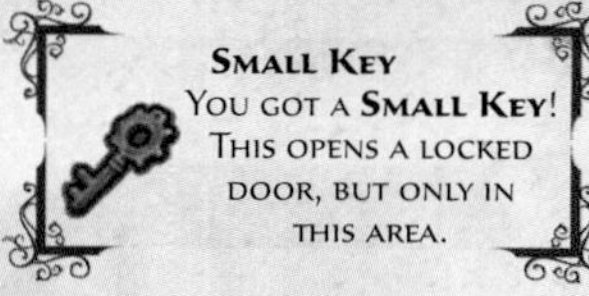
Small Key
You got a Small Key! This opens a locked door, but only in this area.

◄ **Treasure Chest:** With your Small Key in hand (you should have two now; check the screen's bottom-right corner, above your Rupee count), you can inspect this area. Head north. There's a small chest here near a patch of grass you can slice a Heart from. Claim the Rupee prize, then turn directly around and face south. A difficult-to-spot staircase stands in the southwestern corner of this section of the grounds. Head here.

Treasure Chest #7:
Red Rupee (20)

➤ **Treasure Chest:** Run to the top of the steps, and you're on top of a wall between the sections of grounds in this chamber. Break open barrels along this wall for a Heart and a blue (5) and yellow (10) Rupee. When you reach the gap in the wall lip to your left, carefully drop down to a lower ledge and a small chest. Claim a blue Rupee (5) from a barrel on this plinth, and a Red Rupee (20) from the chest.

Treasure Chest #8:
Red Rupee (20)

Enemies Encountered

Bokoblin

Stalfos

King Bulblin

Darknut

Task 3: Exit to the Battlements

Chamber 1: Second Return to Southern Grounds (1F), to Chamber 5: Grand Chandelier Hallway (1F to 2F)

◄ Return to the Southern Grounds, and use the first of your Small Keys to open the main castle door and enter a grand and massive chamber. There's very little time to marvel at the chandeliers and ceiling structures as you're set upon by a gang of Bokoblins! Bring the Master Sword out, and start a variety of your favored techniques. Spin attack the three Lizalfos who join in after you dispatch the first wave of Bokoblins.

➤ **Treasure Chest:** A treasure chest appears on a balcony to the northwest, so run north, smashing the pots here for a Heart, then turn and do the same under the northwestern balcony; there's a Rupee and Heart in the pots here. A pot along the east wall holds a blue Rupee (5). When you're done breaking pottery, climb up the small three-step staircase to the west. This gives you the height to Clawshot up to a chandelier, and dangle down, dropping to the chest. Inside is the Compass. When you've collected it, Clawshot across the chandeliers to the one above the north balcony, and land on it. Open the door.

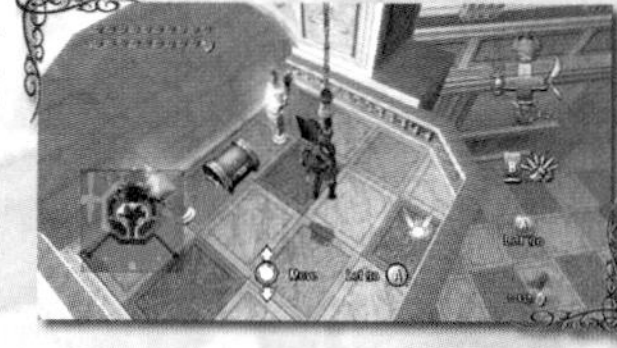

Treasure Chest #9:
Compass

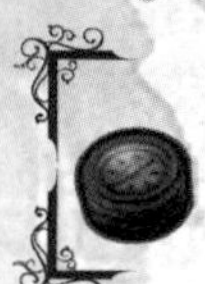
Compass
You got the Compass

Chamber 6: Connecting Corridors (2F)

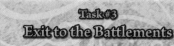

➤ Prepare for a frantic battle, as a Darknut strides toward you in an enclosed combat arena! Don't panic. Remember the technique you used in the Temple of Time: Wait for the Darknut to raise his weapon, leap back, then charge forward and strike, scraping his armor off in stages. Once he's down to his tunic, dodge the blade he throws, then roll around him and execute a back slice, Z targeting constantly! A chest appears on a ledge to the north. Move over and scoop more oil from a bowl into your Lantern.

Missing Links

1. Ball and Chain Bashing

This chamber is surrounded by suits of armor, and they can be bashed if you bring out your Ball and Chain. Expect to find Hearts, a blue Rupee (5), and a Rat in them! Remember to bash all the armor in the Connecting Corridors, too!

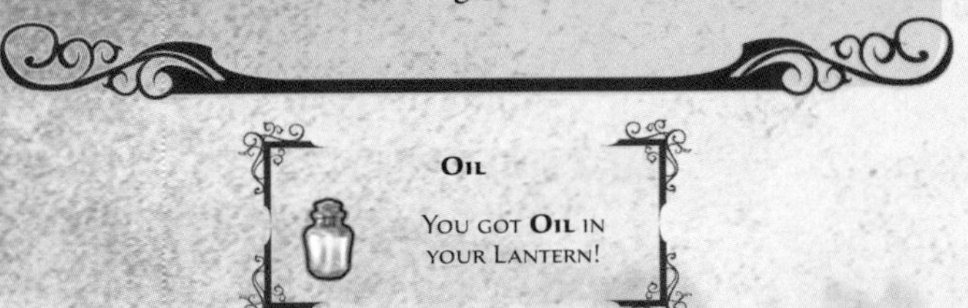

Oil

You got **Oil** in your Lantern!

Treasure Chest: Now light the torches to raise three steps leading to the treasure chest. Unfortunately, once all three are lit, the staircase doesn't ascend all the way to the ledge! Turn and target the torch on the eastern wall adjacent to the Lantern oil bowl. You must be standing on the upper stair (which is at ground level), and bring out your **Gale Boomerang**. Target the torch, snuff the fire, and the stair rises. The chest contains a purple Rupee (50).

Treasure Chest #10: Purple Rupee (50)

Head right from Treasure Chest #10 first, and investigate the corridor rooms to the east. Smash a pot for some arrows, then once through the door, run across the blue carpet and engage two Lizalfos with skull masks, making sure you pick them off one at a time and dodge their attacks. Use Bomb Arrows immediately if you don't want to use your sword. Smash more pots in the chamber for Rupees.

Tip: For a lot of free arrows, try this trick: Smash the pot before you enter the blue carpeted chamber, and collect the arrows. Enter the chamber, then exit back into the initial corridor. The pot has reappeared! Smash it again for more arrows, and keep this up for as long as you want!

The door to the south is still barred, and there seems no way through. Before you begin a fruitless search for keys or enemies, look at this painting of the castle (the only one in the room), and turn into the wolf. Switch on your sense view to see spirits pointing at the wall! Produce your Bomb Arrows, and fire at the painting. The door opens!

Enter this next chamber and strengthen your resolve. Two Darknuts guard this area! You must fight them both, but not at the same time. Edge down the side of the corridor, or fire a Bomb Arrow, and coax one of the Darknuts forward. Then engage him in battle at the north end of the corridor. The second Darknut remains stationary unless you head too far south, so don't! Then attack the other Darknut, and once both are defeated, scour the pots for Hearts and Rupees. There's a blue Rupee (5) in one of the armor suits, too!

Chamber 5: First Return to Grand Chandelier Hallway (2F), back to Chamber 6: First Return to Connecting Corridors (2F)

Treasure Chest: After you defeat the Darknut duo, the doors unseal, allowing you out onto the southeast balcony, where you can open a chest containing a purple Rupee (50). Turn and check the opposite side of the balcony to find a floor switch. Stand on it, and another chest appears, in the northeast balcony that's too high to reach. Return to where you ransacked Treasure Chest #10 and check the other corridors.

Treasure Chest #11: Purple Rupee (50)

Head left from Treasure Chest #10, and you reach a corridor with four unlit torches at the south end. As you reach there and bring out your Lantern, you're set upon by a large flock of Keeses, so bring out the sword and wave it rapidly! Then inspect the torches. Through trial and error, you'll realize they each take a different amount of time to go out. If you get all four lit at once, the locked door to the south opens. Here's the order to light them:

First torch: Southeast. Second torch: Northwest. Third torch: Northeast. Fourth torch: Southwest.

➤ Enter the corridor that's southwest of Chamber 5, and the doors lock and seal. Prepare for a bruising battle against two armored Dynafols! Remember your tactics of dodging around and striking them in the tail, then counterattacking after they swing their axes. The roll and back slice is an excellent technique, too! Smash some pots for Hearts in this room; you may need them!

Chamber 5: Second Return to Grand Chandelier Hallway (2F)

➤ Now open the door leading to the southwest balcony in Chamber 5, and stand on the floor switch. This lowers a chandelier and allows you to reach the chandelier in the northeast corner where you recently summoned a chest.

➤ **Treasure Chest:** Now it's time to claim what's inside; you fought hard enough for it! Drop to the first floor and aim your Clawshot at the chandelier you just lowered. Propel yourself up and to a second chandelier until you're above the northeast balcony. Drop down and claim the huge Rupee prize!

Treasure Chest #12:
Silver Rupee (200)

Chamber 5: Second Return to Connecting Corridors (3F), to Chamber 7: Castle Battlements (3F)

➤ Head back to the Connecting Corridors via chandelier and Clawshot, and exit via the southwest corridor where you fought the Dynafols. You emerge on the Castle Battlements! Head straight forward, toward a large tower at the outer edge of the grounds. An Aeralfos swoops in to intercept you. Remember your takedown technique from the City in the Sky. Wait until it hovers, Clawshot the shield after Z targeting, then hammer him with your sword!

➤ **Treasure Chest:** Once the Aeralfos has been defeated and the energy field lifts, run to the base of the tower, and claim the Small Key from the chest inside. Smash the blue Rupees (5) and Heart out of the barrel, then retrace your steps. Head east, to the middle of the battlements. There's a door to the north, but head down the ramp to the other tower.

Treasure Chest #13:
Small Key

Small Key
You got a **Small Key**! This opens a locked door, but only in this area.

➤ **Treasure Chest:** You wave at your companions, and they wave back. Rusl is carrying his hawk, and they're all here to help. While they secure the grounds, you must fight to the top of the castle, and the chest ahead of you will get you there. Pry it open for the Big Key! Head back and up the exterior ramp to the locked door.

Treasure Chest #14:
Big Key

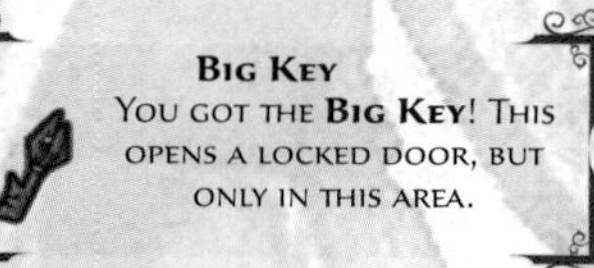

Big Key
You got the **Big Key**! This opens a locked door, but only in this area.

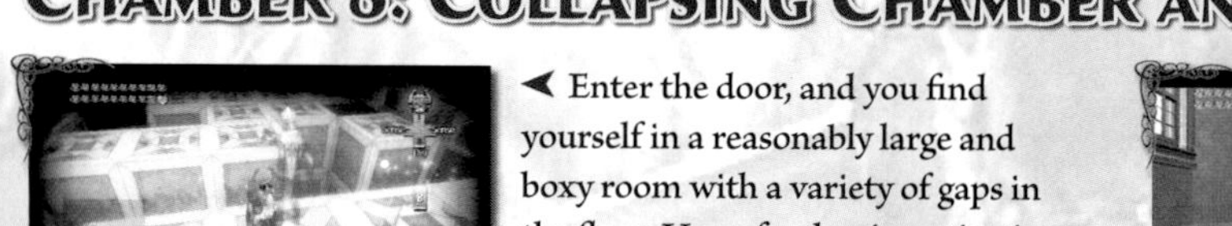

Task 4: Traverse the Collapsing Chamber and Staircases

Chamber 8: Collapsing Chamber and Staircases (3F to 4F)

➤ Enter the door, and you find yourself in a reasonably large and boxy room with a variety of gaps in the floor. Upon further investigation you realize that most of these floor blocks are unsafe and cause you to fall into the bottomless pit beyond! You must call on the spirits to guide you. Change to wolf form and switch on your sense view, and you see a number of spirits. Step only on the blocks they point to, and carefully walk to the subsequent spirit. Keep this up until you reach a half-collapsed staircase.

➤ Change to Link when you reach the steps, then carefully leap across the gaps, all the way to the small connecting chamber. Two Lizalfos are waiting to pounce, but if you stay at the top of the stairs, you can fire a Bomb Arrow and defeat them without brandishing your sword. Or, you can attack them with your preferred combo. Collect one Heart from the crates and barrels, then move to the next staircase up.

Enemies Encountered

Aeralfos

Dynafols

Keese

Lizalfos (Skull-face)

Darknut

Characters Encountered

Princess Zelda

Midna

➤ This staircase is in an even worse state than the previous one! In fact, there are gaps here you cannot jump, so bring out your Double Clawshot, and fire at the sconces clamped to each wall. The pictures adjacent show which sconces to aim at. You must land on the right side of the steps at the top, or you'll fall.

➤ Drop to the top of the steps, and venture into another connecting chamber. Two more Lizalfos are waiting to run in and attack, and once again, you can resort to Bomb Arrows from range, or run in and execute a spin attack and take them both down with a single, well-timed blow! Smash the nearby barrels and debris for a Heart and arrows.

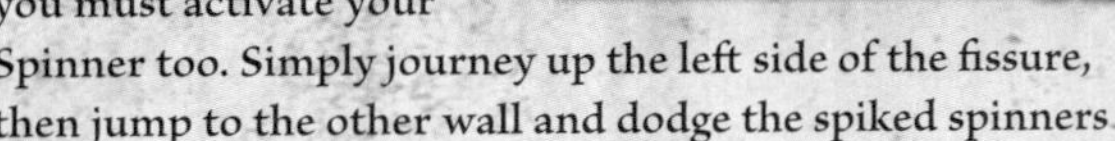

➤ The final staircase isn't really much of a staircase anymore; it's more of a fissure! Spike spinners zip back and forth, and you must activate your Spinner too. Simply journey up the left side of the fissure, then jump to the other wall and dodge the spiked spinners.

➤ The final chamber awaits! Before you reach it however, you must face another Darknut who guards the door that the Big Key fits. Bring your quickest reactions to this combat, defeating the fearsome foe using the techniques you attempted earlier. Remember that there are casks around the perimeter to smash for Hearts.

Task 5: Ransack the Castle's Treasure Trove

Chamber 9: Castle Hyrule Treasure Room

➤ With the Darknut defeated, you can unlock the door with the two Lanterns either side of it. But wait! First check the door to the west, which requires a Small Key. This is also why you should have thoroughly explored the castle (and followed the earlier tactics), because you can make it all the way here without a second key! Check back through the treasure chests and King Bulblin battle to see which one you missed. Or, if you have the key, head on through to fabulous riches!

Treasure Chests: There are Hearts and green (1) and blue (5) Rupees in the pots and crates. In the northwest corner of the room is a pot with a Fairy in it (next to the suit of armor). The following items are available from the large chests in this chamber:

The following items are available from the small chests in this chamber:

Treasure Chest #15	Purple Rupee (50)
Treasure Chest #16	Bomblings (10)
Treasure Chest #17	Silver Rupee (200)
Treasure Chest #18	Seeds (50)
Treasure Chest #17	Silver Rupee (200)
Treasure Chest #19	Orange Rupee (100)
Treasure Chest #20	Blue Rupee (5)
Treasure Chest #21	Yellow Rupee (10)
Treasure Chest #22	Red Rupee (20)
Treasure Chest #23	Water Bombs (15)
Treasure Chest #24	Arrows (20)
Treasure Chest #25	Bombs (20)
Treasure Chest #26	Green Rupee (1)
Treasure Chest #27	Arrows (30)

Task 6: Prepare for Final Combat!

Collapsing Chamber and Staircases (4F), to Chamber 10: Ganon's Inner Sanctum (4F to 5F)

➤ The time has now come! You must venture forward and enter the upper tower of Castle Hyrule. Unlock the heavy chained lock, and step through to face your destiny. The fate of Hyrule rests on your shoulders. Good luck!

Caution

Stop! Save your game right at this point, before you unlock the door. This is the very last opportunity you have to complete any remaining tasks or objectives, or grab items. If you quit, then return to this game, you'll begin at Chamber 1, but all enemies are defeated, chests opened, and doors unlocked. Don't enter this door until you're sure you wish to face the evil puppet master of Zant, and the true power behind the Twilight Throne!

Boss Battle! Ganondorf

Ganondorf:

He's somewhere between 30 and 40 years old. Like Link and Zelda, Ganondorf possesses a true power that only those chosen by the goddesses can obtain. He was once the leader of a tribe of thieves attempting to take over the kingdom, but he was captured by the Sages. At the very moment of his execution, his power woke, and he survived. The Sages concealed Ganondorf's body and power in the Twilight Realm, but it didn't stay hidden for long, and he soon began to control a member of the Twilit King's entourage: Zant. Ganondorf is evil and considerably powerful.

Battle 1: Ganon's Puppet: Zelda

Step 1: The possessed Zelda is your first adversary, and she wields the same power as Ganondorf. She floats about the chamber, creating a triangular field of energy. Flip back out of it as it forms so you aren't stuck in the middle of it. These fields gradually get larger as the combat progresses. Puppet Zelda raises her sword when she is about to conjure, so flip away immediately!

Step 2: After about two of these energy fields (Zelda's attacks are random), Puppet Zelda summons a large white energy ball from her sword, and casts it down at you. Instead of attempting to bounce this back with your shield, Ⓩ target and time a single slash just as the ball reaches you (attempt this early). The ball ricochets and strikes her. Once this strikes her, repeat Step 1. You have to bounce three energy balls back at her, and she can deflect your return up to four additional times before she succumbs.

Threat Meter

Battle 2: Dark Beast Ganon

Step 3: After Midna thrusts light back into Zelda, Ganondorf changes form into a hideous beast with a flailing mane and white eyes. As soon as the beast charges, roll out of the way. He then warps out of existence and creates a series of portals, one at a time, throughout the room. Turn and watch each portal with your **Hero's Bow** primed. When a blue portal is created, Ganon is about to appear. As soon as he charges, fire a single arrow into the white stone between his eyes. Roll to the side immediately to avoid his slide.

Step 4: The farther away Ganon is when you shoot, the less likely you are to be knocked down by his slide. As he slides, bring out your sword, Ⓩ target the white split in his belly, and slash away until he howls in anguish! The best combo is three slices and then a great spin. Repeat this two or three more times.

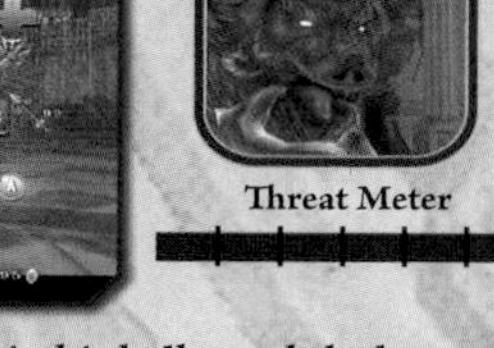

Threat Meter

Step 4: As soon as the arrows stop working, change to wolf form and face down Ganon as he charges out of a blue portal. A second before he strikes you, you're given the option to push with Ⓐ. Do this and Midna's arm extends and grabs Ganon about the head. Press ◀ or ▶ to throw him, as you would a goat—a giant, demonic goat! Once Ganon slides onto his side, transform into Link and Ⓩ target and follow him, and attack his belly as before.

Tip

At this point you might want to secure Hearts and arrows from the pots surrounding the throne room. Run around collecting them, then return to focusing on Ganon.

Enemies Encountered

Lizalfos (Axe-tail)

Darknut

Ganon

Ganondorf

Characters Encountered

Princess Zelda

Midna

Battle 3: Dark Rider Ganondorf

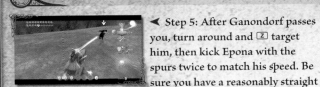

Phantom Rider

Phantom Riders are Ganondorf's conjurations, and they do not attack independently. They are bolts of angry energy that charge and strike you during the battle. React by riding between them or avoiding them completely.

Threat Meter

Threat Meter

➤ Step 5: After Ganondorf passes you, turn around and Ⓩ target him, then kick Epona with the spurs twice to match his speed. Be sure you have a reasonably straight line between yourself and Ganondorf as Zelda prepares a Light Arrow. She fires, and it strikes, unless you're making a sharp turn, or are struck by his attack—the Phantom Riders.

➤ Step 6: If Ganondorf launches an airborne attack, judge where the riders will form, and ride between or around them. If you fall off your horse, get back on, spur a couple of times to speed up, and repeat Step 5. Once Zelda strikes with her arrow, speed up to the side of Ganondorf, and slice at him. A spin attack works well. Now repeat this about three more times until Ganondorf falls from his mount.

Battle 4: Dark Lord Ganondorf

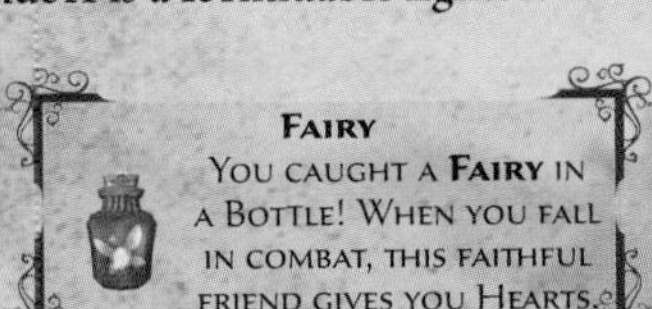

Step 7: Ganondorf rises as the thunder claps. He is prepared to fight you in sword combat, and he seals Zelda out of the battle. When the fight begins, turn right, and begin to slice the skulls around the perimeter of the energy wall. Behind Ganondorf and to the right is a skull containing a Fairy. The rest contain Hearts. As the battle begins, you'll see that Ganondorf is a formidable fighter!

Tip: If ever there was a time to don your Magic Armor with a Giant Wallet holding 1,000 Rupees, now is it! Also remember to continuously Ⓩ target during battle.

Threat Meter

Step 9: But your prime opportunity to defeat Ganondorf is when he raises his sword like this. When a "chance" message appears, press Ⓐ immediately!

Fairy

You caught a **Fairy** in a Bottle! When you fall in combat, this faithful friend gives you Hearts.

Step 8: The key to defeating Ganondorf is to maintain a distance of about 12 feet away from him. If you're too close, you'll be struck by his sword (shield block it). If you're too far, Ganondorf charges you, then executes a roundhouse punch with the sword hilt. If you attack with simple slashes, he blocks, then leaps into the air and slices down at you. Run or roll from him if you can't see him. You can occasionally strike him by rolling around and using a back strike, then land and slash.

Step 10: Your swords entangle, and you both begin to push each other. Tap Ⓐ repeatedly, so you begin to push Ganondorf backward.

Step 11: As soon as you push Ganondorf backward, execute an immediate three slashes then pause for a split-second and finish with a spin attack (a great spin is even better!). Keep pummeling Ganondorf until he falls over. Repeat Steps 9–11 twice more.

Step 12: On the third attempt (or earlier if you connect with a great spin), when Ganondorf falls to the ground, you're given a split-second to "finish" with Ⓐ. Ⓩ target at once and leap into the air, skewering the hated Ganondorf once and for all!